WINDO

—SUPERBOOK—

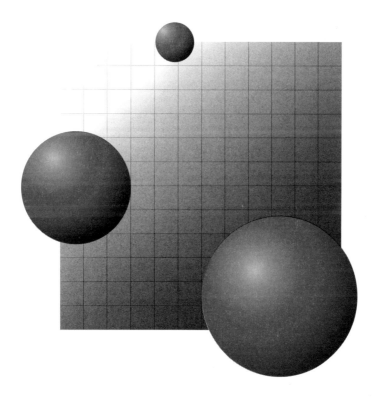

by: maranGraphics' Development Group

Corporate Sales

Contact maranGraphics
Phone: (905) 890-3300
       (800) 469-6616
Fax: (905) 890-9434

Visit our Web site at:
http://www.maran.com

Canadian Trade Sales

Contact Prentice Hall Canada
Phone: (416) 293-3621
       (800) 567-3800
Fax: (416) 299-2529

Windows® 95 Superbook

Copyright© 1997 by maranGraphics Inc.
5755 Coopers Avenue
Mississauga, Ontario, Canada
L4Z 1R9

Canadian Cataloguing in Publication Data

Heilbron, Maarten
        Windows 95 : superbook

(Visual 3-D series)
Includes index.
ISBN 1-896283-33-0

1. Microsoft Windows (Computer file).   2. Operating systems
(Computers).   I. Maran, Ruth, 1970-   . II. Whitehouse, Paul.
III. MaranGraphics Inc. IV. Title. V. Series.

QA76.76.H44   1997   005.4'469   C97-931873-4

Printed in the United States of America

10   9   8   7   6   5   4   3   2

Trademark Acknowledgments

© 1997 maranGraphics, Inc.

The 3-D illustrations are the
copyright of maranGraphics, Inc.

WINDOWS® 95

— S U P E R B O O K —

VISUAL SERIES
3D

maranGraphics™

Every maranGraphics book represents
the extraordinary vision and commitment of a unique family:
the Maran family of Toronto, Canada.

Back Row (from left to right): *Sherry Maran, Rob Maran, Richard Maran, Maxine Maran, Jill Maran.*

Front Row (from left to right): *Judy Maran, Ruth Maran.*

Richard Maran is the company founder and its inspirational leader. He developed maranGraphics' proprietary communication technology called "visual grammar." This book is built on that technology—empowering readers with the easiest and quickest way to learn about computers.

Ruth Maran is the Author and Architect—a role Richard established that now bears Ruth's distinctive touch. She creates the words and visual structure that are the basis for the books.

Judy Maran is the Project Coordinator. She works with Ruth, Richard and the highly talented maranGraphics illustrators, designers and editors to transform Ruth's material into its final form.

Rob Maran is the Technical and Production Specialist. He makes sure the state-of-the-art technology used to create these books always performs as it should.

Sherry Maran manages the Reception, Order Desk and any number of areas that require immediate attention and a helping hand.

Jill Maran is a jack-of-all-trades and dynamo who fills in anywhere she's needed anytime she's back from university.

Maxine Maran is the Business Manager and family sage. She maintains order in the business and family—and keeps everything running smoothly.

CREDITS

Authors:
Maarten Heilbron, Ruth Maran
and Paul Whitehead

Director of Editing and Indexer:
Kelleigh Wing

Project Coordinator:
Judy Maran

Copy Developers and Editors:
Brad Hilderley
Wanda Lawrie
Carol Barclay

Editors:
Peter Lejcar
Tina Veltri
Roxanne VanDamme
Betty Barna

Layout Designers:
Ben Lee
Jamie Bell
Treena Lees

Illustrators:
Chris K.C. Leung
Russell C. Marini

Screen Artist:
Jeff Jones

Screen Captures and Post Production:
Robert Maran

ACKNOWLEDGMENTS

The goal of this book is similar to the goal of Windows itself: to take something powerful and make it simple. I hope that this book will make it easier to accomplish the tasks you bring to your computer.

I am deeply indebted to Ruth Maran for her patience and understanding, and her ability to synthesize complex tasks into clear and easy-to-follow steps. She made my work simple, and our collaboration efficient and harmonious.

I thank the entire staff of maranGraphics for their tireless pursuit of excellence. They have checked every detail and questioned every assertion, and made the book better at every turn.

Finally, I thank my wife Kim, and my children Kieran and Calla for their help and cooperation. This book would not be possible without them.

Maarten Heilbron

Thanks to the dedicated staff of maranGraphics, including Carol Barclay, Betty Barna, Jamie Bell, Francisco Ferreira, Brad Hilderley, Jeff Jones, Wanda Lawrie, Ben Lee, Treena Lees, Peter Lejcar, Chris K.C. Leung, Michael W. MacDonald, Jill Maran, Judy Maran, Maxine Maran, Robert Maran, Russell C. Marini, Roxanne VanDamme, Tina Veltri, Paul Whitehead and Kelleigh Wing.

Finally, to Richard Maran who originated the easy-to-use graphic format of this guide. Thank you for your inspiration and guidance.

Ruth Maran

WINDOWS®95

WHAT'S INSIDE

GETTING STARTED

TABLE OF CONTENTS

5) EXCHANGING DATA

6) MS-DOS PROGRAMS

WINDOWS 95 ACCESSORIES

7) USING WORDPAD

TABLE OF CONTENTS

8) USING PAINT

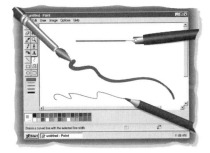

9) MORE ACCESSORIES

CUSTOMIZE WINDOWS 95

10) CUSTOMIZE YOUR COMPUTER

11) CUSTOMIZE THE START MENU

TABLE OF CONTENTS

WORK WITH DISKS

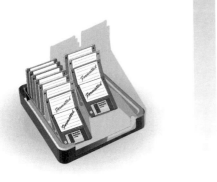

15) BACK UP INFORMATION

V CONNECT TO OTHER COMPUTERS

16) MODEMS

17) DIAL-UP NETWORKING

TABLE OF CONTENTS

VI · SEND E-MAIL AND FAXES

21) SEND FAXES

NETWORKING

22) INTRODUCTION TO NETWORKS

TABLE OF CONTENTS

WINDOWS 95 AND THE INTERNET

TABLE OF CONTENTS

IX INSTALLING AND TROUBLESHOOTING

WHAT'S NEW IN WINDOWS 95

Windows 95 is a true operating system because it does not require any other operating system to run. Previous versions of Windows required MS-DOS to operate. You had to install and start MS-DOS before you could install and start Windows.

Windows 95 looks and works differently from previous versions of Windows. Microsoft tested Windows 95 with groups of beginner and advanced users to make it easier to use and more powerful.

The current version of Windows 95, called OSR2, has been released only to hardware manufacturers and is available only when you buy a new computer.

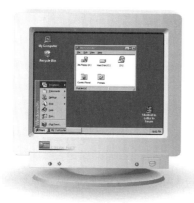

The Desktop

If you have used Windows before, you will see that the Windows 95 screen, called the desktop, has a simpler look. The desktop displays icons, such as the Recycle Bin, windows and other items. The taskbar appears at the bottom of the desktop and allows you to see which programs are running and allows you to switch between open windows. You can access your programs and files by clicking the Start button in the bottom left corner of the taskbar.

Shortcuts

You can create a shortcut to provide a quick way of opening items such as files, folders or programs you use regularly. A shortcut represents a link to the original item. You can add a shortcut icon to the desktop, the Start menu or a folder.

Quick View

You can use the Quick View feature to view the contents of a document without starting the program that created the document. Quick View helps you decide whether the document you selected is the one you want to work with.

Find

If you cannot remember the name or location of a file you want to work with, you can have Windows search for the file using the Find feature. You can specify where you want Windows to search, what file name Windows should search for or have Windows search for files based on the date the file was created.

Shortcut Menus

When you right-click an item, a shortcut menu appears. The shortcut menu contains commands like Open, Print, View, Rename or Delete. From the shortcut menu, you can access an item's Properties panel, which tells you more about the item and lets you adjust its settings.

My Computer and Explorer

You can access your files and settings using My Computer or Explorer. All disk drives and control panels are found in one location in My Computer. My Computer uses multiple windows and large icons to make it easier to browse through information on your computer. Explorer uses a structured view to display your computer's contents so you can manage your files.

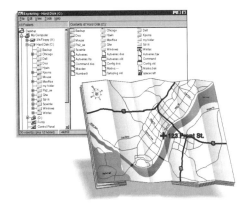

Drag and Drop

You can drag information from its current location and place it in a new location. You can use drag and drop to move or copy files, create shortcuts and print documents. You can also use drag and drop to share information between documents or programs. Windows 95 makes extensive use of drag and drop.

Undo

You can undo an action you performed by right-clicking the desktop and selecting Undo from the menu. You can usually undo several actions.

When you delete a file, Windows moves the file to the Recycle Bin. You can undo the deletion to recover the file from the Recycle Bin.

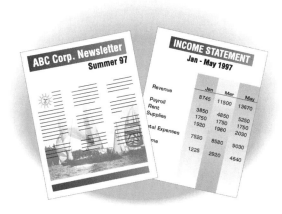

Long File Names

Windows 95, and programs that are designed for Windows 95, can use file names of up to 255 characters, including spaces. Long file names can better describe a file's contents for easier identification later. If you use programs that do not recognize long file names, the name will be shortened to eight characters.

CONTINUED ▶

WHAT'S NEW IN WINDOWS 95
CONTINUED

Plug and Play

Plug and Play simplifies the way that new hardware items are added to your computer. Windows 95 can often detect and help install a hardware device even if it is not a Plug and Play device. With a Plug and Play device, you only need to connect or install the device. The next time you start Windows, Windows asks for the floppy disk or CD-ROM disc containing the software for the device.

Performance

Windows 95 uses the 32-bit capabilities of Intel processors. A 32-bit processor is better able to manage several tasks at the same time. This increases the flexibility and speed of the operating system. With Windows 95, you can format a floppy disk while you are working in a program or start a second program while you are waiting for the first to open.

Programs are now handled separately, so the system will stop less often due to badly behaved programs. You can end a failed task or exit a program without having to restart the computer.

Internet Programs

Windows 95 includes the Internet Explorer 3 Web browser and Mail and News software for sending messages. NetMeeting is also included to allow you to communicate with other people online. Windows 95 includes several other tools and utilities to make it easy to connect to and use the capabilities of the Internet.

You can share a modem with multiple programs using Windows 95. You do not have to disable your fax, e-mail or connection program to connect to the Internet and then restart the program when you are done.

Accessory Programs

Windows 95 includes a basic word processor, a paint program, a calculator, screen savers and several games. Windows 95 also includes software that can check your drives, defragment your files and back up information on your computer. DriveSpace is included with Windows 95. You can use DriveSpace to compress, or squeeze together, the information stored on your hard drive. DriveSpace may be able to double the available free space on your hard drive.

Customization and Personalization

You can customize many elements in Windows 95 to suit your working style, tastes or needs. For example, you can change the color of the desktop, change the way a window displays files or adjust the way you access commands. Windows 95 includes a wide range of accessibility options for people with special needs.

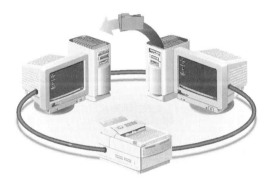

Networking

Windows 95 includes all of the components needed to create and connect to a peer-to-peer network. You can use Windows 95 with all popular networks, including the Internet. You can use Network Neighborhood to display all the computers on your network. You can use Dial-Up Networking to dial in to another computer using a modem.

Help and Wizards

You can access Windows 95's extensive help system by pressing the F1 key. There are many troubleshooters in Help, which can help you identify and fix problems like non-functioning hardware and printer error messages. Many tasks you perform, like adding a printer or installing software, use wizards. Wizards help you perform your task by asking questions about the task that you want to perform so you will not make a mistake.

CD-ROMs and Multimedia

Windows 95 allows a program provided on a CD-ROM disc to start itself. When you insert a CD-ROM disc with a multimedia program, Windows either starts the program automatically or displays a menu. Windows 95 includes support for enhanced CDs, which include graphics and other multimedia components in addition to music. Standard audio CDs start to play automatically when they are inserted.

Mobile Users

Windows 95 has special capabilities to make it easy to coordinate and transfer files between portable and desktop computers. Support for direct cable connections, Plug and Play and delayed printing allows portables to work in many different situations without having to reconfigure the computer. There are also power management features to help increase battery life.

PARTS OF THE
WINDOWS 95 SCREEN

The Windows 95 screen uses icons to display the tools, documents and devices you can work with on your computer. Each icon is used to access a specific item. The available items depend on how your computer is set up.

Title Bar

Displays the name of an open window. The title bar of the window you are currently using is a different color than other open windows.

Menu Bar

Provides access to lists of commands available in a window.

My Computer

Lets you view all the folders, files and tools stored on your computer.

Toolbar

Contains buttons that provide quick access to frequently used menu commands.

Network Neighborhood

Lets you view all the folders and files available on your local network.

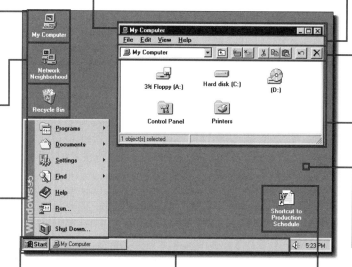

Window

A rectangle on your screen that displays information. A window can be moved and sized.

Recycle Bin

Stores deleted files and lets you recover them later.

Desktop

The background area of your screen.

Start Button

Gives you quick access to programs, files, Windows Help and the settings on your computer.

Taskbar

Displays a button for each open window on your screen. You can use these buttons to switch between the open windows.

Shortcut

Allows you to quickly access a document or program you use regularly. You can place a shortcut to a file or program on your desktop.

USING THE MOUSE

A mouse is a hand-held device that lets you select and move items on your screen. When you move the mouse on your desk, the mouse pointer on your screen moves in the same direction.

The mouse pointer assumes different shapes, such as ⬚ or I, depending on its location on the screen and the task you are performing.

Click

Press and release the left mouse button. A click is used to select an item on the screen.

Double-Click

Quickly press and release the left mouse button twice. A double-click is used to open a document or start a program.

Right-Click

Press and release the right mouse button. A right-click is used to display a list of commands you can use to work with an item.

Drag and Drop

Position the mouse pointer over an item on the screen and then press and hold down the left mouse button. Still holding down the button, move the mouse to where you want to place the item and then release the button. Dragging and dropping makes it easy to move an item to a new location.

Cleaning the Mouse

You should occasionally remove the small cover on the bottom of the mouse and clean the ball inside the mouse. Make sure you also remove dust and dirt from the inside to help ensure smooth motion of the mouse.

Mouse Pads

A mouse pad provides a smooth, non-slip surface for moving the mouse. A mouse pad also reduces the amount of dirt that enters the mouse and protects your desk from scratches. Hard plastic mouse pads attract less dirt and provide a smoother surface than fabric mouse pads.

START WINDOWS

You start Windows when you turn on your computer. You may need to enter a user name and password before you can use Windows. If you share your computer with other people, a password enables each person to have a personalized working environment. The password can also identify you to a network and verify that you have permission to access and use network services.

When your computer starts, you may be asked to choose which hardware setup you are using. This process is commonly used for portable computers that may or may not be connected to an office network or other devices.

If your computer was not shut down properly the last time it was used, Windows will automatically launch ScanDisk to check your files. For information on ScanDisk, see page 290.

The Welcome dialog box appears and provides you with a tip about using Windows. You can turn off the Welcome dialog box so it does not appear every time you start Windows.

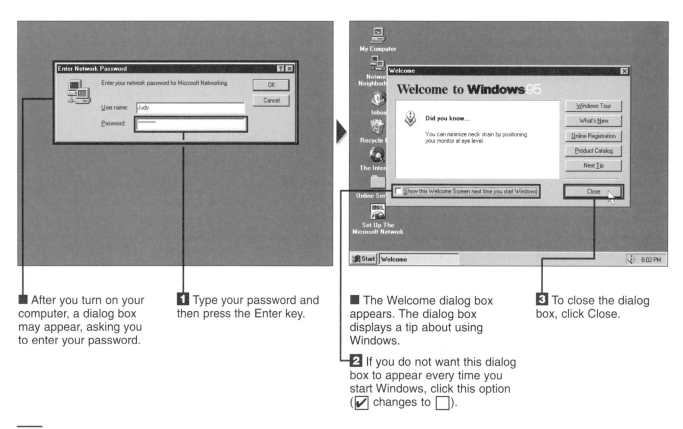

■ After you turn on your computer, a dialog box may appear, asking you to enter your password.

1 Type your password and then press the Enter key.

■ The Welcome dialog box appears. The dialog box displays a tip about using Windows.

2 If you do not want this dialog box to appear every time you start Windows, click this option (☑ changes to ☐).

3 To close the dialog box, click Close.

SHUT DOWN WINDOWS

Y ou should always shut down Windows before you turn off your computer. Turning off your computer before Windows indicates it is safe to do so may cause you to lose data. Shutting down properly allows Windows to save and close your documents, close programs, disconnect from

the network and warn you about users who may be accessing your files.

There are several options you can choose from. The Shut down option shuts down your computer so you can turn off the power. The Restart option is useful when your computer is operating strangely or a

program stopped working unexpectedly. The restart process gives the computer memory and resources a fresh start. For information about MS-DOS mode, see page 142. For information about logging on as a different user, see page 234.

1 Click Start.

2 Click Shut Down.

■ The Shut Down Windows dialog box appears.

3 Click the option you want to use (○ changes to ◉).

4 Click Yes.

Note: To quickly restart Windows without restarting the computer, select the Restart the computer option in step 3. Then press and hold down the Shift key as you perform step 4.

■ Do not turn off your computer until a message appears, saying that it is safe to do so.

START A PROGRAM

You can start a program by using the Start button. The Start button appears on the taskbar and is a good starting place for you to find and start your programs.

When you click the Start button, the Start menu appears, providing quick access to your programs. You can also use this menu to find documents, get help and shut down Windows.

You can use the Start button while you are working in another program. The Start button allows you to quickly start a new program without having to close or minimize the current program.

You can access the Start menu using the mouse or the keyboard.

When you start a program, a button for the program appears on the taskbar.

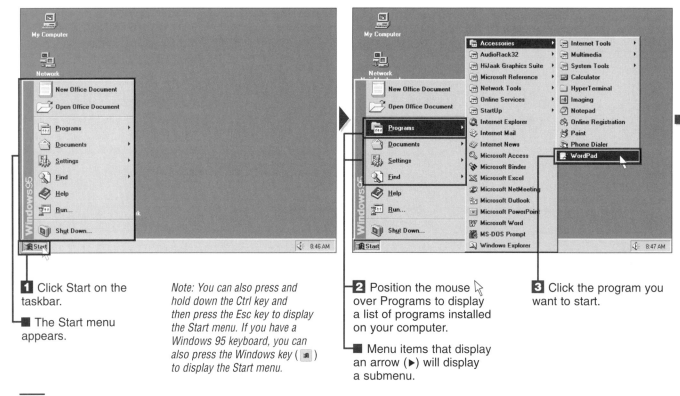

1 Click Start on the taskbar.

■ The Start menu appears.

Note: You can also press and hold down the Ctrl key and then press the Esc key to display the Start menu. If you have a Windows 95 keyboard, you can also press the Windows key (🔲) to display the Start menu.

2 Position the mouse ⬉ over Programs to display a list of programs installed on your computer.

■ Menu items that display an arrow (▶) will display a submenu.

3 Click the program you want to start.

When I clicked on a program in the Start menu, it did not start. What is wrong?

The program may start as a minimized button on the taskbar. Look for the button on the taskbar and then click the button to display the program's window.

Can I add a program to the Start menu?

To add a program to the main Start menu, you can drag and drop the icon for the program over the Start button on the taskbar. If you want to place the program in a submenu on the Start menu, see page 250.

How can I find a program not on the Start menu?

You can try to locate the program using either My Computer, Explorer or the Find feature on the Start menu. For information on the Find feature, see page 76.

Can I rearrange the Start menu?

If you right-click the Start button and select Explore, you can view all the items in the Start menu and rearrange them. See page 256.

How do I close the Start menu?

To close the Start menu, press the Esc key or click outside the menu area. You may have to press the Esc key more than once if submenus are displayed.

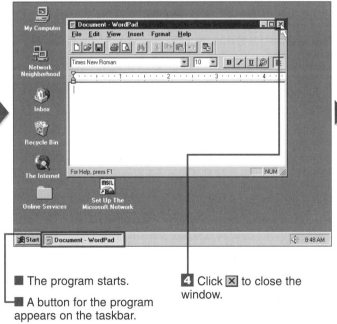

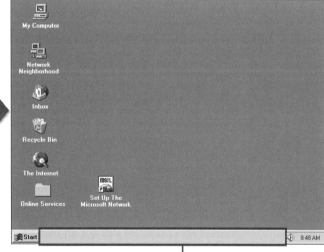

■ The program starts.

■ A button for the program appears on the taskbar.

4 Click ⊠ to close the window.

■ The window disappears from your screen.

■ The button for the window disappears from the taskbar.

USING RUN TO START A PROGRAM

You can use the Run command to start a program that does not appear on the Start menu.

There are many programs that Windows does not display in the Start menu, such as programs that can be used to change the settings on your computer. This helps to avoid the accidental misuse of system programs.

There are also several utility programs that Windows does not display in the Start menu.

You may have MS-DOS and older Windows programs on your computer, such as games, that are also not displayed on the Start menu. You can use the Run command to access these types of programs.

You can also display a list of programs you have recently started using the Run command and then choose a program from the list.

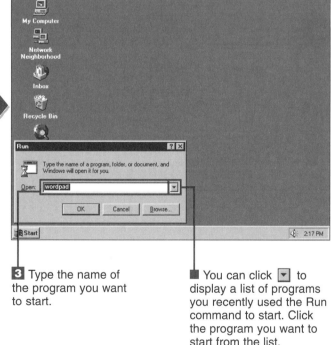

1 Click Start.

2 Click Run.

■ The Run dialog box appears.

3 Type the name of the program you want to start.

■ You can click ▼ to display a list of programs you recently used the Run command to start. Click the program you want to start from the list.

What if I do not know the name of the program I want to open?

You can use the Browse button to find a program, file or folder you want to open.

Is there another way to start a program?

You can drag programs, folders and files to the Start button from an open window or your desktop. You can then click the Start button and select the item you want to open. For more information, see page 251.

Can I use the Run command to open other items?

The Run command can open many types of items. For example, if you type the address of a page on the World Wide Web, Windows will connect to the Internet, open your Web browser and display the Web page. You can also type the name, including the path, of a file or folder to open the item. You cannot use the Run command to open a file or folder if the item name contains a space, like Start Menu.

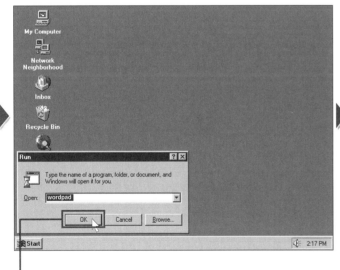

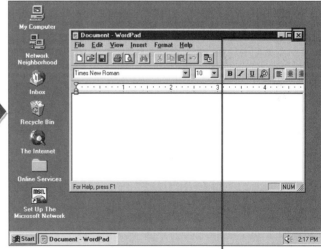

4 Click OK to start the program.

■ The program starts.

■ Click ☒ to close the program.

MAXIMIZE OR MINIMIZE A WINDOW

You may want to enlarge a window to fill your screen so you can see more information or you can put the window aside while you concentrate on another task.

When you maximize a window, you enlarge the window to fill your screen. This allows you

to view more of the contents of the window.

When you are not using a window, you can minimize the window to remove it from your screen. When you minimize a window, the window reduces to a button on your taskbar. To once again display the window,

click the button on the taskbar. The window will appear in its original location and in the same size it was displayed before you minimized the window.

If you have a lot of open windows on your screen, you can save time by minimizing all of the windows at once.

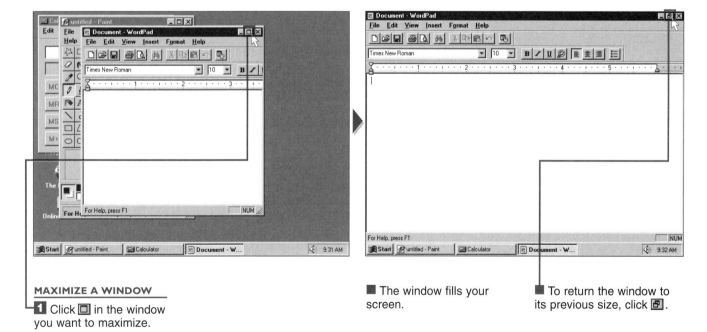

MAXIMIZE A WINDOW

1 Click 🗖 in the window you want to maximize.

■ The window fills your screen.

■ To return the window to its previous size, click 🗗.

TIPS

I keep clicking the wrong button when I try to maximize a window. Is there an easier way to maximize a window?

If you double-click the title bar of a window, the window fills your screen. You can also increase the size of the buttons at the top right corner of a window by using the Display Properties Appearance tab. See page 204.

How can I read the name of a taskbar button if the whole name is not displayed?

Position the mouse pointer over the button. After a few seconds, a box appears, displaying the full name of the window the button represents.

Can I automatically minimize a program when it starts?

You can have a program automatically appear minimized on the taskbar each time you start the program. See page 90.

Can I make the taskbar disappear so it does not cover the bottom of a maximized window?

You can change the way the taskbar behaves. For more information, see page 196.

GETTING STARTED

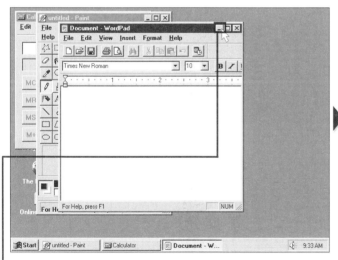

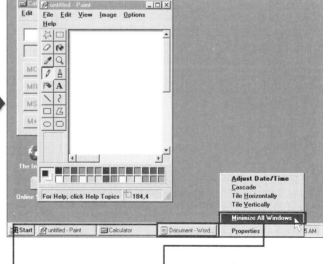

MINIMIZE A WINDOW

1 Click ⬜ in the window you want to minimize.

■ The window reduces to a button on the taskbar. To redisplay the window, click the button.

MINIMIZE ALL WINDOWS

1 To minimize all windows displayed on your screen, right-click an empty area on the taskbar. A menu appears.

2 Click Minimize All Windows.

15

MOVE OR SIZE A WINDOW

You can have many windows open on your desktop at one time. Adjusting the location and size of windows can help you work with their contents more easily.

You can move a window to a new location if it covers important items on your screen. If you have more

than one window open, you can adjust the position of the windows to ensure that you can view the contents of each window. You can click on any open window to bring it to the front.

You can increase the size of a window to see more of its contents. You can reduce the

size of a window to view more of the items it covers.

Just as you can move and size windows on your desktop, you can also move and size windows in open programs.

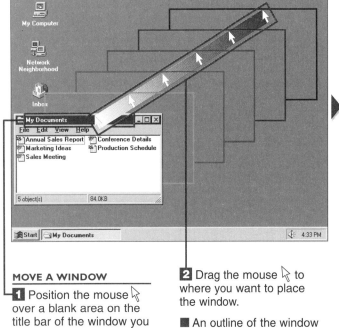

MOVE A WINDOW

1 Position the mouse ⌖ over a blank area on the title bar of the window you want to move.

2 Drag the mouse ⌖ to where you want to place the window.

■ An outline of the window indicates the new location.

■ The window moves to the new location.

TIPS

How can I see the contents of a window I am moving or sizing?

Microsoft Plus! includes a feature called Full Window Drag which shows the contents of a window while it is being moved or sized. See page 618.

Can I move or size a maximized window?

You will not be able to move or size a window that has been maximized. Restore the window first and then move or size it. To restore a window, see page 14.

Can I move an entire window off the screen?

You can move most of a window off the screen but some of the window will still be visible. This allows you to put a document aside, as you might on a real desk.

Can all programs be sized?

Some programs, like Calculator, cannot be sized.

GETTING STARTED

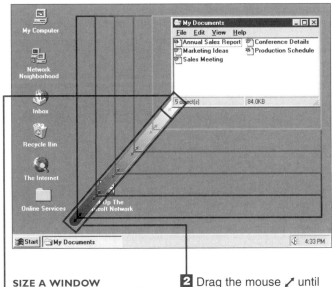

SIZE A WINDOW

1 Position the mouse ⊾ over an edge of the window you want to size (⊾ changes to ↗ or ↘).

2 Drag the mouse ↗ until the outline of the window displays the size you want.

■ The window changes to the new size.

17

SWITCH BETWEEN WINDOWS

When you have more than one window open, you can switch between all of the open windows.

Although you are able to have several windows open, you can only work in one window at a time. This window is called the active window. The active window appears in front of all the other windows. The title bar

of the active window is a different color than the title bar of the other open windows.

The taskbar displays a button for each open window on your screen. Each taskbar button displays all or part of the name of the window it represents.

You can make a window active by clicking its button on the taskbar. You can also use your

keyboard to switch between open windows.

The ability to have multiple windows open and switch between them is very useful. Switching between windows allows you to consult a report while you answer your e-mail, or verify a budget when you are preparing a presentation.

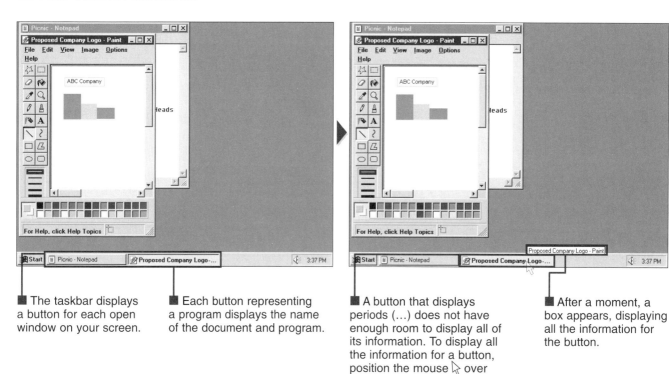

■ The taskbar displays a button for each open window on your screen.

■ Each button representing a program displays the name of the document and program.

■ A button that displays periods (...) does not have enough room to display all of its information. To display all the information for a button, position the mouse ▷ over the button.

■ After a moment, a box appears, displaying all the information for the button.

How can I use a program's taskbar button to display a document?

Select the document you want to display and then drag the document to the program's button on the taskbar. The program's window opens. Still holding down the mouse button, drag the document into the window.

Is there another way to make an open window active?

You can click any part of an open window to make it the active window.

The taskbar is not displayed on my screen. How do I get the taskbar to appear?

If you have turned on Auto hide, move your mouse pointer to the bottom of the screen to display the taskbar. You can also press the Ctrl and Esc keys at the same time to display the taskbar.

What can I do if my taskbar will not reappear?

Your taskbar may have been resized. Move the mouse pointer to the edge of the screen where it was last seen. When the pointer changes to a double-headed arrow, drag the taskbar back onto the screen.

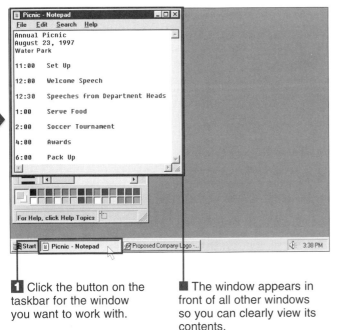

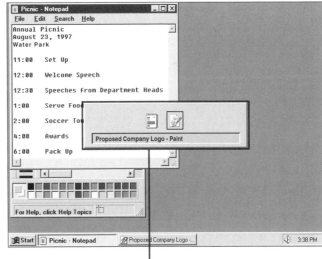

1 Click the button on the taskbar for the window you want to work with.

■ The window appears in front of all other windows so you can clearly view its contents.

USING THE KEYBOARD

1 Press and hold down the Alt key.

2 Still holding down Alt, press the Tab key.

■ A box appears, displaying an icon for each open program.

3 Still holding down Alt, press the Tab key until the box displays the name of the window you want to work with. Then release Alt.

ARRANGE WINDOWS

Y ou can arrange your open windows to make them easier to use or display more of their contents.

You can have several windows open at the same time. Similar to a real desk, you can have many items, such as an agenda, a letter and a budget, all open on your desktop at once. Windows allows you to arrange and

organize these items so they are easier to use.

You can choose to cascade your open windows. Cascade displays windows one on top of the other so that you can see the title bar of each window. This is useful if you are working with My Computer and have many windows open. You can move between the open windows by

clicking the title bar of the window you want to view.

You can use the Tile commands to see two or more windows side by side or one above the other. Tiling allows you to compare the contents of your windows and drag information from one window to another.

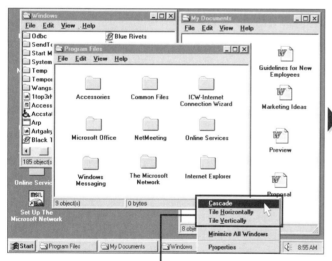

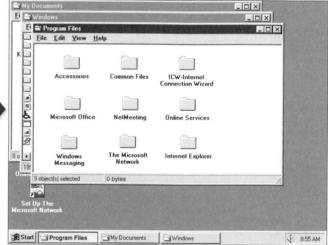

1 Right-click an empty area on the taskbar. A menu appears.

2 Click the way you want to arrange the windows.

CASCADE

■ The windows neatly overlap each other. You can clearly see the title bar of each window.

■ You can click the title bar of the window you want to work with. The window will appear in front of all other windows.

TIPS

How do I make a window appear in front of all other windows?

Click any part of the window. You can also click the window's button on the taskbar.

How can I change back to the previous window arrangement?

To change back to the previous window arrangement, right-click the taskbar and then select Undo.

Why are some of my programs not tiling correctly?

Some programs with a fixed window size, like Calculator, cannot be tiled.

Why can't I see a difference between Tile Vertically and Tile Horizontally?

Tiled windows are displayed the same way on your screen when there are four or more windows open.

How do I tile or cascade only some of the windows I have open?

Minimize the windows you do not want included before you use the tile or cascade commands.

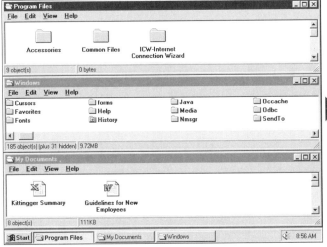

TILE HORIZONTALLY

■ The windows appear one above the other. You can view the contents of each window.

■ You can compare the contents of the windows and exchange information between the windows.

■ You can click anywhere in the window you want to work with to make that window active.

TILE VERTICALLY

■ The windows appear side by side. You can view the contents of each window.

■ You can compare the contents of the windows and exchange information between the windows.

■ You can click anywhere in the window you want to work with to make that window active.

SCROLL THROUGH INFORMATION

A scroll bar lets you browse through information in a window. This is useful when a window is not large enough to display all the information it contains. Some dialog boxes with lists also display scroll bars that you can use to view all of the items in a list.

The location of the scroll box on the scroll bar indicates which part of the window you are viewing. For example, when the scroll box is halfway down the scroll bar, you are viewing information from the middle of the window. The size of the scroll box varies, depending on the amount of information the window contains.

Some programs show new information as you drag the scroll box. Other programs display new information only when you release the scroll box.

The Microsoft IntelliMouse has a wheel between the left and right mouse buttons. Moving this wheel allows you to scroll through information in the most recent versions of some Microsoft programs.

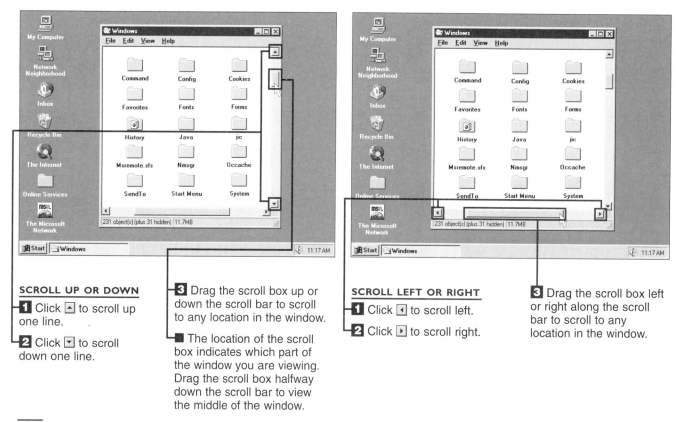

SCROLL UP OR DOWN

1 Click ▲ to scroll up one line.

2 Click ▼ to scroll down one line.

3 Drag the scroll box up or down the scroll bar to scroll to any location in the window.

■ The location of the scroll box indicates which part of the window you are viewing. Drag the scroll box halfway down the scroll bar to view the middle of the window.

SCROLL LEFT OR RIGHT

1 Click ◄ to scroll left.

2 Click ► to scroll right.

3 Drag the scroll box left or right along the scroll bar to scroll to any location in the window.

SHORTCUT MENUS

Most items in Windows have a shortcut menu that appears when you right-click the item. The shortcut menu includes actions and commands appropriate for the item.

The shortcut menu for a file includes commands to Cut, Copy, Delete and Rename the file. Some programs may add additional commands to the shortcut menu.

Almost every item displays the Properties command in the shortcut menu. The Properties command provides access to a dialog box with information and settings that allow you to customize the selected item.

On the shortcut menu, the default action for the item is listed in bold. When you double-click an item, the default action is performed. For example, when you right-click a document, the Open command in the shortcut menu is bold. If you double-click the document, Windows will open the document. The default action for a sound or movie file is Play. For a screen saver file, the default action is Test.

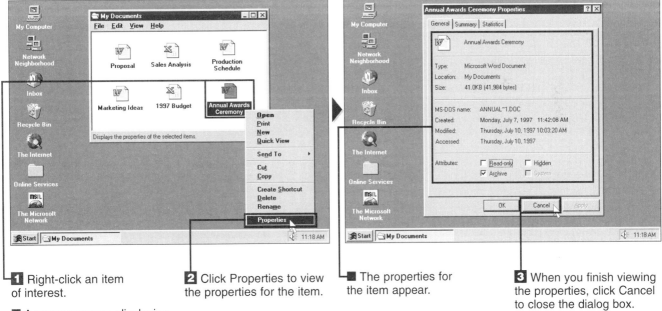

1 Right-click an item of interest.

■ A menu appears, displaying the most frequently used commands for the item.

2 Click Properties to view the properties for the item.

■ The properties for the item appear.

3 When you finish viewing the properties, click Cancel to close the dialog box.

SELECT COMMANDS

Windows programs provide menus and dialog boxes so you can access their commands and features. Most Windows programs share similar commands, which makes the programs easier to learn and use. You can use your mouse or the keyboard to select commands.

Each menu contains a group of related commands. Some menu commands, like Save or Undo, perform an action when they are selected.

You can use some menu commands to turn an option on or off. If an option is on, a check mark (✔) or a dot (●) appears to the left of the command.

If a small arrow (▶) appears to the right of a menu command, the command will open another menu with more commands.

Some menu commands, like Open or Print, open a dialog box. These commands are usually followed by three dots (...). A dialog box appears when a program needs more information from you to perform an action. Dialog boxes have areas where you can enter text or select options from a list.

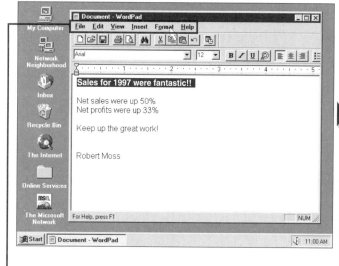

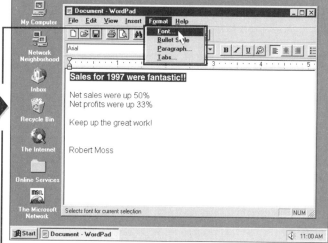

1 Click the name of the menu you want to display.

■ To select a menu with the keyboard, press the Alt key followed by the underlined letter in the menu name (example: o for Format).

2 Click the name of the command you want to select.

■ To select a command with the keyboard, press the underlined letter in the command name (example: F for Font).

■ To close a menu without selecting a command, click outside the menu or press the Alt key.

TIPS

Why do some menu commands have a dimmed appearance?

Commands that have a dimmed appearance are currently not available. You must perform a specific task before you can access the command. For example, you must select text to make the Cut and Copy commands in the Edit menu available.

Are there shortcut keys for menus?

Many menu commands offer keyboard shortcuts you can use to quickly select commands. For example, Ctrl+S saves the current document. If a keyboard shortcut is available, it appears beside the command in the menu.

What is the difference between an option button (○) and a check box (☐)?

When a list of choices displays round option buttons (○), you can select only one option. The selected option displays a dark center (●). When a list of choices displays check boxes (☐), you can select as many options as you want. Selected options display a check mark (☑).

Are there shortcuts for dialog boxes?

In some dialog boxes, double-clicking an item selects both the item and the OK button. For example, you can double-click a file in an Open dialog box to quickly open the file.

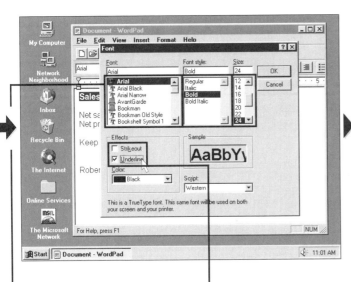

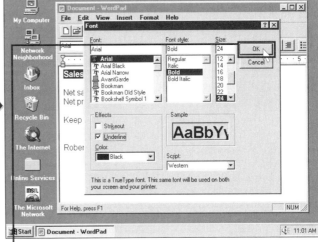

3 Click an item you want to select from a list.

■ To move through the options in a dialog box with the keyboard, press the Tab key. Press the up or down arrow keys to select an item from a list.

4 Click a check box to turn an option on (☑) or off (☐).

■ Press the Spacebar to turn an option on (☑) or off (☐).

5 Click OK or press the Enter key to save the changes you made.

■ You can click Cancel or press the Esc key to leave the dialog box without making any changes.

SAVE DOCUMENTS

You can save a document you have created to keep a permanent copy of the document. Your document is saved as a file on your hard drive.

To save a document, you must name the document. In Windows 95, you can use up to 255 characters to name a document, including spaces and special characters. The only

characters you cannot use to name a document are the \ / : * ? " < > or | characters. If you will be sharing the document with people who do not use Windows 95, the document name should use no more than 8 letters, with no spaces and no special characters.

You can use the Save As dialog box to move through folders and

drives on your computer and store the document exactly where you want. You can organize your work in folders so it is easier to find a document when you need it again. You can also view information about your saved documents, such as the date and time the document was last changed.

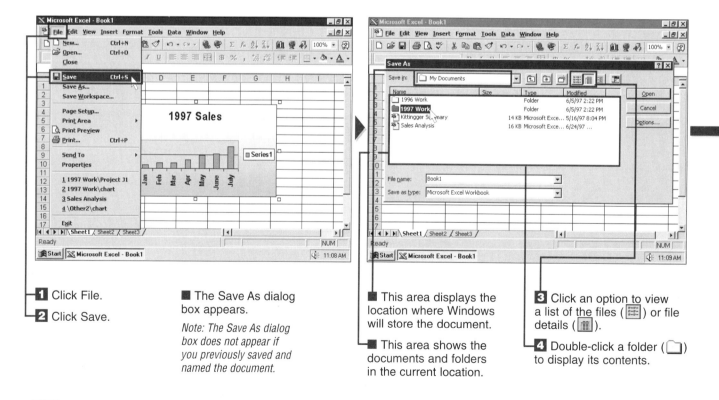

1 Click File.

2 Click Save.

■ The Save As dialog box appears.

Note: The Save As dialog box does not appear if you previously saved and named the document.

■ This area displays the location where Windows will store the document.

■ This area shows the documents and folders in the current location.

3 Click an option to view a list of the files ( ) or file details ( ).

4 Double-click a folder ( ) to display its contents.

How often should I save the document I am working on?

You should save the document frequently. This will ensure that all the changes you make to the document are saved. Frequent saving also reduces the amount of work that could be lost in the event of a power loss or computer failure.

Can I manage files from the Save As dialog box?

You can right-click any file in the Save As dialog box. A menu appears containing many commands, including Delete and Rename.

How can I change the default folder so that files are automatically saved in the folder I want?

Some programs allow you to change the default folder. Right-click the Start button and select Open or Explore. Then locate the shortcut to the program you use. Right-click the program shortcut and select Properties from the menu that appears. Then select the Shortcut tab. In the Start in text box, type the path to the folder where you want to store documents created with the program. For example, type **c:\my documents\letters** to save documents in the Letters folder located in the My Documents folder on your hard drive.

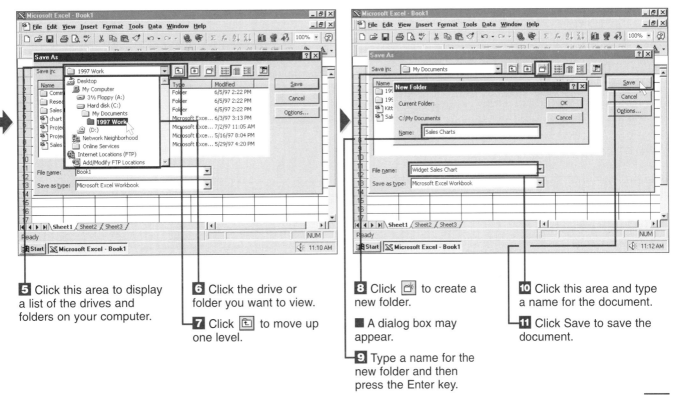

5 Click this area to display a list of the drives and folders on your computer.

6 Click the drive or folder you want to view.

7 Click 🔁 to move up one level.

8 Click 🗁 to create a new folder.

■ A dialog box may appear.

9 Type a name for the new folder and then press the Enter key.

10 Click this area and type a name for the document.

11 Click Save to save the document.

GETTING HELP
Where to Get Help

If you have a problem using Windows, there are many sources of help available. You can refer to Windows Help, the Microsoft Technical Support Knowledge Base and Internet newsgroups to find help. If you prefer more personal help, you can use help options such as telephone support, friends and professional consultants.

When you are using Windows, the most convenient source of help is Windows Help. The Windows Help feature is automatically installed with Windows and is free to use.

There are several ways you can use Windows Help to find the information you are looking for. You can browse through help topics by category, search Windows Help files for the information you need or use the alphabetical index of help topics.

Windows Help is available for the operating system and all Windows programs. Windows Help works the same way in all programs, so it is easy to learn and use. Windows Help is a good source of general information and can answer most of your questions.

Windows Help does not include information about problems, or bugs, that were identified after Windows 95 was released.

You can use the Microsoft Technical Support Knowledge Base to obtain the latest information about Windows. The Microsoft Technical Support Knowledge Base can be found on the Internet at:

www.microsoft.com/kb

The Knowledge Base contains known problems and solutions to the problems that have been identified by Windows users and the Microsoft technical support staff. The Knowledge Base is constantly being updated as new problems are discovered and solved.

If you have a question or problem, you can search the Knowledge Base for the information you need. The Knowledge Base is not comprehensive and you may have to read many pages before you find the information you want.

You can use Internet newsgroups as a source of information and help.

Deja News maintains a list of messages posted to newsgroups. You can search through these messages to find the answers you need. You may have to spend a great deal of time reading messages to find one that answers your question. Deja News can be found on the Internet at:

www.dejanews.com

If you cannot find the information you need in the messages, you can post a message to an appropriate newsgroup asking a specific question. Other readers may read your question and e-mail you the answer or post it in the newsgroup.

Keep in mind that the information you receive from Internet newsgroups may not always be reliable or may not work with the setup of your computer.

You can receive help over the phone from an experienced user who has the latest information.

You can speak to a Microsoft support technician who will try to solve your problem over the phone. Depending upon your location, and how and when you purchased Windows, the Microsoft telephone support may be free.

Windows has many fee-based telephone support options that are explained to you when you call the appropriate number for your region. The number for your region is usually included with your license information.

If you purchased Windows pre-installed on a new computer, your manufacturer or vendor may provide telephone support.

Telephone support can sometimes be a frustrating experience. You may spend a long time on hold and if you are paying long-distance charges, it can be expensive.

When you have a problem, you can use friends and colleagues as a source of help.

With so many people using Windows 95, you probably know someone who has experienced a similar problem. Every office or neighborhood has a computer guru who can provide information and help less experienced users solve problems.

Friends and colleagues may not always be able to help solve your computer problems. Your friends and colleagues are usually not experts and may not understand how the setup of your computer differs from their own. A procedure that worked on your friend's computer may create more problems on your computer.

Consultants are experienced professionals who provide expert on-location help and advice. Consultants are trained in specific areas of computer hardware or software. You can have a consultant come to your home or office to solve your problem.

You should ask for recommendations from your friends, colleagues or other knowledgeable computer users when looking for a consultant.

Before you hire a consultant, make certain that the consultant's area of expertise is in the area where you need help. For example, a consultant experienced in accounting software may not be able to help you with your Windows 95 problems.

GETTING HELP
Using the Contents Tab

You can use the Contents tab to browse through Windows help topics by subject.

The Contents tab contains categories of help topics arranged into books. The books contain general help, specialized information, tips and problem solving techniques on a wide range of Windows topics. Even experienced users will find useful information on the Contents tab.

The Introducing Windows book is useful if you are using Windows 95 for the first time or if you are upgrading from a previous version of Windows.

The How To book contains step by step procedures to help you complete tasks. You can find shortcut buttons that open dialog boxes and access other items to help you complete tasks faster.

The Tips and Tricks book contains valuable and interesting information to help you use Windows effectively. This book is a good source of timesaving tips.

The Troubleshooting book contains a list of specific issues and can help you identify and resolve a problem.

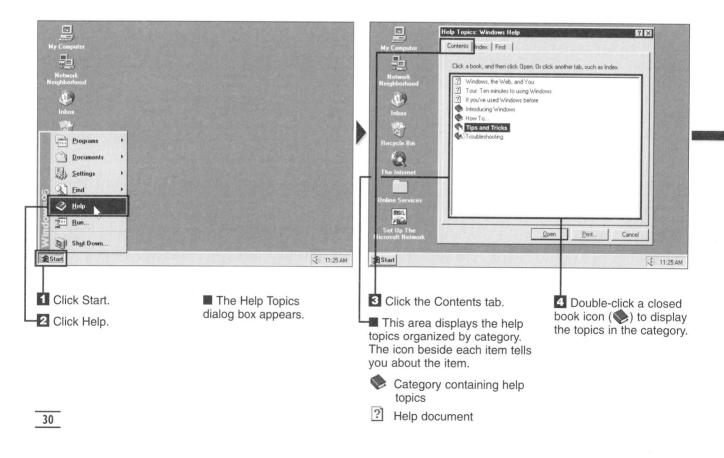

■1 Click Start.

■2 Click Help.

■ The Help Topics dialog box appears.

■3 Click the Contents tab.

■ This area displays the help topics organized by category. The icon beside each item tells you about the item.

◆ Category containing help topics

? Help document

■4 Double-click a closed book icon (◆) to display the topics in the category.

Is there a shortcut to Help?

Pressing the F1 key will open the Help feature in Windows and nearly every Windows program.

Is there a quick way to access the Help Topics dialog box after I finish reading the information in a Help window?

Click the Help Topics button in the Help window to redisplay the Help Topics dialog box.

I opened the Help Topics dialog box and now the Help window is frozen. Why?

When you open the Help Topics dialog box, you cannot use the Help window until you choose another topic.

Why does the Help Topics dialog box seem to disappear when I leave it open?

The Help Topics dialog box hides behind other open windows. If you close or minimize your open windows and programs, you will see the Help Topics dialog box again.

Does the Help Topics dialog box have a button on the taskbar?

Only open windows have a button on the taskbar. The Help Topics dialog box is not a window so it does not have a button on the taskbar.

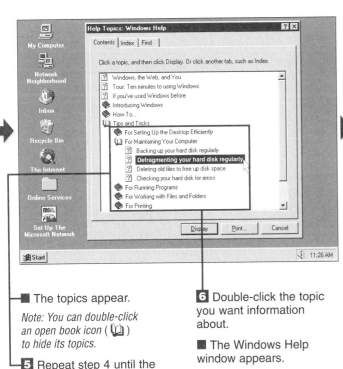

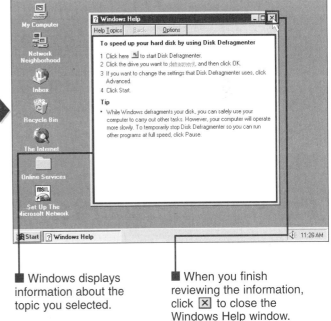

■ The topics appear.

Note: You can double-click an open book icon (📖) to hide its topics.

5 Repeat step 4 until the topic of interest appears.

6 Double-click the topic you want information about.

■ The Windows Help window appears.

■ Windows displays information about the topic you selected.

■ When you finish reviewing the information, click ☒ to close the Windows Help window.

GETTING HELP

Using the Index Tab

The Index tab contains an alphabetical listing of all the items in Windows help topics.

You can use the Index tab to find information the same way you would use the index of a book.

When you type the first few characters of the item you want to find, Windows will take you to the item's location in the index.

Windows categorizes items so you can quickly find the information you need. For example, if you want to add an item to your computer, you can type the word **adding**. Listed under "adding", you will find help topics for adding applications, fonts, printers and

Windows components to your computer.

Windows lists most items in non-technical terms. For example, you can type **X** to find information about what the X in the top right corner of a window does.

After you find the help topic you want, you can display the help information for the topic.

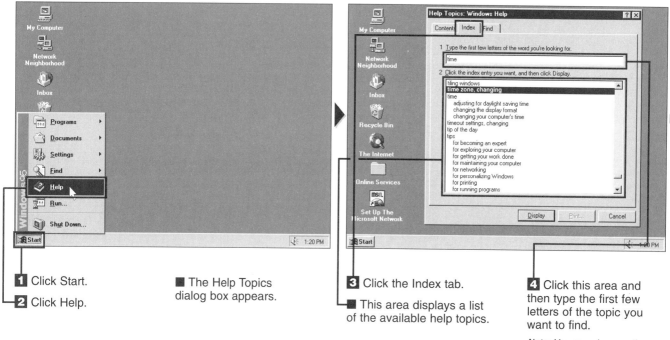

1 Click Start.

2 Click Help.

■ The Help Topics dialog box appears.

3 Click the Index tab.

■ This area displays a list of the available help topics.

4 Click this area and then type the first few letters of the topic you want to find.

Note: You can also use the scroll bar to browse through the help topics.

TIPS

What can I do if the Help window that opened does not contain the information I need?

Some Help windows contain a button that lets you display related topics. You can also click the Help Topics button to return to the Help Topics dialog box. From the Help Topics dialog box, you can select a new topic.

The text in the Help window is too small. Can I increase the size?

Click the Options button and then select Font. You can make the font size larger or smaller.

The Help window is in the way. Can I move it?

Click the Options button. Click the Keep Help on Top option and then select Not On Top. The Not On Top setting allows you to place another window or dialog box on top of the Help window. You can also minimize the Help window as you would minimize any window.

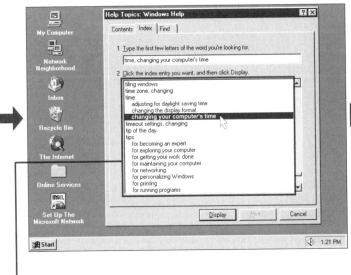

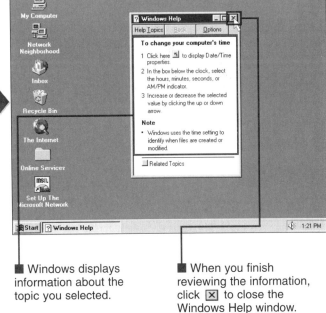

■ This area displays topics beginning with the letters you typed.

5 Double-click the topic of interest to get information about the topic.

■ The Windows Help window appears.

■ Windows displays information about the topic you selected.

■ When you finish reviewing the information, click ☒ to close the Windows Help window.

GETTING HELP

Using the Find Tab

You can use the Find tab to search all of the words in Windows help topics.

The Find tab contains a list of all the words used in the help topics. You can type one or more words and have Windows search the list to find matches for the words.

Windows searches the list after you type each letter, so you can find matches even if you do not know the correct spelling of an entire word.

Windows displays the matching topics and tells you how many help topics it has found. If a lot of help topics are displayed, you can narrow your search by adding

another word or searching for a more specific word.

Windows displays the help topics containing all of the words you typed, regardless of the order of the words.

After you find the help topic you want, you can review the help information for the topic.

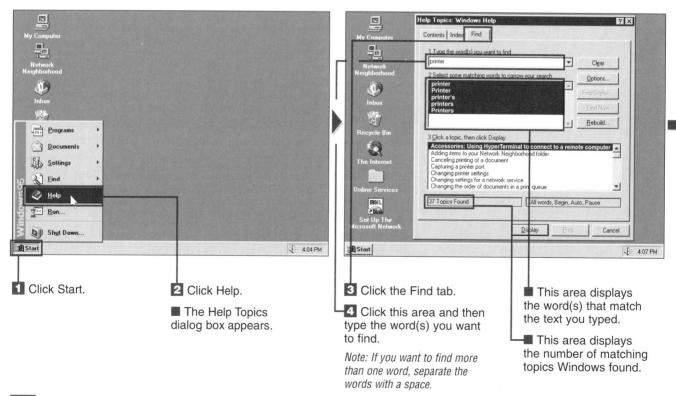

1 Click Start.

2 Click Help.

■ The Help Topics dialog box appears.

3 Click the Find tab.

4 Click this area and then type the word(s) you want to find.

Note: If you want to find more than one word, separate the words with a space.

■ This area displays the word(s) that match the text you typed.

■ This area displays the number of matching topics Windows found.

Why did the Find Setup Wizard dialog box appear when I clicked the Find tab?

The first time you use the Find tab, Windows needs to create a list of all the words used in the help topics. Follow the instructions in the dialog box to have Windows create the word list.

Why doesn't Windows display matching words when I type the word I am looking for?

All of the words in the help topics may not have been added to the list. Click the Rebuild button and then select the Maximize search capabilities option.

Can I change the way the Find tab works?

You can use the Options button to change the way the Find tab works. You can have Windows search for topics containing any of the words you type instead of all the words you type.

You can have Windows find matches for only part of the word you type. You can also tell Windows when you want the search to begin.

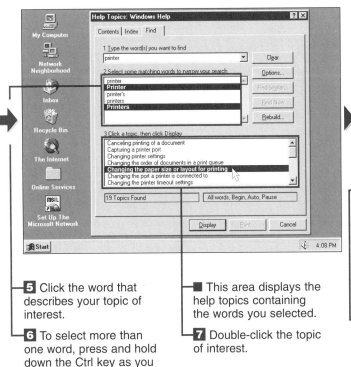

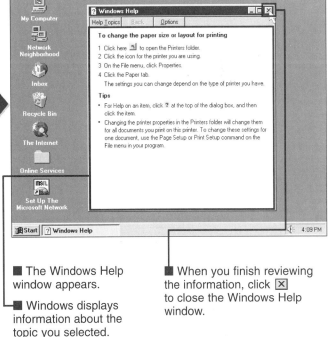

■5 Click the word that describes your topic of interest.

■6 To select more than one word, press and hold down the Ctrl key as you click each word.

■ This area displays the help topics containing the words you selected.

■7 Double-click the topic of interest.

■ The Windows Help window appears.

■ Windows displays information about the topic you selected.

■ When you finish reviewing the information, click ☒ to close the Windows Help window.

GETTING HELP
Print a Help Topic

You can print a paper copy of the help topic displayed on your screen. Printing a help topic can be very useful because it is often difficult to remember all of the information in a Help window.

A printed copy of a help topic allows you to review a procedure from beginning to end before you start a task. You can also use

a printed copy when you want to refer to other sources about a specific help topic.

It is not always possible to view the information in a Help window. If you are completing a task that requires you to restart your computer, you will not be able to refer to the help information while the computer is turned off. A printed copy of

the topic will help you complete the task.

A printed reference of a help topic can also help you learn about Windows features more easily. For example, although it can take a long time to become familiar with all of the Windows shortcut keys, a printed reference can help you memorize them.

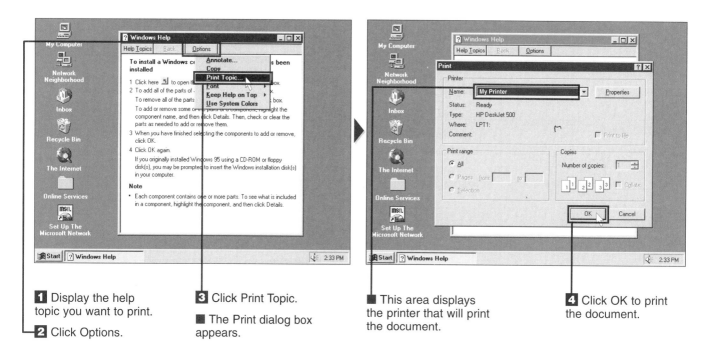

1 Display the help topic you want to print.

2 Click Options.

3 Click Print Topic.

■ The Print dialog box appears.

■ This area displays the printer that will print the document.

4 Click OK to print the document.

GETTING HELP
Add Notes to Help Topics

Y ou can add a note to a help topic to display details or explanations. Windows stores the note with the help topic so the note will be available when you need the information again.

Windows allows you to personalize a help topic with

your own comments so the topic is easier for you to use. You can use notes to store information about company procedures, the setup of your computer or further details about how the help topic works.

A help topic displays a paper clip when there is a note

attached to it. You can click the paper clip to display the note.

You can remove a note you no longer need or copy a note into a program, such as WordPad. Notes you have added do not appear when you print a help topic.

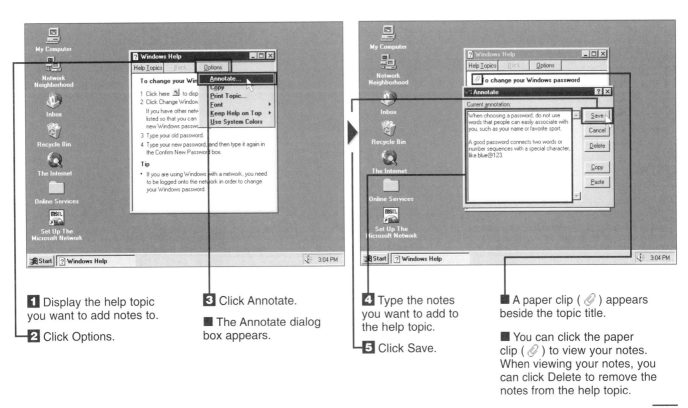

1 Display the help topic you want to add notes to.

2 Click Options.

3 Click Annotate.

■ The Annotate dialog box appears.

4 Type the notes you want to add to the help topic.

5 Click Save.

■ A paper clip (⬚) appears beside the topic title.

■ You can click the paper clip (⬚) to view your notes. When viewing your notes, you can click Delete to remove the notes from the help topic.

37

GETTING HELP
Copy Help Information

You can create your own help documents by copying Windows help information into a document in your word processor. Using a word processor, you can edit, format and print your help document so it will be available even when you do not have access to Windows help

topics or your computer is turned off.

You can use the information displayed in a Help window to create a specialized help document containing the step by step procedure for a specific task you must perform. A specialized document containing Windows

help information is useful when you are performing a complex task such as connecting to the Internet.

You can create a general help document by gathering Windows tips and suggestions into one document. This type of general help document can help you improve your Windows skills.

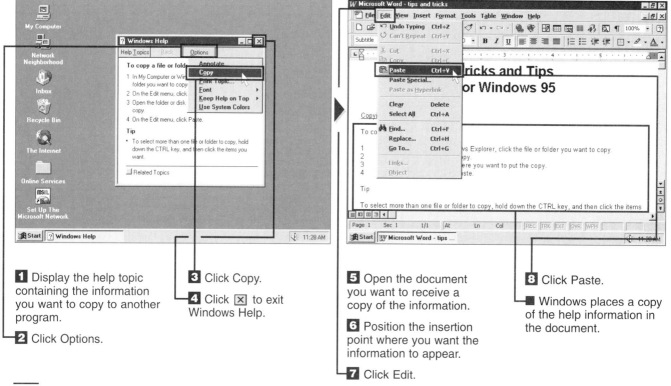

1 Display the help topic containing the information you want to copy to another program.

2 Click Options.

3 Click Copy.

4 Click ☒ to exit Windows Help.

5 Open the document you want to receive a copy of the information.

6 Position the insertion point where you want the information to appear.

7 Click Edit.

8 Click Paste.

■ Windows places a copy of the help information in the document.

GETTING HELP
Getting Help in a Dialog Box

You can find information about a dialog box you are using.

If you are unfamiliar with a dialog box, you can use the **?** button to display Windows help information. The **?** button provides you with details concerning the options in a dialog box.

When you click the **?** button and then click an option in a

dialog box, a box containing Windows help information appears. The help information explains what the option you selected does and how you can use the option. The help information stays on the screen while you learn about the option.

You must click the **?** button each time you want to display help information for an option.

If the **?** button is not available in the dialog box you are working in, you can press the F1 key to find general information about the dialog box. You can right-click an option and then click the What's This button to display specific information about an option in most dialog boxes.

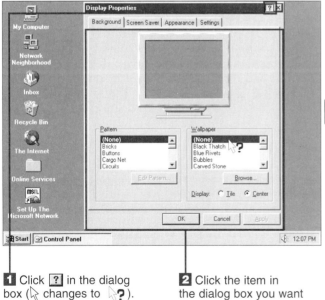

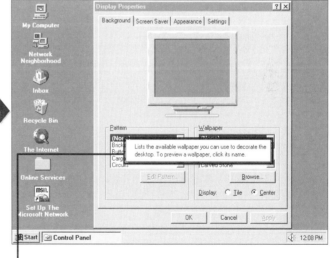

1 Click **?** in the dialog box (changes to **?**).

2 Click the item in the dialog box you want information about.

■ Help information appears for the item you selected.

■ You can click anywhere to hide the help information.

COMPUTER HARDWARE
Devices You Attach to a Computer

Monitor

A monitor displays text and images on the screen that were generated by the computer. The size of a monitor is measured diagonally across the screen. Common monitor sizes range from 14 to 21 inches.

Keyboard

A keyboard is used to enter information and instructions into a computer.

Speakers and Headphones

Speakers and headphones are used to listen to sounds created by a sound card. Headphones let you listen to sounds privately. Computer speakers must be shielded to prevent the magnets inside the speakers from distorting the image on a monitor. Most computer speakers include an amplifier and run on batteries or other power sources.

Printer

A printer produces a paper copy of documents created on the computer. Laser printers produce high-quality, black and white pages. Inkjet printers make color printing affordable. Dot matrix printers are often used to print multi-part forms.

Microphone

A microphone is used with a sound card to record speech and other sounds. Not all sound cards are compatible with all types of microphones.

Mouse

A mouse is a hand-held device that lets you select and move items on your screen. There are many different types of mouse alternatives, including trackballs, touch-sensitive pads and tablets that use pens. Some mice have a wheel between the buttons to simplify the task of scrolling up and down through information in a window.

Video Camera

A video camera is used for video conferencing or to create video files.

Removable Drive

A removable drive is a combination of a hard drive and floppy drive. The disks you use with a removable drive can contain from 100 MB to 1.5 GB of information. You can use a removable hard drive to transfer large amounts of information between computers.

Scanner

A scanner reads graphics and text into a computer. Scanners range in size from small hand-held scanners to large flatbed scanners that can scan full pages.

Port

A port is a connector at the back of a computer where you plug in an external device, such as a printer or modem. This allows instructions and data to flow between the computer and the device. A parallel port has 25 holes and connects a printer, removable drive or tape drive. The computer uses LPT to identify a parallel port. A serial port has either 9 or 25 pins and is used to connect many devices, such as a mouse or modem. The computer uses COM to identify a serial port. Your system also has additional ports to connect devices like your monitor, joystick, speakers and a phone line. A Universal Serial Bus (USB) port provides a way to connect several devices using only one port.

Scan Convertors

Scan convertors are used to convert computer images so they can be displayed on a television. Scan convertors are sometimes built into a video card.

Modem

A modem lets computers exchange information through telephone lines. You can use a modem to connect to the Internet and to send and receive e-mail messages and faxes. There are two types of modems. Internal modems are circuit boards that fit inside your computer. External modems plug into the back of your computer.

The speed of a modem determines how fast it can send and receive information through telephone lines. The most common modem speed is 28.8 Kbps.

You can use an Integrated Services Digital Network (ISDN) terminal adapter as an alternative to a modem for connecting to the Internet using digital ISDN phone lines.

Tape Drive

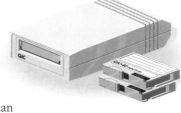

A tape drive stores and retrieves information on tape cartridges. You can use a tape drive to back up files, archive old or rarely used files or transfer large amounts of information. There are many types of tape drives available, including the Travan drive, the QIC (Quarter-Inch Cartridge) drive, and the DAT (Digital Audio Tape) drive.

CONTINUED ▶

COMPUTER HARDWARE CONTINUED

Inside a Computer

Floppy Drive

A floppy drive stores and retrieves information on floppy disks. A double-density (DD) floppy disk can store 720 K of information. This disk has only one hole at the top of the disk. A high-density (HD) floppy disk can store 1.44 MB of information. This disk has two holes at the top of the disk. You can prevent erasing information on a floppy disk by sliding the tab to the write-protected position.

CD-ROM Drive

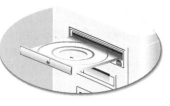

A CD-ROM drive reads information stored on compact discs. You can use a CD-ROM drive to install programs, play games on CD-ROM discs and listen to music CDs. Currently the most common CD-ROM speed is 12x. Some CD-ROM drives can hold several disks at once. CD-ROM discs can store up to 720 MB of information. You cannot record on a CD-ROM drive. CD-Recordable (CD-R) drives are available if you want to store your own information on a disc. You can also use the CD-R drive to play CD-ROM discs. Digital Video Disc (DVD) is a type of CD-ROM disc that can store up to 17 GB of information.

Expansion Slot

An expansion slot is a socket where you plug in an expansion card to add a new feature to your computer. The number of expansion slots your computer has indicates how many features you can add to the computer.

Hard Drive

A hard drive is the primary device that a computer uses to store information. Most computers have one hard drive, named drive C. Most hard drives have 1 GB or more of storage space.

Bytes

Bytes are used to measure the amount of information a device can store.

One byte is one character.

One kilobyte (K) is 1,024 characters. This is approximately equal to one page of double-spaced text.

One megabyte (MB) is 1,048,576 characters. This is approximately equal to one novel.

One gigabyte (GB) is 1,073,741,824 characters. This is approximately equal to 1,000 novels.

Motherboard

A motherboard is the main circuit board of a computer. All of the computer's electronic components plug into the motherboard.

TV and Radio Tuner Cards

TV tuner cards are used to listen to or watch television on your computer. The TV image appears in a window on the desktop. You can listen to the radio on your computer with the radio tuner card.

Central Processing Unit (CPU)

The Central Processing Unit (CPU) is the main chip in a computer. The CPU processes instructions, performs calculations and manages the flow of information through a computer system. Intel CPU chips are the most popular. Each new generation of CPUs is more powerful than the one before. Intel CPU generations include Intel486™ processor, Pentium®, Pentium® Pro and Pentium® II processors.

Each CPU generation is available in several speeds, which are measured in megahertz (MHz). The faster the speed, the faster the computer operates. CPUs with MMX™ technology have additional capabilities to process large data types like photographic images, audio and video. Programs must be specially designed to take advantage of MMX™ technology capabilities.

Bus

The bus is the electronic pathway in a computer that carries information between devices. Common bus structures include ISA (Industry Standard Architecture), VL-Bus (VESA Local Bus) and PCI (Peripheral Component Interconnect). SCSI (Small Computer Systems Interface) is an additional bus structure used to connect some types of drives and scanners.

Memory

Memory, also known as Random Access Memory (RAM), temporarily stores information inside a computer. The information stored in RAM is lost when you turn off the computer. The amount of memory a computer has determines the number of programs a computer can run at once and how fast programs will operate. Most computers have eight or 16 MB of RAM.

Network Interface Card

A network interface card physically connects each computer to a network. This card controls the flow of information between the network and the computer. A network is a group of connected computers that allows people to share information and devices like printers and modems.

Video Card

A video card translates instructions from the computer into a form the monitor can understand. Some computers have video capabilities included on the motherboard.

Video Capture Card

A video capture card is used to transform video from a video camera or a VCR into files that can be used by a computer.

Sound Card

A sound card lets a computer play and record sounds. A sound card allows you to record from a microphone or other audio device. Sound cards are also used to play music CDs and MIDI files as well as narration, music and effects during games. Some computers have sound capabilities included on the motherboard.

USING MY COMPUTER

My Computer provides access to all of the drives, files and folders on your computer. It also contains all of the tools you need to set up, manage and control your computer, printer and connections to other computers. Each item in a My Computer window is represented by an icon.

You can use My Computer to browse through the files and folders on your computer. You can double-click a file or folder to open it and display its contents. A folder can contain items such as documents, programs and other folders. Arranging items into folders makes items easy to find and use.

My Computer can help you manage and organize your files and folders. You can create, rename or delete files and folders in a My Computer window. You can also copy or move files and folders between windows you open using My Computer.

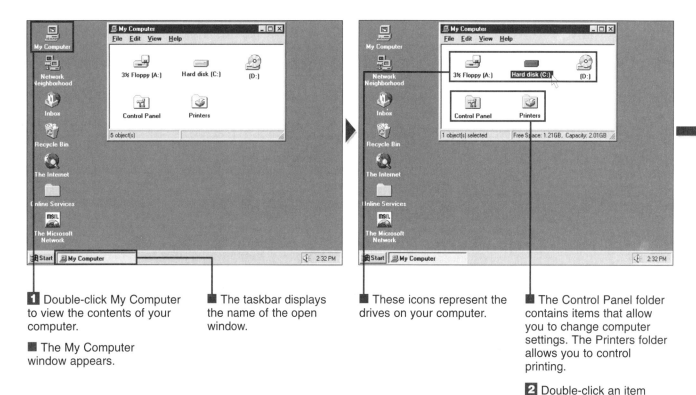

■ Double-click My Computer to view the contents of your computer.

■ The My Computer window appears.

■ The taskbar displays the name of the open window.

■ These icons represent the drives on your computer.

■ The Control Panel folder contains items that allow you to change computer settings. The Printers folder allows you to control printing.

2 Double-click an item to display its contents.

TIPS

How can I open an item if I have trouble double-clicking?

Right-click the drive, file or folder and then select Open from the menu that appears.

Is it possible to see all my open windows at the same time?

Right-click the taskbar and then select Tile Horizontally or Tile Vertically to arrange all of your open windows.

Can I change the way items look in a My Computer window?

You can change the appearance of items in your windows to make them easier to view and work with. See page 48.

How can I see the overall folder structure of the computer?

The Explorer window has two panes. One pane displays the folder structure and the other pane displays the contents of the currently selected folder. See page 58.

How can I retrace my steps?

The Backspace key lets you move back through all your open windows. You can also bring an open window to the front by clicking any part of the window or its button on the taskbar.

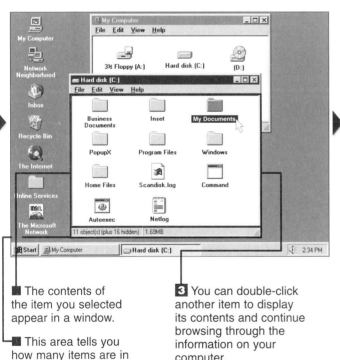

■ The contents of the item you selected appear in a window.

■ This area tells you how many items are in the window and the size of the items.

3 You can double-click another item to display its contents and continue browsing through the information on your computer.

■ The contents of the item you selected appear in a window.

4 Click ☒ to close a window.

GETTING STARTED

45

CHANGE BROWSING OPTIONS

As you browse through the files and folders on your computer, each item you open appears in a new window. You may find it difficult to locate an item you want to work with when there are many open windows. You can change the browsing options so that all items open in the same window. This prevents your screen from becoming cluttered with windows.

TIPS

Can I open a folder in the same window without changing the browsing options?

Press and hold down the Ctrl key and then double-click the folder. If you have changed the browsing options, you can use this procedure to open a folder in a new window.

Can I open a folder in an Explorer window from a My Computer window?

Select the folder you want to open. Press and hold down the Shift key and then double-click the folder.

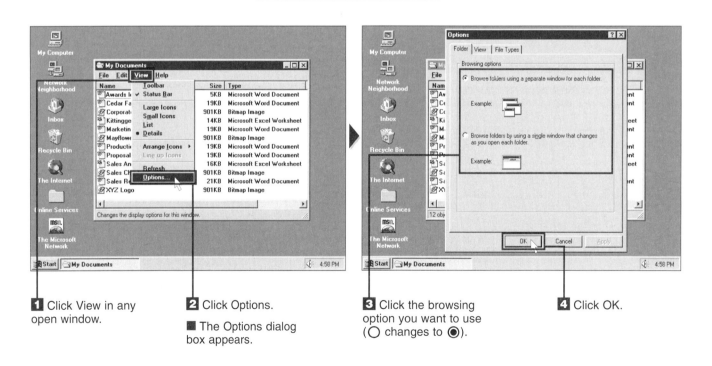

1 Click View in any open window.

2 Click Options.

■ The Options dialog box appears.

3 Click the browsing option you want to use (○ changes to ●).

4 Click OK.

SORT ITEMS

You can sort the items displayed in a window. This can help you find files and folders more easily.

Windows allows you to sort items by name, type, size or date.

Name sorts items alphabetically, from A to Z. If you know the name of the item you want to find, try sorting by name.

Type sorts items alphabetically according to their extension. If you are looking for a program, try sorting by type.

Size sorts items by their size, from smallest to largest. To find a large file, try sorting by size.

Date sorts items according to the date they were last saved, from newest to oldest. If you

know when the file you want to find was last saved, try sorting by date.

Regardless of how you sort items, Windows sorts files and folders separately and displays the folders before the files.

If a window displays column headings, you can also use the column headings to sort items.

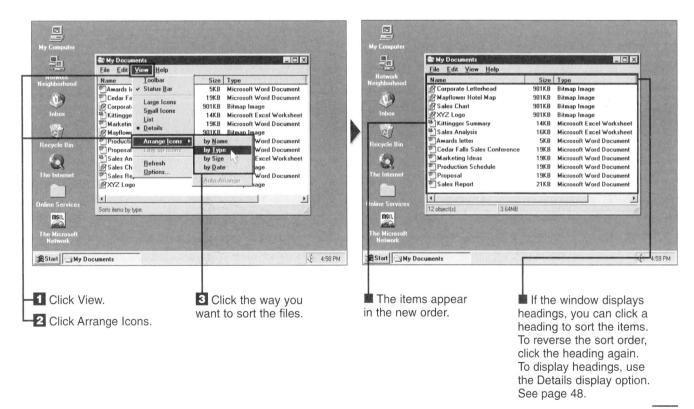

1 Click View.

2 Click Arrange Icons.

3 Click the way you want to sort the files.

■ The items appear in the new order.

■ If the window displays headings, you can click a heading to sort the items. To reverse the sort order, click the heading again. To display headings, use the Details display option. See page 48.

CHANGE VIEW OF ITEMS

You can change the view of items in a window. The view you select depends on the information you want to see in the window.

Windows displays a picture, or icon, to represent each type of item in a window. For example, the ☐ icon indicates the item is a folder. Documents created in Word display the 🐶 icon. Pictures created with the Paint program display the 🎨 icon.

When you first use Windows, items are displayed as large icons. The Large Icons view makes it easy to see the types of items available in the window.

You can choose the Small Icons view or List view to see more items in a window.

The Details view displays the items in a column and displays information such as the file

name and size. You can change the width of the columns in the Details view to make the information easier to view.

Changing the view of items affects only the open window. Each window remembers the view you selected and displays the items in that view the next time you open the window.

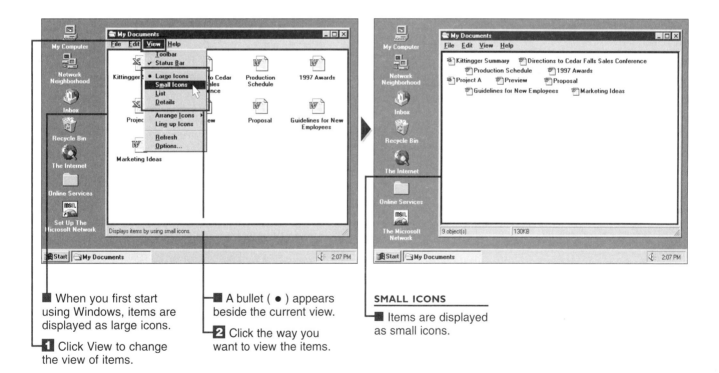

■ When you first start using Windows, items are displayed as large icons.

1 Click View to change the view of items.

■ A bullet (•) appears beside the current view.

2 Click the way you want to view the items.

SMALL ICONS

■ Items are displayed as small icons.

What is the difference between the Small Icons and List views?

The Small Icons view displays items from left to right in a window. You can arrange the items any way you like in the Small Icons view. The List view displays items from top to bottom in a window. You cannot arrange the items in the List view.

Can I refresh the items displayed in a window?

You can press the F5 key to update the items displayed in a window. This is useful if you are viewing the contents of floppy disks. When you switch disks, you can press F5 to display the contents of the second disk.

Is there a shortcut for changing views?

Choose the View menu and then select Toolbar. A toolbar appears, displaying buttons to help you change views. Click the 🔳 button to display large icons. Click the 🔳 button to display small icons. Click the 🔳 button to display items in the List view. Click the 🔳 button to display items in the Details view.

LIST

■ Items are displayed as small icons in a list.

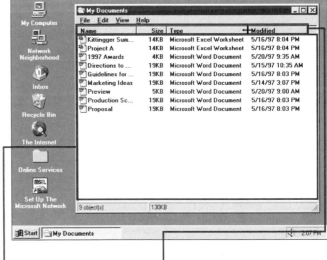

DETAILS

■ Information about each item is displayed, such as the name, size and type of item.

■ To change the width of a column, position the mouse ▷ over the right edge of a column heading (▷ changes to ◀▶) and then drag the column to a new width.

Note: To resize a column to fit the longest item, double-click the right edge of the column heading.

CHANGE VIEW OPTIONS

You can change the files and information displayed in your windows.

You can view hidden system files in your windows. Windows uses system files to control hardware devices such as printers, to save settings like the date and time and to perform tasks such as displaying mouse pointers.

Windows hides system files from view so they cannot be accidentally deleted or moved. Deleting or moving system files may affect the way your computer operates. Windows also hides system files to reduce the number of files displayed in certain folders.

You can display the path of the current folder in the title bar of the window. This is a quick way to see

the location of the folder you are viewing.

You can hide or display the MS-DOS file extension in file names. An extension is three letters following the final period in a file name. Extensions help Windows identify the program that created the file. Hiding file extensions can help reduce clutter in a window.

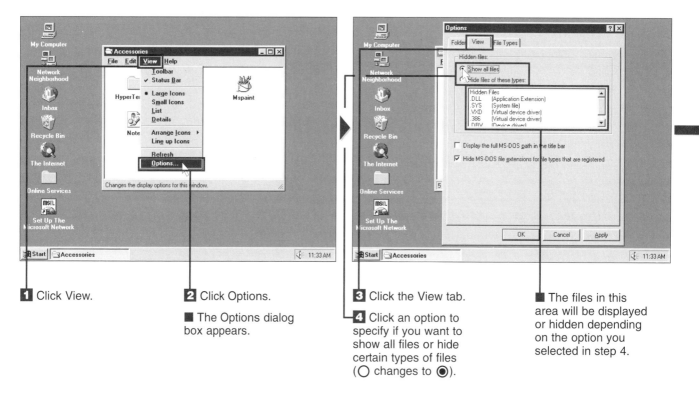

1 Click View.

2 Click Options.

■ The Options dialog box appears.

3 Click the View tab.

4 Click an option to specify if you want to show all files or hide certain types of files (○ changes to ●).

■ The files in this area will be displayed or hidden depending on the option you selected in step 4.

What is a path?

A path is a list of folders you must travel through to find a file or folder. A path starts with a drive letter and is followed by folder names. Each folder name is separated by a backslash (\). For example, the path to the StartUp folder is C:\WINDOWS\Start Menu\Programs

How can I determine the file type when file extensions are not displayed?

You can determine the file type by looking at the icon for the file. Each type of file is represented by a different icon.

Why does a warning appear when I try to change a file extension?

If you change a file extension, Windows will not know which program to associate with the file. A file without a program associated with it may not open.

The Options dialog box in Windows Explorer displays an extra option. What is it for?

In Windows Explorer, you can choose to display or hide the description bar. The description bar provides information, such as the path for the current folder, for both panes of an Explorer window.

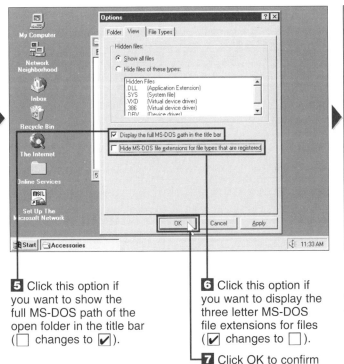

5 Click this option if you want to show the full MS-DOS path of the open folder in the title bar (☐ changes to ☑).

6 Click this option if you want to display the three letter MS-DOS file extensions for files (☑ changes to ☐).

7 Click OK to confirm your changes.

■ The title bar displays the MS-DOS path for the window if you selected the MS-DOS path option in step 5.

■ The files in the window display MS-DOS extensions if you selected the file extension option in step 6.

VIEW TOOLBAR AND STATUS BAR

Windows provides a toolbar and status bar to help you work with items in a window and display information. You can hide or display these bars to suit your needs.

The toolbar appears at the top of a window and contains buttons that help you select commonly used menu commands such as

Cut, Copy and Paste. Selecting a button on the toolbar saves you from searching for a command in a menu. If you want to find out what a button does, position the mouse pointer over the button and a description will appear.

The toolbar's drop-down list can help you find your position in the folder structure of your computer.

You can also use the list to display the contents of another item.

The status bar appears at the bottom of a window and provides information about the selected item in a window. For example, if you select a drive, the status bar will display the amount of free space on the drive, as well as the total capacity of the drive.

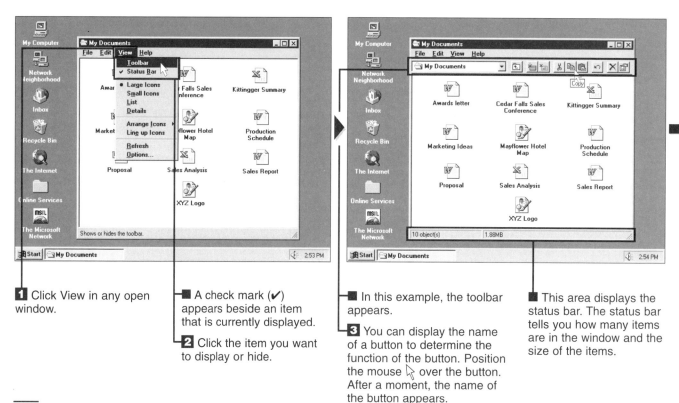

1 Click View in any open window.

■ A check mark (✔) appears beside an item that is currently displayed.

2 Click the item you want to display or hide.

■ In this example, the toolbar appears.

3 You can display the name of a button to determine the function of the button. Position the mouse ⟍ over the button. After a moment, the name of the button appears.

■ This area displays the status bar. The status bar tells you how many items are in the window and the size of the items.

TIPS

GETTING STARTED

When I display the toolbar in a window, why doesn't the next window I open also display the toolbar?

The toolbar and status bar settings must be changed for each window. By default, the status bar is displayed and the toolbar is not. When you change these settings for a window, the settings you choose will be used each time the window is opened.

Can I change the default settings for new folders I create?

Set up a My Computer window with the settings you want to display in the new folder's window. Press and hold down the Ctrl key and then click ☒ to close the My Computer window. Each new folder you create will display these settings.

Can I change the way items are displayed in a window?

You can click ▣ to display items as large icons and ▣ to display items as small icons. You can use the ▣ button to display the items as small icons in a list and the ▣ button to provide details about each item, such as size and type.

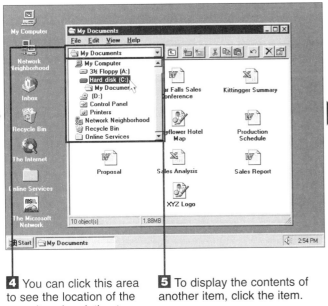

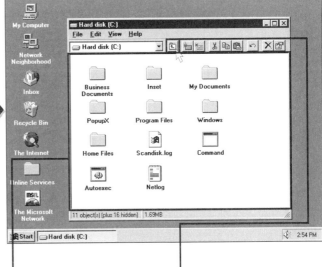

4 You can click this area to see the location of the open item in relation to other items on your computer.

5 To display the contents of another item, click the item.

■ The contents of the item you selected appear.

6 Click ▣ to move back through the series of folders.

ARRANGE ICONS AUTOMATICALLY

You can have Windows automatically arrange your icons to fit neatly in a window. If your icons are scattered or piled one on top of another, arranging your icons will make the contents of your window easier to view.

The Auto Arrange feature places your icons at a fixed distance

from one another in neat rows and columns. The icons will remain neatly arranged even if you resize the window or add and remove icons.

When the Auto Arrange feature is on, you can move an icon to a new location in a window. The other icons will shift to make space for the icon but will stay

in the rows and columns. You cannot move an icon to a blank area of the window.

Just as you can arrange the icons in a window, you can also arrange icons on your desktop. Windows will arrange all the icons on your desktop in columns, starting at the left edge of your screen.

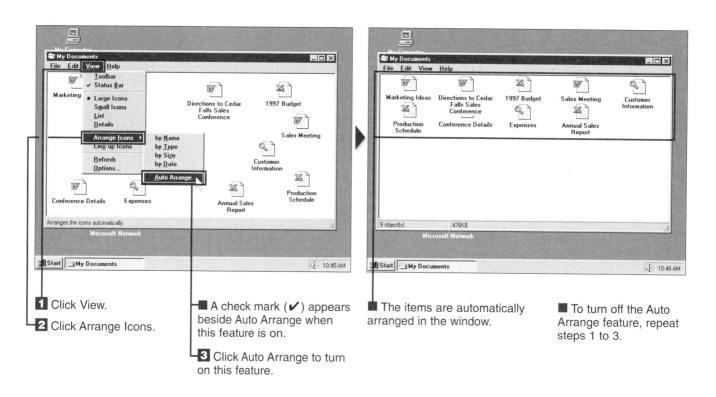

1 Click View.

2 Click Arrange Icons.

■ A check mark (✔) appears beside Auto Arrange when this feature is on.

3 Click Auto Arrange to turn on this feature.

■ The items are automatically arranged in the window.

■ To turn off the Auto Arrange feature, repeat steps 1 to 3.

TIPS

Is there another way to neatly line up the icons in a window?

Choose the View menu and then select Line up Icons to have Windows move the icons to the nearest row or column. Unlike Auto Arrange, the icons will not shift if other icons are added or removed in the window.

Why is the Auto Arrange feature not available?

The Auto Arrange feature is not available when your icons are displayed in the List or Details view. For information on changing the view, see page 48.

I placed a folder icon on top of another folder icon and it disappeared. Why?

Windows thought you wanted to store one folder inside the other. From the Edit menu, select the Undo Move command to restore the folder that disappeared.

If you place a document icon on top of a program icon, the program starts and opens the document.

How can I move icons closer together or farther apart?

You can change icon spacing by changing the Appearance settings in the Display Properties dialog box. For information on Appearance settings, see page 204.

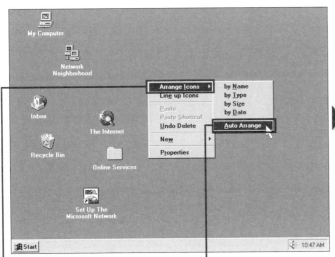

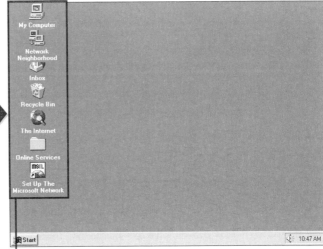

ARRANGE DESKTOP ITEMS

1 Right-click an empty area on the desktop. A menu appears.

2 Click Arrange Icons.

3 Click Auto Arrange.

■ The items are automatically arranged on the desktop.

PRINT CONTENTS OF A FOLDER

You can create, edit and print a list of the files stored in any folder on your computer. This can include a folder on your hard drive, a removable drive, a floppy disk or a tape.

A printed listing can help you organize information on your computer. You can create a printed index of the contents of your floppy or removeable disks.

A listing is helpful when you are trying to create more free disk space. You can see which files you no longer need and which files are duplicated in several folders.

Although the ability to print the contents of a folder is not included in either My Computer or Explorer, you can use the MS-DOS directory (dir) command. This command displays a listing on your screen. Additional

commands are used to save the listing in a file that you can open, edit and print.

MS-DOS commands require strict attention to detail. Carefully note the spelling, punctuation and spaces that are used or the command will not work.

When you double-click the file, it will open as a Notepad document. If the listing is large, you will be able to use WordPad instead.

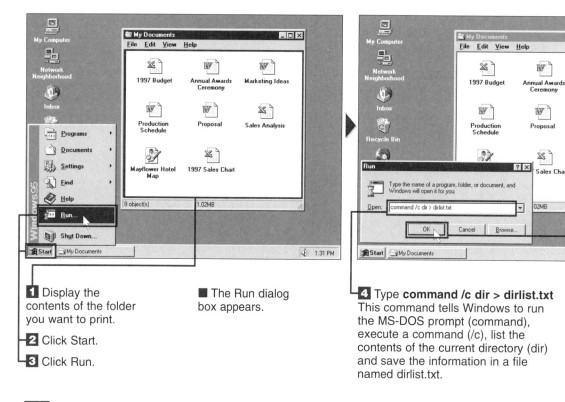

1 Display the contents of the folder you want to print.

2 Click Start.

3 Click Run.

■ The Run dialog box appears.

4 Type **command /c dir > dirlist.txt** This command tells Windows to run the MS-DOS prompt (command), execute a command (/c), list the contents of the current directory (dir) and save the information in a file named dirlist.txt.

5 Click OK.

How can I create a listing of all the files in the folders contained in the current folder?

Use the /s command. For example, type **command /c dir /s > dirlist.txt**

Can I save the listing in a different file?

Instead of typing **dirlist.txt**, type the name of the file you want. For example, type **command /c dir > files.doc**

How do I create a listing of all the folders and files on my hard drive?

Type **command /c dir c:\ /s > dirlist.txt** You can replace c: with any drive letter.

Can I print the listing without saving it?

At the command prompt, type **command /c dir > lpt1** This command will only work if you have a printer that is connected to your parallel port and can print plain text.

Is it possible to sort the listing?

To sort by name, type the **/on** command. To sort by date, type the **/od** command. For example, type **command /c dir /od > dirlist.txt** You can type **command /k dir /?** to view all the options you can use with the dir command.

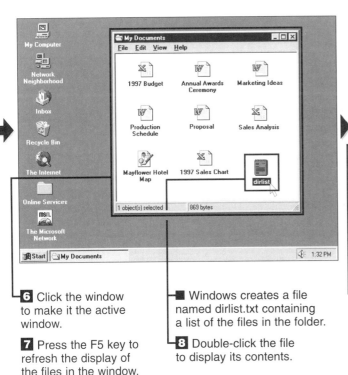

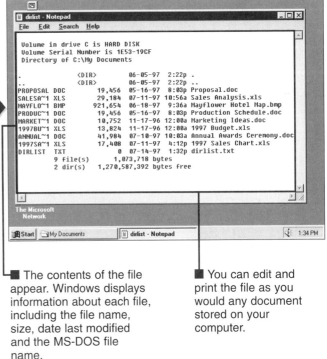

■6 Click the window to make it the active window.

■7 Press the F5 key to refresh the display of the files in the window.

■ Windows creates a file named dirlist.txt containing a list of the files in the folder.

■8 Double-click the file to display its contents.

■ The contents of the file appear. Windows displays information about each file, including the file name, size, date last modified and the MS-DOS file name.

■ You can edit and print the file as you would any document stored on your computer.

USING WINDOWS EXPLORER

Like a map, Windows Explorer shows you the location of every file and folder on your computer. The Explorer window helps you understand the relationship between files and folders on your computer. You can use Explorer to find and view drives and folders on your computer,

including the Control Panel, Printers and Dial-Up Networking.

The Explorer window has two panes. The left pane shows the structure of your drives and folders. The right pane shows the contents of the drive or folder selected in the left pane. You can expand the information available in the left pane to show some or

all of the drives and folders available on your computer. You can also reduce the information in the left pane to provide an overview of the items available on your computer.

You can use Explorer to manage and organize files, start programs and open documents.

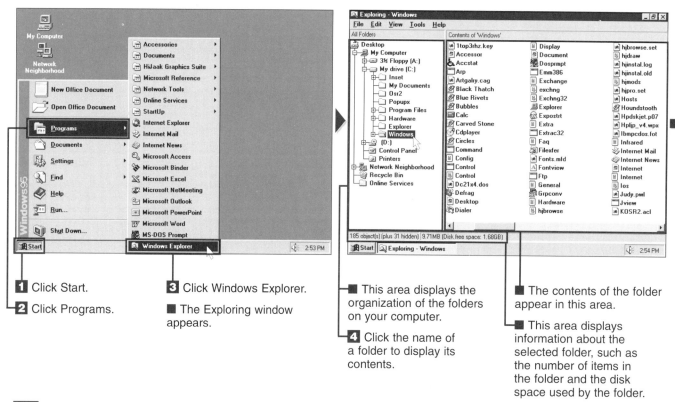

1 Click Start.

2 Click Programs.

3 Click Windows Explorer.

■ The Exploring window appears.

■ This area displays the organization of the folders on your computer.

4 Click the name of a folder to display its contents.

■ The contents of the folder appear in this area.

■ This area displays information about the selected folder, such as the number of items in the folder and the disk space used by the folder.

Can I start Explorer without using the Start menu?

Right-click My Computer or the Start button and then select Explore.

How do I list all the drives and folders without clicking each plus sign ([+])?

To list all the drives and folders, hold down the Alt key and press the [*] key on the numeric keypad. You can list all the items within a folder by selecting a folder and then pressing the [*] key on the numeric keypad. To again display only the main folder, click the minus sign ([-]) beside the top folder and then press the F5 key.

How do I open a file or folder using Explorer?

You can double-click a file or folder in the right pane.

How can I see all the files in a folder, including the hidden files?

Choose the View menu and then select Options. See page 50.

Can I see how much disk space is available on my drives?

Select My Computer in the left pane. Choose the View menu and then click Details. The column headings will change to display the Total Size and Free Space on each drive.

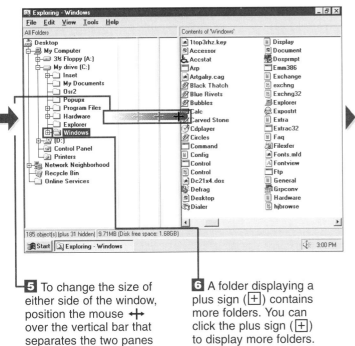

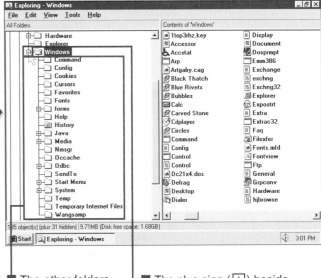

5 To change the size of either side of the window, position the mouse ↔ over the vertical bar that separates the two panes and drag the bar to a new location.

6 A folder displaying a plus sign ([+]) contains more folders. You can click the plus sign ([+]) to display more folders.

■ The other folders appear.

■ The plus sign ([+]) beside the folder changes to a minus sign ([-]). This indicates that all the folders within the folder are displayed.

■ You can click the minus sign ([-]) to once again display only the main folder.

59

SELECT FILES

Before you can work with a file or folder, you must select the item. For example, you can copy, move, delete or open a file or folder you select. When you select a file or folder, Windows highlights the item.

You can select and work with multiple files and folders.

This lets you perform the same procedure on several files and folders at the same time. Working with multiple files and folders saves you from repeating the same tasks over and over.

You can select files and folders using different techniques. The best way to select a group of files will depend on which view you

use to display the items. For example, when you are working in the Large or Small Icons view, you can drag the mouse to form a rectangle around the group of files you want to select. For information on the ways to view items, see page 48.

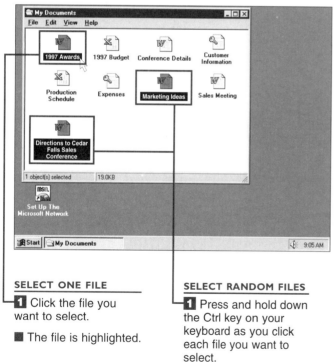

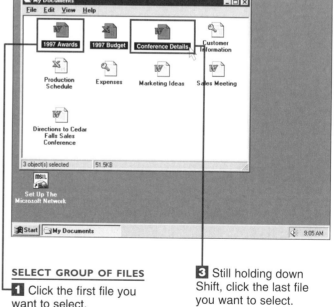

SELECT ONE FILE

■1 Click the file you want to select.

■ The file is highlighted.

SELECT RANDOM FILES

■1 Press and hold down the Ctrl key on your keyboard as you click each file you want to select.

SELECT GROUP OF FILES

■1 Click the first file you want to select.

■2 Press and hold down Shift on your keyboard.

■3 Still holding down Shift, click the last file you want to select.

TIPS

How do I deselect files or folders and start over?

Select any file or folder that is not currently selected.

I am trying to select multiple files, but the wrong files are being selected. What is the problem?

The way files are displayed in a window can affect the way they are selected. In the Small Icons view, files are selected by rows first, starting at the top of the window. In the List view, files are selected by columns first, from the left side of the window.

Is there an easy way to select all but a few files in a folder?

You can select all the files in a folder and then hold down the Ctrl key while you click the files you do not want. You can also select the files you do not want and then choose the Edit menu and select Invert Selection.

How do I remove one file or folder from a group I have selected?

Hold down the Ctrl key while you click on the file or folder you want to deselect.

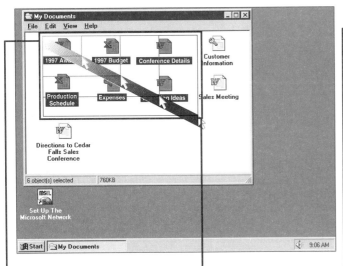

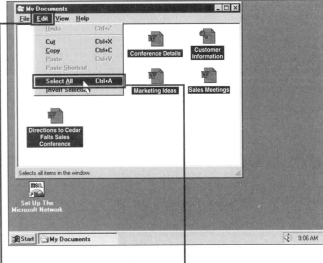

SELECT GROUP OF FILES

You can also select a group of files by dragging the mouse.

1 Position the mouse to the left of the first file you want to select.

2 Drag the mouse to form a rectangle around the files you want to select.

SELECT ALL FILES

1 Click Edit to select all items in a window.

2 Click Select All.

MOVE AND COPY FILES

You can move or copy your files when you want to take work home, share documents with a colleague or reorganize files on your hard drive. Copying files is also useful for making backup copies.

When you move a file, you delete the file from its original location.

When you copy a file, you create a second file that is exactly the same as the first. You can place the copy in another folder on your computer, a network drive or on a floppy or removable disk. If you create a copy in the same folder, Windows will add "Copy of" to the file name.

You can also move and copy folders. When you move or copy a folder, all files in the folder are also moved or copied.

When you drag and drop a file, the result depends on the file's destination. When you drag a file onto a different folder on the same drive, Windows moves the file. When you drag a file onto a different drive, Windows copies the file.

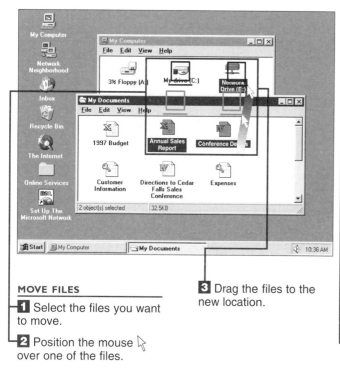

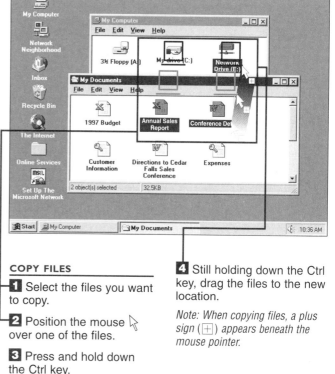

MOVE FILES

1 Select the files you want to move.

2 Position the mouse ⌖ over one of the files.

3 Drag the files to the new location.

COPY FILES

1 Select the files you want to copy.

2 Position the mouse ⌖ over one of the files.

3 Press and hold down the Ctrl key.

4 Still holding down the Ctrl key, drag the files to the new location.

Note: When copying files, a plus sign (⊞) appears beneath the mouse pointer.

TIPS

How do I move a file to a different drive?

When you drag a file to a different drive, a plus sign (⊞) appears, indicating Windows will make a copy. To move the file, hold down the Shift key.

I tried to move an application, but Windows created a shortcut instead. What should I do?

To move an application, hold down the Shift key as you drag the application. To copy an application, hold down the Ctrl key as you drag the application. If you move programs from the directory where they were created, they may not function properly.

I frequently move files to the same folder. How can I simplify this procedure?

To add a folder you use frequently to the Send To menu, see page 216. To place a shortcut to the folder on your desktop, see page 88.

My computer screen is crowded when I try to view two open folders. How else can I move and copy files?

Select the files you want to move or copy. Right-click one of the files. To move the files, click Cut. To copy the files, click Copy. Open the folder where you want the files to appear. Right-click a blank area of the folder and then click Paste.

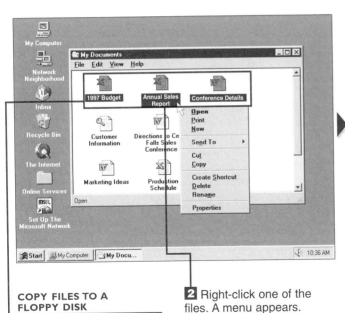

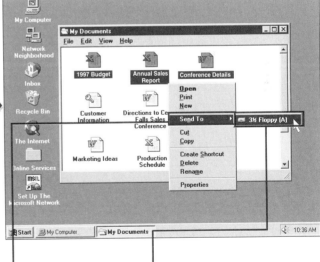

COPY FILES TO A FLOPPY DISK

1 Select the files you want to copy to a floppy disk.

2 Right-click one of the files. A menu appears.

3 Click Send To.

4 Click the drive you want to receive a copy of the files.

OPEN FILES

You can open a file directly from My Computer or Windows Explorer to display its contents on your screen.

Each file on your computer is associated with an application. When you open a file, the associated application starts automatically. For example, bitmap files with the extension

.bmp are usually associated with the Paint application. When you open a file with the .bmp extension, the Paint application starts and the file is opened.

If Windows does not know which application to start, the Open With dialog box appears. You can then choose which application you want to use to display the file. For example, a

software company may include an information file named readme.1st on their installation disks. Although readme.1st is a text file, the extension (.1st) is not associated with any Windows application. Windows does not know which application to start to open the file. You can use the Open With dialog box to specify the application you want to start to display the file.

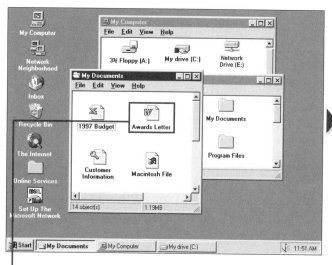

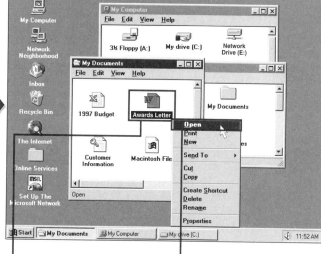

1 Locate the file you want to open.

■ You can use My Computer or Windows Explorer to browse through the contents of your computer to find a file you want to open.

2 Right-click the file you want to open. A menu appears.

3 Click Open.

Note: You can double-click the file instead of performing steps 2 and 3.

TIPS

Where are my files stored?

Your files are stored in the folders where they were created. The Open and Save As dialog boxes for each application display the name of the folder where your files are stored.

How can I find files created in a specific application?

From the Start menu click Find and then select Files or Folders. Use the Advanced tab to set the Of type option to the application type you are looking for. See page 78.

Can I verify this is the file I want before I open the file?

You can right-click the file and select Quick View to preview the file without opening the application. See page 80.

How do I change the association between a file type and an application?

Press and hold down the Shift key, then right-click the file. Click Open With to select the application you want to associate with the file. Then click Always use this program to open this type of file.

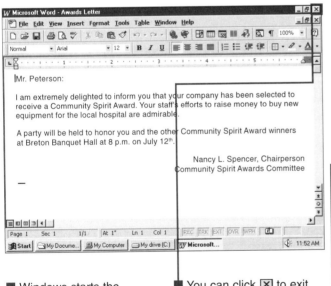

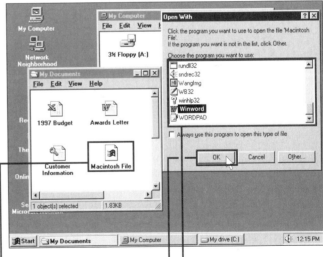

■ Windows starts the appropriate program and displays the contents of the file. You can now review and make changes to the file.

■ You can click ☒ to exit the program.

■ The Open With dialog box appears if Windows does not know which program to use to open a file you selected.

■ In this example we open a Macintosh file.

1 Click the program you want to use to open the file.

■ Windows will use the program you select to open this file.

2 Click OK to open the file.

OPEN RECENTLY USED FILES

Windows helps you quickly find and open a file you recently worked with.

Windows remembers the last files you opened or saved and displays the names of the files in a list on the Start menu. You can quickly open any of these files to review or make changes to the file.

When you select a file from the list in the Start menu, the program starts and the file opens. Selecting a file from the list saves you from searching through folders on your computer to find the file you want to open.

Windows displays the files in the Start menu in alphabetical order to make it easier to find

the file you are looking for. A small icon appears beside each file to indicate which program was used to create the file.

You can clear the list of recently used files at any time. Clearing the list is useful when the list becomes cluttered or contains many files you no longer need to work with.

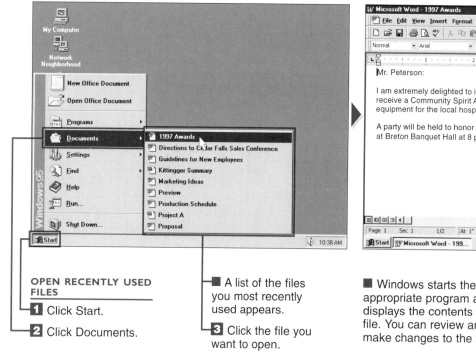

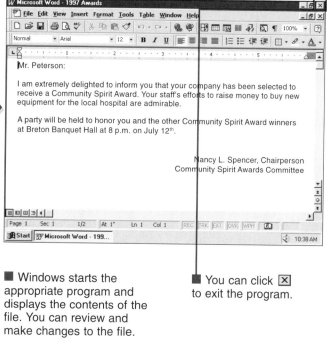

OPEN RECENTLY USED FILES

1 Click Start.

2 Click Documents.

■ A list of the files you most recently used appears.

3 Click the file you want to open.

■ Windows starts the appropriate program and displays the contents of the file. You can review and make changes to the file.

■ You can click ☒ to exit the program.

TIPS

How can I add files to the list of recently used files?

You can add a file to the list in the Start menu by opening the file. There is no procedure that will place a file on the list permanently.

Can I have Windows automatically clear the list in the Start menu?

You can use Tweak UI from the PowerToy collection to automatically clear the list of files from the Start menu every time you restart the computer. For information on the PowerToy utilities, see page 602.

Why is a file not listed in the Start menu?

A file will not appear on the list of recently used files if you use a program that was not designed for Windows 95. A file also may not appear in the Start menu list if you drag and drop the file on a program icon. If you open a file in an e-mail message, the file will also not appear in the list.

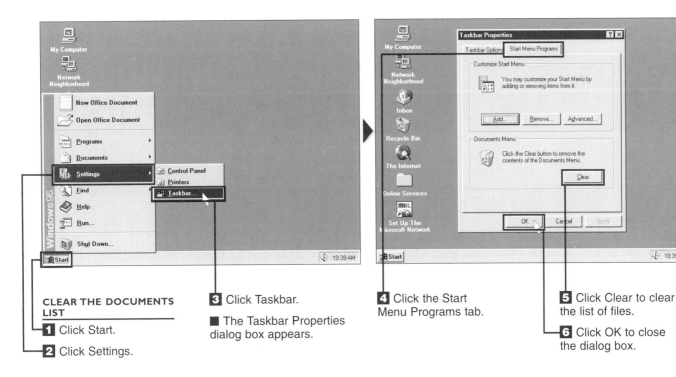

CLEAR THE DOCUMENTS LIST

1 Click Start.

2 Click Settings.

3 Click Taskbar.

■ The Taskbar Properties dialog box appears.

4 Click the Start Menu Programs tab.

5 Click Clear to clear the list of files.

6 Click OK to close the dialog box.

RENAME FILES

You can change the name of a file to better describe its contents. This makes it easier for you to find the file later. When naming your files, use a keyword that will identify the file, such as the name of a client, a project or an event.

In Windows 95, you can use up to 255 characters to name a file. You can also include spaces and periods. The only characters you cannot use to name a file are the symbols \ / : * ? | " < or >. If you use periods in the file name, only the letters after the last period will be used as the file's extension.

An MS-DOS name has eight characters and a three-character extension. To shorten the name, Windows takes the first six letters, inserts the tilde (~) character and a number. You can see the shortened name used by older programs in the file's Properties dialog box.

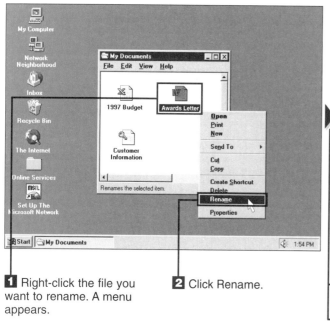

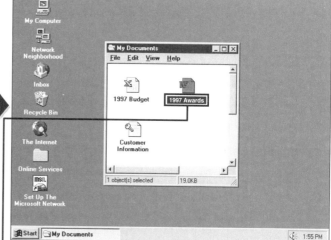

1 Right-click the file you want to rename. A menu appears.

2 Click Rename.

■ A box appears around the file name.

3 Type a new name and then press the Enter key.

Note: You can edit the file name instead of replacing it. Click the file name where you want to make the change.

■ If you change your mind while typing a name, press the Esc key to return to the original name.

TIPS

Can I rename folders?

You can rename folders, but make sure you only change the names of folders that contain documents. If you change the names of program or system folders, Windows will not be able to find the files it needs to operate.

Can I use both upper and lower case letters to name a file?

You can type upper and lower case letters to make file names easier to read, but Windows does not recognize the difference between upper and lower case letters. For example, Windows sees ReadMe.txt, README.TXT and readme.txt as identical names.

Can I use the same file name for two different files?

You can use the same file name for two different files if the files are located in different folders.

Are long file names compatible with all programs?

Some programs, such as older backup programs and other disk utility programs, do not support long file names. If you use these programs, you must save all your files with an MS-DOS file name.

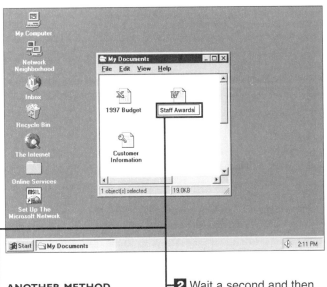

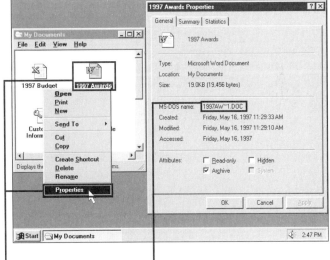

ANOTHER METHOD

1 Click the name of the file you want to rename.

2 Wait a second and then click the name of the file again. You can also press the F2 key.

Note: If you accidentally double-click the file, the file will open.

3 Type a new name and then press the Enter key.

DISPLAY MS-DOS FILE NAME

1 Right-click the file. A menu appears.

2 Click Properties.

■ The Properties dialog box appears.

■ This area displays the file name in MS-DOS format. Some programs use this format for your files.

DELETE FILES

You can remove documents, folders and applications you no longer need to free up space on your computer. If you delete a folder, Windows erases all the files and folders inside the folder. To protect you from accidentally erasing files, Windows stores deleted files in the Recycle Bin.

As a precaution, Windows asks you to confirm the files you are erasing. Additional confirmations appear if the files you are deleting are programs or system files. Make sure you do not delete system files required to run Windows or files required by programs you still use. Do not delete any file unless

you are certain you no longer need the file.

Before you delete documents, consider the value of your work. You may want to save a copy on a floppy disk or a backup tape or drive. The cost of blank disks and tapes is small compared to the cost of recreating a document.

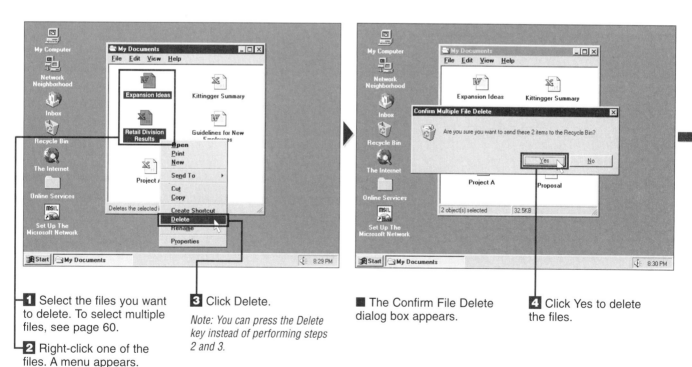

1 Select the files you want to delete. To select multiple files, see page 60.

2 Right-click one of the files. A menu appears.

3 Click Delete.

Note: You can press the Delete key instead of performing steps 2 and 3.

■ The Confirm File Delete dialog box appears.

4 Click Yes to delete the files.

How do I delete a sensitive file so it cannot be recovered?

Select the file and then press the Shift and Delete keys. The file will be deleted from your computer and will not appear in the Recycle Bin.

Which files are safe to delete?

You can safely erase any files and folders in the c:\windows\temp folder. Restart your system and then delete all files and folders in this folder. Your computer may also contain many documents which start with "Backup of." Once you have finished working on a document, you may safely delete the backup.

Can I turn off the Confirm File Delete dialog box?

The Recycle Bin provides many options, including turning off the confirmations. See page 74 .

Is there another way to delete a file?

You can drag and drop a file to the Recycle Bin to delete the file. When you drag and drop the file to the Recycle Bin, the confirmation dialog box does not appear.

Are all files saved in the Recycle Bin?

Files deleted from floppy disks or other removable disks are not saved in the Recycle Bin and cannot be recovered.

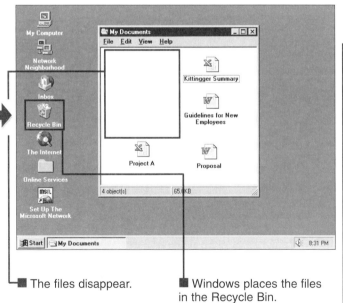

■ The files disappear.

■ Windows places the files in the Recycle Bin.

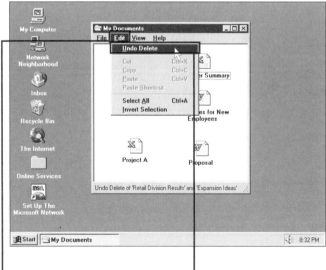

■ You can immediately restore files you just accidentally deleted.

1 Click Edit.

2 Click Undo Delete.

RESTORE DELETED FILES

The Recycle Bin is a special folder that stores the files you have deleted. If you have accidentally deleted a file, you will probably find it in the Recycle Bin. You can then restore the file to its original location on your computer. You cannot restore files deleted from a floppy disk, removable disk or network drive. Files deleted from these items are not stored in the Recycle Bin.

When you are certain that you no longer need the files in the Recycle Bin, you can use the Empty Recycle Bin command to remove all the files and increase the available disk space on your computer. When you empty the Recycle Bin, all the files are removed from your computer.

When the Recycle Bin fills up with deleted files, the Recycle Bin will permanently remove older and larger files without warning you.

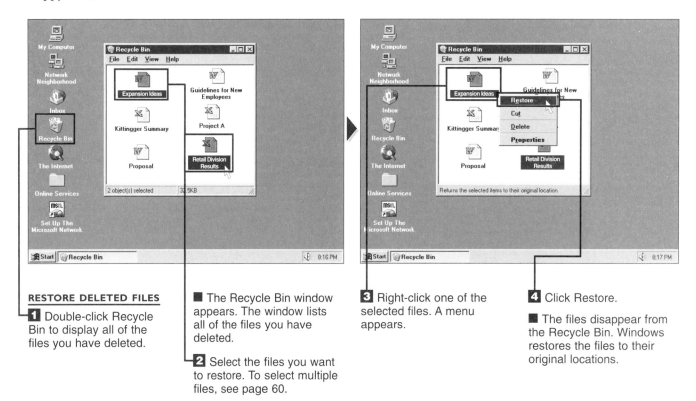

RESTORE DELETED FILES

1 Double-click Recycle Bin to display all of the files you have deleted.

■ The Recycle Bin window appears. The window lists all of the files you have deleted.

2 Select the files you want to restore. To select multiple files, see page 60.

3 Right-click one of the selected files. A menu appears.

4 Click Restore.

■ The files disappear from the Recycle Bin. Windows restores the files to their original locations.

TIPS

How can I see the files listed and sorted by their original folder locations?

You can list and sort Recycle Bin files just like other windows by choosing the View menu and selecting Details. The Original Location column in the Recycle Bin shows where the deleted files came from.

How do I restore a deleted folder?

A deleted folder will not appear in the Recycle Bin. When you restore one of the files that was in the deleted folder, the folder is also restored to its original location.

How do I restore a file to a different folder?

Use My Computer or Explorer to open the folder where you want to place the files. Then drag the files from the Recycle Bin to the open folder.

I deleted a file and it is not in the Recycle Bin. What happened to my file?

If you delete a large file or many files at once, the files may bypass the Recycle Bin and be permanently deleted. Files deleted at the DOS prompt are not saved in the Recycle Bin.

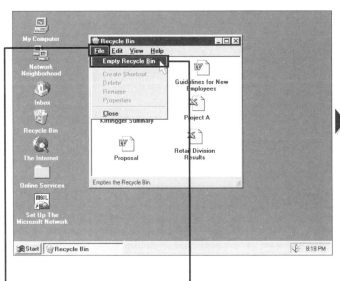

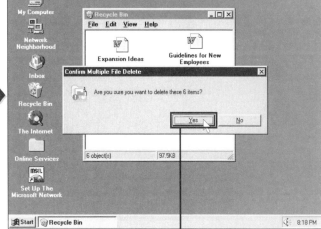

EMPTY THE RECYCLE BIN

1 Click File in the Recycle Bin window.

2 Click Empty Recycle Bin.

■ A dialog box appears, confirming the deletion.

3 Click Yes to permanently remove all the files from the Recycle Bin.

■ The files disappear and are permanently removed from your computer.

CHANGE RECYCLE BIN PROPERTIES

The Recycle Bin protects you from accidents, by temporarily saving the files you delete. Files cannot be saved in the Recycle Bin forever. You can change the properties of the Recycle Bin to give you the kind of protection you want.

The Recycle Bin normally uses up to 10% of your hard drive's space to store deleted files. On a 1 GB drive this means as much as

100 MB may be used by the Recycle Bin. By checking the status of files in the Recycle Bin for a week or two, you can estimate how much space is needed to safeguard a day's, week's or month's worth of work. You can then adjust the settings accordingly.

If you have more than one drive on your computer, each drive can

have its own Recycle Bin settings. If you use one drive to store your applications and the other for documents, you may want to use a larger setting for the document drive and a smaller setting for the applications' drive.

You can delete files more quickly by removing confirmation dialog boxes.

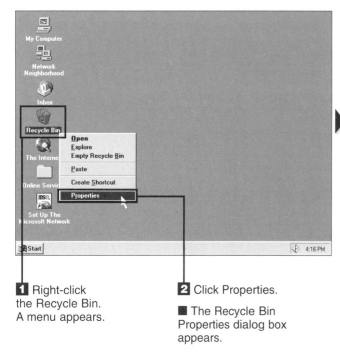

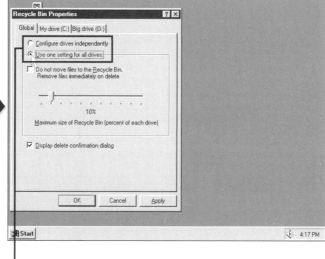

1 Right-click the Recycle Bin. A menu appears.

2 Click Properties.

■ The Recycle Bin Properties dialog box appears.

3 You can choose to use different Recycle Bin settings for each drive or use the same settings for all of your drives. Click the option you want to use (○ changes to ◉).

TIPS

How can I find out how much space the Recycle Bin is using?

Right-click the Recycle Bin and then click Properties. On the Global tab, Windows displays the amount of space it uses for the Recycle Bin.

How do I adjust the size of the Recycle Bin for drives that do not have a tab, like my removable hard drive?

The Recycle Bin does not store files you delete from these types of drives.

How can I bypass the Recycle Bin and delete a sensitive or private document immediately without changing the settings for all files?

To delete a selected file or group of files permanently, hold down the Shift key while you press the Delete key. A dialog box will confirm your deletion. If the file is already in the Recycle Bin, just delete the file as you would delete any file.

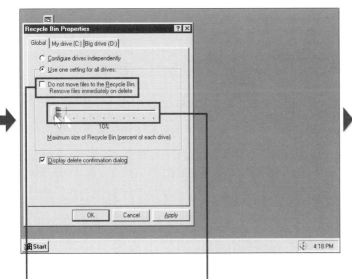

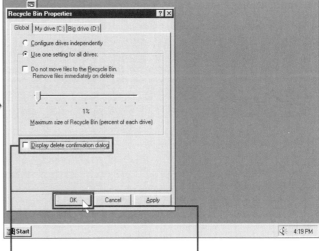

4 Files you delete are sent to the Recycle Bin. You can click this option if you want to permanently remove files you delete rather than send them to the Recycle Bin (☐ changes to ✔).

5 To change the size of the Recycle Bin, drag the slider (⬇) to a new location.

6 Windows displays a warning message when you delete files. You can click this option if you do not want the warning message to appear (✔ changes to ☐).

Note: This option is not available if you selected "Do not move files to the Recycle Bin" in step 4.

7 Click OK to confirm all of your changes.

FIND FILES

If you cannot remember the name or location of a file you want to work with, you can have Windows search for the file.

You can have Windows search for a specific word in the file name. For example, a search for a file named "report" will find every file or folder that contains the word "report" in its name. This is useful if you know all or part of the name of the file.

You can specify where you want Windows to search for a file. If you do not limit the search to a specific drive or folder, Windows will search all of the drives on your computer. This is useful if you cannot remember where the file is located.

You can also search for files based on the date the file was created or last changed. This is useful if you know the file was saved during a specific time period.

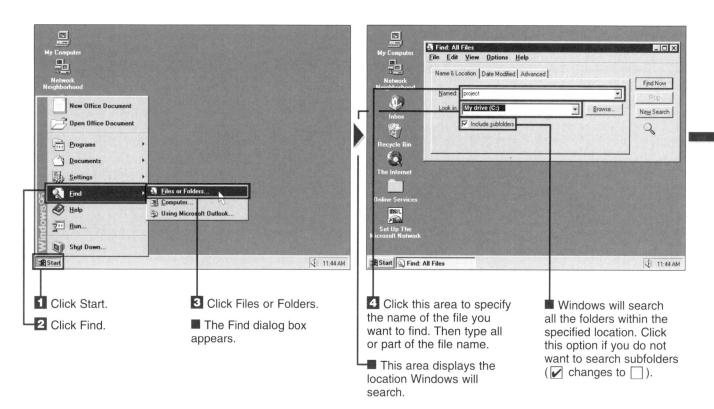

1 Click Start.

2 Click Find.

3 Click Files or Folders.

■ The Find dialog box appears.

4 Click this area to specify the name of the file you want to find. Then type all or part of the file name.

■ This area displays the location Windows will search.

■ Windows will search all the folders within the specified location. Click this option if you do not want to search subfolders (☑ changes to ☐).

TIPS

Can I use wildcards to find files with specific characters in their names?

You can use the asterisk (*) or a question mark (?) to find files. The asterisk (*) represents many characters. The question mark (?) represents a single character. For example, type d*.xls to find all Microsoft Excel files with names beginning with the letter d.

Can I enter two words in the Named field?

If you enter two words in the Named field, Windows will locate every file that has at least one of the words in its name.

If I only remember the date I saved a file, can Windows locate the file?

You can find a file by searching for the date the file was created. If you leave the Named field blank, Windows will search for all files that meet other characteristics you select.

Can I list all the files on my drive?

To see a list of all the files in all the folders on a drive, use the Find feature without specifying any information in the fields.

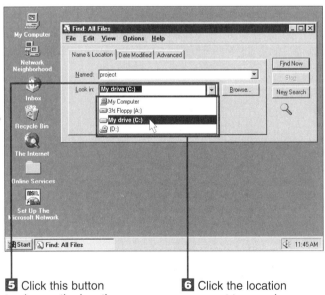

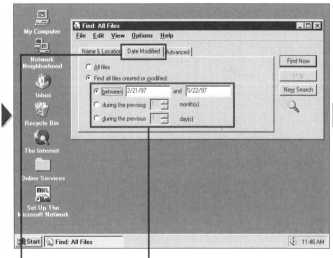

5 Click this button to change the location where Windows will search for the file.

6 Click the location you want to search.

7 Click the Date Modified tab to narrow your search to a specific time period.

8 Click one of these options to find all files that were created or changed during a specific time period (○ changes to ●).

9 Enter the appropriate information.

CONTINUED

77

FIND FILES CONTINUED

Windows allows you to narrow your search to find the file you want.

You can search for a specific type of file. This is useful if you want to locate a file such as an application or screen saver.

If you know a word or phrase that the file contains, you can have Windows search for this information. Searching by file content slows down the search.

Windows can search for a file based on size. This is helpful if you want to find large files that are taking up a lot of drive space. You can search for files that are exactly the size you specify, larger or smaller than the size you specify.

Windows displays all the matching files and information about each file, such as its name, location, size and type. You can open and work with any files Windows finds just as you would open and work with files in a My Computer or Explorer window.

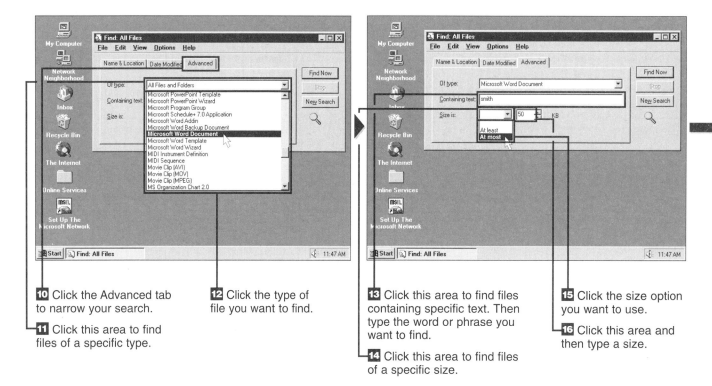

10 Click the Advanced tab to narrow your search.

11 Click this area to find files of a specific type.

12 Click the type of file you want to find.

13 Click this area to find files containing specific text. Then type the word or phrase you want to find.

14 Click this area to find files of a specific size.

15 Click the size option you want to use.

16 Click this area and then type a size.

TIPS

Can I stop Find once it has found the file I am looking for?

You can click the Stop button at any time to end the search.

How can I have Windows only find files where the word "Report" is capitalized?

From the Options menu, select Case Sensitive. Windows will only find words in the document that appear exactly as the word you typed.

Can I save a search to use the same settings again?

From the File menu, select Save Search. The search appears as an icon on your desktop. Double-click the icon to display the Find dialog box with your saved search settings. You can also save the files Windows finds along with the settings you specified. Before starting the search, choose the Options menu and select Save Results.

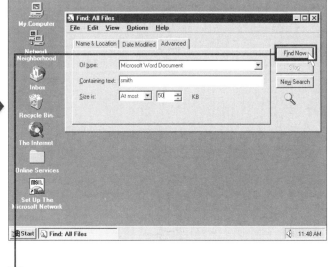

17 Click Find Now to start the search.

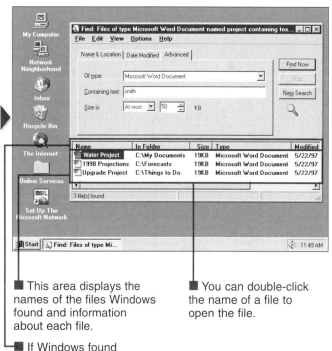

■ This area displays the names of the files Windows found and information about each file.

■ If Windows found several files, you can click a heading to sort the files.

■ You can double-click the name of a file to open the file.

PREVIEW A FILE

You can use the Quick View feature to view the contents of a file without starting the program that created the file. Quick View helps you quickly decide whether the file you selected is the one you want to work with.

You cannot use Quick View to edit a file. Once you have found the file you are looking for, you can use Quick View to start the application and open the file so you can edit it.

When you are viewing a text document, you can change the font size in Quick View to make the text easier to read. When you change the font size of your document in Quick View, the font size of the original file does not change.

You can select the Page View mode to see a full page of your image or document in the Quick View window. The Page View mode simulates what the document will look like. For an accurate view of the document, you must open the document.

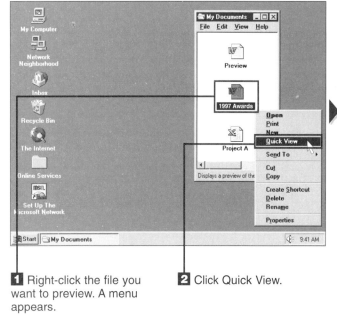

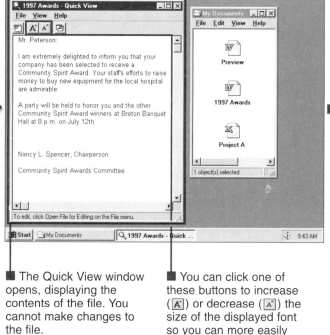

1 Right-click the file you want to preview. A menu appears.

2 Click Quick View.

■ The Quick View window opens, displaying the contents of the file. You cannot make changes to the file.

■ You can click one of these buttons to increase (A⁺) or decrease (A⁻) the size of the displayed font so you can more easily view the information.

Why is Quick View not an option on my right-click menu?

If Quick View is not available, either you cannot preview the type of file you selected or you must install the Quick View component. To add Windows components, see page 580.

How can I preview more types of documents?

You can purchase a utility called Quick View Plus, created by the same developers, to view more types of documents.

My image is upside-down. How can I fix it?

If your saved fax files or other images are upside-down, choose the View menu and select Rotate to turn the images right-side up. This command is not available when Page View is selected.

How can I view my documents in a single window?

Each document will appear in a new Quick View window. If you choose the Replace Window option, Quick View will open new documents using a single window. You can also drag and drop a file into the open Quick View window to preview the file.

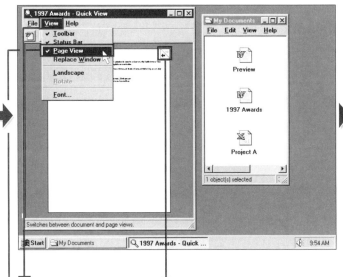

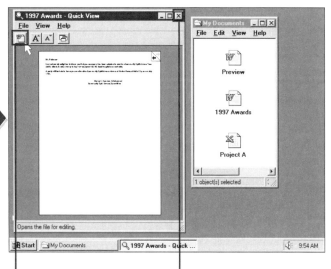

3 To display an entire page, click View.

4 Click Page View.

■ If the file contains more than one page, arrows appear in this area. You can click the arrows to move back and forth between the pages.

Note: To once again view just a portion of the page, repeat steps 3 and 4.

5 To open the file so you can make changes, click 📝.

Note: The appearance of the button varies, depending on the type of file you are viewing.

■ To close the Quick View window without opening the file, click ☒.

UNDO YOUR LAST ACTION

When you change your mind or make a mistake, Windows can help you undo what you have done.

You can undo commands such as delete and rename from your desktop or in a My Computer or Explorer window. You can also undo dragging and dropping you performed to move or copy an item. The Undo command indicates which action is available to undo. You may be able to undo up to the last 10 actions.

You cannot undo all actions. For example, if you move a document to a folder that already has a document with the same name, Windows asks if you want to replace the original document. If you replace the original document and then decide to undo, Windows will only undo the move. The original document will not be restored. You cannot undo an undo or a save. You also cannot undo a delete command after you empty the Recycle Bin.

Many programs also have Undo commands.

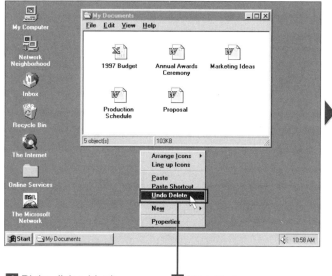

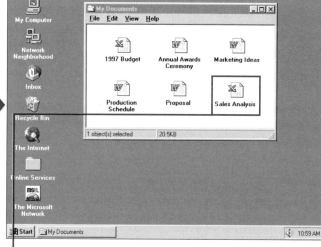

1 Right-click a blank area on your desktop or a blank area in a window. A menu appears.

2 Click Undo.

Note: You can also click Edit and then select Undo in an open window.

■ Windows reverses your last action.

Note: In this example, the Sales Analysis file reappears.

CLOSE MISBEHAVING PROGRAMS

Y ou can close a program that is no longer working properly without closing Windows. You can close a program even when you do not have access to the program's menus or commands.

You can stop any active task on your computer. An active task can be a program, a utility or the software that controls your mouse.

When a program fails to check for mouse or keyboard commands, Windows identifies the program as not responding. Windows may detect that a program is not responding before you do and display a warning message. You may also discover, while using a program, that it is not behaving as it should.

When you close a program that is not responding, you will lose all the unsaved information in the program. Closing a misbehaving program should not affect your other open programs or Windows.

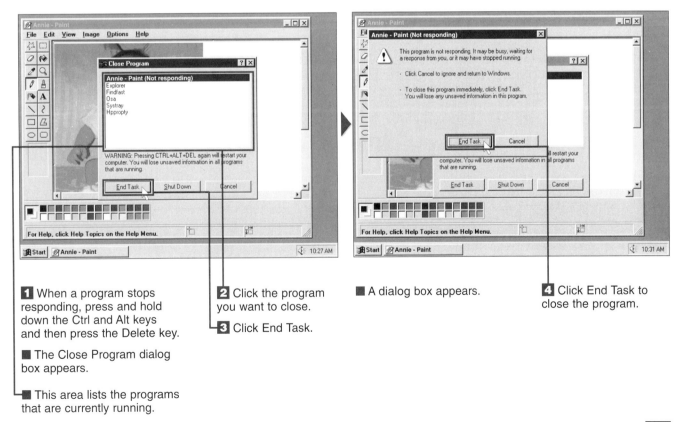

1 When a program stops responding, press and hold down the Ctrl and Alt keys and then press the Delete key.

■ The Close Program dialog box appears.

■ This area lists the programs that are currently running.

2 Click the program you want to close.

3 Click End Task.

■ A dialog box appears.

4 Click End Task to close the program.

CREATE A NEW FOLDER

You can create a new folder to better organize the information stored on your computer. Creating a new folder is like placing a new folder in a filing cabinet.

When you begin using your computer, you should create new folders to store your work. Storing documents in personalized folders will help

you quickly locate your documents.

You can create folders inside other folders to help further organize information. For example, you can create a folder named "letters" to store folders named "clients," "colleagues" and "personal." You can also create folders on your desktop to organize your shortcuts.

You can create as many folders as you need to organize your documents by date, project or type. Use a system that makes sense to you and will help you find your documents.

A folder name can use up to 255 characters and can include spaces. Folder names cannot contain the \ / : * ? " < > or | characters.

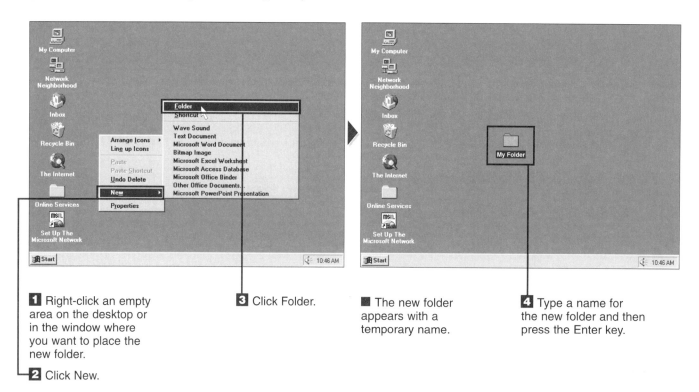

1 Right-click an empty area on the desktop or in the window where you want to place the new folder.

2 Click New.

3 Click Folder.

■ The new folder appears with a temporary name.

4 Type a name for the new folder and then press the Enter key.

CREATE A NEW FILE

You can create, name and store a new file in the appropriate folder without having to start the programs. This allows you to focus on your work, rather than the programs you need to accomplish your tasks.

Before writing a letter or creating a new spreadsheet,

you can first determine where you want to store the new file. By selecting the location of the file you can organize your work and later find the file more easily.

Once you decide on the location of a new file, you can give the file a name. A file name can use up to 255 characters and

can include spaces. File names cannot contain the \ / : * < > or | characters.

The types of new files you can create depend on the programs installed on your computer. Programs not designed for Windows 95 may require you to start the program before you can create a new file.

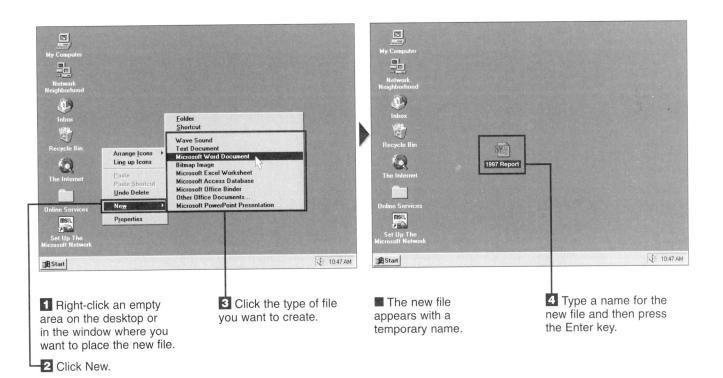

1 Right-click an empty area on the desktop or in the window where you want to place the new file.

2 Click New.

3 Click the type of file you want to create.

■ The new file appears with a temporary name.

4 Type a name for the new file and then press the Enter key.

DISPLAY AND CHANGE FILE PROPERTIES

You can find information about a file or folder by reviewing its properties. In addition to the file's name in both Windows 95 and MS-DOS format, you can find information about the file's type, location and size. You can also find the date the file was created, last changed and last opened.

A file has attributes which you can verify or change. The Read-only attribute prevents you from saving changes to the file. The Archive attribute is used to determine if the file has changed since the last backup. Windows uses the Hidden and System attributes to identify, hide and protect files it needs to operate.

When you select a multimedia file such as a sound or video file, the Properties dialog box displays additional tabs. You can view details such as copyright information and the length and format of the file. You can use the Preview tab to play the sound or video.

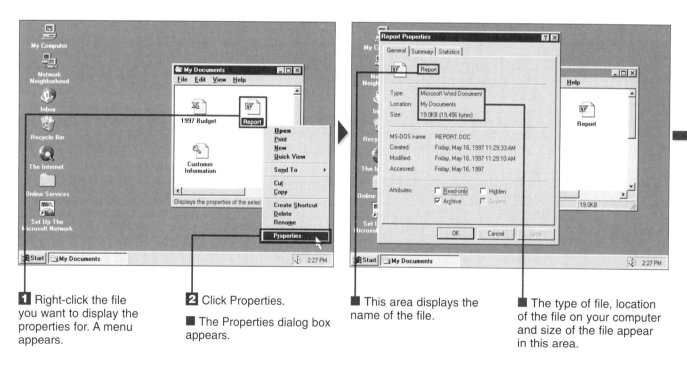

1 Right-click the file you want to display the properties for. A menu appears.

2 Click Properties.

■ The Properties dialog box appears.

■ This area displays the name of the file.

■ The type of file, location of the file on your computer and size of the file appear in this area.

TIPS

I turned the Hidden attribute on. Why is the file still visible?

There is a master setting which determines whether hidden files are displayed or not. From the View menu, select Options to adjust the setting. See page 50.

Can I protect a file so it cannot be erased?

There are no attributes in the Properties dialog box that will protect your file from being erased. You can save the file on a floppy disk and use the write-protect tab to prevent the file from being erased.

What does the Read-only attribute do?

The Read-only attribute prevents an original file from being changed. You can open a Read-only file, but if you change it you must save the file with a new name. This is useful for files such as letterhead or blank forms that you do not want altered.

Why does the Properties dialog box show two different numbers for the file size?

The Properties dialog box shows the file size in both bytes and kilobytes (KB). 1024 bytes are equal to 1KB.

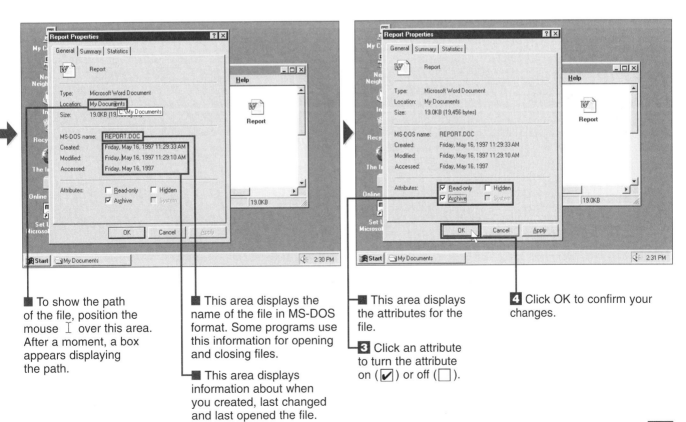

■ To show the path of the file, position the mouse I over this area. After a moment, a box appears displaying the path.

■ This area displays the name of the file in MS-DOS format. Some programs use this information for opening and closing files.

■ This area displays information about when you created, last changed and last opened the file.

■ This area displays the attributes for the file.

3 Click an attribute to turn the attribute on (☑) or off (☐).

4 Click OK to confirm your changes.

CREATE A SHORTCUT

You can create a shortcut to provide a quick way of opening items you use regularly.

A shortcut icon resembles the original item, but displays an arrow (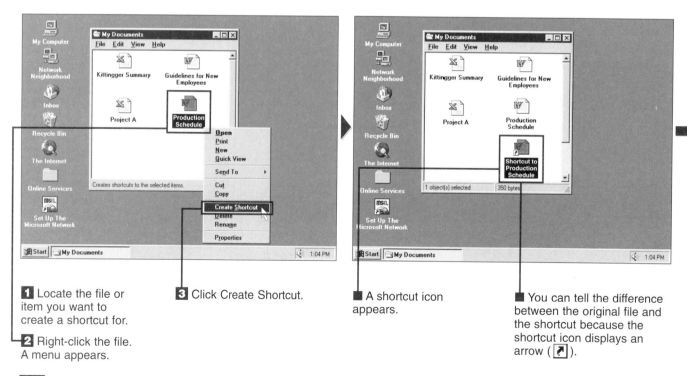) in the bottom left corner. A shortcut is a link to the original item.

You can place a shortcut icon on the desktop, inside a folder or on the Start menu. A shortcut icon on the desktop provides quick access to a program, document, folder or drive you use frequently.

Shortcuts make working with files easier. For example, you can use shortcuts to place all of the documents for a project in one folder, instead of moving all the documents and later returning them when the project is complete. This is particularly useful if some of the files are stored on other computers on a network.

You can create shortcuts for files, folders and other items, such as Dial-up Networking connections, Control Panel icons and printers.

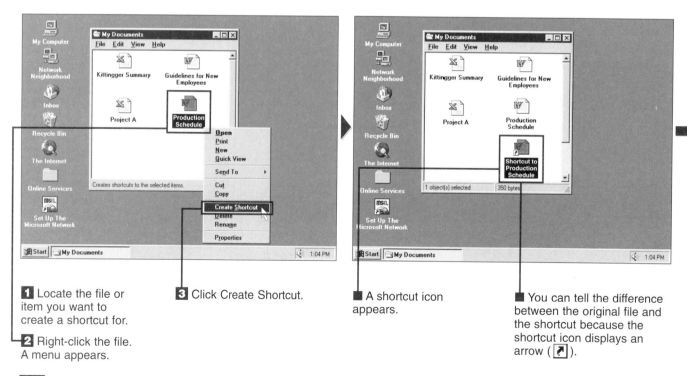

1 Locate the file or item you want to create a shortcut for.

2 Right-click the file. A menu appears.

3 Click Create Shortcut.

■ A shortcut icon appears.

■ You can tell the difference between the original file and the shortcut because the shortcut icon displays an arrow ( ).

Can I rename a shortcut?

The name of a shortcut usually starts with "Shortcut to." To rename a shortcut, click the shortcut name and press the F2 key. Type a new name for the shortcut and then press Enter on your keyboard.

If I delete a shortcut, will the original file also be deleted?

A shortcut contains the information needed to find the file, but it does not contain the information from the file itself. If you delete a shortcut icon, the file remains on your computer.

What happens if I try to use a shortcut to a file that has been moved or deleted?

If Windows cannot find the file a shortcut refers to, a message appears, telling you there is a problem with the shortcut. Windows will try to help you find the file the shortcut icon refers to.

Is there a faster way to create a shortcut?

Right-click the item you want to create a shortcut for. Drag the item to the location you want to place the shortcut. From the menu that appears, select Create Shortcut(s) here.

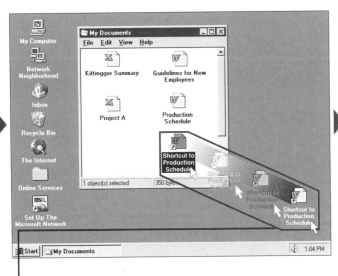

4 Drag the shortcut icon to the location where you want the shortcut to appear.

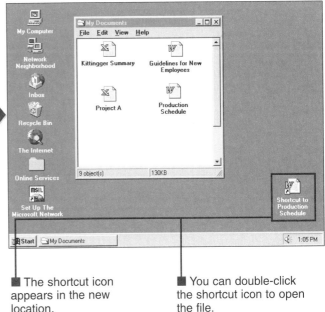

■ The shortcut icon appears in the new location.

■ You can double-click the shortcut icon to open the file.

CHANGE SHORTCUT PROPERTIES

A shortcut has properties that show you what the shortcut does and allow you to change the way it works. As with most Windows items, you can find information about the shortcut in the Properties dialog box. You can see where the shortcut is stored, its size and when it was created.

When viewing shortcut properties, you can find the location of the item that the shortcut opens. You can also use the Properties dialog box to change the way the shortcut works.

You can choose where you would like to save files related to the specific program or file.

The location you choose to save files is the location that automatically appears when you use the Open or Save commands.

You can specify a shortcut key that allows you to press a single key or combination of keys to open the program or file the shortcut points to.

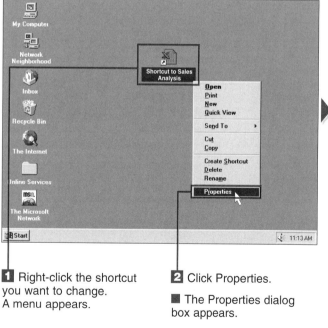

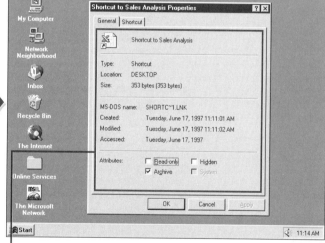

1 Right-click the shortcut you want to change. A menu appears.

2 Click Properties.

■ The Properties dialog box appears.

■ This area displays information about the shortcut, including the location, size, MS-DOS name and the date and time you created the shortcut.

TIPS

Can I use a shortcut key to open a program or file?

You can create a shortcut key to open any program or file that has a shortcut. A shortcut key only works if the shortcut that uses it is on the Start menu or the desktop. For example, if you create a shortcut on your desktop to a screen saver (.scr) file and create a shortcut key, you can press the shortcut key to instantly activate the screen saver.

How can I quickly find the location of the original file?

In the Properties dialog box, select the Shortcut tab and click the Find Target button. The folder containing the original file opens and the file is selected.

Which are good shortcut keys to use?

The best shortcut keys are any combination of the Ctrl and Alt keys and a letter, such as Ctrl+Alt+Y. You can also use some of the function keys, like F9 through F12. When you select a function key for a shortcut, the shortcut cancels whatever function the key had. For example, if you use the F2 key as a shortcut key, you will no longer be able to use F2 to rename files.

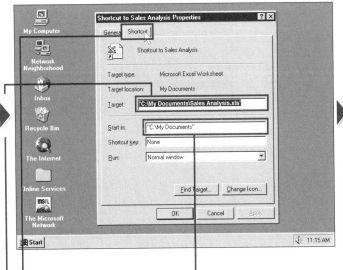

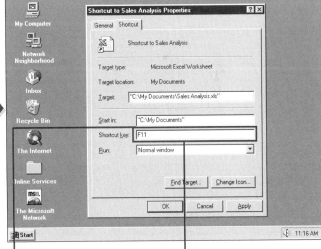

3 Click the Shortcut tab.

■ This area displays the location of the item the shortcut points to. You can change this information.

■ This area displays the location of the folder where the program will automatically save the files. You can change this information.

4 Click this area if you want to create a keyboard shortcut that will instantly activate the shortcut.

5 Press the keyboard keys you want to assign to the shortcut.

CONTINUED ▶

CHANGE SHORTCUT
PROPERTIES CONTINUED

You can change the appearance of a shortcut icon to show the purpose of the program or file the shortcut refers to. Windows provides a selection of icons you can choose from. When you change a shortcut icon, the appearance of the

original item's icon does not change.

You can change the properties for a program's shortcut to choose how you want the program to appear when it starts. You can have the program open in a normal window. If a program

requires the full screen area, you can choose to display the program as a maximized window when it opens. If you have a program that opens automatically every time you start Windows, you can also choose to display the program minimized as a button on the taskbar until you need it.

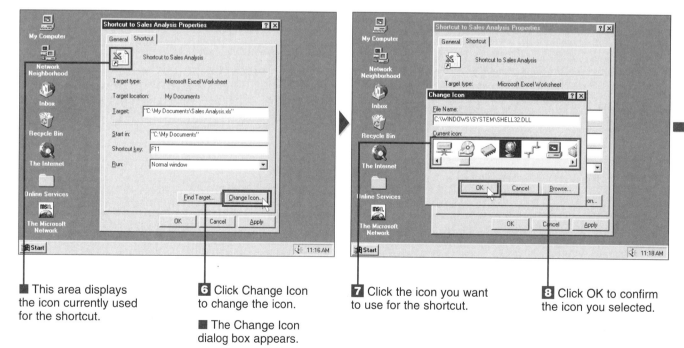

■ This area displays the icon currently used for the shortcut.

6 Click Change Icon to change the icon.

■ The Change Icon dialog box appears.

7 Click the icon you want to use for the shortcut.

8 Click OK to confirm the icon you selected.

Can I change the default icon used for a specific type of file?

You can change the default icon used for a specific type of file by modifying the file type. See page 246.

Are there more icons that I can choose on my computer?

You can use the Browse button to find files containing icons on your computer. Additional Windows icons are located in the c:\windows\moricons.dll and c:\windows\system\shell32.dll files. Most program files also contain more than one icon that you can use. Program files usually have the .exe, .com or .dll extensions.

I wanted a program to open maximized when I select the shortcut, but it is not working. What is wrong?

Not all programs are capable of opening in a different window size. This may be a result of the program's design. The program also may not be able to work with these settings if the program was created to work with an older version of Windows.

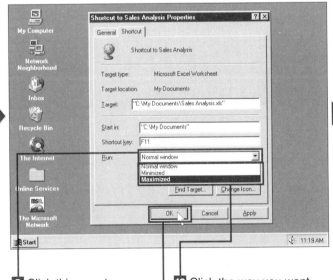

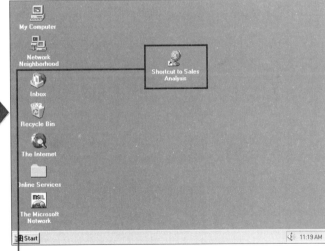

9 Click this area to specify how you want the window to appear when you open the item.

10 Click the way you want the window to appear. The window can appear in a normal window, minimized as a button on the taskbar or maximized to fill the screen.

11 Click OK to confirm all of your changes.

■ If you selected a new icon for the shortcut, the appearance of the shortcut changes.

PRINT FILES

You can produce a paper copy of a file from a My Computer or Explorer window. This allows you to print a file even if the file or the program that created the file is not open.

Windows can print most types of files. You can select many different types of files and print them all at the same time.

When you print a file, Windows starts the program associated with the file you want to print and displays the program on your screen. Windows may also display the file and the Print dialog box on your screen.

Windows closes the program when the file has been sent to the printer.

You can also create a shortcut for a printer on your desktop. A shortcut lets you quickly print by dragging a file onto the shortcut icon.

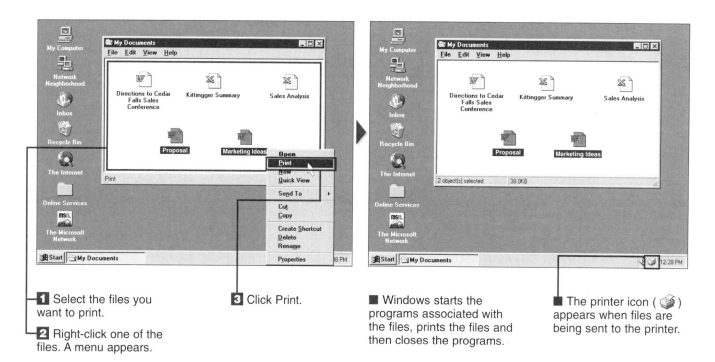

1 Select the files you want to print.

2 Right-click one of the files. A menu appears.

3 Click Print.

■ Windows starts the programs associated with the files, prints the files and then closes the programs.

■ The printer icon (🖨) appears when files are being sent to the printer.

TIPS

Which printer will the file be sent to?

When you use the Print command, Windows sends the file to your default printer. If you are using printer shortcuts, you can drag the file to the shortcut icon for the printer you want to use.

Why does a message appear, telling me to create an association when I drag a file to my printer's shortcut icon?

Windows does not recognize the file type and does not know which program to open to print the file. To create an association between a file and a program, see page 64.

If I delete a printer's shortcut icon, can I still use the printer?

You can still use the printer even if you delete the shortcut icon for the printer. The shortcut contains only the information needed to quickly access the printer. When you delete the shortcut icon, the printer is not removed from your computer.

How do I select multiple files for printing?

Click the first file you want to select. Hold down the Ctrl key and then click the other files you want to select.

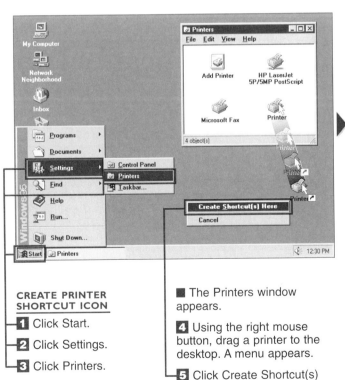

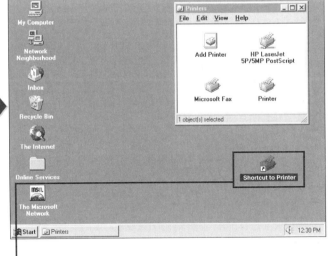

CREATE PRINTER SHORTCUT ICON

1 Click Start.

2 Click Settings.

3 Click Printers.

■ The Printers window appears.

4 Using the right mouse button, drag a printer to the desktop. A menu appears.

5 Click Create Shortcut(s) Here.

■ A shortcut icon for the printer appears.

■ You can now drag files to the printer's shortcut icon to print files.

VIEW PRINTING STATUS

You can view information about a printer and the files you send to the printer.

Each of your printers has its own print manager window. A print manager window displays information about the current status of the printer and the documents waiting to print.

The title bar for a print manager window displays the name of the

printer and indicates its status. This information lets you know if the printer is paused or if an error has occurred.

Each document that is printing or waiting to print is listed in the print manager window. Each column in the window lists information about the document, including the name, status and which network station or user sent the document.

The Progress column indicates the size of the print job. While the document is printing, the Progress column keeps track of how much of the document has been sent to the printer.

The Started At column tells you the date and time a file was sent to the printer. This information is useful if you have a long list of print jobs.

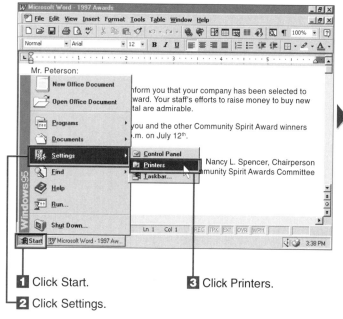

1 Click Start.

2 Click Settings.

3 Click Printers.

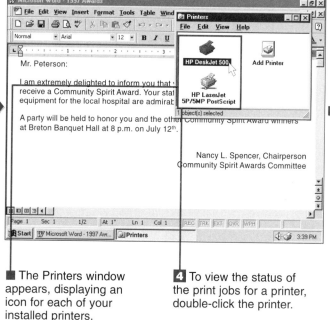

■ The Printers window appears, displaying an icon for each of your installed printers.

4 To view the status of the print jobs for a printer, double-click the printer.

TIPS

Can I sort the print jobs by clicking the column headings in the print manager window?

Windows does not support sorting in the print manager window. Print jobs are listed in the order they will print.

How can I view information about all available printers at once?

Open the Printers folder. Choose the View menu and then select Details. Windows will display information about the status and number of documents printing on each printer. Viewing information on all the printers at once enables you to decide which printer to use.

How can I change the order of print jobs?

Open the print manager window and then drag a file to a new location in the list of print jobs. You cannot change the order of files other people have sent to a network printer.

What happens when I close the print manager window?

Closing the print manager window has no effect on the files that are currently printing. The printer icon ( ) remains on the taskbar until the files are finished printing.

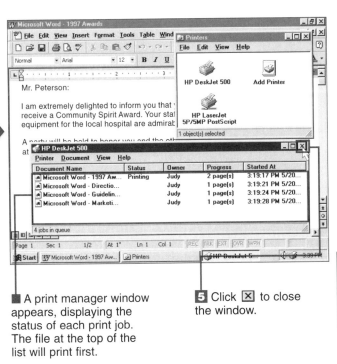

■ A print manager window appears, displaying the status of each print job. The file at the top of the list will print first.

5 Click ☒ to close the window.

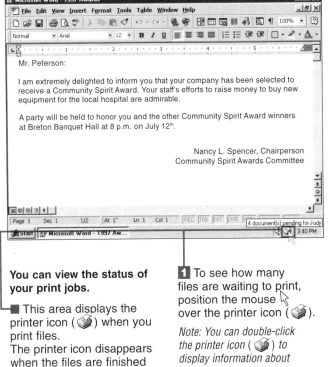

You can view the status of your print jobs.

■ This area displays the printer icon ( ) when you print files.
The printer icon disappears when the files are finished printing.

1 To see how many files are waiting to print, position the mouse ⤢ over the printer icon ( ).

Note: You can double-click the printer icon ( ) to display information about the files you are printing.

PAUSE PRINTING

You can pause the printer to temporarily hold all print jobs. Pausing the printer is useful when you want to change the toner or add more paper to the printer. You can also pause the printer until all of your files are ready so you can pick all the files up from the printer at one time.

You can also use the Pause Printing command to pause the printing of a specific file. Pausing a file is useful to hold the file so more important documents can print first.

When you print a document, Windows creates a file and

sends it to the printer. You can intercept the file while Windows is performing this task and pause the document before it prints. The length of time you have to pause the document depends on the number and size of files waiting to print and the speed of the printer.

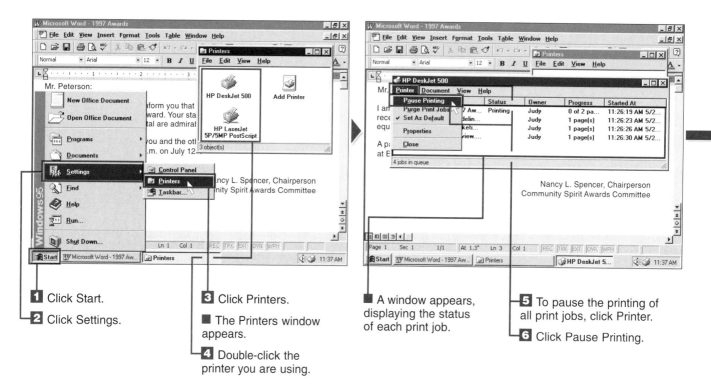

■1 Click Start.

■2 Click Settings.

■3 Click Printers.

■ The Printers window appears.

■4 Double-click the printer you are using.

■ A window appears, displaying the status of each print job.

■5 To pause the printing of all print jobs, click Printer.

■6 Click Pause Printing.

If I unpause a file, when will it print?

When you pause a file, it keeps its place in the print queue. When you unpause a file, the file will print according to its location in the print queue. The print queue is the order in which documents are printed.

What happens if I pause the document that is currently printing?

If you pause a document while it is printing, there may be problems with the next print job or the printer may freeze. The printer will not print other jobs until the paused job is unpaused or canceled.

Can I pause the files of others on a network?

You cannot pause files printed by other people on a network unless you are a network administrator.

Can I pause the printer while files are printing?

You should not pause the printer while it is printing. If you need to pause the printer, you should first pause all the jobs in the queue except the one currently printing or wait until there are no print jobs in the queue.

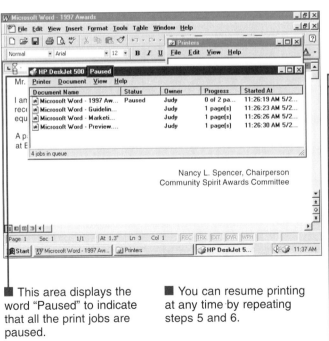

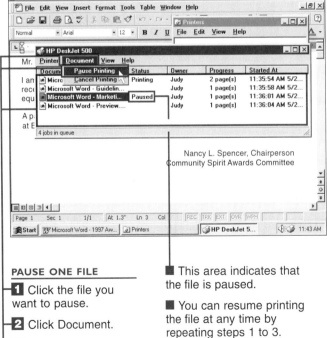

■ This area displays the word "Paused" to indicate that all the print jobs are paused.

■ You can resume printing at any time by repeating steps 5 and 6.

PAUSE ONE FILE

-1 Click the file you want to pause.

-2 Click Document.

-3 Click Pause Printing.

■ This area indicates that the file is paused.

■ You can resume printing the file at any time by repeating steps 1 to 3.

CANCEL PRINTING

Yo u can stop a document from printing if you have made a mistake and need to make a correction. The Cancel Printing command is available even if a document has already started to print.

Windows allows you to cancel a single print job or cancel the entire print queue. A print queue

is a listing of documents waiting to be printed. When using a network printer, you can only cancel your own print jobs. The network administrator is the only person who can cancel the print jobs of others on a network.

When you cancel printing a document or cancel all print jobs, Windows will not offer

you a warning or an undelete option. Do not cancel any print jobs unless you are sure you do not want to print the document. It may be wise to pause the printer first and then decide if you want to cancel the print jobs.

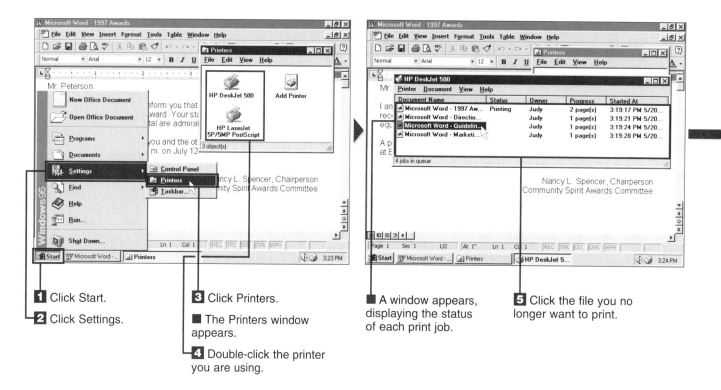

1 Click Start.

2 Click Settings.

3 Click Printers.

■ The Printers window appears.

4 Double-click the printer you are using.

■ A window appears, displaying the status of each print job.

5 Click the file you no longer want to print.

TIPS

How can I get quick access to a printer?

In the Printers window, right-click the printer you are using and then drag the icon to your desktop. Select Create Shortcut(s) Here from the menu.

When you are printing a file, you can double-click the printer icon that appears on the taskbar.

Can I cancel all jobs while the printer is printing?

You can cancel all print jobs while documents are printing, but this can cause problems and the printer may have to be reset.

What happens if I shut down Windows while there are paused print jobs?

When you restart the computer, you will see a dialog box providing you with three options. You can choose Yes to start printing, No to continue to pause the print jobs or Cancel to delete the print jobs.

Can I cancel a document while it is printing?

You can cancel a document if the file has already started printing, but this can cause problems with the next print job. The printer may have to be reset.

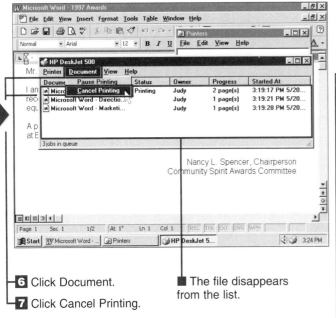

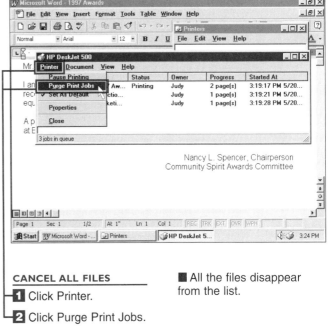

6 Click Document.

7 Click Cancel Printing.

■ The file disappears from the list.

CANCEL ALL FILES

1 Click Printer.

2 Click Purge Print Jobs.

■ All the files disappear from the list.

SET THE DEFAULT PRINTER

If you have access to more than one printer, you can choose which one you want to print your documents. You should choose the printer you use most often. The printer you choose is referred to as the default printer. Windows will automatically use the default printer to print your files unless you specify otherwise.

You may occasionally want to print your document on another printer. In Windows and programs such as Word, you must use the program's Print dialog box to select a different printer.

Some programs, such as Notepad, do not provide a Print dialog box and send

your document directly to the default printer. A Print dialog box is also not available when you right-click a file and select the Print command. In these cases, changing the default printer is the only way you can choose a different printer.

You can change the default printer as often as you need.

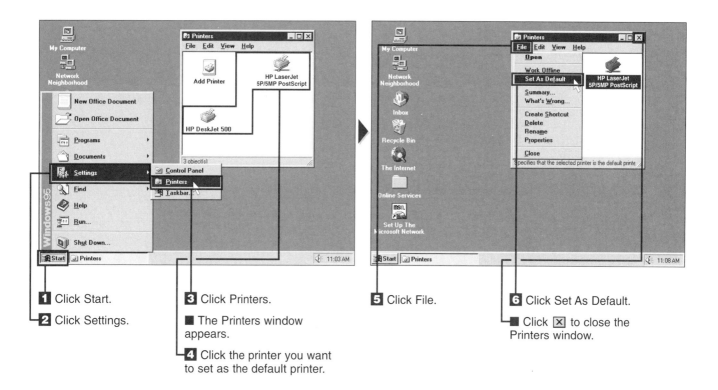

1 Click Start.

2 Click Settings.

3 Click Printers.

■ The Printers window appears.

4 Click the printer you want to set as the default printer.

5 Click File.

6 Click Set As Default.

■ Click ☒ to close the Printers window.

WORK OFFLINE

You can tell Windows that you are offline. This will allow you to save your print jobs and print them at a later date. Working offline is useful when you are not connected to a printer.

You can work offline when you are traveling and your portable computer is not connected to the network

or when a network printer is unavailable because it needs paper, toner or maintenance. In both cases, Windows will save your print jobs until you are back in the office or the problem is fixed. Your documents will be sent to the printer as soon as you tell Windows you are no longer offline.

By working offline, you save the time of having to reopen the document and print it later. You also eliminate the chance that you will forget which documents you wanted to print.

Working offline is only available for network printers. This feature is also called deferred printing.

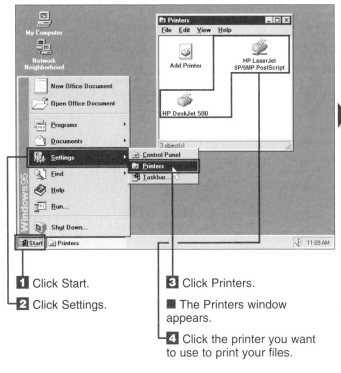

1 Click Start.

2 Click Settings.

3 Click Printers.

■ The Printers window appears.

4 Click the printer you want to use to print your files.

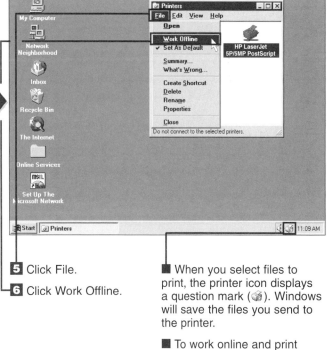

5 Click File.

6 Click Work Offline.

■ When you select files to print, the printer icon displays a question mark (🖨). Windows will save the files you send to the printer.

■ To work online and print the files, repeat steps 1 to 6.

RENAME A PRINTER

You can change the name of a printer to help you identify its type and location.

Printer names can be up to 31 characters long, including letters, numbers and special characters. Long, descriptive printer names make it easier to choose the right printer and locate your printed documents.

For example, a printer named "Kim's color printer in room 204" is much easier to identify than a printer named "Printer 2".

When you rename your printer, the new name will appear in the Print dialog boxes in all of your programs. This helps you select the correct printer when printing a document.

Renaming the printer will not have any effect on the list of documents currently waiting to print.

The Printers window displays an icon for each printer connected to your computer, with the name of the printer below the icon.

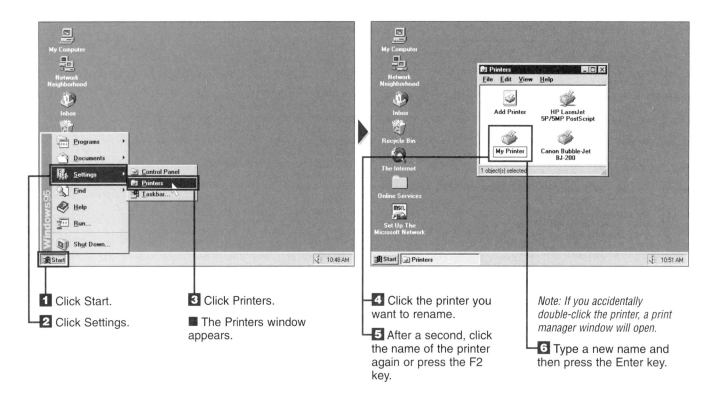

1 Click Start.

2 Click Settings.

3 Click Printers.

■ The Printers window appears.

4 Click the printer you want to rename.

5 After a second, click the name of the printer again or press the F2 key.

Note: If you accidentally double-click the printer, a print manager window will open.

6 Type a new name and then press the Enter key.

DELETE A PRINTER

If you no longer use a printer, you should delete the printer, as well as disconnecting it from your computer.

When you delete a printer, you remove the printer's settings from your computer. Windows will no longer display the printer in the Print dialog boxes of your programs.

When you are replacing an old printer with a new one, problems can occur if the commands and instructions designed for the old printer are sent to your new printer. Deleting the old printer from your computer will eliminate these problems.

If Windows detects that it no longer needs the files it used to communicate with the printer,

Windows offers to remove the files for you. If you are removing the printer permanently, you should delete the old printer files to free up storage space on your computer. If you intend to reconnect the printer later, you should keep the files, especially if they were provided on a floppy disk or CD-ROM disc with the printer, or downloaded from the Internet.

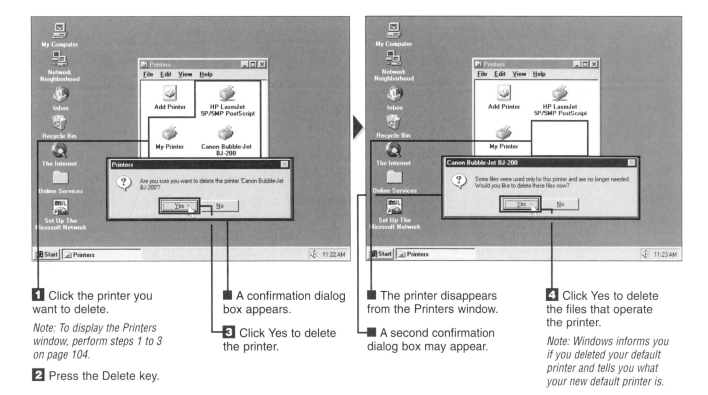

1 Click the printer you want to delete.

Note: To display the Printers window, perform steps 1 to 3 on page 104.

2 Press the Delete key.

■ A confirmation dialog box appears.

3 Click Yes to delete the printer.

■ The printer disappears from the Printers window.

■ A second confirmation dialog box may appear.

4 Click Yes to delete the files that operate the printer.

Note: Windows informs you if you deleted your default printer and tells you what your new default printer is.

CHANGE PRINTER OPTIONS

You can change your printer's settings to suit your working environment. Changing a printer's settings will affect all the documents it prints. The printer you are using determines the available settings.

Changing your printer's General settings can be useful when the printer is shared with other people on a network. You can add a

comment about your printer that will be seen by other people on the network when they install the printer.

If your printer is used by many people, you can have the printer insert a separator page between each document that is printed. The separator page prints before the document and helps to identify who printed the document. The

Full separator page uses a large font and displays graphics. The Simple separator page uses the printer's default font and contains only text. You can only change the Separator page setting if the printer is attached to your computer. If you are using a printer connected to a network, you cannot change this setting.

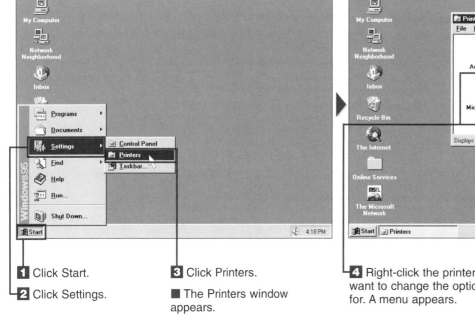

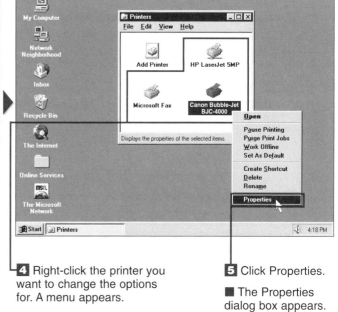

1 Click Start.

2 Click Settings.

3 Click Printers.

■ The Printers window appears.

4 Right-click the printer you want to change the options for. A menu appears.

5 Click Properties.

■ The Properties dialog box appears.

Should I print a test page?

The printer test page confirms that the printer is working properly and provides information about the printer's driver. You can use this information if you want to check for an updated printer driver at the manufacturer's Web site.

My printer is not working properly. Can Windows help me?

From the Start menu, select Help and then click the Contents tab. Double-click the Troubleshooting book and select the If you have trouble printing topic.

Can I create a custom separator page?

You can use files in Windows metafile (.wmf) format as separator pages. Advanced graphics programs, like CorelDRAW!, can save files in the .wmf format. When you use a custom page, Windows does not print the name of the user on the separator page. Use the Browse button to find the .wmf file you want to use.

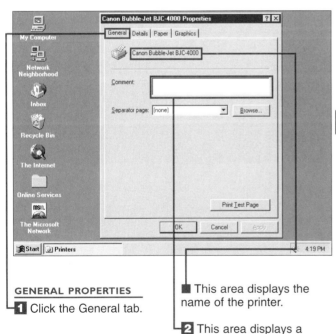

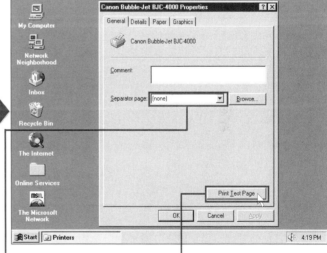

GENERAL PROPERTIES

■1 Click the General tab.

■ This area displays the name of the printer.

■2 This area displays a comment about the printer. You can click this area and type a comment.

■3 This area specifies if a separator page will print between each printed document. You can click ▾ in this area to select a separator page.

Note: You can only select a separator page if the printer is attached to your computer.

■4 You can click this button to print a test page to make sure your printer is set up correctly.

CONTINUED ▶

CHANGE PRINTER OPTIONS
CONTINUED

You can specify how your computer works with your printer. Your printer must be attached to your computer to adjust some of the Details settings.

You can view which port is used to connect the printer to your computer. You can also view the printer driver. A driver is a program that helps your computer communicate with the printer. The driver also determines which

settings are available for your printer.

The spool settings determine how and when information is sent to the printer. When you print a document, the program you are working in creates a print file. When the program has finished creating the print file, you can resume working with your computer. Windows then sends the print file to the printer. This process is called

spooling and means that you do not have to wait for the printer to print your documents before using your computer to perform another task.

If your printer is capable of communicating with your computer in both directions, you should leave the bi-directional option enabled. This feature will allow Windows to provide additional information about your print jobs.

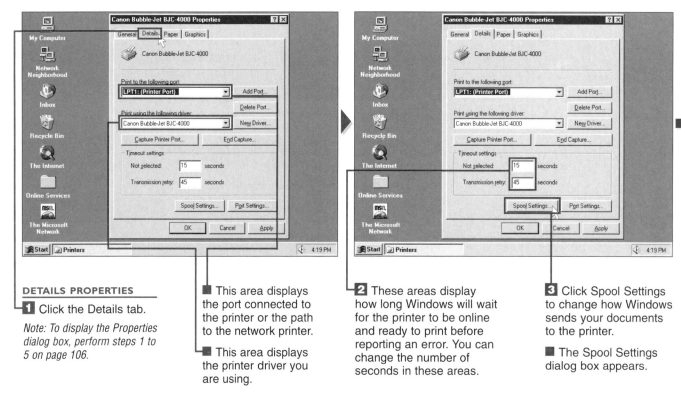

DETAILS PROPERTIES

■1 Click the Details tab.

Note: To display the Properties dialog box, perform steps 1 to 5 on page 106.

■ This area displays the port connected to the printer or the path to the network printer.

■ This area displays the printer driver you are using.

■2 These areas display how long Windows will wait for the printer to be online and ready to print before reporting an error. You can change the number of seconds in these areas.

■3 Click Spool Settings to change how Windows sends your documents to the printer.

■ The Spool Settings dialog box appears.

What are the Timeout settings used for?

The Not selected setting indicates the amount of time it takes your printer to be ready to print after you turn it on. The Transmission retry time reflects how long Windows will wait before sending your printer more data. This setting may need to be increased for printers using Postscript.

Which spool settings should I choose?

If you want your document printed quickly, select the Print directly to the printer and RAW format settings. If you want to be able to use your computer quickly, select the Spool print jobs so program finishes printing faster setting, the Start printing after last page is spooled setting and the EMF format setting.

What are spool data formats?

Spool data formats control the way information is saved in a print file. The EMF format creates an EMF file and then frees up your computer. The print file is created from the EMF file in the background. Postscript printers cannot use this format and some programs also may not be able to use this format properly. The RAW format creates the print file directly.

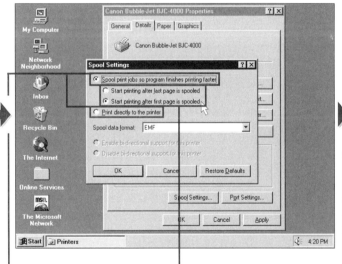

■4 Click an option to specify if you want to spool documents you print or print directly to the printer (○ changes to ●).

■5 If you selected to spool documents, click an option to specify when you want Windows to start printing (○ changes to ●).

■6 This area displays the format that Windows uses to store information waiting to be printed. Click this area to select another format.

■7 Click an option to specify if you want Windows to communicate with the printer in both directions (○ changes to ●). If the bi-directional option is available, you should leave it enabled.

■8 Click OK to close the Spool Settings dialog box.

CONTINUED

CHANGE PRINTER OPTIONS
CONTINUED

You can use different sizes of paper to print your documents. The available paper settings depend on the printer you are using.

You can print on legal size paper, envelopes or custom paper like letterhead. You can also change the orientation of the pages you print. Portrait is the standard orientation. Landscape is the orientation

often used to print certificates and tables. The Paper source setting allows you to specify where the paper you want to use is located in your printer.

Because the paper settings you choose will affect all the documents you send to the printer, it is often better to change the paper settings in the program you are printing from. Changing the paper

settings in the program allows you to leave the printer's settings at those you use most often.

You may also have settings that control how graphics are printed. You can change the resolution and improve the color of a graphic. You can also have a graphic print lighter or darker on a page.

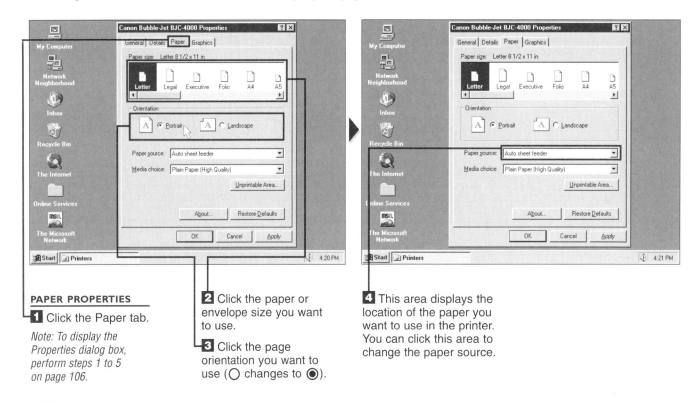

PAPER PROPERTIES

1 Click the Paper tab.

Note: To display the Properties dialog box, perform steps 1 to 5 on page 106.

2 Click the paper or envelope size you want to use.

3 Click the page orientation you want to use (○ changes to ◉).

4 This area displays the location of the paper you want to use in the printer. You can click this area to change the paper source.

TIPS

I print envelopes frequently. How can I avoid changing my printer's settings each time?

You can install another copy of your printer and name the copy "envelopes". Specify the settings required to print envelopes on the new "virtual" printer and then select the virtual printer whenever you want to print an envelope.

How many "virtual" printers can I create?

You can create as many virtual printers as you need. You may want to create one virtual printer to print using a high resolution for graphics and another to print using the letterhead tray.

What is resolution?

Resolution is the number of dots printed per inch. A high resolution setting produces better quality images, but your documents take longer to print.

What is dithering?

Dithering is the technique of using dots of a few pure colors to create the illusion of a wide spectrum of colors. This technique is used by most kinds of printers to create full-color images.

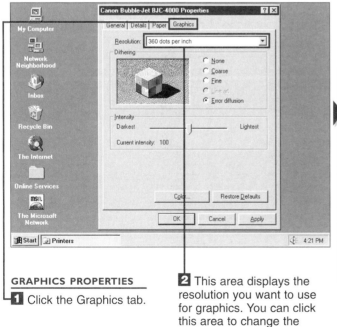

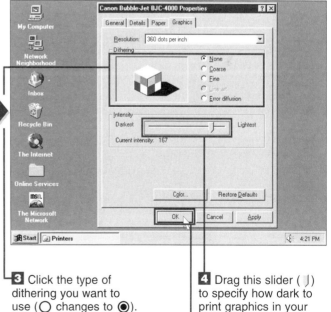

GRAPHICS PROPERTIES

1 Click the Graphics tab.

2 This area displays the resolution you want to use for graphics. You can click this area to change the resolution.

3 Click the type of dithering you want to use (○ changes to ◉). Windows shows you how a document will print.

4 Drag this slider ( ) to specify how dark to print graphics in your documents.

5 Click OK to confirm all of your changes.

INSTALL A PRINTER

You can install a new printer on your computer. The Add Printer Wizard helps ensure that your new printer is installed correctly and working properly. The wizard asks a series of questions and then sets up the printer according to the information you provide.

Windows has a driver for most printer models. A driver is a program that helps your computer communicate with the printer. You may need to use your Windows 95 CD-ROM disc or floppy disks to add the correct driver for the printer you are installing.

Although Windows supports hundreds of models from nearly 50 different manufacturers, including Hewlett-Packard, Epson and Panasonic, your printer may not be on Windows' list of manufacturers and models. The documentation that came with your printer should contain information indicating that your printer is compatible with a similar model.

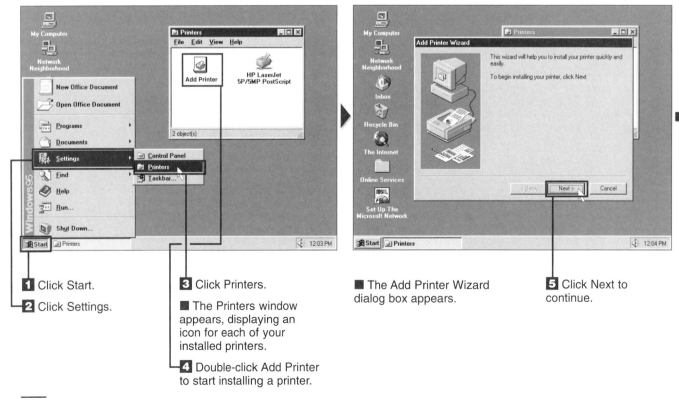

1 Click Start.

2 Click Settings.

3 Click Printers.

■ The Printers window appears, displaying an icon for each of your installed printers.

4 Double-click Add Printer to start installing a printer.

■ The Add Printer Wizard dialog box appears.

5 Click Next to continue.

TIPS

Which driver should I use if no documentation or disk was supplied with the printer?

You can use the Generic driver, but this driver is very limited. To install a laser printer, try the HP LaserJet IIIP. For a dot matrix printer, try the Panasonic KX-P1124.

My printer came with an installation disk. Should I use the disk to install the printer?

If you purchased the printer after 1995, the driver on the disk may be more up-to-date than the driver included with Windows 95. Insert the installation disk and then click the Have Disk button. Windows will find all the necessary information on the disk.

What will happen when I install a printer with Plug and Play capabilities?

Windows will identify a printer with Plug and Play capabilities as soon as you plug it in and restart the computer. Windows will then prompt you to insert the disks supplied with the printer and will install the driver for you.

My printer can print both Postscript and PCL pages. Do I need two drivers?

Yes. Postscript and PCL are printer languages used to describe the information that will appear on a page. For printers that support both languages, you must install one driver for each language.

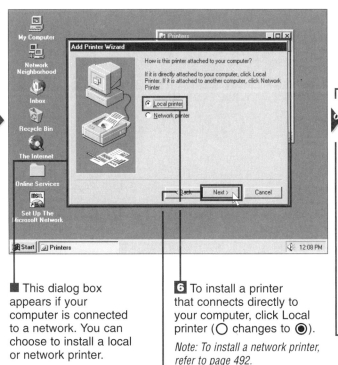

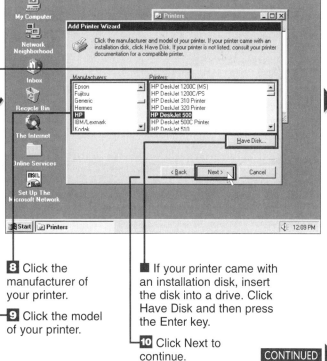

■ This dialog box appears if your computer is connected to a network. You can choose to install a local or network printer.

6 To install a printer that connects directly to your computer, click Local printer (○ changes to ◉).

Note: To install a network printer, refer to page 492.

7 Click Next to continue.

8 Click the manufacturer of your printer.

9 Click the model of your printer.

■ If your printer came with an installation disk, insert the disk into a drive. Click Have Disk and then press the Enter key.

10 Click Next to continue.

CONTINUED

INSTALL A PRINTER
CONTINUED

You must tell Windows how the printer you are installing is connected to your computer. In nearly all cases, the printer is attached to the computer's parallel port, called LPT1.

The wizard asks you to type a name for your printer, which can be up to 31 characters long.

This option is useful if you will be sharing the printer. Using a descriptive name helps other people on a network easily identify the printer's type, location and owner.

If you have only one printer, it will be the default printer. If you have several printers, you must select one to be your default

printer. All of your programs will use the default printer unless you select a different printer.

Windows allows you to print a test page to confirm everything is working properly. The page contains information about the printer. You may want to keep the test page for future reference.

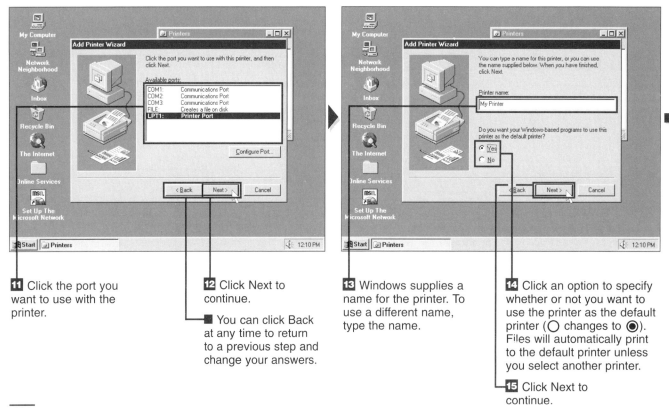

11 Click the port you want to use with the printer.

12 Click Next to continue.

■ You can click Back at any time to return to a previous step and change your answers.

13 Windows supplies a name for the printer. To use a different name, type the name.

14 Click an option to specify whether or not you want to use the printer as the default printer (○ changes to ●). Files will automatically print to the default printer unless you select another printer.

15 Click Next to continue.

Will I be able to use my printer from MS-DOS programs?

Yes. You can click the Configure Port button in the Add Printer Wizard dialog box and then set up your printer for MS-DOS programs. Each MS-DOS program that accesses the printer must also have the correct printer driver to be able to communicate with your printer.

How do I change the default printer after installing a printer?

Open the Control Panel window and then open the Printers folder. Right-click the printer you want to be the default printer and then click Set As Default.

How do I rename a printer after I install it?

Open the Control Panel window and then open the Printers folder. Click the name of the printer you want to change and then press the F2 key. Type the new name and then press the Enter key. If your printer is shared, this will cause other people to lose their connection to the printer.

How can I print another test page?

Open the Control Panel window and then open the Printers folder. Right-click the printer and then click Properties. Click the Print Test Page button.

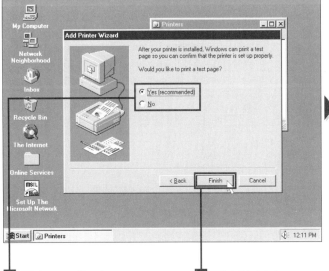

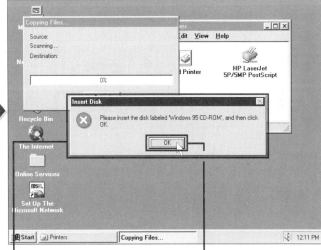

16 Click an option to specify whether or not you want to print a test page (○ changes to ◉). A test page will confirm your printer is set up properly.

17 Click Finish to install the printer.

■ A dialog box appears, asking you to insert the installation CD-ROM disc or a specific floppy disk.

18 Insert the CD-ROM disc or floppy disk into a drive.

19 Click OK.

■ Windows copies the necessary information to your computer.

MOVE OR COPY DATA

You can move or copy data to a different place in a document or from one document to another.

You can select text, numbers or images in a document and share the data with other documents, without having to retype or recreate the data. You can also share data between programs. For example, you can move an image created in Paint to a WordPad document.

The Clipboard is a temporary storage area for data you are moving or copying.

When you move data, Windows removes the data from the original document and places the data in the Clipboard. The data disappears from the original document.

When you copy data, Windows makes a copy of the data and places the copy in the Clipboard. The data remains in its place in the original document.

When you paste data into a document, Windows places the data from the Clipboard into the document. The data appears in the document where you positioned the insertion point.

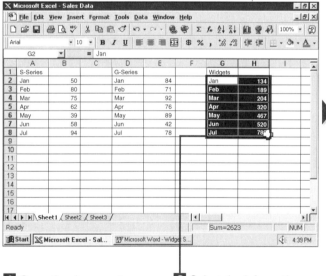

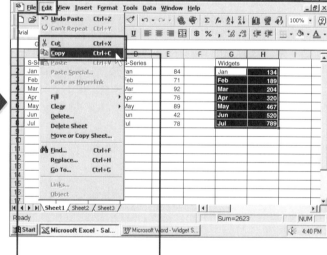

■1 Open the document containing the information you want to appear in another document.

■2 Select the information.

■3 Click Edit.

■4 Click one of the following options.

Cut - Move the information. The information disappears from the document.

Copy - Copy the information. The information remains in the document.

■ Windows places the information in the Clipboard.

How do I select the data I want to move or copy?

In most programs, you can drag the mouse over the data you want to select. Selected data usually appears highlighted on your screen.

Is there a faster way to move or copy data?

Many programs provide toolbar buttons you can use to quickly cut, copy and paste data.

Can I put several items in the Clipboard and then paste them all?

The Clipboard can hold only one item at a time. When you place a new item in the Clipboard, the previous item is replaced.

Can I move or copy data in a dialog box?

Most Windows programs allow you to use the keyboard to move or copy data whenever you do not have access to menus or toolbars. To move data, select the data and then press Ctrl+X on your keyboard. To copy data, select the data and then press Ctrl+C on your keyboard. To paste data, position the insertion point where you want the data to appear and then press Ctrl+V on your keyboard.

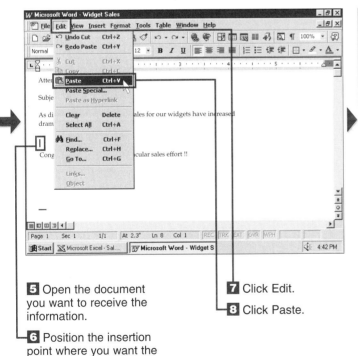

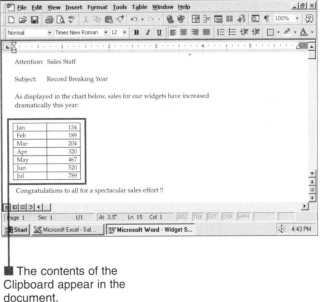

5 Open the document you want to receive the information.

6 Position the insertion point where you want the information to appear.

7 Click Edit.

8 Click Paste.

■ The contents of the Clipboard appear in the document.

USING DRAG AND DROP TO EXCHANGE DATA

You can use the mouse to drag information from its current location to a new location.

You can drag and drop information within a document or between two documents.

If both documents are displayed on the screen, select the information you want and drag it to the new location.

If you want to move or copy information to a program that is minimized on the taskbar, you can select the information and drag it to the program's button on the taskbar. The program window opens and you can then drag and drop the information where you want it to appear.

If you see a black circle with a slash through it ($\bigcirc$) when you try to drag and drop information,

you cannot place the information where the mouse pointer is. For example, you cannot drag files or folders into the Control Panel.

Drag and drop will not work for all programs. If you are having trouble dragging and dropping, you can check your program's manual or Help to see if the program supports the feature.

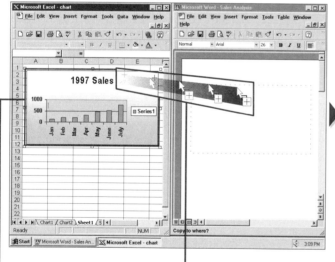

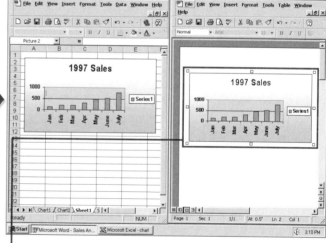

1 Open the documents you want to exchange information.

2 Select the information you want to appear in the other document.

3 Position the mouse over the information.

4 Press and hold down the Ctrl key as you drag the information to the other document.

■ A box indicates where the information will appear.

■ The information appears in the new location.

Note: To move the information instead of copying it, do not hold down the Ctrl key in step 4.

COPY SCREEN OR
WINDOW CONTENTS

You can take a picture of the entire desktop or just the active window. This is useful if you are trying to explain a problem or procedure and you need an example of what you are explaining.

When you copy the desktop or active window, the image is stored in the Clipboard. You can then

place the image in a program like Paint or WordPad.

You can open the Clipboard Viewer to verify that the image is the one you want before pasting it into a program. You can also use the Clipboard Viewer to save your pictures.

You can buy programs that provide options the Print Screen

key does not offer. For example, some programs can include the mouse pointer appearance and location in the picture. There are also programs like Lotus ScreenCam and Microsoft Camcorder that can record a series of movements on your screen and save them as a movie.

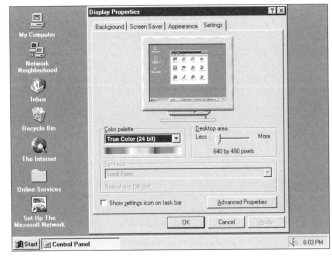

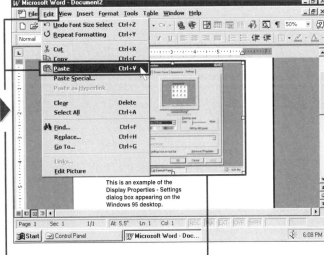

1 Press the Print Screen key to copy the entire screen.

■ To copy just the active window or dialog box, press and hold down the Alt key as you press the Print Screen key.

■ Windows places a copy of the image in the Clipboard.

2 Open the document you want to receive a copy of the image.

3 Click Edit.

4 Click Paste.

■ The image appears in the document.

VIEW CONTENTS OF CLIPBOARD

You can use the Clipboard Viewer to view and save the text, image or other item currently stored in the Clipboard.

The Clipboard is an area of your computer's memory that temporarily stores information. Many different types of programs can access and use the information stored in the Clipboard.

What you see in the Clipboard Viewer depends on the type of item you placed in the Clipboard. When you place an item such as an image or text in the Clipboard, you can view the entire item. When you place an item such as a file or folder in the Clipboard, you can only view the path of the item. The contents of the item are not displayed.

When you place a multimedia item such as a sound or video file in the Clipboard, you can only view the icon that represents the item.

You can save information stored in the Clipboard and reuse the information later. The information you save in the Clipboard will be saved in a file with the .clp extension.

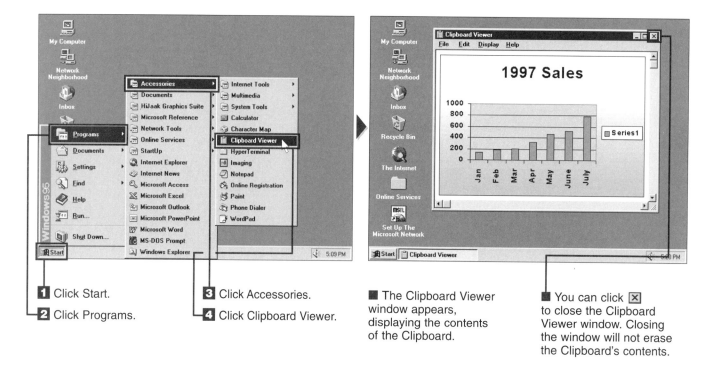

■1 Click Start.

■2 Click Programs.

■3 Click Accessories.

■4 Click Clipboard Viewer.

■ The Clipboard Viewer window appears, displaying the contents of the Clipboard.

■ You can click ⊠ to close the Clipboard Viewer window. Closing the window will not erase the Clipboard's contents.

TIPS

Why can't I find the Clipboard Viewer on my computer?

The Clipboard Viewer may not be installed. The Clipboard Viewer is located in the Accessories group on the Windows 95 CD-ROM disc. See page 580.

Why does the image appear distorted in the Clipboard Viewer?

The Clipboard Viewer automatically sizes items to fit the window. In some cases, you can choose the Display menu and then select the DIB Bitmap or Bitmap commands to display the image at the original size.

How long does information stay in the Clipboard?

The Clipboard stores one item at a time. You can paste the item as many times as you want. As soon as you move or copy a new item, the new item replaces the item currently stored in the Clipboard. When you shut down Windows, the item in the Clipboard is deleted.

How do I open a Clipboard file I saved?

You can open a Clipboard file you saved by choosing the File menu and then selecting the Open command.

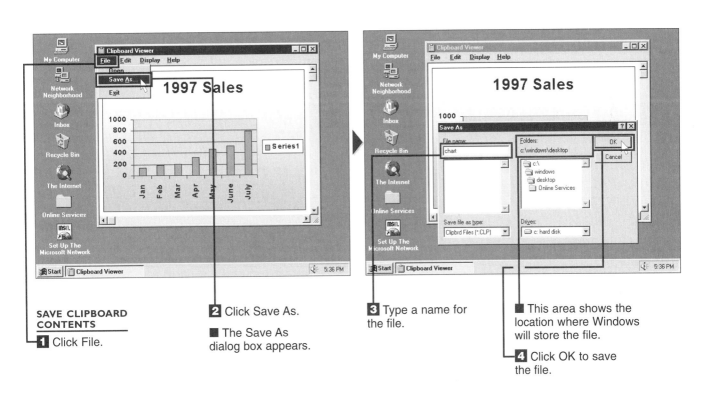

SAVE CLIPBOARD CONTENTS

1 Click File.

2 Click Save As.

■ The Save As dialog box appears.

3 Type a name for the file.

■ This area shows the location where Windows will store the file.

4 Click OK to save the file.

PUT PART OF DOCUMENT ON THE DESKTOP

You can place frequently used information on your desktop. This gives you quick access to the information. Information you place on the desktop is called a scrap.

Document scraps save you time since you do not have to retype the information over and over. For example, you can create a

scrap containing your name, address and phone number. You can then drag the scrap into a document whenever you need the information.

You can also create a scrap for images, like your company logo. A scrap can also be a sound file that plays a message.

Using scraps is the easiest way to gather selections from many documents to create a new document.

Scraps are usually available for programs that allow you to drag and drop information and that support Object Linking and Embedding (OLE).

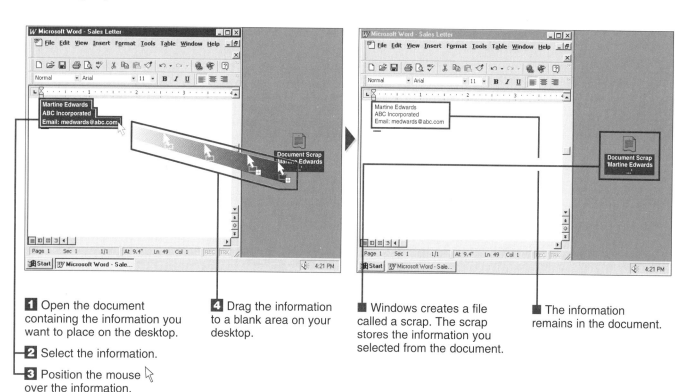

1 Open the document containing the information you want to place on the desktop.

2 Select the information.

3 Position the mouse over the information.

4 Drag the information to a blank area on your desktop.

■ Windows creates a file called a scrap. The scrap stores the information you selected from the document.

■ The information remains in the document.

How can I remove a scrap I no longer need?

You can work with a scrap as you would work with any file on your desktop. To remove a scrap you no longer need, drag the scrap to the Recycle Bin.

Can I view or edit the contents of a scrap?

When you double-click a scrap, the program you used to create the original document opens and displays the contents of the scrap. You can edit the scrap as you would any document.

How do I create a scrap from a program that does not support Object Linking and Embedding (OLE)?

You must first copy the information to a program that does support OLE. For example, you can copy an image created in Paint to a WordPad document. From the WordPad document, you can drag the image to the desktop to create a scrap.

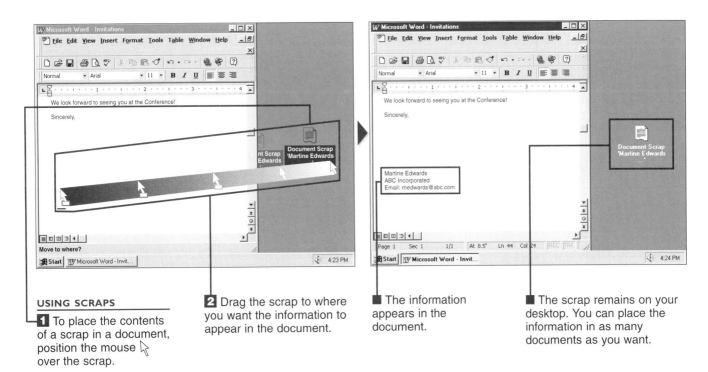

USING SCRAPS

■1 To place the contents of a scrap in a document, position the mouse ⌖ over the scrap.

■2 Drag the scrap to where you want the information to appear in the document.

■ The information appears in the document.

■ The scrap remains on your desktop. You can place the information in as many documents as you want.

EMBED INFORMATION

You can use Object Linking and Embedding (OLE, pronounced oh-lay) to create a document that contains information from several programs. This type of document is called a compound document.

Each piece of information used to create a compound document is called an object. You can use objects such as text, charts, graphs, images, sound and video clips.

Each program on your computer is designed to work with a specific type of object. You can use a specific program to create an object and then embed all the objects you create in a compound document. For example, you can use a spreadsheet to create a graph and an image editing program to create an image. You can then embed these objects in a report created in a word processor.

When you embed objects, the objects become part of the compound document. The objects are not connected to the document they were created in.

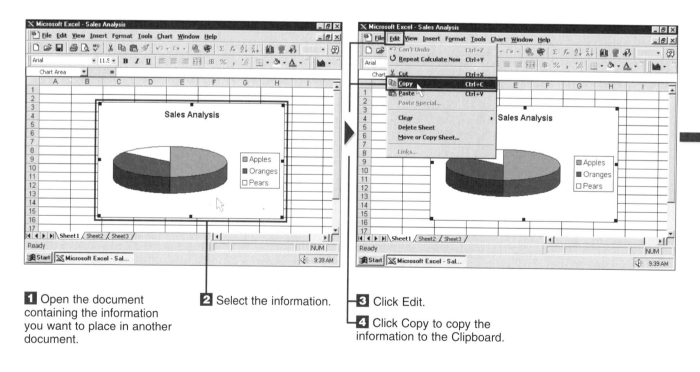

1 Open the document containing the information you want to place in another document.

2 Select the information.

3 Click Edit.

4 Click Copy to copy the information to the Clipboard.

How can I tell if a program supports OLE?

All programs designed for Windows 95 support OLE. If a program has the Paste Special command in the Edit menu, the program supports OLE.

Can I create a new object without first starting the program I want to use?

In the compound document, choose the Insert menu then select the Object command. Select the Create New tab and then click the type of object you want to create. You can use this procedure in the Microsoft, Lotus and Corel Office suites.

Can I use drag and drop to embed objects?

In programs that support drag and drop, you can drag and drop objects to embed them in a compound document.

Can I embed an object I have already created without opening the document?

In the compound document, choose the Insert menu and then select the Object command. Select the Create from File tab and then click the Browse button to find the document you want to embed. You can use this procedure in the Microsoft, Lotus and Corel Office suites.

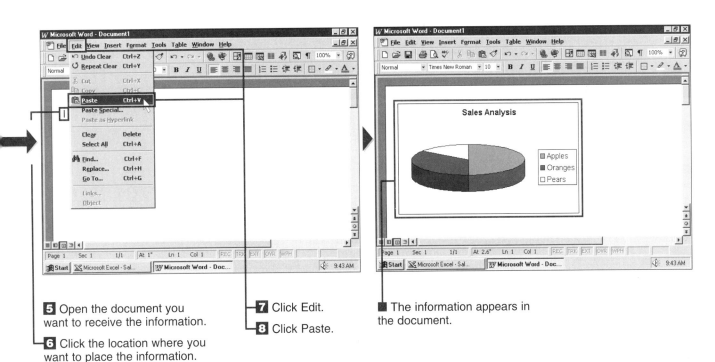

5 Open the document you want to receive the information.

6 Click the location where you want to place the information.

7 Click Edit.

8 Click Paste.

■ The information appears in the document.

EDIT EMBEDDED INFORMATION

You can change an embedded object in a compound document. You can edit the object using the same tools you used to create it, without leaving the compound document.

An embedded object is part of the compound document. When you change an embedded object, the object in the original document does not change.

When you double-click an embedded object, the menus and toolbars of the program you used to create the object appear on your screen. In some circumstances, the embedded object may be displayed in a window and take on the appearance of the original program. For example, a spreadsheet object may appear in a window with rows and columns.

When you finish editing the object, the menus and toolbars from the original program disappear from your screen and you can continue working with the compound document.

A compound document file is often large because it stores information about each embedded object and the program the object was created in.

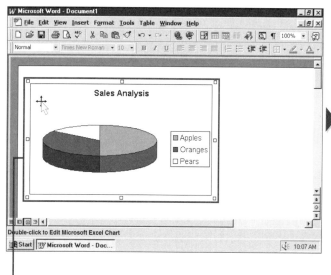

1 Double-click the embedded information you want to change.

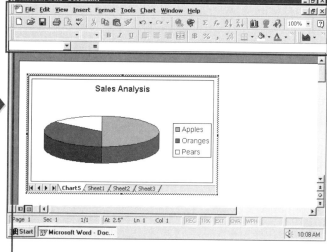

■ The toolbars and menus from the program you used to create the information appear. You can access all the commands you need to make the necessary changes.

Can I work with a compound document that someone else has created?

If you have the programs that were used to create the objects contained in the compound document, you can work with a compound document someone else has created. You will not be able to edit an object if you do not have the appropriate program. You may not even be able to see an object created in a program you do not have installed on your computer.

Why isn't an object I copied and pasted responding to my double-click?

When you copy and paste an object, the object may be only placed in the document, not embedded. You may need to paste the object again using a different procedure. Choose the Edit menu and then select the Paste Special command. In the Paste Special dialog box, select Paste to embed the object.

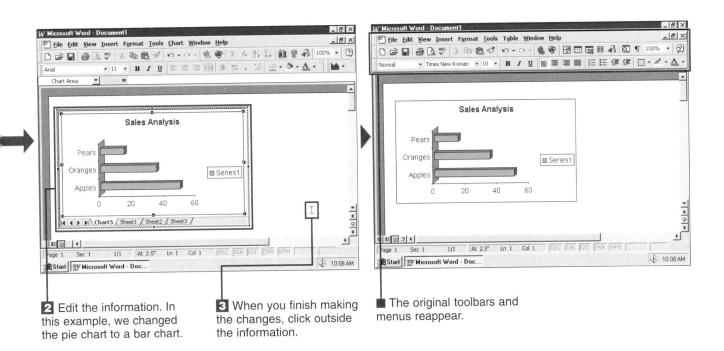

2 Edit the information. In this example, we changed the pie chart to a bar chart.

3 When you finish making the changes, click outside the information.

■ The original toolbars and menus reappear.

LINK INFORMATION

You can use Object Linking and Embedding (OLE) to link the information in one document to several compound documents. A compound document can contain information from several sources.

The information you place in a compound document from another document is called an object and can include items such as text, pictures, charts, spreadsheets and slides. You can link an object between documents in the same program or in different programs. For example, you can link a chart in your spreadsheet to a report, a presentation and a newsletter.

When you link an object, the compound document displays the object but contains only a description of where the object is stored, and not the object itself. The object remains in the original document. Since the linked object is always part of the original document, a connection, or link, exists between the original and compound documents. You should not delete, move or rename the original document containing the object you have linked to compound documents.

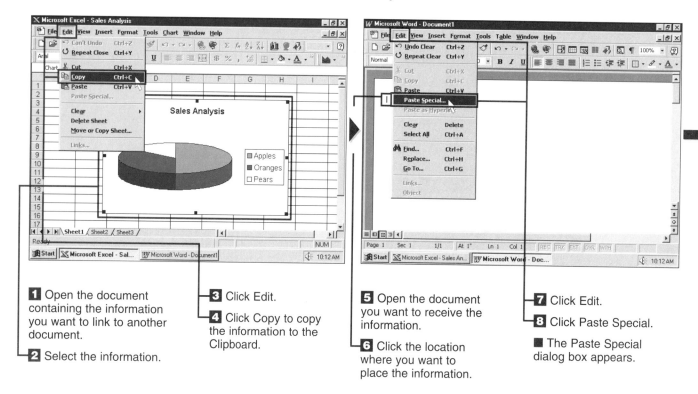

1 Open the document containing the information you want to link to another document.

2 Select the information.

3 Click Edit.

4 Click Copy to copy the information to the Clipboard.

5 Open the document you want to receive the information.

6 Click the location where you want to place the information.

7 Click Edit.

8 Click Paste Special.

■ The Paste Special dialog box appears.

TIPS

The information I linked between two documents created in the same program does not work properly. How can I fix this?

The most reliable way to link information in the same program is to insert the information as an Object in the Paste Special dialog box.

How can I tell if a program supports OLE?

If the program you are pasting an object into has the Paste Special command in the Edit menu, the program supports OLE. If the command is on the menu but not available, the program where you created the object does not support OLE.

Can I use drag and drop to link objects?

When you drag and drop an object, the object is embedded in the new document, not linked. For information on embedding, see pages 124 to 127.

Can I edit a linked object?

You can edit a linked object in the original document. When you edit a linked object, all of the compound documents containing the link are automatically updated to reflect the changes. This helps to ensure that your compound documents always display up-to-date information. See page 130.

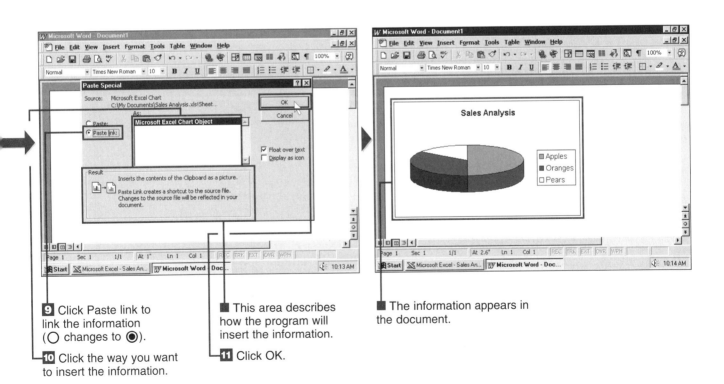

■ **9** Click Paste link to link the information (○ changes to ⊙).

■ **10** Click the way you want to insert the information.

■ This area describes how the program will insert the information.

■ **11** Click OK.

■ The information appears in the document.

EDIT LINKED INFORMATION

When you change a linked object, the original and compound documents both display the changes. If you have linked the same object to several documents, editing the linked object allows you to update all of the compound documents at the same time.

A compound document displays the object, but contains only a description of where the object is stored, and not the object itself. To edit the linked object, the original document must be available on your computer or network, and the program used to create the object must be installed on your computer.

When you double-click a linked object in a compound document, the program used to create the object opens and displays the object in the original document.

You can also go directly to the program to open the original document and display the object. You can then edit the linked object as you would edit any other object. All of the changes you make to the linked object appear in the compound documents.

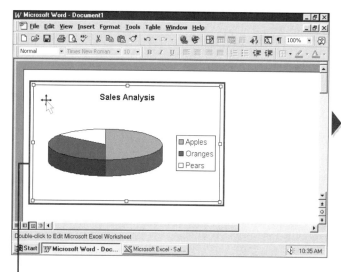

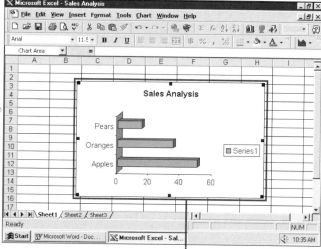

1 Double-click the linked information you want to change.

■ The program you used to create the information opens. You can access all the commands you need to make the necessary changes.

2 Edit the information. In this example, we changed the pie chart to a bar chart.

How long does it take to update a linked object?

After you edit an object, the linked object will update within a few seconds in an open compound document. If a compound document is not open, you will be asked to update the linked object the next time you open the document.

How can I make sure the linked objects are up-to-date before I print a document?

You can choose the Edit menu and then select the Links command to view and update the links.

Can I e-mail a compound document that contains linked objects?

E-mailing a compound document is most useful on a network where people have access to the same programs and the same shared documents. If you e-mail a compound document to someone who does not have access to the original document, they will not be able to receive updates when you change the linked object. If the recipient does not have the program the object was created in, they will not be able to edit the compound document.

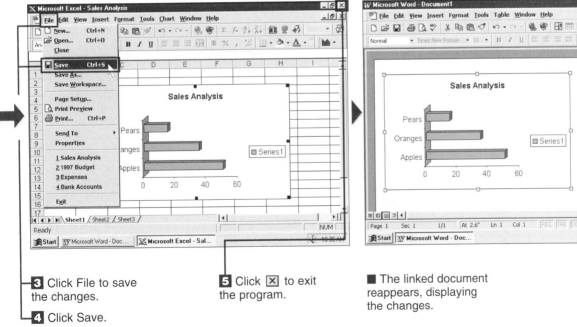

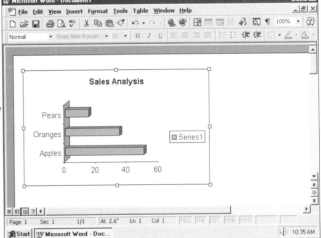

-3 Click File to save the changes.

-4 Click Save.

-5 Click ☒ to exit the program.

■ The linked document reappears, displaying the changes.

START AN MS-DOS PROMPT WINDOW

You can use the MS-DOS command prompt to work with MS-DOS programs and commands in Windows.

Windows can run almost all MS-DOS games and programs without any problem. Some MS-DOS utilities, such as disk defragmenters, backup programs and undelete programs, may not run properly in Windows.

If you want to use these utility programs in Windows, a message may appear indicating that the program is not suitable for use with Windows, or that the program cannot run while other programs are running.

To make the MS-DOS Prompt window easier to use, you can enlarge the window to fill your entire screen. You can

also display text in the window in a different font.

Although you can have several MS-DOS Prompt windows open at the same time, they require some of your computer's resources. Having many MS-DOS windows open may slow down your computer's performance or prevent you from starting other MS-DOS or Windows programs.

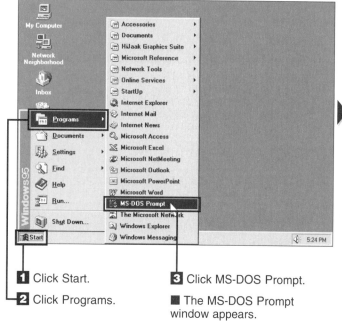

1 Click Start.

2 Click Programs.

3 Click MS-DOS Prompt.

■ The MS-DOS Prompt window appears.

■ You can enter MS-DOS commands and start MS-DOS programs in the window. In this example, we enter the **dir** command to list the contents of the current directory.

4 Click 🔲 to fill the entire screen with the MS-DOS Prompt window.

Note: You can also hold down the Alt key and then press the Enter key.

TIPS

How do I change the size of the MS-DOS Prompt window?

When you choose a new font size, the size of the MS-DOS Prompt window also changes to accommodate the new font size. You can drag the edges of an MS-DOS window, but the window may not adjust to the new size properly.

Is there another way to close an MS-DOS Prompt window?

You can click ☒ to close the window, but a message may appear warning that you will lose any unsaved information.

How can I find out what commands MS-DOS uses?

In the MS-DOS window, type **cd c:\windows\command** to open the folder that contains the MS-DOS commands included with Windows. Then type **dir** to list the commands.

How can I find out what each MS-DOS command does?

Type the name of a command followed by /? For example, you can type **move/?** to find out what the move command does.

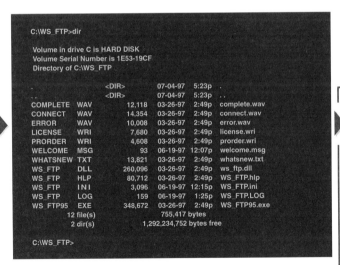

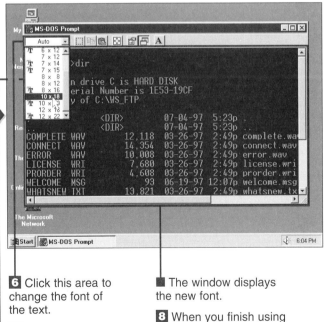

■ The MS-DOS Prompt window fills the entire screen.

5 Hold down the Alt key and then press the Enter key to return the MS-DOS screen to a window.

6 Click this area to change the font of the text.

7 Click the font you want to use.

■ The window displays the new font.

8 When you finish using the MS-DOS Prompt window, type **exit** and then press the Enter key to close the window.

COPY DATA BETWEEN MS-DOS AND WINDOWS PROGRAMS

Y ou can copy and paste information from MS-DOS programs to Windows programs or other MS-DOS programs.

When you begin using Windows, you do not need to abandon your old MS-DOS programs or files. If your new Windows programs cannot open your old files, you can still use your older files in

the MS-DOS program. Copying and pasting information from MS-DOS is not as efficient as in Windows programs, but it is better than having to find a paper copy of the document and then retyping it into a Windows program.

When you copy information from an MS-DOS program, you lose the format of the text and

the word wrap. Any pasted text is displayed in the default font of the program you are copying to.

A paragraph break is inserted at the end of every line.

You can also copy and paste MS-DOS commands and their results. For example, you can copy the listing created using the dir command into a document.

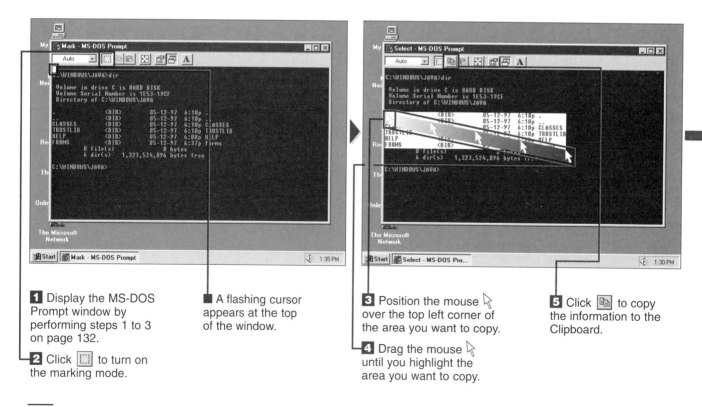

1 Display the MS-DOS Prompt window by performing steps 1 to 3 on page 132.

2 Click 🔲 to turn on the marking mode.

■ A flashing cursor appears at the top of the window.

3 Position the mouse ⬉ over the top left corner of the area you want to copy.

4 Drag the mouse ⬉ until you highlight the area you want to copy.

5 Click 🖻 to copy the information to the Clipboard.

Can I copy a picture of the MS-DOS window?

To copy a picture of the window, click anywhere in the MS-DOS window and then press Alt+Print Scrn. You can then paste the picture of the MS-DOS window in a document.

Can I copy text from an MS-DOS program displayed in full-screen mode?

You cannot copy specific text if an MS-DOS program is displayed in full-screen mode. You can copy all the text from the screen at once by pressing the Print Scrn key. You can then paste the text into a document.

Is there an easier way to select text I want?

You can use the QuickEdit mode for the mouse to select text more easily. Click 🖫 to open the Properties dialog box and select the Misc tab. From the Mouse section, select QuickEdit (☐ changes to ☑). In QuickEdit mode, the mouse is used to highlight text. You cannot use the mouse as a pointing device in the MS-DOS program when the QuickEdit mode is active.

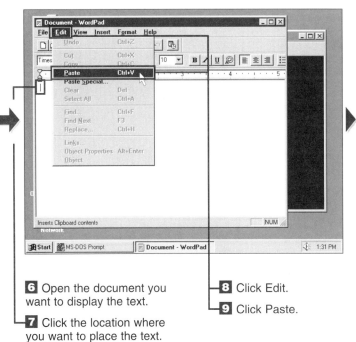

6 Open the document you want to display the text.

7 Click the location where you want to place the text.

8 Click Edit.

9 Click Paste.

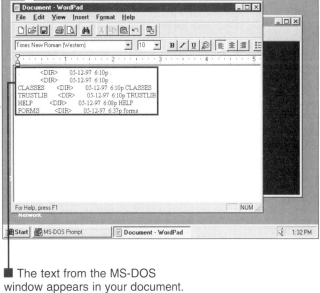

■ The text from the MS-DOS window appears in your document.

INSTALL AND RUN
MS-DOS PROGRAMS

Programs designed to work with MS-DOS can be installed and used in Windows 95.

You must locate and run the installation program for the program you want to install. Many programs provide a file with documentation to help you install the program. These files often

have names such as readme.txt or install.txt

If a documentation file does not exist or does not contain specific installation information, look for the file you need to install the program on your computer. This file may start with the word

install, setup or go, and may also have the .bat extension.

When you install an MS-DOS game, the program will often ask questions about the devices on your computer, like a joystick or sound card. The program can then make adjustments to your computer so the game can run properly.

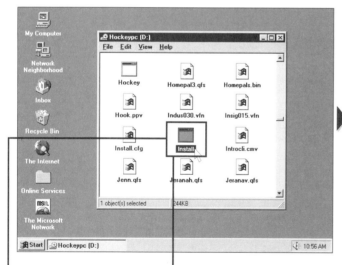

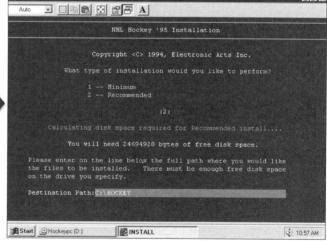

INSTALL A PROGRAM

■1 Locate the installation file for the program you want to install.

■ The installation file may be on your computer if you downloaded a program from the Internet, or the file may be stored on a floppy disk.

■2 Double-click the installation file.

■ The installation program starts.

■3 Follow the instructions on your screen. Every program will set itself up differently. In this example, we are installing a game named Hockey 95.

TIPS

Can I place the program on the Start menu?

From a My Computer or Explorer window, drag the file you use to start the program onto the Start menu. See page 250 for more information.

How can I delete an MS-DOS program?

To delete an MS-DOS program, drag the program folder to the Recycle Bin. Make sure the folder does not contain any documents you still need. You should also remove any shortcuts to the program on the desktop and the Start menu.

What can I do if there is no installation program or documentation provided?

Create a new folder on your computer and copy all the files from the disk(s) into the folder. Use the program file to start the program. If you are not sure which is the program file, look for a file with a .bat, .com or .exe extension.

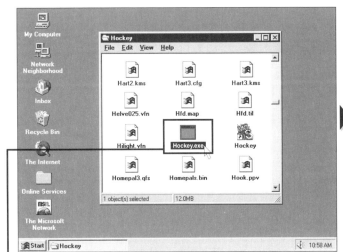

RUN A PROGRAM

1 Locate the file that runs the program.

2 Double-click the file.

■ The program starts.

OPTIMIZE MS-DOS PROGRAMS

General and Font Settings

You can change the General and Font settings to maximize performance when running MS-DOS programs. When you encounter problems with an MS-DOS program, you can adjust the settings so the program will operate properly.

The General tab displays information about a program, including the size, the MS-DOS name and the date and time the file was created. You can also check the attributes for a file. Attributes include Read-only, Archive, Hidden and System. You should not have to change the attributes that Windows sets for the program.

You can use the Font settings in the MS-DOS Properties dialog box to select the font type and size you want to use for the program. The font you select also determines the size of the window displaying the program. You can see a preview of the font and the way the program will appear on your screen.

If you make changes to the General or Font settings, the new settings are saved and used when you run the program again.

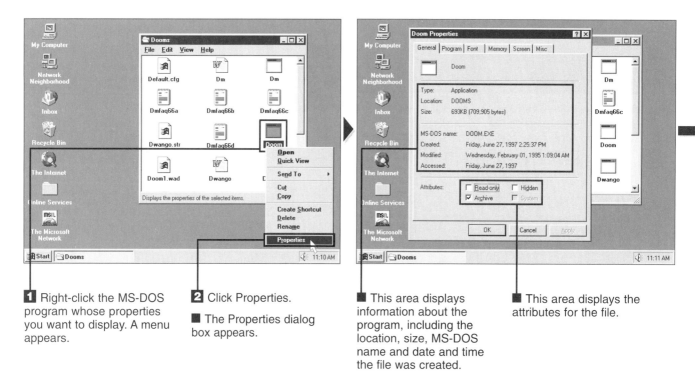

1 Right-click the MS-DOS program whose properties you want to display. A menu appears.

2 Click Properties.

■ The Properties dialog box appears.

■ This area displays information about the program, including the location, size, MS-DOS name and date and time the file was created.

■ This area displays the attributes for the file.

TIPS

Why isn't the General tab shown in the Properties dialog box?

If you are displaying the Properties dialog box for a program that is currently running, the General tab is not available.

I selected a different font size. Why doesn't the font change in a full-screen MS-DOS window?

In a full-screen MS-DOS window, your computer's hardware font is used.

Which is the appropriate font to use?

Each font creates a window of a different size. You may find some font sizes and types easier to read than others. If you leave the font setting at Auto, Windows will use the appropriate font for the window size you use.

GETTING STARTED

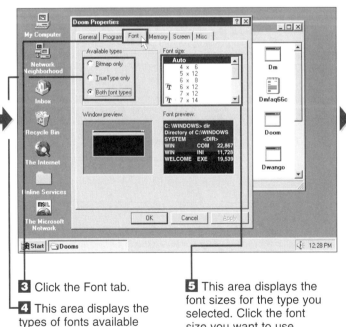

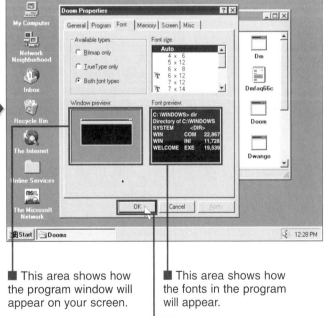

3 Click the Font tab.

4 This area displays the types of fonts available for the program. Click the type of font you want to use (○ changes to ◉).

5 This area displays the font sizes for the type you selected. Click the font size you want to use.

■ This area shows how the program window will appear on your screen.

■ This area shows how the fonts in the program will appear.

6 Click OK to confirm your changes.

OPTIMIZE MS-DOS PROGRAMS

Change Program Settings

You can control the way an MS-DOS program starts. You should only adjust the Program settings if the program does not start properly.

You can view the program name and icon, as well as the command that starts the program. There are additional icons you can choose from to represent the program.

You can specify the folder where you want the program to open and save files.

If the program needs to run a batch file, you can specify the name of the batch file. A batch file is a text file that contains commands the program requires to run properly.

If you use the program regularly, you may want to give the program

a keyboard shortcut so you can start the program using the keyboard.

When you start the program, you can have the program appear as a window, a minimized button on the taskbar or enlarged to fill your entire screen.

You can have the MS-DOS window close automatically or stay open after you close the program.

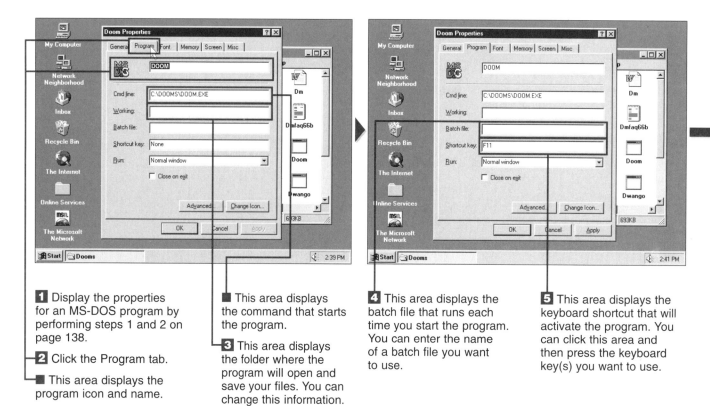

■1 Display the properties for an MS-DOS program by performing steps 1 and 2 on page 138.

■2 Click the Program tab.

■ This area displays the program icon and name.

■ This area displays the command that starts the program.

■3 This area displays the folder where the program will open and save your files. You can change this information.

■4 This area displays the batch file that runs each time you start the program. You can enter the name of a batch file you want to use.

■5 This area displays the keyboard shortcut that will activate the program. You can click this area and then press the keyboard key(s) you want to use.

How do I know if a program needs to run a batch file?

You can consult your computer's manual, the hardware's manual or the program's manual for more information about batch files the program may need.

What shortcut key combination should I use?

You should use a combination made up of Ctrl, Alt and another key, such as Ctrl+Alt+Y. You may also use a function key that is not assigned to another task.

Why won't my shortcut keys start the program?

A shortcut key will only start the program if the program is on the desktop or on the Start menu. Your shortcut keys will also not work if they are assigned to another task in Windows.

Will I need to change any of these settings?

The shortcut key is the only setting you may want to change.

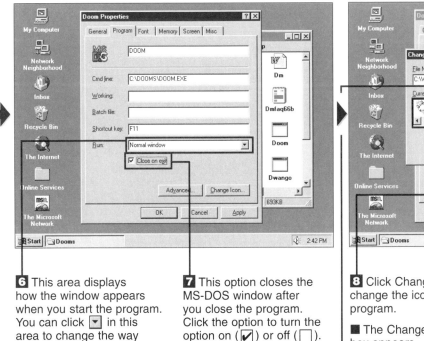

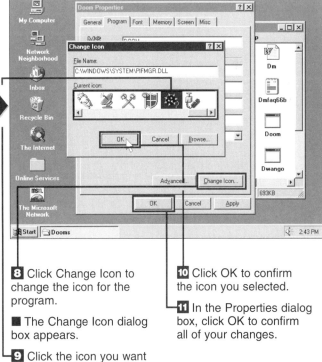

6 This area displays how the window appears when you start the program. You can click ▼ in this area to change the way the window appears.

7 This option closes the MS-DOS window after you close the program. Click the option to turn the option on (✔) or off (☐).

8 Click Change Icon to change the icon for the program.

■ The Change Icon dialog box appears.

9 Click the icon you want to use for the program.

10 Click OK to confirm the icon you selected.

11 In the Properties dialog box, click OK to confirm all of your changes.

OPTIMIZE MS-DOS PROGRAMS
Change Advanced Program Settings

When you encounter problems with an MS-DOS program, you can adjust the Advanced Program settings so the program will operate properly.

Some programs may not run properly or not run at all if they detect that Windows is running on the computer at the same time.

You can choose to prevent the MS-DOS program from detecting Windows or have Windows determine whether the program must use MS-DOS mode to run properly. You can allow the MS-DOS program to shut down Windows and take complete control of your computer.

When running a program in MS-DOS mode, you can have a warning appear before your other programs are shut down and the computer restarts.

In MS-DOS mode, a program can use its own personalized set of startup configuration files that enable the program to run properly.

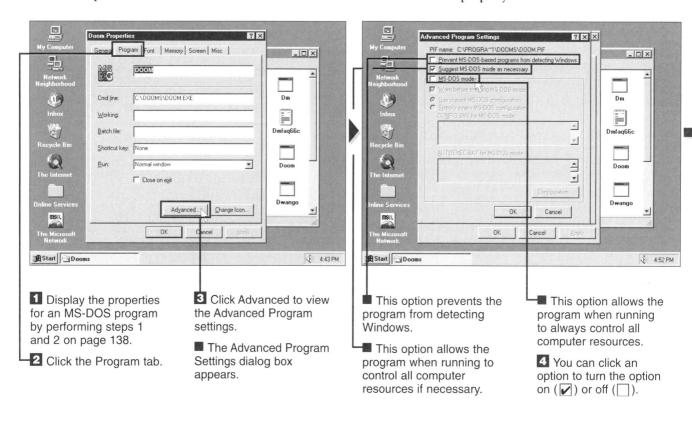

■1 Display the properties for an MS-DOS program by performing steps 1 and 2 on page 138.

■2 Click the Program tab.

■3 Click Advanced to view the Advanced Program settings.

■ The Advanced Program Settings dialog box appears.

■ This option prevents the program from detecting Windows.

■ This option allows the program when running to control all computer resources if necessary.

■ This option allows the program when running to always control all computer resources.

■4 You can click an option to turn the option on (☑) or off (☐).

When should I change the Advanced Program settings?

You should change the Advanced Program settings only as the last resort for unwilling and uncooperative programs.

What settings should I use in the Config.sys and Autoexec.bat files?

Use the minimum amount of settings in the configuration files to make the program work. You can usually find details on the best settings for the configuration files in the MS-DOS program's manual. Help files or other instruction files on the program's disk or CD-ROM disc may also contain configuration information.

How do I set up the mouse in an MS-DOS program?

In the Advanced Program Settings dialog box, click the Configuration button to display the Select MS-DOS Configuration Options dialog box. If a warning dialog box appears, click Yes to continue. Select Mouse from the list (☐ changes to ☑) and then click OK. The mouse is not available for all programs.

Note: You may have to select MS-DOS mode and Specify a new MS-DOS configuration for the Configuration button to be available.

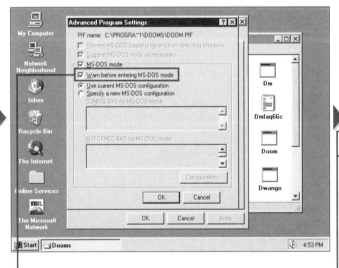

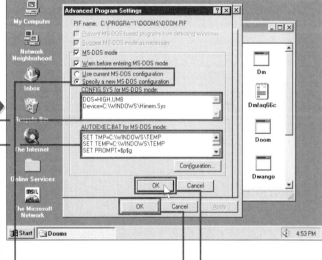

5 This option will display a warning before closing all other programs and running the program. Click the option to turn the option on (☑) or off (☐).

Note: You can only perform steps 5 to 7 if you selected MS-DOS mode in step 4.

6 You can choose to use the current Config.sys and Autoexec.bat file settings or choose to create new settings for this program. Click the appropriate option (○ changes to ◉).

7 You can use this area to edit the Config.sys and Autoexec.bat files used by this program.

8 Click OK.

9 Click OK in the Properties dialog box to confirm your changes.

OPTIMIZE MS-DOS PROGRAMS
Change Memory Settings

You can manage the memory requirements of an MS-DOS program. You should leave the memory requirements set at Auto unless the program is not working properly. Before changing any memory settings, you should consult the program's manual to find the specific settings the program requires. Memory settings are saved and used each time you start the program.

If the amount of conventional memory needs to be adjusted, you can specify a new amount in kilobytes (K) for the program. You can also protect the conventional memory from being altered by the program. The program may run slower when you protect the conventional memory.

You can specify the amount of expanded and extended memory

in kilobytes (K) for the program. You can also specify if the program can use a section of extended memory called the high memory area (HMA).

Windows chooses an amount of MS-DOS protected-mode memory for the program based on the setup of your computer. You can choose a different amount.

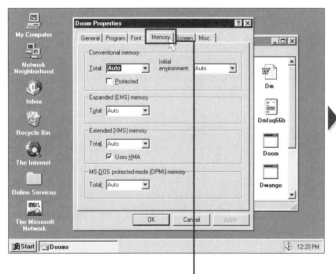

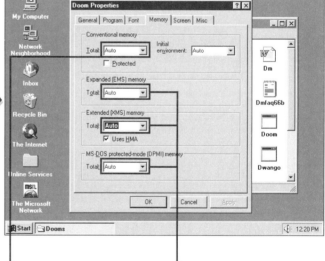

1 Display the properties for an MS-DOS program by performing steps 1 and 2 on page 138.

2 Click the Memory tab.

■ This area displays the amount of conventional memory required by the program.

■ This area displays the maximum amount of expanded, extended and MS-DOS protected-mode memory assigned to the program.

3 You can click ▼ beside a memory type to change the amount of memory assigned to the program.

TIPS

How much conventional memory is available for MS-DOS programs?

In an MS-DOS window, type **mem** and then press Enter to view the amount of memory on your computer available for MS-DOS programs. In most circumstances, there should be about 580 K of conventional memory available. There may be some devices running on your computer that use up a portion of that memory. You can free up some conventional memory by opening the Autoexec.bat and Config.sys files and removing these devices. For information on viewing and editing the Autoexec.bat and Config.sys files, see page 640.

My program is not running properly. How can I fix this?

Some MS-DOS programs do not perform well with access to an unlimited amount of expanded and extended memory. You can set the amount of expanded and extended memory to 8192 K if you are having problems using your program.

Why does the Memory tab indicate that my computer is not set up to use expanded memory?

You may not be able to use expanded memory if your computer's Config.sys file contains the emm386.exe command with the "noems" setting.

GETTING STARTED

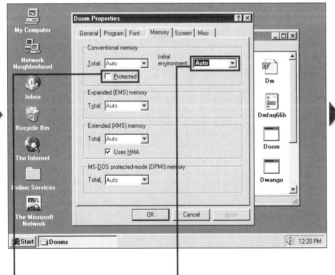

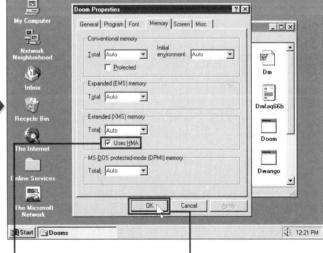

4 This option protects the system memory from program errors. Click the option to turn the option on (☑) or off (☐).

5 This area displays the amount of memory reserved for the MS-DOS interface. You can click ▼ in this area to change the amount of reserved memory.

6 This option specifies if the program can use the high memory area (HMA). Click the option to turn the option on (☑) or off (☐).

7 Click OK to confirm all of your changes.

OPTIMIZE MS-DOS PROGRAMS
Change Screen Settings

You can control the way an MS-DOS program appears on your screen. You should only change the Screen settings if the MS-DOS program is not appearing properly.

Most text-based MS-DOS programs appear in a window. This allows you to share information with other programs. MS-DOS programs that contain

graphics usually fill your entire screen.

You can have the toolbar appear every time you start the program in a window.

You can restore the program's window setting to display certain settings, such as font and window size, every time

you start the program. If you do not restore the window settings, the settings that are displayed when you exit the program will be used the next time you start the program.

You can also adjust the performance settings if the program is not appearing properly on your screen.

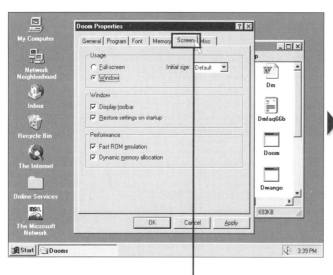

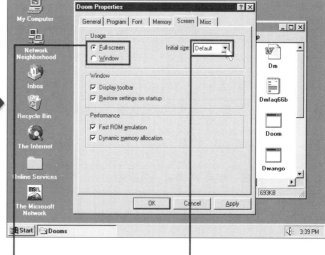

1 Display the properties for an MS-DOS program by performing steps 1 and 2 on page 138.

2 Click the Screen tab.

3 You can choose to display the program using the entire screen or in a window. Click the appropriate option (○ changes to ◉).

4 This area specifies the initial number of lines the screen will display. You can click this area to change the number of lines.

TIPS

Why should I change the number of lines displayed in a screen?

Changing the number of lines allows you to display more information on your screen. For example, you can view 50 lines of a directory listing instead of 25 lines. Some MS-DOS programs will not display a different number of lines.

Can I save the Screen settings when the program fills the entire screen?

Windows automatically saves the settings that are displayed when you exit a program that fills the entire screen. The settings will be used the next time you open the program.

Can I switch between displaying the program in a window and displaying the program using the entire screen?

You can use Alt+Enter to switch back and forth between displaying a program in a window and using the entire screen. If the program can only run when it fills the entire screen, Windows will let you know if it needs to suspend the program when you switch to a window.

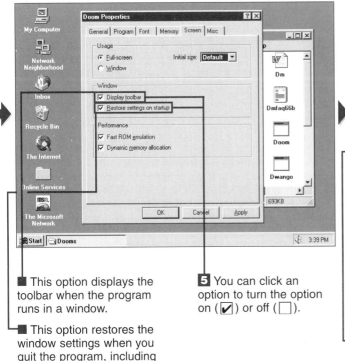

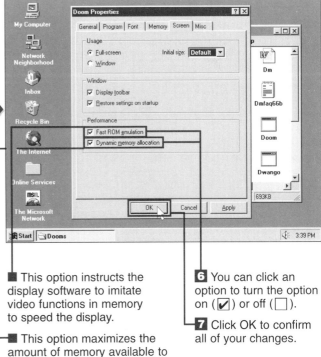

■ This option displays the toolbar when the program runs in a window.

■ This option restores the window settings when you quit the program, including the window size, position and font.

5 You can click an option to turn the option on (✔) or off (☐).

■ This option instructs the display software to imitate video functions in memory to speed the display.

■ This option maximizes the amount of memory available to other programs if the program uses text and graphic modes.

6 You can click an option to turn the option on (✔) or off (☐).

7 Click OK to confirm all of your changes.

OPTIMIZE MS-DOS PROGRAMS
Change Miscellaneous Settings

You can control the way an MS-DOS program works with Windows. You should only adjust the settings on the Misc tab if the program is not working properly.

Idle sensitivity indicates how long the program can be idle before Windows reduces computer resources to the program. Low idle sensitivity lets the program run longer

before computer resources to the program are reduced.

You can also use the Always suspend option to prevent the program from accessing any computer resources when the program is not active.

The Allow screen saver option lets the screen saver start even when the program is active. You may want to turn this option off if your screen saver

interferes with the operation of your program.

The Warn if still active option displays a message on your screen when you try to close the program window while the program is running.

The MS-DOS program may use shortcut keys that exist in Windows. You can turn off the shortcut keys in Windows to use the shortcut keys in the MS-DOS program.

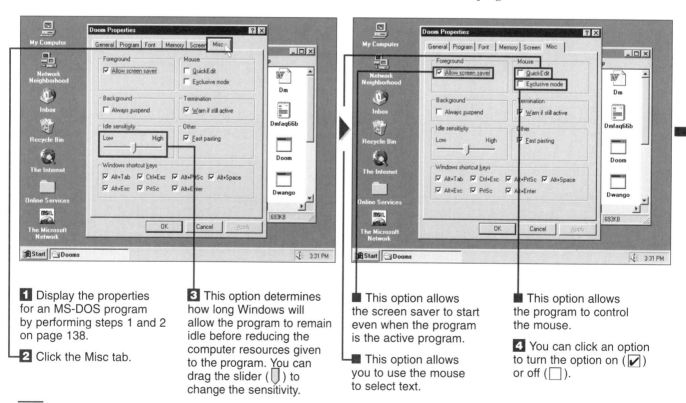

1 Display the properties for an MS-DOS program by performing steps 1 and 2 on page 138.

2 Click the Misc tab.

3 This option determines how long Windows will allow the program to remain idle before reducing the computer resources given to the program. You can drag the slider ( ) to change the sensitivity.

■ This option allows the screen saver to start even when the program is the active program.

■ This option allows you to use the mouse to select text.

■ This option allows the program to control the mouse.

4 You can click an option to turn the option on (✔) or off (☐).

TIPS

Why isn't my mouse working properly?

When you set the mouse to Exclusive mode, you give control of the mouse to the MS-DOS program and you cannot use the mouse as a standard Windows pointer. When the program fills your screen, use Alt+Spacebar+P to access the Properties dialog box. If you want to use the mouse alone to select text for moving and copying, you can turn on the QuickEdit option.

How much of my computer's resources does an MS-DOS window use?

An open MS-DOS window, even when idle, uses 1-2% of your computer's resources and 2-3% of your processor time.

The information I paste into the program does not appear properly? How can I fix this?

You can turn off the Fast pasting option. This will slow down the rate that Windows transfers pasted information to the MS-DOS program.

Where should I set the Idle sensitivity?

You can set the Idle sensitivity to high if the program is waiting for you to enter information. You should set the Idle sensitivity to low if the program performs a regular action or waits for a specific time to perform an action.

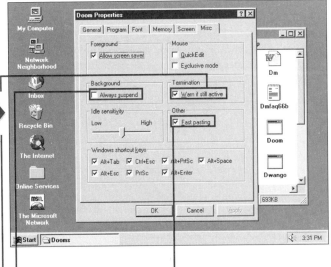

■ This option prevents the program from using any computer resources when it is not active.

■ This option displays a warning message when you try to close the program.

■ This option allows Windows to use a faster method of pasting information into the program.

5 You can click an option to turn the option on (☑) or off (☐).

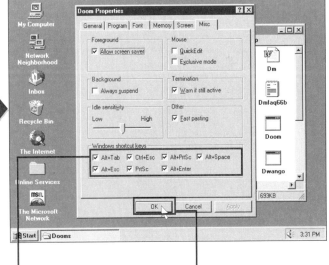

6 This area displays the shortcut keys you want to reserve for Windows instead of the program. Click each shortcut key you want Windows to ignore when using the program (☑ changes to ☐).

7 Click OK to confirm all of your changes.

David C. Thompson
President
Dynamic Advertising Inc.
1223 Lincoln Ave.
New York, N.Y.
10023

Dear Mr. Thompson,

I would like to take this opportunity to congratulate you and your company for winning First Prize in the 1996 Logo Design Contest. It gives me the greatest pleasure to inform you that the Judging Committee's decision was unanimous. Your entry was clearly the best among the hundreds of outstanding entries we received this year.

Enclosed please find a copy of the Judging Committee's remarks. This report states that "the logo designed by Dynamic Advertising Inc. serves to enhance the company's image through the creative use of colors and modern design principles."

The award will be presented on August 20 at the International Design Institute's annual banquet. We hope to see you there.

Once again, please accept my congratulations.

Sincerely,

Karen Davis
Chairperson
Judging Committee

Office Party

- Appetizers
- Drinks
- Games
- Dinner to follow

First Street
Water Street

Who : Everyone!
Where: 80 Water Street
When : June 16th @ 8 p.m.

START WORDPAD

WordPad is a word processing program included with Windows 95. You can use WordPad to create many simple documents, such as letters and memos.

WordPad uses many of the same commands and procedures used in more powerful programs, such as Microsoft Word. You can use WordPad to review and edit files created with other word processing programs.

Word processing is similar to using a typewriter. You use some special keyboard keys, such as the Tab key, just as you do when using a typewriter. One of the advantages of using a word processor such as WordPad is that when you are typing text in a document, you do not need to press the Enter key at the end of each line.

The text automatically moves to the next line.

Entering text in a document is only the beginning of word processing. When you finish typing the text, you can make changes to the content and appearance of your document.

Before performing many tasks in WordPad, you must select the text you want to work with. Selected text appears highlighted on your screen.

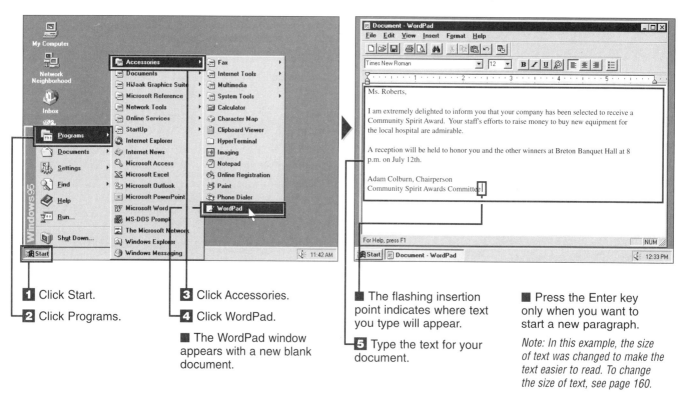

1 Click Start.

2 Click Programs.

3 Click Accessories.

4 Click WordPad.

■ The WordPad window appears with a new blank document.

■ The flashing insertion point indicates where text you type will appear.

5 Type the text for your document.

■ Press the Enter key only when you want to start a new paragraph.

Note: In this example, the size of text was changed to make the text easier to read. To change the size of text, see page 160.

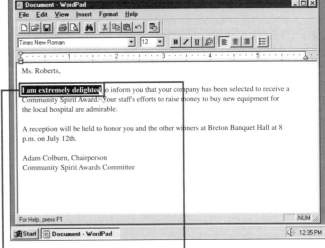

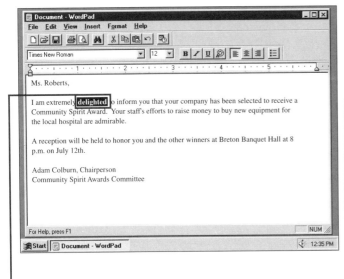

TIPS

How can I select text using the keyboard?

Position the cursor at the start or end of the text you want to select. Hold down the Shift key while you use the arrow keys to select the text.

Why does WordPad sometimes select more text than I want?

When you are selecting part of a word and you include the space before or after the word, WordPad automatically selects the entire word. If you want to select parts of words, choose the View menu and then click the Options command. Select the Options tab and then click the Automatic word selection option (✔ changes to ☐).

Is there a fast way to select text?

To select a word, double-click the word. To select one line of text, click in the left margin beside the line you want to select. To select a paragraph, double-click in the left margin beside the paragraph you want to select. You can also triple-click any word in a paragraph to select the entire paragraph. To select all the text in the document, triple-click anywhere in the left margin of the document. When clicking in the left margin, the mouse I changes to ⇗.

SELECT ONE WORD

1 To select one word, double-click the word.

■ To deselect text, click outside the selected area.

SELECT ANY AMOUNT OF TEXT

1 Position the mouse I over the first word you want to select.

2 Drag the mouse ⇗ until you highlight all the words you want to select. The text appears highlighted.

Note: To select all the text in your document, press Ctrl+A on your keyboard.

EDIT TEXT

The ability to edit a document by changing or adding text makes a word processor a more powerful tool than a typewriter. You can insert, delete and re-organize the text in your document without having to retype the entire document.

You can add new text to a document. The existing text will shift to make room for the text you add.

You can delete text you no longer need from a document. The remaining text will shift to fill any empty spaces.

Moving text lets you try out different ways of organizing the text in a document. You can find the most effective structure for a document by experimenting with different placements of sentences and paragraphs.

You can also place a copy of text in a different location in your document. This will save you time since you do not have to retype the text.

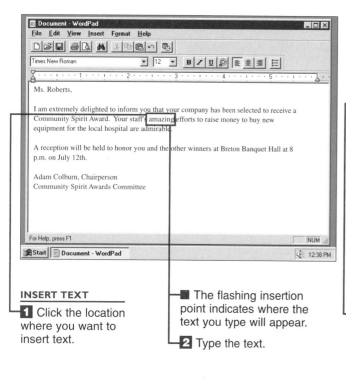

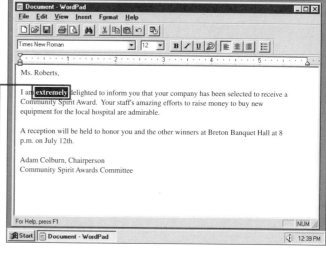

INSERT TEXT

1 Click the location where you want to insert text.

■ The flashing insertion point indicates where the text you type will appear.

2 Type the text.

DELETE TEXT

1 Select the text you want to delete.

2 Press the Delete key to remove the text.

■ To delete one character at a time, click to the left of the first character you want to delete. Press the Delete key to remove the character to the right of the flashing insertion point.

TIPS

Can I cancel a change I made?

WordPad remembers the last change you made. From the Edit menu, select the Undo command to cancel a change that you regret. You can also click the Undo button (↺) on the toolbar to cancel a change.

How can copying text help me edit my document?

If you plan to make major changes to a paragraph, you may want to copy the paragraph before you begin. This gives you two copies of the paragraph - the original paragraph and a paragraph with the changes.

Can I find or change every occurrence of a word in a document?

From the Edit menu, select the Find command to locate every occurrence of a word or phrase in your document. From the Edit menu, choose the Replace command to find text in your document and replace it with new text. These features are useful if you have misspelled a name throughout your document.

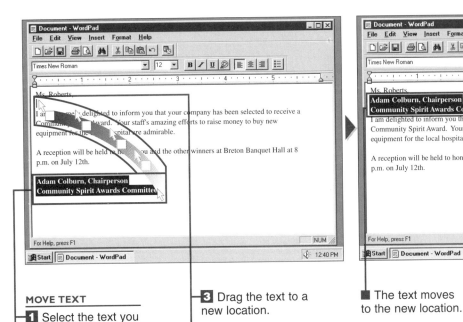

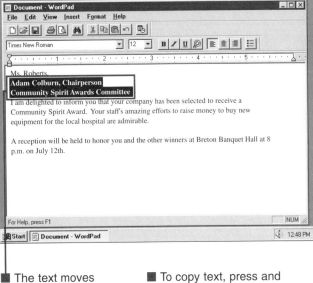

MOVE TEXT

1 Select the text you want to move.

2 Position the mouse I over the text (I changes to ↖).

3 Drag the text to a new location.

■ The text will appear where you position the insertion point on your screen.

■ The text moves to the new location.

■ To copy text, press and hold down the Ctrl key as you perform step 3.

SAVE AND PRINT A DOCUMENT

You should save your document to store it for future use. This lets you later retrieve the document for reviewing or editing. When you save a document, you give the document a name.

You may want to save a document as soon as it has been created. If there is an equipment failure or

power loss before you save your document, you may lose your work.

You should periodically save your document while you are working with it. This will ensure that all the changes you make to the document are saved. You can decide how often you want to save your changes. For example,

if you are prepared to lose an hour of work, save every hour. If you do not want to lose more than five minutes of work, save every five minutes.

You can produce a paper copy of a document. When you print your document, you can print one page, a range of pages or the entire document.

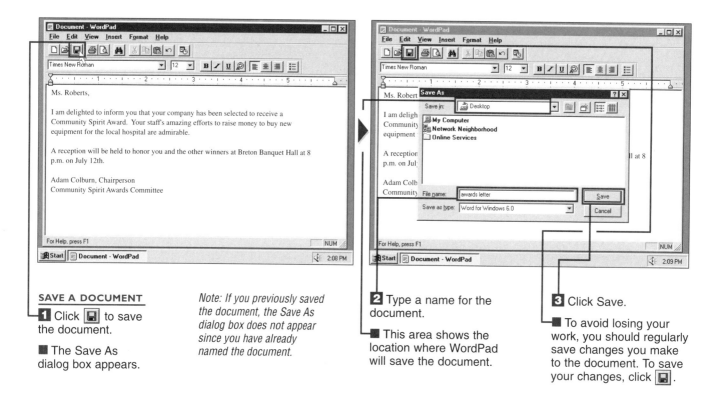

SAVE A DOCUMENT

1 Click 🖫 to save the document.

■ The Save As dialog box appears.

Note: If you previously saved the document, the Save As dialog box does not appear since you have already named the document.

2 Type a name for the document.

■ This area shows the location where WordPad will save the document.

3 Click Save.

■ To avoid losing your work, you should regularly save changes you make to the document. To save your changes, click 🖫.

Can I preview a document before I print it?

If you want to preview a document, click the File menu and then select the Print Preview command. Previewing a document lets you verify that the document will look the way you want it to when printed.

How can I tell if my document is printing?

A printer icon appears on the right side of the taskbar. You can double-click the printer icon for information about your print job. The printer icon disappears from the taskbar when your document has been sent to the printer.

Can I share WordPad documents with people who do not use WordPad?

When saving a document, you can specify a different type of file. In the Save As dialog box, click the Save as type area to display the file types you can use. To keep the document's formatting, such as bold or underline, select Rich Text Format. To save the document without formatting, select Text Document.

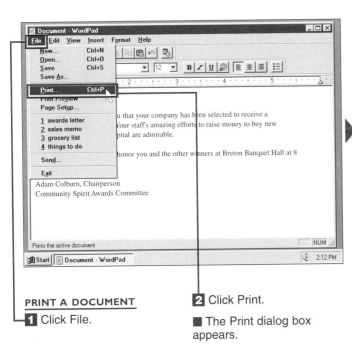

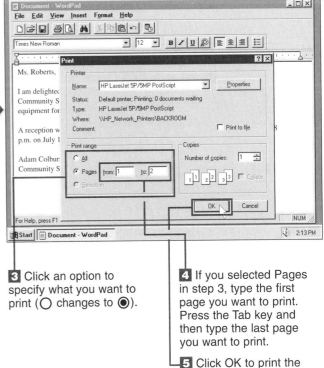

PRINT A DOCUMENT

1 Click File.

2 Click Print.

■ The Print dialog box appears.

3 Click an option to specify what you want to print (○ changes to ●).

4 If you selected Pages in step 3, type the first page you want to print. Press the Tab key and then type the last page you want to print.

5 Click OK to print the document.

OPEN A DOCUMENT

You can open a new document in WordPad to start writing a letter, memo or report.

When you open a new document in WordPad, you must choose the type of document you want to create. The Word 6 Document type is the standard type used for WordPad. You should select this type if you want to share the document with Word for Windows users.

You can also create a document that you can share with people who do not use Windows. The Rich Text Document type can be used by most word processors, including word processors for Macintosh computers. Rich text can contain formatting, such as bold or underline. The Text Document type can also be used by most word processors, but contains no formatting.

You can open a saved document and display it on your screen. This allows you to review and make changes to the document.

WordPad only lets you work with one document at a time. If you are working with a document, save the document before opening another.

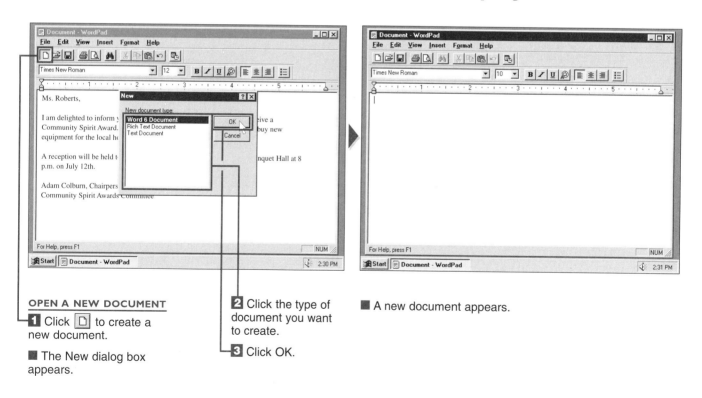

OPEN A NEW DOCUMENT

1 Click ☐ to create a new document.

■ The New dialog box appears.

2 Click the type of document you want to create.

3 Click OK.

■ A new document appears.

TIPS

Is there a faster way to open a saved document?

The last four documents you worked on in WordPad appear on the File menu. You can click any of these documents to open them. Also, the last 15 documents you worked with on your computer appear in the Documents folder on the Start menu. To open a document from the Start menu, see page 66.

Can WordPad display all of the features available in Word for Windows 95?

WordPad does not support all of the features available in Word for Windows 95. If you use WordPad to open a document created in Word for Windows 95, some features may not display properly.

Is there any way to work with two WordPad documents at the same time?

You can start WordPad multiple times to have several documents open at once. Having several documents open at the same time allows you to cut and paste information between documents. You can use the Start menu to start WordPad again. You can also double-click a WordPad document in a My Computer or Explorer window to start WordPad.

WINDOWS 95 ACCESSORIES

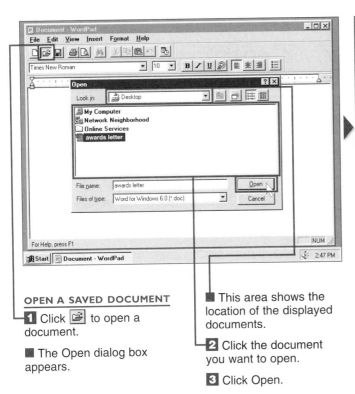

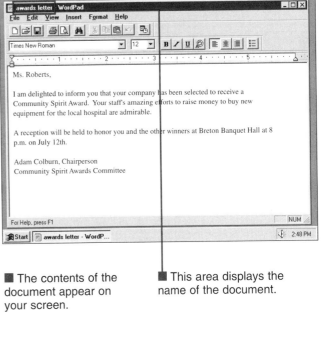

OPEN A SAVED DOCUMENT

1 Click 📂 to open a document.

■ The Open dialog box appears.

■ This area shows the location of the displayed documents.

2 Click the document you want to open.

3 Click Open.

■ The contents of the document appear on your screen.

■ This area displays the name of the document.

159

FORMAT CHARACTERS

You can make text in your document look more attractive by using various fonts, sizes, styles and colors.

When you start WordPad, the text appears in the Times New Roman font. The default size for text is 10 points and the default color is black.

When you install Windows, some other fonts are also installed,

including Arial and Courier. The rest of the available fonts depend on your printer and the setup of your computer.

WordPad measures the size of a character in points. There are 72 points in one inch. Due to differences in design, two fonts may appear to be different sizes even though they are displayed using the same point size.

You can change the style of text using the Bold, Italic and Underline features. These features are used mainly for emphasis, or to set apart different types of text, like the names of books.

You can change the color of text to draw attention to headings or important information in your document.

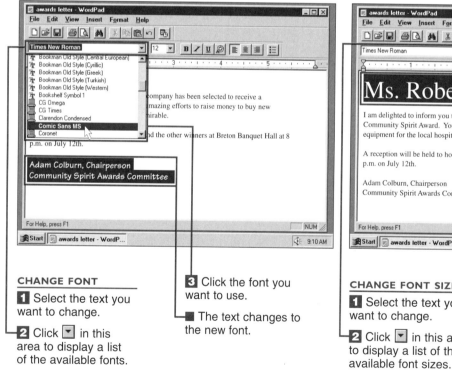

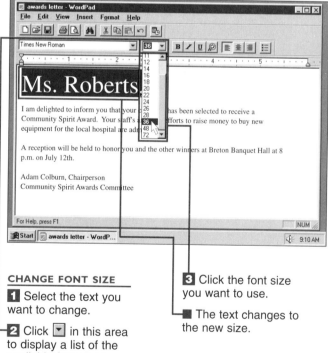

CHANGE FONT

1 Select the text you want to change.

2 Click ▼ in this area to display a list of the available fonts.

3 Click the font you want to use.

■ The text changes to the new font.

CHANGE FONT SIZE

1 Select the text you want to change.

2 Click ▼ in this area to display a list of the available font sizes.

3 Click the font size you want to use.

■ The text changes to the new size.

TIPS

How can I change the format of text while I am typing?

Before you begin typing the text you want to display a different format, change to the new format you want to use. Any text you type after making the change will display the new format.

How can I preview a font?

In the Format menu, select Font. The Font dialog box opens and allows you to change the formatting of your text. The dialog box displays an area where you can preview the settings you choose.

Can I add fonts to my computer?

You can purchase fonts at most computer stores. To install fonts, see page 230. If you have installed other programs on your computer, WordPad can use the fonts provided with these programs.

Can I use colored text if I do not have a color printer?

You can select colors for your text, but they will appear as shades of gray when printed on a black-and-white printer. You can use color effectively in documents that will only be viewed on-screen.

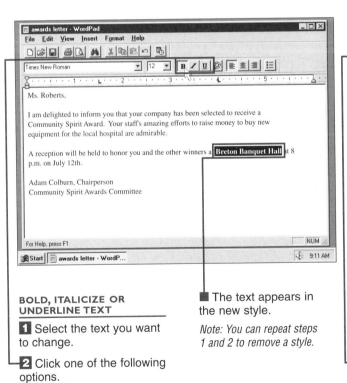

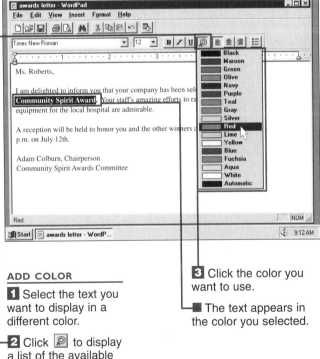

BOLD, ITALICIZE OR UNDERLINE TEXT

1 Select the text you want to change.

2 Click one of the following options.

B Bold

I Italic

U Underline

■ The text appears in the new style.

Note: You can repeat steps 1 and 2 to remove a style.

ADD COLOR

1 Select the text you want to display in a different color.

2 Click 🖉 to display a list of the available colors.

3 Click the color you want to use.

■ The text appears in the color you selected.

FORMAT PARAGRAPHS

You can format the paragraphs in a WordPad document to help organize the document.

Aligning text allows you to line up the edge of a paragraph along a margin. Most documents are left aligned so the edges of the paragraphs line up along the left margin. Right alignment is often used to line up dates or return addresses along the right margin. You can also center paragraphs between the left and right margins. Centering paragraphs is most effective for headings and titles.

You can change the tabs for your document. This is useful for lining up columns of information. By default, WordPad sets a tab every 0.5 inches.

You can indent a paragraph from the left, right or both margins. Indenting paragraphs is often used to identify and set apart quotations. You can indent just the first line of a paragraph so you do not need to press the Tab key at the beginning of every new paragraph.

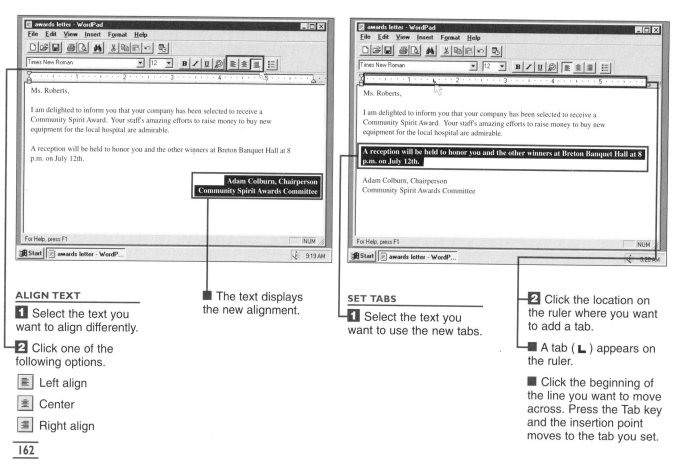

ALIGN TEXT

1 Select the text you want to align differently.

2 Click one of the following options.

≣ Left align

≣ Center

≣ Right align

■ The text displays the new alignment.

SET TABS

1 Select the text you want to use the new tabs.

2 Click the location on the ruler where you want to add a tab.

■ A tab (L) appears on the ruler.

■ Click the beginning of the line you want to move across. Press the Tab key and the insertion point moves to the tab you set.

TIPS

How do I display the ruler on my screen?

From the View menu, select Ruler to display or hide the ruler. When the ruler is displayed, a check mark appears beside Ruler in the menu.

How can I move a tab?

You can drag a tab (**L**) to a new location on the ruler. You can also drag a tab off the ruler to remove the tab. Only tabs in the currently selected paragraphs are changed.

How can I clear all the tabs?

From the Format menu, select Tabs to display the Tabs dialog box. Then click the Clear All button. You can also use this dialog box to set tabs.

Can I format more than one paragraph at a time?

You can format as many paragraphs as you want. WordPad applies your formatting changes to any paragraphs that are currently selected. The entire paragraph does not have to be selected to be included.

Can I align my text along both the left and right margins?

WordPad does not have a full justification feature.

WINDOWS 95 ACCESSORIES

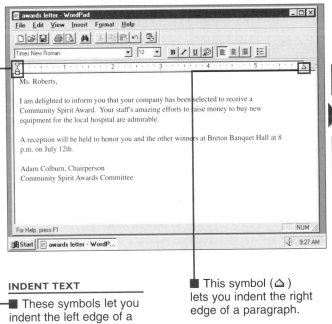

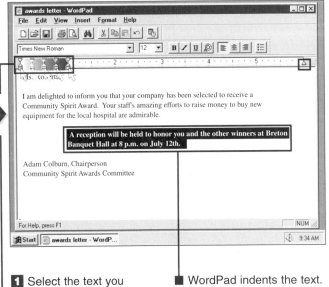

INDENT TEXT

■ These symbols let you indent the left edge of a paragraph.

▽ Indent first line

▤ Indent all but first line

▽ Indent all lines

■ This symbol (△) lets you indent the right edge of a paragraph.

1 Select the text you want to indent.

2 Move the mouse ⬡ over an indent symbol and then drag the symbol to a new location.

■ WordPad indents the text.

FORMAT PAGES

You can adjust the appearance of the pages in your document to suit your needs.

WordPad sets each page in your document to print on letter-sized paper. If you want to use a different paper size, you can change this setting. The available paper sizes depend on the printer you are using.

You can change the orientation of pages in your document. The Portrait orientation prints across the short side of a page and is used for most documents. Certificates and tables are usually printed across the long side of the page, in the Landscape orientation.

A margin is the amount of space between text and the

edge of your paper. You can change the margins to suit your document. Changing margins lets you accommodate letterhead and other specialty paper.

The Page Setup dialog box displays a sample page with all of your changes.

The changes you make affect the entire document.

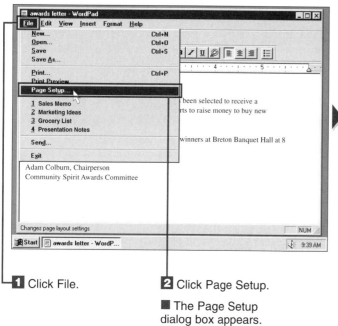

■ Click File.

■ Click Page Setup.

■ The Page Setup dialog box appears.

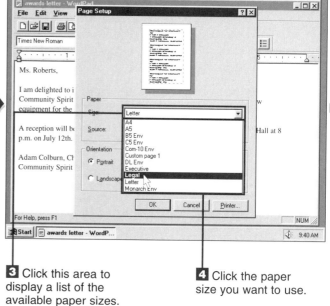

■ Click this area to display a list of the available paper sizes.

■ Click the paper size you want to use.

TIPS

How can I change the units a page is measured in?

From the View menu, select the Options command. Click the Options tab and select your preferred unit of measure. You can choose from inches, centimeters, points and picas. Points and picas are measurement systems used by graphic artists and typesetters.

How do I change the left and right margins for only part of my document?

If you want to change the left and right margins for only part of your document, you must change the indentation of the paragraphs. See page 163.

Can I change the top and bottom margins for only the first page of my document?

WordPad cannot change the top and bottom margins for only part of your document.

How can I see what my pages will look like before I print the document?

From the File menu, select the Print Preview command to preview your document before it is printed.

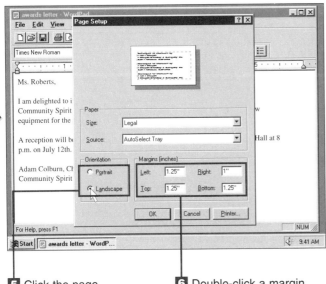

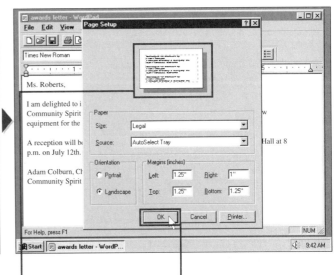

5 Click the page orientation you want to use (○ changes to ◉).

6 Double-click a margin you want to change. Then type the new margin.

7 Repeat step 6 for each margin you want to change.

■ This area displays how your document will appear.

8 Click OK to confirm your changes.

START PAINT

Paint is a simple graphics program included with Windows 95. You can use Paint to create and edit images. Images you create in Paint can be inserted into other programs, printed and displayed on your desktop as wallpaper.

A Paint image is made up of a grid of tiny colored dots, called pixels. The resolution of your screen is also measured in pixels. Paint uses your screen resolution to determine the default size of your images.

Paint files have the .bmp extension.

TIPS

Why would I need a more sophisticated image editing program?

To open and work with high quality photo image files, you need a program like Corel Photopaint or Adobe Photoshop. There are also programs like Corel Draw, Adobe Illustrator and Micrografx Designer that create drawings from objects.

How can I find out what each tool does?

To display a description of a tool, move the mouse pointer over the tool. After a few seconds, the name of the tool appears.

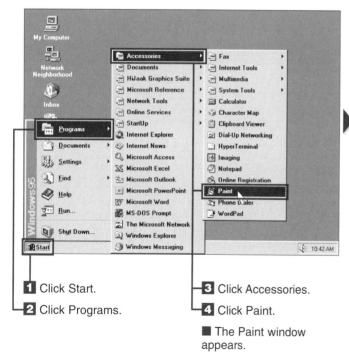

1 Click Start.

2 Click Programs.

3 Click Accessories.

4 Click Paint.

■ The Paint window appears.

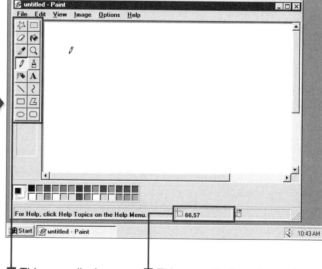

■ This area displays the tools you use to create your painting.

■ This area displays the position of the mouse on your screen to help you line up objects in your painting. The numbers indicate the number of pixels from the left of the painting followed by the number of pixels from the top of the painting.

DRAW SHAPES

You can use Paint's tools to draw shapes such as rectangles, rounded rectangles, ellipses and polygons. You can use the Polygon tool to draw many different kinds of multi-sided shapes, ranging from simple triangles to complex objects.

Before you draw a shape, you can specify whether you want to outline the shape or fill the shape with a color. You can also specify the colors you want to use for the outline and the inside of the shape.

TIPS

How do I draw a circle or a square?

Press and hold down the Shift key as you drag the mouse to draw the shape. To draw a circle, select the Ellipse tool. To draw a square, select the Rectangle tool.

How do I change the width of a shape's outline?

Before drawing the shape, select the ☒ or ☒ tool and then select the width you want to use. For more information, see page 168.

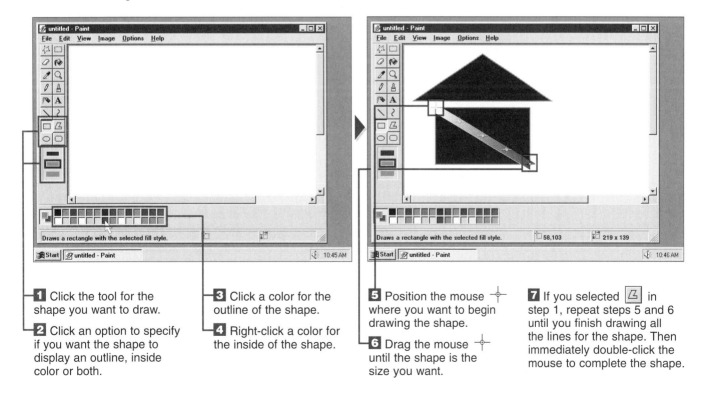

1 Click the tool for the shape you want to draw.

2 Click an option to specify if you want the shape to display an outline, inside color or both.

3 Click a color for the outline of the shape.

4 Right-click a color for the inside of the shape.

5 Position the mouse ⊹ where you want to begin drawing the shape.

6 Drag the mouse ⊹ until the shape is the size you want.

7 If you selected ☒ in step 1, repeat steps 5 and 6 until you finish drawing all the lines for the shape. Then immediately double-click the mouse to complete the shape.

DRAW LINES AND CURVES

Paint can create four different types of lines in your paintings. You can draw straight lines, curved lines, pencil lines and brush strokes.

The Line tool allows you to draw a perfectly straight line when you drag the mouse from one point to another.

When you use the Curve tool, the line begins as a perfectly straight line. You can then bend or twist the line to create the curve you want.

The Pencil and Brush tools allow you more freedom when drawing lines and curves.

The Brush tool has many different styles that you can

choose, including some that work like a calligraphy pen.

You can use the Airbrush tool to spray areas of color onto a painting and create shading effects. When using the Airbrush tool, the slower you drag the mouse, the darker the color appears in your painting.

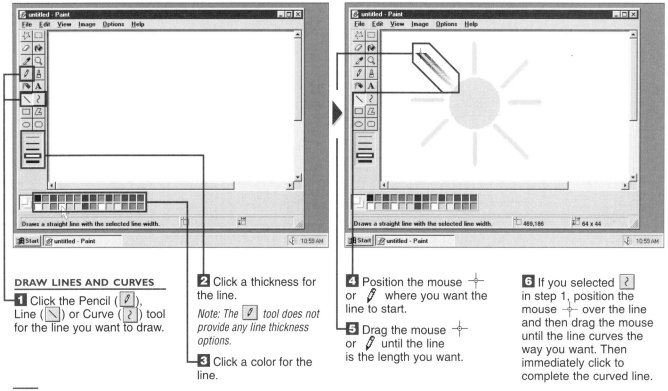

DRAW LINES AND CURVES

1 Click the Pencil (✎), Line (◥) or Curve (ʔ) tool for the line you want to draw.

2 Click a thickness for the line.

Note: The ✎ tool does not provide any line thickness options.

3 Click a color for the line.

4 Position the mouse ╬ or ✎ where you want the line to start.

5 Drag the mouse ╬ or ✎ until the line is the length you want.

6 If you selected ʔ in step 1, position the mouse ╬ over the line and then drag the mouse until the line curves the way you want. Then immediately click to complete the curved line.

How do I zoom in to draw precise lines?

To zoom in on your painting to draw precise lines, click the View menu. Select Zoom and then select Large Size. To view your painting at different zoom levels, click the View menu. Choose Zoom and then select Custom. Choose Show Thumbnail to see the zoomed area in normal view at the same time.

Can I draw a line using the background color?

To draw a line using the background color, use the right mouse button instead of the left.

How do I draw a line that is exactly horizontal?

You can draw perfectly horizontal, vertical or diagonal lines by holding down the Shift key while you draw the line. This works for the Line, Curve and Pencil tools, but not the Brush or Airbrush.

Can I change the line width of the Pencil tool?

You cannot change the line width of the Pencil tool. Because of its thin line width, the Pencil tool is best used for editing detail when you are zoomed in on your painting.

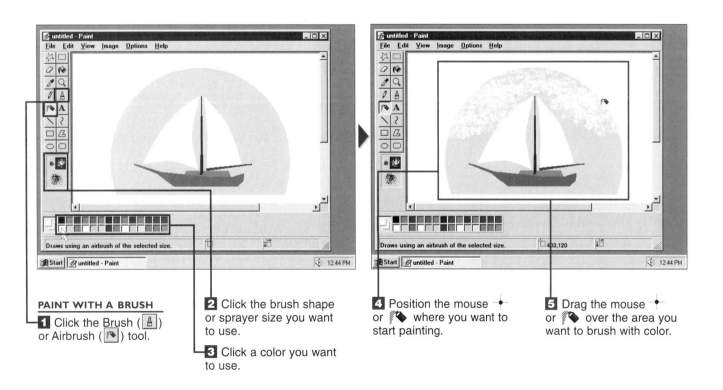

PAINT WITH A BRUSH

■1 Click the Brush (▨) or Airbrush (▨) tool.

■2 Click the brush shape or sprayer size you want to use.

■3 Click a color you want to use.

■4 Position the mouse ✛ or ▨ where you want to start painting.

■5 Drag the mouse ✛ or ▨ over the area you want to brush with color.

ADD TEXT

You can add text to your painting to provide written information or explanations. Adding text to a painting is useful for adding a title to a painting or street names to a map.

You cannot change the text in a text box after you select another tool or click outside the text box.

Paint does not have a spell-checker, so you must make sure the text is correct before you continue creating your painting.

TIPS

Can I use text I have already typed in a document?

Select and copy the text you want to use in the original program. Display the Paint window and create a text box large enough to fit the text. Press Ctrl+V to paste the text into the text box.

How can I make changes to the appearance of text?

When you create a text box, the Text toolbar appears. If the toolbar does not appear, click the View menu and select Text Toolbar. You can use the toolbar to change the size and appearance of the text.

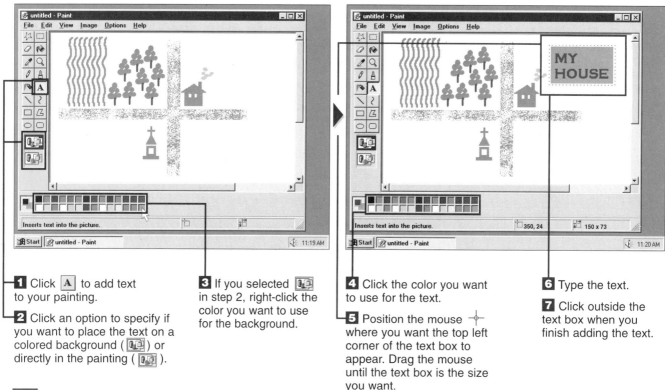

1 Click A to add text to your painting.

2 Click an option to specify if you want to place the text on a colored background ( ) or directly in the painting ( ).

3 If you selected in step 2, right-click the color you want to use for the background.

4 Click the color you want to use for the text.

5 Position the mouse where you want the top left corner of the text box to appear. Drag the mouse until the text box is the size you want.

6 Type the text.

7 Click outside the text box when you finish adding the text.

FILL AREA WITH COLOR

Y ou can change the color of any solid object or any area in the painting that has a solid border.

Filling an area with color is useful if you want to color an entire item, recolor text letter by letter, or create a pattern of colors using lines drawn inside a circle.

You can also change the color of the entire background of your painting by clicking a blank area of your painting.

TIPS

Why did the color of everything change?

If there are breaks or holes in the border of the area you are filling with color, the color will leak out into the surrounding area. Click the Edit menu and select Undo to return to the original colors. Then fix the holes in the object's border using the Pencil ( ) or the Brush ( ) tool before you try filling the area with color again.

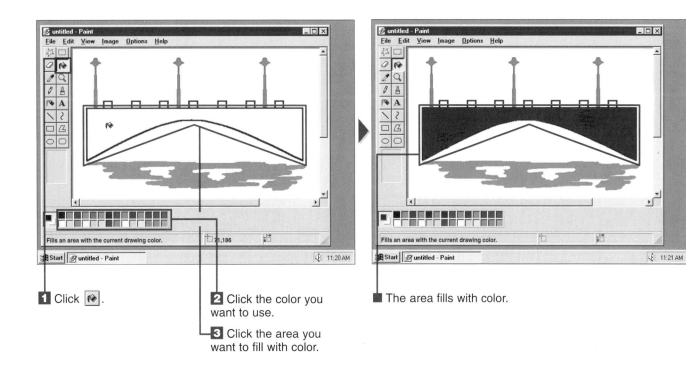

1 Click .

2 Click the color you want to use.

3 Click the area you want to fill with color.

■ The area fills with color.

171

MOVE PART OF A PAINTING

You can rearrange the items in a painting. You can move items with or without their background. The empty space left by the moved item will be filled with the color you specify.

If you are planning to make several changes to a painting, you may want to save the original painting with a new name first. This will give you two copies of the painting – the original and one with all the changes. This is useful in case your changes do not work out the way you expect.

TIPS

Can I move an item back to its original location?

From the Edit menu, select the Undo command to move an item back to its original location. Paint can undo the last three changes you made.

Can I copy an item to a different location in my painting?

Hold down the Ctrl key as you drag the item to place a copy in a new location.

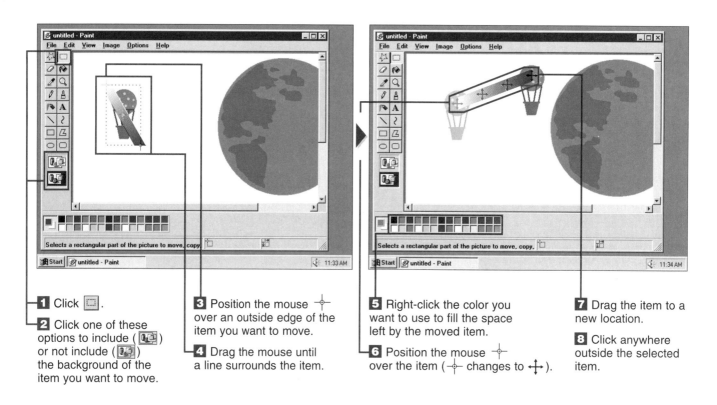

1 Click ▢.

2 Click one of these options to include (▣) or not include (▣) the background of the item you want to move.

3 Position the mouse ┿ over an outside edge of the item you want to move.

4 Drag the mouse until a line surrounds the item.

5 Right-click the color you want to use to fill the space left by the moved item.

6 Position the mouse ┿ over the item (┿ changes to ✛).

7 Drag the item to a new location.

8 Click anywhere outside the selected item.

ERASE PART OF A PAINTING

You can remove an area from your painting. Paint offers four different eraser sizes for you to choose from. Choose the small eraser when you want to be precise in your erasing. Choose the large eraser when you want to erase a large area of your painting.

You can use any color to erase an area of your painting. Use a white eraser when the area you want to erase has a white background. Use a colored eraser when the area you want to erase has a colored background.

TIPS

How can I remove a large area of my painting without erasing?

Perform steps 1 to 5 on page 172 and then press the Delete key. The empty area is filled with the color you specified.

How can I see more detail in the area I am erasing?

From the View menu, select the Zoom command. Click Custom and then select the level of magnification you want.

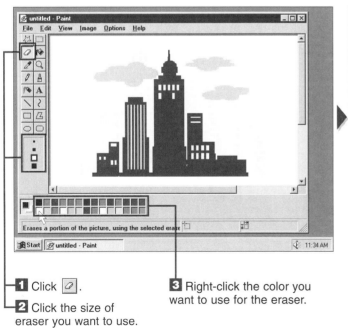

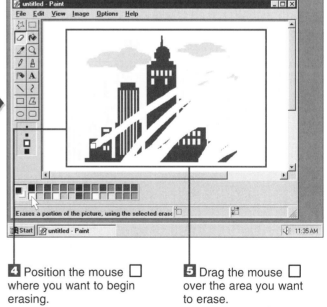

1 Click 🖊️.

2 Click the size of eraser you want to use.

3 Right-click the color you want to use for the eraser.

4 Position the mouse ☐ where you want to begin erasing.

5 Drag the mouse ☐ over the area you want to erase.

SAVE A PAINTING

You can save your painting to store it for future use. This lets you later review and make changes to the painting.

Store your paintings in a folder on your computer where you will be able to easily find them again. If you plan on using your painting as wallpaper on your desktop, store it in the Windows folder.

You should periodically save your painting while you are working. This will ensure that all the changes you make to the painting are saved, in case of a computer problem or power failure.

TIPS

Can I choose the number of colors that are used to save the painting?

You can select the number of colors used to save your painting from the Save as type area. Saving fewer colors results in a smaller file size. If your system can only display 256 colors, there may be no advantage in saving the painting with more colors.

Which formats can I use to save my painting?

Paint can only save files in the Windows bitmap (.bmp) format.

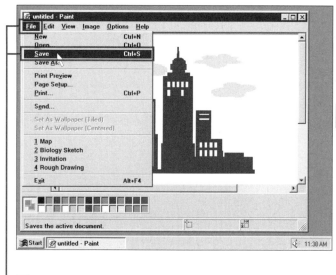

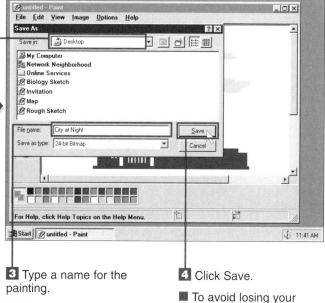

1 Click File.

2 Click Save.

■ The Save As dialog box appears.

Note: If you previously saved the painting, the Save As dialog box does not appear since you have already named the painting.

3 Type a name for the painting.

■ This area shows the location where Paint will store the painting.

4 Click Save.

■ To avoid losing your work, you should regularly save changes you make to the painting. To save your changes, repeat steps 1 and 2.

OPEN A PAINTING

You can open a saved painting and display it on your screen. This allows you to view or make changes to the painting.

You can use Paint to modify wallpaper files and other bitmap (.bmp) files saved on your computer.

Paint only lets you work with one painting at a time. If you are currently working with a painting, save the painting before opening another.

TIPS

Is there any way to work with two paintings at the same time?

You can start Paint several times to have several paintings open at once. You can use the Start menu to start Paint or double-click a Paint file in a My Computer or Explorer window.

Is there a faster way to open a painting?

The last four paintings you worked with in Paint appear on the File menu. You can click any of these paintings to open them.

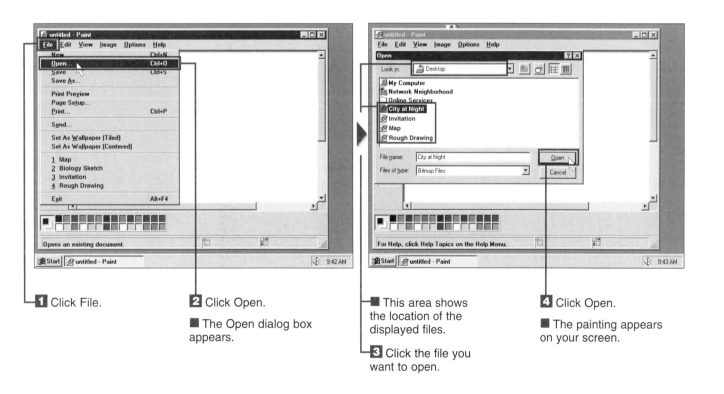

1 Click File.

2 Click Open.

■ The Open dialog box appears.

■ This area shows the location of the displayed files.

3 Click the file you want to open.

4 Click Open.

■ The painting appears on your screen.

PRINT A PAINTING

When you finish creating a painting, you can print a copy of your work.

A color printer prints a copy of your painting in color. If you print your painting using a black-and-white printer, colors appear as shades of gray.

If your painting is too large to fit on one page, it will print on multiple pages. You can choose to print one page, a range of pages or all the pages.

TIPS

How do I e-mail a painting to a friend?

From the File menu, select Send to start Microsoft Exchange. The painting is displayed as an icon in the message and will be sent as an attached file. If the recipient has Windows 95, they can double-click the icon to see the painting.

How do I preview a painting before I print it?

From the File menu, select Print Preview to preview a painting.

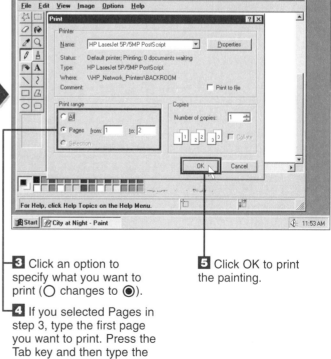

1 Click File.

2 Click Print.

■ The Print dialog box appears.

3 Click an option to specify what you want to print (○ changes to ●).

4 If you selected Pages in step 3, type the first page you want to print. Press the Tab key and then type the last page you want to print.

5 Click OK to print the painting.

USE A PAINTING AS DESKTOP BACKGROUND

Y ou can use any painting created in Paint as background for your desktop. This is an easy way to customize your desktop.

Paint uses the size of your desktop as the default size of your painting. The painting you create will fill the area on your desktop. You can also create a smaller painting. A smaller painting can be centered on your desktop or tiled to cover the entire screen.

TIPS

How do I make a painting smaller?

From the Image menu, select Stretch/Skew to shrink a painting that you already created. Click the Image menu and select Attributes to change the size of a painting before you start. If you use Attributes to change the size of a painting, all the paintings you create will use the new size.

How can I reset my desktop background?

You can use the Display Properties dialog box to remove the painting from your desktop. See page 202.

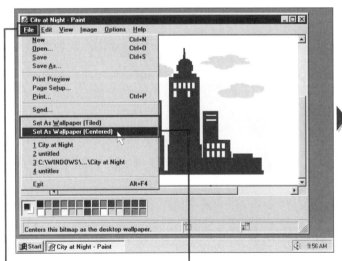

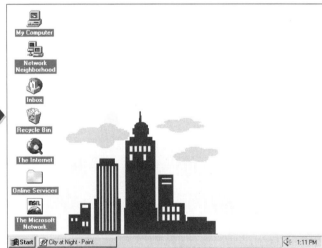

■ You must save a painting before you can use the painting as your desktop background. To save a painting, refer to page 174.

1 Click File.

2 Click the wallpaper option you want to use.

Tiled - Repeat painting to cover desktop.

Centered - Display painting once in center of desktop.

■ The painting appears on your desktop.

INSERT SPECIAL CHARACTERS

You can use Character Map to include special characters in your documents which are not available on the keyboard.

Your computer has many sets of characters, or fonts, for you to choose from. Each font has a selection of up to 255 characters, which can include upper and lower case accented letters, one character fractions like $1/4$ and symbols like the copyright mark ©.

The Character Map window displays all of the characters for each font. You can view an enlarged version of each character a font offers.

Some fonts, like Symbol and Wingdings, contain only special characters. The Symbol font primarily contains symbols used in mathematical equations. The Wingdings font contains bullet characters and arrows.

You can copy the special characters from Character Map and paste them into your documents.

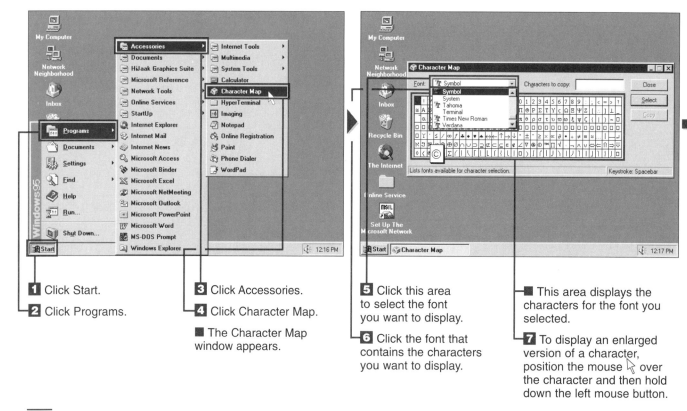

1 Click Start.

2 Click Programs.

3 Click Accessories.

4 Click Character Map.

■ The Character Map window appears.

5 Click this area to select the font you want to display.

6 Click the font that contains the characters you want to display.

■ This area displays the characters for the font you selected.

7 To display an enlarged version of a character, position the mouse over the character and then hold down the left mouse button.

Why isn't Character Map displayed in the Accessories menu?

You may need to install Character Map on your computer. The Character Map is located in the Accessories group on the Windows 95 CD-ROM disc. See page 580.

Can I use special characters without opening Character Map each time?

Each special character has a keystroke combination that appears in the Character Map window. When you enter the keystroke combination, the character appears in your document. For example, to enter the symbol for the English pound (£) in the System font, press and hold down the Alt key as you enter 0163 using the numeric keypad.

Some of the characters I copy and paste do not appear properly. How can I fix them?

Select the characters that appear incorrectly in the document and change them to the same font you selected in the Character Map dialog box.

How can I make Character Map easier to access?

You can move Character Map to the StartUp folder so it will open each time you start Windows. If you use Character Map regularly, you can leave it open on the desktop or minimize it on the taskbar.

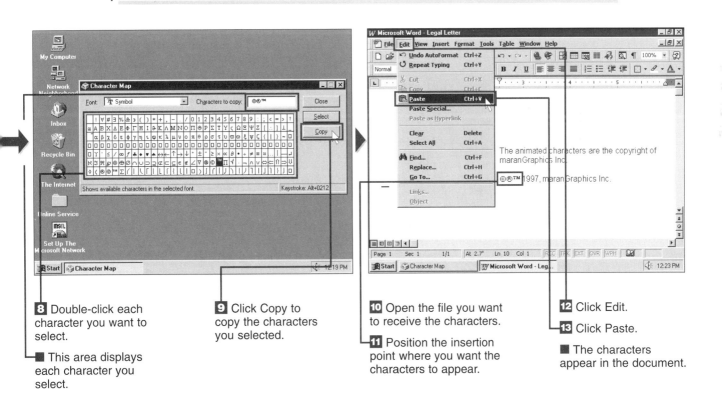

8 Double-click each character you want to select.

■ This area displays each character you select.

9 Click Copy to copy the characters you selected.

10 Open the file you want to receive the characters.

11 Position the insertion point where you want the characters to appear.

12 Click Edit.

13 Click Paste.

■ The characters appear in the document.

USING THE CALCULATOR

Windows provides a calculator to help you perform calculations. You can work with the Calculator in either the Standard or Scientific view.

The Calculator's Standard view allows you to perform basic mathematical calculations. In this view, the Calculator resembles a small hand-held calculator.

You can use the Scientific view to perform more complex mathematical calculations. This view lets you calculate averages, exponents, sines, cosines, tangents and much more.

You can enter information into the Calculator by using your mouse to click the buttons in the Calculator or by pressing the keys on the numeric

keypad on your keyboard. The result of a calculation appears in the Calculator.

Windows allows you to copy numbers to the Calculator from other programs and then paste the result of a calculation in a document. This can save you from having to retype numbers and helps you avoid errors when entering numbers.

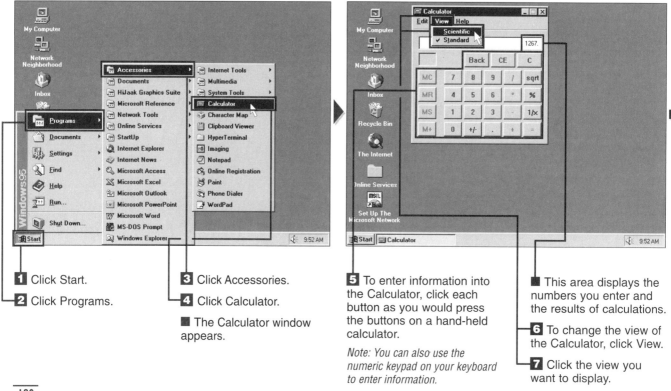

1 Click Start.

2 Click Programs.

3 Click Accessories.

4 Click Calculator.

■ The Calculator window appears.

5 To enter information into the Calculator, click each button as you would press the buttons on a hand-held calculator.

Note: You can also use the numeric keypad on your keyboard to enter information.

■ This area displays the numbers you enter and the results of calculations.

6 To change the view of the Calculator, click View.

7 Click the view you want to display.

TIPS

What is the easiest way to copy the result of a calculation to another program?

To copy the result of a calculation, hold down the Ctrl key as you press C on your keyboard. Switch to the other program and then paste the result by holding down the Ctrl key as you press V on your keyboard. You can also use this technique to copy a selected number into the Calculator.

How can I find out what the Calculator buttons do?

Right-click a button of interest. A box containing the text "What's This?" appears. Click this box to display information about the button.

Why are the number keys on the numeric keypad not working?

Num Lock must be on. To turn this setting on, press the Num Lock key on your keyboard. A status light on your keyboard indicates this setting is on.

Can I keep the Calculator on the screen all the time?

Yes. You can also minimize the Calculator on the taskbar. To have the Calculator open each time you turn on your computer, drag the Calculator into the StartUp folder. See page 258.

WINDOWS 95 ACCESSORIES

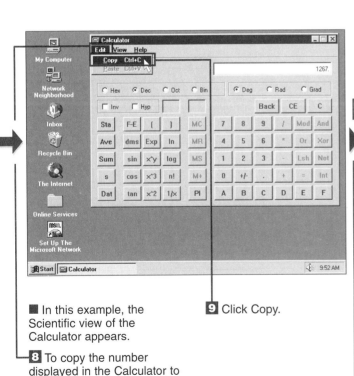

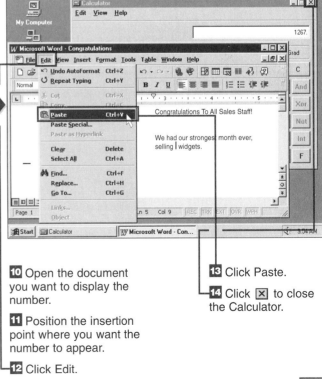

■ In this example, the Scientific view of the Calculator appears.

8 To copy the number displayed in the Calculator to another program, click Edit.

9 Click Copy.

10 Open the document you want to display the number.

11 Position the insertion point where you want the number to appear.

12 Click Edit.

13 Click Paste.

14 Click ⊠ to close the Calculator.

181

USING NOTEPAD

N otepad is a fast and easy text processor, with many uses.

Notepad is a small Windows program that does not require a lot of your computer's resources to run.

You can use Notepad to take notes or create simple documents. Notepad files are small and can

be opened by most word processors and publishing programs.

Notepad is used to create and edit Web pages, MS-DOS batch files and to view .log and .ini files.

Notepad displays each paragraph of a document on one line. To read an entire line you have to scroll from left to right in the

window. You can use Notepad's Word Wrap feature to wrap the text within the width of the window. Wrapping text can make the document easier to read.

You can have Notepad enter the current date and time in your documents. This is useful if you use Notepad to take phone messages and want the messages time stamped.

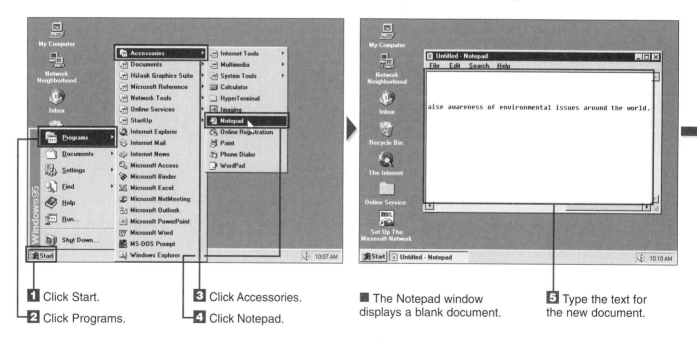

1 Click Start.

2 Click Programs.

3 Click Accessories.

4 Click Notepad.

■ The Notepad window displays a blank document.

5 Type the text for the new document.

How do I open a document I previously created in Notepad?

You can open a Notepad document by choosing the File menu and then selecting the Open command. Notepad only lets you work with one document at a time. If you are currently working with a document, save the document before opening another.

Is there a way to have Notepad automatically enter the time and date in my document?

You can have Notepad display the current time and date at the end of a document each time you open the document. To do so, type **.LOG** on the first line of the document.

Why is Notepad entering the wrong time or date in my documents?

You may need to adjust your computer's clock. See page 198.

How can I find a word in a Notepad document?

From the Search menu, select the Find command to search for a specific word in a document.

How do I save a document I created in Notepad?

You can save a Notepad document by choosing the File menu and then selecting the Save command.

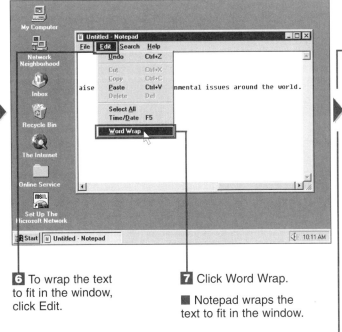

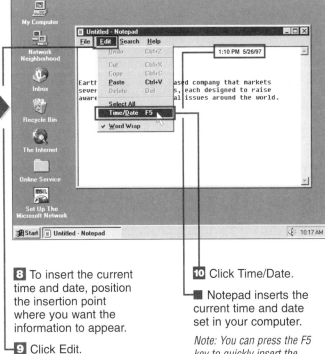

6 To wrap the text to fit in the window, click Edit.

7 Click Word Wrap.

■ Notepad wraps the text to fit in the window.

8 To insert the current time and date, position the insertion point where you want the information to appear.

9 Click Edit.

10 Click Time/Date.

■ Notepad inserts the current time and date set in your computer.

Note: You can press the F5 key to quickly insert the current time and date.

USING PHONE DIALER

If your computer has a modem, you can connect a telephone to the modem and use Phone Dialer to make and keep track of telephone calls for you.

Phone Dialer allows you to enter a phone number in several different ways.

You can enter the phone number using the number keys in the numeric keypad on your keyboard. You can also use the mouse to click the numbers on the dial pad on your screen. You can select a phone number from a list of recently dialed numbers. You can also use the speed-dial buttons to select a phone number you dial frequently.

You can use other Windows 95 telephone programs at the same time you use Phone Dialer. For example, if you also use Microsoft Fax, you do not have to close the program to stop it from accepting faxes before you use the Phone Dialer. Windows coordinates the programs so that both programs can use the modem.

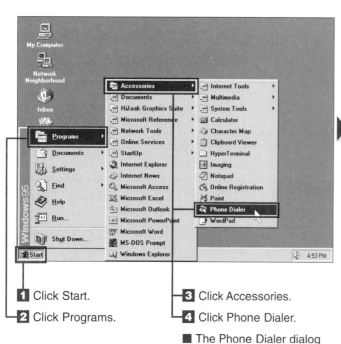

1 Click Start.

2 Click Programs.

3 Click Accessories.

4 Click Phone Dialer.

■ The Phone Dialer dialog box appears.

Note: The Location Information dialog box appears if Windows needs information on how to dial your modem.

5 Type the phone number you want to dial.

Note: You can also click ▼ to display a list of phone numbers you recently used. You can then select the phone number you want to dial from the list.

6 Click Dial to dial the number.

■ The Dialing dialog box appears. The Call Status dialog box also appears.

TIPS

How can I view a list of all my phone calls?

From the Tools menu, select Show Log to display a list of all your phone calls. The phone log displays information about each call you made. You can call any number listed in the log by double-clicking the phone number.

How do I dial a phone number and then an extension?

Insert commas between the phone number and the extension you want to dial. Each comma you insert makes Phone Dialer pause for two seconds. You must insert enough commas to allow Phone Dialer to make the connection before dialing the extension.

Can I use the Phone Dialer if I have voice mail service?

The Phone Dialer cannot call out if you have a special dial tone on your phone line to let you know there is a message waiting. Once the Phone Dialer has placed a call and the connection has been made, you cannot use the program to enter commands.

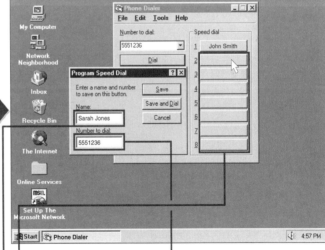

7 When the Phone Dialer has finished dialing the number, lift the receiver of your telephone.

8 Click Talk.

9 When you finish with the call, replace the receiver.

10 Click Hang Up.

11 To store a phone number, click an empty speed-dial button.

■ The Program Speed Dial dialog box appears.

12 Type the name of the person and then press the Tab key.

13 Type the phone number and then press the Enter key.

■ The name appears on the button.

Note: To dial a stored phone number, click the button for the number.

USING IMAGING

You can use Imaging to turn paper documents such as forms, receipts, images and news clippings into documents that can be used on your computer. Once a paper document is an Imaging document, you can save, edit, print and share the document as you would any document on your computer.

You can use a scanner to read a paper document into your computer so you can use the document in Imaging. You can also use a fax machine to fax yourself the document. When you receive a fax using Microsoft Exchange, you can work with the fax in Imaging.

You can change the way an Imaging document appears on your screen. You can increase or decrease the size of the document and rotate the document to the left or right. You can also view a small version of the document, called a thumbnail.

Imaging supports the most popular picture file formats and is an effective tool for converting picture files in formats such as .tif and .jpg to the Windows bitmap (.bmp) format.

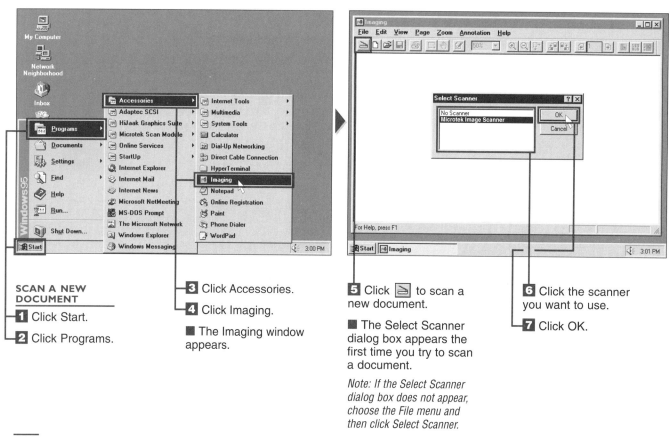

SCAN A NEW DOCUMENT

1 Click Start.

2 Click Programs.

3 Click Accessories.

4 Click Imaging.

■ The Imaging window appears.

5 Click ⬛ to scan a new document.

■ The Select Scanner dialog box appears the first time you try to scan a document.

Note: If the Select Scanner dialog box does not appear, choose the File menu and then click Select Scanner.

6 Click the scanner you want to use.

7 Click OK.

TIPS

Where can I get Imaging?

If Imaging is not already installed on your computer, you can install it from the Windows CD-ROM disc. Imaging is a part of the Accessories component. To install a Windows component, see page 580. If you are not using OSR2, you can get Imaging from Microsoft's Windows 95 Web site at www.microsoft.com/windows95

How do I open faxes in Imaging?

In Microsoft Exchange, save your fax with the .awd extension. You can then open and work with your faxes in Imaging.

How do I size a document to fit my screen?

You can click Zoom and then select the Fit to Width command to see the document from side to side. You can also select the Best Fit command to see the entire document.

How do I create a multiple page document?

In the Page menu, you can select Insert and then click Scan Page to insert a new page before the current page. You can also select Append and then Scan Page to add a new page at the end of the document.

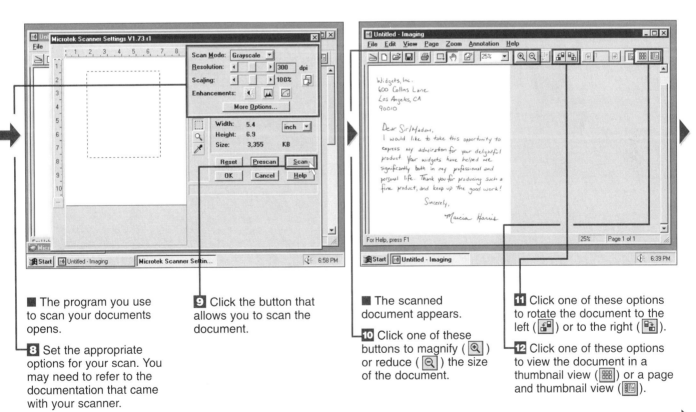

■ The program you use to scan your documents opens.

■ **8** Set the appropriate options for your scan. You may need to refer to the documentation that came with your scanner.

9 Click the button that allows you to scan the document.

■ The scanned document appears.

10 Click one of these buttons to magnify (🔍) or reduce (🔍) the size of the document.

11 Click one of these options to rotate the document to the left (🖼) or to the right (🖼).

12 Click one of these options to view the document in a thumbnail view (🖳) or a page and thumbnail view (🖳).

CONTINUED ▶

USING IMAGING CONTINUED

You can work with an Imaging document as you would work with any paper document. You can fill in a form, add details to a receipt or put a message on a magazine clipping.

You can add text or a note to an Imaging document. The text or note you add is called an annotation. Adding annotations is useful when you want a document to contain your remarks and comments. For example, you can use annotations to fill out a form you received by fax. You can also scan the minutes of a meeting, add your notes and then distribute the document to people who missed the meeting.

You can save an annotation with a document. You can also print or fax a document that contains annotations.

Imaging includes a tool that you can use to rubber stamp a document. You can indicate that the document is a draft, the date the document was received or the date the document was approved or rejected.

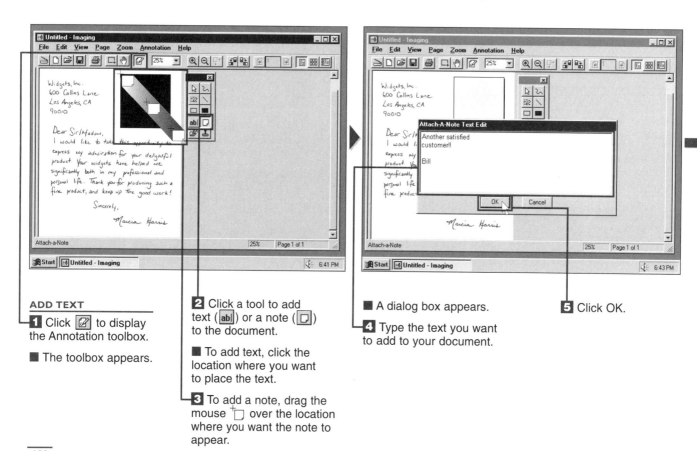

ADD TEXT

1 Click ☑ to display the Annotation toolbox.

■ The toolbox appears.

2 Click a tool to add text (ab|) or a note (☐) to the document.

■ To add text, click the location where you want to place the text.

3 To add a note, drag the mouse ☐ over the location where you want the note to appear.

■ A dialog box appears.

4 Type the text you want to add to your document.

5 Click OK.

Is an annotation part of the document?

An annotation is like a layer of information on top of the document. You can use the Annotations menu to hide or display an annotation. To permanently combine an annotation with a document so the annotation cannot be changed, click Annotation and then select the Make Annotations Permanent command. This command is not available when the annotations are hidden.

Can I move or delete an annotation?

Click the Annotation Selection tool (⬚). To move an annotation, drag the annotation to a new position. To delete an annotation, click the annotation and then press the Delete key.

How do I change the font in an annotation?

Click the Annotation Selection tool (⬚). Right-click the annotation you want to change and then select Properties. The Properties dialog box appears, displaying the options you can change.

Can I print a document without the annotation?

In the File menu, click Print. In the Print dialog box, click the Options button. Then select whether or not you want to print the annotation with your document.

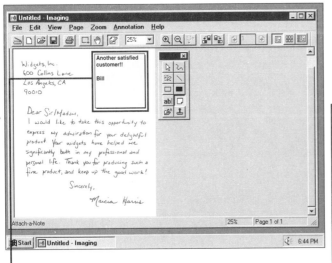

■ The text or note appears on your document.

Note: You can repeat step 1 to hide the Annotation toolbox.

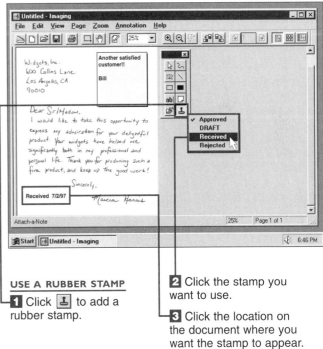

USE A RUBBER STAMP

1 Click ⬚ to add a rubber stamp.

2 Click the stamp you want to use.

3 Click the location on the document where you want the stamp to appear.

PLAY GAMES

Windows includes several games you can play when you need a break from your work. Games are also a fun way to improve your mouse skills, hand-eye coordination and reflexes.

Windows 95 comes with three card games. Solitaire and FreeCell are single-player card games. If you are on a network with other Windows 95 users, up to four people can join in a game of Hearts. You can also play Hearts by yourself, with Windows playing the other three hands.

Minesweeper is a strategy game in which you try to avoid being blown up by mines.

Hover! is available from the Windows 95 CD-ROM disc.

This is a three-dimensional game that demonstrates the graphics capabilities of your computer. Hover! works best when your screen displays 256 colors and the resolution is set at 640x480.

These games are an introduction to the types of games you can play using Windows 95.

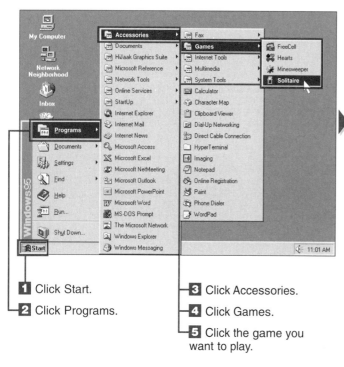

1 Click Start.

2 Click Programs.

3 Click Accessories.

4 Click Games.

5 Click the game you want to play.

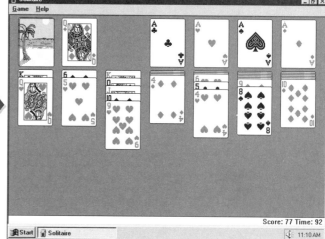

SOLITAIRE

Solitaire is a classic card game that you play on your own. You try to put all the cards in order from ace to king in four stacks, one stack for each suit.

Why aren't there any games available on my computer?

Games may not be installed on your computer. Games are located in the Accessories component on the Windows 95 CD-ROM disc. See page 580.

How do I play a game of Hearts on the network?

One player must choose to be the dealer. Other players can join the game by typing in the name of the dealer. Use the same name that appears for the dealer's computer in your Network Neighborhood.

How do I start Hover!?

To start Hover!, insert the Windows 95 CD-ROM disc into the drive and then select Hover! from the screen that appears.

How do I cheat at Solitaire?

When you are using the Draw three option, you can take only one card by pressing the Ctrl+Alt+Shift keys and then clicking the deck of cards.

How can I improve my score?

Click Help and then select Help Topics. The Contents tab provides information about the game's strategies that can help you improve your skills and score.

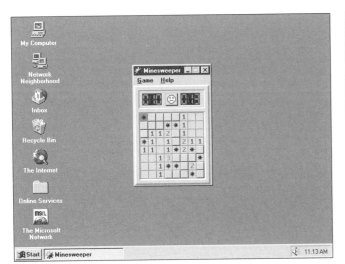

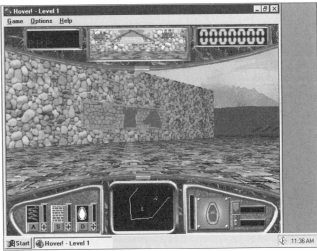

MINESWEEPER

In Minesweeper, you try to locate all of the mines without actually uncovering them.

HOVER!

With Hover!, you steer a hovercraft through a three-dimensional world as you attempt to gather all the enemy flags before the enemy captures yours.

10) CUSTOMIZE YOUR COMPUTER

11) CUSTOMIZE THE START MENU

CUSTOMIZE WINDOWS 95

12) MULTIMEDIA

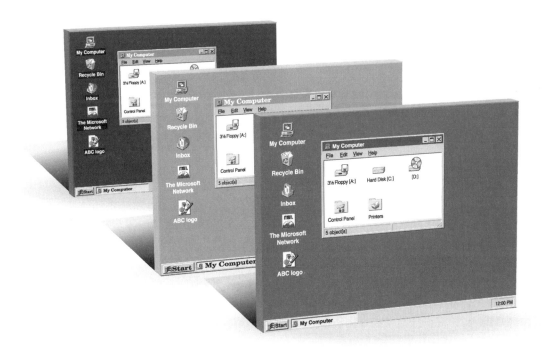

MOVE AND SIZE THE TASKBAR

Y ou can move and size the taskbar to accommodate your preferences and make it easier to use. The taskbar is the starting point for most of the tasks you perform in Windows. The taskbar contains the Start button and displays the name of each open window on your screen as well as the current time.

Windows initially displays the taskbar at the bottom of your screen, but you may want to display the taskbar in a different location on the screen. Windows allows you to move the taskbar to any side of your screen. Since other software programs display their menus at the top of the screen, you

may prefer to have the taskbar appear there too.

You can adjust the size of the taskbar. Increasing the size of the taskbar provides more space for Windows to display information about open windows.

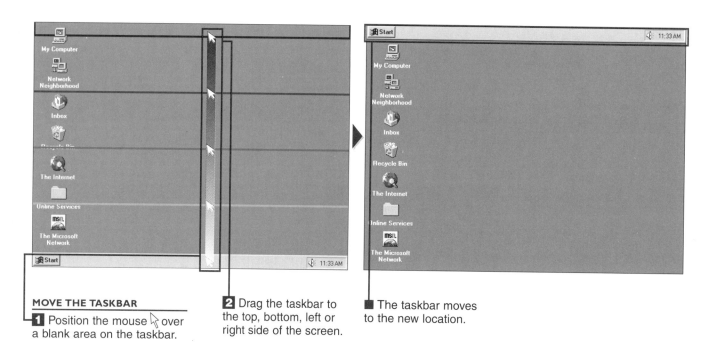

MOVE THE TASKBAR

1 Position the mouse ⌖ over a blank area on the taskbar.

2 Drag the taskbar to the top, bottom, left or right side of the screen.

■ The taskbar moves to the new location.

Why has my taskbar disappeared?

Your taskbar has been accidentally sized. Position the mouse pointer over the edge of the screen where the taskbar was last seen. When the pointer changes to $\updownarrow$, you can drag the mouse to increase the size of your taskbar.

How can I see more information about a small button on the taskbar?

Position the mouse pointer over the button. After a few seconds, a box appears displaying the full name of the window the button represents.

How can I use the taskbar to display the current date?

Position the mouse pointer over the time. After a few seconds, Windows displays the current date in a box.

How do I correct the time displayed on the taskbar?

Double-click the time to open the Date/Time Properties dialog box. This dialog box allows you to change the computer date and time. See page 198.

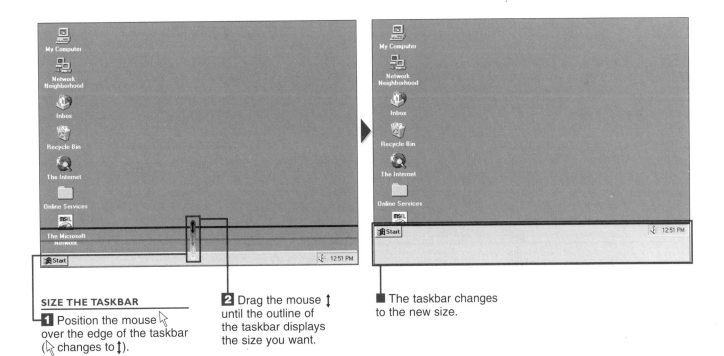

SIZE THE TASKBAR

1 Position the mouse ↘ over the edge of the taskbar (↘ changes to $\updownarrow$).

2 Drag the mouse $\updownarrow$ until the outline of the taskbar displays the size you want.

■ The taskbar changes to the new size.

CUSTOMIZE THE TASKBAR

You can modify the taskbar to suit your needs and make it easier to use.

Software programs designed for Windows 95 have space to accommodate the taskbar. When you use older programs, the taskbar may cover important parts of the screen. You can turn off the Always on top option while using

older programs so you can see the entire screen.

You can use the Auto hide option to hide the taskbar when you are not using it. Hiding the taskbar provides more working area on your desktop. To redisplay the taskbar, move the mouse pointer over the bottom edge of the screen.

The Show small icons in Start menu option reduces the size of the Start menu and the amount of space the menu takes up when it is displayed.

The Show Clock option displays or hides the clock on the taskbar.

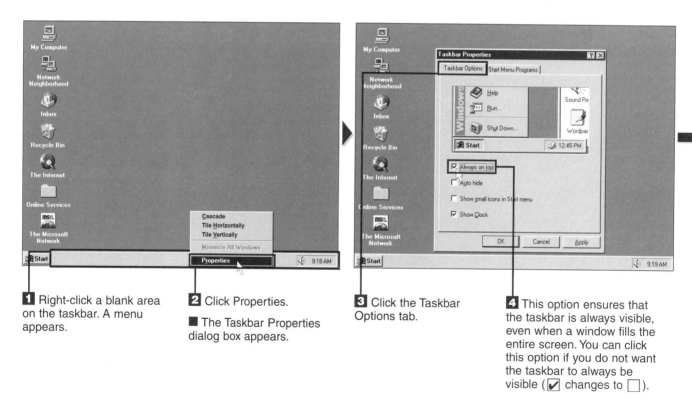

■1 Right-click a blank area on the taskbar. A menu appears.

■2 Click Properties.

■ The Taskbar Properties dialog box appears.

■3 Click the Taskbar Options tab.

■4 This option ensures that the taskbar is always visible, even when a window fills the entire screen. You can click this option if you do not want the taskbar to always be visible (☑ changes to ☐).

How can I make the taskbar appear when I am using a maximized window?

Hold down the Ctrl key and then press the Esc key to display the taskbar and the Start menu. You can also select both the Always on top and Auto hide options to have Windows always display the taskbar over a maximized window.

Can I size an individual taskbar button or remove a button from the taskbar?

Taskbar buttons cannot be sized. To remove a button from the taskbar, you must close the window the button represents.

Are all of my active programs displayed on the taskbar?

Windows may run programs that do not display a button on the taskbar. You can see a complete listing of your active programs in the Close Program dialog box. See page 83.

What happens when I have more windows open than will fit on the taskbar?

Two small arrows appear to the right of the taskbar buttons. You can click these arrows to scroll through buttons not currently displayed on the taskbar.

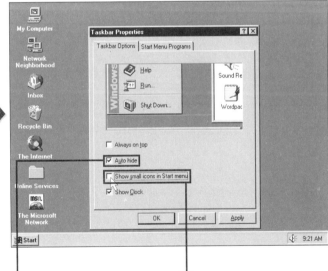

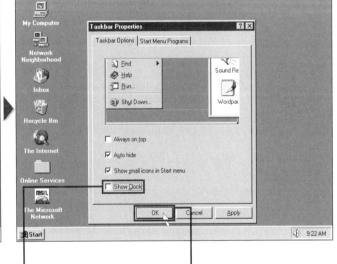

5 You can click this option to hide the taskbar when you are not using the taskbar (☐ changes to ☑).

6 You can click this option to reduce the size of the Start menu (☐ changes to ☑).

7 This option displays a clock on the right side of the taskbar. You can click this option to hide the clock (☑ changes to ☐).

8 Click OK to confirm all your changes.

SET THE DATE AND TIME

You can set the correct date and time in your computer. Setting the correct date and time is important because Windows uses this information to identify when documents are created and updated. If your computer's calendar and clock are accurate, you will be able to find your files more easily.

Your computer maintains the date and time even when the power is turned off. Windows adjusts the date and time automatically to compensate for daylight savings time. When you turn the computer on after a time change, Windows will tell you that your date and time settings have been updated.

If complete accuracy of your computer's clock is important to you, there are programs available that will synchronize your computer's clock with one of the very precise clocks on the Internet.

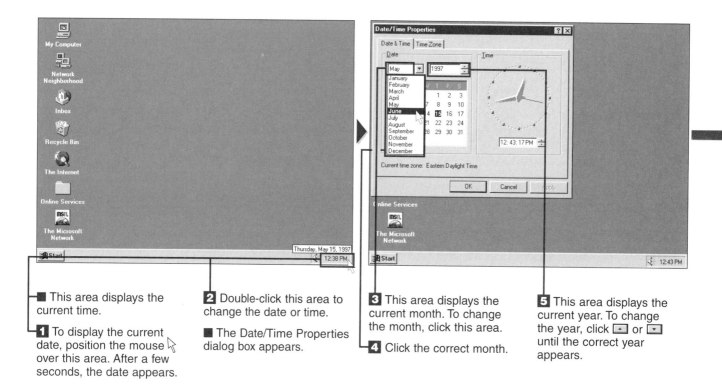

■ This area displays the current time.

■1 To display the current date, position the mouse over this area. After a few seconds, the date appears.

■2 Double-click this area to change the date or time.

■ The Date/Time Properties dialog box appears.

■3 This area displays the current month. To change the month, click this area.

■4 Click the correct month.

■5 This area displays the current year. To change the year, click ▲ or ▼ until the correct year appears.

How can I remove the clock from my taskbar?

In the Taskbar Properties dialog box, turn off the Show Clock feature. See page 196.

How can Windows help me get to my appointments on time?

There are many calendar and time management programs, like Microsoft Outlook and Lotus Organizer, that use the date and time set in your computer to remind you of your appointments. These programs usually provide audio and visual warnings in advance of your scheduled appointments.

I use my laptop in two time zones. Can Windows maintain both times like my watch can?

No, but you can switch back and forth between the time zones as often as you need to.

Will my computer's clock still work in the year 2000?

Some older programs might have difficulty making date calculations that span across both centuries, but Windows is designed to work with dates in the year 2000. You can test this feature by setting your computer clock to 11:59 PM 1999.

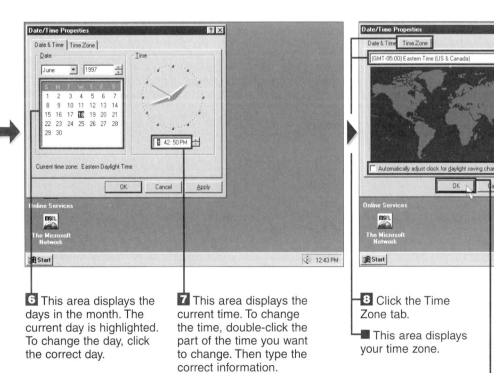

6 This area displays the days in the month. The current day is highlighted. To change the day, click the correct day.

7 This area displays the current time. To change the time, double-click the part of the time you want to change. Then type the correct information.

8 Click the Time Zone tab.

■ This area displays your time zone.

9 Windows will automatically adjust the computer's clock for daylight savings time. You can click this option to turn off this feature (☑ changes to ☐).

10 Click OK to confirm your changes.

CHANGE REGIONAL SETTINGS

You can change the way numbers, currency, dates and times are displayed on your computer to use the settings common to your region of the world.

Most North Americans use a period (.) to indicate the decimal point and a comma (,) to separate larger numbers. These settings are not universal. In fact, in many regions these settings are reversed.

When you select a new region for your computer, Windows changes the settings for all numbers, currency, time and dates.

Each region has its own settings, but you can adjust these settings to your own personal preference. For example, although most North Americans prefer to use 12-hour clocks, some people may prefer to use 24-hour clocks.

When you transfer a document to a computer in a different region, Windows changes the settings used in the document. Each person sees the document with the settings that they are used to.

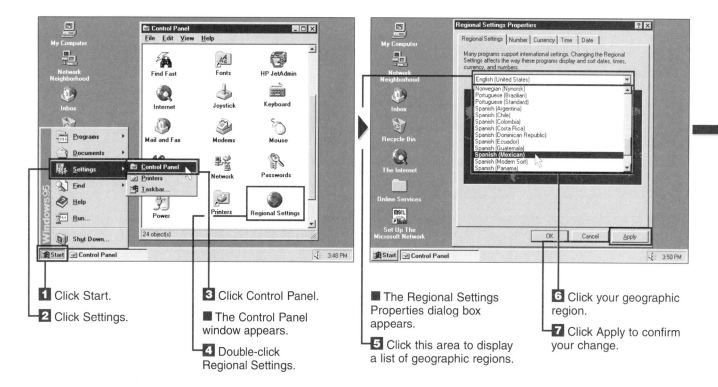

1 Click Start.

2 Click Settings.

3 Click Control Panel.

■ The Control Panel window appears.

4 Double-click Regional Settings.

■ The Regional Settings Properties dialog box appears.

5 Click this area to display a list of geographic regions.

6 Click your geographic region.

7 Click Apply to confirm your change.

How do I change to a 24-hour clock display?

Select a time style where the hours are represented by the capital letter H.

How do I install the font I need to display documents in a foreign alphabet?

To install fonts needed for a foreign alphabet, you should install the Multilanguage Support group. Multilanguage Support installs the specific fonts and other files needed to allow you to work with and create documents in several non-Western alphabets including Greek, Polish and Ukrainian. To install Windows components, see page 580.

How do I change the language used in the Windows menus?

Changing the regional settings only affects numerical, financial, date and time-related options. To change the language displayed in items such as menus and the Help feature, you must buy a copy of Windows in the language you want to use.

Can I change my keyboard for another language?

If you need to type special characters and symbols used in another language that are not available on the standard keyboard, you can change your keyboard language settings. In the Control Panel, select Keyboard. In the Keyboard Properties dialog box, select the Language tab.

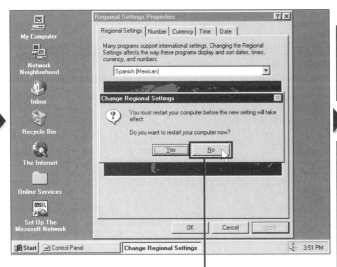

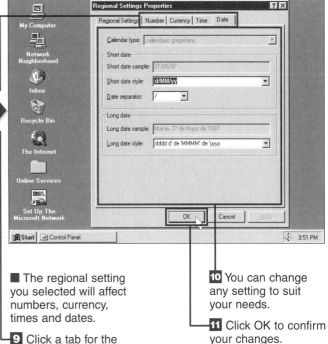

■ The Change Regional Settings dialog box appears, stating you must restart your computer before the new setting will take effect.

8 Click No if you do not want to restart your computer now.

■ The regional setting you selected will affect numbers, currency, times and dates.

9 Click a tab for the settings you want to view.

10 You can change any setting to suit your needs.

11 Click OK to confirm your changes.

CHANGE YOUR DESKTOP BACKGROUND

Like hanging posters on your walls or placing pictures on your desk, you can customize the Windows desktop to create a friendly and personalized working environment.

You can use patterns to add designs to your desktop. A pattern is a simple design made up of dots that alternate between black and the color of the background.

You can also use wallpaper to customize your desktop. Wallpaper is an image you display on your desktop. You can center a large image on the desktop or tile a small image to repeat it over the entire desktop.

Windows includes many different patterns and wallpaper images. There are also additional wallpaper images available on the Windows CD-ROM disc.

You can search the Internet for sites providing free wallpaper images. Collections of clip art and photographs found in computer stores can be used to create wallpaper images. You can also use your scanner to create personal wallpaper images.

You can create or modify wallpaper images using Paint or another program that can save images in the .bmp format.

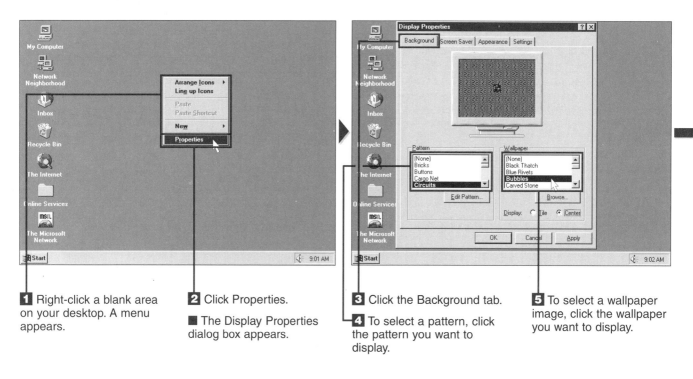

■1 Right-click a blank area on your desktop. A menu appears.

■2 Click Properties.

■ The Display Properties dialog box appears.

■3 Click the Background tab.

■4 To select a pattern, click the pattern you want to display.

■5 To select a wallpaper image, click the wallpaper you want to display.

How do I use clip art, scanned photographs or images I find on the Internet as my wallpaper?

In the c:\windows folder, save the image in the .bmp format so that it will appear on the list of available wallpaper images. If you have saved the image in another folder, you can use the Browse button to locate the image.

Why do the colors in the image I am using look odd?

To display photographic-quality images, your Color palette should be greater than 256. For more information on the Color palette, see page 208.

Does using a wallpaper image have any effect on my computer's performance?

Some of the computer's resources must be devoted to keeping the wallpaper information in memory. On systems with less than 16 MB of RAM, using a wallpaper image may affect the computer's ability to work with and switch between multiple programs. You may want to use a pattern instead, as patterns use fewer resources than a wallpaper image.

Can I modify patterns?

You can use the Edit Pattern button to make changes to patterns.

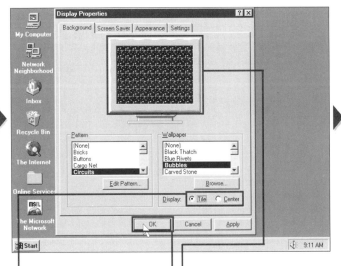

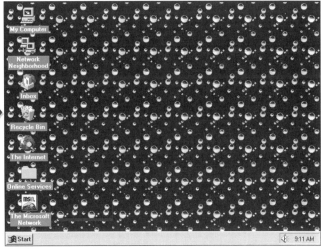

6 If you selected a wallpaper image, click the display option you want to use for the image.

Tile - Repeat image until it fills your entire screen.

Center - Place image in the middle of your screen.

Note: If you tile a wallpaper image, the wallpaper will cover any pattern you selected in step 4.

■ This area displays how your screen will appear.

7 Click OK.

■ The appearance of the screen changes.

■ To remove a wallpaper image or pattern from your screen, repeat steps 1 to 7 selecting (None) in steps 4 or 5.

CHANGE SCREEN COLORS

You can change the Windows screen to personalize and enhance your working environment. This can make your screen more attractive and easier to view.

Windows offers several schemes you can choose from. A scheme is a pre-defined screen appearance, including colors, text sizes and styles. High Contrast schemes are designed for people with vision impairments. High color schemes are designed for use on computers displaying more than 256 colors. VGA schemes are designed for use on computers limited to 16 colors. Choosing a scheme allows you to make multiple adjustments with one choice.

If you find the text on menus and under icons too small to read or have trouble clicking on small buttons, you can change individual items to suit your needs and preferences. You can also change the font, color and size of individual items to create your own unique scheme.

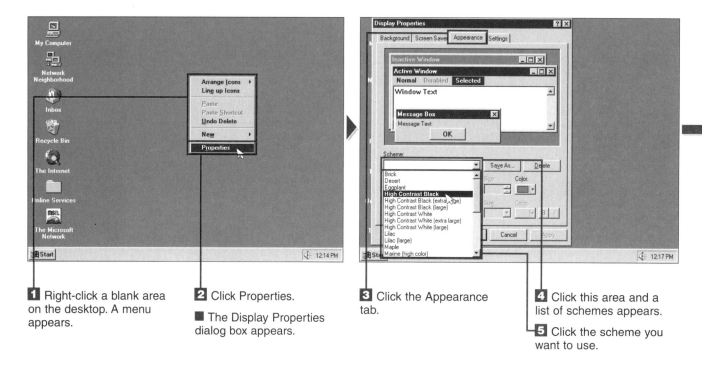

1 Right-click a blank area on the desktop. A menu appears.

2 Click Properties.

■ The Display Properties dialog box appears.

3 Click the Appearance tab.

4 Click this area and a list of schemes appears.

5 Click the scheme you want to use.

TIPS

How can I save the changes I have made to a scheme?

Click Save As to save your scheme with a new name. Windows will not display a warning if this procedure replaces a previously saved scheme.

I chose a large scheme and now a dialog box is too big. How do I cancel?

Some of the schemes do not fit on a 640x480 screen display. Select the Windows Standard scheme to change back to a scheme that will fit.

How do I change my screen back to the way it was?

Select the original scheme for Windows, called Windows Standard.

How do I change the font style and size used in the taskbar or the status bars?

In the Display Properties dialog box, select the Active Title Bar item to make changes to the taskbar settings. Select the ToolTip item to change the status bar settings.

How else can I change my screen appearance?

You can also change the screen appearance by changing the desktop background or by installing Desktop Themes. For information on changing the desktop background, see page 202. For information on Desktop Themes, see page 616.

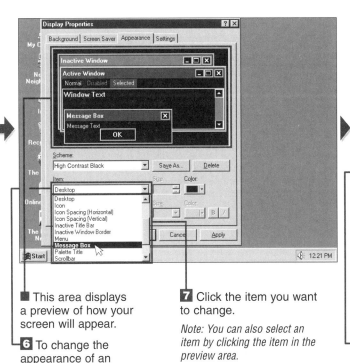

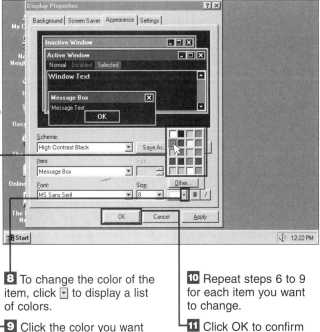

■ This area displays a preview of how your screen will appear.

6 To change the appearance of an individual item, click this area.

7 Click the item you want to change.

Note: You can also select an item by clicking the item in the preview area.

8 To change the color of the item, click ▼ to display a list of colors.

9 Click the color you want to use.

Note: You can also select a different font, size or style for some items.

10 Repeat steps 6 to 9 for each item you want to change.

11 Click OK to confirm your changes.

CHANGE THE SCREEN RESOLUTION

You can change the screen resolution to adjust the size of the image displayed on your screen.

Resolution is measured by the number of horizontal and vertical pixels. A pixel is the smallest element on a screen. The standard screen resolution is 640x480, but most monitors can display resolutions up to 1024x768.

Lower resolutions display larger images so you can see the information on your screen more clearly. Some games are designed to run at a specific screen resolution. You may need to use a lower resolution to have the game fill your entire screen.

Higher resolutions display smaller images so you can view more information on your screen at once. A higher resolution allows you to see more of a word processing document or more cells in a spreadsheet without scrolling. A higher resolution may allow you to display two documents side-by-side and view their contents. In a graphics program, a higher resolution allows you to see more detail without zooming in or out.

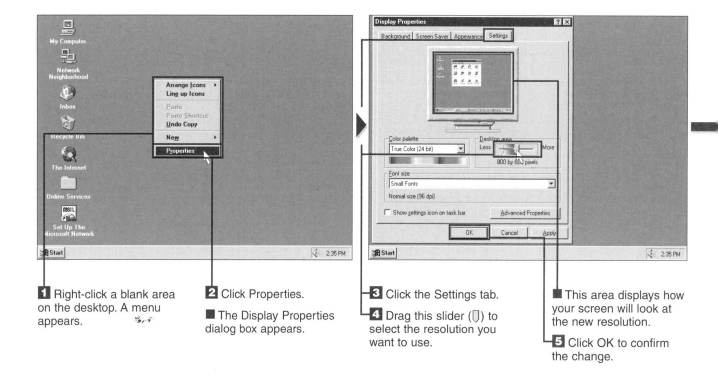

1 Right-click a blank area on the desktop. A menu appears.

2 Click Properties.

■ The Display Properties dialog box appears.

3 Click the Settings tab.

4 Drag this slider (◰) to select the resolution you want to use.

■ This area displays how your screen will look at the new resolution.

5 Click OK to confirm the change.

Why do I have wide black borders around the edge of my screen or lose part of the desktop when I change the resolution?

You may need to make adjustments to your monitor after changing the resolution. Use the manual that comes with your monitor to find the horizontal and vertical size and position controls and then make the necessary adjustments.

Menus and other screen items are too small to read when I change to a higher resolution. What can I do?

You can make the text easier to read in menus and other screen items. From the Display Properties dialog box, click the Settings tab and change the Font size setting from Small Fonts to Large Fonts.

Is there an easier way to change the resolution?

You can select the Show settings icon on the taskbar option to display the monitor icon on the taskbar. You can then click the monitor icon to display a list of all the available resolutions. This option is only available for OSR2.

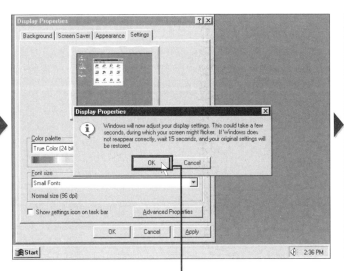

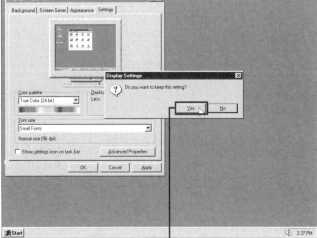

■ The Display Properties dialog box appears. Windows will now adjust the screen resolution.

Note: Some changes may require you to restart your computer. Click Yes to restart the computer.

6 Click OK to continue.

■ Windows changes the size of the information on your screen.

■ A dialog box appears, asking if you want to continue using the new screen resolution.

7 Click Yes to keep the screen resolution.

CHANGE NUMBER OF SCREEN COLORS

You can increase the number of colors your screen displays. Increasing the number of colors not only improves the quality of images, but also improves the general appearance of your screen.

Windows offers several different color palettes. The 16 Color setting displays low-resolution images. The 256 Color setting is ideal for most home, business

and game applications. The High Color setting (16 bit) is ideal for video and desktop publishing. The True Color (24 bit) setting is ideal for high-end graphics programs and photo-retouching. With 256 or more colors you will be able to use some advanced Windows features including the 3-D and animated mouse cursors as well as font smoothing. Some multimedia

programs also work better on computers that display 256 or more colors.

The number of colors your screen can display is directly related to the amount of memory on your computer's video card. A smaller video card memory means you must use a smaller color palette.

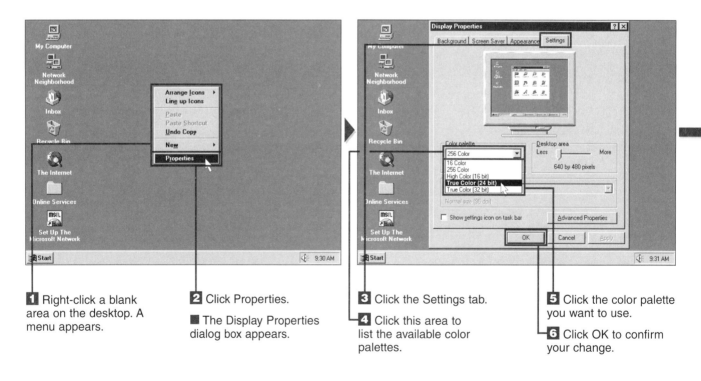

1 Right-click a blank area on the desktop. A menu appears.

2 Click Properties.

■ The Display Properties dialog box appears.

3 Click the Settings tab.

4 Click this area to list the available color palettes.

5 Click the color palette you want to use.

6 Click OK to confirm your change.

TIPS

What is font smoothing?

Font smoothing softens the edges of letters with gray to make them appear to be higher quality than normal letters. Font smoothing makes reading text on your screen for a long period of time easier. Font smoothing can only be used with a High Color (16 bit) or better setting. This feature is included with Microsoft Plus! and is also available from the Microsoft Web site, www.microsoft.com/truetype

Will I need to upgrade my monitor if I increase my color palette?

All modern monitors are capable of using the True Color setting to display millions of colors.

Will a larger color palette affect my computer's performance?

Your computer's performance should not be affected. Although small color palettes are slightly faster than large color palettes, there is only a minor speed difference.

How can I control whether or not Windows will restart when I change the color palette?

Choose the Settings tab. Then click the Advanced Properties button and select the Performance tab. You can now tell Windows what you want it to do when the color palette is changed. This allows you to make changes without having to restart Windows. This feature is only available in OSR2.

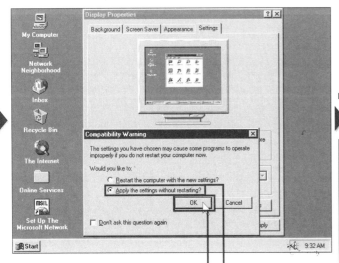

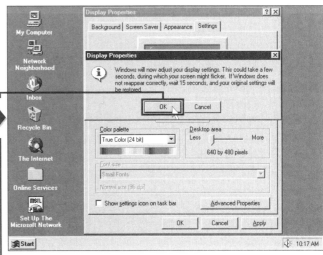

■ The Compatibility Warning dialog box appears. Some programs may operate improperly if you do not restart your computer.

Note: A different dialog box may appear, stating that you must restart your computer. Click Yes to restart your computer.

7 Click this option to apply the setting without restarting your computer (○ changes to ◉).

8 Click OK.

■ The Display Properties dialog box appears. Windows will now adjust the color palette.

9 Click OK to continue.

■ Windows will adjust your screen and display a dialog box asking if you want to continue using the new color palette. Click Yes to keep the setting.

SET UP A SCREEN SAVER

A screen saver is a moving picture or pattern that appears on your screen when you do not use your computer for a period of time. You can use a screen saver to keep your work private while you are away from your desk.

There are many screen savers available that display interesting patterns, personal messages or entertaining images from popular cartoons, movies and television programs.

When you do not use your computer for a certain period

of time, Windows starts the screen saver. You can select the amount of time the computer must be idle before the screen saver appears. Adjusting the time period is useful to prevent the screen saver from disrupting your work while you are reviewing material on your screen.

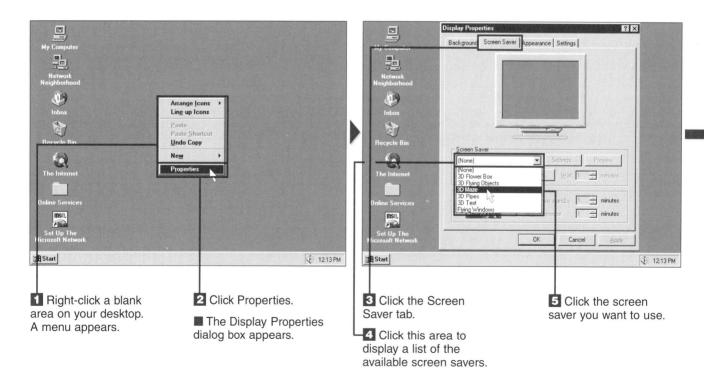

1 Right-click a blank area on your desktop. A menu appears.

2 Click Properties.

■ The Display Properties dialog box appears.

3 Click the Screen Saver tab.

4 Click this area to display a list of the available screen savers.

5 Click the screen saver you want to use.

TIPS

What do screen savers do?

Screen savers were originally designed to prevent screen burn, which occurs when an image appears in a fixed position for a long period of time. Today's monitors are better designed to prevent screen burn, but people still use screen savers.

Do I need to use a screen saver?

You do not need to use a screen saver to protect the screen from damage. Many people now use screen savers for their entertainment value and energy saving features. Some screen savers, such as those provided by the PointCast Network, display news, sports, weather, stock and other information.

Can I customize my screen savers?

You can click the Settings button to customize your screen savers. Each screen saver offers different options you can change.

Where can I get more screen savers?

The Windows CD-ROM disc includes several screen savers. Some camera stores will prepare screen savers from your favorite photographs.

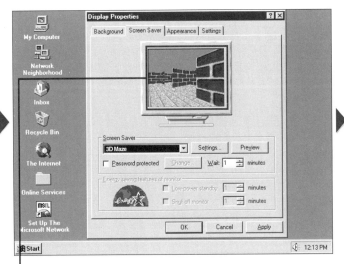

■ This area displays how the screen saver will look on your screen.

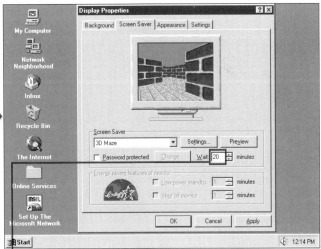

6 To change the length of time the computer must be inactive before the screen saver will appear, double-click this area. Then type a new number.

CONTINUED ▶

SET UP A SCREEN SAVER
CONTINUED

Most screen savers can add a level of security and privacy to your work.

You can use the screen saver password feature to prevent other people from using your computer when you are not at your desk. This protects your work from unauthorized changes and keeps your documents private.

If you assign a password for your screen saver, you must enter the password correctly to remove the screen saver and use your computer. This makes it difficult for people to use your computer without your permission.

When you choose a password, do not use words that people can associate with you, such as your name or favorite sport. The most effective passwords connect two words or numbers with a special character (example: blue@123). To keep your password secure, do not write down your password in an area where people can find it. You may also want to change your password every few weeks.

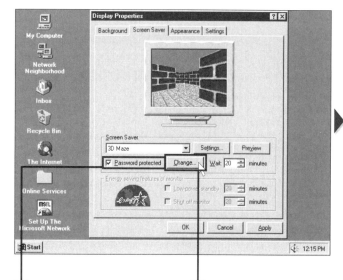

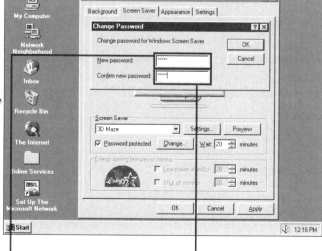

7 Click Password protected to assign a password that must be entered to remove the screen saver (☐ changes to ☑).

Note: If you do not want to assign a password, skip to step 12.

8 Click Change.

■ The Change Password dialog box appears.

9 Type a password and then press the Tab key. An asterisk (*) appears for each character you type to prevent others from seeing your password.

10 Type the password again to confirm the password and then press the Enter key.

TIPS

CUSTOMIZE WINDOWS 95

How do I stop the screen saver?

Press the Shift key or move your mouse to stop the screen saver. While the screen saver is on, you still have open programs on your computer. If you press a different key, you might affect the open program. If you use a password, you need to enter the password to turn off the screen saver.

What impact do screen savers have on my computer?

Screen savers can cause your computer to operate slower because they constantly monitor the activity of your computer. You may also have to wait while the computer switches from the screen saver back to your work.

How secure is the screen saver password feature?

Your screen saver password is not very secure. Other people can access your computer simply by restarting it. You can buy commercial screen savers that are more secure and do not allow access by restarting the computer.

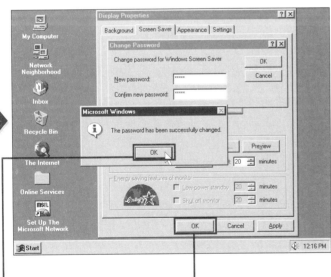

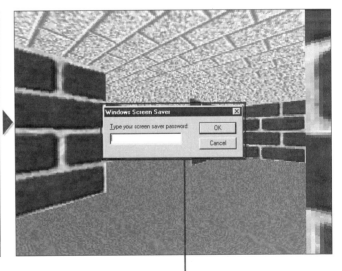

■ A dialog box appears, indicating that the password was successfully changed.

11 Click OK to close the dialog box.

12 Click OK to close the Display Properties dialog box.

■ The screen saver appears when you do not use your computer for the amount of time specified.

■ You can move the mouse or press a key on the keyboard to remove the screen saver.

■ If you selected a password in step 12, the Windows Screen Saver dialog box appears, asking for your password. Type your password and then click OK.

HAVE MONITOR
TURN OFF AUTOMATICALLY

You may be able to save energy and increase the life of your monitor by using its energy-saving features. Monitors that have energy-saving features usually display the Energy Star symbol. When you do not use an Energy Star computer for a period of time, you can have the monitor enter an energy-saving mode. You can specify the length of time that

must pass before the energy-saving mode begins.

The low-power standby mode reduces the power to the monitor but keeps the monitor turned on and ready to use. You can reactivate the monitor by pressing a key on your keyboard or moving the mouse.

The shut off mode turns off the power to the monitor. When you press a key on your keyboard or move the mouse, the monitor turns back on. The screen reappears more slowly than in the low-power standby mode. The shut off mode conserves more energy than the low-power standby mode.

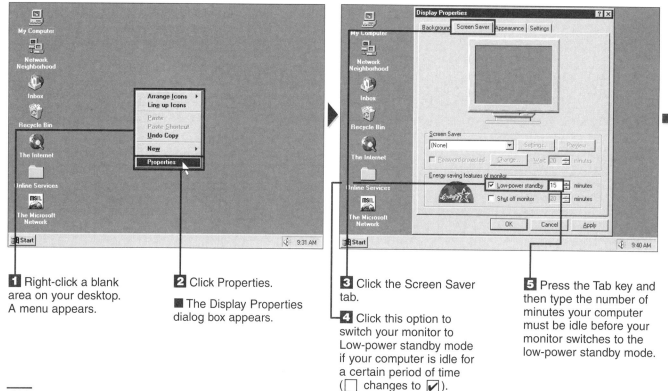

1 Right-click a blank area on your desktop. A menu appears.

2 Click Properties.

■ The Display Properties dialog box appears.

3 Click the Screen Saver tab.

4 Click this option to switch your monitor to Low-power standby mode if your computer is idle for a certain period of time (☐ changes to ☑).

5 Press the Tab key and then type the number of minutes your computer must be idle before your monitor switches to the low-power standby mode.

Does Windows have any other energy-saving features?

If you are using OSR2, Windows will place your hard drive in a low-power mode after a 30 minute period of inactivity. In the Control Panel, select the Power icon to adjust the amount of time that must pass before the drive will enter the low-power mode.

Why aren't the energy-saving features available for my Energy Star monitor?

Windows may not know you have an Energy Star monitor. Click the Settings tab and then click the Advanced Properties or Change Display Type button. Click the Monitor tab and select the Monitor is Energy Star compliant option.

Are there times when I should not use an energy-saving mode?

If you work in the graphics industry, and your monitor has been adjusted for exact colors, you should not use an energy-saving mode.

Can I use the energy-saving features with a screen saver?

You can use the energy-saving features and the screen saver separately or in any combination. For example, you can have the screen saver activate after 5 minutes, the low-power standby mode activate after 10 minutes and the shut off mode activate after 20 minutes.

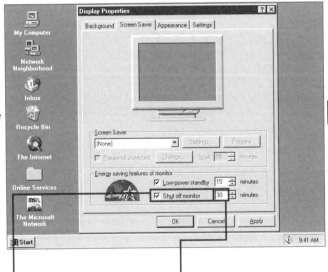

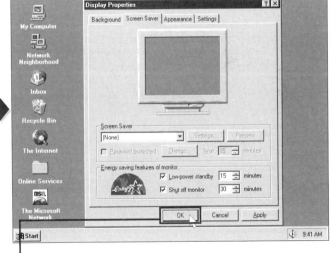

6 Click this option to turn off your monitor if your computer is idle for a certain period of time (☐ changes to ☑).

7 Press the Tab key and then type the number of minutes your computer must be idle before your monitor turns off.

8 Click OK to confirm your changes.

■ When your computer switches to an energy-saving mode, you can press a key on your keyboard or move the mouse to reactivate your monitor.

ADD DESTINATIONS TO SEND TO MENU

The Send To menu allows you to send files to another location. You can customize the Send To menu to include the folders, programs and devices you use most often. Your floppy and removable drives are already in the Send To menu.

You can place shortcuts to folders, programs and devices in the Send To folder. Any item in the Send To

folder appears in the Send To menu.

You can use the Send To menu to open files in a program or move files to a new folder. You can also print, fax or e-mail a file using the Send To menu. Using the Send To menu simplifies procedures because you do not have to open a folder or program or see the device

you are sending a file to before you send the file.

For example, if you place a shortcut to a printer in the Send To menu, you can send a selected file directly to the printer. If you place a shortcut to WordPad in the Send To menu, you can use the Send To menu to open a file using WordPad that does not have a standard extension, like readme.1st

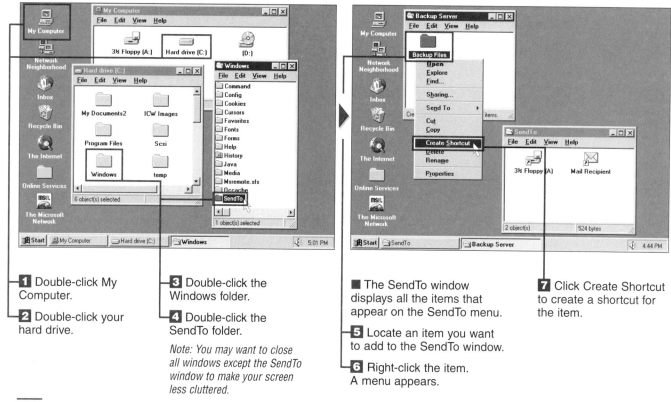

1 Double-click My Computer.

2 Double-click your hard drive.

3 Double-click the Windows folder.

4 Double-click the SendTo folder.

Note: You may want to close all windows except the SendTo window to make your screen less cluttered.

■ The SendTo window displays all the items that appear on the SendTo menu.

5 Locate an item you want to add to the SendTo window.

6 Right-click the item. A menu appears.

7 Click Create Shortcut to create a shortcut for the item.

Can I send files to people on a network using Send To?

You can send files to people on a network if they have shared folders. You can create a shortcut to a shared folder and place the shortcut in your Send To folder.

Can I store items in folders within the Send To folder?

You can create a folder in the Send To folder to store additional options. The folder will appear at the top of the Send To menu with an arrow (▶) indicating there are more choices. You can click on the folder to display another menu with more choices.

I am sending a file to a folder. How do I know if Send To will move or copy the file?

If the folder is on the same drive as the file, the file is moved to the folder and disappears from its current folder. If the folder is on a different drive than the file, the file is copied to the folder. If you are sending a program file, a shortcut is created and the original program file stays in its current folder.

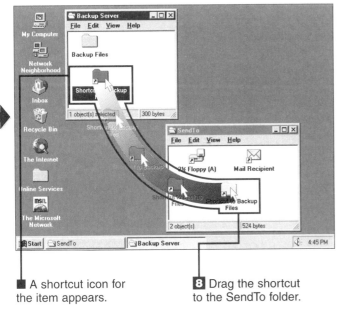

■ A shortcut icon for the item appears.

8 Drag the shortcut to the SendTo folder.

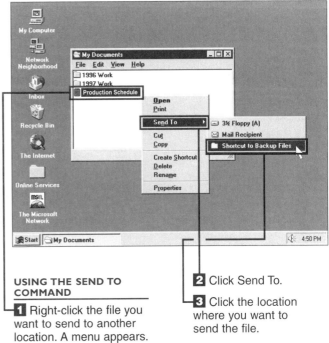

USING THE SEND TO COMMAND

1 Right-click the file you want to send to another location. A menu appears.

2 Click Send To.

3 Click the location where you want to send the file.

217

CHANGE MOUSE SETTINGS

You can change the way your mouse works to make it easier to use. The Mouse Properties dialog box offers many options you can adjust to suit your needs.

The left mouse button is used to select or drag items and activate buttons. The right mouse button is used to

display a list of commands for the selected item. If you are left-handed, you can switch the functions of the left and right mouse buttons to make the mouse easier to use.

Double-clicking is most often used to open an item. You can change the amount of time

that can pass between two clicks of the mouse button for Windows to recognize a double-click. If you are a new mouse user or you have difficulty double-clicking, you may find a slower speed easier to use. You can try out the new double-click speed setting in the Mouse Properties dialog box.

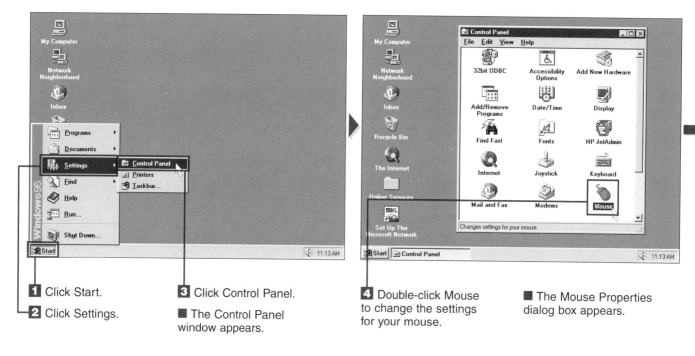

1 Click Start.

2 Click Settings.

3 Click Control Panel.

■ The Control Panel window appears.

4 Double-click Mouse to change the settings for your mouse.

■ The Mouse Properties dialog box appears.

My mouse pointer jumps around or gets stuck on the screen. What can I do?

Your mouse may need to be cleaned. Turn the mouse over and remove and clean the roller ball. Use a cotton swab to remove the dirt from the rollers inside the mouse. You can refer to the manual that came with your mouse for further instructions.

Why should I use a mouse pad?

A mouse pad provides a smooth surface for moving the mouse on your desk. You should choose a mouse pad with a hard plastic surface that is easy to keep clean. Fabric covered mouse pads collect dirt, which may stick to the roller ball of the mouse.

I have made adjustments to the double-click speed setting, but I still have difficulty double-clicking. What are my alternatives?

After you click an item, you can press the Enter key to perform the same action as double-clicking. You can also right-click an item and then click the first option in the menu that appears. Some manufacturers make mice with three buttons so you can set one of the buttons to act as a double-click button.

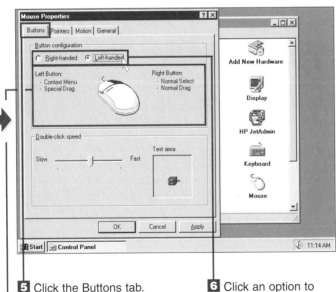

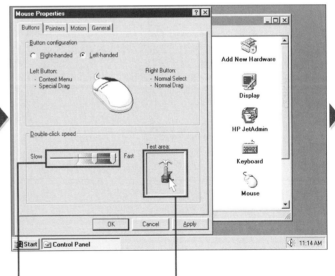

5 Click the Buttons tab.

■ This area describes the functions of the left and right mouse buttons.

6 Click an option to specify if you are right-handed or left-handed (○ changes to ⦿). Changing the option will switch the functions of the left and right mouse buttons.

7 Drag this slider (⬚) to a new position to change the double-click speed.

8 Double-click this area to test the double-click speed. A jack-in-the-box appears if you double-click at the correct speed.

CONTINUED ▶

CHANGE MOUSE SETTINGS
CONTINUED

You can personalize your mouse by changing the look of the pointers and the way the pointer moves on your screen.

The mouse pointer assumes different shapes, depending on its location on your screen and the task you are performing. For example, the standard mouse pointer turns into an hourglass when the computer is busy,

or a double-headed arrow when you are adjusting the size of a window.

Windows includes several sets of pointers including animated, three-dimensional and oversized pointers. You can choose to display a different set of mouse pointers or change the appearance of just one mouse pointer.

You can make the mouse pointer on your screen move faster or slower.

You can leave a trail of mouse pointers as you move the mouse around your screen. Displaying mouse trails can help you follow the movement of the mouse pointer on your screen. This is especially useful on portable computer screens, where the mouse pointer can be difficult to follow.

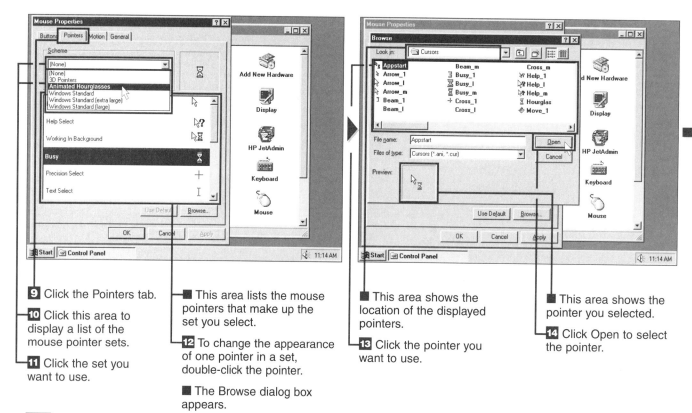

■9 Click the Pointers tab.

■10 Click this area to display a list of the mouse pointer sets.

■11 Click the set you want to use.

■ This area lists the mouse pointers that make up the set you select.

■12 To change the appearance of one pointer in a set, double-click the pointer.

■ The Browse dialog box appears.

■ This area shows the location of the displayed pointers.

■13 Click the pointer you want to use.

■ This area shows the pointer you selected.

■14 Click Open to select the pointer.

How do I install the additional sets of pointers included in Windows 95?

In the Control Panel, select Add/Remove Programs to add mouse pointers. The mouse pointers are part of the Accessories group. See page 580.

Where can I find more mouse pointer schemes?

Microsoft Plus! and Plus! for Kids contain themes which include coordinated mouse pointer schemes, wallpaper images and sounds.

How do I save my set of customized mouse pointers?

After you have customized a set of mouse pointers, you can use the Save As button to name and save your set of mouse pointers.

Why does my Mouse Properties dialog box have additional options?

If you are using a specialized mouse, such as Microsoft IntelliMouse, you will find additional options in the Mouse Properties dialog box.

Why didn't my mouse pointers change their appearance?

Some mouse pointers, such as the three-dimensional and animated pointers, are only available when your color palette is set at 256 or more colors. To change the color palette, see page 208.

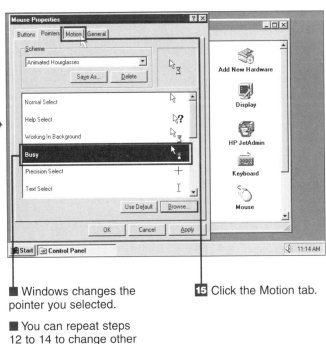

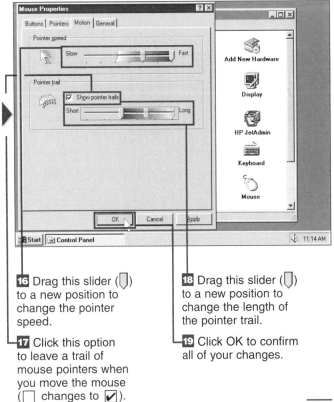

■ Windows changes the pointer you selected.

■ You can repeat steps 12 to 14 to change other pointers in the set.

15 Click the Motion tab.

16 Drag this slider (⬜) to a new position to change the pointer speed.

17 Click this option to leave a trail of mouse pointers when you move the mouse (☐ changes to ☑).

18 Drag this slider (⬜) to a new position to change the length of the pointer trail.

19 Click OK to confirm all of your changes.

CHANGE KEYBOARD SETTINGS

You can change the way your keyboard responds to your commands.

Repeated characters appear on your screen when you hold down a key on your keyboard. If you use repeated characters to underline, separate or emphasize text, you may want to adjust the Repeat delay and Repeat rate settings.

The Repeat delay setting adjusts the length of time a key must be held down before it starts to repeat.

The Repeat rate determines how quickly characters appear on your screen while a key is held down. You can test the settings while making adjustments.

You can also change the speed at which the cursor blinks. The cursor, or insertion point, indicates where the text you type will appear. The cursor should blink fast enough so it is easy to find, but slow enough so it is not distracting. You can preview your Cursor blink rate to find a setting you prefer.

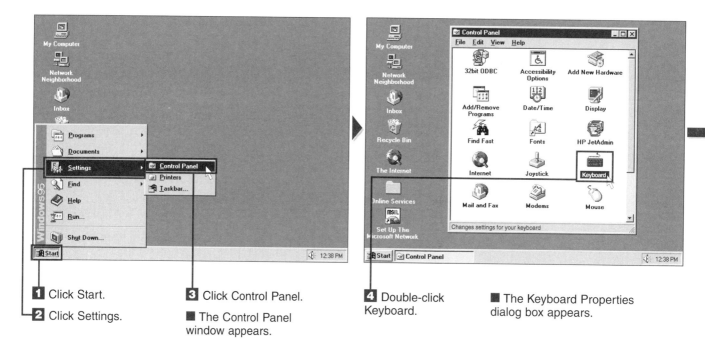

1 Click Start.

2 Click Settings.

3 Click Control Panel.

■ The Control Panel window appears.

4 Double-click Keyboard.

■ The Keyboard Properties dialog box appears.

TIPS

What is the correct typing posture to help avoid wrist strain?

You should keep your elbows level with the keyboard. Always keep your wrists straight and higher than your fingers while working on the keyboard. You can use a wrist rest with your keyboard to elevate your wrists and ensure they remain straight at all times. If you start to experience any pain, tingling or numbness while working, take a break. If the sensation continues, you should see a doctor.

I find it difficult to hold down two keys and then press a third. Can I make my keyboard easier to use?

The Accessibility options can make your keyboard easier to use. The Accessibility options are located in the Control Panel window. See page 224.

How do I clean my keyboard?

To remove dust, use a small paintbrush. To clean away dirt, use a cloth dampened with soapy water or a window-cleaning solution.

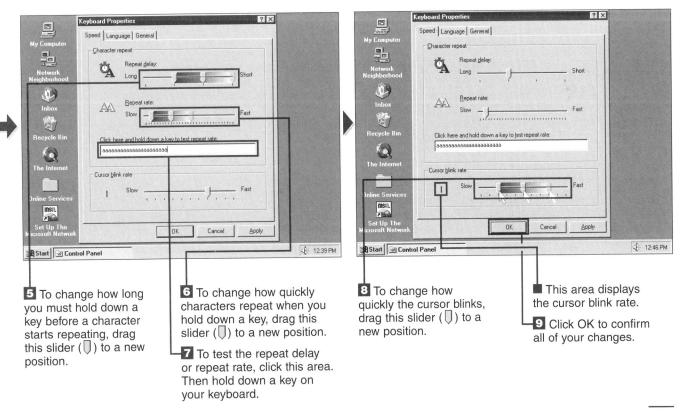

5 To change how long you must hold down a key before a character starts repeating, drag this slider (⬇) to a new position.

6 To change how quickly characters repeat when you hold down a key, drag this slider (⬇) to a new position.

7 To test the repeat delay or repeat rate, click this area. Then hold down a key on your keyboard.

8 To change how quickly the cursor blinks, drag this slider (⬇) to a new position.

■ This area displays the cursor blink rate.

9 Click OK to confirm all of your changes.

ACCESSIBILITY OPTIONS

The operation of your computer can be adjusted to accommodate special needs and situations. Windows' accessibility options allow you to make a computer easier to use if you have physical restrictions, or when using a mouse is not practical.

Windows offers several options designed to improve the usability of your keyboard.

StickyKeys help users who have difficulty pressing two keys at the same time. When you press Shift, Ctrl or Alt on your keyboard, the key will remain active while you press the second key. FilterKeys reduce the keyboard's sensitivity to brief or repeated keystrokes. ToggleKeys allow you to hear a tone when the Caps Lock, Num Lock or Scroll Lock keys are pressed.

Windows also allows you to replace sound cues with visual ones. SoundSentry flashes window borders or caption bars as a visual signal. ShowSounds provides on-screen captions for some speech and sound events.

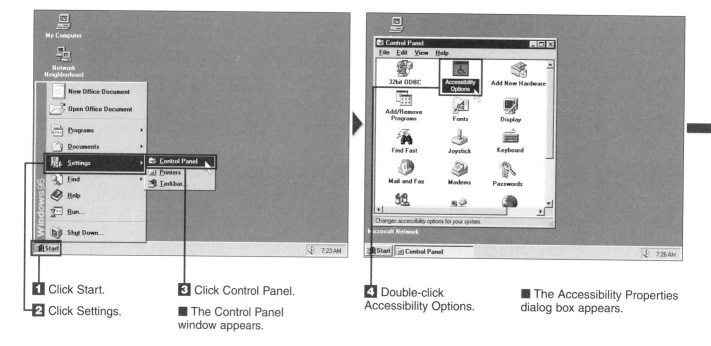

1 Click Start.

2 Click Settings.

3 Click Control Panel.

■ The Control Panel window appears.

4 Double-click Accessibility Options.

■ The Accessibility Properties dialog box appears.

TIPS

There is no Accessibility Options icon in my Control Panel. How can I add this feature?

In the Control Panel, use the Add/Remove Programs icon to install the Accessibility Options group from your Windows 95 CD-ROM disc. See page 580.

What shortcut keys can I use to turn on the keyboard features?

You can activate StickyKeys by pressing the Shift key five times. You can turn on FilterKeys by holding down the right Shift key for eight seconds. You can activate ToggleKeys by holding down the Num Lock key for five seconds.

How can I activate the shortcut keys to turn on the keyboard features?

To activate the shortcut keys, click the Settings button beside a feature and then click Use shortcut.

How do I know a feature is turned on?

Some features, like StickyKeys, display an icon on your taskbar to indicate they are turned on.

My keyboard is still too sensitive, even with FilterKeys turned on. What should I do?

Use the Settings button to adjust and test the FilterKeys option. The Settings dialog box provides access to even more settings for further fine-tuning.

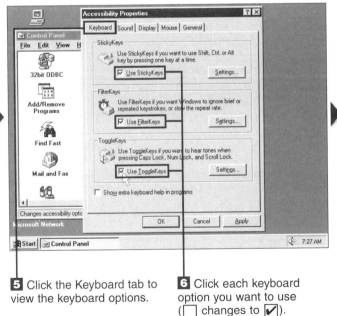

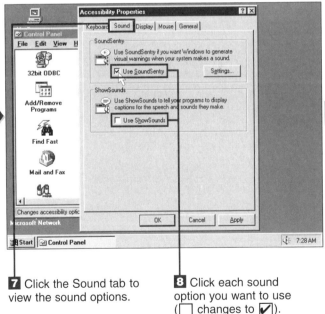

5 Click the Keyboard tab to view the keyboard options.

6 Click each keyboard option you want to use (☐ changes to ☑).

7 Click the Sound tab to view the sound options.

8 Click each sound option you want to use (☐ changes to ☑).

CONTINUED ▶

ACCESSIBILITY OPTIONS
CONTINUED

The accessibility options can make your screen easier to read and allow you to perform mouse actions using your keyboard.

If you find the screen difficult to read, you can change the screen display. Windows will change the colors of text and other items to increase the contrast and make the screen easier to read.

MouseKeys allow you to control the mouse pointer using the numeric keypad instead of the mouse. This can be useful in situations where a mouse is impractical or inappropriate, such as when using a laptop. Graphic artists who need finer and more accurate control of mouse pointer movements may also want to use MouseKeys.

If you share a computer with several users who do not all use the accessibility options, you can turn off these features when they are not in use. You can use optional warning messages to let you know when a feature is active.

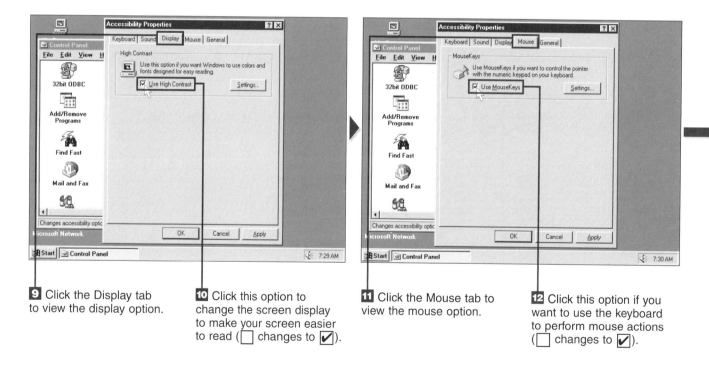

9 Click the Display tab to view the display option.

10 Click this option to change the screen display to make your screen easier to read (☐ changes to ☑).

11 Click the Mouse tab to view the mouse option.

12 Click this option if you want to use the keyboard to perform mouse actions (☐ changes to ☑).

How can I use shortcut keys to change the screen display?

In the Display tab, click the Settings button and then click Use shortcut. You can then press the left Alt key, the left Shift key and the Print Screen key at the same time to activate High Contrast display. Pressing the same keys resets the screen to its previous settings.

The MouseKeys feature is not working. How do I activate it?

The Num Lock key must be on to use MouseKeys. A light on your keyboard indicates the status of the Num Lock key. You can also click the Settings button to change the settings for this feature.

What keys can I use to control my mouse pointer?

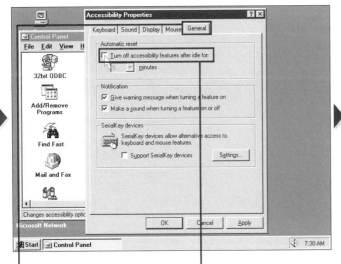

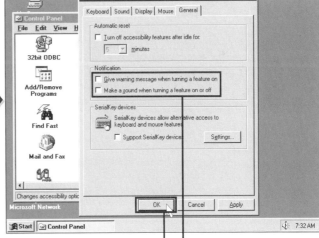

13 Click the General tab to view the settings for all the accessibility options.

■ Windows will turn off the accessibility options if you do not use your computer for a certain period of time.

14 If you want the accessibility options to remain on at all times, click this option (✓ changes to ☐).

■ Windows will display a message and sound a tone when you use a shortcut key to turn an accessibility option on or off. For examples of shortcut keys, see page 225.

15 If you want to turn off a notification option, click the option (✓ changes to ☐).

16 Click OK to confirm all the accessibility options you selected.

VIEW FONTS ON YOUR COMPUTER

Y ou can view the fonts on your computer to see what they look like before using the fonts in your documents.

A font is a set of characters with a particular design and size. There are a wide variety of fonts you can use. Fonts can be serious and corporate or fancy and funny.

Viewing the fonts on your computer allows you to choose the right font for a document.

Most of the fonts included with Windows are TrueType fonts. A TrueType font generates characters using mathematical formulas. You can change the size of a TrueType font without distorting the font.

A TrueType font will print exactly as it appears on the screen.

Windows displays information about each font on your computer as well as samples of each font in various sizes. You can print a copy of this font information and save it for later reference.

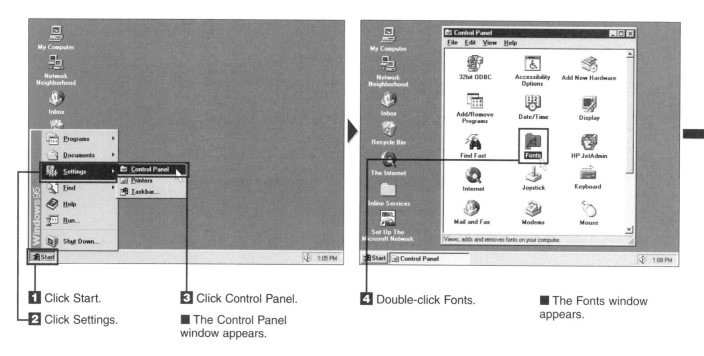

1 Click Start.

2 Click Settings.

3 Click Control Panel.

■ The Control Panel window appears.

4 Double-click Fonts.

■ The Fonts window appears.

TIPS

What are printer fonts?

Printer fonts are fonts stored in a printer's memory. Nearly all printers include printer fonts. Unlike TrueType fonts, printer fonts may not be accurately represented on your screen. Printer fonts are not displayed in the Fonts window. This type of font may appear in a program's font list and is indicated by a printer icon.

Why do many font names appear more than once in the Fonts window?

Windows displays variations of many fonts, such as bold and italic. In the View menu, click Hide Variations to remove the variations and display only the basic style for each font in the window.

Why do some fonts in the Fonts window display a red A?

Fonts displaying a red A are system fonts. Windows uses system fonts to display text in menus and dialog boxes. These fonts are only available in specific sizes. Although system fonts may appear in a program's font list, they are not suitable for most printing tasks.

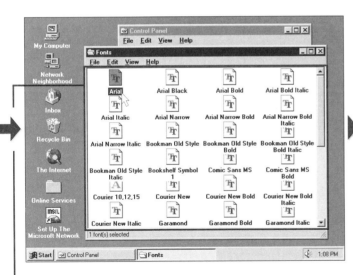

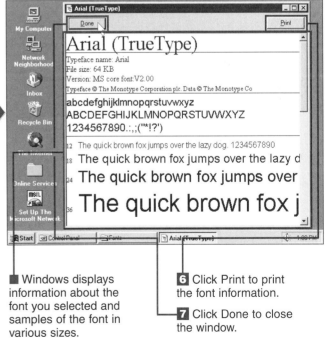

■ Each icon in the Fonts window represents a font installed on your computer. The icon for a TrueType font displays two letter Ts.

5 Double-click a font you want to view.

■ A window appears.

■ Windows displays information about the font you selected and samples of the font in various sizes.

6 Click Print to print the font information.

7 Click Done to close the window.

ADD AND DELETE FONTS

You can add fonts to your computer to give you more choices when creating documents. You can add special fonts to create maps and print music using your computer.

Windows includes a few standard fonts. The standard Windows fonts and any other fonts you install can be used in all programs on your computer.

There are thousands of fonts available. If you want to add more fonts to your computer, you can install them from the Windows 95 CD-ROM disc or floppy disks. You can also buy fonts wherever software is sold. You can search for free fonts on the Internet. Simply search for "TrueType fonts".

When you buy or download fonts, choose the Windows version of TrueType fonts. A TrueType font generates characters using mathematical formulas. This type of font will print exactly as it appears on your screen.

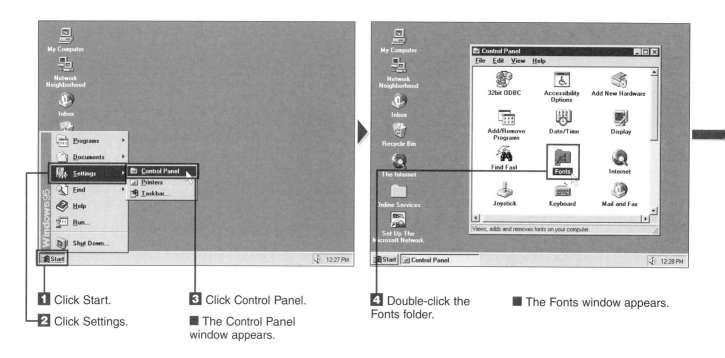

1 Click Start.

2 Click Settings.

3 Click Control Panel.

■ The Control Panel window appears.

4 Double-click the Fonts folder.

■ The Fonts window appears.

How many fonts can I install?

There is no limit to the amount of fonts you can install, but keep in mind that fonts take up storage space on your computer. You may also find a long list of fonts becomes too cluttered and difficult to use.

Can I change the way items appear in the Fonts window?

To change the view of the items in the Fonts window, select the option you want from the View menu. You can view large or small icons, icons grouped by their similarity to the selected font, or details about each item.

Is there an easy way to manage fonts?

There are several programs, such as Adobe Type Manager, that can arrange fonts in groups. The fonts can then be installed or used as a group on your computer. You may want to group fonts that you only use for specific projects.

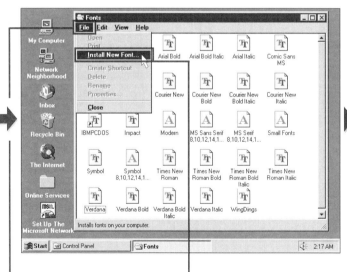

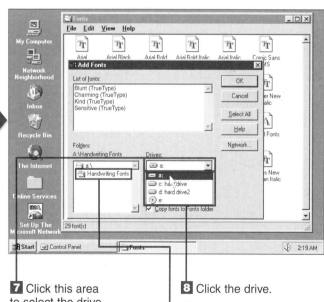

■ The Fonts window displays a list of the fonts installed on your computer.

5 Click File to add a new font.

6 Click Install New Font.

■ The Add Fonts dialog box appears.

7 Click this area to select the drive containing the fonts you want to add.

8 Click the drive.

9 Double-click the folder containing the fonts.

ADD AND DELETE FONTS
CONTINUED

When adding fonts, you can select one font or all the available fonts in the folder.

You can organize your fonts and store them in the Fonts folder or other folders on your computer.

You can remove fonts you no longer use from your computer.

Any font that is required by Windows displays a red A on its icon. You should not delete these fonts.

Before you delete a font you do not recognize, make sure the font is not part of a program that requires specific fonts. Reference programs like dictionaries, maps and encyclopedias often require special fonts.

If you delete a font that is used by Windows or a Windows program, a different font will be used to replace the one you deleted. You may not like the substitution Windows makes.

Deleted fonts are sent to your Recycle Bin. To be safe, you may want to make a backup copy of the font before you delete it.

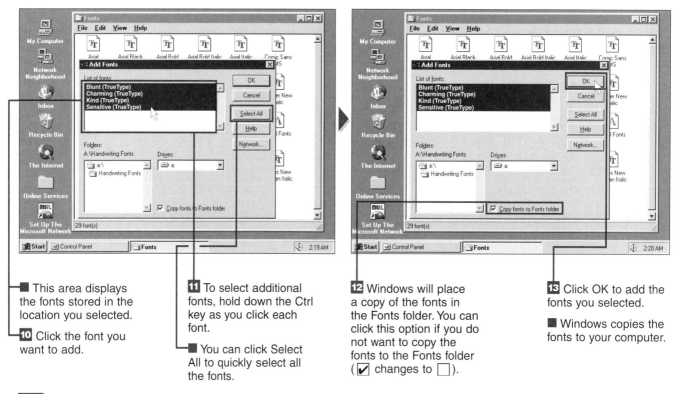

■ This area displays the fonts stored in the location you selected.

■10 Click the font you want to add.

■11 To select additional fonts, hold down the Ctrl key as you click each font.

■ You can click Select All to quickly select all the fonts.

■12 Windows will place a copy of the fonts in the Fonts folder. You can click this option if you do not want to copy the fonts to the Fonts folder (☑ changes to ☐).

■13 Click OK to add the fonts you selected.

■ Windows copies the fonts to your computer.

Is there another way to delete fonts?

You can drag and drop the font's icon to your Recycle Bin.

How can I get a font back that I accidentally deleted?

You can open your Recycle Bin and retrieve a font you deleted by mistake. See page 72.

How can I copy fonts from another computer on the network?

In the Add Fonts dialog box, click the Network button to install fonts from the Fonts folder on a colleague's computer.

Can I move any file into the Fonts folder?

You can only place font files in the Fonts folder. If you try to place another type of file in the Fonts folder, Windows will display an error message.

I moved some fonts into the Fonts folder. Why are the fonts still in the original folder?

When you drag and drop a font file into the Fonts folder, Windows places a copy of the file in the Fonts folder. The original file stays in its location on your computer.

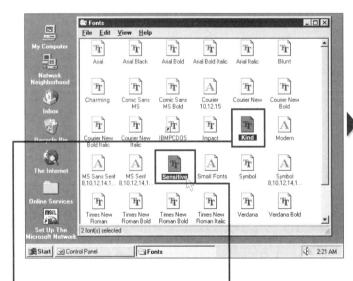

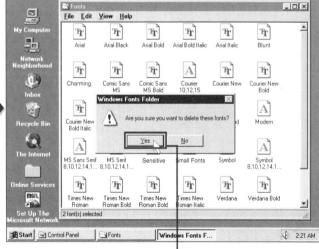

DELETE FONTS

1 Click a font you want to delete.

Note: To display the Fonts folder, perform steps 1 to 4 on page 230.

2 To select additional fonts, hold down the Ctrl key as you click each font.

3 Press the Delete key.

■ Windows displays a warning dialog box.

4 Click Yes to delete the fonts.

■ Windows sends the fonts to your Recycle Bin.

CREATE CUSTOM SETTINGS FOR EACH PERSON

I f you share a computer with one or more people, you can create user profiles to allow each person to customize their own settings.

Customized settings can include the desktop background, screen saver, Start menu items, desktop icons and much more.

Windows stores the customized settings for each person with

their user name and password. Each time Windows is started or restarted, a login dialog box appears. When you enter your user name and password, Windows displays your customized settings.

Custom settings are useful when there are people with special needs using the computer, like children. Custom settings are

also useful when one person requires two or more custom settings. For example, if you use your computer to perform demonstrations, you may like people to see the demonstration on a computer using default settings. When you are finished, you can change the computer back to your own personalized settings.

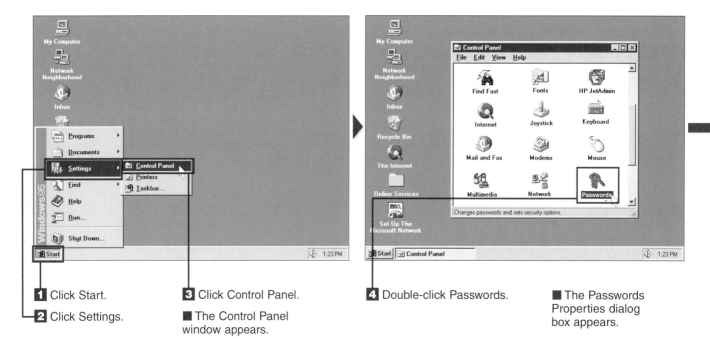

1 Click Start.

2 Click Settings.

3 Click Control Panel.

■ The Control Panel window appears.

4 Double-click Passwords.

■ The Passwords Properties dialog box appears.

TIPS

Can I use the computer even if I do not have a user name and password?

In the login dialog box, select Cancel to use the computer.

When I finish using the computer, how can another person access their settings?

From the Start menu, select Shut Down when you are finished using the computer. In the Shut Down Windows dialog box, click Close all programs and log on as a different user. This restarts Windows without restarting the computer. The login dialog box appears so the next person can enter their name and password.

I do not want to use a password anymore. How do I remove the user profiles?

From the Passwords Properties dialog box, select the User Profiles tab to remove the user profiles. Click All users of this PC use the same preferences and desktop settings (○ changes to ◉). You will no longer need to enter a password, but everyone must use the same settings.

How do I create a new profile?

In the login dialog box, type in a user name and password to create a new profile. When Windows asks if you want to retain your individual settings, click Yes.

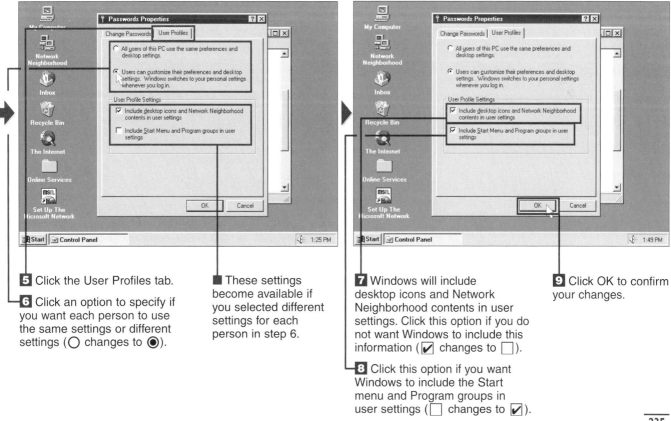

5 Click the User Profiles tab.

6 Click an option to specify if you want each person to use the same settings or different settings (○ changes to ◉).

■ These settings become available if you selected different settings for each person in step 6.

7 Windows will include desktop icons and Network Neighborhood contents in user settings. Click this option if you do not want Windows to include this information (☑ changes to ☐).

8 Click this option if you want Windows to include the Start menu and Program groups in user settings (☐ changes to ☑).

9 Click OK to confirm your changes.

CHANGE WINDOWS PASSWORD

You can change your Windows password as often as you like.

There are many reasons to use a password in Windows. You can use a password to protect your computer and your files from unauthorized access. If you share a computer with other people, Windows identifies you by your user name and password and displays your customized

settings. If your computer is connected to a network, you must enter a password to access the network.

You can have Windows use the same passwords for many activities such as logging on to a network and deactivating your screen saver. This is useful because you only have to remember and change one

password instead of many passwords.

When you change your Windows password, other passwords on your computer may be lost. Make sure you know all of the other passwords used on your computer. For example, you should know the passwords for your Microsoft Network or your Internet service provider's Dial-Up Networking account.

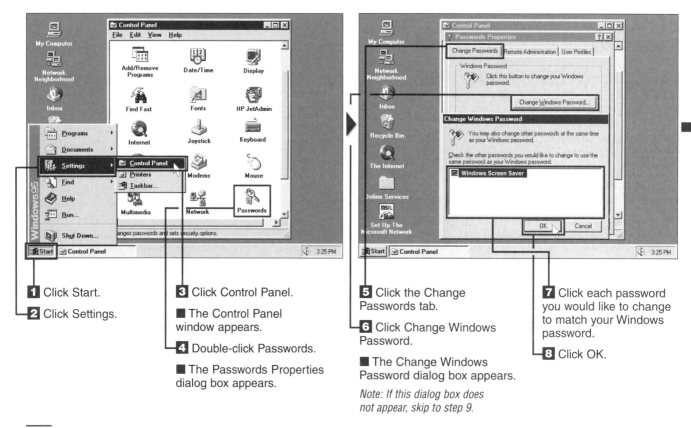

1 Click Start.

2 Click Settings.

3 Click Control Panel.

■ The Control Panel window appears.

4 Double-click Passwords.

■ The Passwords Properties dialog box appears.

5 Click the Change Passwords tab.

6 Click Change Windows Password.

■ The Change Windows Password dialog box appears.

Note: If this dialog box does not appear, skip to step 9.

7 Click each password you would like to change to match your Windows password.

8 Click OK.

TIPS

How do I pick a good password?

When choosing a password, do not use words that people can associate with you, such as your name or favorite sport. A good password connects two words or number sequences with a special character, like blue@123.

How can I prevent unauthorized people from accessing my computer and my files?

You can assign passwords to the files you share with other people on a network. Only give your passwords to authorized people, and change your passwords regularly.

Why do I need to change my password?

A Windows password does not protect your files, but it does make it difficult for people to use your computer without your permission. If you continually change your password, it is more difficult for other people to access your computer.

Why can't I see my password when I type it?

When you type a password, Windows displays an asterisk (*) for each character you type. The asterisks protect the secrecy of your password.

CUSTOMIZE WINDOWS 95

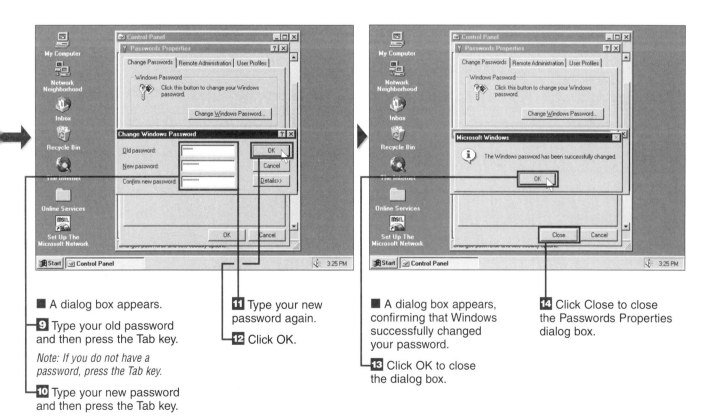

■ A dialog box appears.

9 Type your old password and then press the Tab key.

Note: If you do not have a password, press the Tab key.

10 Type your new password and then press the Tab key.

11 Type your new password again.

12 Click OK.

■ A dialog box appears, confirming that Windows successfully changed your password.

13 Click OK to close the dialog box.

14 Click Close to close the Passwords Properties dialog box.

237

CHANGE SHUT DOWN SCREENS

You can use Paint to change the screens that appear when you shut down your computer. The shut down screens simply remind you not to turn off your computer while Windows is shutting down and indicate when it is safe to turn off the computer.

The screen that displays the message "Please wait while your computer shuts down" is stored as a file called Logow.sys. The screen

that displays the message "It's now safe to turn off your computer" is stored as a file called Logos.sys. Both of these files are found in the windows folder on your hard drive. Computers that turn themselves off automatically do not display the Logos.sys screen.

Although these files do not have the .bmp extension, you can open and change the screens using Paint. You can customize the shut

down screens with a corporate logo, a funny message or your name.

Before you make any changes to the shut down screens, you should save a backup copy of the files. Save the backup copies as Logow.bmp and Logos.bmp. Creating a backup is useful in case you want to return to the original screens later.

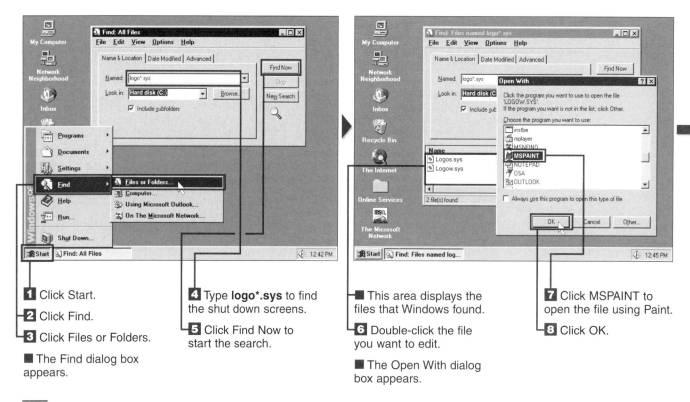

1 Click Start.

2 Click Find.

3 Click Files or Folders.

■ The Find dialog box appears.

4 Type **logo*.sys** to find the shut down screens.

5 Click Find Now to start the search.

■ This area displays the files that Windows found.

6 Double-click the file you want to edit.

■ The Open With dialog box appears.

7 Click MSPAINT to open the file using Paint.

8 Click OK.

Can I give copies of my customized shut down screens to my friends?

Once you have made the changes, you can copy your customized screens to a floppy disk and transfer them to other computers.

How do I change the screen that appears while Windows is starting?

The screen that appears while Windows starts is stored in the c: folder in a file called Logo.sys. This file may not appear on all Windows systems. If you accidentally delete the Logo.sys file, the file called Io.sys contains a copy that is used instead.

Can I edit the text?

You cannot edit the text. You can use the painting tools to remove the existing text and then use the Text tool to add new text.

Can I create new images instead of changing the existing screens?

You can use any new image you create, as long as it is in the Windows bitmap (.bmp) format, saved in 256 colors and sized to 320x400. Windows stretches the image horizontally, so it will look wider when it appears on your screen. Save the file as "Logow.sys" or "Logos.sys" in the windows folder.

■ The Logow.sys file opens. This is the first screen that appears when you shut down your computer. You can use the tools in Paint to edit this screen.

■ You can also open the Logos.sys file and use the tools in Paint to edit this screen.

CHANGE ROLE OF COMPUTER

You can tell Windows how you normally use your computer. This can improve your computer's use of Random Access Memory (RAM) and your hard drive by helping your computer better manage cache and virtual memory.

The cache is an area of your computer's memory where Windows stores information it has recently retrieved from your hard drive. Storing information in the cache allows Windows to retrieve the information without having to look on your hard drive.

Virtual memory is an area on your hard drive that Windows sets aside as an extension of RAM. When more memory is needed, Windows moves information from RAM to the virtual memory on your hard drive. When the information is needed again, Windows retrieves the information from the virtual memory.

The role you specify for your computer also indirectly controls the number of paths and file names Windows keeps in memory. The more paths and file names that are kept in memory, the less time Windows has to spend searching for them on your hard drive.

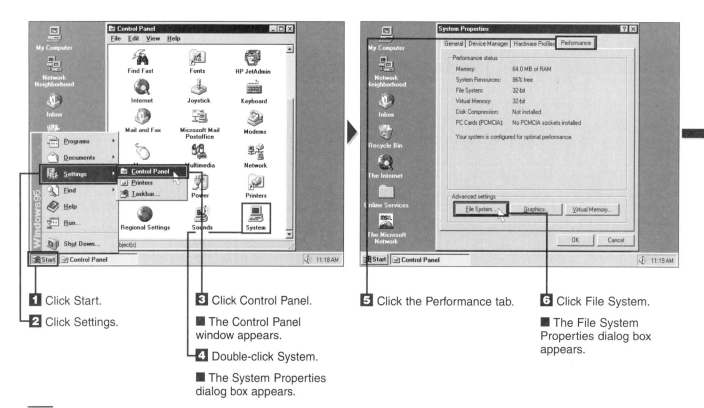

1 Click Start.

2 Click Settings.

3 Click Control Panel.

■ The Control Panel window appears.

4 Double-click System.

■ The System Properties dialog box appears.

5 Click the Performance tab.

6 Click File System.

■ The File System Properties dialog box appears.

TIPS

When is the Network server setting appropriate?

You should use this setting when your computer has more than 16 MB of RAM. This setting is useful if you are on a network and share your files with other people. The Network setting retains the largest number of paths and file names in memory.

When should I choose the Desktop computer setting?

You should choose this setting when your computer has more than 4 MB of RAM and is not using battery power.

When should I use the Mobile or docking system setting?

You should use this setting when your computer has the minimum amount of memory and uses battery power, such as when you are using a portable computer. When using this setting, Windows frequently empties the cache to prevent data loss and reduce battery drain. The Mobile or docking system setting keeps very few paths and file names in memory.

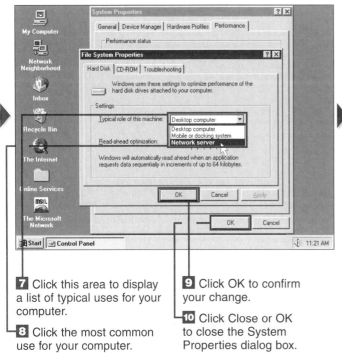

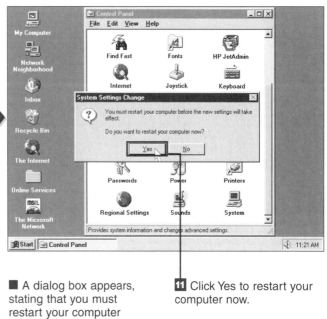

7 Click this area to display a list of typical uses for your computer.

8 Click the most common use for your computer.

9 Click OK to confirm your change.

10 Click Close or OK to close the System Properties dialog box.

■ A dialog box appears, stating that you must restart your computer before the new settings will take effect.

11 Click Yes to restart your computer now.

CREATE A
NEW FILE TYPE

You can create a new file type and tell Windows how you want to work with files of that type.

You can give your file type a description so you can identify it later.

You must give the new file type an extension. Windows uses

extensions to associate a file type with a program. For example, you can create a file type for all of your letters, using the .let extension. You can tell Windows to always open files of this type with the WordPad program. Every time you double-click a file with

the .let extension, WordPad will open and display the file.

If you do not create a file type to tell Windows the association between a file type extension and program, you will not be able to open a file of that type by double-clicking the file.

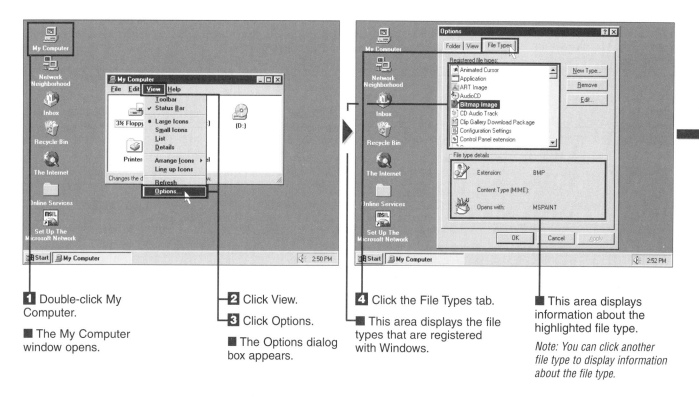

1 Double-click My Computer.

■ The My Computer window opens.

2 Click View.

3 Click Options.

■ The Options dialog box appears.

4 Click the File Types tab.

■ This area displays the file types that are registered with Windows.

■ This area displays information about the highlighted file type.

Note: You can click another file type to display information about the file type.

Is there a faster way to register a new file type?

You can use the Open With dialog box to register a file type. To specify the program you want to use to open the file type, click the program. Then click the Always use this program to open this type of file option. For information on the Open With dialog box, see page 64.

Can I remove a file type I created?

Click the file type you want to remove in the Registered file types list. Click the Remove button and then click Yes to remove the file type. Keep in mind that when you remove a registered file type, you will not be able to open a file of that type by double-clicking the file.

Can I use more than three letters in a file type extension?

You can create longer extensions, such as .budget. Extensions cannot contain any spaces or periods. Longer extensions may not display fully in some dialog boxes. If you share files with people who do not use Windows 95, longer extensions may not work correctly.

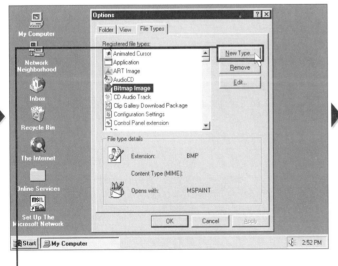

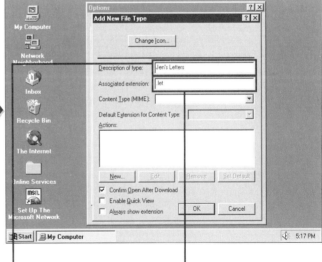

5 Click New Type to register a new file type.

■ The Add New File Type dialog box appears.

6 Click this area and then type a description for the file type.

7 Click this area and then type the extension for the file type.

CONTINUED ▶

CREATE A
NEW FILE TYPE CONTINUED

You can add an action to a file type you create. You can also specify what will happen when the action is selected.

When you right-click a file, Windows displays the available actions for the file in a menu.

For every file type you create, you should add the Open action.

The Open action lets you start a program and open the selected file in one step.

You can choose a name for the action. An action name is usually one word that describes the action, such as Open or Edit.

You can select the program you want to use to perform the action.

You may also want to add the Quick View command to your file type. Quick View allows you to view a file without opening the file. Quick View is not available for all file types. For more information about Quick View, see page 80.

You can also choose to hide or display the extension for the file type.

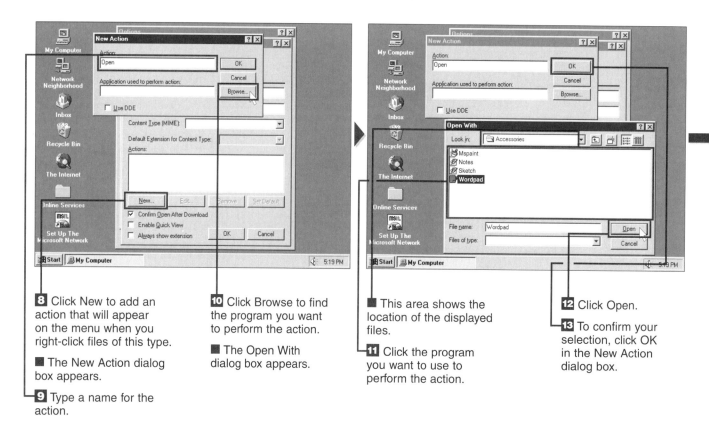

8 Click New to add an action that will appear on the menu when you right-click files of this type.

■ The New Action dialog box appears.

9 Type a name for the action.

10 Click Browse to find the program you want to perform the action.

■ The Open With dialog box appears.

■ This area shows the location of the displayed files.

11 Click the program you want to use to perform the action.

12 Click Open.

13 To confirm your selection, click OK in the New Action dialog box.

I used Browse to select a program, but Windows cannot find the program. Why?

You may have selected the program's shortcut. Shortcuts only contain the information needed to find a program. When you create a file type, you must select the original program file. Program files have the .exe extension.

I created a new extension, but when I saved a file, it displayed two periods and two extensions. How can I avoid this?

Some programs make it very difficult to save using a non-standard extension. Type the name of the file inside quotation marks (""). For example, type "new fall products.let" as the file name.

Can I create two actions for one file type?

You can create several actions for one file type. For example, you can have one action to open the file and another action to edit the file. Name the first action Open and select a program to open the file. Name the second action Edit and select a program to edit the file.

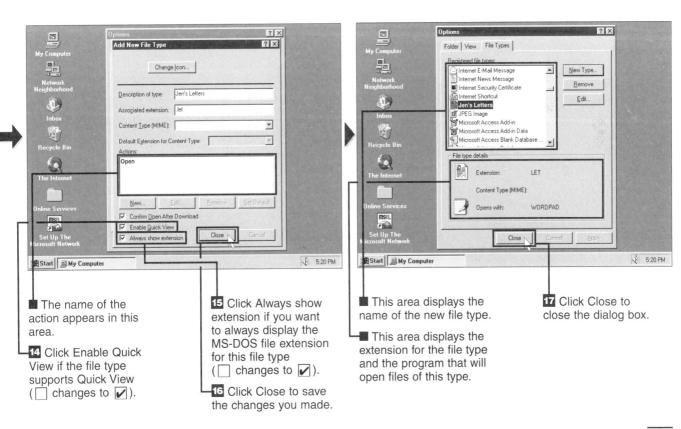

■ The name of the action appears in this area.

14 Click Enable Quick View if the file type supports Quick View (☐ changes to ✔).

15 Click Always show extension if you want to always display the MS-DOS file extension for this file type (☐ changes to ✔).

16 Click Close to save the changes you made.

■ This area displays the name of the new file type.

■ This area displays the extension for the file type and the program that will open files of this type.

17 Click Close to close the dialog box.

CHANGE ICON
FOR A FILE TYPE

Each type of file on your computer is represented by a specific icon. Icons help you identify each file and the type of information a file contains. You can change the icon Windows displays for a file type. Windows displays a list of icons you can choose from.

In addition to identifying the contents of a file, the icon beside the file name normally indicates the program that will be used to open the file. For example, if WordPad is used to open a file, Windows will display the WordPad icon beside the name of the file. If you create your own file type, you may want to change the icon to one that better represents it.

Make sure you only change the icons for file types you have created. Changing a file type Windows created can cause problems.

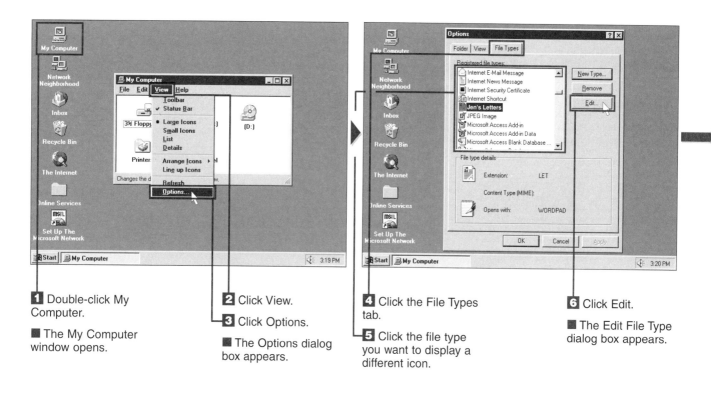

1 Double-click My Computer.

■ The My Computer window opens.

2 Click View.

3 Click Options.

■ The Options dialog box appears.

4 Click the File Types tab.

5 Click the file type you want to display a different icon.

6 Click Edit.

■ The Edit File Type dialog box appears.

TIPS

Are there more icons that I can choose on my computer?

You can use the Browse button to find files containing icons on your computer. Additional Windows icons are located in the c:\windows\moricons.dll and c:\windows\system\shell32.dll files. Most program files also contain more than one icon that you can use. Program files usually have the .exe extension.

Are there any other sources of icons?

Microsoft Plus! and Plus! for Kids contain collections of coordinated icons, wallpaper and sounds.

Can I create my own icons?

There are several programs available to create your own icons. Microangelo from Impact Software (www.impactsoft.com) and Icon Editor from NeoSoft (www.neosoftware.com) are both available as shareware programs and can be downloaded from the Internet.

Why isn't the Edit button available when I select the Application or MS-DOS Application file types?

These file types cannot be modified. You cannot change their icons.

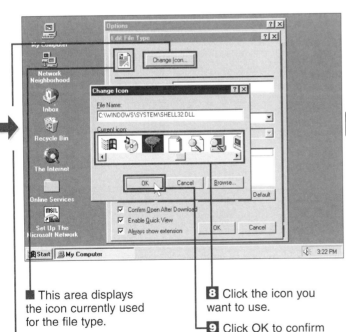

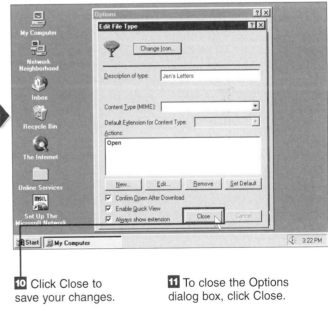

■ This area displays the icon currently used for the file type.

7 Click Change Icon to change the icon.

■ The Change Icon dialog box appears.

8 Click the icon you want to use.

9 Click OK to confirm your selection.

10 Click Close to save your changes.

11 To close the Options dialog box, click Close.

EDIT A FILE TYPE

You can change the options for a file type. You should only edit the file types that you have created.

You can change the program that opens a file when you double-click the file. For example, if a file type is currently opened by Notepad,

you can change the Open action and choose another program, such as WordPad to open files of that type.

You can also add new actions to a file type. For example, besides Open, you may want to add actions such as Edit or Print to a file type.

You can change the description of your file type to one that better suits your file type. For example, you may want to change the description of a file type from Letters to Business Letters to make it easier to identify the file type.

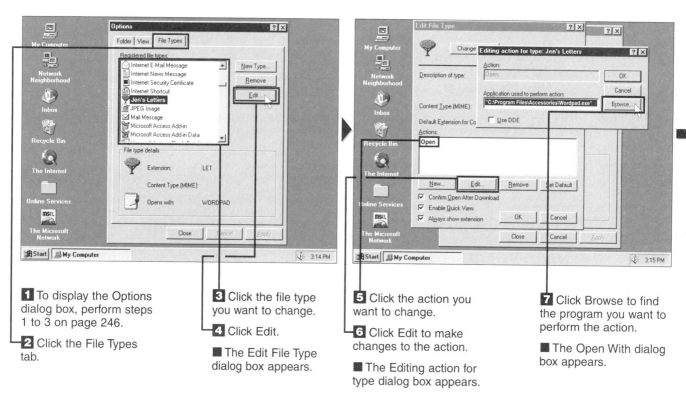

1 To display the Options dialog box, perform steps 1 to 3 on page 246.

2 Click the File Types tab.

3 Click the file type you want to change.

4 Click Edit.

■ The Edit File Type dialog box appears.

5 Click the action you want to change.

6 Click Edit to make changes to the action.

■ The Editing action for type dialog box appears.

7 Click Browse to find the program you want to perform the action.

■ The Open With dialog box appears.

TIPS

How do I add an action like Print to a file type?

In the Options dialog box, you can select the Edit button to see how an existing file type performs an action you want to add. This is especially useful for actions such as Print, that need special instructions added to the program name. For example, if you want to include an action that prints a file using WordPad, look at the Print action for the WordPad file type. You can use your keyboard to copy information from an existing file type to a new file type. To copy information, use Ctrl+C. To paste information, use Ctrl+V.

How do I change the extension for a file type?

You cannot change an extension. You can remove the file type and then create a new file type with the extension you want to use.

How do I remove an action that I no longer need?

Select the action you want to remove. Click the Remove button and then click Yes in the confirmation dialog box.

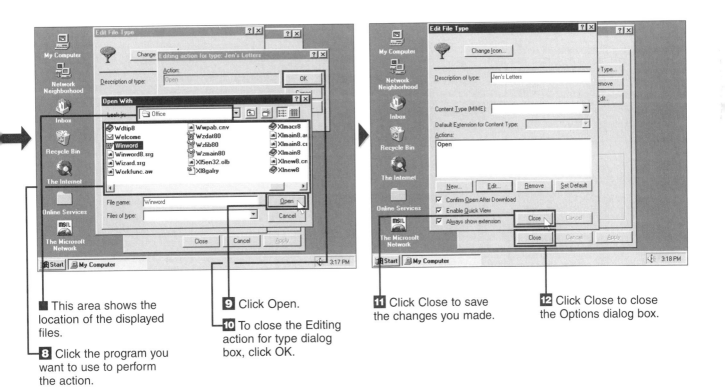

■ This area shows the location of the displayed files.

■8 Click the program you want to use to perform the action.

■9 Click Open.

■10 To close the Editing action for type dialog box, click OK.

■11 Click Close to save the changes you made.

■12 Click Close to close the Options dialog box.

ADD PROGRAM TO THE START MENU

You can add your favorite programs to the Start menu so you can quickly open them. You can also add files and folders you frequently use to the Start menu for quick access. Having items you frequently use on the Start menu saves you the time of having to look for them on your computer.

Most programs designed for Windows will place a shortcut on the Start menu while they are being installed. Windows does not add all of the programs and utilities available on your computer to the Start menu. If Windows does not add an item you want to access, you must

manually add the item to the Start menu.

When you add an item to the Start menu, Windows creates a shortcut to the program, file or folder. The original program, file or folder stays in the same place on your computer.

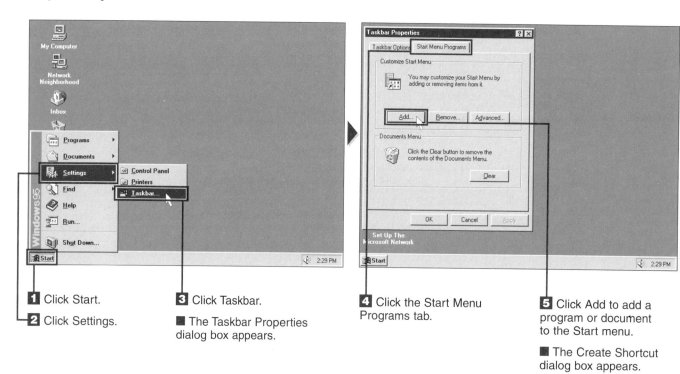

■1 Click Start.

■2 Click Settings.

■3 Click Taskbar.

■ The Taskbar Properties dialog box appears.

■4 Click the Start Menu Programs tab.

■5 Click Add to add a program or document to the Start menu.

■ The Create Shortcut dialog box appears.

The Browse dialog box is only showing my programs. Where are my files?

To view all of your files in the Browse dialog box, change the File of type option from Programs to All files.

How do I add a printer to the Start menu?

From the Start menu, select Settings and then click Printers. Drag the printer you want to add from the Printers window to the Start button. The printer will appear on the first level of the Start menu.

Can I add items on the network to the Start menu?

Click the Browse button and use the Look in list to display the Network Neighborhood. You can then add network items to the Start menu.

Can I add an item to the Start menu from a My Computer or Explorer window, or the desktop?

To add an item from any window or the desktop, simply drag the item to the Start button. The item will appear on the first level of the Start menu.

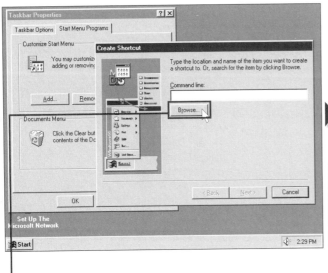

6 Click Browse to search for the program or document you want to add to the Start menu.

■ The Browse dialog box appears.

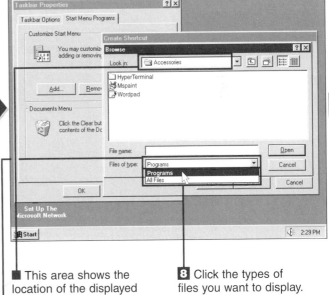

■ This area shows the location of the displayed folders and files.

7 Click this area to specify the types of files you want to show in the dialog box.

8 Click the types of files you want to display.

CONTINUED ▶

ADD PROGRAM TO
THE START MENU CONTINUED

You can choose the Start menu folder where you want a program, file or folder to appear.

The Start menu contains several levels and folders. You can place an item on the first level of the

Start menu or inside one of the many folders on the Programs menu. If you want an item to open automatically when Windows is started, you can place the item in the StartUp folder.

You can also give the program, file or folder a descriptive name.

Windows will suggest a name for the item based on the name of the original program, file or folder. The name you choose will only appear on the Start menu item and will not affect the name of the original program, file or folder.

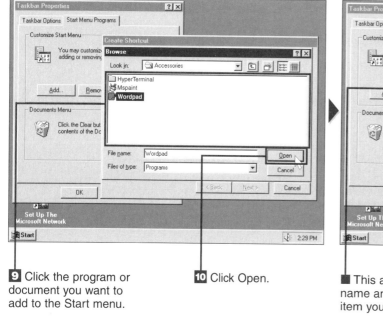

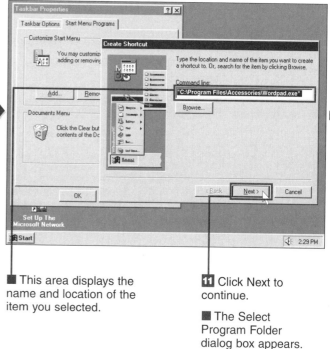

■9 Click the program or document you want to add to the Start menu.

■10 Click Open.

■ This area displays the name and location of the item you selected.

■11 Click Next to continue.

■ The Select Program Folder dialog box appears.

TIPS

Can I add another folder to the Start menu?

If you cannot find an appropriate folder on the Start menu, you can create a new folder. In the Select Program Folder dialog box, select the New Folder button.

Can I change the way Windows displays items in the Start menu?

Windows always displays folders first, followed by files. Each group of items is sorted in alphabetical order. If you want an item to appear first, put an **a** or **1** in front of the name. For example, use the name **A WinFax** or **1 WinFax** to have the item appear at the top of the list.

Are there any limitations on what I name a program, file or folder?

Windows has several rules you must obey when naming an item. A name can contain up to 255 characters, including spaces. A name cannot contain the \ / : * ? " < > or | characters. Use a short name so the Start menu will not take up too much space when displayed on your screen.

Why does Windows ask me to choose an icon for the program?

If you are adding an MS-DOS program that Windows does not recognize, Windows asks you to select the icon you want to use to represent the program.

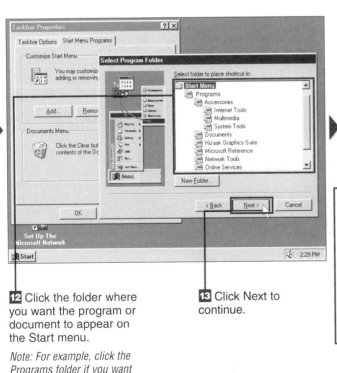

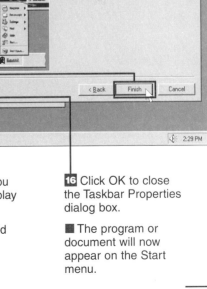

12 Click the folder where you want the program or document to appear on the Start menu.

Note: For example, click the Programs folder if you want a program to appear on the Programs menu.

13 Click Next to continue.

14 Type the name you want the item to display on the Start menu.

15 Click Finish to add the item to the Start menu.

16 Click OK to close the Taskbar Properties dialog box.

■ The program or document will now appear on the Start menu.

REMOVE PROGRAM FROM THE START MENU

You can remove a program you no longer want to appear in the Start menu. Removing items you do not need reduces clutter in the Start menu.

Most programs designed for Windows will place a shortcut on the Start menu while they are being installed. Even after you delete the program from your computer, the Start menu may still display the program. You can remove programs you no longer need or only use once in a while to make the Start menu easier to use.

You can also remove files or folders from the Start menu. When you remove a folder from the Start menu, all of the items in the folder are removed as well. Before removing a folder from the Start menu, you should view the contents of the folder to make sure you will not remove items you frequently work with.

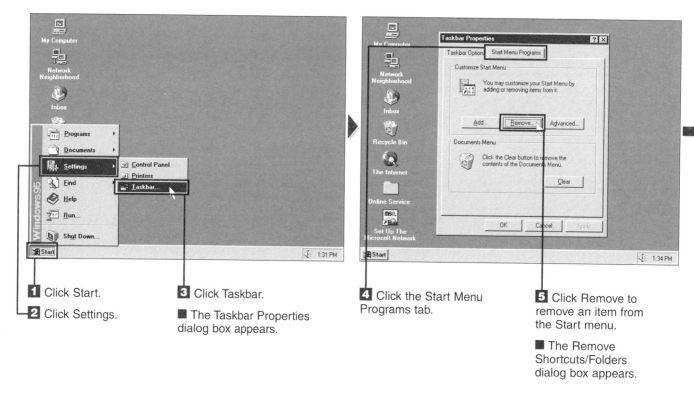

1 Click Start.

2 Click Settings.

3 Click Taskbar.

■ The Taskbar Properties dialog box appears.

4 Click the Start Menu Programs tab.

5 Click Remove to remove an item from the Start menu.

■ The Remove Shortcuts/Folders dialog box appears.

TIPS

Can I organize my items into folders on the Start menu?

In the Taskbar Properties dialog box, click the Advanced button to organize items into folders. See page 256.

How can I bring back an item I accidentally removed from the Start menu?

You can use the Recycle Bin to restore any items you accidentally removed from the Start menu. See page 72. If the item is not available from the Recycle Bin, you can add the item to the Start menu again. See page 250.

Does removing a program from the Start menu delete the program from my computer?

Removing a program from the Start menu does not delete the program from your computer. The Start menu only displays shortcuts to the programs, not the programs themselves. You can delete a program from your computer by choosing the Control Panel and then selecting the Add/Remove Programs icon. See page 580.

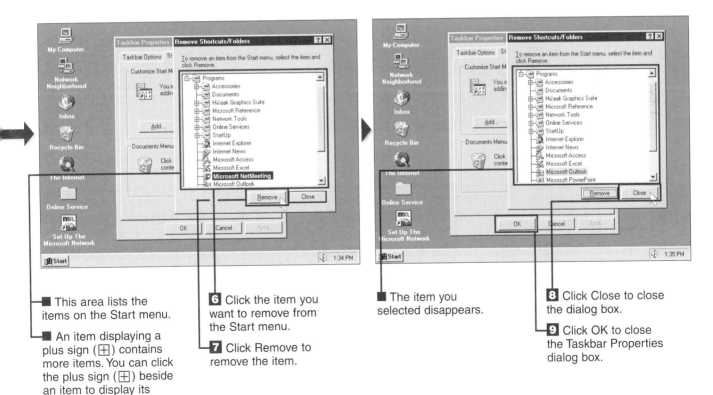

■ This area lists the items on the Start menu.

■ An item displaying a plus sign (⊞) contains more items. You can click the plus sign (⊞) beside an item to display its contents.

6 Click the item you want to remove from the Start menu.

7 Click Remove to remove the item.

■ The item you selected disappears.

8 Click Close to close the dialog box.

9 Click OK to close the Taskbar Properties dialog box.

ORGANIZE THE START MENU

Y ou can create folders to organize and store shortcuts on the Start menu. Each new folder will appear as a submenu on the Start menu.

When you install a new program, a shortcut to the program is placed on the Start menu. When you drag

an item to the Start button, a shortcut for the item appears on the first level of the menu. Eventually the Start menu may become cluttered and difficult to use.

You can use the folders you create to organize your program and item shortcuts into logical groups. Shortcuts

organized into folders are easy to find and use. For example, you can create a new folder named Utilities to store the shortcuts to the utility programs you frequently use. You can also create a folder named Reports to store the shortcuts to your report documents.

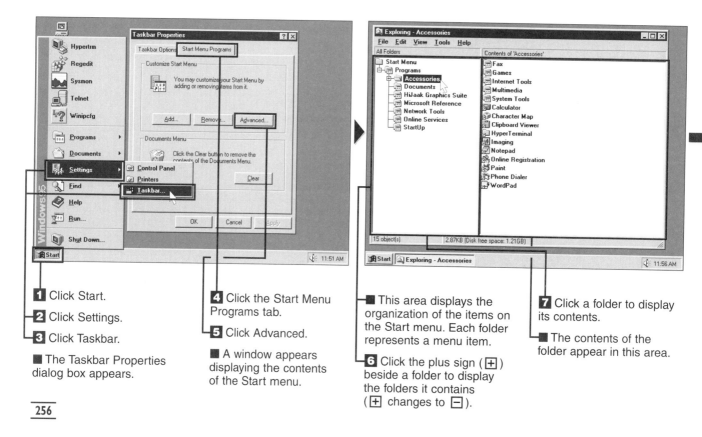

1 Click Start.

2 Click Settings.

3 Click Taskbar.

■ The Taskbar Properties dialog box appears.

4 Click the Start Menu Programs tab.

5 Click Advanced.

■ A window appears displaying the contents of the Start menu.

■ This area displays the organization of the items on the Start menu. Each folder represents a menu item.

6 Click the plus sign (⊞) beside a folder to display the folders it contains (⊞ changes to ⊟).

7 Click a folder to display its contents.

■ The contents of the folder appear in this area.

Can I create a folder for the Control Panel?

Creating a folder for the Control Panel allows you to select an item you want to use from a submenu without having to open the Control Panel window. Create a folder and name the folder for the submenu: **Control Panel.{21EC2020-3AEA-1069-A2DD-08002B30309D}**

You can also create a submenu for Dial-Up Networking by naming the new folder: **Dial Up Net.{992CFFA0-F557-101A-88EC-00DD010CCC48}** and Printers by naming the new folder: **Printers.{2227A280-3AEA-1069-A2DE-08002B30309D}**

How do I move a shortcut to a different menu?

Drag the shortcut from the right pane to the folder in the left pane where you want to place the shortcut.

How can I delete shortcuts I no longer need from the Start menu?

Click the item you want to remove and then press the Delete key. This does not remove the item from your computer, but you can no longer access it using the Start menu.

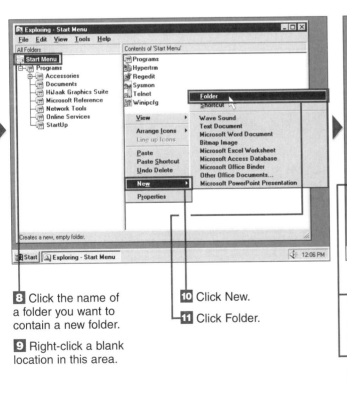

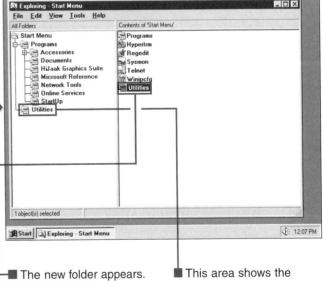

8 Click the name of a folder you want to contain a new folder.

9 Right-click a blank location in this area.

10 Click New.

11 Click Folder.

■ The new folder appears. This folder will appear as a new submenu on the menu you selected.

12 Type a name for the new folder and then press the Enter key.

■ This area shows the location of the folder on the Start menu.

■ You can drag items to the new folder that you want to appear on the submenu.

257

START PROGRAM AUTOMATICALLY

You can have Windows automatically start programs each time you turn on your computer.

Having a program start automatically is useful for frequently used applications, such as e-mail software, and for items you want to be able to access immediately, like a daily organizer or the Calculator. You can also have documents you work with daily open automatically when you start

Windows. This is useful for documents such as an order form.

Having a program start automatically saves not only the time required for you to locate the program on the Start menu, but also the time Windows takes to load the program from your hard drive.

Your StartUp folder may already contain several programs. Examples of programs that

can appear in the StartUp folder include utility programs that speed file access, check for viruses or set up your modem to receive faxes.

When you no longer want a program to start automatically, you can move the program to another folder or delete it from the StartUp folder.

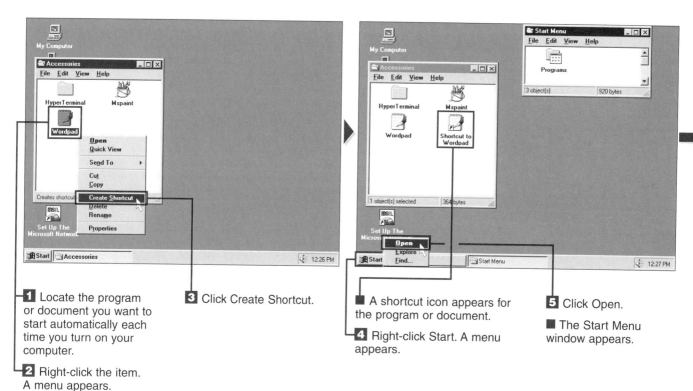

■1 Locate the program or document you want to start automatically each time you turn on your computer.

■2 Right-click the item. A menu appears.

■3 Click Create Shortcut.

■ A shortcut icon appears for the program or document.

■4 Right-click Start. A menu appears.

■5 Click Open.

■ The Start Menu window appears.

258

TIPS

How do I find applications on my computer?

In the Find window, select the Advanced tab to search for applications. To use the Find feature, see page 76. From the View menu, you can also select Details in Explorer or a window you have opened using My Computer. Then sort the items in the window by Type.

What is the easiest way to add programs to the StartUp folder?

Create a shortcut to the StartUp folder and place it in the Send To menu. See page 216.

Can I stop the program from opening on the desktop and have it appear only on the taskbar?

Right-click the shortcut for the program in the StartUp window. On the Shortcut tab, click Properties and then click Run: Minimized.

Should I add all my favorite programs to the StartUp folder?

Loading too many programs will cause your computer to slow down and place a strain on the computer's resources. This may cause your computer to become unstable or behave unpredictably.

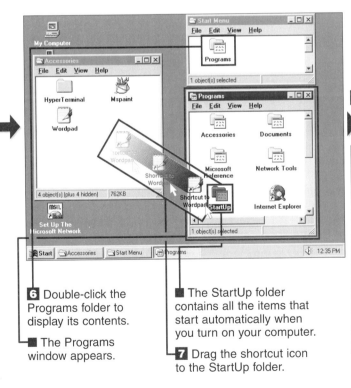

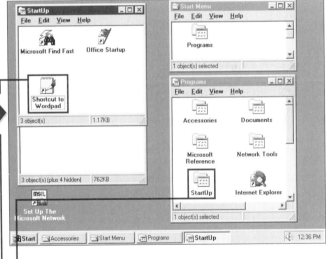

6 Double-click the Programs folder to display its contents.

■ The Programs window appears.

■ The StartUp folder contains all the items that start automatically when you turn on your computer.

7 Drag the shortcut icon to the StartUp folder.

8 To display the contents of the StartUp folder, double-click the folder.

■ The StartUp window appears, displaying the shortcut icon you added.

■ If you no longer want a program or document to start automatically, delete the shortcut icon from the StartUp window. To delete a file, see page 70.

ASSIGN SOUNDS TO PROGRAM EVENTS

You can have Windows play sounds when you perform certain tasks on your computer. Assigning sounds can make Windows more fun and interesting.

You need a sound card and speakers on your computer to hear sounds. If your sound card and speakers are set up properly, you will hear a short musical introduction each time Windows starts.

The sounds on your computer can provide information about what Windows is doing, alert you to the appearance of a dialog box or let you know that e-mail has arrived.

You can add or change many sounds at once on your computer by choosing a sound scheme. A sound scheme is a set of related sounds that usually have a theme, such as jungle sounds, musical instruments or sounds from a favorite cartoon or movie.

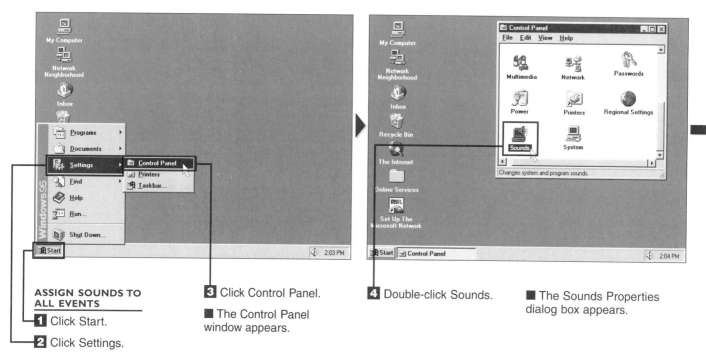

ASSIGN SOUNDS TO ALL EVENTS

1 Click Start.

2 Click Settings.

3 Click Control Panel.

■ The Control Panel window appears.

4 Double-click Sounds.

■ The Sounds Properties dialog box appears.

Does Windows provide additional sound schemes?

The Windows CD-ROM disc includes sound schemes that contain music and effects with animal, new age and other themes. You can add these additional sound schemes from the Multimedia component. See page 580.

Where can I get other sound schemes?

You can get other sound schemes from Microsoft Plus! and Plus! for Kids. These programs have collections of coordinated sounds, wallpapers, screen savers and mouse pointers.

How can I create my own sound files?

There are many different ways to create sound files. You can record sound from audio CDs playing in your CD-ROM drive. You can also connect a microphone or a cassette recorder to your sound card to create sound files. You can use the Sound Recorder to record sounds from any of these devices. See page 276 for information on using Sound Recorder.

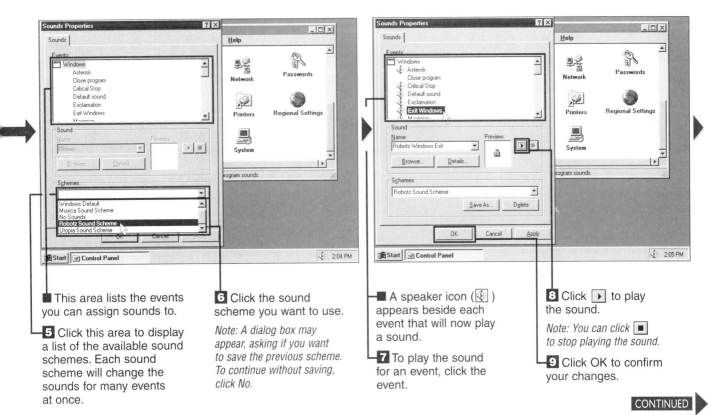

■ This area lists the events you can assign sounds to.

5 Click this area to display a list of the available sound schemes. Each sound scheme will change the sounds for many events at once.

6 Click the sound scheme you want to use.

Note: A dialog box may appear, asking if you want to save the previous scheme. To continue without saving, click No.

■ A speaker icon (🔊) appears beside each event that will now play a sound.

7 To play the sound for an event, click the event.

8 Click ▶ to play the sound.

Note: You can click ■ to stop playing the sound.

9 Click OK to confirm your changes.

CONTINUED

ASSIGN SOUNDS TO PROGRAM EVENTS CONTINUED

You can assign a sound to a specific event. You may like to play familiar music from the end of a cartoon when Windows closes, or hear a sigh of relief when you restore a window. You can mix and match sound files to create a

personalized scheme for your computer.

You can use sound files you have purchased, the Windows 95 CD-ROM disc or the Internet. You can also use sound files you created yourself. The sound files you use must be saved in the

.wav format. Windows 95 does not include a tool that lets you convert other types of sound files into the .wav format.

When you assign a sound to an event, you can listen to a preview of the sound.

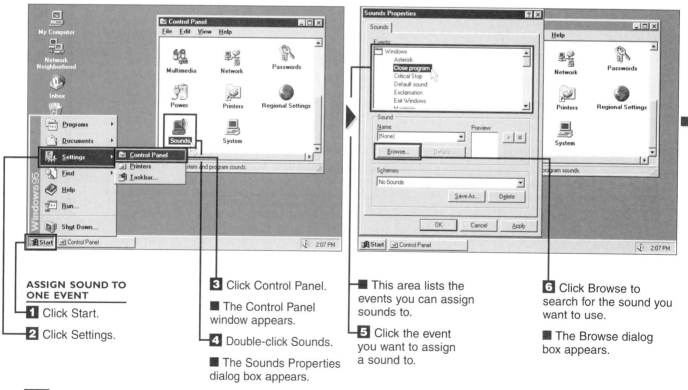

ASSIGN SOUND TO ONE EVENT

1 Click Start.

2 Click Settings.

3 Click Control Panel.

■ The Control Panel window appears.

4 Double-click Sounds.

■ The Sounds Properties dialog box appears.

■ This area lists the events you can assign sounds to.

5 Click the event you want to assign a sound to.

6 Click Browse to search for the sound you want to use.

■ The Browse dialog box appears.

TIPS

Can I save the sound settings I have created?

You can save your sound settings in a sound scheme. This will enable you to use other schemes and return to your personalized scheme. From the Sounds Properties dialog box, click the Save As button. Type a name for the scheme and then click OK.

Is there another way to add a sound?

To assign a sound to an event, you can drag and drop a sound file from any open window onto the event in the sound files list.

Where are my sound files saved?

The sound files that appear in the sound files list are stored in the c:\windows\media folder. You can use the Browse button to find files in other folders on your computer.

How do I adjust the volume of the sounds?

You can adjust the volume of the sounds by clicking on the speaker icon on the taskbar. A volume control box will appear. If you want additional volume controls, double-click the speaker icon on the taskbar. For more information, see page 264.

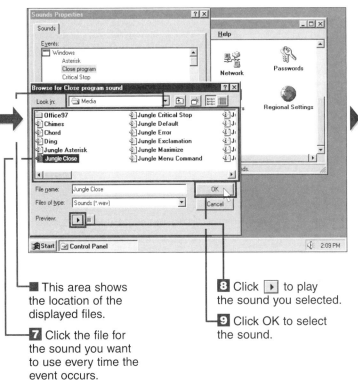

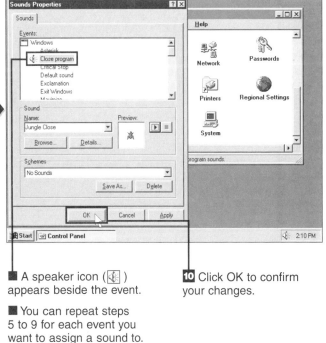

■ This area shows the location of the displayed files.

7 Click the file for the sound you want to use every time the event occurs.

8 Click ▶ to play the sound you selected.

9 Click OK to select the sound.

■ A speaker icon (🔊) appears beside the event.

■ You can repeat steps 5 to 9 for each event you want to assign a sound to.

10 Click OK to confirm your changes.

USING VOLUME CONTROL

You can adjust the volume of sound coming from your speakers.

You can use the Volume Control window to adjust the overall volume on your computer or mute all the sound.

You can use the Volume Control window to change the volume of specific items on your computer. For example, if your CD player is too loud, you can lower the volume of the CD player without affecting the volume of other items.

You can also make adjustments to the balance. Adjusting the balance makes one speaker louder than the other. If one speaker is further away from your preferred listening position, you can make that speaker louder.

You can have the Volume Control window display controls to adjust the balance and volume for either recording or playing back sounds.

You can also specify which devices you want to appear in the Volume Control window, such as the microphone or CD player.

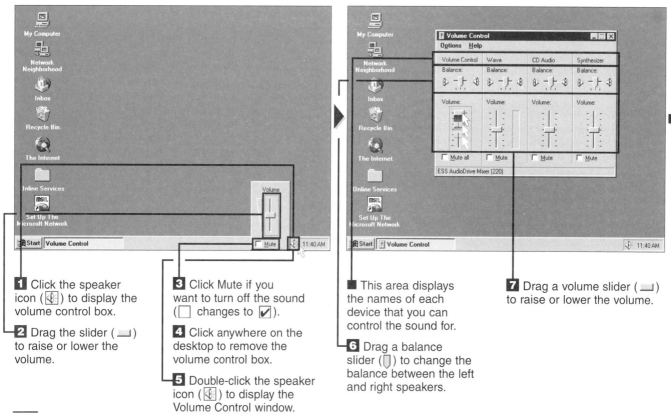

1 Click the speaker icon (🔊) to display the volume control box.

2 Drag the slider (▭) to raise or lower the volume.

3 Click Mute if you want to turn off the sound (☐ changes to ☑).

4 Click anywhere on the desktop to remove the volume control box.

5 Double-click the speaker icon (🔊) to display the Volume Control window.

■ This area displays the names of each device that you can control the sound for.

6 Drag a balance slider (▯) to change the balance between the left and right speakers.

7 Drag a volume slider (▭) to raise or lower the volume.

There is no speaker icon on my taskbar. How can I get it back?

From the Control Panel window, double-click Multimedia. On the Audio tab, select the Show volume control on the taskbar option (☐ changes to ☑).

I adjusted the volume, but Windows did not make the change. What is wrong?

With some older sound cards, you cannot adjust the volume using Windows. These older sound cards have a control that lets you manually adjust the volume.

Why does my computer make beeping sounds even after I have muted the sound?

The beeping sounds are coming from the computer's internal speaker. Windows cannot control this speaker. You may have to physically disconnect the internal speaker if you want it muted.

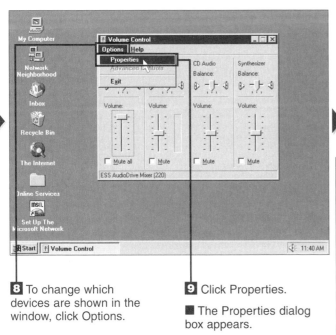

8 To change which devices are shown in the window, click Options.

9 Click Properties.

■ The Properties dialog box appears.

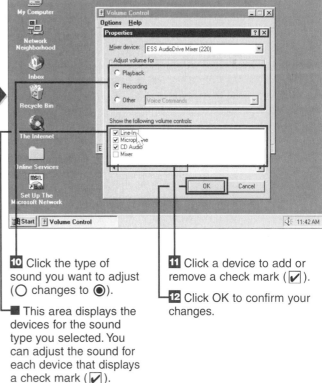

10 Click the type of sound you want to adjust (○ changes to ●).

■ This area displays the devices for the sound type you selected. You can adjust the sound for each device that displays a check mark (☑).

11 Click a device to add or remove a check mark (☑).

12 Click OK to confirm your changes.

USING CD PLAYER

You can use your computer's CD-ROM drive to play audio CDs while you work.

You need a CD-ROM drive, a sound card and speakers to play audio CDs.

The CD Player has many of the same controls as a standard CD player and can be used in the same way.

The CD Player has controls to stop, start and pause the disc. Other buttons are used to skip backwards and forwards from selection to selection. You can also move forwards or backwards to other parts of the same selection. The CD Player also has an option to play the selections on your CD in random order.

Once the CD has started playing, you can continue to work on your computer. The CD Player uses only a small amount of resources on your computer and should have no effect on the speed of your programs.

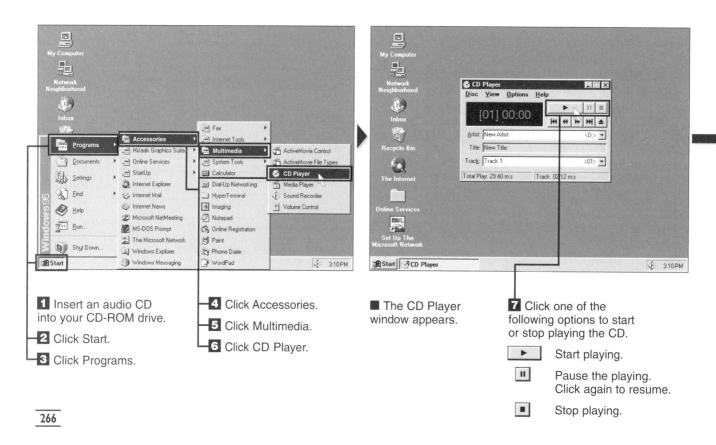

1 Insert an audio CD into your CD-ROM drive.

2 Click Start.

3 Click Programs.

4 Click Accessories.

5 Click Multimedia.

6 Click CD Player.

■ The CD Player window appears.

7 Click one of the following options to start or stop playing the CD.

▶ Start playing.

❚❚ Pause the playing. Click again to resume.

■ Stop playing.

TIPS

Why does the CD Player start automatically when I put in a CD?

Windows is set to automatically open the CD Player and start playing when a CD is inserted in the CD-ROM drive.

How can I listen to a CD with headphones?

You can plug headphones into the CD-ROM drive's headphone jack. If the CD-ROM drive does not have a headphone jack, you can plug the headphones into the back of the computer, where the speakers plug in.

How can I adjust the volume?

In the CD Player window, choose the View menu and then select Volume Control. To adjust your computer's master volume, double-click the speaker icon on the taskbar. See page 264. If you are using headphones, you can adjust the volume using the volume control on the front of the CD-ROM drive.

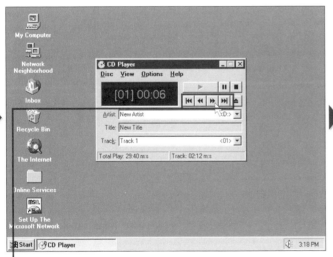

8 Click one of the following options to move through the tracks on the CD.

⏮ Go to the previous track.

⏪ Skip backwards through the current track.

⏩ Skip forwards through the current track.

⏭ Go to the next track.

9 To play the tracks in random order, click Options.

10 Click Random Order.

Note: To once again play the tracks in order, repeat steps 9 and 10.

CONTINUED

USING CD PLAYER CONTINUED

You can use the CD Player to create a catalog of your audio CDs. You can enter the title of the disc, the name of the artist and the title of each selection on the CD.

When you have entered the information for a CD, Windows will recognize the disc each time

it is inserted and display the information for the disc.

The information you enter for a CD will help you when you want to create a play list for the disc. A play list tells the CD Player which selections you would like to listen to and in what order. Creating a play

list is useful because you can eliminate the selections that you dislike and rearrange the order of the selections you want to hear.

When you create or edit the play list, the CD Player saves your changes and recalls them the next time you insert the disc.

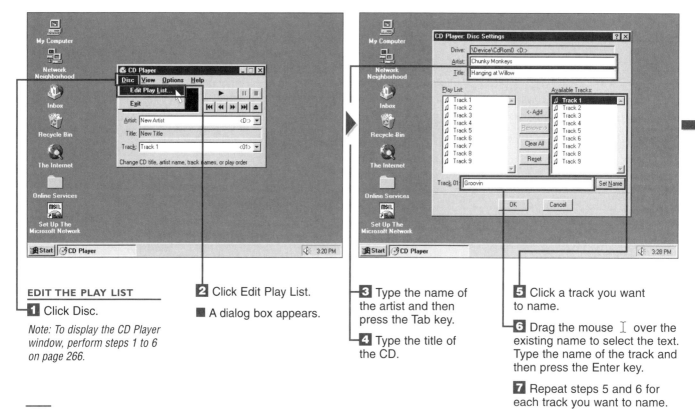

EDIT THE PLAY LIST

1 Click Disc.

Note: To display the CD Player window, perform steps 1 to 6 on page 266.

2 Click Edit Play List.

■ A dialog box appears.

3 Type the name of the artist and then press the Tab key.

4 Type the title of the CD.

5 Click a track you want to name.

6 Drag the mouse I over the existing name to select the text. Type the name of the track and then press the Enter key.

7 Repeat steps 5 and 6 for each track you want to name.

TIPS

Can I pause the CD Player from the taskbar?

Normally, you cannot pause the CD Player from the taskbar. If you have the FlexiCD utility from the PowerToys collection, an icon appears on the taskbar ( ) when you play an audio CD. When you right-click this icon, you can pause, play, stop your CD and more. See page 266.

How can I reset the play list so that the entire CD plays?

You can click the Reset button to return the play list to its original order and listen to the entire CD.

Can I access the CD catalog in another program?

You can open the CD catalog with any word processor, including WordPad. This is useful if you want to print a listing of all the selections on your CDs. The catalog is saved in the Windows folder as a text file named cdplayer.ini

Can I record from an audio CD?

When playing a CD, you can record and create standard Windows sound files using the Sound Recorder. See page 276.

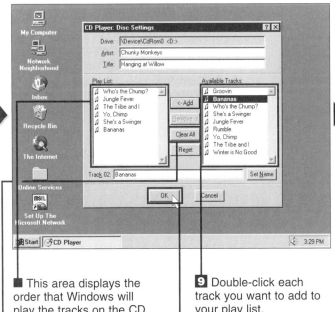

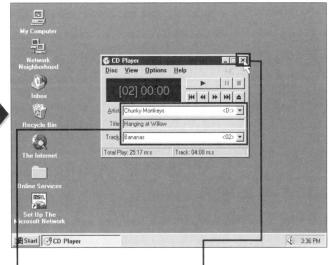

■ This area displays the order that Windows will play the tracks on the CD.

8 Click Clear All to clear the play list so you can create your own.

9 Double-click each track you want to add to your play list.

Note: To remove a track from your play list, double-click the track in the Play List area.

10 Click OK to confirm your changes.

■ This area displays the information you entered for the artist name, album title and current track.

11 Click ✕ to close the CD Player window when you finish listening to the CD.

CHANGE PROPERTIES OF A CD-ROM DRIVE

Y ou can change the way Windows works with your CDs.

The Auto insert notification option allows Windows to automatically detect a CD you place in your computer's CD-ROM drive. If it is a Windows 95 program CD with AutoPlay capabilities, the opening screen will appear. If it is a music CD, the music will start to play.

Windows also displays the name of the CD below the CD-ROM drive icon in the My Computer window. You can turn off the Auto insert notification option if you do not want Windows to detect your CDs.

On most computers, the CD-ROM drive is assigned the letter "D". If your computer has a removable drive, the CD-ROM drive letter will be "E". When the removable

drive is turned off or is unavailable, the CD-ROM drive letter may change. A program that uses the CD-ROM may not be able to find the files it needs when the CD-ROM drive letter changes. To eliminate this problem, you can reserve a drive letter for the CD-ROM. You must select a higher letter than is currently assigned.

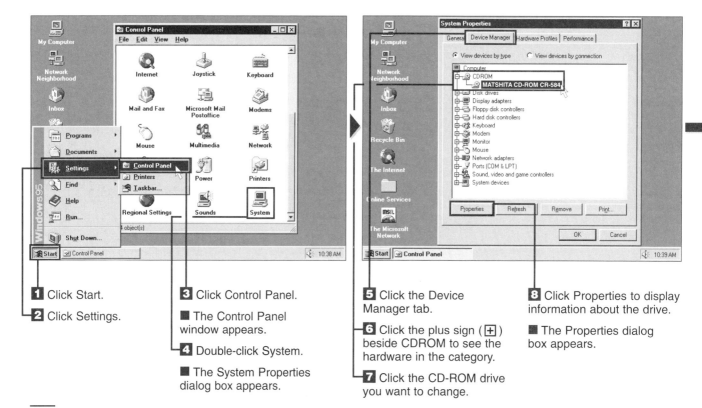

1 Click Start.

2 Click Settings.

3 Click Control Panel.

■ The Control Panel window appears.

4 Double-click System.

■ The System Properties dialog box appears.

5 Click the Device Manager tab.

6 Click the plus sign (⊞) beside CDROM to see the hardware in the category.

7 Click the CD-ROM drive you want to change.

8 Click Properties to display information about the drive.

■ The Properties dialog box appears.

How do I stop an AutoPlay CD from playing when I put it in the drive?

If you do not want to turn off Auto insert notification for all CDs, hold down the Shift key while you insert the CD you do not want to automatically play.

Can I add AutoPlay to older CDs?

An AutoPlay CD contains an autorun command file. Since you cannot record on a CD-ROM disc, it is not possible to add the autorun command file later.

Can I improve the performance of my older CD-ROM?

If you have 16 MB of RAM or more, you can make sure that the CD-ROM's cache is set to the highest setting. The cache stores information from the CD-ROM disc in memory where it can be accessed more quickly than from the disc. In the System Properties dialog box, select the Performance tab and then click the File System button. Then click the CD-ROM tab and adjust the settings.

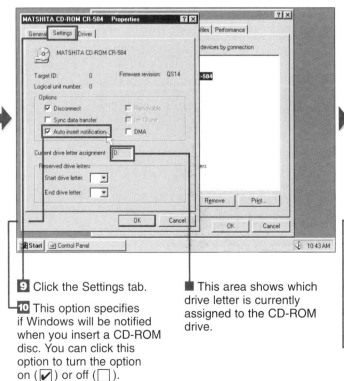

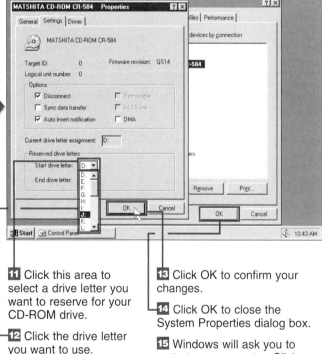

9 Click the Settings tab.

10 This option specifies if Windows will be notified when you insert a CD-ROM disc. You can click this option to turn the option on (✔) or off (☐).

■ This area shows which drive letter is currently assigned to the CD-ROM drive.

11 Click this area to select a drive letter you want to reserve for your CD-ROM drive.

12 Click the drive letter you want to use.

13 Click OK to confirm your changes.

14 Click OK to close the System Properties dialog box.

15 Windows will ask you to restart your computer. Click Yes to restart your computer.

USING MEDIA PLAYER

Play a Video

Media Player lets you play sound, video and animation files on your computer. Media Player is a combination VCR, CD player and cassette deck.

The setup of your computer determines the types of multimedia files you can play. You can identify the type of file by the three-letter extension. You need a sound card and speakers to play digital audio (.wav) and musical instrument (.mid) files. You need a CD-ROM drive to play audio CDs.

Media Player has the same controls you would find on a VCR. These controls allow you to start, stop, rewind or fast forward a video.

A timeline indicates the length of the video. A slider on the timeline indicates your current position in the video. You can use the slider to move through a video.

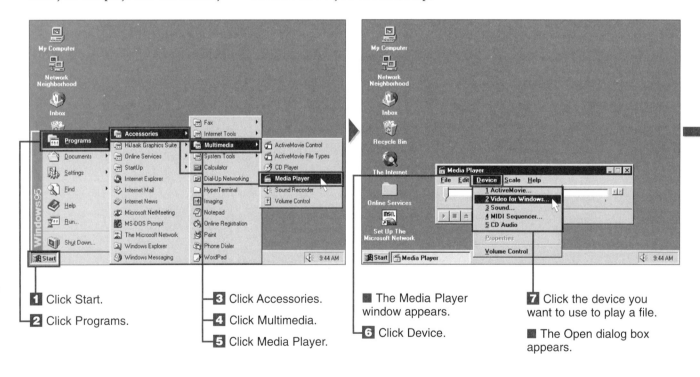

1 Click Start.

2 Click Programs.

3 Click Accessories.

4 Click Multimedia.

5 Click Media Player.

■ The Media Player window appears.

6 Click Device.

7 Click the device you want to use to play a file.

■ The Open dialog box appears.

How can I tell how long a CD is?

When using Media Player to play an audio CD, the timeline displays the tracks on the CD. From the Scale menu, select the Time option to view the amount of time it will take to play a CD.

What kind of videos can I play?

OSR2 can play files in the Video for Windows (.avi), MPEG (.mpg) and QuickTime (.mov) formats. If you use an older version of Windows 95, you may need to install ActiveMovie to play MPEG and QuickTime files. To install a program, see page 584.

The Media Player window is covering the viewing window. How can I make Media Player temporarily disappear?

You can double-click the title bar of Media Player to integrate it into the viewing window. You can double-click the title bar of the viewing window to restore Media Player.

Where can I get sample files?

The Windows 95 CD-ROM disc includes several sample video files you can play.

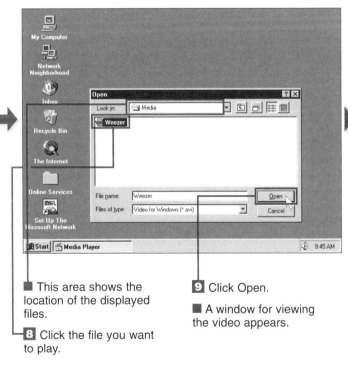

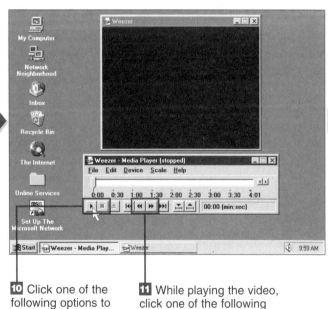

■ This area shows the location of the displayed files.

8 Click the file you want to play.

9 Click Open.

■ A window for viewing the video appears.

10 Click one of the following options to start or stop playing the video.

▶ Start playing

■ Stop playing

11 While playing the video, click one of the following options to move through the video.

◀◀ Rewind

▶▶ Fast forward

Note: You can also drag the slider ( ) to move through a video.

CONTINUED

USING MEDIA PLAYER CONTINUED

Change Play Options

You can change the way Media Player plays a video. Windows uses the settings you select for every video you play.

Videos automatically play at their original size. You can reduce the size of the viewing window if the video is jerky or the sound stops and starts. A smaller viewing

window may help make the video run more smoothly.

You can also have the video play on a larger area of the screen. You can increase the size of the viewing window or have the video take up the entire screen. If you enlarge a video beyond its original size, the video may

display large blocks of color or other visual distortions.

You can have a multimedia file automatically rewind when it is finished playing. You can also have a multimedia file play continuously. This is useful if you are using a multimedia file in a demonstration.

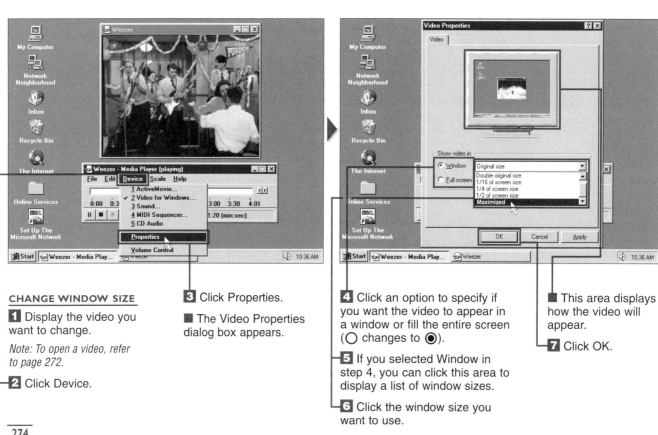

CHANGE WINDOW SIZE

1 Display the video you want to change.

Note: To open a video, refer to page 272.

2 Click Device.

3 Click Properties.

■ The Video Properties dialog box appears.

4 Click an option to specify if you want the video to appear in a window or fill the entire screen (○ changes to ⦿).

5 If you selected Window in step 4, you can click this area to display a list of window sizes.

6 Click the window size you want to use.

■ This area displays how the video will appear.

7 Click OK.

How do I pause or stop Media Player when a video is playing full screen?

You can press the ESC key to pause the video and access the Media Player window.

Why does ActiveMovie start when I double-click a video?

The default association for most kinds of video files is ActiveMovie. The default association for sound files with the .wav extension is Sound Recorder. The default player for audio CDs is CD Player. You can change the program associations so these types of files always play in Media Player. See page 248.

Can I copy part of a video to a word processing document?

You can paste a multimedia clip into a program that supports Object Linking and Embedding (OLE). You can use the Start ([▣]) and End ([▣]) Selection buttons to select a portion of the file. You can then copy the item and paste it into the word processing document.

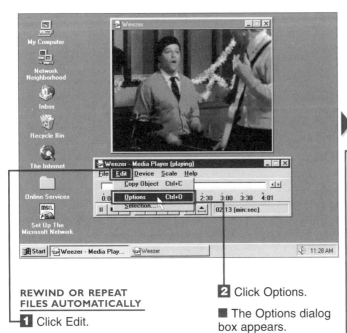

REWIND OR REPEAT FILES AUTOMATICALLY

1 Click Edit.

2 Click Options.

■ The Options dialog box appears.

3 Click this option to automatically rewind a video when it finishes playing (☐ changes to ☑).

4 Click this option to play a video continuously (☐ changes to ☑).

5 Click OK to confirm your changes.

USING SOUND RECORDER

You can use the Sound Recorder to record, playback and edit sounds from a microphone, CD player, stereo, VCR, tape recorder or any other sound device you connect to your computer.

You need a sound card and speakers to record and play sounds.

You can use a sound to make a document or presentation unique. For example, a presentation at a sales meeting can be more interesting if energetic music is playing while you present the agenda.

You can also record sounds, effects or comments and have them play when specific events occur in Windows, such as when you close a window. This can help personalize your computer.

The Sound Recorder lets you complete basic work with sound files. There are many other more sophisticated sound recording and editing programs.

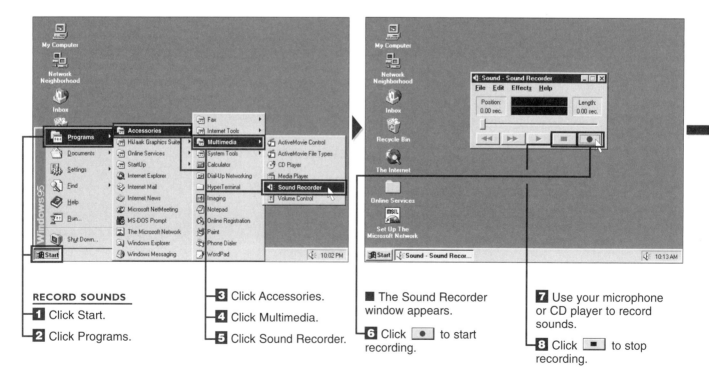

RECORD SOUNDS

1 Click Start.

2 Click Programs.

3 Click Accessories.

4 Click Multimedia.

5 Click Sound Recorder.

■ The Sound Recorder window appears.

6 Click ● to start recording.

7 Use your microphone or CD player to record sounds.

8 Click ■ to stop recording.

TIPS

The recording is too quiet, or too loud and distorted. Can I change the recording volume?

In the Sound Recorder window, the green line shows the level of the volume of your recording. If the green line barely moves, you need to increase the recording level. If the green line reaches to the top and bottom of the box, the sound is too loud and will be distorted. In the Edit menu, select Audio Properties to adjust the recording volume.

How can I begin a new recording?

Choose the File menu and then select New to begin a new recording.

How do I save my recording?

From the File menu, select Save As to save your recording. You can also choose the Edit menu, select Copy and then paste the recording directly into a document or message. When you save the document or message, the recording will be saved with it.

How can I change the volume of the playback?

Use the speaker icon on the taskbar to change the volume of the playback. See page 264.

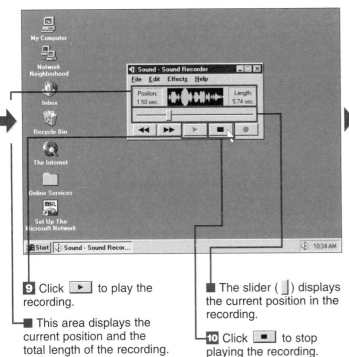

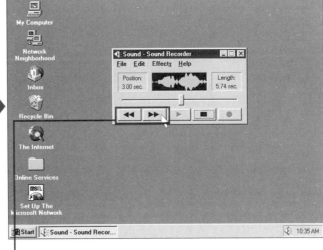

9 Click ▶ to play the recording.

■ This area displays the current position and the total length of the recording.

■ The slider ( ) displays the current position in the recording.

10 Click ■ to stop playing the recording.

11 Click one of these buttons to move through the recording.

◀◀ Move to the beginning.

▶▶ Move to the end.

Note: You can also drag the slider ( ) to move through a recording.

CONTINUED ▶

USING SOUND RECORDER
CONTINUED

The Sound Recorder has several effects you can use to change your recording. You can adjust the volume of your recording to make it softer or louder. You can also speed up your recording to create a chipmunk effect or slow it down to create a spooky and mysterious effect. There is an echo option that can create a large room sound and an option to play your recording backwards.

The size of your sound recording file depends on the quality of the recording. High-quality sound files are larger than lower-quality sound files.

The Sound Recorder has three quality settings for recording:

CD Quality, Radio Quality and Telephone Quality. Each setting is used for different types of recordings. For example, if you are recording music to play over a high-quality speaker system, you will want to use the CD Quality setting. If you are creating sound documents for a Web site, use the Telephone Quality setting so the file will be able to transfer quickly.

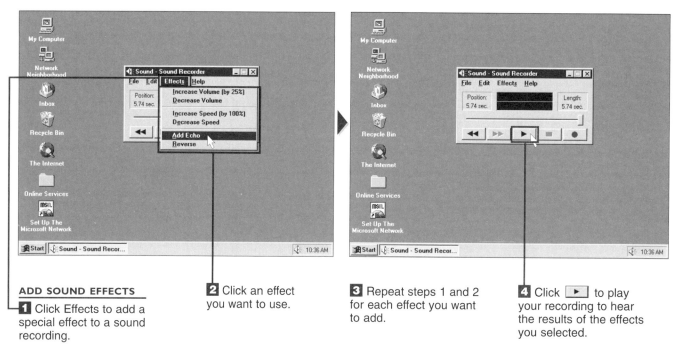

ADD SOUND EFFECTS

1 Click Effects to add a special effect to a sound recording.

2 Click an effect you want to use.

3 Repeat steps 1 and 2 for each effect you want to add.

4 Click ▶ to play your recording to hear the results of the effects you selected.

TIPS

Can I insert a recording in the middle of another recording?

From the Edit menu, select the Copy and Paste commands. The sound file will be inserted into the other sound file at the current slider position.

How do I undo a mistake?

The Sound Recorder has no Undo option. You should save your recording every time you make a successful change. If you make a mistake, display the File menu and select Revert to return to the last saved version of your recording.

Can I mix two files together?

You can combine two sound files together to form one file. From the Edit menu, select Mix with File. The first sound file will be mixed into the other file at the slider position. Mixing two files together is useful if you are adding music background to a voice recording.

Why is the sound quality poor?

Some older computers cannot record properly even at the best quality settings. Your microphone or speakers also may not be able to provide the sound quality you want.

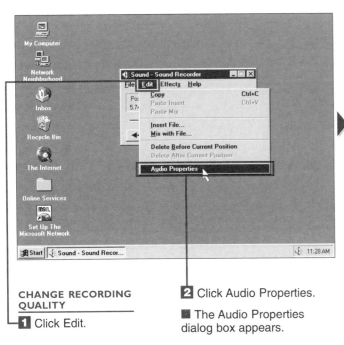

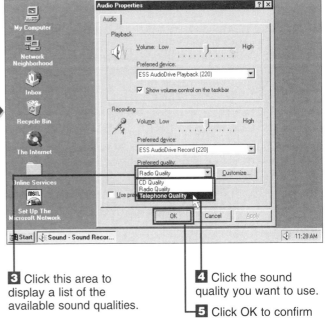

CHANGE RECORDING QUALITY

1 Click Edit.

2 Click Audio Properties.

■ The Audio Properties dialog box appears.

3 Click this area to display a list of the available sound qualities.

4 Click the sound quality you want to use.

5 Click OK to confirm your change.

CUSTOMIZE WINDOWS 95

WORK WITH DISKS

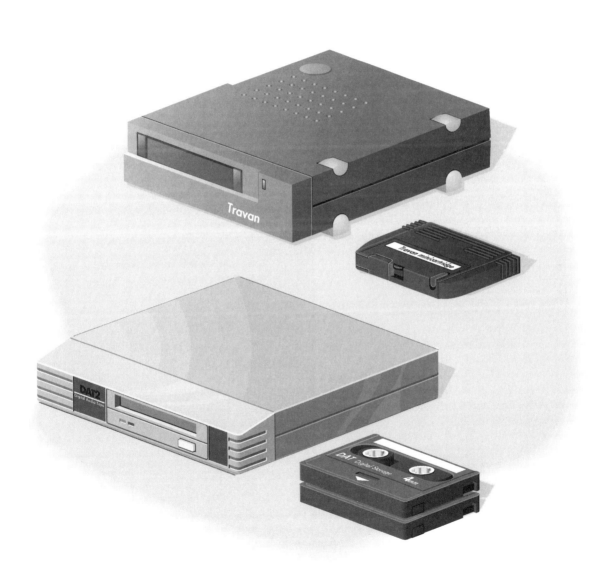

COPY FLOPPY DISKS

Windows makes it easy to copy a floppy disk. Copying a floppy disk is useful when you want to give a copy of a disk to a friend or colleague. You may also want to copy a floppy disk to make a backup copy of important information.

You can copy floppy disks even if your computer has only one floppy drive. Windows makes a temporary copy of the

information from the original disk on your hard drive. When you insert the second disk, Windows copies the information to the disk.

Make sure the floppy disk receiving the copy does not contain information you want to keep. Copying will remove all the old information from the disk.

The original disk and the disk that will receive the copy must

be able to store the same amount of information. A double-density disk has one hole and can store 720 KB of information. A high-density disk has two holes and can store 1.44 MB of information. You can copy information from a double-density disk to a high-density disk, but Windows will reformat the second disk as a double-density disk.

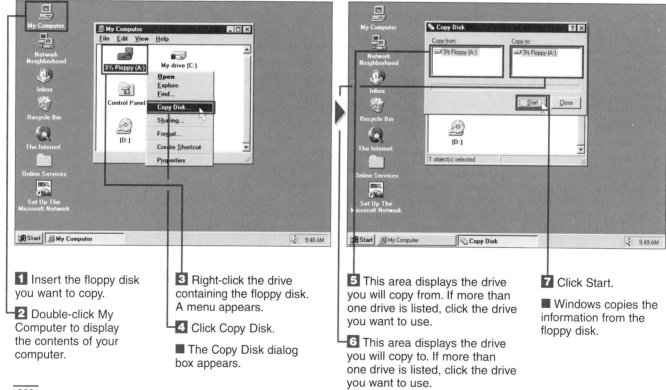

1 Insert the floppy disk you want to copy.

2 Double-click My Computer to display the contents of your computer.

3 Right-click the drive containing the floppy disk. A menu appears.

4 Click Copy Disk.

■ The Copy Disk dialog box appears.

5 This area displays the drive you will copy from. If more than one drive is listed, click the drive you want to use.

6 This area displays the drive you will copy to. If more than one drive is listed, click the drive you want to use.

7 Click Start.

■ Windows copies the information from the floppy disk.

TIPS

Do I need to format the disk I want to receive the copy?

If the disk is unformatted, Windows will format the disk as part of the copy process.

Why did Windows display a message saying the floppy disk could not be formatted?

If the disk is inserted properly, check that the write-protect tab on the disk is closed. An error message also appears if you are copying the contents of a high-density disk onto a double-density disk.

I made a copy from a double-density disk to a high-density disk, but the file names are not displayed correctly in the window. What should I do?

Remove the disk from the drive and then reinsert it. Press the F5 key to refresh the window.

How can I make several copies of a floppy disk without having to reinsert the disk each time?

It may be faster to copy the contents of the disk to a folder on the desktop. Then copy the information onto the disks from the desktop.

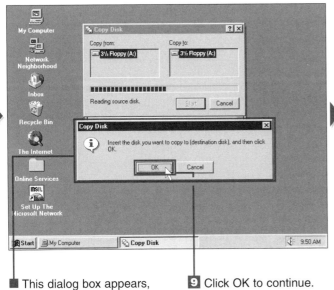

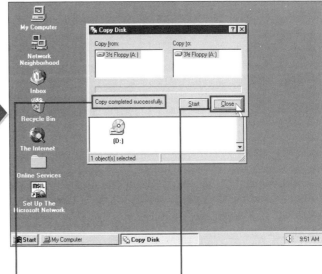

■ This dialog box appears, asking you to insert the floppy disk you want to receive the copy.

8 Remove the floppy disk from the drive and then insert the disk you want to receive the copy.

9 Click OK to continue.

■ This message appears when the copy is complete.

■ You can click Close to close the Copy Disk dialog box.

Note: To copy another floppy disk, insert the disk into the drive and then click Start.

FORMAT FLOPPY DISKS

A floppy disk must be formatted before you can use it to store information.

When you purchase a new box of blank disks, you will probably need to format the disks so they can be used to store files. You can also buy formatted disks.

If the disk has already been used, make sure the disk does not contain information you want

to keep. Formatting will remove all the information on a disk.

Disks are available in two capacities. A double-density disk can hold 720 KB of information. This is approximately equal to 50 two-page documents. A high-density disk can contain twice that amount, or 1.44 MB.

The Quick (erase) format option removes all files but does not check the disk for damaged areas. This option is useful for a disk

that was previously formatted. You should only use this option if you are sure the disk is not damaged.

The Full format option removes all files and checks the disk for damaged areas. If Windows finds bad areas on the disk, the areas are marked so they will not be used to store information.

Windows allows you to label the disk so you can easily identify it later.

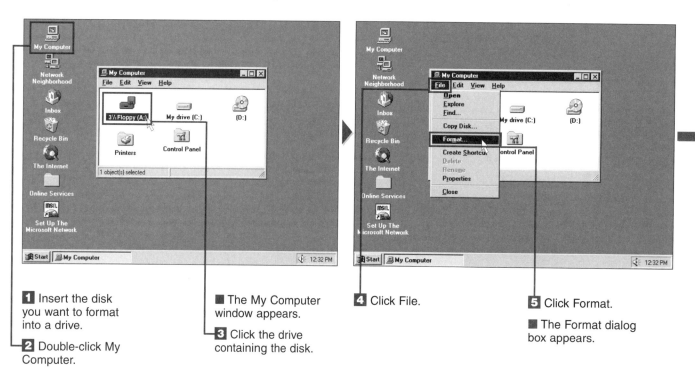

■ Insert the disk you want to format into a drive.

■ Double-click My Computer.

■ The My Computer window appears.

■ Click the drive containing the disk.

■ Click File.

■ Click Format.

■ The Format dialog box appears.

How can I tell if a disk is formatted?

Windows will tell you if a disk is not formatted when you try to open the disk. You cannot tell if a disk is formatted just by looking at it.

A friend gave me a disk with documents on it, but Windows tells me it is blank and suggests I format it. What is wrong with the disk?

Either the disk has been formatted using a different file system, like the Macintosh, or the disk has been damaged.

How can I protect my disks from damage?

You can help protect your disks by keeping them away from moisture, heat and magnets.

When should I use the Copy system files only format option?

You can use this option if you want to add system files to a disk. This is useful if you want to be able to use the disk to start your computer. This option does not format the disk and does not erase any existing files on the disk.

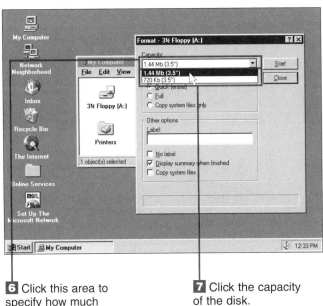

6 Click this area to specify how much information the disk can hold.

7 Click the capacity of the disk.

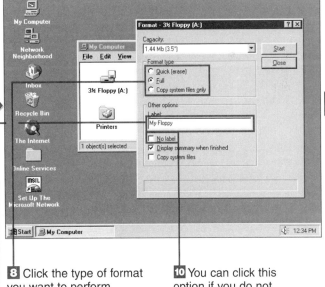

8 Click the type of format you want to perform (○ changes to ◉).

9 Click this area to name the disk. Then type a name for the disk.

10 You can click this option if you do not want to name the disk (☐ changes to ☑).

CONTINUED ▶

FORMAT FLOPPY DISKS
CONTINUED

You can have Windows display summary information about the disk when the format is complete. The Format Results dialog box contains information about the disk, such as the total amount of disk space, the amount of space used by the system files, the amount of space in bad sectors and the total available space on the disk.

A disk with system files can be used to start the computer.

You can have Windows copy system files to the disk you are formatting or you can add the files to a disk that has already been formatted.

You should not copy the system files to every disk you format. System files take up space and make your computer more vulnerable to viruses.

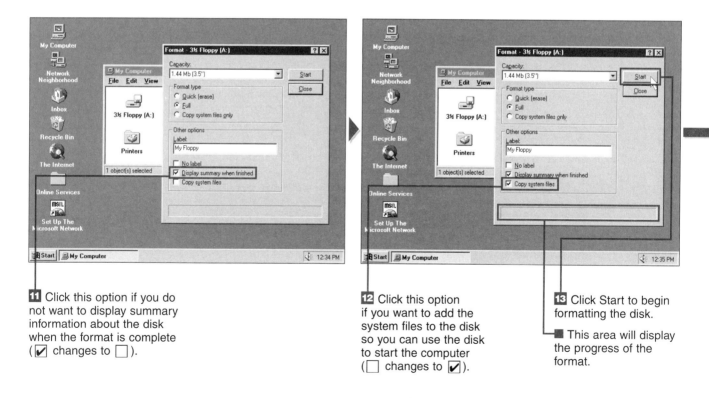

11 Click this option if you do not want to display summary information about the disk when the format is complete (☑ changes to ☐).

12 Click this option if you want to add the system files to the disk so you can use the disk to start the computer (☐ changes to ☑).

13 Click Start to begin formatting the disk.

■ This area will display the progress of the format.

TIPS

Instead of formatting the disk, I get an error message. What is wrong?

If you get an error message, you may be currently using the files on the disk or have its files open in a My Computer or Explorer window. Windows will not format a disk when the disk's files are in use. You should also check the capacity settings you selected for the disk.

Can I format disks from an Explorer window?

You can format a disk from an Explorer window by right-clicking the drive containing the disk and then selecting Format. If the files are displayed in the right pane of the window, Format will not start.

What should I do if a disk has bad sectors?

A few damaged sectors are normal, even on a new disk. If you have one or two damaged sectors, you can still use the disk to store information. If a new disk has many damaged sectors, you should return the disk to the manufacturer for a replacement. If the disk has many damaged sectors and it is an old disk, throw it out.

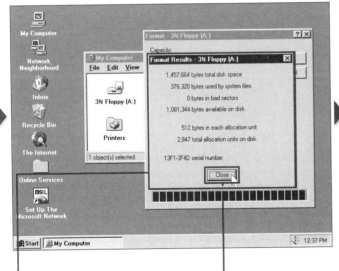

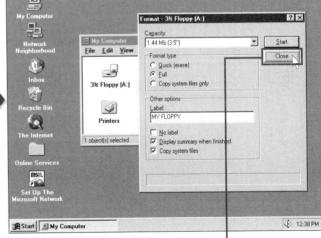

■ The Format Results dialog box appears when the format is complete. The dialog box displays information about the formatted disk.

Note: The dialog box does not appear if you turned off the Display summary option in step 11.

14 Click Close to close the Format Results dialog box.

■ To format another disk, insert the disk and then repeat steps 6 to 13 starting on page 285.

15 Click Close to close the Format dialog box.

VIEW AMOUNT OF DISK SPACE

You can view the amount of used and free space on any disk, including hard disks, floppy disks, removable disks and CD-ROM discs.

The amount of space on a disk is measured in bytes, megabytes (MB) and gigabytes (GB). A byte equals one character. One MB equals approximately one million characters, or one novel. A GB equals one billion characters, or one thousand novels.

You should check the amount of available disk space on your computer at least once a month, when you run ScanDisk and check the defragmentation status of your computer. You should also check the amount of available disk space before you install a new program.

You should have at least 10% of your hard disk free. For example, if you have a 2 GB hard disk, make sure you have at least 0.2 GB free. This will help improve virtual

memory performance as well as decrease fragmentation.

If you want to increase the amount of free space on your hard disk, you have many choices. You can empty the Recycle Bin to free up disk space. You can also save older files you no longer use onto a floppy disk and delete the files from your hard disk. You can also delete programs you no longer use.

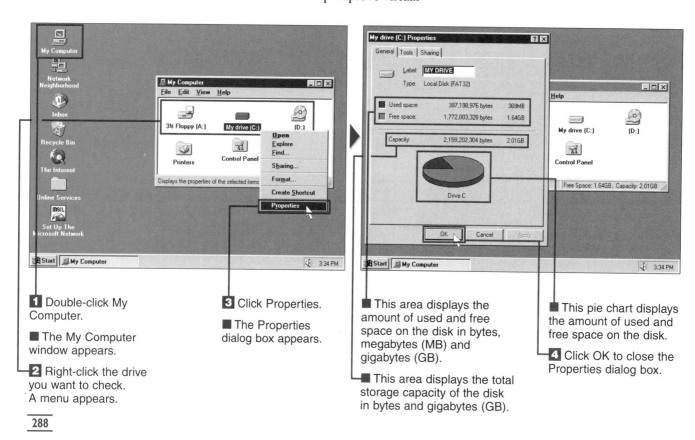

■1 Double-click My Computer.

■ The My Computer window appears.

■2 Right-click the drive you want to check. A menu appears.

■3 Click Properties.

■ The Properties dialog box appears.

■ This area displays the amount of used and free space on the disk in bytes, megabytes (MB) and gigabytes (GB).

■ This area displays the total storage capacity of the disk in bytes and gigabytes (GB).

■ This pie chart displays the amount of used and free space on the disk.

■4 Click OK to close the Properties dialog box.

RENAME A DISK

You can rename your hard disk, removable disk or floppy disks. Renaming a disk allows you to more easily identify the disk. You cannot rename a CD-ROM disc or network drive.

You can use up to 11 letters or numbers to rename a disk.

The name can contain spaces, but cannot contain the \ / : * ? " < > or | characters.

If you are renaming a floppy disk, you can label the disk by date, project name or whatever other information will help you to identify it quickly.

The new name of the floppy disk will only appear in the Properties dialog box.

When you label a disk, you can use both upper and lower case letters. The Properties dialog box displays all names in capital letters.

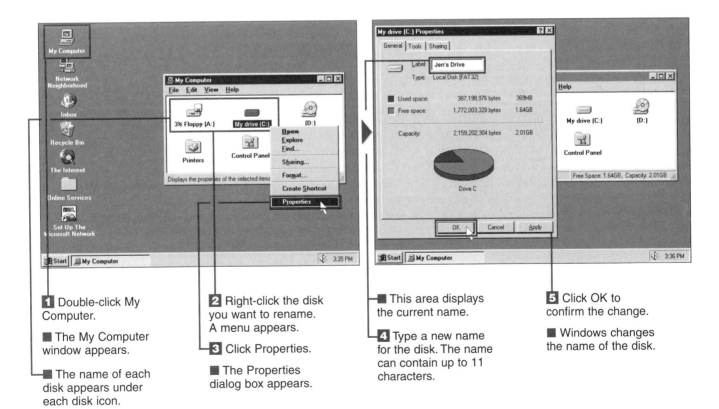

1 Double-click My Computer.

■ The My Computer window appears.

■ The name of each disk appears under each disk icon.

2 Right-click the disk you want to rename. A menu appears.

3 Click Properties.

■ The Properties dialog box appears.

■ This area displays the current name.

4 Type a new name for the disk. The name can contain up to 11 characters.

5 Click OK to confirm the change.

■ Windows changes the name of the disk.

CHECK FOR DISK ERRORS

ScanDisk is a program included with Windows that detects and repairs disk errors.

ScanDisk can check for errors on hard or floppy drives and removable hard drives. ScanDisk cannot check CD-ROM drives or network drives.

The standard test checks for errors in files and folders. The thorough test performs the same check as the standard test and also checks the disk surface for physically damaged areas that can no longer be used to store information.

You can have ScanDisk automatically fix the errors it finds.

When ScanDisk is finished checking a drive, a summary appears, displaying information about the drive. You can have ScanDisk display the summary only when errors are found.

You can save the summary for each check. You can store the summaries in a log to keep track of the errors that occur over time.

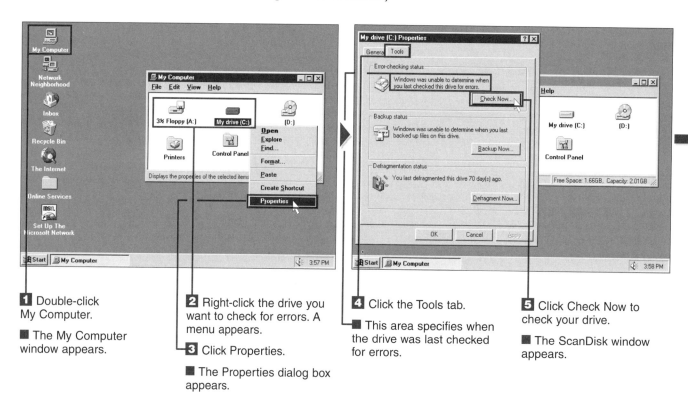

1 Double-click My Computer.

■ The My Computer window appears.

2 Right-click the drive you want to check for errors. A menu appears.

3 Click Properties.

■ The Properties dialog box appears.

4 Click the Tools tab.

■ This area specifies when the drive was last checked for errors.

5 Click Check Now to check your drive.

■ The ScanDisk window appears.

Why does another version of ScanDisk sometimes run automatically when I start Windows?

If Windows was not shut down properly the last time you used it, Windows will automatically run the command prompt version of ScanDisk to check for errors in your files and folders.

How often should I use ScanDisk?

You should perform the thorough test once a month. If you experience problems opening or saving files, you should perform the test more often. You can perform the standard test as often as you like.

How long does the thorough test take?

The thorough test can be time-consuming, especially on large disks. While the standard test takes about a minute, the thorough test may take about twenty minutes on a one gigabyte drive.

Can I speed up the thorough test?

You can change the options for the thorough test to perform the test more quickly. You can specify which areas you want ScanDisk to check: the system and data areas, the system area only or the data area only. ScanDisk can check the system area very quickly.

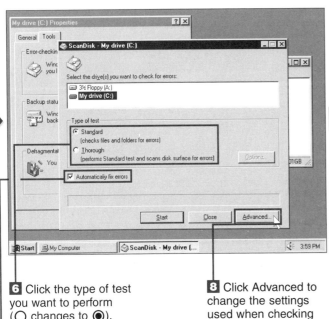

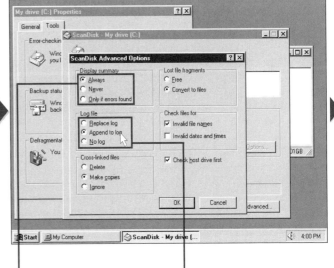

6 Click the type of test you want to perform (○ changes to ◉).

7 Click Automatically fix errors if you want ScanDisk to automatically repair errors it finds (☐ changes to ☑).

8 Click Advanced to change the settings used when checking for errors.

■ The ScanDisk Advanced Options dialog box appears.

9 Click an option to specify if you want to display a summary when ScanDisk finishes checking a drive (○ changes to ◉).

10 Click an option to specify if you want to save the results of the ScanDisk check (○ changes to ◉).

CONTINUED ▶

CHECK FOR DISK ERRORS
CONTINUED

You can change the settings that ScanDisk uses when checking your files and folders for errors. You can specify what you want ScanDisk to do when it finds errors.

Cross-linked files are two or more files stored in the same area of a disk. The data in cross-linked files is often

correct for only one of the files. The Make copies setting provides the best chance of recovering information from cross-linked files.

Lost fragments are pieces of data that have become detached from a file. Lost fragments cannot be recovered and simply take up disk space. You can use the Convert to files setting to

view information the lost fragments contain.

You can check for files with invalid names. You may be unable to open, move or delete files with invalid names. You can also check for invalid dates and times. Files with invalid dates and times can be difficult to back up.

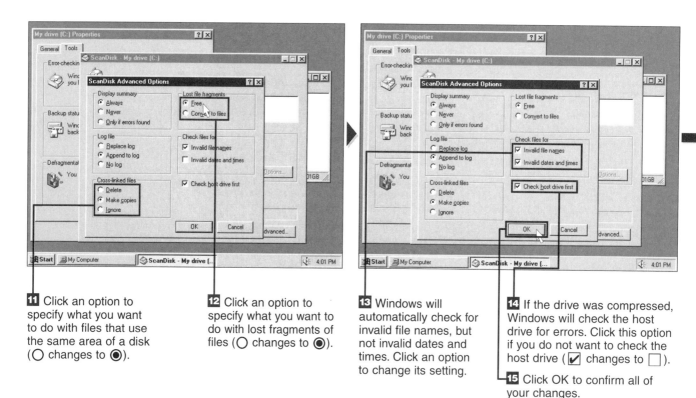

11 Click an option to specify what you want to do with files that use the same area of a disk (○ changes to ◉).

12 Click an option to specify what you want to do with lost fragments of files (○ changes to ◉).

13 Windows will automatically check for invalid file names, but not invalid dates and times. Click an option to change its setting.

14 If the drive was compressed, Windows will check the host drive for errors. Click this option if you do not want to check the host drive (☑ changes to ☐).

15 Click OK to confirm all of your changes.

TIPS

Can I use ScanDisk on a compressed disk?

ScanDisk can check and repair disks that have been compressed using the compression program included with Windows 95. For information on compressed disks, see pages 310 to 325.

Can I program ScanDisk to run at a specified time?

The Microsoft Plus! System Agent program can be used to start ScanDisk automatically at a time and date you specify.

Can I use my computer while ScanDisk is running?

You can use your computer while ScanDisk is running, but the check may slow down. ScanDisk will restart if the disk being checked is accessed. The use of screen savers may also affect a thorough check. You should run ScanDisk when you do not need to use your computer.

Can I stop ScanDisk before it's finished?

You can click the Cancel button to stop ScanDisk at any time.

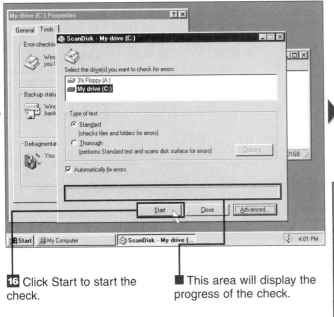

16 Click Start to start the check.

■ This area will display the progress of the check.

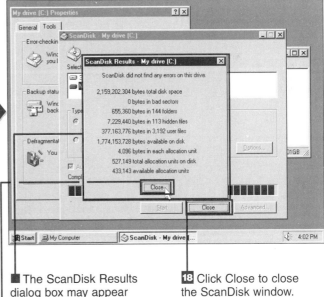

■ The ScanDisk Results dialog box may appear when the check is complete. The dialog box displays information about the drive.

17 Click Close to close the ScanDisk Results dialog box.

18 Click Close to close the ScanDisk window.

19 Click OK to close the Properties dialog box.

DEFRAGMENT YOUR HARD DRIVE

You can improve the performance of your computer by using the Disk Defragmenter program.

Over time, the files on a hard drive become more and more fragmented. To retrieve or save a file, the computer must use many different areas on the hard

drive. The Disk Defragmenter reorganizes your files to reduce fragmentation and improve the performance of your drive.

For best performance, you should defragment your hard drive regularly.

If you decide to work while Disk Defragmenter is running,

your computer will operate more slowly. It is best to defragment at a time when you do not need your computer.

When you start Disk Defragmenter, Windows advises you whether defragmenting the hard drive will improve the performance of your computer.

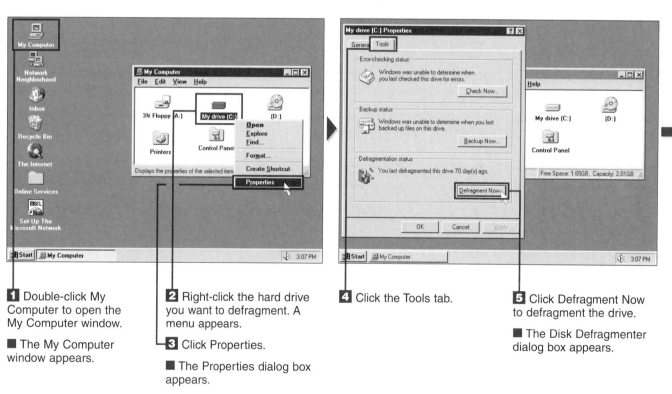

1 Double-click My Computer to open the My Computer window.

■ The My Computer window appears.

2 Right-click the hard drive you want to defragment. A menu appears.

3 Click Properties.

■ The Properties dialog box appears.

4 Click the Tools tab.

5 Click Defragment Now to defragment the drive.

■ The Disk Defragmenter dialog box appears.

TIPS

How long will the defragmentation process take?

The amount of time it takes to defragment the hard drive depends on several factors including how badly the files are fragmented and the amount of free space on your hard drive.

What drives cannot be defragmented by Windows?

Windows cannot defragment a CD-ROM drive or a network drive. Windows also cannot defragment a hard drive that has been compressed using a compression program Windows does not support.

Are there other defragmentation programs with more features available?

Some defragmentation programs can move specific files to faster areas of the hard drive or defragment files that Disk Defragmenter does not affect. The System Agent in Microsoft Plus! lets you specify the time and date you want to automatically defragment your hard drive.

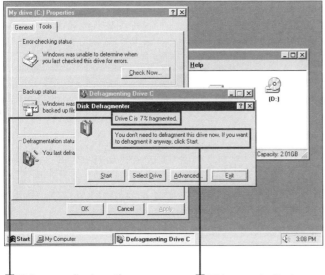

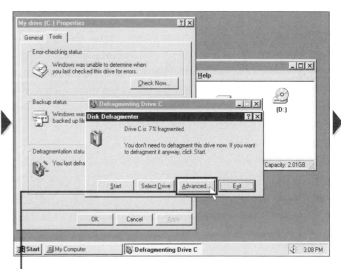

■ This area displays the percentage of the drive that is fragmented.

■ This area indicates whether defragmenting the drive will improve its performance.

6 Click Advanced to select how you want to defragment the drive.

■ The Advanced Options dialog box appears.

CONTINUED ▶

DEFRAGMENT YOUR HARD DRIVE CONTINUED

Windows offers several options for the way you can defragment a drive.

The Full defragmentation option places all the parts of a file together and places any empty clusters together. The Defragment files only option is a faster method. This option places all parts of a file together. Files currently stored on the drive will be defragmented, but files you store in the future may be fragmented. The Consolidate free space only option places empty clusters together. Files currently stored on the drive remain fragmented.

If your drive contains any errors, Windows cannot defragment the drive. You can have Windows check the drive for errors before starting the defragmentation.

You can tell Windows whether you want to save the options you selected for the defragmentation. Saving your options lets you avoid having to select the same options the next time you defragment your hard drive.

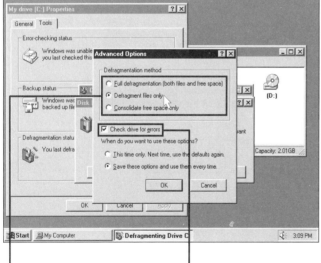

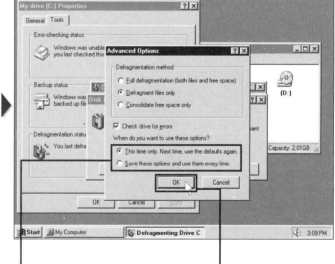

7 Click the way you want to defragment the drive (○ changes to ●).

8 Windows will check the files and folders on the drive for errors before defragmenting the drive. Click this option if you do not want to check the drive for errors (☑ changes to ☐).

9 Click the setting that specifies when you want to use the options you selected (○ changes to ●). Saving the options stores the options and uses them each time you defragment a drive unless you change the options.

10 Click OK to confirm your changes.

Can I pause the defragmentation?

You can pause the defragmentation by clicking the Pause button. Click the Resume button to continue defragmenting your drive. Pausing is useful if you need to finish another task immediately. The defragmentation will start over if you access the disk while Disk Defragmenter is paused.

Can I stop the defragmentation while it is running?

You can click the Stop button to stop defragmenting your drive. The defragmentation process will not be completed. There will be no effect on your files or their locations on your hard drive.

What does the details window show me?

The details window shows the details of the defragmentation. Click the Show Details button to display the details window. To understand the various colored squares in the details window, click the Legend button. Click the Hide Details button to close the window.

Will I have more free space after defragmenting my drive?

Defragmenting your drive only reorganizes your files to make them easier to find and access. No additional free space will be created on your computer.

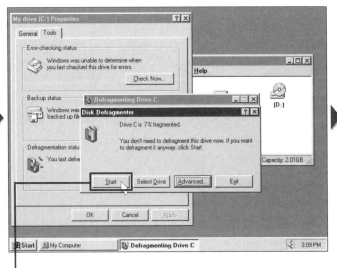

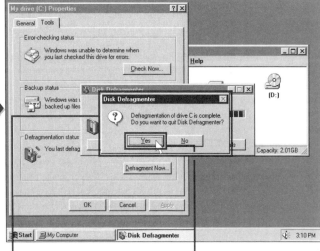

11 Click Start to begin the defragmentation process.

■ Windows will display the progress of the defragmentation.

■ This dialog box appears when the defragmentation is complete.

12 Click Yes to exit Disk Defragmenter.

DISPLAY REGISTRATION AND VERSION NUMBER

You can find out information about Windows and your computer by displaying the System Properties dialog box.

The version of Windows you are currently using is the first item displayed in the System Properties dialog box.

Microsoft has released three versions of Windows 95. The first version is identified by the number 4.00.950. This version is

sold as the Microsoft Windows 95 upgrade. The second version is identified by the letter "a" following the same number (4.00.950 a). This version is created by installing an upgrade kit called Service Pack 1, which is available from the Microsoft Web site. Some computers were sold with this version installed. The most recent version is identified by the letter "B" (4.00.950 B). This version is also called OSR2

(OEM Service Release 2). OSR2 has been released only to hardware manufacturers and may be available when you purchase a new computer.

The System Properties dialog box also displays the user name which was entered when the operating system was installed, your Windows registration number, some basic information about your processor, as well as the amount of RAM installed.

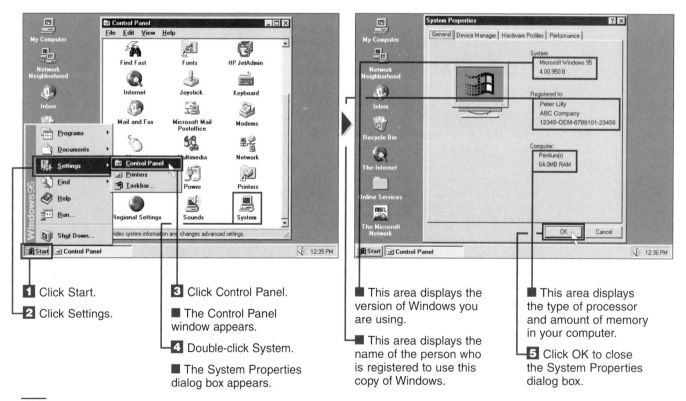

1 Click Start.

2 Click Settings.

3 Click Control Panel.

■ The Control Panel window appears.

4 Double-click System.

■ The System Properties dialog box appears.

■ This area displays the version of Windows you are using.

■ This area displays the name of the person who is registered to use this copy of Windows.

■ This area displays the type of processor and amount of memory in your computer.

5 Click OK to close the System Properties dialog box.

CHECK PERFORMANCE STATUS

You can check the performance of your computer by viewing the six items displayed on the Performance tab in the System Properties dialog box.

The first item, Memory, displays the amount of physical memory (RAM) in your computer. This amount will not change unless you add or remove memory from your computer. More memory means better performance.

The second item, System Resources, displays a percentage that will change while you are working. When there is less than 30% free, you should close some programs or restart Windows to avoid potential problems.

The third and fourth items, File System and Virtual Memory, should both be set at 32-bit for the best performance. There are only some isolated cases where this might not be true.

The fifth item, Disk Compression, indicates if you have any disk compression software installed on your computer. This may affect system performance, depending on processor speed, disk speed and the amount of memory installed.

PC Cards is the last item and applies to portable computers. This area indicates the type of PC Cards installed on your computer.

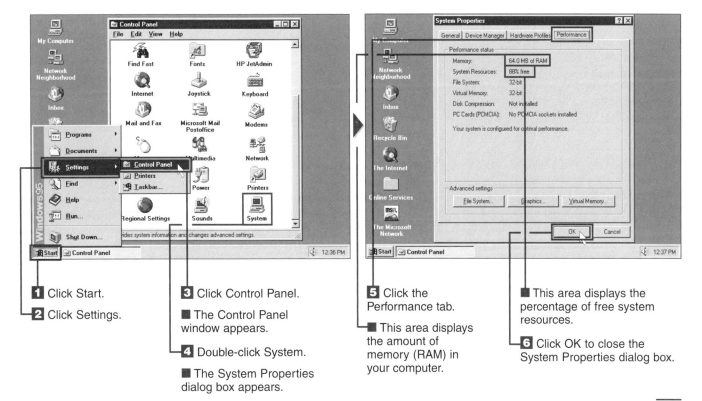

■1 Click Start.

■2 Click Settings.

■3 Click Control Panel.

■ The Control Panel window appears.

■4 Double-click System.

■ The System Properties dialog box appears.

■5 Click the Performance tab.

■ This area displays the amount of memory (RAM) in your computer.

■ This area displays the percentage of free system resources.

■6 Click OK to close the System Properties dialog box.

CREATE MORE DISK SPACE

As you create documents and install programs, the available space on your hard drive decreases. You should always have at least 20 MB of available disk space. There are many ways to increase the amount of free space on your hard drive.

You should run ScanDisk before you attempt to create more space on your hard drive. ScanDisk locates errors such as lost file fragments on your hard drive. Lost file fragments are saved on your hard drive with a name such as "FILE0000.CHK". You can delete these file fragments.

Back Up and Delete Files

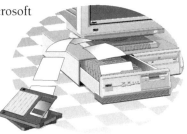

You can use Microsoft Backup to copy files you rarely use to floppy disks. You can then remove these files from your hard drive to create more storage space on your computer. Even if you save the backup set on your hard drive, there will be more space available because the files are compressed.

Remove Unused Programs and Components

You can delete programs and components you no longer use to free up space on your hard drive. In the Control Panel, use Add/Remove Programs and select the Install/Uninstall tab to delete programs. Select the Windows Setup tab to remove Windows components.

Empty the Recycle Bin

You can create more space on your computer by permanently removing all the files from the Recycle Bin. You can also adjust the Recycle Bin properties so it will use less space. If you have not changed the default settings, the Recycle Bin could be storing as much as 100 MB of files on a 1 GB drive.

Empty the Internet Explorer Cache

Internet Explorer saves Web pages you have opened in a cache, so Explorer can display the pages more quickly the second time. When you delete the contents of the cache from the Temporary Internet Files folder, you will have more available disk space. You can reduce Internet Explorer's default cache size.

Delete E-Mail Messages and Faxes

You can delete e-mail messages and faxes you no longer need. Messages with attached files can be particularly large. Once you save the attachment, you probably do not need to keep the message. The disk space recovered by deleted messages and faxes may not appear immediately. Microsoft Exchange saves all messages and faxes in one file. Exchange may take a day or more to adjust the file and remove the messages and faxes you deleted.

Upgrade to FAT32

If you have OSR2 and do not have the FAT32 file system installed, you can upgrade your hard drive to FAT32. The FAT32 file system provides additional free space on drives larger than 512 MB. On a 1 GB drive, FAT32 may free up over 200 MB. When you upgrade to the FAT32 file system, you must back up all of the files on your hard drive, format the hard drive and then reinstall Windows.

Install a New Drive

When all other options fail, you can add a second hard drive or replace your current drive with a larger one. You may also consider a removable hard drive or a CD-Recordable drive to increase your storage capacity.

Compress a Drive

You can use DriveSpace to compress, or squeeze together, the information stored on your hard drive. Compression may be able to double the amount of information the drive can store. Compression is not possible with FAT32. Microsoft Plus! contains several compression enhancements. If you do not have OSR2 or Microsoft Plus! the compressed drives you create cannot hold more than 512 MB.

Delete Temporary and Backup Files

When Windows is not closed properly, temporary files are not deleted. To remove temporary files, restart Windows and then delete any files in the c:\windows\temp folder. You may also find temporary files in other folders. Temporary files usually have the extension .tmp or start with the tilde (~) character.

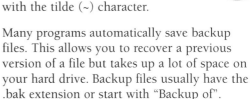

Many programs automatically save backup files. This allows you to recover a previous version of a file but takes up a lot of space on your hard drive. Backup files usually have the .bak extension or start with "Backup of".

You can use the Find feature to look for temporary and backup files.

USING FDISK

You can use FDISK to change the size or type of partitions on your hard drive. A partition is a part of the drive that is assigned a drive letter and acts as a separate hard drive. Most drives have only one partition.

OSR2 includes a new version of FDISK, which enables you to create partitions larger than 2 GB.

This version of FDISK also enables you to install the FAT32 file system, which will use a large drive more efficiently than previous versions. FAT32 provides about 200 MB more free space on a 1 GB drive.

Partitioning will remove all of the information stored on a drive.

Before you start, you should perform a complete backup of your hard drive using the Full system backup set in the Backup program. See page 332.

To reinstall your information, you will need to reinstall Windows and then restore the backup set. To reinstall Windows, see page 588.

1 Insert the Windows 95 startup disk into drive A.

2 Turn on your computer.

3 Type **fdisk** and then press the Enter key.

■ You are asked if you want to use the FAT32 file system.

Note: This screen does not appear if you are using a non-OSR2 startup disk.

4 To use the FAT32 file system, press **Y** (for Yes) and then press the Enter key.

■ If you want to use the FAT16 file system, press **N** (for No) and then press the Enter key.

TIPS

If I change my computer to FAT32, will others be able to access my files on the network?

People on a network who do not have OSR2 will be able to access the files on a FAT32 partition.

My computer has OSR2. Why wasn't the FAT32 file system installed when I bought my computer?

The FAT32 file system in OSR2 requires updated versions of disk utility programs and is incompatible with some programs. Some computer sellers choose not to install FAT32.

Where can I get a startup disk?

You can create your own startup disk using Windows. See page 636.

How can I get a copy of OSR2 or FAT32?

You may get a copy of OSR2 when you buy a new computer. Microsoft may make the FAT32 file system available as an upgrade. FAT32 will be included in the next version of Windows. PartitionMagic is a program developed by PowerQuest that can create FAT32 partitions. For information on PartitionMagic, see page 607.

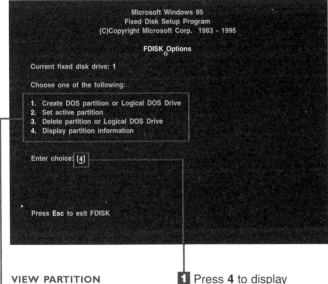

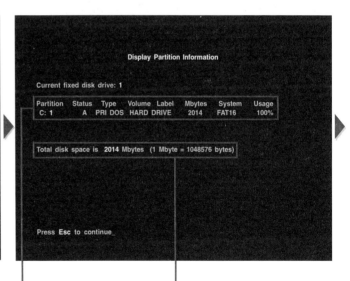

VIEW PARTITION INFORMATION

■ This area displays a list of FDISK options that you can choose from.

1 Press **4** to display partition information and then press the Enter key.

■ This area displays information about each partition on the drive.

■ This area displays the total space on the entire drive.

2 Press the Esc key to return to the list of FDISK options.

CONTINUED

USING FDISK CONTINUED

You can delete partitions to reorganize your hard drive. When you delete a partition, you will lose all information stored in the partition.

There are two types of DOS partitions. Each hard drive has a primary partition. A primary partition can be the same size as the hard drive or just a portion of it.

An extended partition is the second partition on a hard drive. You must create an extended partition if you want to use two partitions. The extended partition will use any space on the hard drive that is not used by the primary partition.

If you want to create more partitions on a hard drive, you must create logical drives. Logical drives can be created in

the extended partition. The size of all logical drives cannot be larger than the size of the extended partition.

You may also have a non-DOS partition on your hard drive created by another operating system, such as Unix. You can use FDISK to remove non-DOS partitions.

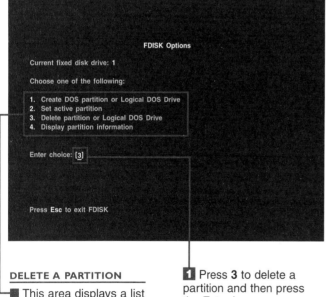

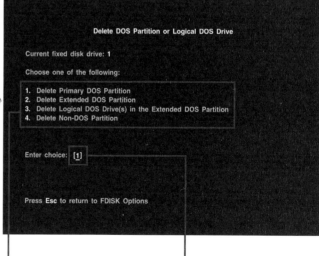

DELETE A PARTITION

■ This area displays a list of FDISK options that you can choose from.

1 Press **3** to delete a partition and then press the Enter key.

■ This area displays the types of partitions that you can delete.

2 Press **1** to delete the primary partition and then press the Enter key.

■ A message appears, warning that you will lose the data in the partition.

Why would there be more than one partition on a hard drive?

Many people use partitions to organize the information on their hard drive. For example, you can use one partition to store programs, one partition for data and one partition for your operating system files.

I have more than one partition. How do I delete all the partitions?

If you have more than one partition, you must delete the partitions in order. First, you must delete the logical drives. Then you can delete the extended partition. Finally, you can delete the primary partition.

Why must I delete a partition?

If you want to set up your hard drive to use FAT32, you must delete all partitions. You must also delete partitions before you can create new ones.

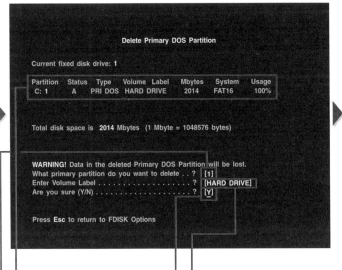

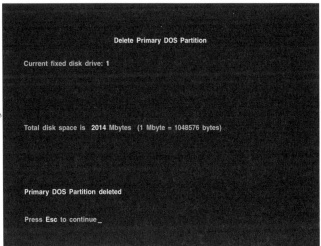

■ This area displays information such as the number and name of the existing partitions.

3 Press the number of the partition you want to delete and then press the Enter key.

4 Type the name of the partition and then press the Enter key.

5 To delete the partition, press **Y** (for Yes) and then press the Enter key.

■ The partition is deleted.

6 Press the Esc key to return to the list of FDISK options.

CONTINUED

USING FDISK CONTINUED

You can create multiple partitions to organize your data or prepare a new disk for use.

Before creating any new partitions, you may have to delete any existing partitions, including the primary partition. The primary partition is used to start the computer and load the Windows 95 operating system.

When you create partitions, you can use the entire drive or leave space for other partitions. Each partition is assigned a drive letter.

You can create a second partition to hold specific groups of files. This can simplify your backup procedure. You can also use a second partition to contain a drive that is shared on a network. Multiple partitions help you separate the public and private areas of your computer.

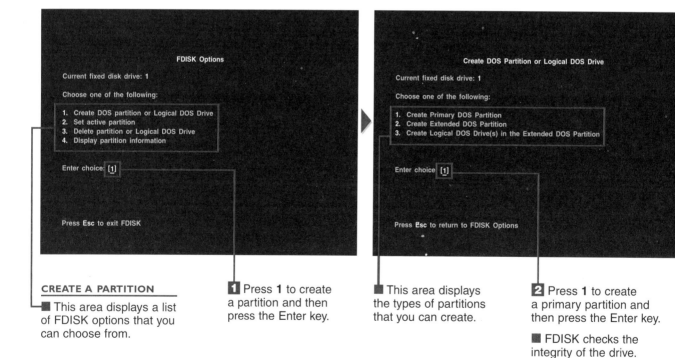

CREATE A PARTITION

■ This area displays a list of FDISK options that you can choose from.

1 Press **1** to create a partition and then press the Enter key.

■ This area displays the types of partitions that you can create.

2 Press **1** to create a primary partition and then press the Enter key.

■ FDISK checks the integrity of the drive.

How can I create more than one partition?

To create more than one partition, you must select No when you are asked if you want to use the entire drive for the partition. You can then specify the size of the primary partition you want. Repeat steps 1 and 2 on page 306, pressing **2** in step 2 to create an extended partition. You must specify the size of the extended partition you want. You are then asked to specify the amount of space you want to assign to a logical drive. You can enter this amount as a percentage of the hard drive available or in megabytes.

Can I return to FAT16?

If you want to switch back to FAT16, you can follow the steps on page 302, selecting No when you are asked if you want to use the FAT32 file system. You will lose all data on the drive when you switch back to FAT16.

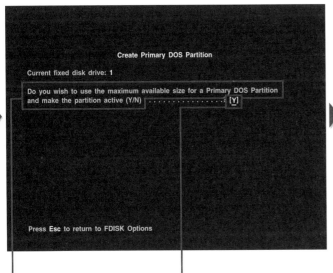

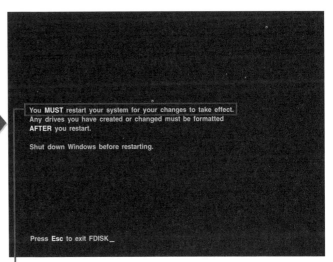

■ You are asked if you want to use the entire drive for the partition.

3 Press **Y** (for Yes) and then press the Enter key.

■ FDISK checks the integrity of the drive again.

■ You are instructed to restart your computer for the changes to take effect.

4 Press and hold down the Ctrl and Alt keys as you press the Delete key to restart your computer.

■ You can now format the drive to prepare it for use. See page 308.

FORMAT A HARD DRIVE

Formatting a hard drive organizes the space available on the drive so Windows can save and read files from the drive. A drive must be formatted before Windows can use the drive.

Before Windows is installed, you must format the drive from the command prompt. It will take

approximately 15 minutes to format a 2 GB drive.

You can format a hard drive to remove all of the files from the drive before giving it to another person.

When you format a hard drive, you have the option of naming

your hard drive. A hard drive name can be up to 11 letters long. If you do not want to name your hard drive, simply press the Enter key when prompted for a name.

After Windows is installed on your hard drive, you can use Windows to format floppy disks or additional hard drives.

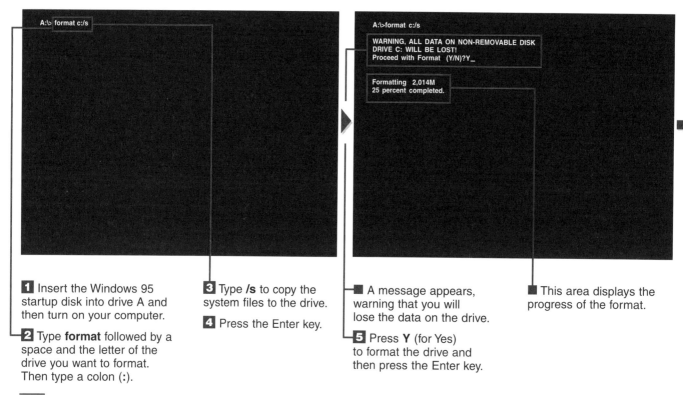

1 Insert the Windows 95 startup disk into drive A and then turn on your computer.

2 Type **format** followed by a space and the letter of the drive you want to format. Then type a colon (:).

3 Type **/s** to copy the system files to the drive.

4 Press the Enter key.

■ A message appears, warning that you will lose the data on the drive.

5 Press **Y** (for Yes) to format the drive and then press the Enter key.

■ This area displays the progress of the format.

Is formatting the hard drive a secure way to remove confidential information?

No. There are programs and drive recovery companies that will allow determined people to recover information from a formatted drive.

Can I copy the system files to a drive after it is formatted?

If the system files did not copy properly during the format of your hard drive, you can copy the system files to the hard drive using your startup disk. Insert the startup disk, and at the A: prompt type **sys c:** and then press the Enter key.

Can I install Windows on an unformatted hard drive?

To install Windows on an unformatted hard drive, you must have a startup disk and the Windows installation disks. If you have Windows on a CD-ROM disc, you must also have a floppy disk that can load the software required to access the CD-ROM drive. Once you start the Windows setup program, Windows will offer to partition and format your drives.

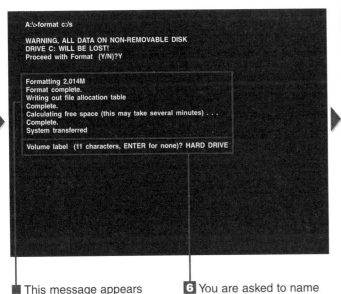

■ This message appears when the format is complete.

6 You are asked to name the drive. Type a name for the drive and then press the Enter key.

■ This area displays information about the drive, such as the total disk space.

■ You can now store data on the drive.

COMPRESS A DRIVE

You can use DriveSpace to compress, or squeeze together, the information stored on your hard drive.

As you install new programs and create new files, you may find that you need more space on your hard drive. You should first try to upgrade or add another hard drive to increase the space. If this is not possible, DriveSpace can provide the additional space you need.

DriveSpace estimates that it will double the amount of information the drive can store. The actual amount of free space that will be available on the drive depends on the size of the drive and the types of information stored on your drive. Text and graphics files compress significantly, whereas program files compress very little.

When DriveSpace is compressing a drive, you cannot use your computer. Because compressing your hard drive may take several hours, you should compress your hard drive when you will not need your computer.

If you have OSR2 and currently use the FAT32 file system, you cannot use DriveSpace to compress your hard drive.

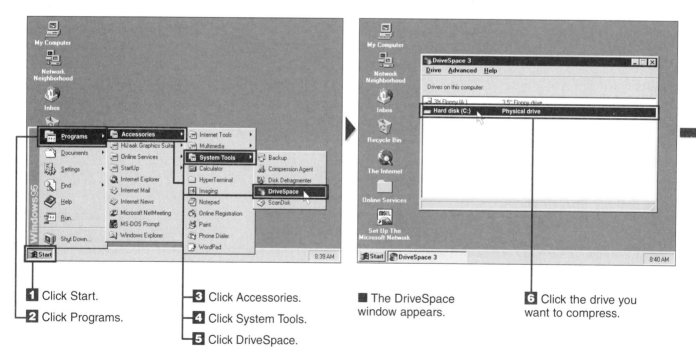

1 Click Start.

2 Click Programs.

3 Click Accessories.

4 Click System Tools.

5 Click DriveSpace.

■ The DriveSpace window appears.

6 Click the drive you want to compress.

Why isn't DriveSpace listed in my System Tools menu?

DriveSpace may not be installed. DriveSpace is located in the Disk Tools group on the Windows 95 CD-ROM disc. To install Windows components, see page 580.

Is it best to compress the whole hard drive, or just part of the hard drive?

Some kinds of files, like the document files created by programs, will compress more than others. You may get the maximum benefit from compression by creating a compressed drive in your disk's free space and using it to store your document files. See page 318.

Can I compress a floppy disk or removable drive?

You can compress any disk or removable drive that appears in the DriveSpace window. You cannot compress a floppy disk that does not have at least 512 K of free space or that contains a file larger than half the disk's capacity. To access a compressed floppy disk or removable drive on another computer system, the other computer must have DriveSpace and Windows 95.

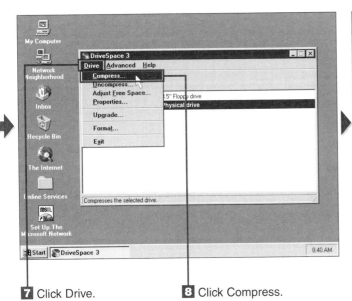

7 Click Drive.

8 Click Compress.

■ The Compress a Drive dialog box appears.

■ This area displays the amount of free and used space before and after you compress your drive.

CONTINUED ▶

COMPRESS A DRIVE CONTINUED

When you compress a drive, DriveSpace creates a drive-sized file, called a Compressed Volume File (CVF), on your hard drive. The CVF is assigned a letter and can be accessed like any other drive.

Your hard drive becomes a host drive that stores the CVF and is assigned a new drive letter. The host drive contains the software needed to start and access the compressed drive. You can hide the host drive so that the CVF cannot be accidentally deleted.

If you have OSR2, DriveSpace can use up to 1 GB of space to store from 1 to 2 GB worth of files. If you do not have OSR2 or Microsoft Plus!, the largest drive you can compress is 256 MB, which can store up to 512 MB of files.

DriveSpace saves space by storing all your old files in one large file. DriveSpace also looks for repeated elements in your files. When repeated elements are found, they are replaced with a shorter element.

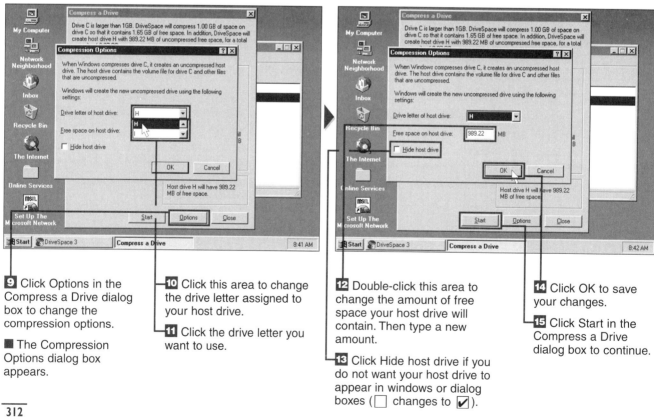

9 Click Options in the Compress a Drive dialog box to change the compression options.

■ The Compression Options dialog box appears.

10 Click this area to change the drive letter assigned to your host drive.

11 Click the drive letter you want to use.

12 Double-click this area to change the amount of free space your host drive will contain. Then type a new amount.

13 Click Hide host drive if you do not want your host drive to appear in windows or dialog boxes (☐ changes to ☑).

14 Click OK to save your changes.

15 Click Start in the Compress a Drive dialog box to continue.

Why should I create a new startup disk?

If you are having trouble starting Windows, you can use a startup disk to start your computer. You should create a new startup disk if you have installed DriveSpace since the last time you created a startup disk. The updated startup disk will recognize the compressed drive and allow you access to the drive.

How can I compress all of a large drive?

If your drive is larger than the maximum size you can compress, you can create multiple compressed drives on your host drive.

What letter should I use for the host drive?

The letter DriveSpace suggests should be fine, unless you require that letter for another drive, such as a new hard drive or a mapped network drive.

Can I hide or unhide the host drive later?

In the DriveSpace window, select the Drive menu and then select Properties. Then click Hide the host drive.

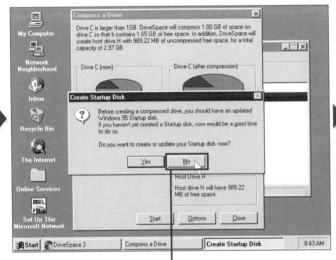

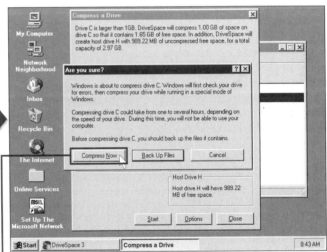

■ Windows may ask you to update your startup disk before compressing your drive.

16 Click No if you have an updated startup disk and do not need to create the disk.

Note: Click Yes to create a startup disk. For information on creating a startup disk, refer to page 636.

■ Windows is about to compress the drive. Windows asks you to back up your files before compressing your drive.

17 Click Compress Now if you have backed up your files and want to start the compression.

Note: Click Back Up Files if you want to back up your files now. For information on backing up files, refer to page 328.

CONTINUED ▶

COMPRESS A DRIVE CONTINUED

DriveSpace checks your drive by running ScanDisk before it starts. ScanDisk checks for errors on the drive you want to compress.

The DriveSpace setup procedure takes care to protect your files. You will be able to recover your files even if a power outage occurs while DriveSpace is working.

After the compressed drive is created, DriveSpace compresses each file and moves it to the compressed drive.

When the compression is finished, DriveSpace estimates the amount of free space available on your drive. DriveSpace estimates that it doubles the amount of information the drive can store.

The actual amount of free space may be less, depending on the types of files stored on your drive.

When you use a file from a compressed drive, it is retrieved from the disk and decompressed. When you save a file on a compressed drive, the file is compressed and then saved.

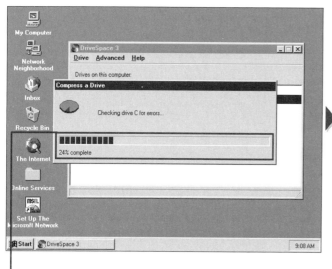

■ The Compress a Drive dialog box shows the progress of the compression.

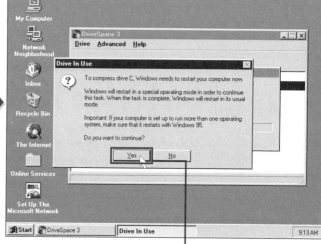

■ A dialog box appears when Windows needs to restart your computer.

🔢 Click Yes to continue.

Where will I find the compressed drive?

Unless the host drive is hidden, you can find the compressed volume file (CVF) on the host drive. Open a My Computer or Explorer window, display the View menu and click Options. Select the View tab and select the Show all files option. Then double-click the host drive. The CVF is named Drvspace.000. If you compressed the drive before you installed Windows 95, the CVF may be named Dblspace.000

Will using compressed files slow down my computer?

As long as you have 8 MB of RAM and your computer is reasonably fast, using compressed files should not affect the speed of your computer. The time required to save or retrieve a file is balanced by the smaller file size. If there is a delay in saving or retrieving files, it should be a minor delay.

Can I uncompress my drive?

You can undo the compression and return your drive to an uncompressed state. See page 322.

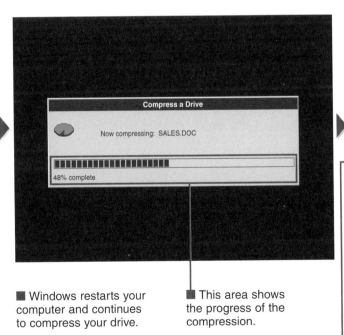

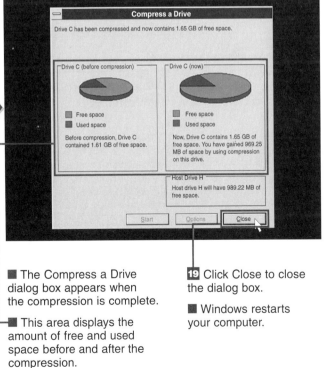

■ Windows restarts your computer and continues to compress your drive.

■ This area shows the progress of the compression.

■ The Compress a Drive dialog box appears when the compression is complete.

■ This area displays the amount of free and used space before and after the compression.

19 Click Close to close the dialog box.

■ Windows restarts your computer.

ADJUST FREE SPACE ON A COMPRESSED DRIVE

You can adjust the amount of available disk space between your compressed drive and its host drive.

If you need more space on the compressed drive and there is space available on your host drive, you can increase the free space for your compressed drive. You can also increase the amount of free space for your host drive if

you are not using all the space on your compressed drive.

When you increase the amount of free space on one drive, you decrease the amount of free space on your other drive.

The maximum size of a compressed drive on a computer with OSR2 is 2 GB. The maximum size of a compressed drive for a computer with Windows 95 is 512 MB.

The larger the adjustment you make to the amount of free space, the longer the resizing process will take.

After you finish adjusting the free space on a compressed drive, you must restart the computer. You should save all your files and quit all other programs before you begin to adjust the free space.

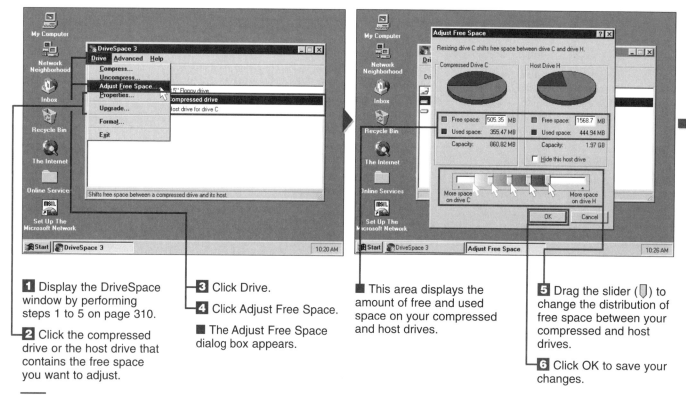

■1 Display the DriveSpace window by performing steps 1 to 5 on page 310.

■2 Click the compressed drive or the host drive that contains the free space you want to adjust.

■3 Click Drive.

■4 Click Adjust Free Space.

■ The Adjust Free Space dialog box appears.

■ This area displays the amount of free and used space on your compressed and host drives.

■5 Drag the slider (⬚) to change the distribution of free space between your compressed and host drives.

■6 Click OK to save your changes.

Will defragmenting my compressed drive increase available space?

Defragmenting your compressed drive will not increase the amount of free space.

The slider is not very accurate. How can I enter the exact size I want?

You can enter the exact size into the Free space text area for either the compressed or the host drive. You can also place the slider (⬇) in approximately the right spot and then use the cursor arrow keys to make more precise adjustments.

I am trying to copy a file to my compressed drive. Why does Windows tell me there is not enough free space?

The amount of free space on a compressed drive is only an estimate, based on files being able to compress to half of their original size. Some types of files, such as program files, compress less than other types of files. The file you want to copy to the compressed drive may not fit, even if it looks like there is enough free space.

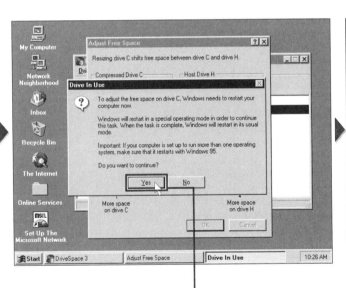

■ Windows needs to restart your computer to adjust the free space on your drive.

7 Click Yes to restart your computer.

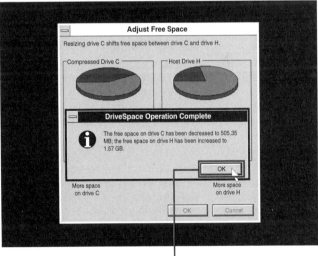

■ The DriveSpace Operation Complete dialog box appears when the operation is complete.

8 Click OK to close the dialog box.

■ Windows restarts your computer.

COMPRESS PART OF A DRIVE

You can use DriveSpace to turn the unused space on your hard drive into a new compressed drive. This allows you to increase the available space for storing information by one-and-a-half to two times. Your hard drive and the files on your hard drive are unaffected by the new compressed drive.

The compressed drive is actually a file called a compressed volume file (CVF). Your hard drive

becomes a host drive and stores the CVF. DriveSpace treats the CVF like a drive and assigns it a drive letter.

You can specify the amount of space that is used to create your compressed drive. If you have OSR2, DriveSpace can use up to 1 GB of available space to create a compressed drive.

You should close all of your programs before creating the new

compressed drive. DriveSpace will need to restart your computer when the compression process is complete.

You cannot compress unused space on a hard drive that is already compressed. If you have OSR2, you cannot use DriveSpace to compress any drives that use the FAT32 file system.

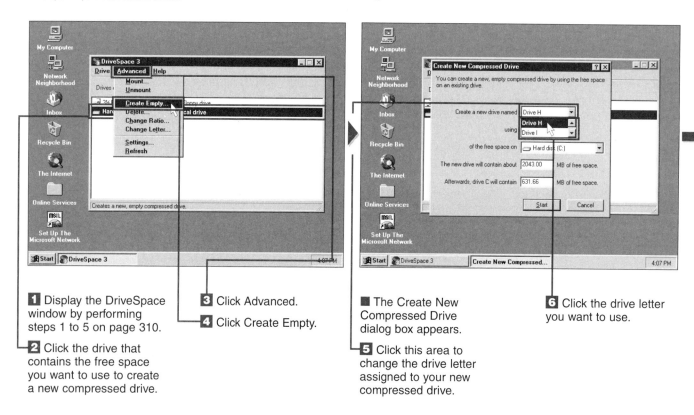

■1 Display the DriveSpace window by performing steps 1 to 5 on page 310.

■2 Click the drive that contains the free space you want to use to create a new compressed drive.

■3 Click Advanced.

■4 Click Create Empty.

■ The Create New Compressed Drive dialog box appears.

■5 Click this area to change the drive letter assigned to your new compressed drive.

■6 Click the drive letter you want to use.

TIPS

How does compressing part of a drive differ from compressing an entire drive?

Compressing the unused space on a drive does not compress any of the files that currently exist on your drive. Compressing unused space is often safer because the Windows files are not on a compressed drive and can be accessed without special software.

Can I change the size of the compressed drive after the drive is created?

In the Drive menu, you can use the Adjust Free Space command to make adjustments to the amount of space available on your compressed and host drives. See page 316.

What letter should I use for the new compressed drive?

You should use the letter DriveSpace suggests. The new drive letter should be out of the range of your current hard drives, CD-ROM drives, removable drives, network drives and any drives you plan to add.

Can I change the drive letter after the compressed drive is created?

In the Advanced menu, you can use the Change Letter command to change the drive letter. You should not change the drive letter if you have installed any programs on the compressed drive.

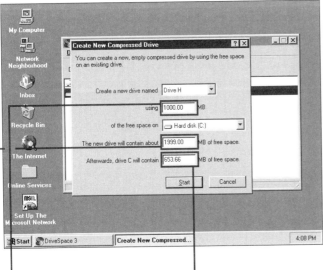

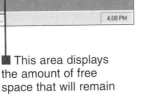

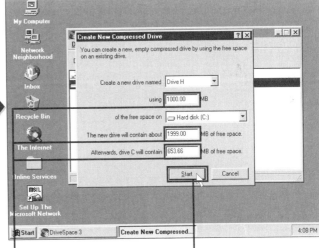

7 Double-click this area to change the amount of free space Windows will use to create your new drive. Then type a new amount.

■ This area displays the approximate amount of free space your new drive will contain.

■ This area displays the amount of free space that will remain on your hard drive.

■ When you change the number displayed in one of these areas, Windows updates the numbers in the other two areas.

8 Click Start to start the compression.

CONTINUED

COMPRESS PART
OF A DRIVE CONTINUED

Once you have created a new compressed drive, you can store files on the compressed drive just as you would on an uncompressed drive. If you have at least 8 MB of RAM, using compressed files should not affect the performance of your computer.

You can create several compressed drives to store different types of

files. This is useful if you want to organize your files into specific drives for backup purposes.

When you move or save a file to the compressed drive, DriveSpace compresses the file. When you retrieve a compressed file, DriveSpace decompresses the file for you. DriveSpace works in the background so you do not notice

DriveSpace compressing and decompressing your files.

A compressed file takes up less space on your drive. Some files compress more than others. Text and graphics files compress significantly. Program files compress very little. Files that are already compressed, such as files with the .zip extension, may not compress at all.

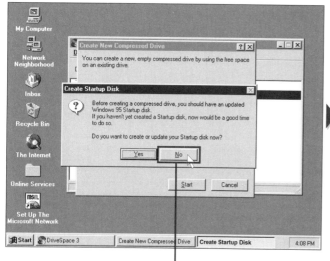

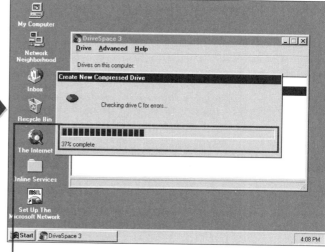

■ Windows may ask you to update your startup disk before creating a compressed drive.

9 Click No if you have an updated startup disk and do not need to create the disk.

Note: Click Yes to create a startup disk. For information on creating a startup disk, refer to page 636.

■ A dialog box appears, displaying the progress of the compression.

Should I create a new startup disk?

A startup disk allows you to start Windows when Windows will not start normally. You should create a new startup disk if you have installed DriveSpace since you created the last startup disk.

Can I move my programs to the compressed drive?

Most programs will not work properly if they are moved to a different drive. You should uninstall the program to remove it from the current drive. You can then install the program on the compressed drive.

Why do I have less space available on my compressed drive than I expected?

DriveSpace estimates how much information will fit on a compressed drive. The estimate may not be accurate because some types of files compress more than others. To change the estimate to reflect the type of files you are storing on the compressed drive, choose the Advanced menu and then select the Change Ratio command.

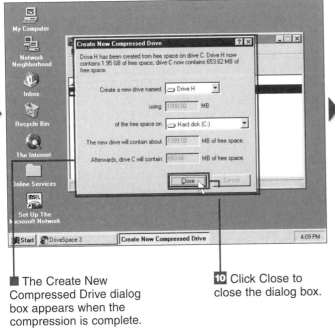

■ The Create New Compressed Drive dialog box appears when the compression is complete.

10 Click Close to close the dialog box.

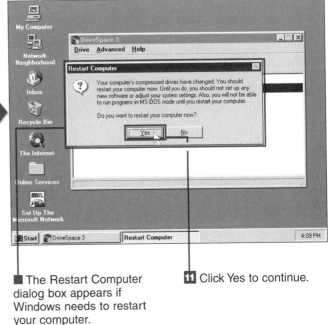

■ The Restart Computer dialog box appears if Windows needs to restart your computer.

11 Click Yes to continue.

UNCOMPRESS A DRIVE

When you no longer need a compressed drive, you can uncompress the drive.

DriveSpace verifies that you will have enough space on the drive to store the compressed files when they are uncompressed. If there is not enough space to store the uncompressed files,

DriveSpace will warn you and show you how much free space is needed. You can delete files, move them to another drive or archive them in a backup set to make space on the drive.

DriveSpace is careful to protect your files during the uncompression process, but you should make sure you create a

backup set of your files before you begin to uncompress a drive.

The uncompression process requires you to restart your computer. You should save all your documents and exit your programs before starting to uncompress a drive.

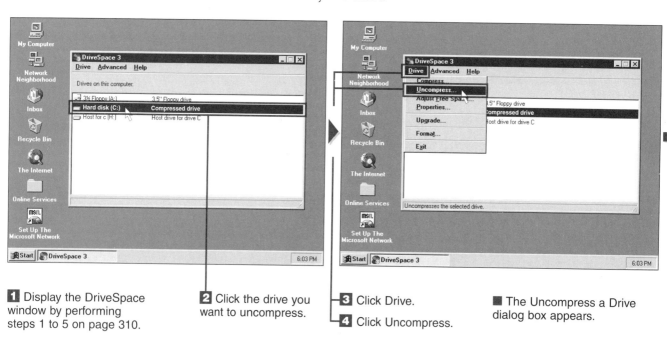

1 Display the DriveSpace window by performing steps 1 to 5 on page 310.

2 Click the drive you want to uncompress.

3 Click Drive.

4 Click Uncompress.

■ The Uncompress a Drive dialog box appears.

TIPS

Do I need to unhide the host drive before I can uncompress a drive?

DriveSpace will unhide the host drive for you. DriveSpace will also return the host to its original drive letter.

How do I remove all of the files from a compressed drive without deleting the drive?

Choose the Drive menu and then select the Format command to remove all of the files in a compressed drive. You can also open a My Computer or Explorer window for the drive and use Ctrl+A to select all files and folders. Then press the Delete key to move all the files to the Recycle Bin.

Can I reduce the size of a compressed drive without uncompressing it?

In the Drive menu, click the Adjust Free Space command. See page 316.

Can I delete a compressed drive I no longer need?

You can delete a compressed drive and all of the information it contains by choosing the Advanced menu and then selecting the Delete command.

IV WORK WITH DISKS

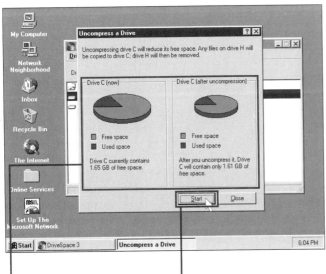

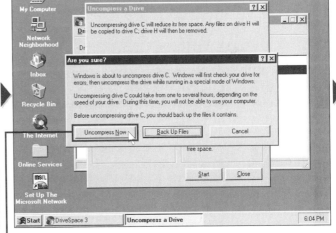

■ This area displays the amount of free and used space before and after you uncompress the drive.

5 Click Start to continue.

■ Windows is about to uncompress the drive. Windows asks you to back up your files before uncompressing the drive.

6 Click Uncompress Now if you have backed up your files and want to start the uncompression.

Note: Click Back Up Files if you want to back up your files now. For information on backing up files, refer to page 328.

CONTINUED ▶

UNCOMPRESS A DRIVE CONTINUED

When you uncompress a drive, all of the files on the drive are moved back to the uncompressed drive. DriveSpace removes the compressed drive from your computer and returns the host to its original drive letter.

The uncompression process may take several hours to complete. You will not be able to use your computer while DriveSpace is uncompressing a drive. You may want to wait and uncompress a drive at a time when you will not need your computer, like after work.

When the last compressed drive is removed from your computer, DriveSpace may ask if you want to remove the software used to access compressed drives, called the compression driver. If you still intend to use compressed floppy or removable disks, do not remove the compression driver.

You cannot uncompress a drive if it will change the letter of the drive that contains Windows. This may happen if you installed Windows on a drive after you installed your disk compression software.

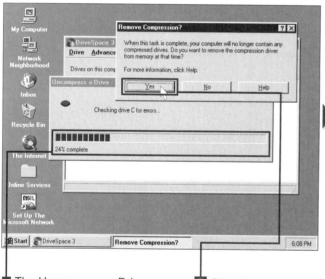

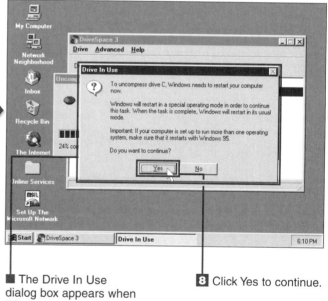

■ The Uncompress a Drive dialog box shows the progress of the uncompression.

■ Windows may ask if you want to remove the compression driver from memory. You may want to remove the driver if you have only one compressed drive and you do not plan to use any compressed floppy disks.

7 Click Yes to remove the compression driver from memory.

■ The Drive In Use dialog box appears when Windows needs to restart your computer.

8 Click Yes to continue.

I uncompressed my hard drive. Why can't I access a compressed floppy disk?

If you removed the compression driver when you uncompressed your hard drive, you will only see a file named readthis.txt when you try to access a compressed floppy disk. You can open this file to read instructions on how to access the files on a compressed disk.

Should I defragment a drive I uncompressed?

You should check the defragmentation of a drive after you have uncompressed or deleted a compressed drive. To check the defragmentation of a drive, perform steps 1 to 5 on page 294. If you need to defragment the drive, click Start.

Can I uncompress a floppy disk?

You can uncompress a floppy disk as long as there is enough space on the floppy disk to store the files it contains when they are uncompressed. If you do not have enough space, you can move the files to a folder on your hard drive, uncompress the floppy disk and then move the files you need from your hard drive back to the floppy disk.

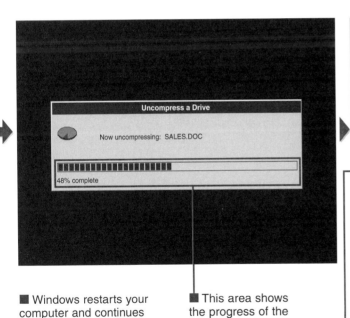

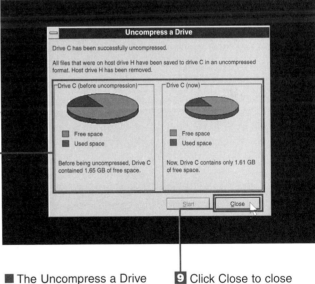

■ Windows restarts your computer and continues to uncompress your drive.

■ This area shows the progress of the uncompression.

■ The Uncompress a Drive dialog box appears when the operation is complete.

■ This area displays the amount of free and used space before and after the uncompression process.

9 Click Close to close the dialog box.

■ Windows restarts your computer.

INTRODUCTION TO MICROSOFT BACKUP

You should regularly make backup copies of the files stored on your computer to protect them from theft, computer failure and viruses. To determine how often you should back up your work, consider the time it may take to re-install your software on the computer and recreate your documents. If you cannot afford to lose the work you accomplish in a day, back up your files once a day. If your work does not change much during the week, back up once a week.

You can save your backup sets on floppy disks, a second hard drive, a network drive, a recordable CD or a tape cartridge. Using tape cartridges is an inexpensive and fast way to back up large amounts of information, such as all the files on your hard drive. A tape drive is easy to use because, unlike using floppy disks, you do not have to keep switching tapes while backing up your files.

If your tape drive was produced prior to 1995, you can probably use it with Backup. You can check the help files in Microsoft Backup to verify your tape drive will work with Backup. You should not use backup software created before Windows 95 because the software will not work with the long file names used in Windows 95.

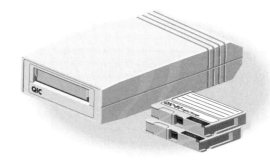

If the backup device you use includes its own software, the software will likely be more powerful and better suited to the device. However, Microsoft Backup is useful for transferring files between computers that do not share compatible backup devices. Microsoft Backup also compresses files and can use multiple disks. These features make Backup useful for transferring files that will not fit on one disk or for sending multiple documents in one file.

You can also use Backup to copy older files and files you rarely use in a compressed format. Once you create the backup, you can delete the original files. This can create more storage space on your computer, but still allow you to access the files if necessary.

Types of Backups

A full system backup is a copy of every file on your system. The full system backup can be used to restore all the files and folders on your hard drive. A full system backup can be very large and time-consuming. You can re-install all your software using the original floppy disks and CD-ROM discs instead of using a full system backup. If you choose to do a full system backup, you may want to back up only when you install a new program or when you change your computer's settings.

After performing a full system backup, you can save incremental backups. An incremental backup saves only the files that have changed since the last full backup. When you restore the files and folders, use the full backup set to restore all your files and then use the most recent incremental backup to restore the latest changes.

You may want to create a separate backup set just for your documents. The backup set for your documents will be smaller than the full system backup and will be faster to back up and restore. You can create a complete backup set to back up all your documents once a week. You can then create an incremental backup set to back up the documents you use each day. When creating your document backup set, do not forget the files that are saved automatically. For example, make sure to include the files or folders that contain the faxes and e-mail messages you receive.

Backup Strategies

Create and then strictly follow a backup schedule. Set regular dates and times to make your full system, incremental and document backups. Hard drive disasters always seem to happen right after you miss a scheduled backup. Simplify the backup process as much as possible. For example, your backup strategy can be as simple as making a copy of your valuable or important files on a floppy disk once a week.

BACKUP *Calendar*

Sun	Mon	Tue	Wed	Thu	Fri	Sat
1	2	3	4	5	6	7
8	9	10	11	12	13	14
15	16	17	18	19	20	21
22	23	24	25	26	27	28
29	30	31				Backup Schedule

Minimize your chances of losing important information by making at least two sets of backup copies. Keep one set near your computer and the second set in another location where it will not be affected by fire or theft. You should also alternate between two or more sets of backup copies. If today's backup set fails, you should be able to use yesterday's backup set to restore your work.

BACK UP FILES

Microsoft Backup helps you copy important information stored on your computer to floppy disks or tape cartridges for safekeeping.

To perform a backup, you must select the drives, folders and files you want to back up. The items you select to back up are grouped together in a file called a backup set.

When you have selected the backup set, Windows counts the number of items and determines the total size of the backup set. You can use this information to determine if you have enough disks or tapes to store the information.

If you are using disks to store the files, the disks must be

formatted before you start the backup.

By default, Backup compresses information so you can store more files on a disk. The amount a file compresses depends on the type of file it is, but you should be able to store an average of 2 MB of information on a high-density (1.44 MB) disk.

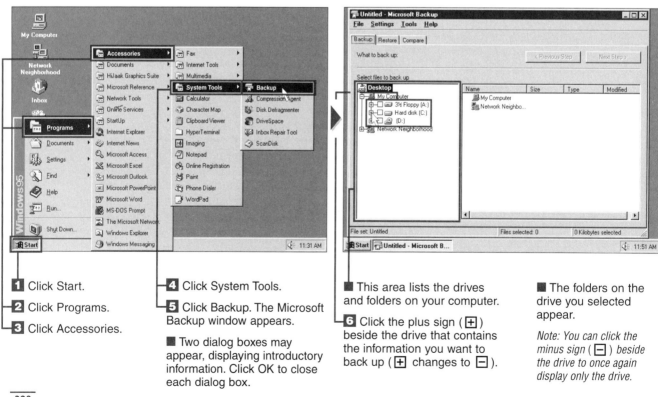

1 Click Start.

2 Click Programs.

3 Click Accessories.

4 Click System Tools.

5 Click Backup. The Microsoft Backup window appears.

■ Two dialog boxes may appear, displaying introductory information. Click OK to close each dialog box.

■ This area lists the drives and folders on your computer.

6 Click the plus sign (⊞) beside the drive that contains the information you want to back up (⊞ changes to ⊟).

■ The folders on the drive you selected appear.

Note: You can click the minus sign (⊟) beside the drive to once again display only the drive.

Why isn't Backup listed on my Start menu?

Microsoft Backup may not be installed on your computer. Backup is located in the Disk Tools group on the Windows 95 CD-ROM disc. To install Windows components, see page 580.

When I start Backup, I see a dialog box saying there is something wrong with my tape drive. What should I do?

If you are not using a tape drive, you can ignore the dialog box. Click OK and continue with the backup. If you are using a tape drive, Backup does not recognize your tape drive. The dialog box that appears provides some helpful suggestions.

Can I back up all the items in a folder without selecting the files and folders one at a time?

To select all the contents of a folder at once, click the minus sign (☐) beside the folder containing the items you want to back up. Click the box beside the folder (☐ changes to ✔). A check mark in a white box (✔) means that all the files and folders within the folder are selected. A check mark in a gray box (✔) means that some items in the folder are not selected.

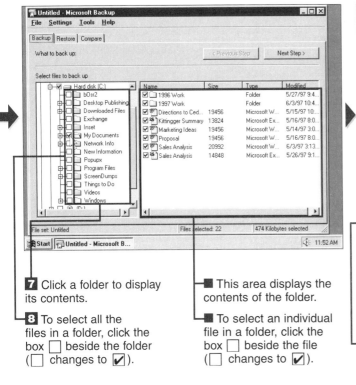

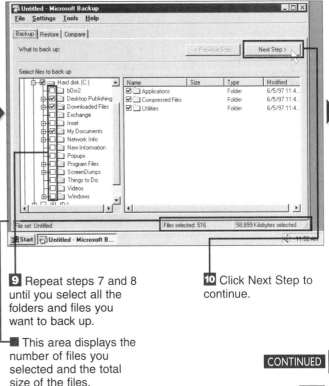

7 Click a folder to display its contents.

8 To select all the files in a folder, click the box ☐ beside the folder (☐ changes to ✔).

■ This area displays the contents of the folder.

■ To select an individual file in a folder, click the box ☐ beside the file (☐ changes to ✔).

9 Repeat steps 7 and 8 until you select all the folders and files you want to back up.

■ This area displays the number of files you selected and the total size of the files.

10 Click Next Step to continue.

CONTINUED ▶

BACK UP FILES CONTINUED

When you back up files, you must decide where you want to save the backup set. You can save the backup set on any of your computer's drives, including a hard drive, floppy drive, tape drive, removable drive or network drive.

You must name the backup set so you can find your files when you need them. It is best to select a name that describes the contents of your backup set and the date you backed up the files. The name can be about 40 characters long including spaces.

You can select a password to protect your files from unauthorized access. A password prevents people from opening your backup set and reviewing your information. Store your password carefully. If you forget your password, you will not be able to restore the files in your backup set.

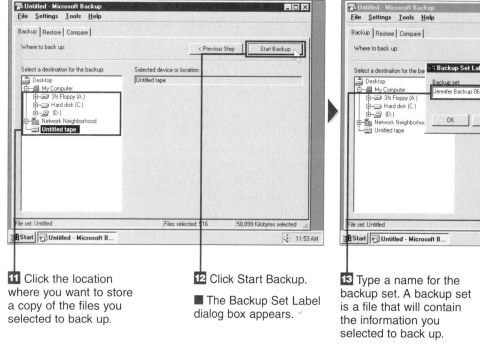
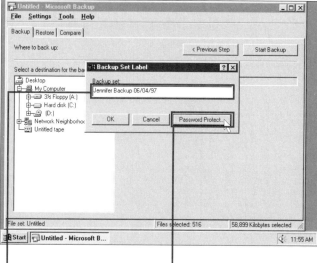

11 Click the location where you want to store a copy of the files you selected to back up.

12 Click Start Backup.

■ The Backup Set Label dialog box appears.

13 Type a name for the backup set. A backup set is a file that will contain the information you selected to back up.

14 Click Password Protect if you want to assign a password to your backup set.

Note: If you do not want to assign a password, skip to step 17.

■ The Password Protect Backup Set dialog box appears.

TIPS

Can I use a disk that already contains files?

Windows will add the backup file to a disk without erasing any of the other files on the disk. If there is very little or no free space on the disk, Windows will warn you that the disk contains data before erasing all of the files.

Backup warned me that my disk contains data. How can I check the contents of the disk?

You can use the Start menu to open an Explorer window. You can then check the contents of the disk. Before continuing, see page 58.

Can I use Backup to copy a large file to another computer?

If you want to transfer a file to another computer, but the file is too large to fit on a single floppy disk, you can use Backup to copy the file on more than one disk. Microsoft Backup will tell you when another disk is required. You can restore the backed up file onto another computer running Windows 95. For information on restoring files, see page 336.

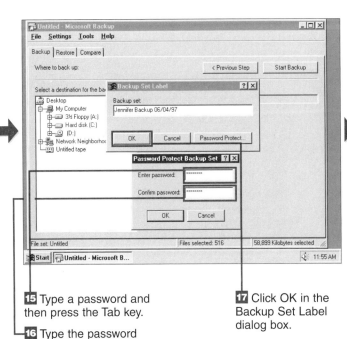

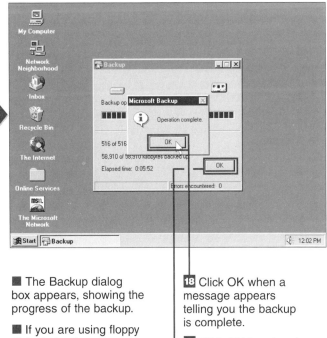

15 Type a password and then press the Tab key.

16 Type the password again to confirm the password and then press the Enter key.

17 Click OK in the Backup Set Label dialog box.

■ The Backup dialog box appears, showing the progress of the backup.

■ If you are using floppy disks to back up the information, a message will appear if you need to insert another disk.

18 Click OK when a message appears telling you the backup is complete.

19 Click OK to return to the Microsoft Backup window.

SAVE FILE SETS

You can create a file set to make your backups as fast and easy as possible. A file set is a file that contains information about the folders and files you want to back up, as well as the options you want to use when you back up these files.

When you want to back up your files, you do not have to select every folder and file separately.

You can start the file set to have Microsoft Backup select the items you want to back up, with all the options you specified.

You may find it useful to save two versions of a backup file set. One version will be the full backup option and the other will be the incremental option.

Windows includes a Full System Backup file set, which can be used to back up everything your computer needs to run properly. You should do a full system backup on a regular basis, depending on how much information has been changed.

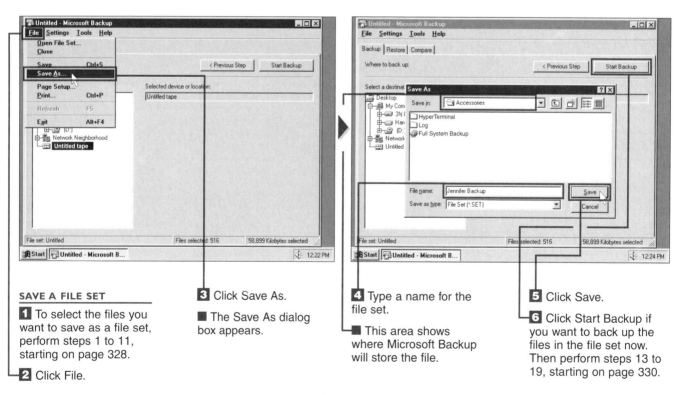

SAVE A FILE SET

1 To select the files you want to save as a file set, perform steps 1 to 11, starting on page 328.

2 Click File.

3 Click Save As.

■ The Save As dialog box appears.

4 Type a name for the file set.

■ This area shows where Microsoft Backup will store the file.

5 Click Save.

6 Click Start Backup if you want to back up the files in the file set now. Then perform steps 13 to 19, starting on page 330.

TIPS

Why did I get an error message after the backup was completed?

You can have Microsoft Backup compare the backed up files to the original files and report any inconsistencies. If you have selected this option and you change or create files during the backup, you may see an error message. For information on changing Backup options, see page 340.

Is there a faster way to back up a file set?

You can double-click a backup file set to open the Backup program and back up your files. If the Backup program is already open on your computer, double-clicking the file set will not work.

How do I make sure new documents are included in a file set?

When you back up a file set, Microsoft Backup backs up all the folders and files you selected. If a folder is selected with a check mark in a white box (✔), all the files and folders in that folder will be included in the backup, even if they did not exist when you created the file set.

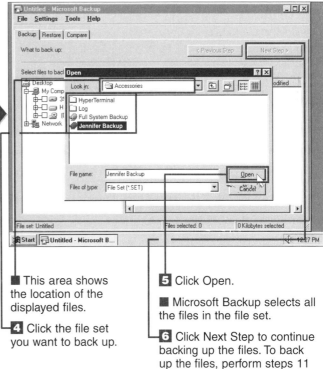

OPEN A FILE SET

1 To start Microsoft Backup, perform steps 1 to 5 on page 328.

2 Click File.

3 Click Open File Set.

■ The Open dialog box appears.

■ This area shows the location of the displayed files.

4 Click the file set you want to back up.

5 Click Open.

■ Microsoft Backup selects all the files in the file set.

6 Click Next Step to continue backing up the files. To back up the files, perform steps 11 to 19, starting on page 330.

VERIFY BACKUP FILES

You can compare the files in the backup set to the original files on your computer to make sure that all of the files on your computer were backed up correctly. When you verify a backup set, you make sure that the backup set is usable and matches your original files.

You can have Microsoft Backup compare files any time you want to verify the accuracy of a backup set. You can verify your entire backup set or only certain files. You should compare backup files to the original files whenever you use a new disk or tape to store a backup set.

If you created a password for the backup set you want to verify, you must enter the password before you begin comparing the files.

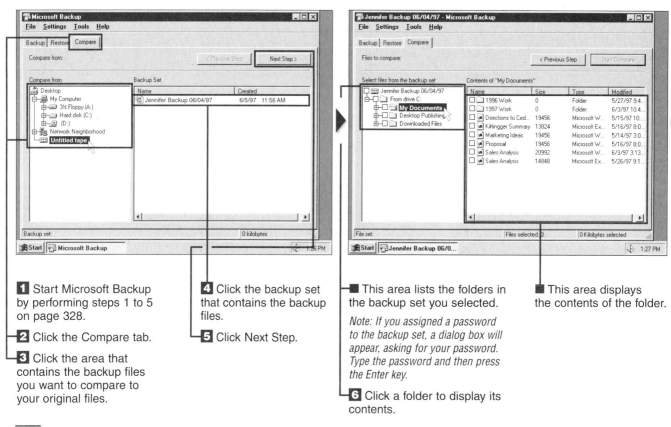

■1 Start Microsoft Backup by performing steps 1 to 5 on page 328.

■2 Click the Compare tab.

■3 Click the area that contains the backup files you want to compare to your original files.

■4 Click the backup set that contains the backup files.

■5 Click Next Step.

■ This area lists the folders in the backup set you selected.

Note: If you assigned a password to the backup set, a dialog box will appear, asking for your password. Type the password and then press the Enter key.

■6 Click a folder to display its contents.

■ This area displays the contents of the folder.

TIPS

What should I do if an error is found?

You can perform another backup so that all of the latest files are included in the backup set.

Can I find out if a file on my computer has been changed since the last backup?

You can compare a single file on your computer to the same file in the backup set. Verifying the backup file will tell you if the file on your computer has changed since the backup set was created.

When I verify my backup set, will an error be found?

The possibility of an error occurring in your backup set is low. When errors do occur, they are usually caused by faulty disks or tapes. You should replace your backup disks or tapes as often as necessary to reduce the chance of errors. If you changed files on your computer between the time the backup set was created and when the comparison was done, you can expect to find some errors.

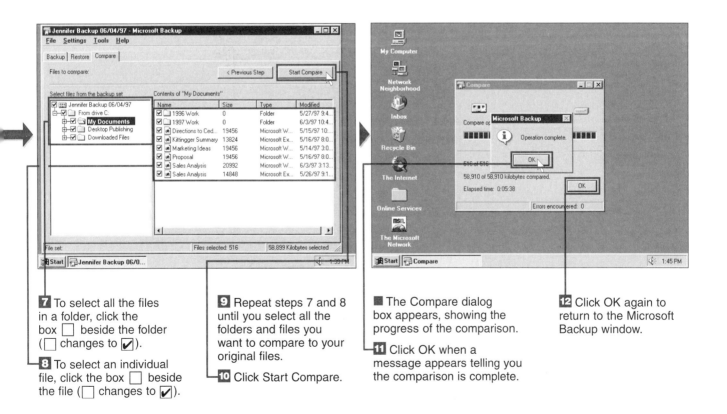

7 To select all the files in a folder, click the box ☐ beside the folder (☐ changes to ☑).

8 To select an individual file, click the box ☐ beside the file (☐ changes to ☑).

9 Repeat steps 7 and 8 until you select all the folders and files you want to compare to your original files.

10 Click Start Compare.

■ The Compare dialog box appears, showing the progress of the comparison.

11 Click OK when a message appears telling you the comparison is complete.

12 Click OK again to return to the Microsoft Backup window.

RESTORE FILES

I f files on your computer are lost or damaged, you can use the backup set to restore the files. A backup set contains the files and folders you copied from your computer when you performed a backup.

You will need to locate the backup disks, tapes or files you created. If you created both full and incremental backup sets,

you will need to use the most recent full backup and the most recent incremental backup to restore all your files.

If your backup set is stored on more than one floppy disk or tape, you must insert the last disk or tape first.

If you created a password for your backup set, you must

enter the password before you can begin restoring files.

If you do not need to restore all the files in a backup set, you can select only the files you want to restore.

When you restore files, they are restored to their original location on your computer.

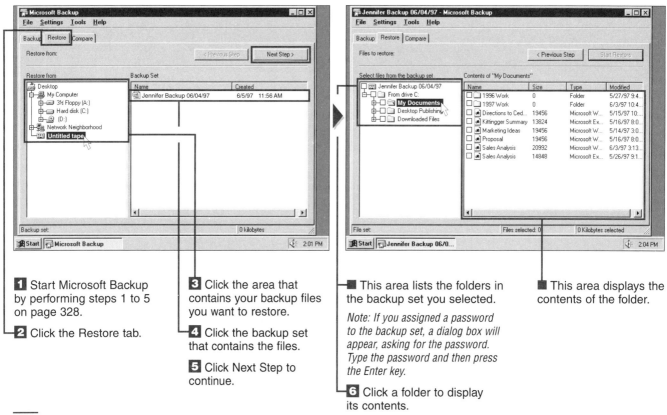

■1 Start Microsoft Backup by performing steps 1 to 5 on page 328.

■2 Click the Restore tab.

■3 Click the area that contains your backup files you want to restore.

■4 Click the backup set that contains the files.

■5 Click Next Step to continue.

■ This area lists the folders in the backup set you selected.

Note: If you assigned a password to the backup set, a dialog box will appear, asking for the password. Type the password and then press the Enter key.

■6 Click a folder to display its contents.

■ This area displays the contents of the folder.

Can I restore my files if I cannot find the last disk?

You can restore the files and folders contained on the disks you can find.

How do I restore a folder?

When you restore one or more files from a folder, Microsoft Backup will recreate the folder in its original location on your computer.

Can I use Microsoft Backup to transfer all of my files and programs to another computer?

You can use the full system backup to transfer all of your files and programs to another computer that has Windows 95 and Microsoft Backup installed. After you have restored the full system backup, you must restart the computer. The full system backup does not restore your computer's hardware settings.

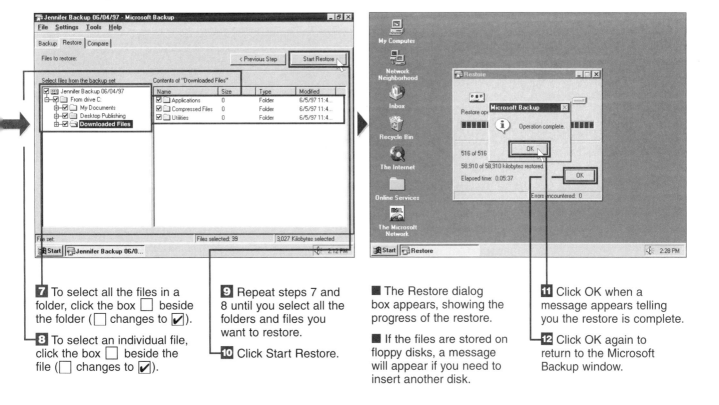

7 To select all the files in a folder, click the box ☐ beside the folder (☐ changes to ✔).

8 To select an individual file, click the box ☐ beside the file (☐ changes to ✔).

9 Repeat steps 7 and 8 until you select all the folders and files you want to restore.

10 Click Start Restore.

■ The Restore dialog box appears, showing the progress of the restore.

■ If the files are stored on floppy disks, a message will appear if you need to insert another disk.

11 Click OK when a message appears telling you the restore is complete.

12 Click OK again to return to the Microsoft Backup window.

BACK UP FILES
FROM THE DESKTOP

You can create a shortcut to a file set and place the shortcut icon on your desktop. A file set stores information about the files you want to back up.

You can use the shortcut to back up your file set. You can start a backup by double-clicking the file set shortcut icon.

The file set shortcut icon also helps remind you to perform the backup.

There are several options you can choose to customize the way Microsoft Backup works. You can have Microsoft Backup start, perform the backup and close in the background, while you

continue to work on your computer.

You can work uninterrupted while Microsoft Backup is running, unless you are backing up files onto a device that requires you to change disks or tapes. Microsoft Backup will remind you each time it needs a new disk or tape.

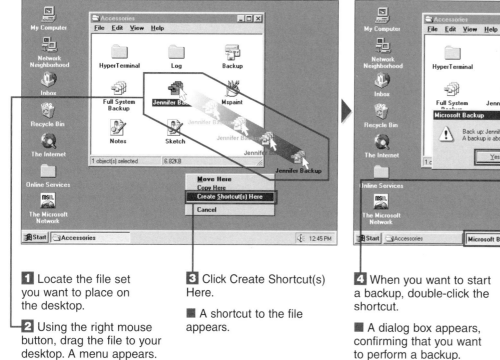

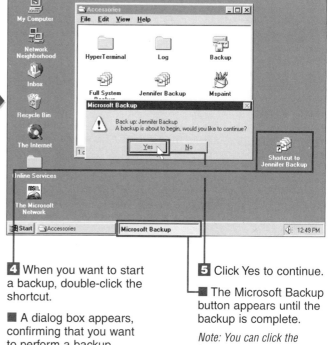

1 Locate the file set you want to place on the desktop.

2 Using the right mouse button, drag the file to your desktop. A menu appears.

3 Click Create Shortcut(s) Here.

■ A shortcut to the file appears.

4 When you want to start a backup, double-click the shortcut.

■ A dialog box appears, confirming that you want to perform a backup.

5 Click Yes to continue.

■ The Microsoft Backup button appears until the backup is complete.

Note: You can click the button at any time to view the status of the backup.

TIPS

Can I save the backup options I specify with the file set?

You can save the options you specify with the file set so the options will be used every time your file set is backed up. From the File menu, click the Save command after you specify the options you want to use and select a drive to back up the files to.

Why doesn't Microsoft Backup start when I double-click the file set shortcut icon?

You cannot double-click a file set shortcut icon to start a backup when Microsoft Backup is already open.

Where can I find my file sets?

File sets are stored in the c:\program files\accessories folder. In the Find dialog box, select the Advanced tab to search for file sets. File sets have the .set extension. To find files, see page 76.

Can I stop a backup?

Click the Microsoft Backup button on the taskbar. A dialog box appears, displaying the status of the backup and the Cancel button. Click Cancel and then click Yes in the confirmation box to stop the backup.

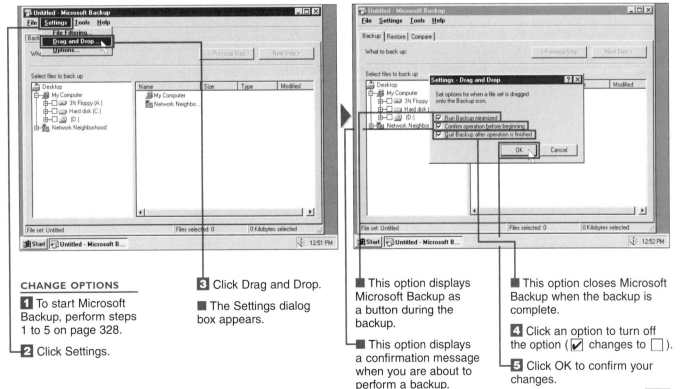

CHANGE OPTIONS

1 To start Microsoft Backup, perform steps 1 to 5 on page 328.

2 Click Settings.

3 Click Drag and Drop.

■ The Settings dialog box appears.

■ This option displays Microsoft Backup as a button during the backup.

■ This option displays a confirmation message when you are about to perform a backup.

■ This option closes Microsoft Backup when the backup is complete.

4 Click an option to turn off the option (✔ changes to ☐).

5 Click OK to confirm your changes.

CHANGE BACKUP OPTIONS

Microsoft Backup offers several options you can change to simplify the backup process. The options you choose will be used every time you perform a backup.

You can choose from two types of backup. Full backups save all selected files. Incremental backups save files that have changed since the last full backup.

Windows can verify the accuracy of a backup once the backup is complete. If you select this option, Windows will compare the files in the backup with the original files to ensure that they are identical.

You can select the data compression option to reduce the size of the backup file so it takes up less space.

If you save the backup file on a tape drive, you can choose to

have Windows format new tapes when necessary.

Windows can also erase used tapes or floppy disks. This option deletes any existing information on the tape or disk before the backup file is saved. If you choose not to erase your tapes or disks, the new backup file will be placed on the tape or disk after the existing data.

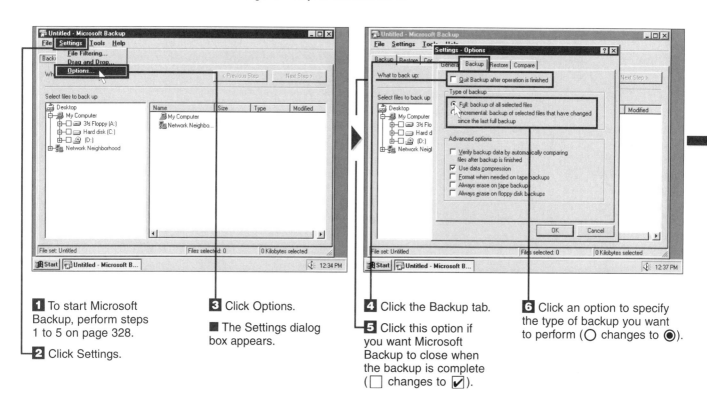

1 To start Microsoft Backup, perform steps 1 to 5 on page 328.

2 Click Settings.

3 Click Options.

■ The Settings dialog box appears.

4 Click the Backup tab.

5 Click this option if you want Microsoft Backup to close when the backup is complete (☐ changes to ✔).

6 Click an option to specify the type of backup you want to perform (○ changes to ◉).

Can I create both a full and incremental backup for the same set of files?

Yes, this is highly recommended. If you perform full and incremental backups on the same file set, select the appropriate type of backup but keep all other options identical.

Why does my incremental backup contain all the files instead of just the ones that have changed?

You must do a full backup before you can do an incremental backup. The incremental backup will then save all files that have changed since the last full backup. If you have not done a full backup first, the incremental backup will contain all the files.

Can I create a compressed backup file on my hard drive to archive old documents?

This process allows you to keep the documents close at hand but use less disk space. Make sure the data compression option is turned on. Copy the files you want to archive into a separate folder and then create a backup from the folder. Compare the files and then delete them from the original location.

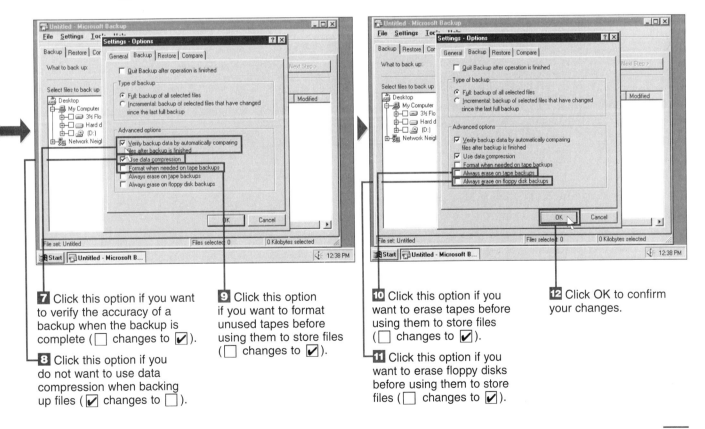

7 Click this option if you want to verify the accuracy of a backup when the backup is complete (☐ changes to ✔).

8 Click this option if you do not want to use data compression when backing up files (✔ changes to ☐).

9 Click this option if you want to format unused tapes before using them to store files (☐ changes to ✔).

10 Click this option if you want to erase tapes before using them to store files (☐ changes to ✔).

11 Click this option if you want to erase floppy disks before using them to store files (☐ changes to ✔).

12 Click OK to confirm your changes.

CHANGE RESTORE OPTIONS

You can change the way Microsoft Backup restores files. The settings you select will be used every time you restore files.

You can have Microsoft Backup close when it has finished restoring your files.

You can specify whether you want to place the restored files in the same location or in an alternate location. The alternate location can be another drive or another folder on the current drive. When you restore files to an alternate location, you can also have all your files restored to a single directory. The original folders are not recreated when files are restored to a single directory.

You can tell Microsoft Backup what to do when it finds a file in the backup set with the same name as a file already on your computer. When this type of conflict occurs, you can choose to never overwrite files, overwrite only if the file on your computer is older than the file in the backup set, or always overwrite the files on your computer. If you choose to always overwrite files, you can have Microsoft Backup display a message before a file is overwritten.

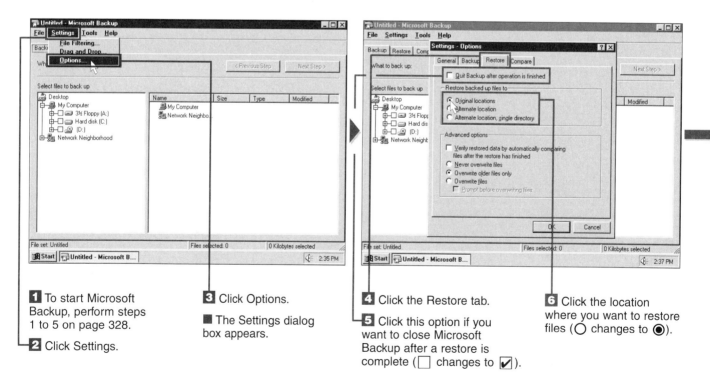

1 To start Microsoft Backup, perform steps 1 to 5 on page 328.

2 Click Settings.

3 Click Options.

■ The Settings dialog box appears.

4 Click the Restore tab.

5 Click this option if you want to close Microsoft Backup after a restore is complete (☐ changes to ✔).

6 Click the location where you want to restore files (○ changes to ◉).

How can I restore an older file from the backup set and keep the newer file on my hard drive?

You can rename the newer file on your hard drive so there will not be a conflict with the restored file.

Is it necessary to do a comparison after files are restored?

Although it is not necessary, comparing the files on your computer against the files in the backup set allows you to verify that all of your files were restored correctly.

Why would I want to restore files to an alternate location?

You can restore files to an alternate location to avoid conflicts between the files in the backup set and the files on a computer. You can create a new folder and restore files to the folder to ensure your files are restored without conflict.

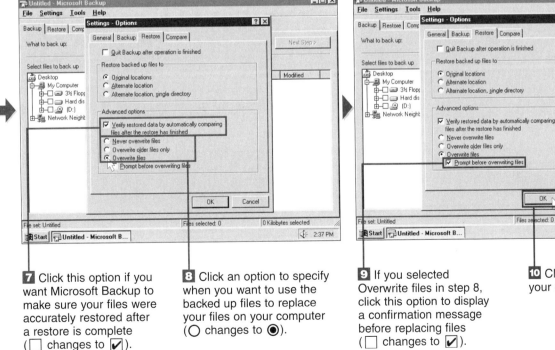

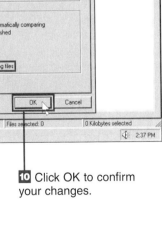

7 Click this option if you want Microsoft Backup to make sure your files were accurately restored after a restore is complete (☐ changes to ✓).

8 Click an option to specify when you want to use the backed up files to replace your files on your computer (○ changes to ◉).

9 If you selected Overwrite files in step 8, click this option to display a confirmation message before replacing files (☐ changes to ✓).

10 Click OK to confirm your changes.

EXCLUDE FILES OF A SPECIFIC TYPE OR DATE

You can tell Microsoft Backup to exclude certain folders and files when a backup is performed.

By excluding files from a backup, you reduce the time it will take to perform the backup. The size of the backup set will be smaller, so the number of disks required

to store the backup set will also be reduced.

You can specify two dates and exclude any files that were created between the dates. This is useful if you want to back up files created before a certain date for archive purposes. Specifying dates also allows you to back up files after

a certain date and then add the files to a full system backup set.

You can exclude certain types of files that you do not need to back up. For example, you may wish to exclude program files with the .exe and .dll extensions because you can restore them from the original disks or CD-ROM disc.

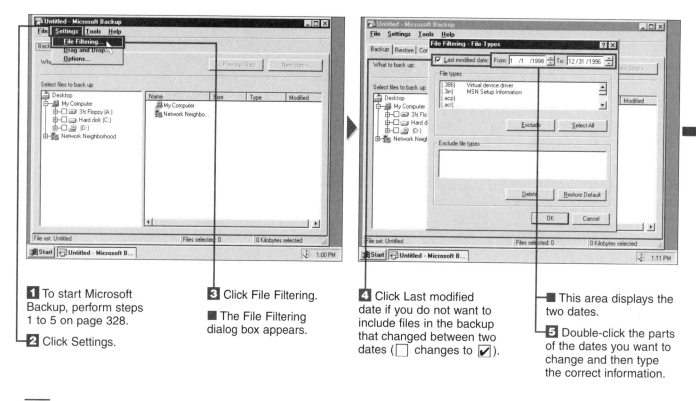

1 To start Microsoft Backup, perform steps 1 to 5 on page 328.

2 Click Settings.

3 Click File Filtering.

■ The File Filtering dialog box appears.

4 Click Last modified date if you do not want to include files in the backup that changed between two dates (☐ changes to ☑).

■ This area displays the two dates.

5 Double-click the parts of the dates you want to change and then type the correct information.

How do I exclude all but a few file types from the backup?

Click the Select All button and then click the Exclude button. In the Exclude file types list, select the file types you want to back up and then click the Delete button.

How can I restore all the excluded file types?

You can restore all of the excluded file types by clicking the Restore Default button. To stop excluding files by date, click the Last modified date option (☑ changes to ☐). Date and file type settings are reset each time you start Microsoft Backup.

Why aren't there any files displayed on the Backup tab?

Excluded files do not appear on the Backup tab. If you have excluded files by date, you should check to make sure that you have not specified dates that exclude all files.

Why are the wrong files excluded when I exclude files by date?

When excluding files by date, it is important to make sure your computer's clock is set correctly. To change the date or time in your computer, see page 198.

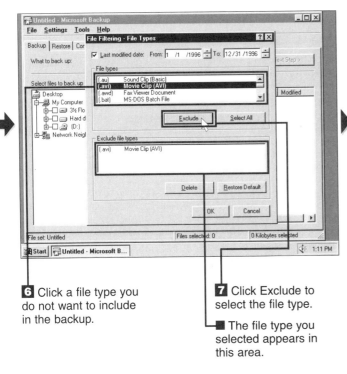

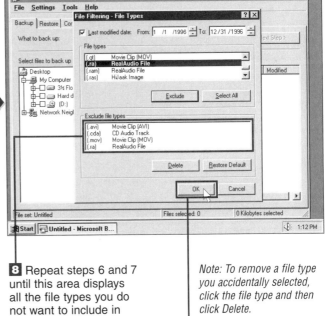

6 Click a file type you do not want to include in the backup.

7 Click Exclude to select the file type.

■ The file type you selected appears in this area.

8 Repeat steps 6 and 7 until this area displays all the file types you do not want to include in the backup.

Note: To remove a file type you accidentally selected, click the file type and then click Delete.

9 Click OK to confirm your changes.

ERASE TAPES

When you no longer need the information stored on a backup tape, you can erase the tape. Erasing a tape removes all the backup sets from the tape. You cannot choose to remove only the backup sets you no longer need.

When you erase a tape, only the directory information from the

beginning of the tape is removed. You do not actually erase the whole tape. The information on the tape cannot be read when the directory information is removed, so you can use the tape as if it were blank.

Tapes wear out and should be replaced regularly. You should replace a tape when it starts to

produce errors when Backup compares files. When erasing a tape, Windows does not check the tape for damage or possible problems.

You should store tapes away from monitors and speakers. The electromagnetic radiation (EMR) from a monitor can damage information on the tape.

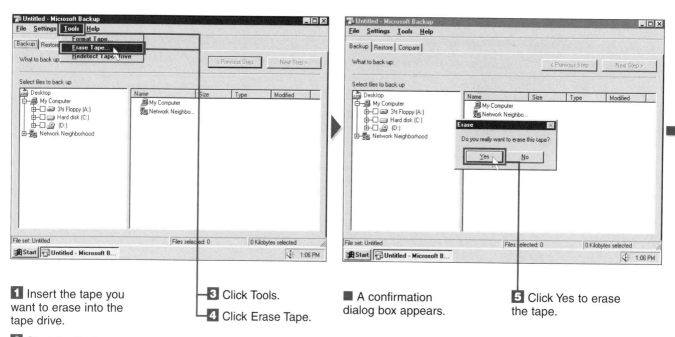

1 Insert the tape you want to erase into the tape drive.

2 Start the Backup program by performing steps 1 to 5 on page 328.

3 Click Tools.

4 Click Erase Tape.

■ A confirmation dialog box appears.

5 Click Yes to erase the tape.

Can I automatically erase a tape before I back up files?

You can automatically erase a tape before backing up your files. In the Backup window, choose the Settings menu. Select Options and then select the Backup tab. Click the Always erase on tape backups option (☐ changes to ✔).

How can I make the Erase Tape option available?

From the Tools menu, select Redetect Tape Drive if the option is not available. This may allow Backup to detect the tape drive. A dialog box may appear with some other helpful suggestions.

How do I format a tape before I use it?

Formatting prepares a tape for use and checks the tape for damage. Most backup tapes are sold already formatted, so this process is usually not necessary. From the Tools menu, select Format Tape when you do have to format a tape. Type a name for the tape and click OK.

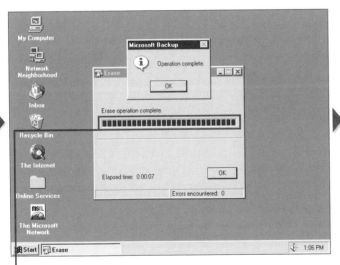

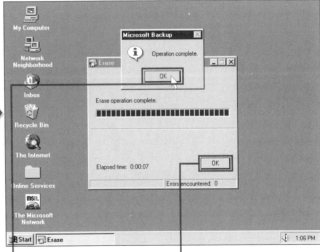

■ This area displays the progress of the erase procedure.

■ A dialog box appears when the erase procedure is complete.

6 Click OK to close the dialog box.

7 Click OK in the Erase window to return to the Microsoft Backup window.

CONNECT TO OTHER COMPUTERS

19) PORTABLE COMPUTERS

INSTALL A MODEM

You can install a modem on your computer. When installing a modem, Windows asks you a series of questions and then sets up the modem according to the information you provide.

A modem is a device that allows computers to exchange information using telephone lines. A modem allows you to connect to the

Internet, send and receive e-mail messages and faxes as well as exchange information with another computer.

A modem translates computer information into a form that can transmit over phone lines. The receiving modem translates the information it receives back into a form the computer can understand.

There are two types of modems. An external modem attaches to a computer using a cable. Many people use external modems because they are more portable and are easier to fix when problems develop. An internal modem is installed inside a computer. Internal modems are less expensive than external modems. Both types of modems provide the same features.

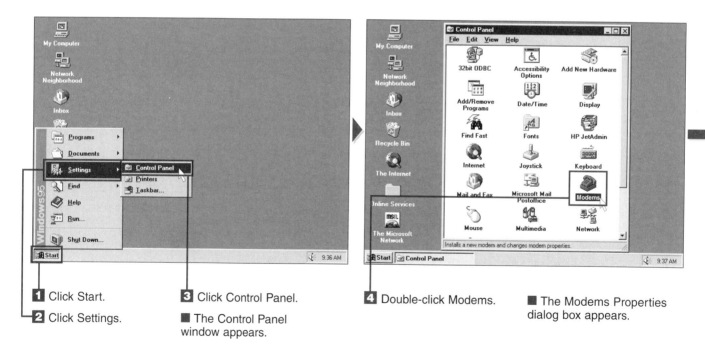

1 Click Start.

2 Click Settings.

3 Click Control Panel.

■ The Control Panel window appears.

4 Double-click Modems.

■ The Modems Properties dialog box appears.

CONNECT TO OTHER COMPUTERS

Can I install more than one modem?

Yes. Windows allows you to install more than one modem on your computer. Most computers have only one modem installed.

What speed should my modem be?

The types of information your modem will send and receive should determine what modem speed you require. A slow modem, such as a 14.4 Kb/s modem, may be suitable for transferring e-mail messages to a computer at work, but it may be too slow if it were used for transferring large files.

Can I have Windows automatically detect my modem?

Windows may be able to automatically detect your modem and install the appropriate software that enables you to use the modem. Follow the procedure shown below, but do not select the Don't detect my modem option in step 6. Windows may not be able to automatically detect some modems.

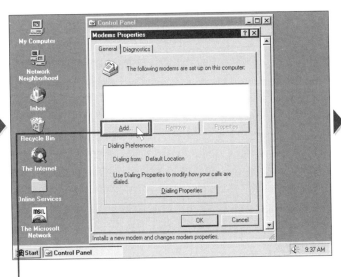

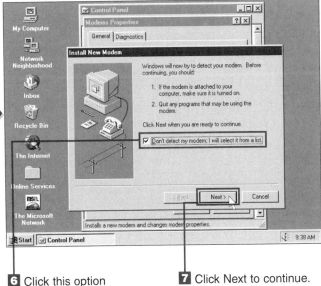

5 Click Add to add a new modem.

■ The Install New Modem wizard appears.

6 Click this option if you want to select your modem from a list (☐ changes to ☑).

7 Click Next to continue.

INSTALL A MODEM CONTINUED

When installing a modem, you must select the name of the manufacturer and the model of the modem you want to install.

Make sure you specify the correct modem type when installing a new modem, otherwise your modem may not work properly.

You must also tell Windows which port the modem will use. A port is a connector that allows instructions and data to flow between the computer and the modem. Most modems use a COM port. A COM port is another name for a computer's serial port. A computer usually has two COM ports, but some computers may have up to four COM ports.

An LPT port is commonly used to connect a printer to a computer. Some modems connect to a computer using an LPT port.

When you install a modem, Windows installs the necessary driver. A driver is a program that helps your computer communicate with the new modem. Windows comes with a driver for most modem models.

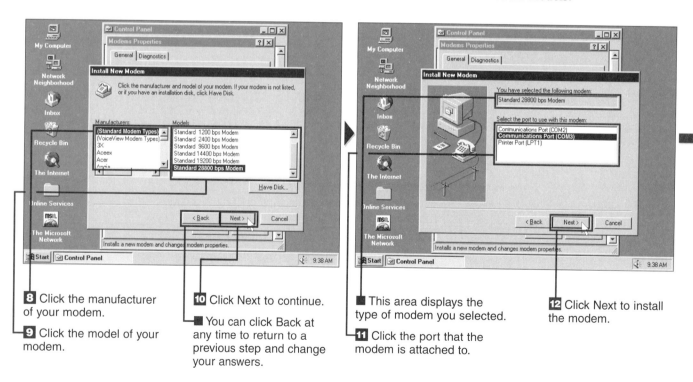

8 Click the manufacturer of your modem.

9 Click the model of your modem.

10 Click Next to continue.

■ You can click Back at any time to return to a previous step and change your answers.

■ This area displays the type of modem you selected.

11 Click the port that the modem is attached to.

12 Click Next to install the modem.

TIPS

How can I tell which model my modem is?

Check the documentation that came with the modem. You can also tell which modem model you are using by inspecting the modem. You may need to remove the cover of your computer to inspect an internal modem.

What should I do if Windows does not have the driver I need for my modem?

If Windows does not have the driver for your modem, you may have to obtain the driver from the manufacturer of the modem.

My modem is not on Windows' list of manufacturers and models. Which modem should I choose?

The documentation that came with your modem should contain information indicating that your modem is compatible with a similar model. If you are still unsure, click Standard Modem Types in the Manufacturers list and then click a modem in the Models list. Many options may not be available with the standard setting, but the modem should work.

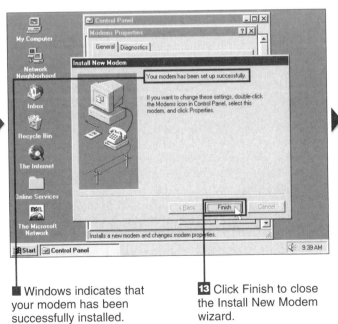

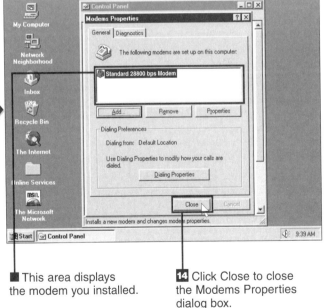

■ Windows indicates that your modem has been successfully installed.

13 Click Finish to close the Install New Modem wizard.

■ This area displays the modem you installed.

14 Click Close to close the Modems Properties dialog box.

CHANGE THE MODEM DIALING PROPERTIES

Y ou can change the dialing properties for your modem. Dialing properties are settings that determine how your modem will dial phone numbers. This is helpful when dialing out using a program such as HyperTerminal or when using

your modem to connect to an Internet Service Provider (ISP).

Windows sets up your modem dialing properties when you install Windows. These settings are named "Default Location". You can change the name to a more descriptive name.

When changing the modem dialing properties, you can tell Windows which area code and country you are calling from. Your modem may dial a different phone number, depending on whether you are making a local call or a long-distance call.

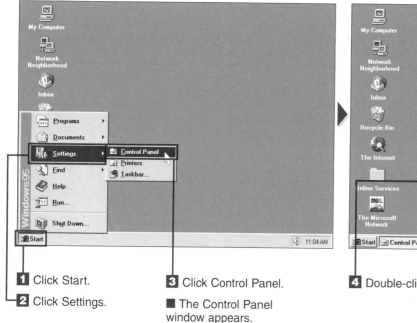

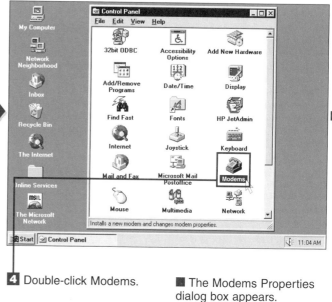

1 Click Start.

2 Click Settings.

3 Click Control Panel.

■ The Control Panel window appears.

4 Double-click Modems.

■ The Modems Properties dialog box appears.

TIPS

What name should I use for a set of dialing properties?

You should use a descriptive word or phrase when naming a set of dialing properties. For example, if you have a portable computer, you could name the set of dialing properties that you use when dialing from home "Home Office". You could name the dialing properties you use while you are traveling "Boston Hotel". A descriptive name can help avoid confusion if you have created several sets of dialing properties on your computer.

Can I set dialing properties for different locations?

Windows allows you to specify different dialing properties for each location where you plan to use your computer. For example, dialing from the office requires different dialing properties than does dialing from a hotel room. Click New in the Dialing Properties dialog box, type a name for the new location and then click OK. You can now enter the properties for the new location.

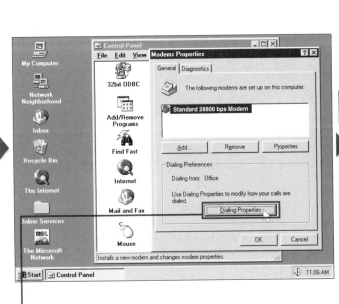

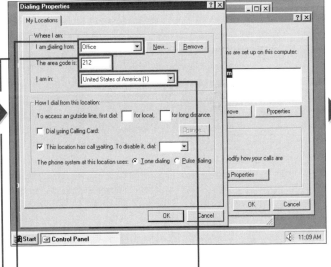

■ **5** Click Dialing Properties to change how your calls are dialed.

■ The Dialing Properties dialog box appears.

■ This area displays the name for the set of dialing properties currently displayed. You can click ▼ in this area to display the dialing properties for another location.

■ This area displays your area code. You can double-click this area to change this information.

■ This area displays your country. You can click this area to change this information.

CONTINUED ▶

CHANGE THE MODEM
DIALING PROPERTIES CONTINUED

When changing the modem dialing properties, you can specify any special numbers you use to dial local or long-distance numbers. This information is useful if you will be making calls from a hotel room and you must dial a number to get an outside line.

You can set up the modem to use a calling card. A calling card is a card that allows you to make long-distance telephone calls and have the charges billed to the owner of the calling card. Calling cards can also be used where toll calls are not permitted.

If you have the call waiting feature, you can have Windows automatically disable the feature when you use your modem. You should turn off the call waiting feature when using your modem, since this feature could disrupt the modem connection.

You can also specify whether you wish to use tone or pulse dialing. Tone dialing is the most common type of dialing used by phone companies.

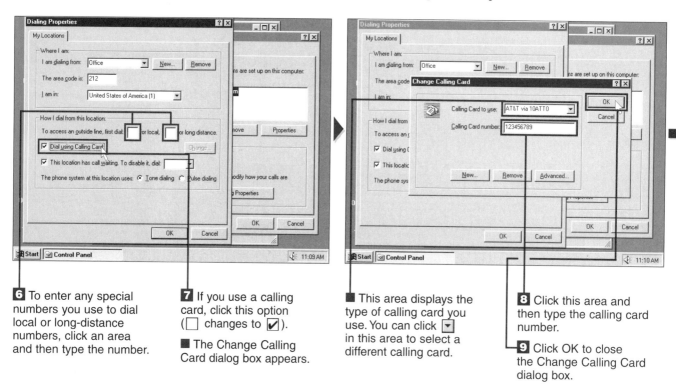

■6 To enter any special numbers you use to dial local or long-distance numbers, click an area and then type the number.

■7 If you use a calling card, click this option (☐ changes to ☑).

■ The Change Calling Card dialog box appears.

■ This area displays the type of calling card you use. You can click ▼ in this area to select a different calling card.

■8 Click this area and then type the calling card number.

■9 Click OK to close the Change Calling Card dialog box.

How do I choose the set of dialing properties I want to use?

When you use your modem to communicate with another computer, Windows often displays a dialog box. The dialog box displays a list of your sets of modem dialing properties. You can select the set of dialing properties you want to use.

How do I disable call waiting?

If you have call waiting, you can disable the feature by dialing a special code before you dial a phone number. You should check with your local phone company to find out what code you should use to disable call waiting. The most common code used to disable call waiting is *70.

Where can I get a calling card?

Most phone companies offer calling cards to their customers. There are many types of calling cards available. Some cards offer incentives, such as discount rates, to attract new customers. Many businesses and organizations use calling cards to track toll calls.

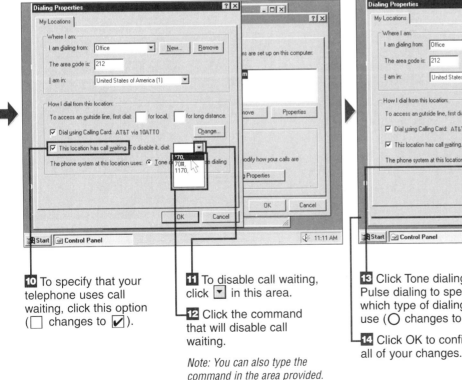

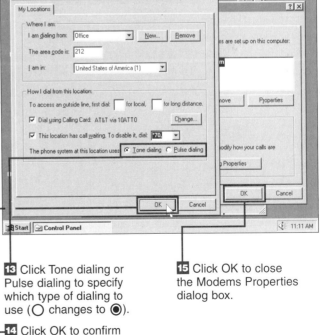

10 To specify that your telephone uses call waiting, click this option (□ changes to ✔).

11 To disable call waiting, click ▼ in this area.

12 Click the command that will disable call waiting.

Note: You can also type the command in the area provided.

13 Click Tone dialing or Pulse dialing to specify which type of dialing to use (○ changes to ⦿).

14 Click OK to confirm all of your changes.

15 Click OK to close the Modems Properties dialog box.

CHANGE THE MODEM SETTINGS

You can change the settings for a modem installed on your computer. Changing the settings can help a modem operate more efficiently.

When you installed a modem, you selected which port you wanted the modem to use. A port is a connector that allows instructions and data to flow between the computer and the modem. Most modems connect

to a COM port. A COM port is another name for a computer's serial port. Some modems connect to a computer using an LPT port.

Most modems have a speaker that lets you hear the modem as it dials and connects to another modem. If your modem has a speaker, you may be able to use the modem settings to adjust the speaker volume.

You can specify the maximum speed setting for your modem, which determines how fast your modem can send and receive information. The speed of a modem is measured in Kilobits per second (Kb/s). The maximum speed setting should match the fastest speed setting of your modem. Check your modem documentation to determine the modem's maximum speed.

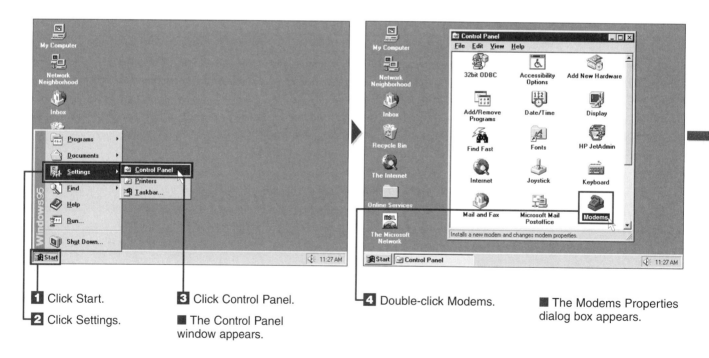

1 Click Start.

2 Click Settings.

3 Click Control Panel.

■ The Control Panel window appears.

4 Double-click Modems.

■ The Modems Properties dialog box appears.

Why are some modem settings not available?

The settings you can change depend on the type of modem you use. One modem may have different features and capabilities than another modem. Also, some settings may not be available if the correct driver is not installed on your computer. Installing the correct driver may allow you to change modem settings that are currently not available.

Why is my modem very slow even though I specified a high maximum speed?

Modems must use the same speed when exchanging information. A fast modem can connect to a slower modem, but they will transfer information at the slower speed.

How do I lock the modem speed?

Many phone lines are affected by interference that may result in slow transmission speeds. If you tell Windows to only connect at a specific speed, a connection will not be made with another modem until Windows can connect at the speed you specified. To lock the modem speed, click the Only connect at this speed option in the Properties dialog box.

CONNECT TO OTHER COMPUTERS

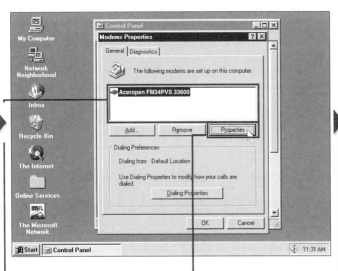

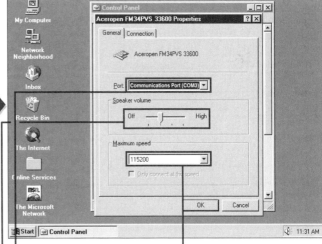

■ This area displays the modems installed on your computer.

5 Click the modem you want to change the settings for.

6 Click Properties.

■ The Properties dialog box appears.

7 This area displays the port your modem uses. You can click this area to change the port.

8 Drag the slider ( ) to raise or lower the speaker volume for your modem.

9 This area displays the maximum speed of your modem. You can click this area to change the maximum speed.

CHANGE THE MODEM SETTINGS
CONTINUED

You can change the connection settings for a modem. Changing a modem's connection settings helps the modem communicate with other modems.

Before two modems can exchange information, the modems must use the same data bit, parity bit and stop bit settings. You will see unreadable text on your screen if the settings are different.

The data bits represent the actual information exchanged between computers. The parity bits determine whether errors occur during the transfer of information. The stop bits indicate when each data bit begins and ends.

You can specify whether you want to wait for a dial tone before the modem starts dialing. You can also tell Windows how long you

want to wait before canceling or disconnecting a call. Having Windows disconnect calls when your modem is idle for a period of time can help prevent the accumulation of online charges.

Most modems are already set up to use the most common options, so it is unlikely that you will have to change the connection settings for your modem.

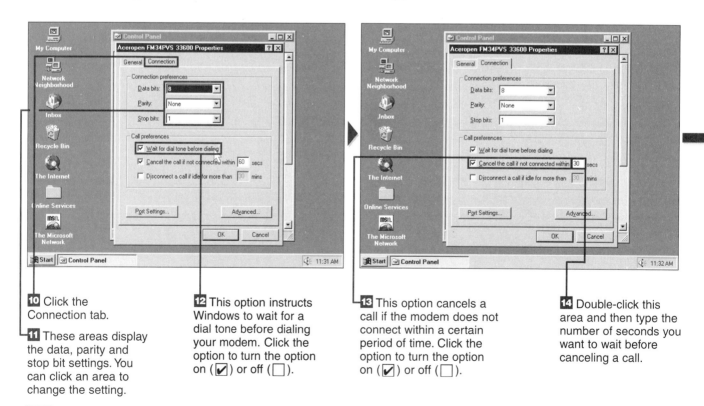

■10 Click the Connection tab.

■11 These areas display the data, parity and stop bit settings. You can click an area to change the setting.

■12 This option instructs Windows to wait for a dial tone before dialing your modem. Click the option to turn the option on (☑) or off (☐).

■13 This option cancels a call if the modem does not connect within a certain period of time. Click the option to turn the option on (☑) or off (☐).

■14 Double-click this area and then type the number of seconds you want to wait before canceling a call.

TIPS

What are the most common bit settings?

Before computers can communicate with each other, they must be set to use the same number of data, parity and stop bits. The most common settings are 8 data bits, no parity bits and 1 stop bit.

Why is my call not connecting?

There are many reasons that a call may not connect. Problems sometimes occur with the phone system or the other modem may not be set to answer calls. Usually 60 seconds is an adequate length of time to wait before disconnecting from an uncompleted call.

Why should my modem wait for a dial tone before dialing?

In many office buildings that use sophisticated phone systems, your modem may not receive a dial tone as soon as it connects to the phone system. Having your modem wait for a dial tone before dialing helps ensure it will be able to dial the number.

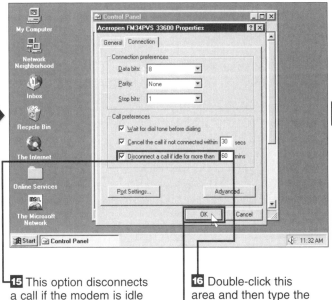

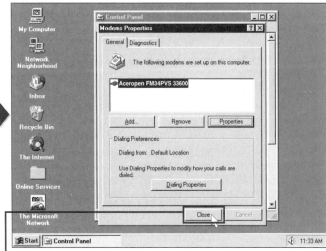

15 This option disconnects a call if the modem is idle for a certain period of time. Click the option to turn the option on (☑) or off (☐).

16 Double-click this area and then type the number of minutes you want to wait before disconnecting a call.

17 Click OK to confirm all of your changes.

18 Click Close to close the Modems Properties dialog box.

CHANGE THE ADVANCED MODEM SETTINGS

Windows allows you to change several advanced settings for a modem. Changing the advanced settings can help a modem operate more efficiently and exchange information faster.

You may need to adjust the advanced settings for your modem if you are experiencing problems while using the modem. For example, if you have trouble

connecting to other computers or you are losing information when transferring data using your modem, you can adjust the advanced settings to attempt to fix the problem.

The hardware and software you use will determine which advanced settings you must change. When most modems are installed, the advanced settings are properly set for the modem.

You can adjust the error control and compression settings. Error control settings let you control how Windows checks for errors when transmitting information. Compression is the process of squeezing data to speed the transfer of information between two computers. If your modem supports error control and can compress data, you should leave these options on.

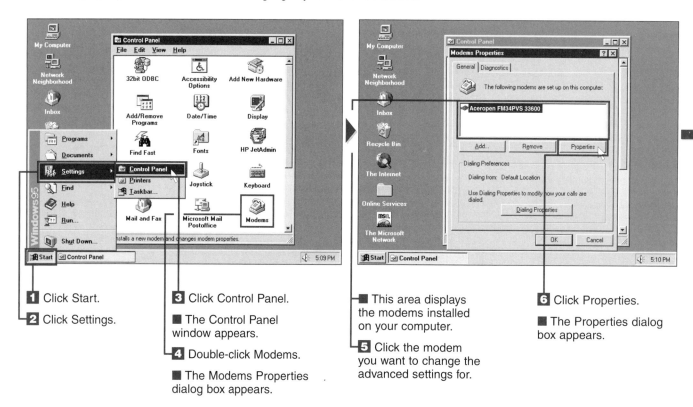

1 Click Start.

2 Click Settings.

3 Click Control Panel.

■ The Control Panel window appears.

4 Double-click Modems.

■ The Modems Properties dialog box appears.

■ This area displays the modems installed on your computer.

5 Click the modem you want to change the advanced settings for.

6 Click Properties.

■ The Properties dialog box appears.

Why are some advanced settings not available for my modem?

The advanced settings you can change depend on the model and type of modem you are using. Settings that cannot be adjusted have a dimmed appearance in the Advanced Connection Settings dialog box.

What does the cellular protocol do?

Some modems, often those in portable computers, can use cellular telephones to communicate with other modems. Because the cellular phone system is prone to errors, special error correction settings are needed when information is being transferred. If you have a cellular modem in your computer, you should turn on the cellular protocol option.

Why does the modem I want to change the advanced settings for not appear in the list of modems?

You may be using an older communications program that was originally intended to operate using MS-DOS. Your modem may not have been set up for Windows 95. If you want to be able to adjust the advanced settings, you must first set up the modem so the device can communicate with Windows 95. To install a modem, see page 350.

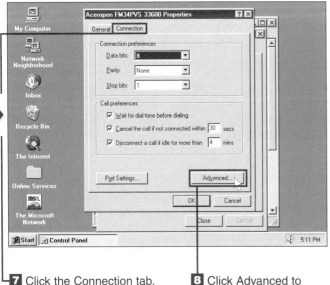

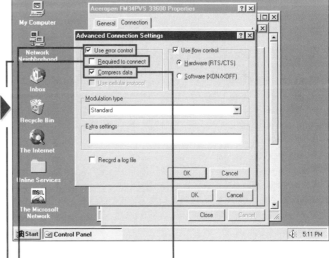

7 Click the Connection tab.

8 Click Advanced to display the advanced modem settings.

■ The Advanced Connection Settings dialog box appears.

■ This option instructs your modem to use error control to make your connections more reliable.

■ This option instructs your modem to connect to other computers only if the connections are reliable.

■ This option instructs your modem to compress data to increase the speed that information transfers.

9 You can click an option to turn the option on (☑) or off (☐).

CONTINUED ▶

CHANGE THE ADVANCED
MODEM SETTINGS CONTINUED

You can change the advanced settings for a modem to adjust the performance of the modem.

The flow control settings determine how data transfers between a computer and the modem. Most modems use hardware flow control.

You can choose a modulation type, which refers to the signals sent between modems. Both computers must use the same type of modulation to successfully exchange information. Most modems use standard modulation. It is unlikely that you will have to change the modulation settings.

You can use extra settings to send special commands to a modem before it starts communicating with another modem. For example, you may be able to type ATM0 to turn the modem speaker off. These extra settings are often referred to as an initialization string. Your modem's manual will explain which extra settings, if any, you can use with your modem.

You can also have Windows keep track of all your modem activities in a log file.

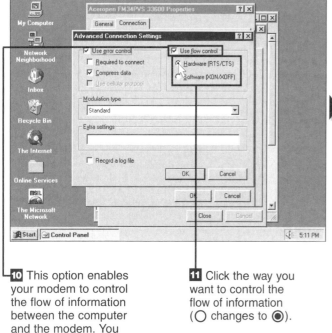

■10 This option enables your modem to control the flow of information between the computer and the modem. You can click this option to turn the option on (☑) or off (☐).

■11 Click the way you want to control the flow of information (○ changes to ⦿).

■12 This area displays the type of signals sent between modems. You can click this area to change the modulation type to match the modem of the computer you are connecting to.

■13 You can type additional settings in this area that you want the modem to use.

V

TIPS

When would I use extra settings?

Some software programs, such as games that let you play against other opponents, require you to use extra settings before you can correctly connect to another computer.

How can I view the log file?

The log file is located in the Windows folder on your hard drive and is called "ModemLog.txt". You can use a text editor such as Notepad to view the log file.

Why should I create a log file?

A log file can help you keep track of the time you spend connected to other computers. You can use the log to monitor charges you acquire from dialing toll calls or from dialing in to your Internet service provider. The log can also help you fix problems with your modem by showing you which commands are causing errors to occur.

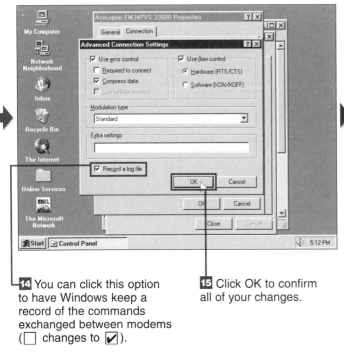

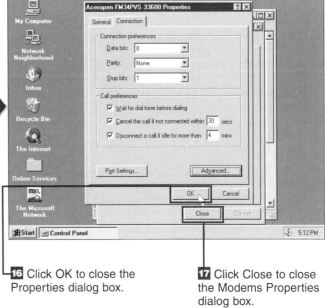

14 You can click this option to have Windows keep a record of the commands exchanged between modems (☐ changes to ☑).

15 Click OK to confirm all of your changes.

16 Click OK to close the Properties dialog box.

17 Click Close to close the Modems Properties dialog box.

365

SET UP A CONNECTION TO ANOTHER COMPUTER

Y ou can use Dial-Up Networking to connect to another computer using a modem. When two computers are connected, you can work with files on the other computer as if they were stored on the computer you are currently using. You can also retrieve your e-mail, print files, send faxes and access information on a network.

Connecting to another computer is useful when you are at home or traveling and you need information on your computer at work. The computer you want to contact must be turned on if you want to connect.

Before connecting to another computer, you must tell Windows about the computer

you want to contact. Windows will store the information you enter about the other computer. This will help you connect to the computer again.

You only need to set up a connection to another computer once. After the connection is set up, Windows displays an icon for the connection in the Dial-Up Networking window.

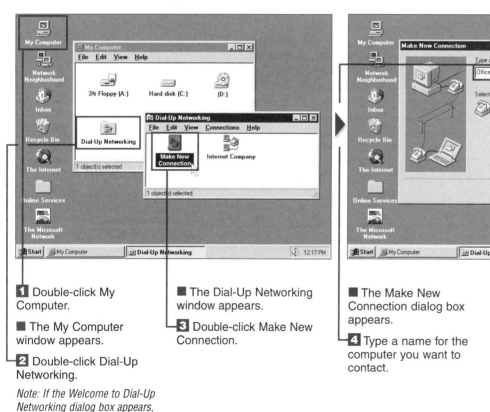

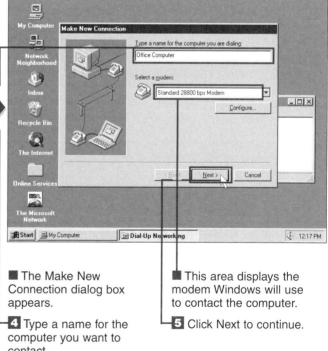

1 Double-click My Computer.

■ The My Computer window appears.

2 Double-click Dial-Up Networking.

Note: If the Welcome to Dial-Up Networking dialog box appears, click Next and then skip to step 4.

■ The Dial-Up Networking window appears.

3 Double-click Make New Connection.

■ The Make New Connection dialog box appears.

4 Type a name for the computer you want to contact.

■ This area displays the modem Windows will use to contact the computer.

5 Click Next to continue.

TIPS

Windows does not display the Dial-Up Networking folder on my computer. Why not?

The Dial-Up Networking component must be installed on your computer before you can use Dial-Up Networking. To install components, see page 580.

The modem I want to use is not displayed. What should I do?

Before you can use Dial-Up Networking, you must have a modem installed on your computer. If you do not see a modem in the list, you may have to install a modem. To install a modem, see page 350.

Is there another way to open the Dial-Up Networking folder?

Click Start, Programs, Accessories, Dial-Up Networking. The Dial-Up Networking folder appears.

Are there any other settings I must specify before dialing in to the computer?

You need to change the settings for the dial-up connection to match the settings of the computer you want to connect to. These settings include the type of server you connect to and the network protocols required to exchange information with the computer. See page 540.

CONNECT TO OTHER COMPUTERS

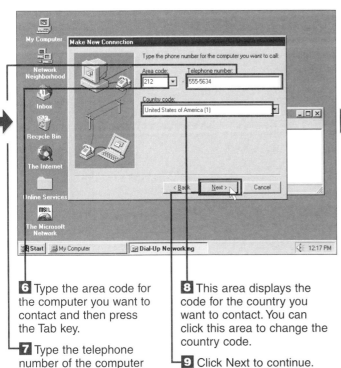

6 Type the area code for the computer you want to contact and then press the Tab key.

7 Type the telephone number of the computer you want to contact.

8 This area displays the code for the country you want to contact. You can click this area to change the country code.

9 Click Next to continue.

■ A message appears, telling you the connection to the computer has been successfully set up.

10 Click Finish.

■ An icon for the connection will appear in the Dial-Up Networking window.

DIAL IN TO ANOTHER COMPUTER

After you set up a connection to another computer, you can dial in to the computer to access information. For example, you can dial in to a computer at work to access files you need while you are away from the computer, such as when you are at home or traveling. You can exchange files and e-mail, send

faxes and access information on a network as if you were directly connected to the office computer.

Windows displays an icon in the Dial-Up Networking window for each connection you set up to other computers. To set up a dial-up connection to another computer, see page 366.

When you start to connect to another computer, Windows displays information such as your user name and the telephone number your modem will dial. You may need to enter a password to connect to the other computer.

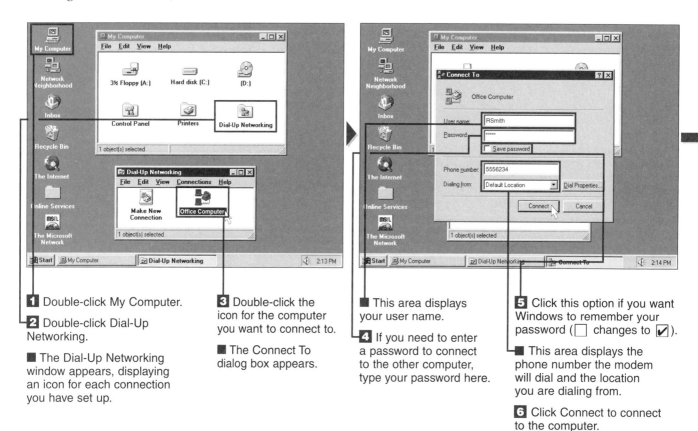

1 Double-click My Computer.

2 Double-click Dial-Up Networking.

■ The Dial-Up Networking window appears, displaying an icon for each connection you have set up.

3 Double-click the icon for the computer you want to connect to.

■ The Connect To dialog box appears.

■ This area displays your user name.

4 If you need to enter a password to connect to the other computer, type your password here.

5 Click this option if you want Windows to remember your password (☐ changes to ☑).

■ This area displays the phone number the modem will dial and the location you are dialing from.

6 Click Connect to connect to the computer.

TIPS

Why did my modem disconnect from the other computer?

Many phone lines are affected by interference. Although interference may cause only a brief break in a normal telephone call, interference can cause a computer's modem to disconnect from another computer. Try connecting again to try for a better phone line connection. Your local phone company may be able to help you eliminate phone line interference. Your modem may also disconnect from another computer if you do not type anything for a long period of time or the computer you are trying to contact is not turned on.

What will happen if I enter the wrong information when I try to dial in to another computer?

If you enter the wrong information, such as the wrong user name or password, you will not be allowed to connect to the other computer. Some computers may take a few moments before they disconnect you, so it may appear that you are briefly connected before you are disconnected.

CONNECT TO OTHER COMPUTERS

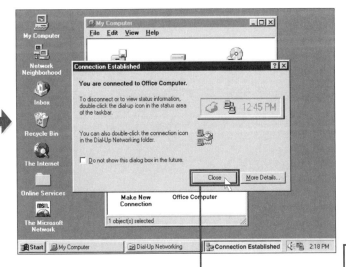

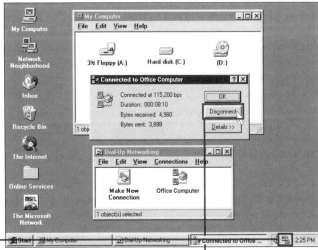

■ A dialog box appears when you are successfully connected.

Note: This dialog box may look different.

■ You can now access information on the other computer as if you were directly connected to the computer.

7 Click Close to close the dialog box.

Note: If there is no Close button, click ▭ to minimize the window.

END THE CONNECTION

-1 Double-click this icon when you want to end the connection with the other computer.

Note: If you minimized the window, click the button for the window on the taskbar.

■ The Connected to dialog box appears.

-2 Click Disconnect.

CHANGE SETTINGS FOR DIALING OUT

You can change the way your computer dials and connects to other computers.

When the redial option is turned on, Windows continually redials a phone number until it establishes a connection. You can specify how many times Windows should redial the number and the amount of time in minutes and seconds Windows should wait between redial attempts.

When you are establishing a connection to another Windows 95 computer, you can have Windows dial and connect to the other computer without prompting you. This is useful if you have mapped the drive of the computer you want to connect to. You can then double-click the mapped drive's icon in a My Computer or Explorer window to establish a connection.

Some additional options are available when you have OSR2

installed on your computer. You can display a Dial-Up Networking icon on the taskbar, which you can use to view the status of a connection. You can by-pass the Connect To dialog box when you connect to another computer by turning off the prompt for information before dialing option. You can also have OSR2 confirm when you have successfully connected to another computer.

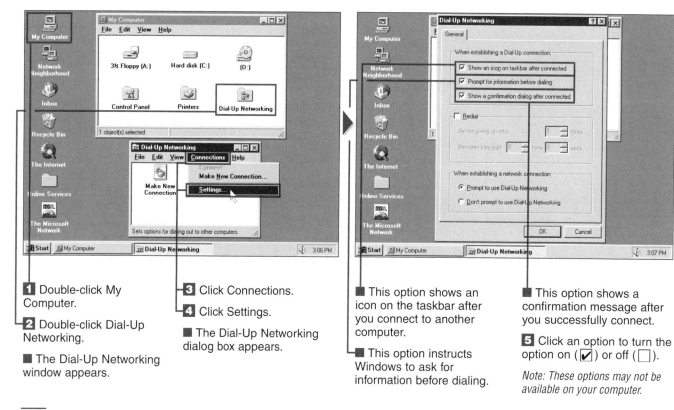

■ Double-click My Computer.

■ Double-click Dial-Up Networking.

■ The Dial-Up Networking window appears.

■ Click Connections.

■ Click Settings.

■ The Dial-Up Networking dialog box appears.

■ This option shows an icon on the taskbar after you connect to another computer.

■ This option instructs Windows to ask for information before dialing.

■ This option shows a confirmation message after you successfully connect.

■ Click an option to turn the option on (☑) or off (☐).

Note: These options may not be available on your computer.

TIPS

How long should I have Windows wait before each redial attempt?

You should set the time between redial attempts as low as possible. When you leave this setting at 0 minutes and 0 seconds, Windows will continuously redial until it connects or reaches the number of specified redials.

Which connections will the new settings effect?

When you change the settings in the Dial-Up Networking dialog box, the new settings take effect immediately and affect all of the connections that you have created.

Why would I want Windows to confirm that I have successfully connected to another computer?

On most computers, the sounds the modem makes while it is connecting to another computer tell you when you have successfully connected. If you have turned off the sound for your modem, you can have Windows tell you when you are connected.

How many times should I have Windows redial?

You should set this option to 100 times so Windows will keep redialing until a connection is made.

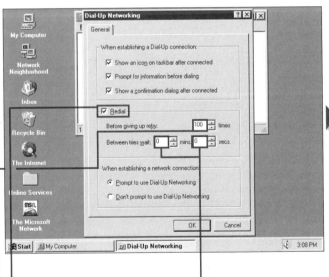

6 Click this option if you want Windows to redial if the other computer is busy, does not answer or you lose the connection (☐ changes to ☑).

7 Double-click this area and then type the number of times you want Windows to redial.

8 Double-click these areas and specify the amount of time you want Windows to wait between each redial attempt.

9 Click an option to specify if you want Windows to ask you to use Dial-Up Networking each time you want to access information on another computer (○ changes to ●).

10 Click OK to confirm your changes.

SET UP A DIAL-UP SERVER

Y ou can set up a computer so you can dial in to the computer from another location. Setting up a dial-up server is ideal for people who use a laptop computer at home, or when traveling and want to access information stored on their desktop computer at the office. A modem must be installed on the dial-up server before you can dial in to the computer.

You can dial in to the office computer to access information stored on the computer and the network attached to the computer. Connecting to the office computer also allows you to exchange e-mail and print documents on printers located at the office.

You can assign a password so only people who know the password can access the dial-up server.

Many networks have a dedicated dial-up server that accepts calls from computers that require access to the network. These dedicated dial-up servers are often called remote access servers.

After you set up a dial-up server, you need to set up a connection to the server on your laptop or home computer. See page 366 to set up a connection.

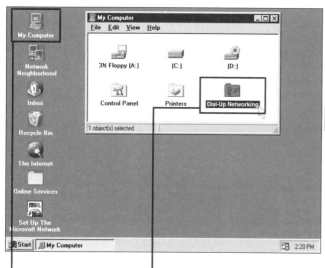

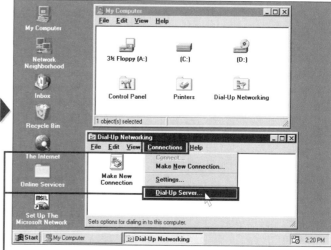

1 Double-click My Computer.

■ The My Computer window appears.

2 Double-click Dial-Up Networking.

■ The Dial-Up Networking window appears.

Note: If the Welcome to Dial-Up Networking or Make New Connection dialog box appears, press the Esc key to close the dialog box.

3 Click Connections.

4 Click Dial-Up Server.

■ The Dial-Up Server dialog box appears.

Why is the Dial-Up Server option not available in my Dial-Up Networking folder?

This option was not included with the original release of Windows 95. You can add this feature by downloading and installing the Dial-Up Networking Upgrade 1.2 or by purchasing and installing the Microsoft Plus! software. For more information, see page 603.

What information will be available on the dial-up server?

Before you can use a computer as a dial-up server, you must share the information you want to be able to access from another location. You can share files as well as printers and other devices. See pages 484 to 503 to share information.

Do I need to change the settings on the dial-up server?

If you plan to use a Windows 95 computer to connect to your dial-up server, you do not need to change the settings on the server. If you plan to connect to your dial-up server using a computer with an older operating system, such as Windows 3.1, you may need to change the settings on the server. To change the settings, click the Server Type button in the Dial-Up Server dialog box.

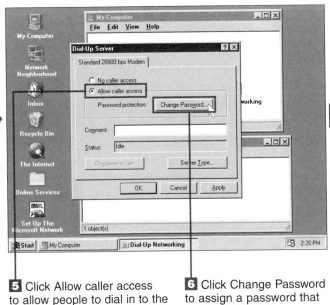

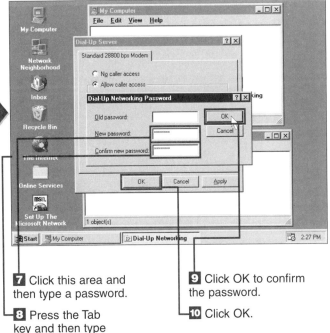

5 Click Allow caller access to allow people to dial in to the computer (○ changes to ⦿).

6 Click Change Password to assign a password that must be entered to access the computer.

■ A dialog box appears.

7 Click this area and then type a password.

8 Press the Tab key and then type the password again.

9 Click OK to confirm the password.

10 Click OK.

373

CONNECT TO ANOTHER COMPUTER USING HYPERTERMINAL

You can connect to another computer by using HyperTerminal. HyperTerminal is included with Windows 95 and allows you to use a modem to communicate with another computer.

You can use HyperTerminal to connect to a friend's computer, a university, a company, a Bulletin Board Service (BBS) or an online service, such as CompuServe.

Before you can contact another computer, you need to set up a connection to the computer. HyperTerminal will guide you through the process of creating a connection and will ask for information such as the computer's area code and telephone number. After you use HyperTerminal to connect two computers, you can transfer information from one computer to the other.

HyperTerminal provides connections to popular online services, including AT&T Mail, CompuServe and MCI Mail. You will find these connections in the HyperTerminal window.

If you have not yet set up your modem, HyperTerminal will ask you to set up the modem when you start the program.

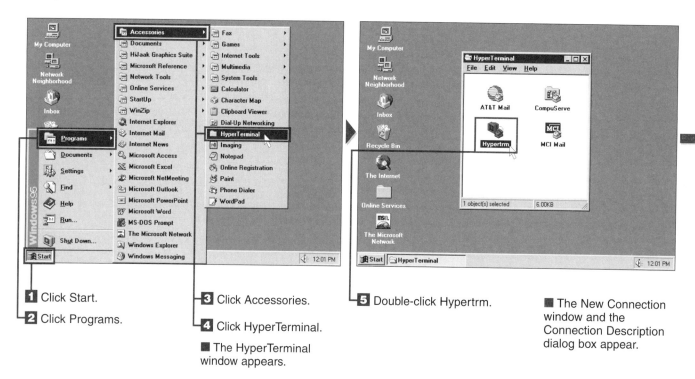

1 Click Start.

2 Click Programs.

3 Click Accessories.

4 Click HyperTerminal.

■ The HyperTerminal window appears.

5 Double-click Hypertrm.

■ The New Connection window and the Connection Description dialog box appear.

Can I access the Internet using HyperTerminal?

Some Internet Service Providers (ISPs) and Bulletin Board Services (BBSs) allow you to use HyperTerminal to connect to the Internet. Once connected, you can then use Internet services, including e-mail, chatting and browsing the Web, although you will not be able to view any graphics.

When shouldn't I use HyperTerminal to connect to another computer?

Most people use HyperTerminal to connect to local bulletin board services. If you want to connect to another computer running Windows 95, such as your computer at work, you should use Dial-Up Networking rather than HyperTerminal. See page 366 for information on Dial-Up Networking.

Where can I get the latest version of HyperTerminal?

Windows 95 includes HyperTerminal. HyperTerminal is continuously updated to add more features. The latest version allows you to quickly recover information when you lose a connection during a file transfer as well as communicate with other computers on the Internet. You can get the latest version of HyperTerminal on the Web at www.hilgraeve.com

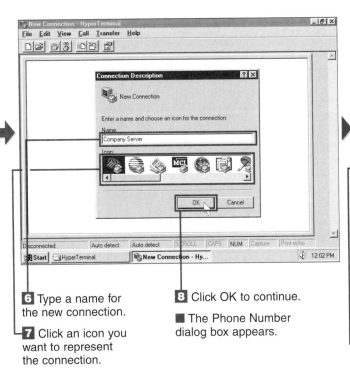

6 Type a name for the new connection.

7 Click an icon you want to represent the connection.

8 Click OK to continue.

■ The Phone Number dialog box appears.

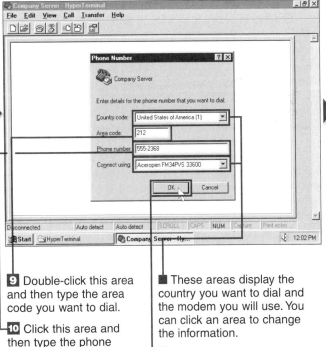

9 Double-click this area and then type the area code you want to dial.

10 Click this area and then type the phone number you want to dial.

■ These areas display the country you want to dial and the modem you will use. You can click an area to change the information.

11 Click OK to continue.

CONTINUED

CONNECT TO ANOTHER COMPUTER USING HYPERTERMINAL CONTINUED

After you connect to another computer using HyperTerminal, you can have Windows save the information you entered about the computer. This prevents you from having to enter the same information each time you want to connect to the computer.

The HyperTerminal window displays an icon for the connection you set up. You can use this icon to connect to the computer at any time.

HyperTerminal can make a computer you connect to believe that your computer is a terminal that allows your computer to connect to mainframe computers. Mainframe computers are large computers that are found in banks, schools, universities and large organizations.

There are many different types of terminals and each offers a different set of features. If the computer you connect to can only

communicate with a specific type of terminal, HyperTerminal will automatically adjust so you will be able to communicate with the computer.

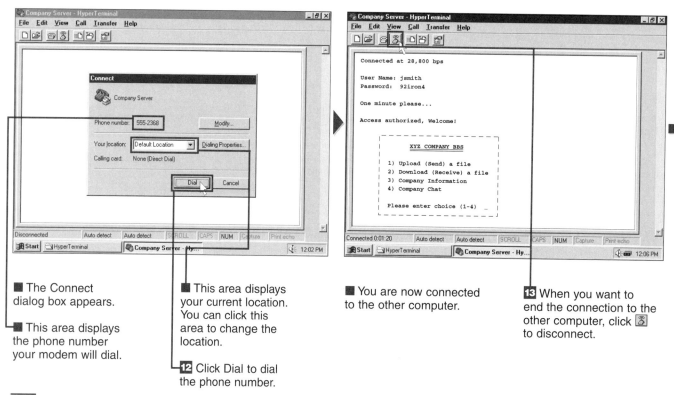

■ The Connect dialog box appears.

■ This area displays the phone number your modem will dial.

■ This area displays your current location. You can click this area to change the location.

12 Click Dial to dial the phone number.

■ You are now connected to the other computer.

13 When you want to end the connection to the other computer, click ⧄ to disconnect.

TIPS

Can I change the phone number for an existing connection?

Most phone numbers for bulletin board services and online services rarely change, but you may have to change the number you dial when calling from a different location, such as when you are traveling. Right-click the connection in the HyperTerminal window and then click Properties. The Phone Number tab allows you to change the phone number for the connection.

Can I view images using HyperTerminal?

HyperTerminal is only capable of displaying text. You will not be able to view images using HyperTerminal, but you can transfer image files to your computer and then use another program to view the images.

Why doesn't anything happen when I connect to another computer?

The computer you connect to must be set up to receive incoming calls. Although a modem may answer your call, the computer connected to the modem must be properly set up to establish a connection.

How do I delete an existing connection?

Over time, you may find the HyperTerminal window fills up with connections that you create. You may want to remove connections you no longer need to make the window less cluttered. Click a connection you want to delete and then press the Delete key to remove the connection.

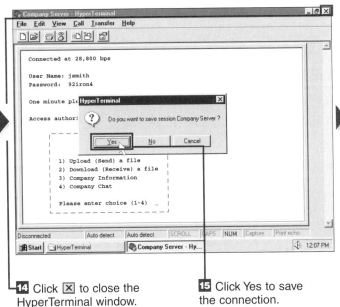

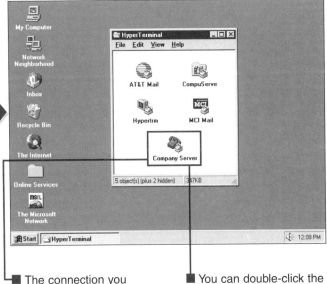

14 Click ☒ to close the HyperTerminal window.

■ A message appears, asking if you want to save the information you entered for the connection.

15 Click Yes to save the connection.

■ The connection you created appears in the HyperTerminal window.

■ You can double-click the connection to reconnect to the computer at any time.

CHANGE FONTS

You can change the font of text displayed in the HyperTerminal window to make the information easier to read. HyperTerminal allows you to change the font, style and size of text.

Some fonts can be difficult to read if you are using HyperTerminal for an extended period of time. When

choosing another font, select a font that you find easy to read.

You may also want to choose a different font style. HyperTerminal offers regular, italic, bold and bold italic styles.

A smaller font size can allow you to fit more information on your screen. A larger font size can make

text easier to read. When you change the font size, HyperTerminal automatically changes the size of the frame that surrounds the text to fit the new font size.

HyperTerminal will remember the font you selected and will use this font the next time you connect to the computer.

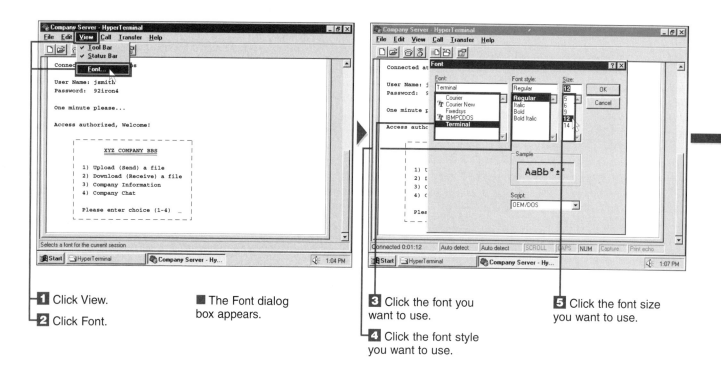

■ Click View.

■ Click Font.

■ The Font dialog box appears.

■ Click the font you want to use.

■ Click the font style you want to use.

■ Click the font size you want to use.

Can I change the color of the font?

You cannot change the color of the fonts by using commands in HyperTerminal, but you can adjust your Windows settings to change the color. Many people find white text on a blue background easier to read. See page 204 to adjust the color of screen elements.

If I change the font, will my captured text be affected?

You can capture text displayed in the HyperTerminal window to send the text to a file or to your printer. Changing the font of text will not affect the way text appears in the file or on your printouts. See page 380 to capture text.

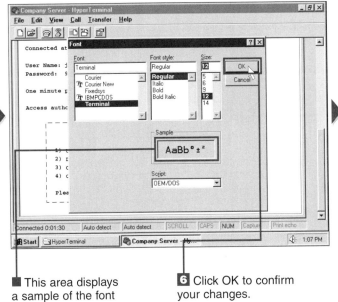

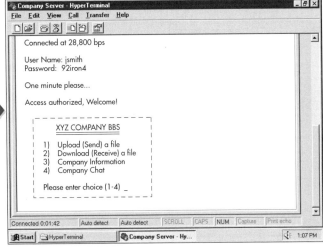

■ This area displays a sample of the font you selected.

6 Click OK to confirm your changes.

■ The text in the window appears in the new font.

CAPTURE TEXT

apturing text allows you to send information you see on your screen to a file or to your printer. You can then review and work with the information later.

Capturing information can save you money because some bulletin board services charge you for the time you spend connected to their service.

Instead of reading information while you are connected to the service, you can capture the text and review the information when you are no longer connected.

Information may appear very quickly on your screen. The information at the top of the screen may scroll off before you have time to read the text.

Capturing text is useful since you may not be able to scroll back to text you previously viewed.

You can stop capturing text at any time. If you are capturing text to a file, you can stop or pause the capture when you know the information will be of no interest in the future.

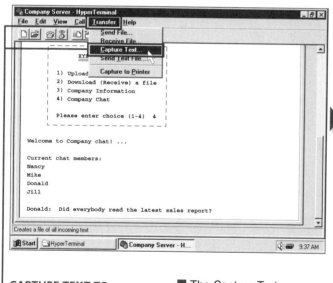

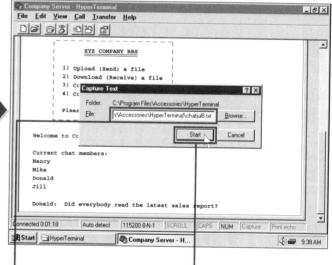

CAPTURE TEXT TO A FILE

1 Click Transfer.

2 Click Capture Text to create a file of all incoming text.

■ The Capture Text dialog box appears.

3 Type a name for the file. Make sure you end the file name with the .txt extension so a text editor can open the file.

4 Click Start to begin capturing the text to a file.

TIPS

How do I view a captured file?

HyperTerminal will save the captured text in a text file so you can use any text editor or word processor to view the file. Even though you can display color and special symbols in HyperTerminal, this information will appear as unreadable text in a text editor or word processor.

How can I stop captured text from printing?

If you want to cancel the printing of captured text, you will have to remove the captured text from the print queue. See page 100.

How else can I capture text?

You can also use the Windows Copy and Paste features to copy information from your HyperTerminal window to another program such as WordPad. This is ideal for small sections of text you want to capture.

How much information can I save in a captured file?

There is no limit to the size of your captured files, except the amount of storage space available on your computer. You should only capture information you plan to review later because captured files can take up a lot of storage space.

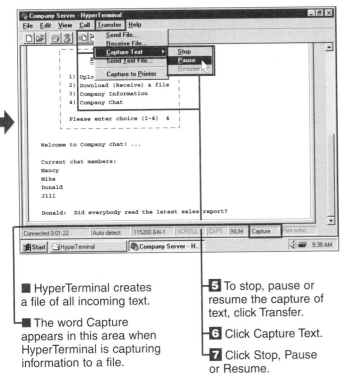

■ HyperTerminal creates a file of all incoming text.

■ The word Capture appears in this area when HyperTerminal is capturing information to a file.

5 To stop, pause or resume the capture of text, click Transfer.

6 Click Capture Text.

7 Click Stop, Pause or Resume.

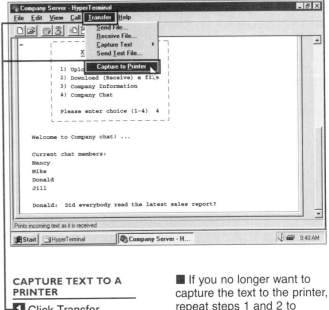

CAPTURE TEXT TO A PRINTER

1 Click Transfer.

2 Click Capture to Printer to print incoming text as it is received.

■ If you no longer want to capture the text to the printer, repeat steps 1 and 2 to remove the check mark (✔) beside Capture to Printer.

381

RECEIVE A FILE

HyperTerminal allows you to receive a file from another computer. One of the primary uses of HyperTerminal is to transfer files from other computers and copy the files to your computer.

Bulletin board services often have a wide variety of text files, pictures and programs that you can transfer to your computer.

Before you can receive a file from another computer, you need to

instruct the other computer to send a file. Each computer you contact will vary in the way you instruct it to transfer a file. You can usually instruct the computer to send a file by selecting commands from a menu offered by the computer.

When transferring files to your computer, you need to specify which protocol to use. A protocol is a language that computers use to communicate with each other.

Both computers must use the same protocol before they can exchange information. HyperTerminal can use several types of protocols, including Xmodem, Ymodem, Zmodem and Kermit. The most common type of protocol is Zmodem.

If you are using Zmodem, you may not have to perform all the steps below.

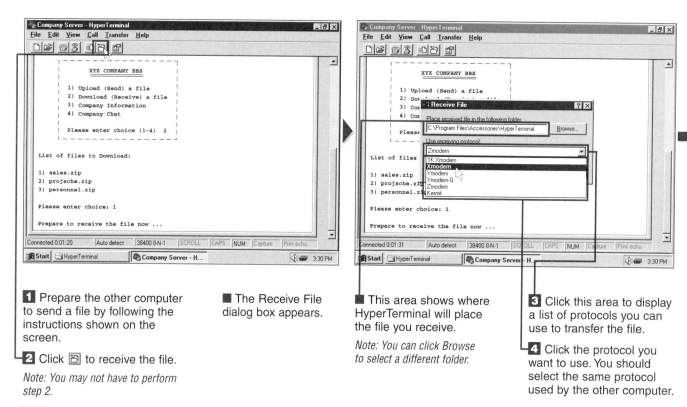

1 Prepare the other computer to send a file by following the instructions shown on the screen.

2 Click 🖻 to receive the file.

Note: You may not have to perform step 2.

■ The Receive File dialog box appears.

■ This area shows where HyperTerminal will place the file you receive.

Note: You can click Browse to select a different folder.

3 Click this area to display a list of protocols you can use to transfer the file.

4 Click the protocol you want to use. You should select the same protocol used by the other computer.

CONNECT TO OTHER COMPUTERS

What does downloading mean?

Transferring a file from another computer to your computer is called downloading. When you are downloading, you are transferring a file down to your computer. When you send a file from your computer to another computer, you are uploading the file.

What is throughput?

Throughput measures the speed that information transfers. When you are receiving a file, HyperTerminal displays the throughput of the file as it receives the file. HyperTerminal measures throughput using Characters Per Second (CPS).

Should I check programs I receive for viruses?

Programs you get from bulletin board services can contain viruses. Viruses can cause a variety of problems on your computer, such as the appearance of annoying messages on your screen or the destruction of information on your hard drive. You should use anti-virus software to scan any programs you receive before running the programs.

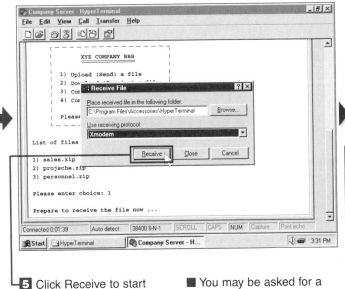

5 Click Receive to start transferring the file.

■ You may be asked for a file name. Type a name for the file and then press the Enter key.

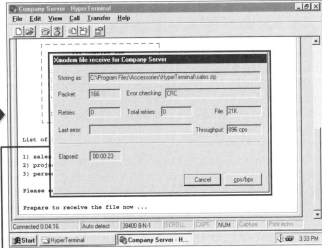

■ A dialog box shows the status of the file transfer. The dialog box that appears depends on the protocol you selected.

SEND A FILE

You can use HyperTerminal to send a file to another computer. Exchanging files between computers using a modem is convenient.

You can use HyperTerminal to transfer any type of file stored on your computer, including images, sounds, programs and text files.

The computer you send a file to must use HyperTerminal or a similar program to receive files.

When sending a file to another computer, you need to specify which protocol to use. A protocol is a language that computers use to communicate with each other. Both computers must use the same protocol before they can exchange

information. Protocols usually compress, or squeeze, the files you send to speed the transfer of information.

The speed that files transfer to another computer depends on the speed of your modem and the modem on the other computer. The faster the modems, the faster the information will transfer.

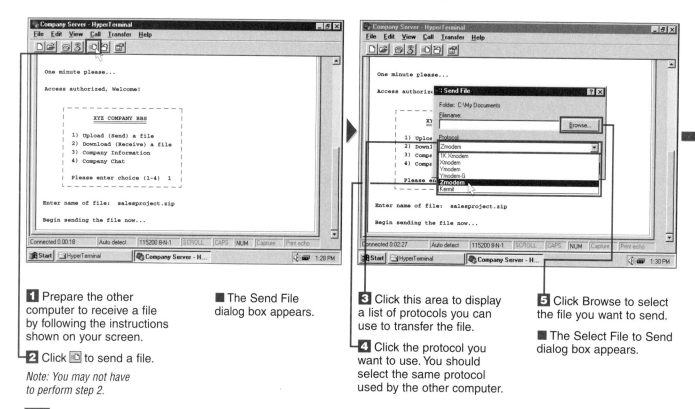

1 Prepare the other computer to receive a file by following the instructions shown on your screen.

2 Click 📋 to send a file.

Note: You may not have to perform step 2.

■ The Send File dialog box appears.

3 Click this area to display a list of protocols you can use to transfer the file.

4 Click the protocol you want to use. You should select the same protocol used by the other computer.

5 Click Browse to select the file you want to send.

■ The Select File to Send dialog box appears.

What happens if a connection is interrupted while I am transferring a file?

If an interruption occurs while transferring a file, you will have to send the entire file again. An interruption can occur because of problems with the phone line. If you are using the latest version of HyperTerminal with the Zmodem protocol, HyperTerminal can automatically recover from a broken connection and continue sending your file. You can get the latest version of HyperTerminal on the Web at www.hilgraeve.com

Does HyperTerminal restrict the size of files I can send?

HyperTerminal does not restrict the size of files you can send. If you are sending a large file, you should make sure the computer receiving the file has enough hard drive space to store the file.

What protocol should I use?

The most commonly used protocol is Zmodem. Almost all online services and Bulletin Board Services (BBSs) allow you to transfer files using Zmodem.

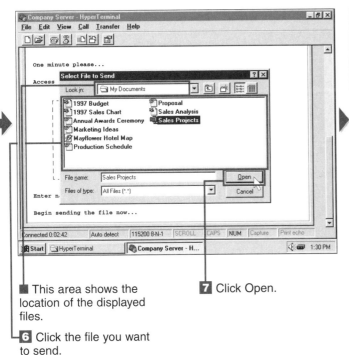

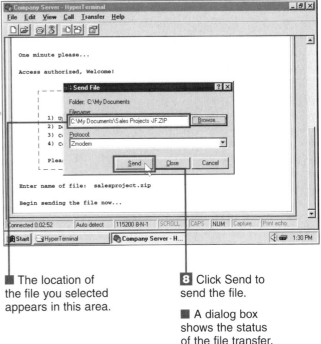

■ This area shows the location of the displayed files.

6 Click the file you want to send.

7 Click Open.

■ The location of the file you selected appears in this area.

8 Click Send to send the file.

■ A dialog box shows the status of the file transfer.

CHANGE SETTINGS FOR A CONNECTION

You can change the settings for any connection you have set up. Changing the settings for a connection gives you more control over how HyperTerminal communicates with another computer.

You can tell HyperTerminal to send certain keyboard commands to the other computer or to use these keyboard commands for tasks on your computer. These

keys include the function keys F1 to F12, the arrow keys and the Ctrl keys. For example, F1 will either be sent to the other computer or display help information on your computer.

HyperTerminal will automatically detect and choose which terminal emulation you need to use to communicate with another computer. Terminal emulation makes a computer you connect

to believe that your computer is a terminal. Your computer must use the same type of terminal emulation as the other computer you are connecting to.

You can have your computer beep three times to notify you when HyperTerminal connects to or disconnects from a computer. You can turn this feature on or off at any time.

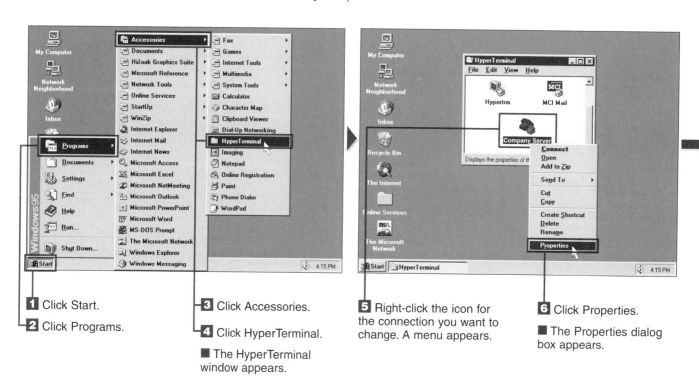

■1 Click Start.

■2 Click Programs.

■3 Click Accessories.

■4 Click HyperTerminal.

■ The HyperTerminal window appears.

■5 Right-click the icon for the connection you want to change. A menu appears.

■6 Click Properties.

■ The Properties dialog box appears.

TIPS

When should I change the terminal emulation used by HyperTerminal?

You may have to choose a different terminal emulation if you have problems displaying information from a computer you connect to. You should contact the administrator of the other computer to determine which type of terminal emulation you should use.

Is there another way that I can access the properties for a connection?

You can also change the properties for a connection when you are connected to another computer. Click the Properties button () in the HyperTerminal window to display the properties for the connection.

What is the backscroll buffer value?

When connected to another computer, the backscroll buffer stores the information displayed on your screen. The buffer allows you to use the scroll bar or the Page Up key to scroll back through the information that scrolled off the top of your screen. You can specify the number of lines you want to be able to view again. The default number of lines is 500, which allows you to scroll back through about 21 screens of information.

CONNECT TO OTHER COMPUTERS

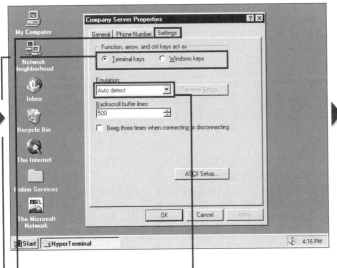

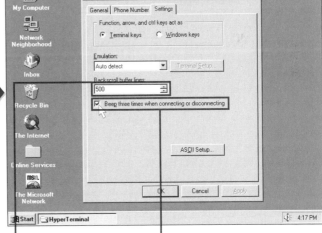

7 Click the Settings tab.

8 Click an option to determine if the function, arrow and Ctrl keys are sent to the other computer or used for tasks on your computer (○ changes to ◉).

9 This area displays the current terminal emulation used by HyperTerminal. You can click this area to select a different terminal emulation.

10 This area displays the number of lines you can see when you scroll back. You can change this number.

11 Click this option if you want your computer to beep three times when connecting to and disconnecting from the other computer (☐ changes to ✔).

CONTINUED ▶

387

CHANGE SETTINGS FOR
A CONNECTION CONTINUED

The ASCII settings in HyperTerminal determine how text transfers between your computer and the computer you are connected to.

Some of the ASCII settings affect the way information you enter is sent to the other computer. If pressing the Enter key moves you to the beginning of the current line instead of starting a new line, you can have HyperTerminal tell the

other computer each time you start a new line. You can turn on the Echo typed characters locally option if you cannot see the characters you type or turn this option off if characters appear twice. You can also tell HyperTerminal how long you want to wait before sending information. If the other computer loses some of the information you send, you can increase the line and character delay settings.

You can also change the settings to adjust the way your computer receives information. You can include line feeds to ensure each line of text appears on a new line. Using 7-bit ASCII text is helpful if your computer is displaying unreadable characters. You can also wrap the text that appears on your screen so the text will not scroll off the screen.

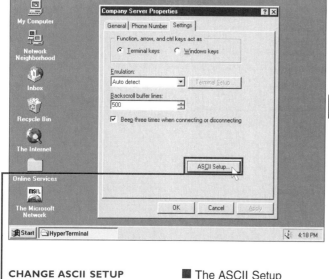

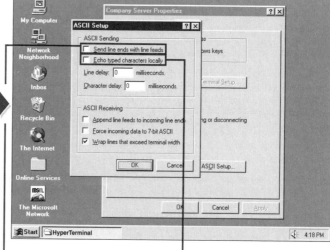

CHANGE ASCII SETUP

1 Click ASCII Setup to set options for the way text transfers between computers.

■ The ASCII Setup dialog box appears.

2 Click this option to let the other computer know each time you send a new line of text (☐ changes to ☑).

3 Click this option to display each character you type before sending the character to the other computer (☐ changes to ☑).

Why am I unable to see what I type?

When you type a character in HyperTerminal, the character is sent to the computer you are connected to and then sent back to HyperTerminal before it is displayed on your screen. If you select the Echo typed characters locally option, HyperTerminal will display each character you type before sending the character to the computer you are connected to.

Why does all the text appear on one line at the bottom of my screen?

Some computers may not be able to determine when a new line of text is being displayed. You can select the Append line feeds to incoming line ends option to fix this problem.

What is 7-bit ASCII text?

7-bit ASCII text is a collection of 128 characters that most computers can understand, such as 3, a, B, @ and $. If HyperTerminal is displaying unrecognizable characters, you should select the Force incoming data to 7-bit ASCII option.

What does ASCII stand for?

ASCII is an acronym for American Standard Code for Information Interchange.

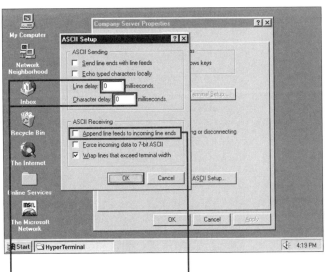

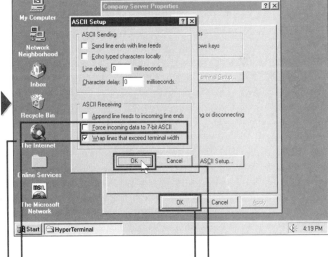

4 These areas indicate the amount of time HyperTerminal will wait before sending each line of text and each character you type. You can double-click these areas to change the amount of time.

5 Click this option to let your computer know each time you receive a new line of text (☐ changes to ✔).

6 Click this option to translate 8-bit characters you receive to 7-bit characters if some of the text appears unreadable (☐ changes to ✔).

7 Click this option to wrap long lines of text to the next line (☐ changes to ✔).

8 Click OK to confirm your changes.

9 Click OK to close the Properties dialog box.

DIRECT CABLE CONNECTION

Set Up Direct Cable Connection

You can use a special cable to connect two computers to share files and resources. This is useful if you want to connect a portable computer to a desktop computer. Unlike a regular network, neither computer needs a network adapter card.

You must designate a host computer and a guest computer.

The host is the computer that provides the resources such as drives and printers. The guest is a computer that can access files and resources on the host and on the network attached to the host.

Make sure you plug the cable into both computers before you begin. You can choose from several types of cable. A serial cable allows you to connect the computers over a long distance but transfers information slowly. A parallel cable transfers information faster than a serial cable. A parallel cable is the best choice for most direct cable connections. You can get direct connection cable at most computer hardware stores.

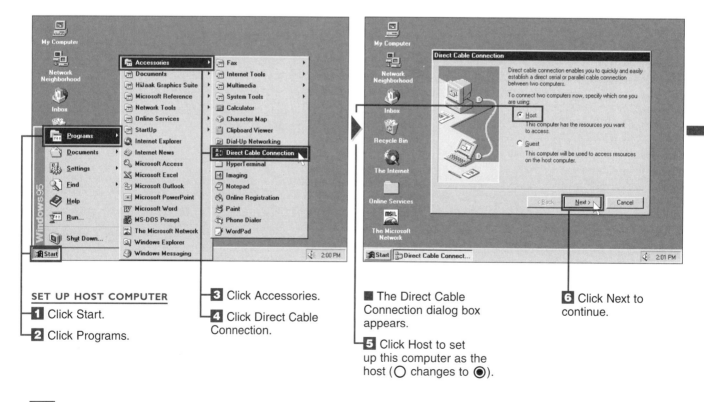

SET UP HOST COMPUTER

1 Click Start.

2 Click Programs.

3 Click Accessories.

4 Click Direct Cable Connection.

■ The Direct Cable Connection dialog box appears.

5 Click Host to set up this computer as the host (○ changes to ◉).

6 Click Next to continue.

TIPS

TIPS

Why isn't Direct Cable Connection available in the Accessories menu?

Direct Cable Connection may not be installed. You must also install Dial-Up Networking to use Direct Cable Connection. Direct Cable Connection and Dial-Up Networking are located in the Communications group on the Windows 95 CD-ROM disc. To install Windows components, see page 580. When you install Direct Cable Connection, you may be asked to provide a computer and workgroup name. You should use the same workgroup name for the host and guest computers.

Is there anything else I have to do to access the information and resources on the host computer?

Before setting up the direct cable connection, you must prepare the host computer to share its files and resources. To turn on sharing, see page 484. To share files, see page 486. To share printers, see page 490.

How can I prevent unauthorized people from accessing the host?

You can set a password to prevent unauthorized people from accessing the host. In the last Direct Cable Connection dialog box, click the Use password protection option. Click Set Password and then specify the password that a guest must enter to access the host.

CONNECT TO OTHER COMPUTERS

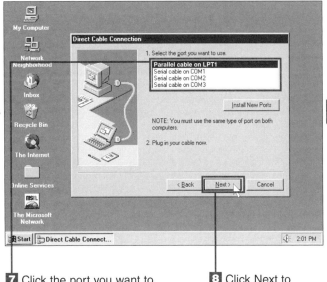

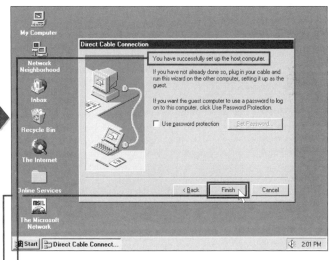

7 Click the port you want to use on the host computer for the connection.

8 Click Next to continue.

■ This message appears when you have successfully set up the host computer.

9 Click Finish.

■ A dialog box appears, telling you the status of the connection.

■ You are now ready to set up the guest computer.

CONTINUED ▶

DIRECT CABLE CONNECTION
Set Up Direct Cable Connection (Continued)

You must set up the guest computer before using it to access files and resources on the host and on the network attached to the host.

You must specify the port you want to use for the guest computer. You must select the same type of port you chose for the host computer.

Once you set up a direct cable connection between two computers, you can exchange files. The host and guest computers will be able to access each other's shared items. If the host computer is part of a network, the guest will also be able to access the network and all shared items on the network.

If any of the shared files or resources on the host computer are password-protected, you will need to enter a password to access the files or resources.

You cannot use a direct cable connection to share an Internet or any TCP/IP network connection.

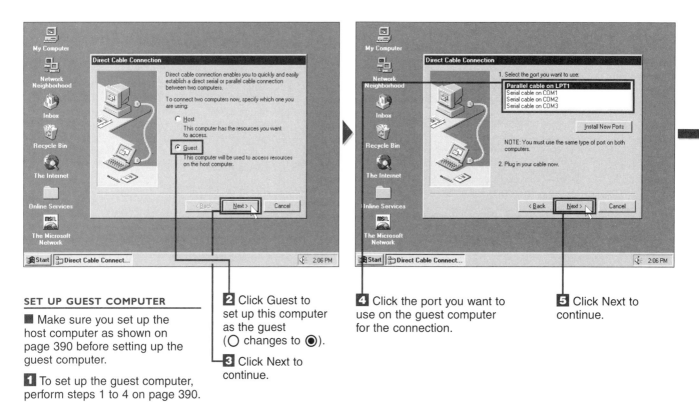

SET UP GUEST COMPUTER

■ Make sure you set up the host computer as shown on page 390 before setting up the guest computer.

1 To set up the guest computer, perform steps 1 to 4 on page 390.

■ The Direct Cable Connection dialog box appears.

2 Click Guest to set up this computer as the guest (○ changes to ◉).

3 Click Next to continue.

4 Click the port you want to use on the guest computer for the connection.

5 Click Next to continue.

Can I use the host computer to access the guest computer?

You can double-click the Network Neighborhood icon on your desktop and then select the guest computer. You can access only the shared items on the guest computer.

How do I print using the host's printer?

Right-click the shared printer in the window that contains the host's shared items. From the menu that appears, select Install. In the Print dialog box of your program, choose the shared printer when you want to print.

I had to disconnect the printer from the host to plug in the cable for the direct cable connection. How can I print my documents?

From the Control Panel, select the Printers folder and then click the printer you want to use. Choose the File menu and then select Pause Printing. Windows will store any documents you send to the printer. When you re-connect to the printer, select the Pause Printing command again to print the documents.

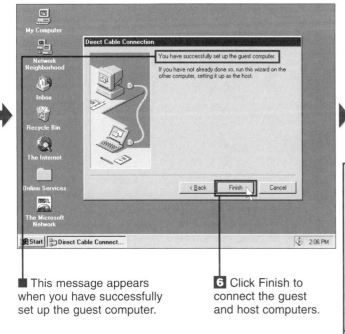

■ This message appears when you have successfully set up the guest computer.

6 Click Finish to connect the guest and host computers.

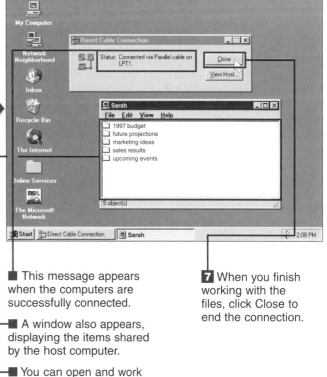

■ This message appears when the computers are successfully connected.

■ A window also appears, displaying the items shared by the host computer.

■ You can open and work with the folders and files as if the information were stored on the guest computer.

7 When you finish working with the files, click Close to end the connection.

DIRECT CABLE CONNECTION
Re-establish Direct Cable Connection

You only need to set up a direct cable connection once. After you set up a connection, you can re-connect the host and guest computers at any time. Windows uses the last successful connection settings to re-establish the connection.

You can leave the cable connected to the host computer

all the time. You can re-attach the cable to the guest computer whenever you need to connect the computers.

You must make sure that the information and resources you want to access on the host computer are still shared. You can open and work with all the

shared information and resources as if they were on the guest computer. Besides opening files and folders, you may be able to run programs that are located on the host computer. You can run programs that do not require special files to be stored on the guest computer.

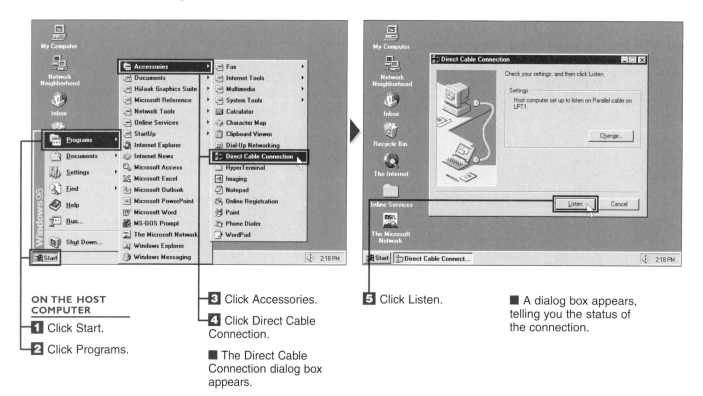

ON THE HOST COMPUTER

1 Click Start.

2 Click Programs.

3 Click Accessories.

4 Click Direct Cable Connection.

■ The Direct Cable Connection dialog box appears.

5 Click Listen.

■ A dialog box appears, telling you the status of the connection.

Can I create a desktop shortcut to re-establish the direct cable connection?

Right-click the Start button and select Open. Double-click the Programs folder and then the Accessories folder. Use the right mouse button to drag the Direct Cable Connection shortcut icon to the desktop. Then select Copy Here in the menu that appears.

How can I change the settings for the direct cable connection?

In the Direct Cable Connection dialog box, click the Change button to make changes to the settings. You can change the ports you are using or the password you set for the host computer.

Why can't I re-establish the connection?

Make sure the cable is plugged in correctly. In Windows Help, click the Contents tab to consult the Troubleshooting book. Select the "If you have trouble using Direct Cable Connection" topic.

Can I have Windows update my files so that both computers have the same information?

You can use the Briefcase feature to update your files. For information on the Briefcase feature, see page 396.

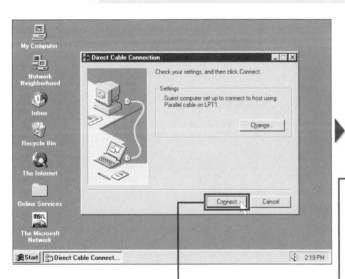

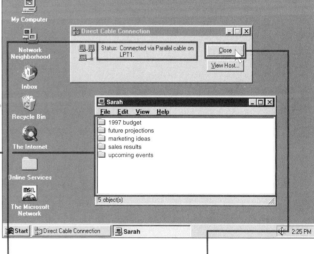

ON THE GUEST COMPUTER

1 Perform steps 1 to 4 on page 394 on the guest computer.

■ The Direct Cable Connection dialog box appears.

2 Click Connect to connect the guest and host computers.

■ This message appears when the computers are successfully connected.

■ A window also appears, displaying the items shared by the host computer.

■ You can open and work with the folders and files as if the information were stored on the guest computer.

3 When you finish working with the files, click Close to end the connection.

USING BRIEFCASE

The computer you use most often may be the one in your office, but you may also use a home computer or a portable computer. When you place a document in your Briefcase, you can transport it back and forth. Briefcase ensures that you are always working with the most up-to-date version of a document, regardless of the computer you use to edit it.

If you place a folder in the Briefcase, all of the documents in the folder are added to the Briefcase. The Briefcase contains a copy of your document or folder. The original document or folder remains on your main computer.

You can move a Briefcase to a floppy disk so you can transfer the documents you want to work with to another computer. A Briefcase on a floppy disk can contain up

to 1.44 MB of information. You can also move a Briefcase to any type of removable or network drive.

When at home or traveling, you can work with Briefcase documents as you would work with any document. Make sure you close all open Briefcase documents before removing the disk containing the Briefcase from the computer's drive.

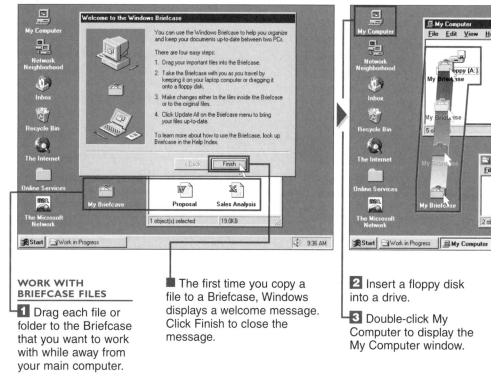

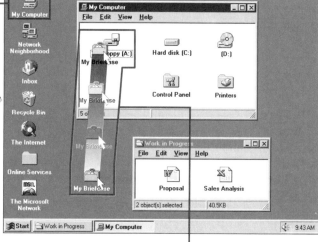

WORK WITH BRIEFCASE FILES

1 Drag each file or folder to the Briefcase that you want to work with while away from your main computer.

■ The first time you copy a file to a Briefcase, Windows displays a welcome message. Click Finish to close the message.

2 Insert a floppy disk into a drive.

3 Double-click My Computer to display the My Computer window.

4 Drag the Briefcase to the drive that contains the floppy disk.

■ Windows moves the Briefcase to the floppy disk. You can now transfer the Briefcase to your portable computer.

Why isn't there a Briefcase icon on my desktop?

Briefcase is only installed automatically on portable computers. You can install Briefcase from the Accessories component. To add Windows components, see page 580.

Why isn't Briefcase listed in the Accessories component?

Briefcase is already installed on your computer but may have been removed from the desktop. Right-click the desktop, click New and then select Briefcase. You can use this procedure to create as many new Briefcases as you need.

Is there another way to place documents in the Briefcase?

You can right-click the document or folder and select Send To. Then click My Briefcase.

Is there a faster way to access a Briefcase on a disk?

Double-click the drive that contains the disk to display the Briefcase. Use the right mouse button to drag the Briefcase to the desktop and select Create Shortcut Here. You will only be able to use the shortcut to access the Briefcase when the disk is in the drive. When you use the shortcut, press the F5 key to update the contents of the Briefcase window.

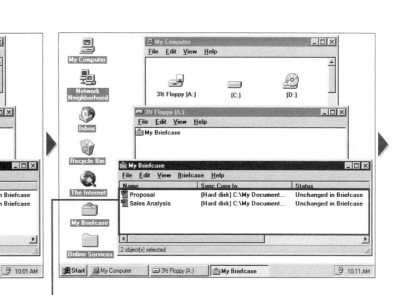

5 Insert the floppy disk into a drive on your portable computer.

6 Double-click My Computer to display the My Computer window.

7 Double-click the drive that contains the floppy disk.

8 Double-click the Briefcase to display its contents.

■ The Briefcase window opens.

■ You can open and edit the files in the Briefcase as you would open and edit any files.

9 When you finish working with the files, remove the floppy disk and return the disk to your main computer.

CONTINUED

USING BRIEFCASE CONTINUED

Briefcase lets you work with documents while you are away from your main computer. When you change the Briefcase copy of a document, the original document is out-of-date. Briefcase will update the documents you changed. You can update all documents or only specific documents.

The update process ensures that the original documents and the Briefcase copies are the same. Briefcase compares the documents it contains with the documents on your main computer and shows you which documents need to be updated. You can have Briefcase replace the original document, the Briefcase version of the document or skip replacing the document completely.

Briefcase replaces the older version of the document with the newer version of the document by default. If both the original and Briefcase copies have been changed, Briefcase will indicate this and not update the document. Do not rename or move the original documents or the documents in the Briefcase. If you do, Briefcase will not be able to update the documents.

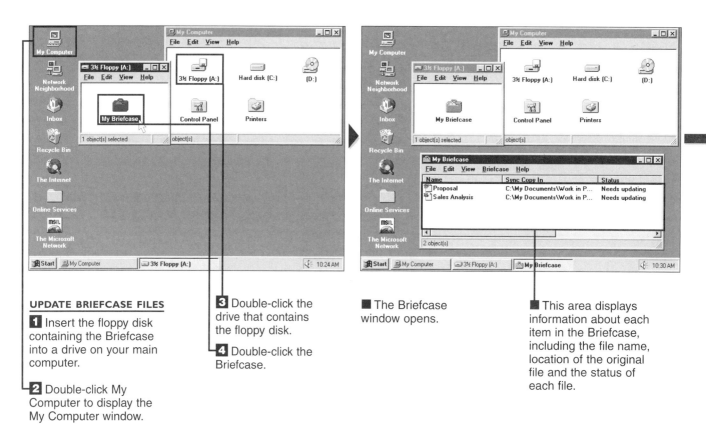

UPDATE BRIEFCASE FILES

1 Insert the floppy disk containing the Briefcase into a drive on your main computer.

2 Double-click My Computer to display the My Computer window.

3 Double-click the drive that contains the floppy disk.

4 Double-click the Briefcase.

■ The Briefcase window opens.

■ This area displays information about each item in the Briefcase, including the file name, location of the original file and the status of each file.

Can I add a document to the Briefcase from the second computer?

The document you add will not be updated to the main computer. You may prefer to create a second Briefcase containing the documents that are located on the second computer.

Can I permanently stop a Briefcase document from updating?

In the Briefcase window, select the document you do not want to update. Click the Briefcase menu and then select the Split From Original command. This lets you keep both the original and changed versions of a document.

How do I use Briefcase to update my documents when I have a network or direct cable connection between my portable and desktop computer?

Make sure sharing is turned on for your desktop computer and the documents and folders you want to use in the Briefcase are shared. To turn on sharing, see page 484. To share information, see page 486. When the computers are connected, move the documents you want to work with into the Briefcase on the portable. You can reconnect the computers when you want to update the documents.

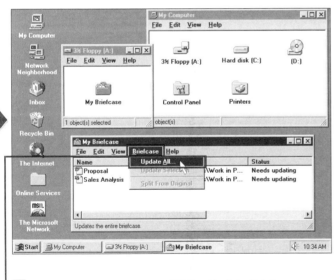

5 Click Briefcase to update the files.

6 Click Update All.

■ The Update Briefcase dialog box appears.

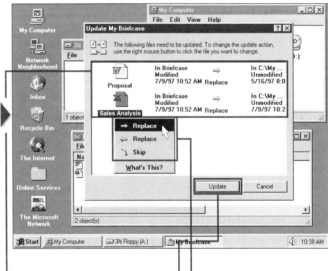

■ This area displays the name of each file that needs to be updated.

7 You can right-click a file to change the way Windows updates the file. A menu appears.

8 Click the update action you want to perform.

9 Click Update to update the files.

■ Windows updates the files.

SET POWER MANAGEMENT OPTIONS

Windows can help you extend the life of a portable computer's battery or conserve energy on a desktop computer. The available power management features depend on your computer.

A portable computer can usually run on battery power for about two hours. When you use Windows power management features, you may be able to increase the amount of time you can use a battery to power the computer. For example, the power management features can conserve power by shutting down your hard drive when you are not using it. This is useful if you are traveling or not near a power outlet.

You can use the icons that appear on the right side of the taskbar to display information about the power source. If you are using battery power, you can view the amount of remaining power.

Although the power management features are useful when you have a limited power supply, you may prefer to keep the hard drive active when the computer is connected to a power outlet.

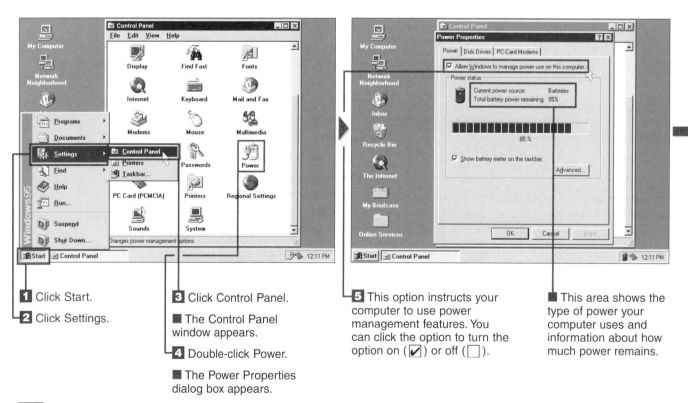

1 Click Start.

2 Click Settings.

3 Click Control Panel.

■ The Control Panel window appears.

4 Double-click Power.

■ The Power Properties dialog box appears.

5 This option instructs your computer to use power management features. You can click the option to turn the option on (☑) or off (☐).

■ This area shows the type of power your computer uses and information about how much power remains.

Why does the Power Properties dialog box on my computer look different?

You may be using an earlier version of Windows 95. The power management features were updated for OSR2.

Is it okay to leave my computer on all day?

There is no significant advantage to turning your computer on and off several times a day. If you choose to leave your computer on, but will not be using it for an extended period of time, you may want to turn off the monitor.

Why aren't the power management features available on my portable computer?

The power management features may not be available if the appropriate hardware devices were not detected when Windows was installed. If you have OSR2, you may be able to add the power management features by using the Add New Hardware Wizard to detect your hardware. See page 576. Otherwise, you may have to reinstall Windows, making sure that you select the portable installation. See page 590.

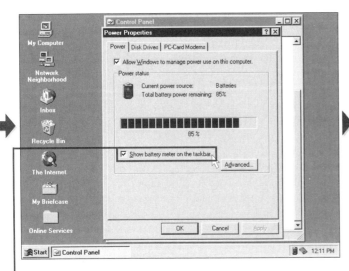

6 This option displays the battery meter on the taskbar. You can click the option to turn the option on (☑) or off (☐).

7 You can double-click the battery meter (🔋) at any time to see information about your computer's power supply.

■ The Battery Meter dialog box appears.

8 Click ☒ to hide the information.

CONTINUED

SET POWER MANAGEMENT
OPTIONS CONTINUED

Most portable computers and an increasing number of desktop computers include power management features that allow you to conserve power without turning off your computer.

You can suspend your portable computer when you are not using it. When you return to the computer, you can resume

working exactly where you left off. You do not have to wait for the computer to restart or reopen all your documents. You can have Windows display the Suspend command in the Start menu all the time or only when your portable computer is not attached to a docking station.

You can have Windows switch a disk drive to low power mode

after the drive has been idle for a specific amount of time. You can specify the amount of time the drive is idle before low power mode starts. You may want to specify a longer time period when you are connected to a power outlet (AC power) and a shorter period of time when you are using battery power.

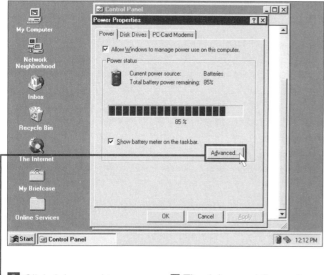

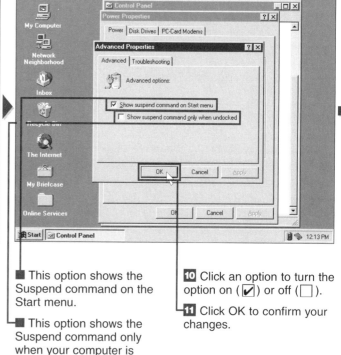

■ 9 Click Advanced to select advanced options for managing power on your computer.

■ The Advanced Properties dialog box appears.

■ This option shows the Suspend command on the Start menu.

■ This option shows the Suspend command only when your computer is undocked.

■ 10 Click an option to turn the option on (✔) or off (☐).

■ 11 Click OK to confirm your changes.

Why are the power management features not working properly on my portable computer?

Your portable computer may have built-in, power-saving strategies that override Windows power management features. You should consult your computer's documentation for more information.

How do I use the Suspend command?

Click the Start button and then select Suspend. You should save all your open documents before you use the Suspend command. To resume working, simply touch any key.

Why are there delays accessing my hard drive when it is in low power mode?

Low power mode shuts down your hard drive after a period of inactivity. It may take a few seconds for the drive to become active again.

How long should I have Windows wait before switching the hard drive to low power mode?

When specifying the amount of time, you should consider how often the programs you use access the hard drive and your working style.

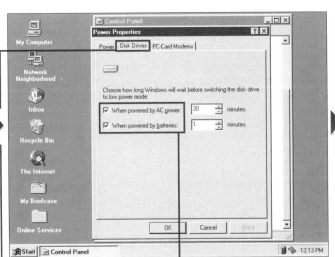

■12 Click the Disk Drives tab.

■13 These options switch the disk drives to low power mode when your computer is powered by an electrical outlet or by a battery. You can click an option to turn the option on (☑) or off (☐).

■14 You can double-click these areas and then type the number of minutes Windows will wait before switching to low power mode.

■15 Click OK to confirm all of your changes.

CREATE HARDWARE PROFILES

You can create a new hardware profile for your portable computer. A profile tells Windows which hardware devices you want to use. To create a new profile, you copy an existing profile and then make changes to the copy.

A portable computer can be used in several different situations. For example, you may use the portable computer at an office where you connect to a docking station to access a network. At home, you may use the portable computer with a printer, monitor, keyboard and mouse. When traveling, you may use the portable computer with no additional hardware. Each situation requires a different setup to make the attached hardware devices work properly with the portable computer.

To avoid the task of having to set up your computer each time you change locations, you can save the hardware settings for each situation in a profile.

Windows automatically creates hardware profiles for portable computers with Plug and Play capabilities and for certain types of docking stations.

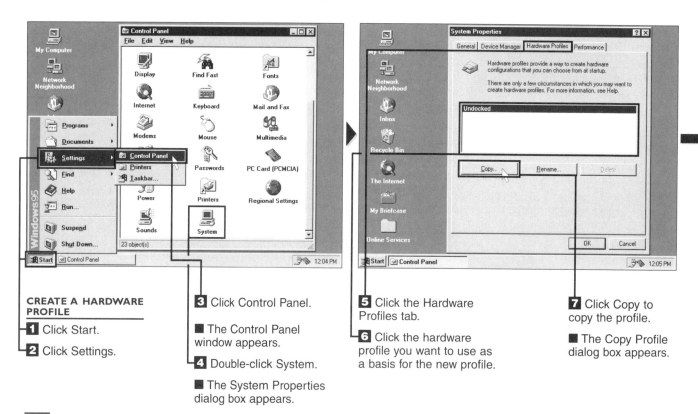

CREATE A HARDWARE PROFILE

1 Click Start.

2 Click Settings.

3 Click Control Panel.

■ The Control Panel window appears.

4 Double-click System.

■ The System Properties dialog box appears.

5 Click the Hardware Profiles tab.

6 Click the hardware profile you want to use as a basis for the new profile.

7 Click Copy to copy the profile.

■ The Copy Profile dialog box appears.

Which existing hardware profile should I copy as the basis for my new profile?

 You should choose a profile that has a large number of devices already installed since it is much easier to remove a device than it is to install one. The profile with the most installed devices is probably the docked, networked profile.

Can I rename a profile I created?

In the System Properties dialog box, select the profile you want to rename and then click the Rename button. Type a new name for the profile and then click OK.

Will I ever need to use hardware profiles on my desktop computer?

It may be beneficial for a desktop computer to have different hardware profiles in some situations. For example, if your computer does not have enough resources to handle all of your add-in cards, you can use a hardware profile to switch between cards.

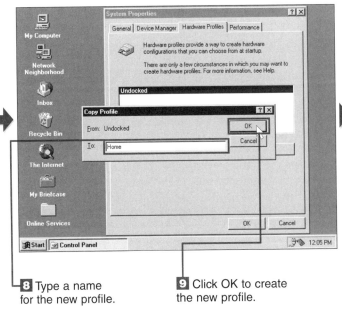

8 Type a name for the new profile.

9 Click OK to create the new profile.

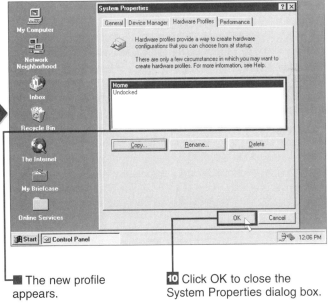

■ The new profile appears.

■ You can now make changes to the new profile to accommodate another situation.

10 Click OK to close the System Properties dialog box.

CONTINUED ▶

CREATE HARDWARE PROFILES
CONTINUED

You create a new hardware profile by copying an existing profile and then changing the copied profile to suit your needs. Changing a profile you have created does not affect any of the other profiles on your computer.

When you start your computer, Windows automatically uses the correct profile for the hardware

it detects. If Windows does not know which profile to use, you can choose a profile from the list it displays.

If you are using OSR2, you can only make changes to the profile you used to start the computer. If you are using Windows 95, you can change any of the profiles available on your computer.

You can disable or enable devices for a hardware profile. Disabling a device for a profile stops Windows from loading the software needed to communicate with the device. You need to disable each device you do not want to use in the profile.

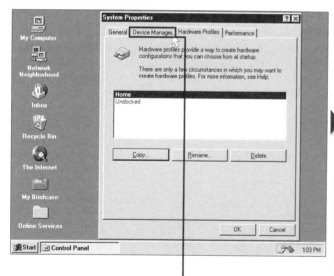

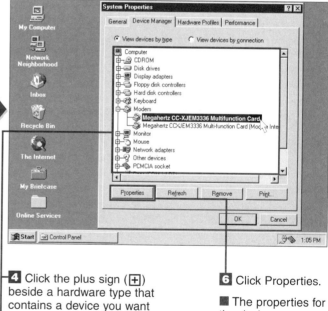

CHANGE A HARDWARE PROFILE

1 Start your computer using the hardware profile you want to change.

2 Display the System Properties dialog box by performing steps 1 to 4 on page 404.

3 Click the Device Manager tab to display the hardware on your computer.

4 Click the plus sign (⊞) beside a hardware type that contains a device you want to add or remove from the profile.

5 Click the hardware device you want to add or remove.

6 Click Properties.

■ The properties for the device appear.

Do I have to add my monitor to the new profile?

The first time you use a new profile, Windows detects and automatically sets up the video display and monitor for you.

Should I disable the printer?

It is not necessary to disable the printer. If you send documents to a printer that is not currently connected to your computer, Windows stores the print job until you reconnect to the printer. If you will not be using the printer in any of your profiles, you can remove the printer. For information on removing a printer, see page 105.

How do I delete a profile I no longer need?

On the Hardware Profiles tab, click the profile you want to remove and then click the Delete button. Then click Yes in the Confirm Profile Delete dialog box.

Can each hardware profile have its own screen resolution?

When you change the screen resolution, it is automatically saved as part of the profile you are currently using. For information on changing your screen resolution, see page 206.

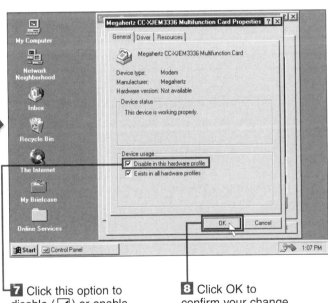

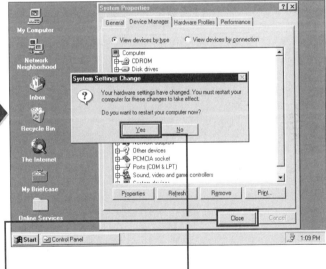

7 Click this option to disable (☑) or enable (☐) the device in this hardware profile.

8 Click OK to confirm your change.

9 Repeat steps 4 to 8 for each device you want to add or remove from the profile.

10 Click OK or Close to close the System Properties dialog box.

■ You may be asked to restart your computer. Click Yes to restart the computer.

SECTION VI

INSTALL EXCHANGE

Y ou can use Exchange to send and receive network e-mail messages and faxes. The Inbox Setup Wizard will help you successfully install Exchange's e-mail and fax components. The Inbox on your desktop starts Exchange and will store the messages and faxes you send and receive.

You can choose to install one or more of Exchange's components. The Microsoft Network is an online service. The Microsoft Network provides access to the Internet, including e-mail, for a monthly fee.

You can use Microsoft Mail to exchange e-mail messages within your corporate network.

Microsoft Fax allows you to send and receive faxes directly from your computer. To send and receive faxes, you must have a fax modem installed on your computer. You should install the fax modem before you begin installing Exchange. If you want to use Microsoft Fax and have not installed a fax modem, the wizard will prompt you to do so.

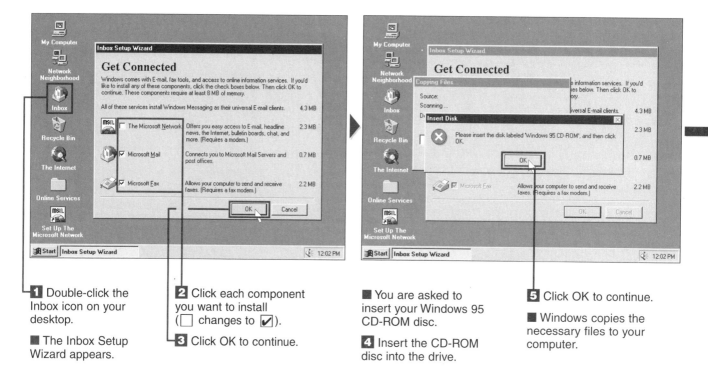

■1 Double-click the Inbox icon on your desktop.

■ The Inbox Setup Wizard appears.

■2 Click each component you want to install (☐ changes to ☑).

■3 Click OK to continue.

■ You are asked to insert your Windows 95 CD-ROM disc.

■4 Insert the CD-ROM disc into the drive.

■5 Click OK to continue.

■ Windows copies the necessary files to your computer.

TIPS

What about my Internet Mail?

If you want to exchange messages
on the Internet, you can add the
Internet Mail service after you
finish installing Exchange. To add
a service to Exchange, see page 416.

Is Exchange my only option for
Internet Mail?

You can also use Internet Explorer
for your Internet Mail. Internet
Explorer is included with OSR2.
If you do not have OSR2, you can
download the latest version of
Internet Explorer from Microsoft's
Web site at www.microsoft.com/ie

What is Microsoft Exchange? What
is Windows Messaging? What is the
Inbox?

They are all the same thing. If you
have Windows 95 or Microsoft Office
97 installed, Microsoft Exchange refers
to the components that allow you to
exchange network e-mail and faxes. If
you have OSR2, the components are
referred to as Windows Messaging.
The Inbox is the desktop icon that
starts Exchange.

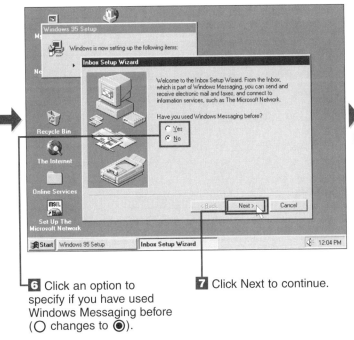

6 Click an option to
specify if you have used
Windows Messaging before
(○ changes to ◉).

7 Click Next to continue.

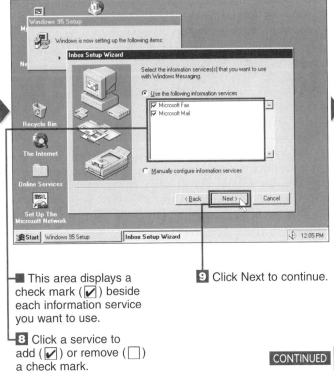

■ This area displays a
check mark (✔) beside
each information service
you want to use.

8 Click a service to
add (✔) or remove (☐)
a check mark.

9 Click Next to continue.

CONTINUED ▶

INSTALL EXCHANGE CONTINUED

You can tell Exchange how you want to send and receive your faxes.

You can choose whether or not you want to have Microsoft Fax answer all the incoming calls on your phone line. If you also use the line to receive voice calls, you should select No. Selecting No allows you to use the same line

to receive both fax and voice calls, but you must be at your computer to receive a fax.

When installing Exchange, you can enter the name and fax number you want to appear on the cover page of your faxes. This information lets the recipient know who sent the fax.

To set up Microsoft Mail for your network e-mail, you must specify the location of your workgroup Postoffice. You may need to ask your network administrator for the name of the computer where the Postoffice is stored. For more information on the Postoffice, see pages 446 to 451.

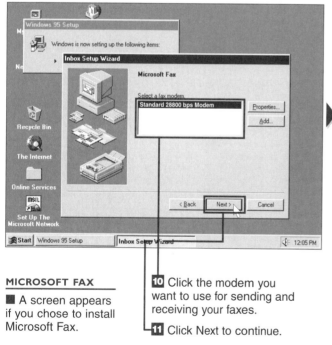

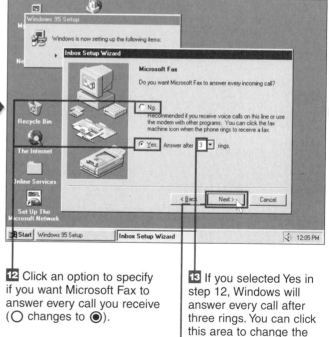

MICROSOFT FAX

■ A screen appears if you chose to install Microsoft Fax.

10 Click the modem you want to use for sending and receiving your faxes.

11 Click Next to continue.

12 Click an option to specify if you want Microsoft Fax to answer every call you receive (○ changes to ◉).

13 If you selected Yes in step 12, Windows will answer every call after three rings. You can click this area to change the number of rings.

14 Click Next to continue.

I have chosen not to have Microsoft Fax answer all my incoming calls. How do I receive a fax?

When Exchange is running, a small fax icon appears on the right side of the taskbar. When you answer the phone and hear fax tones, click on the fax icon. Then click the Answer Now button in the Microsoft Fax Status window and hang up the phone.

How can I have Microsoft Fax answer all calls after I have set up Exchange?

Right-click the fax icon on the taskbar and then click Modem Properties. In the Fax Modem Properties dialog box, select the answer mode you want to use.

Can I use a shared fax modem on the network to send and receive faxes?

When the Inbox Setup Wizard asks you to select a fax modem, click the Add button to connect to a shared fax modem. Then perform steps 9 to 12 on page 502. You can connect to a shared modem on the network to send faxes, but you will not be able to receive faxes directly at your computer.

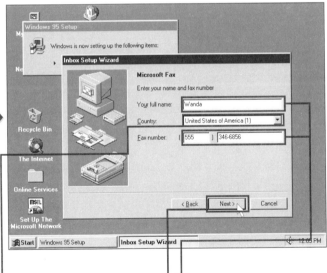

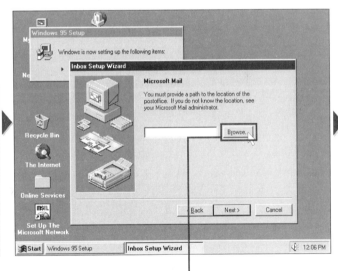

■ Microsoft Fax will use the information in this screen on your fax cover pages.

15 This area displays your country. You can click this area to change the country.

16 These areas display your name and fax number. Double-click each area and then type the appropriate information.

17 Click Next to continue.

MICROSOFT MAIL

■ A screen appears if you chose to install Microsoft Mail.

■ You are asked for the location of your Postoffice.

18 Click Browse to search for the Postoffice.

■ The Browse for Postoffice dialog box appears.

CONTINUED

INSTALL EXCHANGE CONTINUED

When setting up Microsoft Mail, you must tell Exchange where to locate your mailbox in the workgroup Postoffice. To do so, select your name from the list of users. The network administrator usually sets up the Postoffice and is responsible for adding users.

You must also specify the password for your Postoffice

mailbox. If you do not know your password, you can consult your network administrator. You should change your mailbox password after you finish installing Exchange so that your password will be private.

When you have finished installing Exchange, you can use Microsoft Fax and Microsoft Mail. Exchange must be running in order for you

to send and receive faxes and exchange e-mail with people on your network.

The first time you double-click the Inbox, you will find a message waiting.

You can now add additional services to Exchange, such as Internet Mail and CompuServe. To add a service, see page 416.

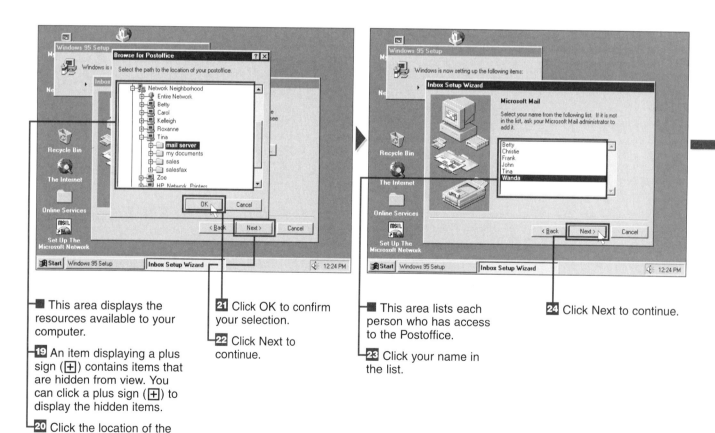

■ This area displays the resources available to your computer.

19 An item displaying a plus sign (⊞) contains items that are hidden from view. You can click a plus sign (⊞) to display the hidden items.

20 Click the location of the Postoffice.

21 Click OK to confirm your selection.

22 Click Next to continue.

■ This area lists each person who has access to the Postoffice.

23 Click your name in the list.

24 Click Next to continue.

SEND E-MAIL AND FAXES

VI

Is there a way to ensure Exchange will run every time I start my computer?

You can place a shortcut to the Inbox in your StartUp folder. This will ensure that Exchange starts every time you start Windows. To place an item in the StartUp folder, see page 258.

How can I find the Postoffice without the network administrator's help?

The Postoffice is normally stored in a shared folder called Postoffice or wgpo0000. You may need to search through all the computers in your workgroup to find the Postoffice.

What do I do if my name does not appear on the Postoffice list?

You can ask the network administrator to add your name. The network administrator must also provide you with the password you need to access your mailbox.

How do I change my password?

In the Exchange window, select the Tools menu. Click Microsoft Mail Tools and then click Change Mailbox Password.

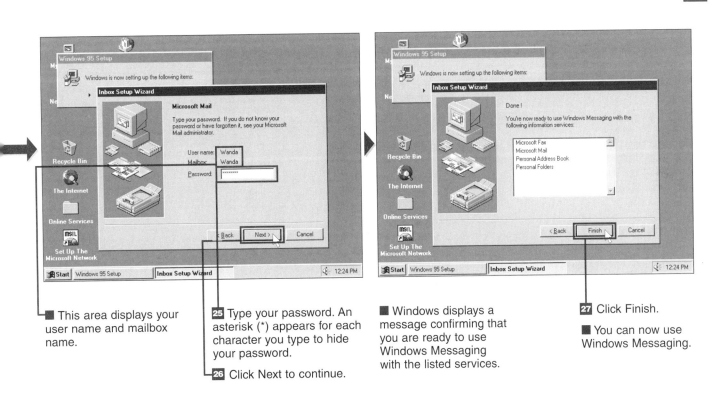

■ This area displays your user name and mailbox name.

25 Type your password. An asterisk (*) appears for each character you type to hide your password.

26 Click Next to continue.

■ Windows displays a message confirming that you are ready to use Windows Messaging with the listed services.

27 Click Finish.

■ You can now use Windows Messaging.

415

ADD A SERVICE TO EXCHANGE

After installing Exchange, you can add a service that you did not select during the initial installation. You can also add a service that was not available when you installed Exchange, such as Internet Mail.

You will need to install the Internet Mail Service on your computer before you can add the service to Exchange. If you have OSR2, you can use the Control Panel's Add/Remove Programs icon to install Internet Mail from the Windows Messaging component. See page 580. If you do not have OSR2, you can download the Internet Mail Service from the Microsoft Web site at www.microsoft.com/windows95/info/inetmail.htm. You can also use the Internet Mail component included in Microsoft Plus!.

When adding the Internet Mail Service, Exchange requires you to enter information about yourself and your e-mail account, including your name, your e-mail address, the mail server that receives your messages, your account name and your password. Your Internet Service Provider (ISP) can supply you with this information.

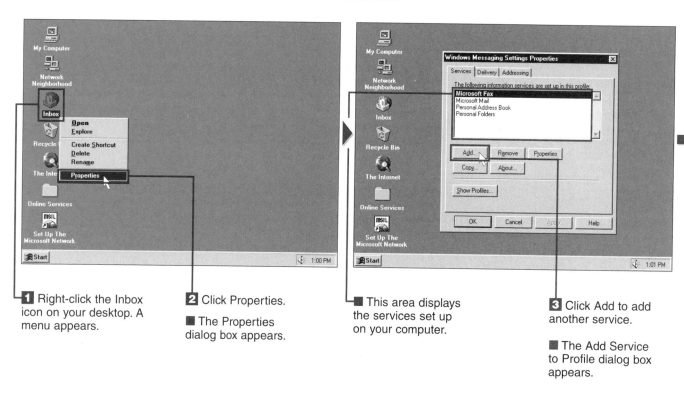

■1 Right-click the Inbox icon on your desktop. A menu appears.

■2 Click Properties.

■ The Properties dialog box appears.

■ This area displays the services set up on your computer.

■3 Click Add to add another service.

■ The Add Service to Profile dialog box appears.

Can I use this procedure to add Internet Mail if I have not installed Exchange?

If you have not installed Exchange, adding the Internet Mail Service will start a wizard to set up both Exchange and Internet Mail.

Should I be concerned about entering my password?

Exchange uses the password you enter when you add the Internet Mail Service to automatically retrieve mail from your Internet mailbox. To ensure that unauthorized users cannot access your Internet mail, make sure you do not save the password with your Dial-Up Networking account.

Can I set up Exchange for my America Online or CompuServe mail?

Yes. Exchange supports both of these services. In OSR2, the Online Services folder contains setup information for these services. You can double-click the service you want to add. If you do not use OSR2, the Windows 95 Upgrade CD-ROM disc has a CompuServe mail setup program in the drivers\other\exchange\compusrv folder.

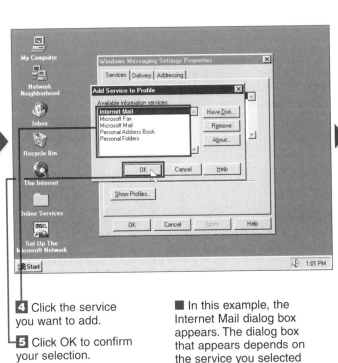

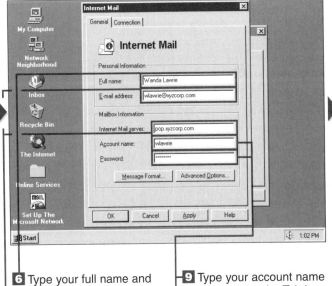

4 Click the service you want to add.

5 Click OK to confirm your selection.

■ In this example, the Internet Mail dialog box appears. The dialog box that appears depends on the service you selected in step 4.

6 Type your full name and then press the Tab key.

7 Type your e-mail address and then press the Tab key.

8 Type the mail server that receives your messages and then press the Tab key.

9 Type your account name and then press the Tab key.

10 Type your password.

CONTINUED

ADD A SERVICE TO EXCHANGE
CONTINUED

Internet service providers may use two different computers, or servers, to process mail. One server handles messages you receive, called inbound mail. The other server handles messages you send, called outbound mail. If your service provider uses a separate outbound mail server, you may need to enter the name of the server. This information is

usually included with the information you receive from your service provider.

You must indicate how you connect to the Internet. If you use a Dial-Up Networking connection, select the modem option and then tell Exchange the name of the connection you use. If you have not configured your modem or

set up a Dial-Up Networking connection, the wizard will ask you to do so.

If you use a modem to connect to the Internet, Remote Mail enables you to make a connection when it is convenient for you, such as when you have messages to send or are ready to answer your mail.

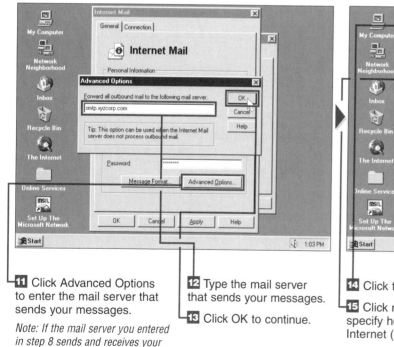

■ Click Advanced Options to enter the mail server that sends your messages.

Note: If the mail server you entered in step 8 sends and receives your messages, you can skip steps 11 to 13.

■ The Advanced Options dialog box appears.

■ Type the mail server that sends your messages.

■ Click OK to continue.

■ Click the Connection tab.

■ Click network or modem to specify how you connect to the Internet (○ changes to ●).

■ If you selected modem in step 15, this area displays the Dial-Up Networking connection you use to connect to the Internet. You can click this area to select another connection.

Why would a modem user choose Remote Mail instead of the scheduled transfer?

The scheduled transfer of messages may fail, causing an error message to appear on your screen. If you are not at the computer, the error may cause you to remain connected to your service provider for a long period of time. Also, the scheduled transfer time may conflict with your need to use the computer. While the Dial-Up Networking connection is being made, you cannot use the computer for other tasks.

Remote Mail can help you save on long-distance charges and connect time, because you only connect when you want to, instead of at regular intervals.

Can I have Exchange automatically connect to my mailbox and retrieve my Internet e-mail messages?

If you decide not to use Remote Mail, you can choose the Connection tab and click the Schedule button to specify how often Exchange connects to your mailbox and transfers messages to your computer.

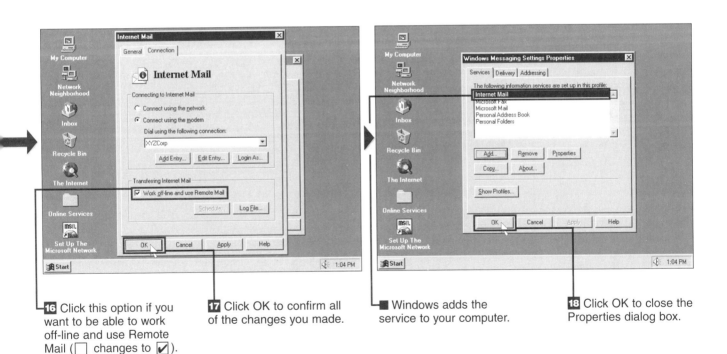

16 Click this option if you want to be able to work off-line and use Remote Mail (☐ changes to ✓).

17 Click OK to confirm all of the changes you made.

■ Windows adds the service to your computer.

18 Click OK to close the Properties dialog box.

CREATE A MESSAGE

You can send an e-mail message to communicate with others.

You can use Microsoft Exchange to send messages to co-workers, other members of The Microsoft Network, members of other online services and anyone using the Internet.

If you want to send a message to several people, you can type each name in the To box. You can use the Cc (carbon copy) box if you want to send a copy of a message to people who would be interested in the message, but are not directly involved.

When you create a message, you should enter a subject that will help the reader quickly identify the contents of your message.

You can indicate the importance of a message by selecting a priority. Windows automatically sends a message as a normal priority. You can specify if you want to send the message as a high or low priority.

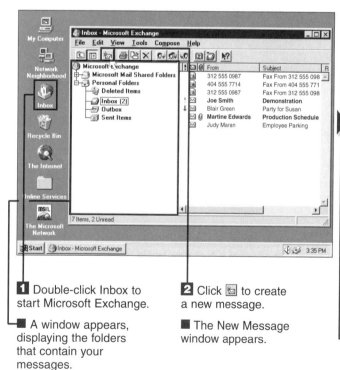

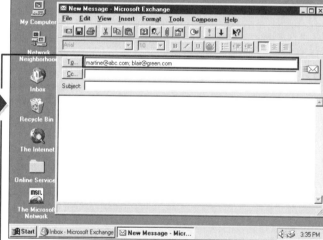

■1 Double-click Inbox to start Microsoft Exchange.

■ A window appears, displaying the folders that contain your messages.

■2 Click 🖾 to create a new message.

■ The New Message window appears.

■3 Type the address of the person you want to receive the message.

■ To send the message to more than one person, separate each address with a semicolon (;).

Note: To select names from your address book, refer to page 426. Then skip to step 5.

Can I format my e-mail messages?

You can use the Format menu commands or the toolbar to change fonts, sizes and other settings for selected text. People outside your workgroup may not be able to see the formatting in your messages.

Can I send a blind carbon copy?

A blind carbon copy lets you send the same message to several people without them knowing that others have also received the message. In the New Message window, choose the View menu and select Bcc Box to turn on this feature.

How soon are messages sent?

Within your corporate network, all messages should be received within 10 minutes. For online services and the Internet, the message will not be sent until you connect and transfer your mail. The message will not be delivered until the recipient transfers their mail to their computer.

How can I find out if the message was received and read?

Exchange can confirm that the message was delivered and opened. From the Tools menu, select Options. Click the Send tab and then choose the option you want. This feature is not supported for messages sent using the Internet.

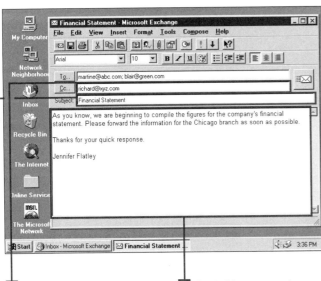

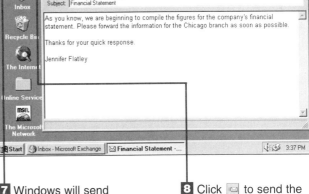

■ **4** Click this area to send a carbon copy of the message to another person. Then type the address for the person.

■ **5** Click this area and then type the subject of the message.

■ **6** Click this area and then type your message.

7 Windows will send the message as a normal priority. Click one of these options if you want to send the message as a high (![]) or low (![]) priority.

■ If the toolbar does not appear on your screen, click View and then click Toolbar.

8 Click ![] to send the message.

■ Windows sends the message and stores a copy of the message in the Sent Items folder.

ADD NAMES TO THE ADDRESS BOOK

Y ou can store the names and e-mail addresses of people you frequently send messages to in an address book.

When you send a message, you can select an e-mail address from the address book. The address book saves you from having to type the same addresses over and over. Using the address book also saves you from having mail

returned due to typing mistakes in the address.

The Personal Address Book contains the names and addresses you add. You can add different types of addresses to the Personal Address Book. For example, you can include Internet e-mail addresses, addresses for online services like The Microsoft Network,

addresses in your network workgroup and fax numbers.

You may find other address books in Exchange. The Postoffice Address List contains the addresses of people in your network workgroup. The Postoffice Address List is set up by the network administrator. You cannot add or remove entries in other address books.

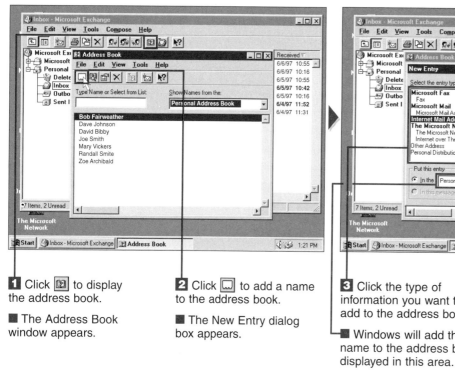

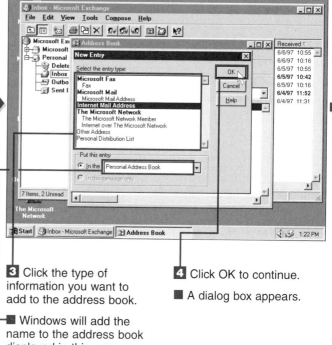

1 Click 📖 to display the address book.

■ The Address Book window appears.

2 Click 📇 to add a name to the address book.

■ The New Entry dialog box appears.

3 Click the type of information you want to add to the address book.

■ Windows will add the name to the address book displayed in this area.

4 Click OK to continue.

■ A dialog box appears.

Can I send the same person different types of messages?

You should create a different entry for each type of message you want to send to a person. For example, you can create one entry to store the person's fax number and another entry to store the person's e-mail address.

Can I send the same message to many people at the same time?

You can create a Personal Distribution List to send the same message to many people at the same time. See page 424.

Can I create a second personal address book to separate my business contacts from friends?

You can only have one Personal Address Book.

How can I find an Internet e-mail address?

To search for an Internet e-mail address, you can use a service like Four11 (www.four11.com). Although there is no comprehensive source of Internet e-mail addresses, Four11 has over six million e-mail addresses in its database.

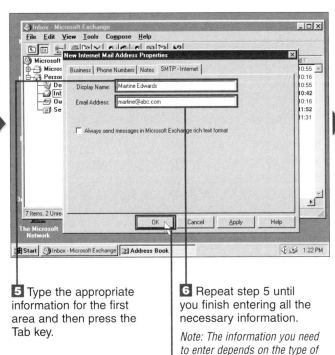

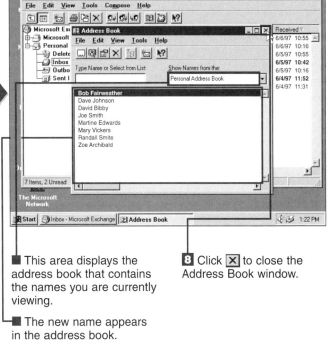

5 Type the appropriate information for the first area and then press the Tab key.

6 Repeat step 5 until you finish entering all the necessary information.

Note: The information you need to enter depends on the type of address you selected in step 3.

7 Click OK to save the information.

■ This area displays the address book that contains the names you are currently viewing.

■ The new name appears in the address book.

8 Click ✕ to close the Address Book window.

ADD GROUPS TO THE ADDRESS BOOK

You can use Exchange to send a message to many people at once by creating a group, called a Personal Distribution List. Creating a group saves you the time of having to enter each person's address into a message.

For example, if you are planning to send a message to your customers advising them of your monthly specials, you can create a group to send the message to all your customers at once.

You can include the addresses from several address books in a group.

One group can contain many different types of messages. For example, you can send the same message by fax, Internet e-mail and Microsoft Mail from one group. Exchange will send each person the message type associated with their address in the address book.

You can create as many groups as you need. Each group appears as a name in an address book.

When you create a new message and select the group you want to send the message to, Exchange will send the message to everyone in the group.

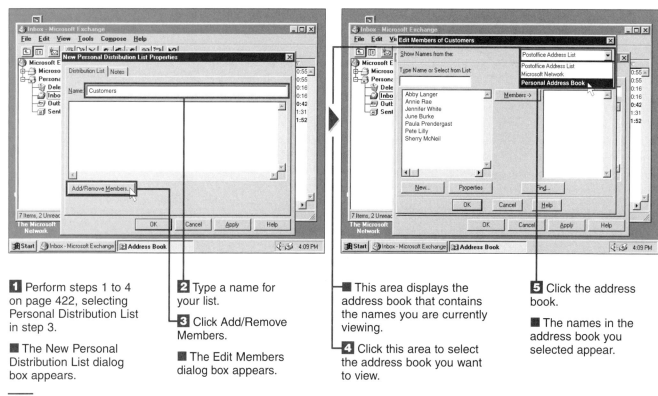

■1 Perform steps 1 to 4 on page 422, selecting Personal Distribution List in step 3.

■ The New Personal Distribution List dialog box appears.

■2 Type a name for your list.

■3 Click Add/Remove Members.

■ The Edit Members dialog box appears.

■ This area displays the address book that contains the names you are currently viewing.

■4 Click this area to select the address book you want to view.

■5 Click the address book.

■ The names in the address book you selected appear.

TIPS

Can I add a name that is not in an address book to a group?

You can click the Add/Remove Members button and then click New to add a name that is not in an address book to a group. This procedure adds the name to your Personal Address Book and the group.

How do I remove a name from a group?

Click the Add/Remove Members button. Select the name you want to remove from the group in the right-hand column and press the Delete key. If necessary, select and delete the semi-colon that followed the name you removed.

How can I tell that all of the messages have been sent?

Exchange transfers the messages that have been sent to the Sent Items folder. If Exchange cannot deliver a message, you will receive a message in your Inbox informing you which people did not receive the message.

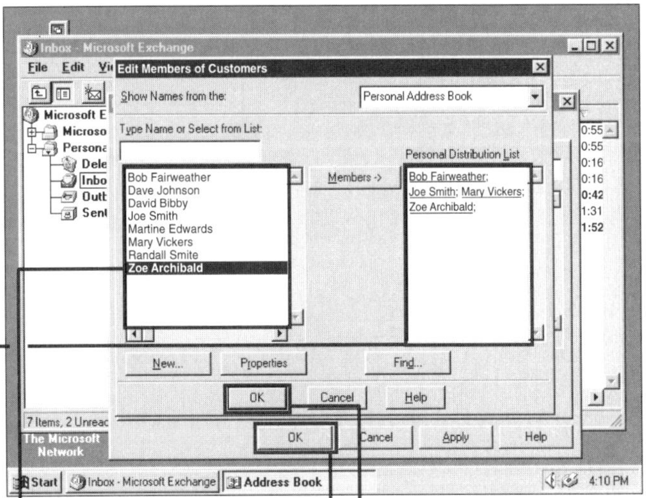

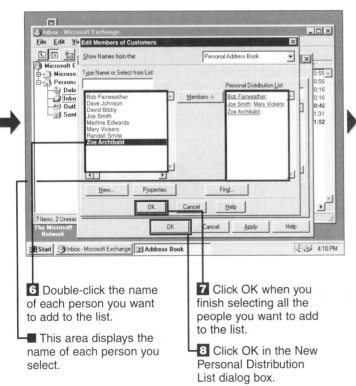

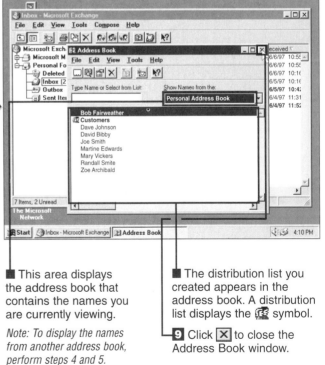

6 Double-click the name of each person you want to add to the list.

■ This area displays the name of each person you select.

7 Click OK when you finish selecting all the people you want to add to the list.

8 Click OK in the New Personal Distribution List dialog box.

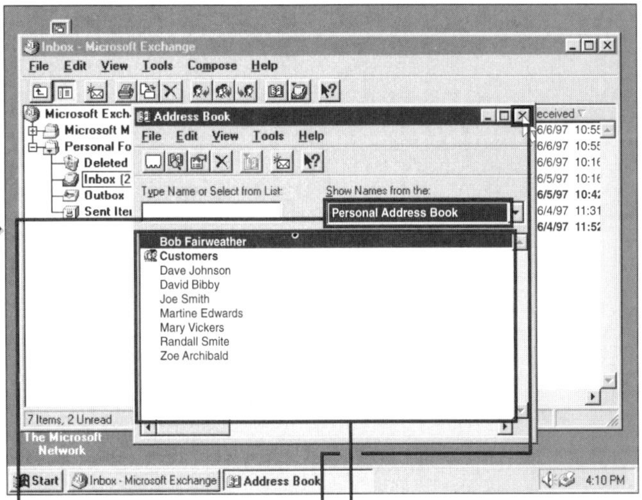

■ This area displays the address book that contains the names you are currently viewing.

Note: To display the names from another address book, perform steps 4 and 5.

■ The distribution list you created appears in the address book. A distribution list displays the symbol.

9 Click ☒ to close the Address Book window.

SELECT NAMES FROM THE ADDRESS BOOK

When sending a message, you can select the name of the person you want to receive the message from an address book. Selecting names from an address book saves you from having to remember and type addresses you use often.

The address book makes it easy to send a message when you do not remember the exact spelling of the recipient's address. The address book also reduces the possibility that the message will be undeliverable because of a typing mistake in the address.

In Exchange, you may find several address books. The Postoffice Address List contains the addresses of people in your network workgroup. The Personal Address Book contains names and addresses you have added. Additional address books may also be available for online services you subscribe to, such as CompuServe.

You can also use the address book to send a copy of a message, called a carbon copy (Cc), to another person. This is useful if you want to send a copy of a message to someone who is not directly involved, but would be interested in the message.

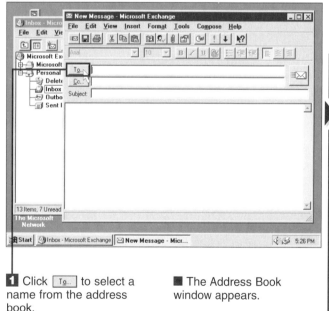

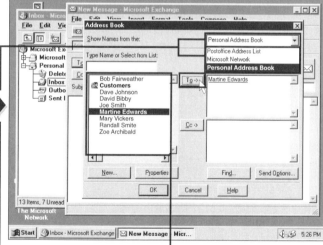

1 Click `To...` to select a name from the address book.

Note: To create a new message, refer to page 420.

■ The Address Book window appears.

2 Click this area to select the address book that contains the addresses you want to view.

3 Click the address book.

■ The names in the address book you selected appear.

4 Click the name of the person you want to receive the message.

5 Click To.

How can I send a blind carbon copy (Bcc)?

A blind carbon copy allows you to send a copy of a message to several people without them knowing that others have also received the same message. In the New Message window, display the View menu and click the Bcc Box command. The Address Book window will then display a Bcc button that you can use to send blind carbon copies.

How do I add names to an address book?

To add names to an address book, see page 422.

Can I mix names selected from the address book with names I type?

You can use names from the address book and names you type to send a message. When you type names in the Address Book window, you must separate the names with a semi-colon.

How do I remove a name from the To area?

To remove a name, select the name and then press the Delete key.

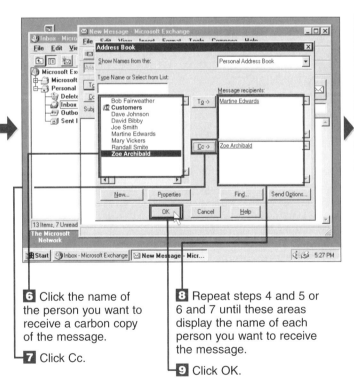

6 Click the name of the person you want to receive a carbon copy of the message.

7 Click Cc.

8 Repeat steps 4 and 5 or 6 and 7 until these areas display the name of each person you want to receive the message.

9 Click OK.

■ These areas display the name of each person you selected from the address book.

■ You can now finish creating the message.

INSERT FILES INTO MESSAGES

You can insert a file into a message. This is useful when you want to include additional information.

You can insert a file created in any application. You can send images, video or sound recordings and even program files. The computer receiving the message must have the necessary software to display

the image or play the video or sound recording.

You can insert a file as text only, which will copy the file's contents and paste them into your e-mail message. You can also insert a file as an attachment. The file keeps all of its formatting and appears as an icon in your message.

You can also send a link to a file on a shared network drive. A shortcut icon to the file appears in the message. When the recipient double-clicks the icon, the file is accessed from the network and opens in the appropriate program. The recipient must have access to the network and the file you send must be in a shared folder.

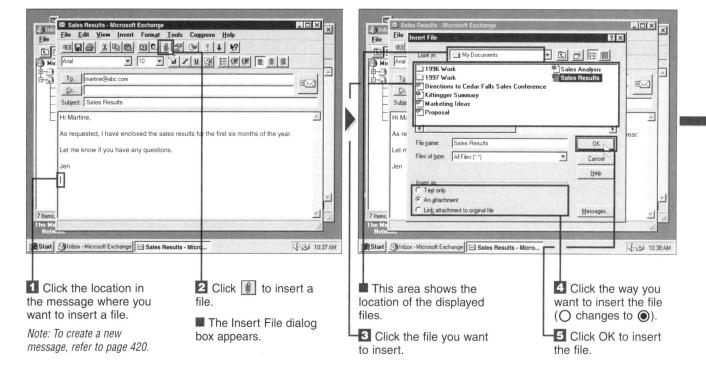

■1 Click the location in the message where you want to insert a file.

Note: To create a new message, refer to page 420.

■2 Click 📎 to insert a file.

■ The Insert File dialog box appears.

■ This area shows the location of the displayed files.

■3 Click the file you want to insert.

■4 Click the way you want to insert the file (○ changes to ●).

■5 Click OK to insert the file.

Can I drag and drop a file into a message?

You can drag and drop a file into a message from the desktop or any open window. An icon appears in the message. This is the easiest way to insert many files into a message.

How can I create a link to a file on my computer?

In the Insert File dialog box, display the contents of the Network Neighborhood. Double-click your own computer and then the drives and folders until you find the file you want to link.

I sent a program in my message. Why doesn't it work on the other computer?

Most programs do not work unless you use the correct method to install them. You should also read your software license agreement carefully to see if there are restrictions on sharing the program.

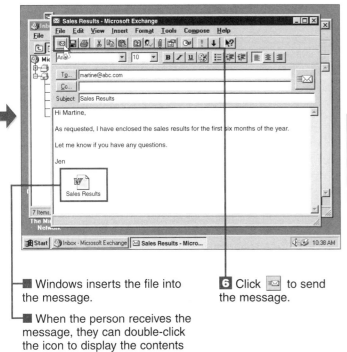

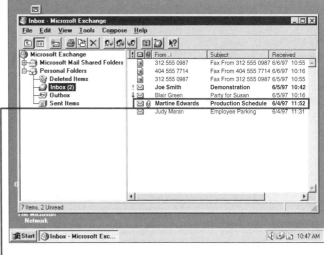

■ Windows inserts the file into the message.

■ When the person receives the message, they can double-click the icon to display the contents of the file.

6 Click to send the message.

VIEW AN ATTACHED FILE

■ When you receive a message with a file, a paper clip ( ) appears beside the message.

READ MESSAGES

Y ou can use Exchange to view many types of messages, such as messages from other people on your network, e-mail messages sent over the Internet, messages sent using services such as The Microsoft Network and faxes.

The name of a folder containing unread messages appears in bold type. Each unread message also appears in bold type. When you

read a message, it changes to regular type.

Exchange has four folders to store your messages. The Inbox folder contains new messages you receive. Messages waiting to be sent are held in the Outbox folder. Messages that have been sent are saved in the Sent Items folder. The Deleted Items folder contains any messages you have deleted.

Fax messages appear in your Inbox as soon as you receive them. Any messages sent using Microsoft Mail on your local network appear in your Inbox shortly after they are sent. To retrieve messages sent by people using online services or the Internet, you must first connect to your online service or the Internet.

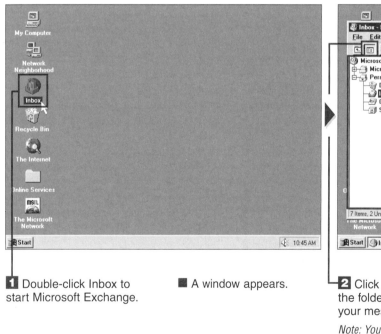

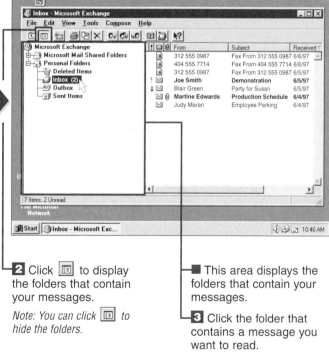

1 Double-click Inbox to start Microsoft Exchange.

■ A window appears.

2 Click 🔳 to display the folders that contain your messages.

Note: You can click 🔳 to hide the folders.

■ This area displays the folders that contain your messages.

3 Click the folder that contains a message you want to read.

TIPS

How do I display the toolbar on my screen?

Display the View menu and select Toolbar.

How can I tell if I have new messages?

You can only receive messages when Exchange is open. When you receive a new message, Exchange displays an envelope icon at the right end of the taskbar. Exchange also lets you specify other ways to indicate you have new mail. From the Tools menu, select Options and then click the options you want from the General tab.

Can I make the message appear bold again, to remind me that I have not replied yet?

You cannot make a message appear bold again using Exchange. If you want to remind yourself that you have not replied to a message, you can create a folder to store the unanswered messages. See page 438.

How can I check for new messages?

From the Tools menu, select Deliver Now to check for new messages. If you have set up multiple services, such as The Microsoft Network or Internet Mail, select the Deliver Now Using command. A dialog box appears, allowing you to check for messages using one or all of your services.

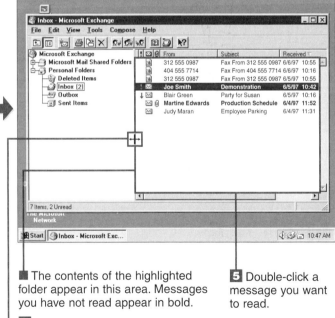

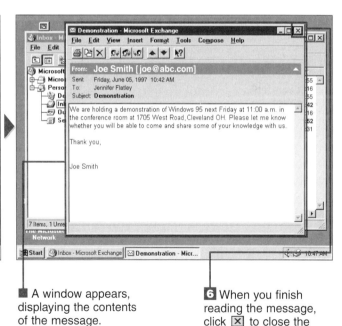

■ The contents of the highlighted folder appear in this area. Messages you have not read appear in bold.

4 To change the size of the two sides of the window, position the mouse ⌖ over the vertical line that separates the two sides (⌖ changes to ↔). Then drag the line to a new location.

5 Double-click a message you want to read.

■ A window appears, displaying the contents of the message.

6 When you finish reading the message, click ✕ to close the window.

431

REPLY TO OR FORWARD A MESSAGE

Y ou can reply to a message to answer a question, express an opinion or supply additional information.

When you reply to a message, you can send your reply to the person who sent the message or to the sender and everyone who received the original message. A new window appears, displaying the name of the recipients and the

subject of the message you are replying to.

The reply includes the contents of the original message so you can refer to it. Including the contents of the original message also helps the reader identify which message you are replying to.

When you send a reply, the text you type appears in blue, to

indicate a different author.

You can also forward, or send, a message to another person. When you forward the message, you can add your own comments to the original message. Forwarding a message is useful if you know that another person would be interested in the contents of the message.

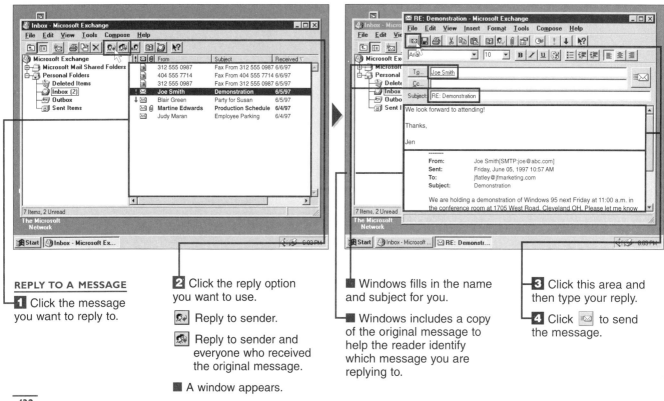

REPLY TO A MESSAGE

1 Click the message you want to reply to.

2 Click the reply option you want to use.

- Reply to sender.

- Reply to sender and everyone who received the original message.

■ A window appears.

■ Windows fills in the name and subject for you.

■ Windows includes a copy of the original message to help the reader identify which message you are replying to.

3 Click this area and then type your reply.

4 Click ✉ to send the message.

TIPS

Can I delete text from the original message?

When you reply or forward a message, you can delete as much of the original text as you want. You may want to delete text if the original message is long or if you are only referring to a specific part of the message.

Can I stop Exchange from including the original message?

If you do not want to include the original message in your replies, choose the Tools menu and then select Options. Select the Read tab and click Include the original text when replying (✔ changes to ☐).

Can I change the color of the reply text, or my comments when I forward a message?

To change the color for all future messages, choose the Tools menu, click Options and select the Read Tab. Then select the Font button for font and color options. You can also use the Formatting toolbar in the message window to change the color of your comments.

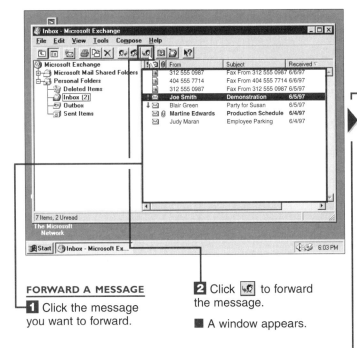

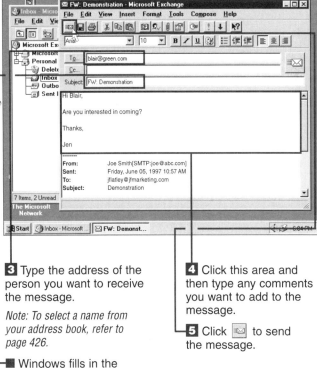

FORWARD A MESSAGE

1 Click the message you want to forward.

2 Click 🔧 to forward the message.

■ A window appears.

3 Type the address of the person you want to receive the message.

Note: To select a name from your address book, refer to page 426.

■ Windows fills in the subject for you.

4 Click this area and then type any comments you want to add to the message.

5 Click ✉ to send the message.

SORT, PRINT OR DELETE MESSAGES

Y ou can sort messages in Exchange so they are easier to find. You can sort by the name of the person who sent or received the message, the subject of the message or the date the message was sent or received. Messages can be sorted in ascending or descending order.

Messages are usually sorted by the date they were sent or received, in descending order.

You can produce a paper copy of a message in Exchange. A printed message is useful when you need a reference copy of the message.

You can delete a message you no longer need. Deleting messages reduces the size of your mail file and makes it easier to manage your messages. When you delete a message in Exchange, the deleted message is placed in the Deleted Items folder.

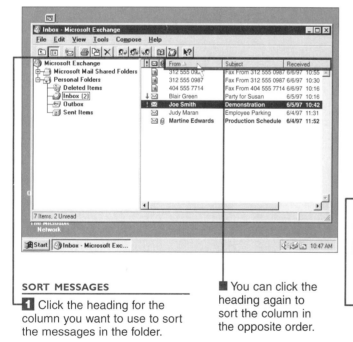

SORT MESSAGES

■1 Click the heading for the column you want to use to sort the messages in the folder.

Note: If you cannot see the heading you want to use to sort the messages, use the horizontal scroll bar to view the heading.

■ You can click the heading again to sort the column in the opposite order.

PRINT MESSAGES

■1 Click the message you want to print.

■2 Click 🖨 to print the message.

■ Windows prints the message.

TIPS

How can I add or delete a column for a folder?

Each folder displays columns in a specific order. In the View menu, select the Columns command to add, remove or change the order of columns in a folder.

Can I change the width of a column?

Place the mouse pointer on the right edge of the column heading you want to change. The mouse pointer changes to a double-headed arrow (↔). Drag the edge of the column until it displays the size you want. You can also double-click the right edge of a column to make the column fit the longest item.

When is the Deleted Items folder emptied?

The Deleted Items folder is automatically emptied every time you close Exchange. You can specify when you want to empty the Deleted Items folder. Choose the Tools menu and click the Options command. Then select the General tab and click Empty the Deleted Items folder upon exiting (☑ changes to ☐). The Deleted Items folder will then only be emptied when you right-click the folder and select Empty Folder.

SEND E-MAIL AND FAXES

VI

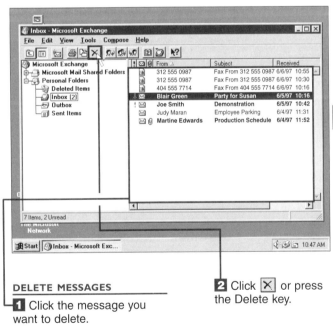

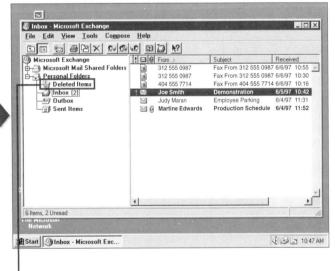

DELETE MESSAGES

◤ 1 Click the message you want to delete.

Note: To delete several consecutive messages at once, click the first message. Press and hold down the Shift key and then click the last message you want to delete.

2 Click ☒ or press the Delete key.

◼ Windows removes the message from the current folder and places the message in the Deleted Items folder.

◼ The messages in the Deleted Items folder are permanently deleted when you close Exchange.

435

FIND MESSAGES

I f you cannot find a message you want to review, you can search for the message.

Exchange has a Find feature that can help you search for and find any message that you have sent or received. This is useful if you cannot remember exactly which message you are looking for.

You can use Find to look in all your folders or in specific folders. For example, if you are looking for a message you have sent, you can save time by searching only the Sent Items folder. You can also search for mail sent to or received from a specific person. If you can only remember a word from the subject of the message, you can

search the subject area of all your messages. You can also find messages containing a specific word.

Exchange will search for messages that match all of the information you specify in the Find window.

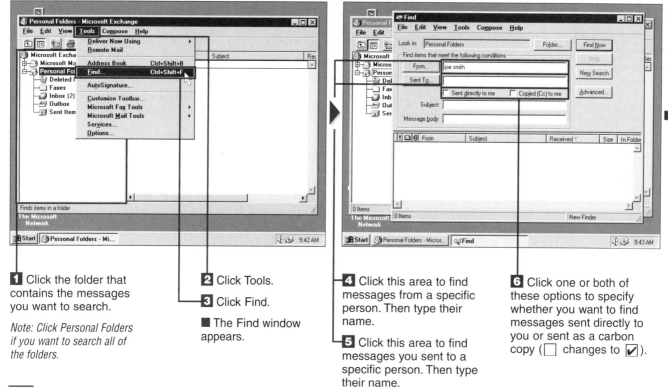

1 Click the folder that contains the messages you want to search.

Note: Click Personal Folders if you want to search all of the folders.

2 Click Tools.

3 Click Find.

■ The Find window appears.

4 Click this area to find messages from a specific person. Then type their name.

5 Click this area to find messages you sent to a specific person. Then type their name.

6 Click one or both of these options to specify whether you want to find messages sent directly to you or sent as a carbon copy (☐ changes to ✔).

Can I save a search?

You cannot save a search, but you can leave the Find window open and have Find update the search results as new messages arrive. For example, if you are trying to finish a sales report, you can set up Find to display only messages from the sales team and then wait for the messages to appear.

How can I better organize my messages?

If you spend a lot of time searching for messages, you can create folders to keep related messages together. See page 438.

How do I find the messages I sent on a specific day?

You can use the Advanced button in Find to search for messages sent on a specific day. You can also choose to look for messages sent between two dates. If all the messages you have sent are in one folder, it may be simpler to use the sort feature. To sort messages, see page 434.

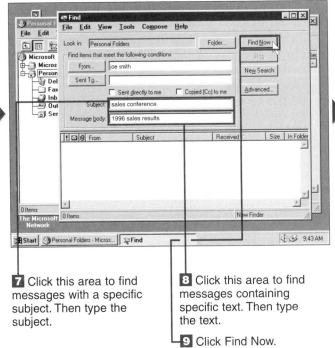

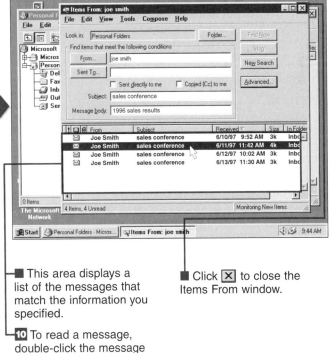

7 Click this area to find messages with a specific subject. Then type the subject.

8 Click this area to find messages containing specific text. Then type the text.

9 Click Find Now.

■ This area displays a list of the messages that match the information you specified.

10 To read a message, double-click the message you want to read.

■ Click ☒ to close the Items From window.

CREATE A MAIL FOLDER

You can create folders in Exchange to keep related messages together and make saved messages easier to find. For example, if you have many messages related to a specific project or client, you can use a folder to organize the messages and keep them together.

You can create a new folder within an existing folder to better organize your messages.

You can use long, descriptive names to label the folders you create, but you may find it easier to manage your folders if you give them shorter names. The Exchange window can

display shorter names more easily. If you can see the full name of a folder in the Exchange window, you will be able to work with the folder more easily.

After you create a folder, you can move messages into the folder.

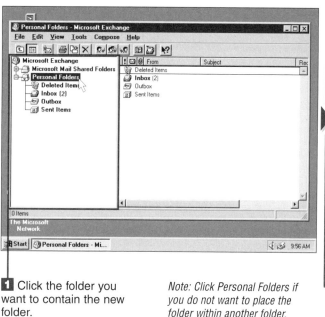

1 Click the folder you want to contain the new folder.

Note: Click Personal Folders if you do not want to place the folder within another folder.

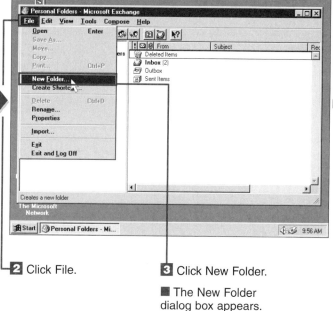

2 Click File.

3 Click New Folder.

■ The New Folder dialog box appears.

How do I rename a folder?

Right-click on the name of the folder you want to change. Select Rename from the menu that appears. Then type the new name and press the Enter key.

How can I delete a folder I no longer need?

Select the folder you want to delete and press the Delete key. You cannot delete the Inbox, Outbox, Deleted Items or Sent Items folders. If you delete a folder that contains messages, the messages will also be deleted. When you delete a folder, it stays in the Deleted Items folder until you close Exchange.

Can I change the columns displayed in a folder?

When you create a new folder, the new folder displays the same column headings as the Inbox. From the View menu, select Columns to change which columns appear in a folder.

Can I rearrange folders?

You can drag and drop folders to a new location. You can also right-click on a folder and use the menu that appears to copy or move the folder to a new location.

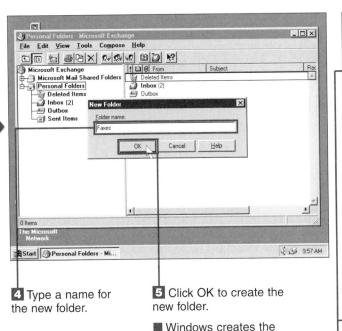

4 Type a name for the new folder.

5 Click OK to create the new folder.

■ Windows creates the new folder.

MOVE MESSAGES TO OTHER FOLDERS

1 Click the message you want to move.

2 Position the mouse over the message.

3 Drag the message to the folder where you want to store the message.

■ Windows moves the message to the folder you selected.

PASSWORD PROTECT YOUR MESSAGES

You can use a password to keep your messages private and confidential. Other people may have access to your computer system, but without a password they cannot read messages you have sent or received.

When choosing a password, do not use words that people can easily associate with you, such as your name or favorite sport. The most effective password connects two words or number sequences with a special character, such as blue@123. If you write down your password, store the password in a safe place where no one will find it.

Once you have selected a password, you must enter the password each time you want to open Exchange to read or send messages. If you forget your password, you will not be able to open Exchange and access your messages.

You can change your password as often as you want. Regularly changing your password makes it more difficult for other people to figure out your password and access your messages.

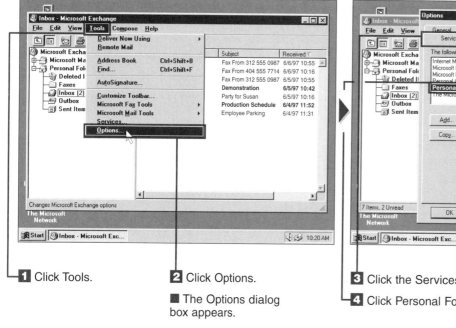

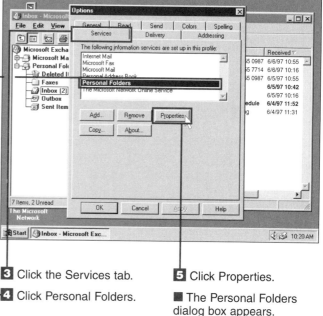

1 Click Tools.

2 Click Options.

■ The Options dialog box appears.

3 Click the Services tab.

4 Click Personal Folders.

5 Click Properties.

■ The Personal Folders dialog box appears.

TIPS

How can I get rid of my other passwords?

In any dialog box that asks for a password, you can select the Remember password option. The password is automatically entered each time it is required. This is useful for other services that use Exchange.

What can I do if I cannot remember my password?

If you cannot remember your password, you will have to delete your Personal Folders and set up Exchange again. All your messages will be lost.

How can I remove my Personal Folders password?

From the Personal Folders dialog box, select Change password. In the dialog box that appears, do not enter any information in the New and Verify password boxes. You can activate and remove the password setting as often as you want. For example, you may only want to set up a password when you will be out of town and other people will be using your computer.

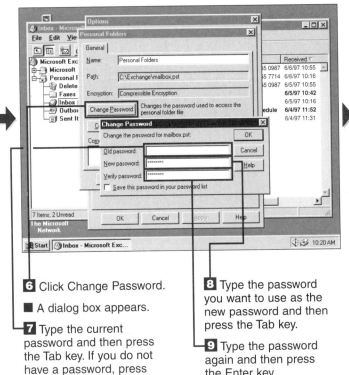

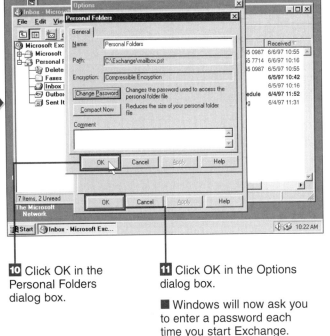

6 Click Change Password.

■ A dialog box appears.

7 Type the current password and then press the Tab key. If you do not have a password, press the Tab key.

8 Type the password you want to use as the new password and then press the Tab key.

9 Type the password again and then press the Enter key.

10 Click OK in the Personal Folders dialog box.

11 Click OK in the Options dialog box.

■ Windows will now ask you to enter a password each time you start Exchange.

CREATE A NEW USER PROFILE

Y ou can use Exchange user profiles on a computer that is used by several people. Each person sharing the computer can have a separate user profile that provides them with their own mail setup, settings and folders for their personal messages.

A user profile stores the settings that provide access

to communication services ranging from Internet mail and online services to fax and office e-mail. When the communication services are set up on a computer, a default user profile, called MS Exchange Settings, is created. When there is only one user profile, the default user profile settings are used each time Exchange starts.

You can also create Exchange user profiles to use on a portable computer. One user profile may include the office network mail component and a corporate online service account. A different user profile may be used at home to access fax capabilities, collect personal Internet e-mail messages and connect to the office network e-mail using Dial-up Networking.

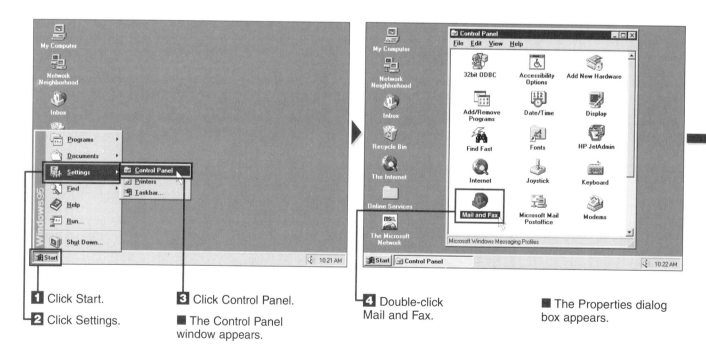

■1 Click Start.

■2 Click Settings.

■3 Click Control Panel.

■ The Control Panel window appears.

■4 Double-click Mail and Fax.

■ The Properties dialog box appears.

TIPS

Can I change my user profile later?

In the Mail and Fax dialog box, you can use the Properties button to make changes to the services or the setup used for the services.

Can I use the Copy feature to create additional profiles?

In the Mail and Fax dialog box, you can use the Copy feature to create additional profiles, but this does not create a Personal Folder or Address Book for the new profile. The same message file is shared between the original user profile and all copies of the profile.

How do I delete a user profile that is no longer needed?

In the Mail and Fax dialog box, select the user profile and then click the Remove button. Be careful when deleting a user profile because there is no undo and the settings are not saved in the Recycle Bin. If you remove all of the profiles, you will have to create a new user profile to use Exchange. Deleting a user profile will not remove the Personal Folder or the Address Book files for the deleted user profile.

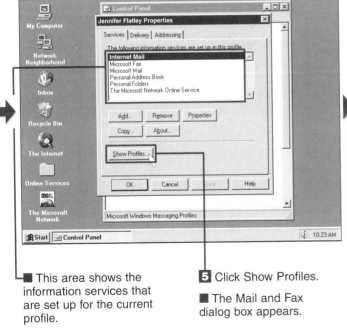

■ This area shows the information services that are set up for the current profile.

5 Click Show Profiles.

■ The Mail and Fax dialog box appears.

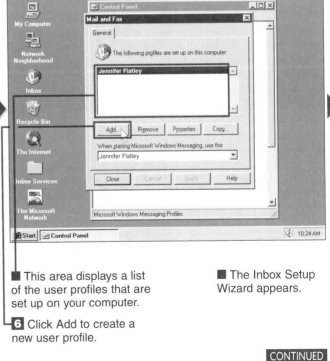

■ This area displays a list of the user profiles that are set up on your computer.

6 Click Add to create a new user profile.

■ The Inbox Setup Wizard appears.

CONTINUED ▶

CREATE A NEW USER PROFILE
CONTINUED

Each Exchange user profile can contain any or all of the settings available on the computer.

You can select the services you want and then name the settings. On a computer with a user profile for each person, use the person's name to name the settings. If you use different user profiles for different locations, use the name of the location like "home", "office" or "hotel room" to name the settings.

The Inbox Setup Wizard sets up the new user profile for you, asking all of the questions needed to set up the communication services for another person. You need the specific information required for each service, including the Internet server's mail address and the location of the network e-mail folder.

Each person should create their own Personal Folder and Address Book files to contain their messages and address book entries.

You can have Exchange ask which user profile you want to use when Exchange is starting or have Exchange use the same profile each time the program opens.

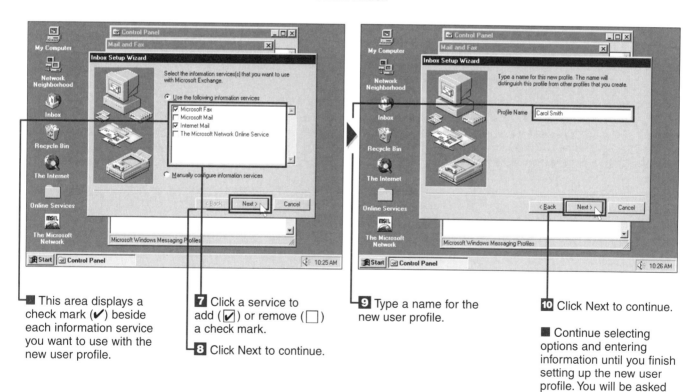

■ This area displays a check mark (✔) beside each information service you want to use with the new user profile.

7 Click a service to add (✔) or remove (☐) a check mark.

8 Click Next to continue.

9 Type a name for the new user profile.

10 Click Next to continue.

■ Continue selecting options and entering information until you finish setting up the new user profile. You will be asked the same questions as when you first installed Microsoft Exchange.

How do we combine Exchange user profiles with computer user profiles?

For information on setting up computer user profiles, see page 234. Each person's login name can have its own Exchange user profile. To set up Exchange user profiles with the computer user profiles, log in and start Exchange. Choose the Tools menu and then select Options. Select the General tab and then click the Always use this profile setting. Choose the user profile you want to use. The next time you log on and open the Inbox, your Exchange profile will be loaded. You only have to set up the settings once for each user profile.

How do we keep each person's messages separate?

Each person's Personal Folder file will contain their personal messages. When you create a new user profile, other people cannot see the messages in the new profile.

I want to configure my computer for several locations. Should I create separate Personal Folder files?

You may prefer to create separate Personal Folder files to keep your personal messages separate from your business messages, but if you are the only person using the computer, this is not necessary.

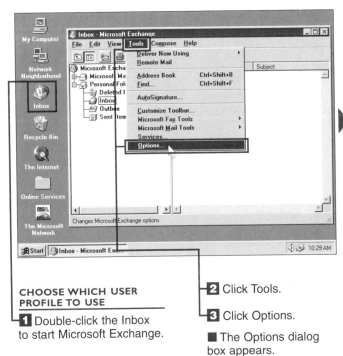

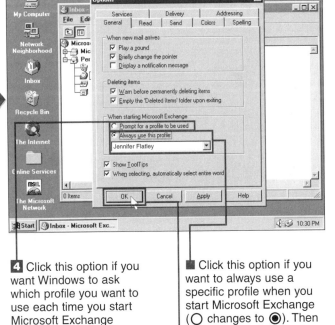

CHOOSE WHICH USER PROFILE TO USE

1 Double-click the Inbox to start Microsoft Exchange.

2 Click Tools.

3 Click Options.

■ The Options dialog box appears.

4 Click this option if you want Windows to ask which profile you want to use each time you start Microsoft Exchange (○ changes to ◉).

■ Click this option if you want to always use a specific profile when you start Microsoft Exchange (○ changes to ◉). Then click this area to select the profile you want to use.

5 Click OK to confirm your selection.

INSTALL THE WORKGROUP POSTOFFICE

In order to use Exchange to send and receive mail on a network, you need to create a Postoffice. The Postoffice stores a mailbox for each person in the workgroup and all of the messages that are sent over the network.

When creating the Postoffice, you must specify where you want Windows to store the Postoffice.

You can store the Postoffice on your computer or specify another computer on the network. You may want to create a specific folder to store the Postoffice. Exchange automatically creates a folder for the Postoffice, called wgpo0000.

Before creating the Postoffice, you must make sure a Postoffice does

not already exist for your workgroup. If there is more than one Postoffice for a workgroup, mail will not be properly transferred on the network.

The Postoffice is usually created and managed by the person responsible for network administration.

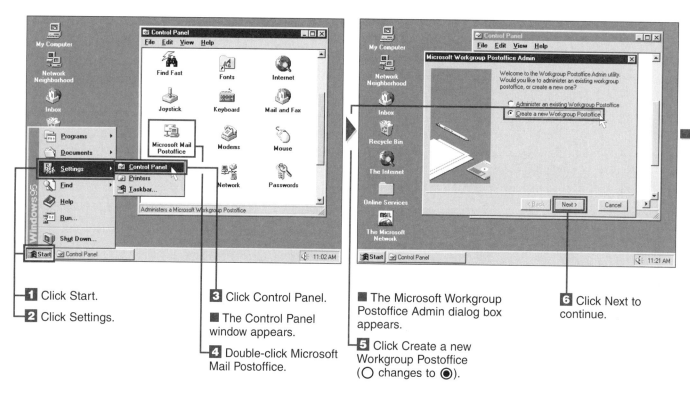

■1 Click Start.

■2 Click Settings.

■3 Click Control Panel.

■ The Control Panel window appears.

■4 Double-click Microsoft Mail Postoffice.

■ The Microsoft Workgroup Postoffice Admin dialog box appears.

■5 Click Create a new Workgroup Postoffice (○ changes to ◉).

■6 Click Next to continue.

TIPS

Why would I create a Postoffice?

You can create a Postoffice if you are on a network and want to use Exchange to send e-mail to people in your workgroup. You do not need to set up the Postoffice to send e-mail using the Internet or services like The Microsoft Network or CompuServe. You also do not need a Postoffice to use Exchange to send faxes.

Why isn't there a Microsoft Mail Postoffice icon in my Control Panel?

If the Microsoft Mail Postoffice icon does not appear, the Microsoft Exchange or Windows Messaging component of Windows 95 may not be installed on your computer. To install a component, see page 580.

Will I have to do anything special if the Postoffice is on my computer?

Your computer must be turned on for the transfer of mail to occur, so you should leave your computer on during all working hours. You should also back up the Postoffice folders regularly, even if only to another drive on the network. For information on how to back up folders and files, see page 328.

SEND E-MAIL AND FAXES

VI

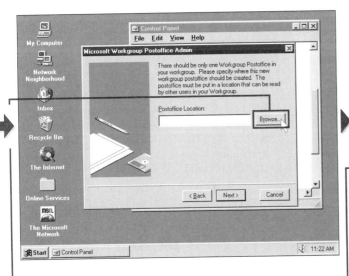

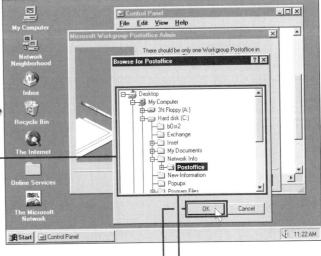

■ Windows wants to know where you want to place the new Postoffice.

7 Click Browse to find the folder where you want to place the Postoffice.

Note: Instead of browsing, you can simply type the location for the Postoffice in the area provided. Then skip to step 11 on page 448.

■ The Browse for Postoffice dialog box appears.

■ This area displays the resources available to your computer.

8 An item displaying a plus sign (⊞) contains more items. You can click the plus sign (⊞) to display the items it contains.

9 Click the location where you want to place the Postoffice.

10 Click OK to confirm your selection.

CONTINUED ▶

INSTALL THE
WORKGROUP POSTOFFICE CONTINUED

When you create the Postoffice, you should create a mailbox for the administrator. You should enter a mailbox name such as Admin, instead of using your own name. This will keep your personal mailbox separate from the administrative mailbox.

The password for the administrative mailbox must be secure. You should carefully choose and protect the administrative password. When choosing a password, do not use words that people can easily associate with you, such as your name or favorite sport. You should make the password easy to remember because without it you will not be able to perform administrative duties.

When you have finished creating the Postoffice, you must share the Postoffice folder so everyone in the workgroup can access the Postoffice.

The administrator has special access rights to the Postoffice. The administrator can create and remove mailboxes for people in the workgroup.

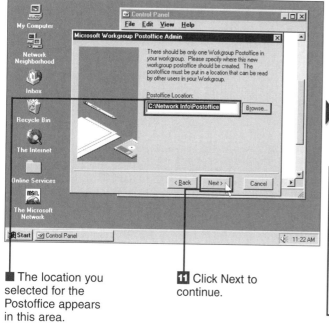

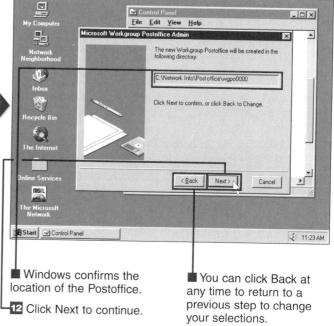

■ The location you selected for the Postoffice appears in this area.

11 Click Next to continue.

■ Windows confirms the location of the Postoffice.

12 Click Next to continue.

■ You can click Back at any time to return to a previous step to change your selections.

Can I change the computer the Postoffice is stored on?

To change the computer the Postoffice is stored on, you must create a new Postoffice with mailboxes for each user on the new computer. You must then have each user change their profile to log on to the new Postoffice. To change a user profile, see page 445.

How do I share the folder that stores the Postoffice?

You must set up your computer to share resources. To do so, choose the Control Panel and select the Network icon. To turn on sharing, see page 484. You can then share the Postoffice folder with the workgroup. To share information, see page 486.

How do I create mailboxes for myself and other people in the workgroup?

In the Control Panel, double-click the Microsoft Mail Postoffice icon and select Administer an existing Workgroup Postoffice. Once you have located the Postoffice folder and entered the administrative mailbox name and password, you will be able to create mailboxes. You can also change passwords for users who have forgotten theirs.

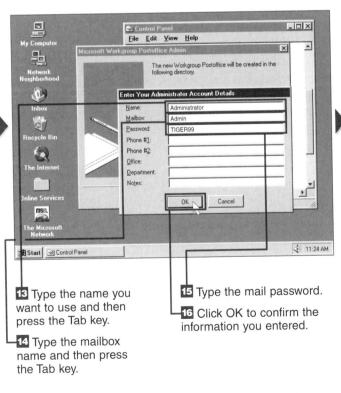

■13 Type the name you want to use and then press the Tab key.

■14 Type the mailbox name and then press the Tab key.

■15 Type the mail password.

■16 Click OK to confirm the information you entered.

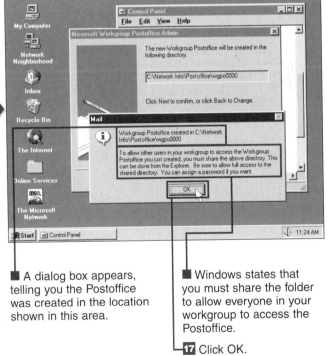

■ A dialog box appears, telling you the Postoffice was created in the location shown in this area.

■ Windows states that you must share the folder to allow everyone in your workgroup to access the Postoffice.

■17 Click OK.

449

ADD POSTOFFICE USERS

You can add users to an existing Postoffice. Before users can exchange e-mail with other users on the network, their names must be added to the Postoffice. This can only be done by a person using the administrator's password.

In order to exchange e-mail within a corporate network, Microsoft Mail must have a Postoffice. There should be only one Postoffice in each workgroup. See pages 446 to 449 for information about installing a Postoffice.

You must enter the user's name, along with the name of their mailbox. Most companies use a combination of either the first name and last initial or first initial and last name for the name of the mailbox.

When adding a user, you can either leave the password as PASSWORD or you can provide the user with a unique password. You must tell each user their password before the user can access their mailbox and retrieve their messages.

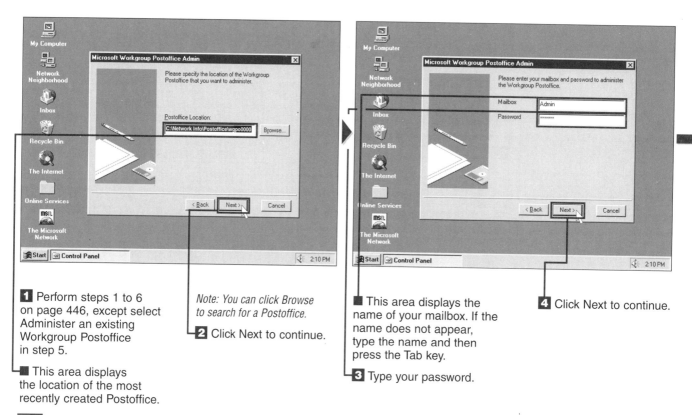

1 Perform steps 1 to 6 on page 446, except select Administer an existing Workgroup Postoffice in step 5.

■ This area displays the location of the most recently created Postoffice.

Note: You can click Browse to search for a Postoffice.

2 Click Next to continue.

■ This area displays the name of your mailbox. If the name does not appear, type the name and then press the Tab key.

3 Type your password.

4 Click Next to continue.

Should a user tell the administrator what their password is?

This is not recommended. Each user should keep their password private so only they have access to their messages. Users should be encouraged to change their password the first time they log on to their mailbox.

What should I do when a user loses their password?

Although you cannot tell what the password is, you can use the Details button to assign a new password. When you reset the password, the user should log on and change the password.

How do users change their mailbox password?

Choose the Tools menu and then select the Microsoft Mail Tools command. Click the Change Mailbox Password command to assign a new password.

Are passwords case-sensitive?

No, upper and lower case letters have the same values when entering passwords.

How do I delete a user?

Select the user's name and then click the Remove User button.

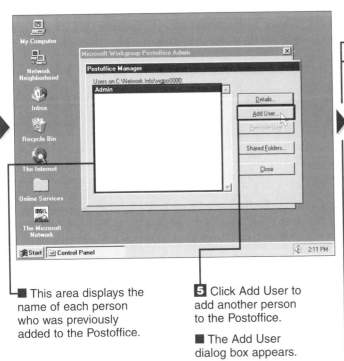

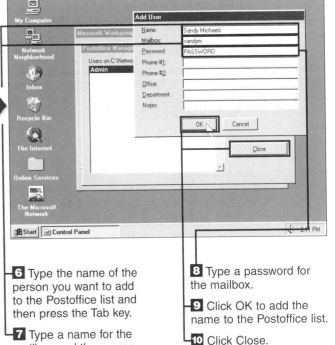

■ This area displays the name of each person who was previously added to the Postoffice.

5 Click Add User to add another person to the Postoffice.

■ The Add User dialog box appears.

6 Type the name of the person you want to add to the Postoffice list and then press the Tab key.

7 Type a name for the mailbox and then press the Tab key.

8 Type a password for the mailbox.

9 Click OK to add the name to the Postoffice list.

10 Click Close.

451

SEND A FAX

You can use Microsoft Fax to send a fax to a friend or colleague across the city or around the world. Sending a fax directly from your computer saves you the time of printing a document and standing in line at the fax machine.

The Microsoft Fax Wizard asks you a series of questions to ensure that you do not forget to include any of the information needed to send a fax. You can go back to any question and change your answer before sending the fax.

The Microsoft Fax Wizard asks you where you are faxing from. Defining your location is useful if you are using a portable computer away from your office.

You can send a fax to one person or to many people at the same time.

You can include a cover page with your fax. Microsoft Fax provides four types of pre-designed cover pages that describe the subject of the fax you are sending. The cover pages Microsoft Fax provides are entitled Confidential!, For your information, Generic and Urgent!.

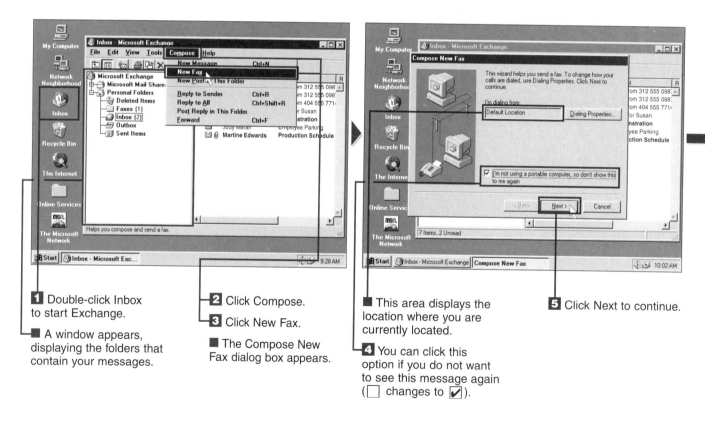

1 Double-click Inbox to start Exchange.

■ A window appears, displaying the folders that contain your messages.

2 Click Compose.

3 Click New Fax.

■ The Compose New Fax dialog box appears.

■ This area displays the location where you are currently located.

4 You can click this option if you do not want to see this message again (☐ changes to ☑).

5 Click Next to continue.

Can I display the Compose New Fax dialog box without starting Exchange?

In the Start menu, select Programs and then click Accessories. Select Fax and then click Compose New Fax to display the Compose New Fax dialog box.

Can I use a name from my Personal Address Book when I send a fax?

Click the Address Book button and then select the Personal Address Book. Click the name of the person you want to send the fax to and then click OK. To add a name to the Personal Address Book, see page 422.

Can I fax a document directly from the program I used to create the document?

You can fax a document from any program that allows you to print. In the File menu, click Print and then select Microsoft Fax as the printer. Then click OK. The Compose New Fax dialog box appears so you can continue sending the fax.

Can I create my own cover pages?

You can modify the cover pages provided by Microsoft Exchange or create new ones using the Cover Page Editor. See page 462.

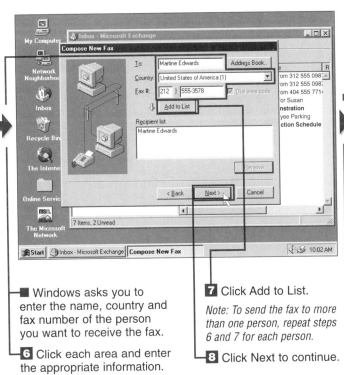

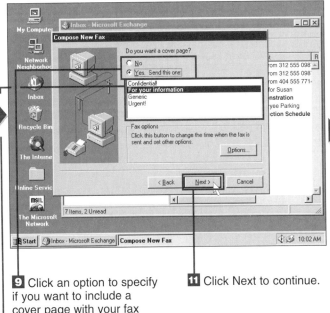

■ Windows asks you to enter the name, country and fax number of the person you want to receive the fax.

6 Click each area and enter the appropriate information.

7 Click Add to List.

Note: To send the fax to more than one person, repeat steps 6 and 7 for each person.

8 Click Next to continue.

9 Click an option to specify if you want to include a cover page with your fax (○ changes to ◉).

10 If you selected Yes in step 9, click the type of cover page you want to include.

Note: To change the fax sending options, refer to page 456.

11 Click Next to continue.

CONTINUED ▶

SEND A FAX CONTINUED

You can include a note with the cover page of your fax. The text on the note is a standard font and size. You cannot format a note you create.

You can attach a file on your computer to a fax. When you attach a file, Microsoft Fax

creates a printed image of the file.

Microsoft Fax sends all of the files you attach at the same time. Sending files by Microsoft Fax is easier and faster than opening and faxing each file individually.

Faxes sent using Microsoft Fax are usually higher quality than those sent by fax machines. There are no smudges or marks on fax pages sent by Microsoft Fax and the pages are not crooked. The quality of fax pages depends in part on the resolution of the receiving fax machine.

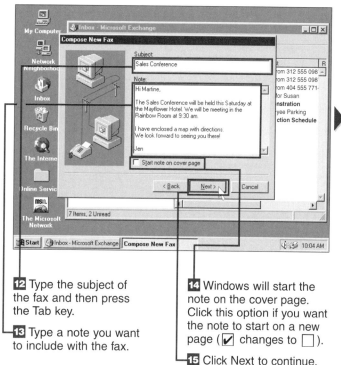

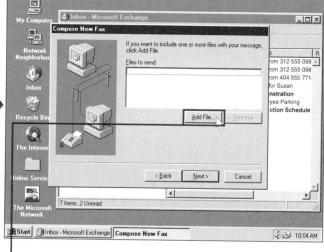

▐12▌ Type the subject of the fax and then press the Tab key.

▐13▌ Type a note you want to include with the fax.

▐14▌ Windows will start the note on the cover page. Click this option if you want the note to start on a new page (☑ changes to ☐).

▐15▌ Click Next to continue.

▐16▌ Click Add File to include a file with your fax.

Note: If you do not want to include a file with your fax, skip to step 19.

■ The Open a File to Attach dialog box appears.

Can I send a fax without a cover page?

You can send a fax without a cover page. If you include a note with the fax, the note will appear on a blank piece of paper. Microsoft Fax does not include page headers when you send a fax. If you do not send a cover page, the recipient may not know who the fax is from.

Can I preview my fax before I send it?

Microsoft Fax does not have a preview feature.

Can I send a picture with my fax?

You may have difficulty sending a good quality picture by attaching it to a fax. You may have more success if you open the picture in a program like Paint. From the File menu, select Send to fax the picture from the program. The quality of faxed pictures is usually not very good.

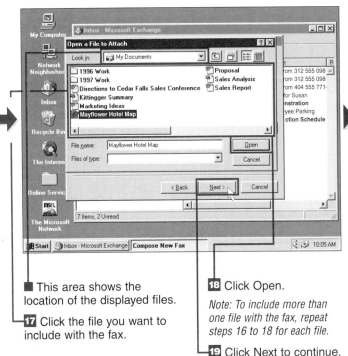

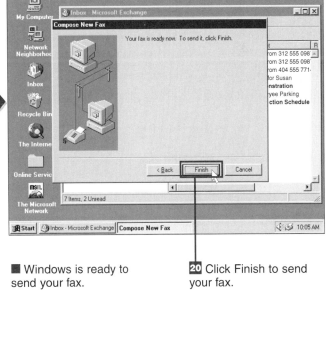

■ This area shows the location of the displayed files.

▬17 Click the file you want to include with the fax.

▬18 Click Open.

Note: To include more than one file with the fax, repeat steps 16 to 18 for each file.

▬19 Click Next to continue.

■ Windows is ready to send your fax.

▬20 Click Finish to send your fax.

CHANGE FAX SENDING OPTIONS

Y ou can tell Microsoft Fax exactly when and how you want to send your faxes.

You can specify when you want to send your fax. If you have prepared a document that is time sensitive, you can have Fax send the fax at a specific time. You can have a fax sent when long-distance charges are lowest. You can also send a fax as soon as

possible. If you delay sending your fax, you must make sure your computer is turned on and Exchange is open when the fax is to be sent.

You can select the format you want to use for your fax. If you know the recipient uses Microsoft Fax, you can send the fax as an editable file. The recipient will be able to open

and make changes to the file. If you are not sure which fax program the recipient uses, you can have Fax determine whether the fax should be sent as an editable or non-editable file. If you do not want the recipient to be able to make changes, you can send the fax as a non-editable file. The recipient will only be able to view the file you send.

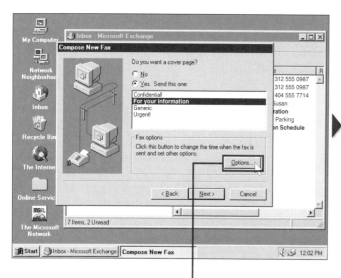

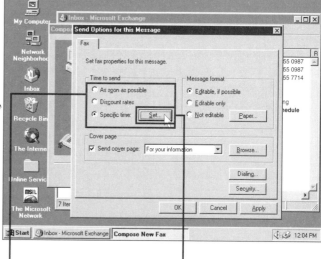

1 Perform steps 1 to 10 on page 452 to start creating a fax.

2 Click Options to change the sending options for the fax.

■ The Send Options for this Message dialog box appears.

3 Click an option to specify when you want to send the fax (○ changes to ◉).

4 If you selected Specific time in step 3, click Set to specify when you want to send the fax.

■ The Set Time dialog box appears.

Which software must the recipient and I use to exchange editable faxes?

To exchange editable faxes, you both must use Microsoft Fax for Windows 95 or Windows for Workgroups 3.11. When the sending and receiving computers use these programs, you can exchange any type of file as an editable fax.

I have created a fax to send at a later time. What will happen if I need to restart my computer?

The fax is stored in the Outbox folder until it is time to send it, even if you restart your computer. As long as your computer is on and Exchange is open, your fax will be sent at the correct time.

Can I change the default properties for all faxes?

The default properties are As soon as possible and Editable, if possible. To change the default properties, right-click the Inbox icon on the desktop. Select Properties and then select Microsoft Fax. Click the Properties button. Exchange will remember the changes you make to the default properties and will apply them to all the faxes you send.

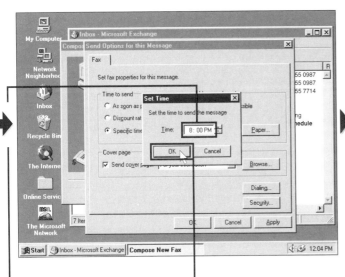

5 Double-click the part of the time you want to change. Then type the correct time.

■ Repeat step 5 until you specify the exact time you want to send the fax.

6 Click OK to confirm the time.

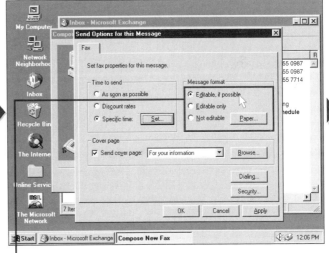

7 Click an option to specify if you want the person receiving the fax to be able to edit the fax (○ changes to ⦿).

CONTINUED ▶

CHANGE FAX
SENDING OPTIONS CONTINUED

You can use a password to protect the files you send using Microsoft Fax. This ensures that only the intended recipient can open the file. The password feature only works with editable faxes.

When you select a security method, the contents of the fax are scrambled so that it cannot be opened or read without the correct password.

The password-protected option requires you to enter a password when you create a fax. The recipient must use the same password to view the fax. Without the password, the recipient cannot open the fax.

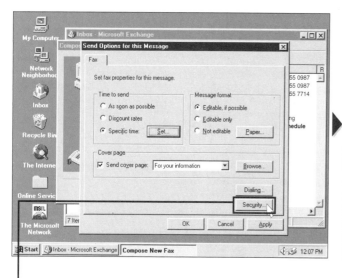

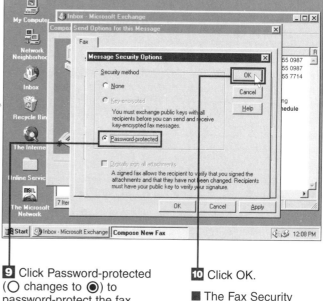

8 Click Security to prevent unauthorized people from reviewing the fax you send.

■ The Message Security Options dialog box appears.

9 Click Password-protected (○ changes to ●) to password-protect the fax.

10 Click OK.

■ The Fax Security dialog box appears.

What is key encryption?

Key encryption enables you to send documents securely without having to provide a password for each document. Key encryption uses a system of codes, called keys, to scramble a document you send and descramble the document when it is received.

To use key encryption, you and the recipient must both create a public key and a private key and then exchange your keys. To create encryption keys, display the Tools menu and select Microsoft Fax Tools. Then select Advanced Security to display the Advanced Fax Security dialog box.

Why can't the recipient open the secure fax I sent?

Passwords are case sensitive. You can use upper and lower case letters when creating a password, but the recipient must type the password exactly the same way when receiving the fax.

I tried to send a secure fax and it failed. What is wrong?

If any of the recipients will be receiving the fax in a non-editable format, the security features will cause the fax to fail.

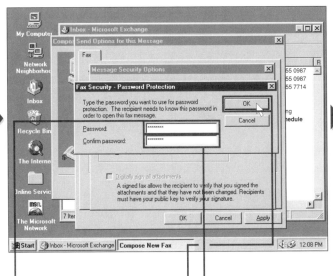

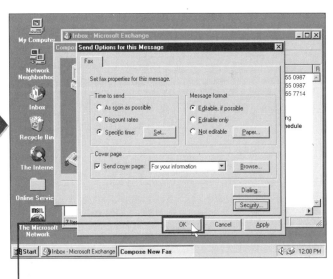

11 Type the password the person receiving the fax must enter to read the fax. Then press the Tab key.

12 Type the password again to confirm the password.

13 Click OK.

14 Click OK to confirm all of the send options you selected.

■ You can now finish creating your fax.

VIEW A FAX

Y ou can display a fax on your screen so you can read the message. Viewing faxes on your computer saves paper.

A fax you receive is a picture of a page. You cannot modify or view the page using a word processing program. Microsoft Fax uses the Windows Imaging

program to display the picture of the page.

When a fax you receive is displayed on your screen, you can scroll back and forth or up and down to see the whole page. You can also reduce a page to see an entire page of the fax on the screen at once

or magnify a page to examine a small area of the page. If a fax contains multiple pages, you can switch from page to page.

A fax may appear upside down or sideways when you receive it. You can rotate the fax to the left or right until it is displayed properly.

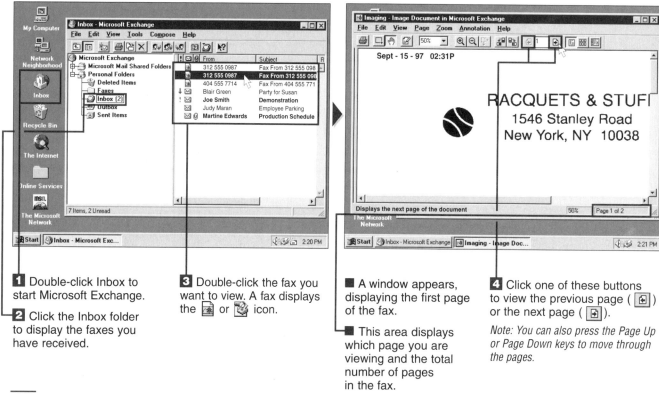

■1 Double-click Inbox to start Microsoft Exchange.

■2 Click the Inbox folder to display the faxes you have received.

■3 Double-click the fax you want to view. A fax displays the 🖼 or 🖼 icon.

■ A window appears, displaying the first page of the fax.

■ This area displays which page you are viewing and the total number of pages in the fax.

■4 Click one of these buttons to view the previous page (🔲) or the next page (🔲).

Note: You can also press the Page Up or Page Down keys to move through the pages.

Can I resize the fax so I do not have to scroll back and forth?

From the Zoom menu, select Fit to Width. The fax page resizes to fit your screen from side to side.

How do I see all the pages in a fax?

From the View menu, select Thumbnails or Page and Thumbnails. Miniature images of all the pages in the fax are displayed along the left side of the screen. To display a different page on your screen, click the miniature page.

How can I organize faxes I receive?

You can create folders to store and organize the faxes you receive. You can also delete, sort and print faxes as you would any e-mail message.

Can I display the fax more clearly?

In the View menu, check that the Scale to Gray option is selected. This option makes a text document easier to read. This option is only available in OSR2.

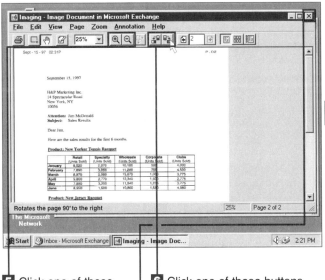

5 Click one of these buttons to magnify (🔍) or reduce (🔍) the page.

6 Click one of these buttons to rotate a page to the left (⬒) or right (⬓) if the page appears sideways or upside down.

Note: The buttons may appear as 🔄 or 🔁 on your screen.

7 Click ✖ when you finish viewing the fax.

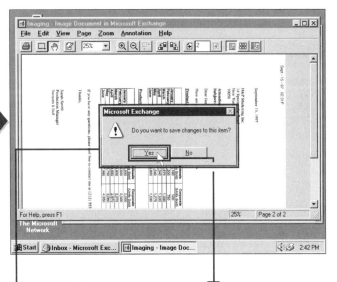

■ This dialog box appears if you changed the way the fax appears.

8 Click Yes to save the changes.

EDIT FAX COVER PAGES

You can create personalized cover pages for your faxes. Windows provides the Urgent!, Confidential!, For your information and Generic fax cover pages for you to use. You can modify the cover pages Windows supplies or create your own cover pages. You can create several versions of a cover page for specific recipients or different types of faxes.

The Cover Page Editor allows you to move items to a different location to customize your cover page. For example, you can place important information at the top of the cover page.

Your cover page should include information about you and your company, as well as your phone and fax numbers so the person receiving the fax can contact you.

The information for many areas on a cover page is entered automatically. Microsoft Fax uses information about you and your company from the information you entered when you set up the program. Information about the recipient is retrieved from your address book. Brackets { } indicate the areas where information is entered automatically.

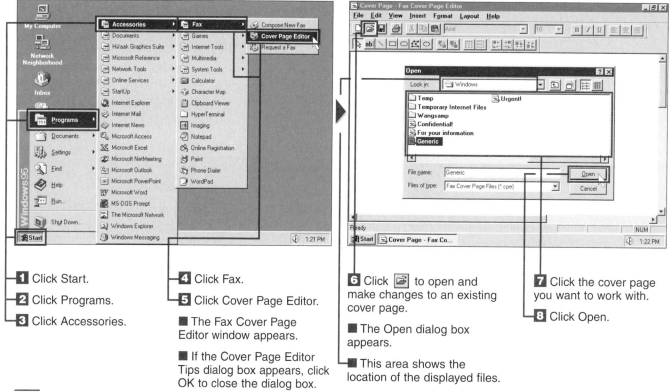

1 Click Start.

2 Click Programs.

3 Click Accessories.

4 Click Fax.

5 Click Cover Page Editor.

■ The Fax Cover Page Editor window appears.

■ If the Cover Page Editor Tips dialog box appears, click OK to close the dialog box.

6 Click 🗁 to open and make changes to an existing cover page.

■ The Open dialog box appears.

■ This area shows the location of the displayed files.

7 Click the cover page you want to work with.

8 Click Open.

Where are the cover pages that Windows provides?

You can find the cover pages in the Windows folder on your hard drive. If you make changes to one of these cover pages, make sure you save the new cover page with a different name. To save a file with a different file name, choose the File menu and select Save As.

Can I delete an item on a cover page?

Click the item you want to delete. Black boxes (■) appear around the item. Click the Delete key to remove the item.

How can I add information about myself or the recipient to the cover page?

Click Insert and select the type of information you want to add. You can then select the information you want to add.

How do I add new text to my cover page?

Click abl on the toolbar and then position the mouse ✛ where you want the top left corner of the text box to appear. Drag the mouse ✛ to create a text box and then type the text you want.

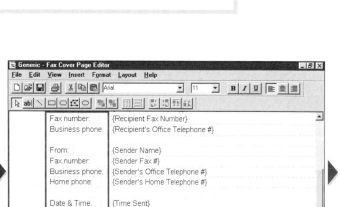

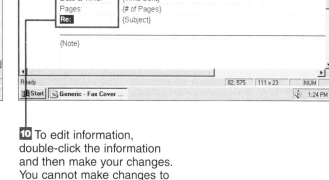

■ The fax cover page you selected appears.

9 To move information on the cover page, click the information you want to move. Black boxes (■) appear around the item. Position the mouse ⬉ over the information (⬉ changes to ✛). Then drag the information to a new location.

10 To edit information, double-click the information and then make your changes. You cannot make changes to information in brackets { }.

CONTINUED ▶

EDIT FAX COVER PAGES CONTINUED

If you want to personalize your fax cover page or project a professional image, you might want to use your company's design. With Cover Page Editor, you can reproduce your letterhead by including your company logo and information on your cover page. Since Microsoft Fax does not add information to the top of

each page of a fax, such as who sent the fax, including your company logo and information can help the recipient identify the fax.

Graphics in a fax are displayed at a low resolution. This means that graphics may appear as blotches when the fax is received. Select the graphics

that you use on your cover page carefully. Sending pages with many large, dark graphics takes much longer than faxing pages with small or no graphics.

You should use graphics saved in the .bmp file format. Before you use a graphic, make sure the graphic does not have copyright restrictions.

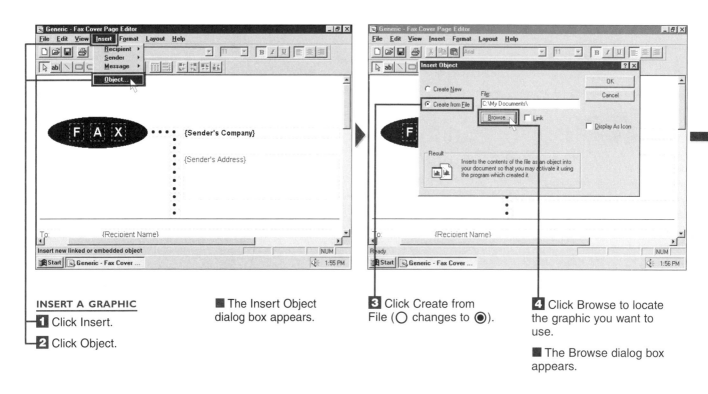

INSERT A GRAPHIC

1 Click Insert.

2 Click Object.

■ The Insert Object dialog box appears.

3 Click Create from File (○ changes to ●).

4 Click Browse to locate the graphic you want to use.

■ The Browse dialog box appears.

How can I get a copy of my logo or create a new logo?

You will need to use a scanner to convert your logo from paper to a .bmp file. To create a new logo, you can use Paint or one of the other painting and drawing packages available for Windows 95.

How can I create new shapes and lines on a cover page?

The toolbar provides several buttons that allow you to create shapes and lines. Click the button for the item you want to create. Position the cursor where you want the top left corner of the item to appear and drag the mouse to create the item.

How do I resize a graphic?

Click the graphic you want to change. Black boxes (■) appear around the graphic. Drag one of the black boxes to resize the object.

Can I use a file format other than the .bmp file format?

Graphics in file formats other than .bmp may appear as icons instead of graphics on the cover page. You can use Imaging to open many types of graphic files and then save them in the .bmp format. For information on Imaging, see pages 186 to 189.

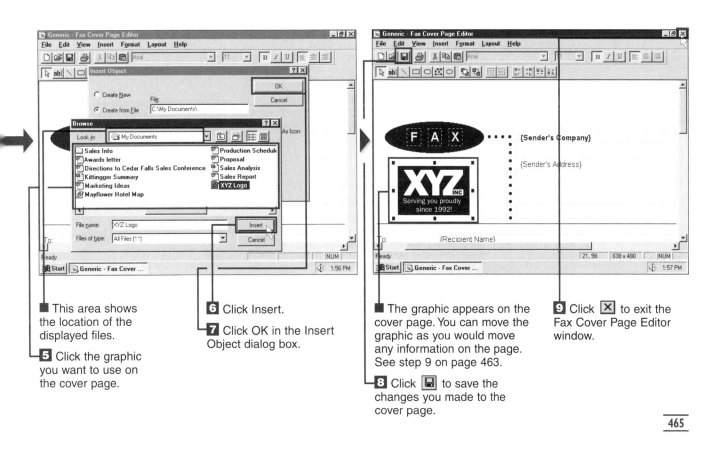

■ This area shows the location of the displayed files.

5 Click the graphic you want to use on the cover page.

6 Click Insert.

7 Click OK in the Insert Object dialog box.

■ The graphic appears on the cover page. You can move the graphic as you would move any information on the page. See step 9 on page 463.

8 Click 🖫 to save the changes you made to the cover page.

9 Click ☒ to exit the Fax Cover Page Editor window.

24) SET UP AND MONITOR A NETWORK

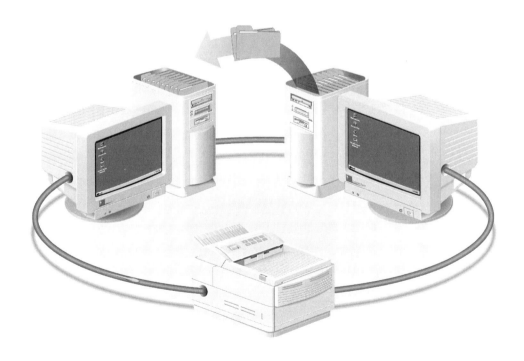

INTRODUCTION TO NETWORKS

A network is a group of computers that are connected together to allow people to share information and equipment.

Before networks, exchanging information between computers was time-consuming. The most common way to transfer information from one computer to another was by saving the information on floppy disks and then carrying the disks to the other computer. Physically carrying information from one computer to another is known as sneakernet. Computer networks eliminate the need for sneakernet. When two computers are connected using a network, they can exchange large amounts of information faster and more reliably than when exchanging information using floppy disks.

Networks allow computers to share equipment such as printers or modems. The ability to share equipment reduces the cost of buying computer hardware. For example, instead of having to buy a printer for each computer, a company can buy just one printer and let everyone access the printer from their own computer.

Once networks became more widespread, many companies started allowing employees to access information on the network while at home or traveling. Employees can now use computers with modems to dial in to the network to access company information.

Many companies use networks to back up information stored on their employees' computers. Backing up information using a network is more reliable and secure than performing a backup on each computer.

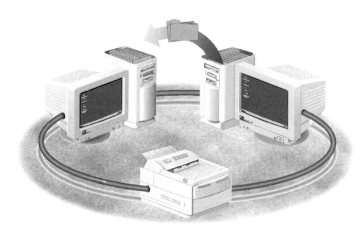

You usually have to enter a user name and password when you want to access information on a network. This ensures that only authorized people can use the information stored on the network.

A system administrator manages the network and makes sure the network functions properly. A system administrator may also be called a network manager, information systems manager or network administrator.

Most businesses and organizations that have computers now use a network to connect their computers. Networks can be used to connect as few as two computers, like in a small business, or millions of computers, like the world's largest network, the Internet.

TYPES OF NETWORKS

There are many different types of networks used by businesses and organizations. The main types of networks are local area networks, metropolitan area networks and wide area networks.

Just as every business and organization is unique, so is every network. The type of network used by a company or organization depends on where the computers that need to be connected are located. The larger the network, the more costly the network is to build, set up and maintain.

Local Area Network (LAN)

A Local Area Network (LAN) connects computers and devices that are located close to each other, such as in one building. Most computers on a local area network are connected using cables. Local area networks connect from as few as two computers to usually no more than 100 computers. LANs are the most common type of network found in businesses.

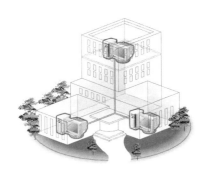

Metropolitan Area Network (MAN)

A Metropolitan Area Network (MAN) is used to connect computers that are located in the same geographic area, such as a town or city. A metropolitan area network is often made up of smaller local area networks that are connected together. For example, a college may use a MAN that connects the local area networks on each campus throughout a city. Networks on a MAN are often connected by radio waves.

Wide Area Network (WAN)

A Wide Area Network (WAN) connects multiple networks together. The networks that make up a wide area network may be located throughout a country or even around the world. Wide area networks are very expensive and complicated to build. Networks in a WAN are often connected by microwave or satellite. A wide area network owned and controlled by one company is often referred to as an enterprise network. The Internet is the largest wide area network in the world.

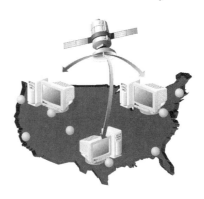

NETWORK HARDWARE

Network hardware is the physical components that make up a network. All networks require special networking equipment.

Computers

The most important job of a network is to link computers together so they can share information. Networks can connect various types of computers, such as IBM-compatible or Macintosh.

Hub

A hub is a device that provides a central location where all the cables on a network come together. All the computers and devices that are connected to a hub can exchange information with each other.

Network Interface Card (NIC)

A Network Interface Card (NIC) physically connects each computer to a network and controls the flow of information between the network and the computer. Most NICs are installed inside a computer. You can see the edge of the card at the back of the computer. An NIC has a port where the network cable plugs in.

Bridge

A bridge is a device that joins two networks together. Both networks can connect to the bridge to allow the computers on each network to exchange information.

Network Resources

A network resource is a device that computers on a network can use. The most common type of network resource is a printer. All people on a network can send documents to a printer that is connected to a network. Other examples of network resources include hard drives, fax machines and tape drives.

Transmission Medium

A transmission medium is anything that lets computers exchange information. Cables are the most popular type of transmission medium and are used to connect computers and equipment to a network. There are four main types of cables — coaxial, Unshielded Twisted Pair (UTP), Shielded Twisted Pair (STP) and fiber optic. The type of cable used on a network depends on the type and size of the network. Some newer transmission technologies allow computers to be connected using radio or infrared waves. These networks are called wireless networks.

NETWORK LAYOUT

Peer-to-Peer Networks

Computers on a peer-to-peer network store files and programs on their own hard drives. Each computer that is connected to the peer-to-peer network is used to perform regular tasks, such as word processing. The computers can also communicate with other computers to share information or devices, such as printers or modems. For example, if a person on the peer-to-peer network has a printer attached to their computer, they may share the printer with other people on the network. Peer-to-peer networks are used to connect fewer than 10 computers.

Client/Server Networks

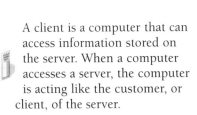

Computers on a client/server network store files on a central computer called a server. There are many types of servers. For example, a file server is a computer that stores a large collection of documents. Storing the documents on one computer makes it easy to manage a large collection of information. Backing up files on one server is easier and faster than backing up the files on each person's computer on the network.

A client is a computer that can access information stored on the server. When a computer accesses a server, the computer is acting like the customer, or client, of the server.

Client/server networks can be any size but are usually used when 10 or more computers need to exchange information.

NETWORK ARCHITECTURE

Network architecture is the term used to describe the method of transferring information on a network. Computers and other devices on a network must all use the same method of transmitting information. If devices use different methods to transfer information, the information may become damaged and unreadable.

The most common type of network architecture is Ethernet. An Ethernet network is inexpensive and easy to set up. Other network architecture types include Token-Ring and Arcnet.

The type of network architecture used on a network determines how fast information transfers across the network.

NETWORK COMPONENTS

There are four main components that allow a Windows 95 computer to communicate, share resources and exchange information with other computers and devices on a network. These components are called adapters, protocols, clients and services.

Adapter

A network adapter is a device that physically connects a computer to a network. When you want to send information such as a document to another computer on a network, the network adapter converts the document into a format that can transfer over the network's transmission media, such as a cable. Most networks connected by cables use Network Interface Cards (NICs) as adapters. Ethernet is a popular type of network adapter.

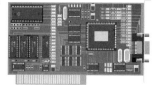

A modem may also be used as a network adapter since it connects a computer to a network using telephone lines. A modem used as a network adapter is referred to as a dial-up adapter.

Protocol

A protocol is a language that computers and other devices on a network use to communicate. Computers and devices on a network must use the same protocol before they can exchange information with each other. For example, if you want to print information on a network printer, your computer and the printer must use the same protocol.

Protocols may be used to perform maintenance tasks such as correcting errors in information transmission or redirecting information around broken connections on a network.

Windows 95 supports the most popular protocols used on computer networks, including IPX/SPX, NetBEUI and TCP/IP.

Service

A service lets you share and access information and resources on a network. Windows provides services that allow you to share files and printers on Microsoft and Novell networks. There are also services that allow you to connect to Hewlett-Packard printers that are directly attached to a network.

Client

A client is software that lets your computer communicate with other computers on a network. The type of network you want to connect to, such as Microsoft or Novell, determines the client you need. Windows 95 includes client software for the most popular networks.

When you save information, the client software determines whether you are saving the information to your own hard drive or to another computer on the network. Because the client determines where information goes, client software is often referred to as a redirector.

THE OSI MODEL

The Open Systems Interconnect (OSI) model is a set of guidelines that companies follow when creating devices and software for networks. Many companies follow the guidelines in the OSI model to make sure all the hardware and software in a network will be able to work together. The OSI model has seven sections, or layers, that describe the tasks that must be performed for information to transfer on a network.

Application Layer

The application layer is responsible for exchanging information between the programs running on a computer and other services on a network, such as a database or print server.

Presentation Layer

The presentation layer formats information so that it can be read by a software program and computer.

Session Layer

The session layer determines how two devices communicate. This layer establishes and monitors connections between computers.

Transport Layer

The transport layer corrects errors in transmission and ensures that the information is delivered reliably.

Physical Layer

The physical layer defines how a transmission medium, such as a cable, connects to a computer. This layer also specifies how electrical information transfers on the transmission medium.

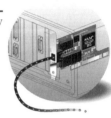

Data Link Layer

The data link layer groups data into sets to prepare the data for transferring over a network.

Network Layer

The network layer identifies computers on a network and determines how to direct information transferring over a network.

NAME YOUR COMPUTER

You can change the name of your computer on a network. Naming your computer is useful if you want other people to be able to access information or use equipment connected to your computer, such as a printer.

Each computer on a network must have a unique name. A descriptive name such as "Johns_Computer" makes a

computer much easier to find and identify than a name like "Computer-10".

A computer name cannot be more than 15 characters in length. A computer name also cannot contain spaces, but you can use an underscore (_) to replace a blank space.

You can change which workgroup your computer belongs to. The workgroup

name cannot be more than 15 characters in length.

You can also assign a description to your computer. Assigning a description lets other people know more detailed information about your computer, such as where the computer is located.

You should check with your system administrator before changing your computer or workgroup name.

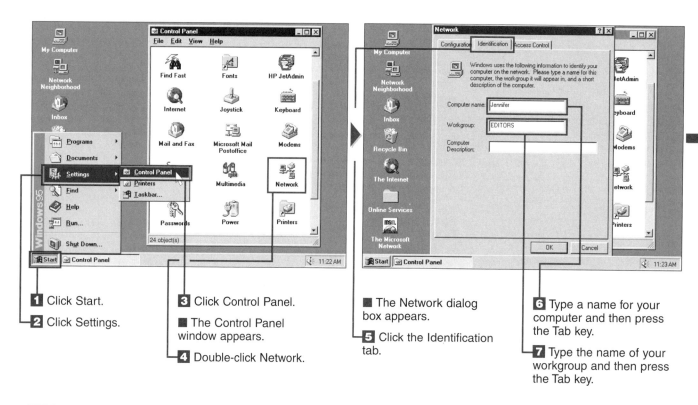

1 Click Start.

2 Click Settings.

3 Click Control Panel.

■ The Control Panel window appears.

4 Double-click Network.

■ The Network dialog box appears.

5 Click the Identification tab.

6 Type a name for your computer and then press the Tab key.

7 Type the name of your workgroup and then press the Tab key.

TIPS

What is a workgroup?

A workgroup is a group of computers on a network that contain most of the resources that you will use. A workgroup often consists of computers located close to each other, such as the accounting or sales department of a business. Since all the computers in the department use the same equipment, such as printers and fax modems, it makes sense to place the computers in the same workgroup. If you do not know the name of your workgroup, ask your system administrator.

After I change the name of my computer, do I need to inform other individuals on the network?

After you change the name of your computer, you should inform the people who use information or equipment on your computer.

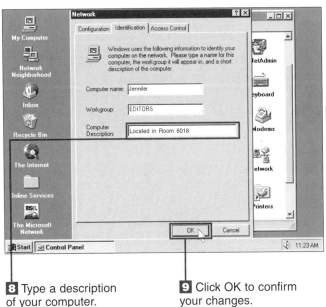

8 Type a description of your computer.

9 Click OK to confirm your changes.

■ The System Settings Change dialog box appears, telling you Windows needs to restart your computer before the new settings will take effect.

10 Click Yes to restart your computer.

BROWSE THROUGH A NETWORK

Network Neighborhood allows you to find and browse through shared resources available on your network. The Network Neighborhood icon appears on your desktop when your computer is set up to use a network.

The most common types of shared network resources include

information such as files and folders, as well as equipment like printers, CD-ROM drives and modems.

Windows displays icons to represent network computers and shared network resources. Using Network Neighborhood to locate resources on a network is very similar to using My Computer or

Explorer to locate information on your own computer.

Some people on the network may require you to enter a password before you can view or access their shared resources. Windows will ask you for the password.

After you find a resource, you can work with the resource as if it was on your computer.

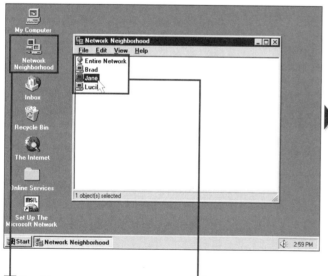

1 Double-click Network Neighborhood.

■ The Network Neighborhood window appears. The window displays the computers in your workgroup.

2 Double-click the computer containing the resources you want to view.

Note: You can double-click Entire Network to view other computers on the network that are not in your workgroup.

■ A list of folders shared by the computer appears.

3 Double-click the folder containing the information you want to view.

VII

TIPS

Why can I no longer access a shared folder on a network?

Folders are stored on computers connected to the network. If the computer that stores the folder is not turned on, or if the owner of the computer decides to stop sharing the folder with other people on the network, you will no longer be able to access the folder.

Can I use Windows Explorer to browse through a network?

In the Explorer window, double-click Network Neighborhood to display a list of computers on the network. The Explorer window shows a structural view of the information stored on the network.

What does an X through an icon mean?

An X through the icon of a shared resource means the resource has a new password or is unavailable. You may have to enter the new password before you can access the resource.

How can I quickly access the shared resources on another computer?

You can create shortcuts to shared files, folders, printers and drives on another computer and then place the shortcuts on your desktop. You can then double-click a shortcut to access the shared resource. For information on creating shortcuts, see page 88.

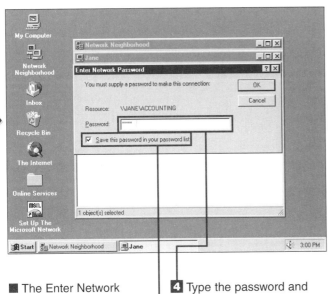

■ The Enter Network Password dialog box appears if a password is required to access the folder.

4 Type the password and then press the Enter key.

■ This option saves the password so you do not have to retype the password the next time you select the folder.

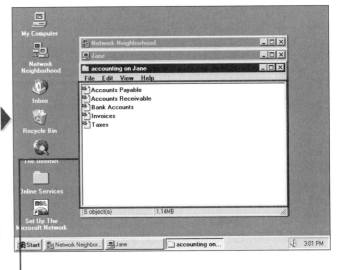

■ The contents of the folder appear.

■ You can work with the files and folders as if they were stored on your computer.

FIND A COMPUTER

You can find a computer on a network. Being able to locate a computer is especially useful if your network consists of hundreds of computers.

You can enter the entire name of the computer you want to find or just a portion of the name. For example, you can type **Jonathan** or **Jon** to find the computer named Jonathan.

If you are searching for a computer on a large network, Windows may take a while to display the names of any computers it finds. You can cancel the search at any time.

After the search is complete, Windows displays a list of all computers with the name you specified. Windows also tells you the location of each computer that was found.

Once you find a computer, you can browse through a list of information and equipment shared by the computer. You can access the information stored on the computer as if it was a folder stored on your own computer. Windows may ask you to enter a password to access some shared items.

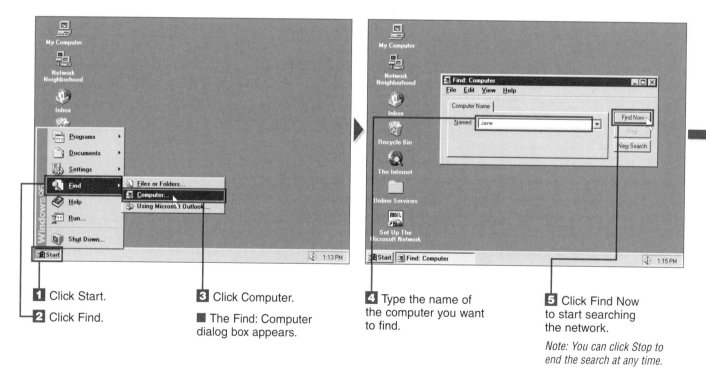

1 Click Start.

2 Click Find.

3 Click Computer.

■ The Find: Computer dialog box appears.

4 Type the name of the computer you want to find.

5 Click Find Now to start searching the network.

Note: You can click Stop to end the search at any time.

How can I change the order Windows lists the computers it finds?

You can sort the list by name, location or comment. Click the heading of the column you want to sort by. Windows will sort the items alphabetically. You can change the order of the items as often as you want.

Why is no comment displayed for some computers?

Windows will only display a comment for a computer if the person who shared the computer typed a comment.

Can I use wildcards to help me search for the computer?

You can use the asterisk (*) or a question mark (?) to find a computer on the network. The asterisk (*) represents many characters. The question mark (?) represents a single character. For example, you can type **Sale*** to find a computer named Sales&Marketing.

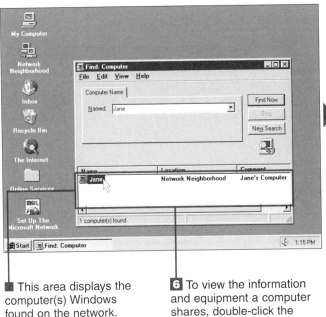

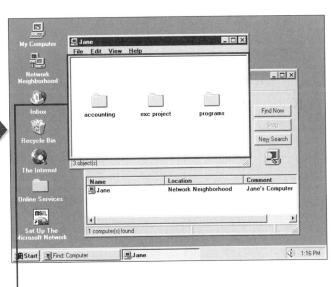

■ This area displays the computer(s) Windows found on the network.

6 To view the information and equipment a computer shares, double-click the computer.

■ A list of the resources shared by the computer appears.

■ You can work with the resources as if they were on your own computer.

Note: You may be asked to type a password to access some shared items.

MAP A NETWORK DRIVE

Mapping a network drive provides a quick way to access the information on another computer on a network. You can access a drive or folder on the other computer as if the drive or folder was on your own computer.

If you frequently use information stored on another computer, mapping can save you time.

Accessing a drive or folder that has not been mapped may require you to type a long path to specify the location of the drive or folder. Windows simplifies this process by assigning a single letter to specify the location of a mapped drive.

You can have Windows connect to a mapped network drive each time you log on to the network.

Mapping network drives is also useful if you are working with DOS or older Windows-based software. These programs may not understand how Windows 95 represents drives and folders that are located on other computers. Mapping helps you access drives and folders while using older programs.

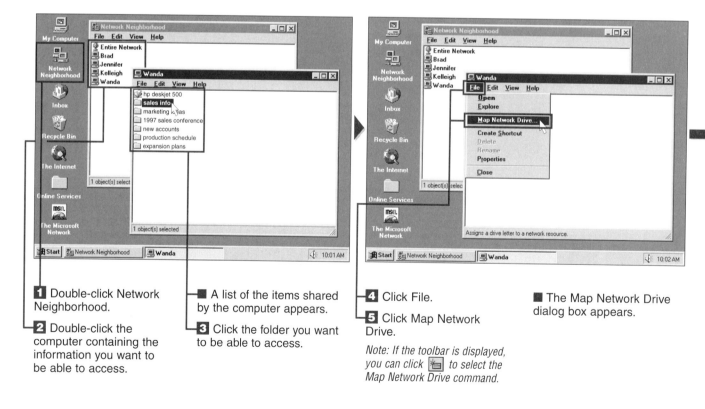

1 Double-click Network Neighborhood.

2 Double-click the computer containing the information you want to be able to access.

■ A list of the items shared by the computer appears.

3 Click the folder you want to be able to access.

4 Click File.

5 Click Map Network Drive.

Note: If the toolbar is displayed, you can click ⬛ to select the Map Network Drive command.

■ The Map Network Drive dialog box appears.

Will Windows remember a password needed to access a mapped network drive?

When you create a mapped network drive, you may be asked for a password. Windows will remember the password so you do not have to type it each time you want to connect to the information.

How do I disconnect a mapped network drive?

In the My Computer window, right-click the mapped network drive you want to disconnect from and then click Disconnect.

Why do some mapped network drives require a password?

The drives you access on a network are shared by other people. When the owner of a computer turns on sharing for the drive, they may assign a password. Only people who know the password can access the information on the drive.

Why does an X appear through a mapped network drive?

An X through the icon of a mapped network drive means the drive is unavailable or the drive has a new password.

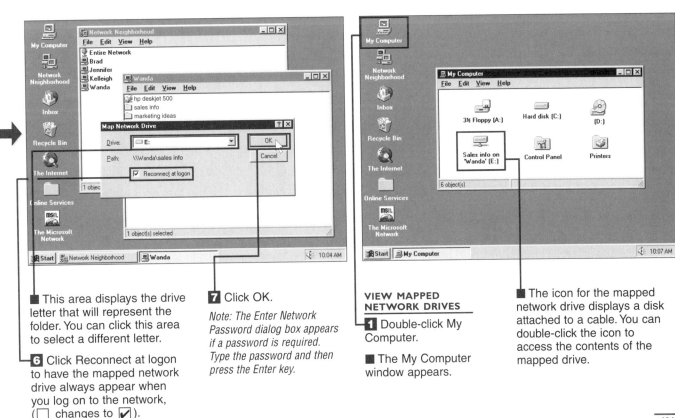

■ This area displays the drive letter that will represent the folder. You can click this area to select a different letter.

6 Click Reconnect at logon to have the mapped network drive always appear when you log on to the network, (☐ changes to ✔).

7 Click OK.

Note: The Enter Network Password dialog box appears if a password is required. Type the password and then press the Enter key.

VIEW MAPPED NETWORK DRIVES

1 Double-click My Computer.

■ The My Computer window appears.

■ The icon for the mapped network drive displays a disk attached to a cable. You can double-click the icon to access the contents of the mapped drive.

EXCHANGE MESSAGES WITH WINPOPUP

You can use WinPopup to exchange short messages with other people on your network. On a Novell network, you may not be able to send a WinPopup message that is longer than 38 characters.

The person you send a message to must be using their computer and have WinPopup open at the time you send the message.

WinPopup is useful for asking questions, expressing ideas and making short announcements. For example, you can use WinPopup to let all the people in your workgroup know when you are about to stop sharing information or a resource, such as a printer.

WinPopup is automatically installed on your computer when you install Microsoft Exchange, Windows Messaging or networking components. To install a Windows component, see page 580.

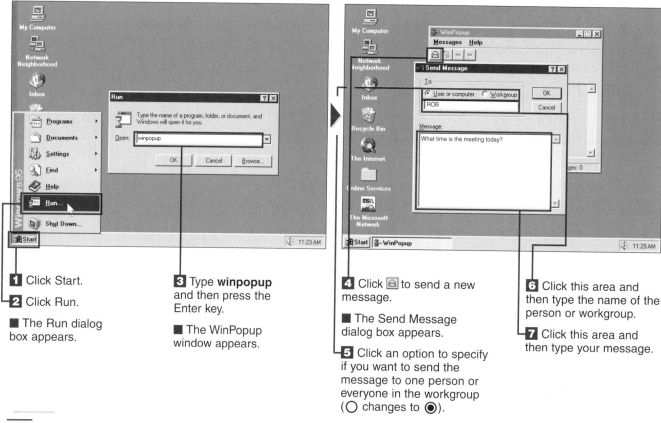

1 Click Start.

2 Click Run.

■ The Run dialog box appears.

3 Type **winpopup** and then press the Enter key.

■ The WinPopup window appears.

4 Click 🖾 to send a new message.

■ The Send Message dialog box appears.

5 Click an option to specify if you want to send the message to one person or everyone in the workgroup (○ changes to ◉).

6 Click this area and then type the name of the person or workgroup.

7 Click this area and then type your message.

Can I have WinPopup open automatically each time I start Windows?

Locate the Winpopup.exe file in the Windows folder and then drag the file to the StartUp folder. See page 258 for more information on starting programs automatically.

Can I save the WinPopup messages I receive?

No. You cannot save WinPopup messages. If you need to keep a WinPopup message, select the text you want to keep, right-click the selected text and then click Copy. You can then paste the information into a document in another program.

Can I make the WinPopup window open automatically each time I receive a message?

In the WinPopup window, choose the Messages menu and then select the Options command. In the Options dialog box, click the Pop up dialog on message receipt option (☐ changes to ✔) and then click OK. You can now minimize the WinPopup window. The window will automatically pop up on your screen when you receive a message.

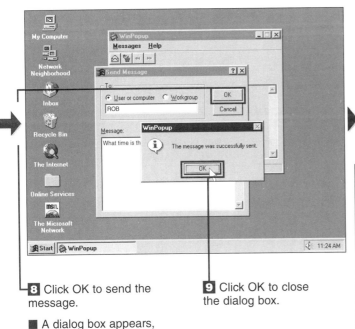

■8 Click OK to send the message.

■ A dialog box appears, telling you the message was successfully sent.

■9 Click OK to close the dialog box.

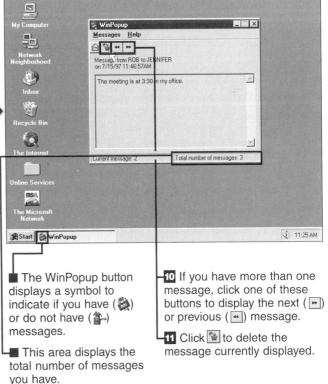

■ The WinPopup button displays a symbol to indicate if you have (🐷) or do not have (🐷→) messages.

■ This area displays the total number of messages you have.

■10 If you have more than one message, click one of these buttons to display the next (►►) or previous (◄◄) message.

■11 Click 🗑 to delete the message currently displayed.

TURN ON SHARING

Before you can share information or a printer with individuals on a network, you must set up your computer to share resources.

You may choose to share files stored on your computer with other people on the network. Sharing files is useful if you

want your colleagues to be able to access information on your computer. You can share many types of files, such as programs, documents, videos, sounds and graphics.

You can also share a printer connected to your computer. After you share your printer,

people can then send print jobs directly to the printer using the network. When sharing a printer, make sure the printer is turned on and contains paper.

You will have to restart your computer before the new sharing settings will take effect.

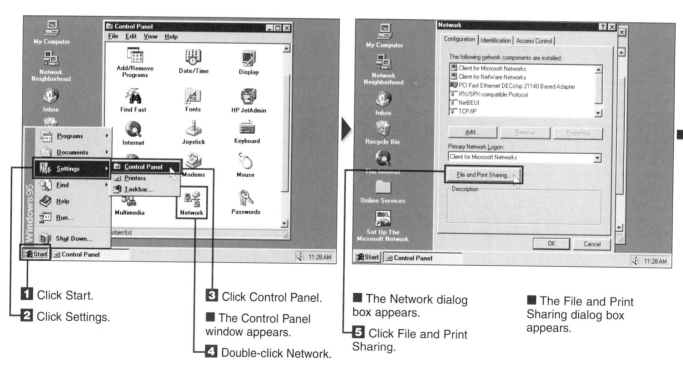

1 Click Start.

2 Click Settings.

3 Click Control Panel.

■ The Control Panel window appears.

4 Double-click Network.

■ The Network dialog box appears.

5 Click File and Print Sharing.

■ The File and Print Sharing dialog box appears.

TIPS

I turned on sharing, but my colleagues still cannot access my files and printer. What is wrong?

Once you turn on sharing, you must specify exactly what you want to share. For information on sharing files, see pages 486 to 489. For information on sharing a printer, see pages 490 to 495.

What happens when I turn off file or print sharing for my computer?

After you turn off file or print sharing, you must restart your computer. Once the computer restarts, other people on the network will no longer be able to access your resources.

If I turn sharing back on, will Windows remember which resources I previously shared?

Windows does not keep track of files and printers that you previously shared. If you wish to share files and printers again, you will have to specify again exactly which files and printers you want to share. To share information, see page 486.

NETWORKING

VII

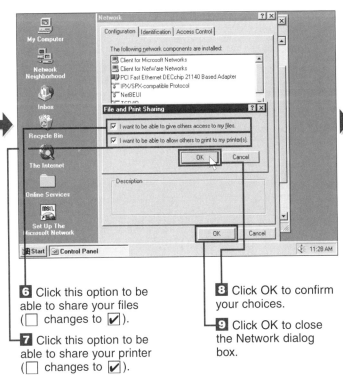

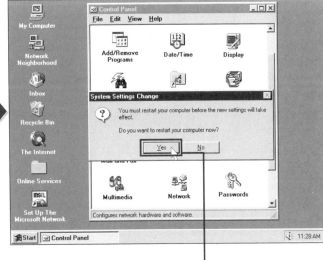

6 Click this option to be able to share your files (☐ changes to ☑).

7 Click this option to be able to share your printer (☐ changes to ☑).

8 Click OK to confirm your choices.

9 Click OK to close the Network dialog box.

■ Windows may ask you to insert the Windows 95 CD-ROM disc. If so, insert the disc into your computer.

■ The System Settings Change dialog box appears, telling you Windows needs to restart your computer before the new settings will take effect.

10 Click Yes to restart your computer.

Note: To later turn off file and printer sharing, repeat steps 1 to 10 (☑ changes to ☐ in steps 6 and 7).

485

SHARE INFORMATION

Y ou can specify exactly what information you want to share with individuals on a network. Sharing information is useful if you and your colleagues are working together on a project and need access to the same files.

File sharing is the most common use for a network. You can choose to share your entire hard drive or specific files on your computer.

Other people can work with your files as if the files were stored on their own computers. You can also let other people access drives that are connected to your computer, such as your floppy drive and CD-ROM drive.

Sharing information using computers connected to a network is very efficient. Computers can exchange information over a

network in a matter of seconds. Before computer networks, people had to either print a copy of the information or transfer the information using floppy disks when they wanted to share information.

Before you can share information, you must set up your computer to share resources. To turn on file and printer sharing, see page 484.

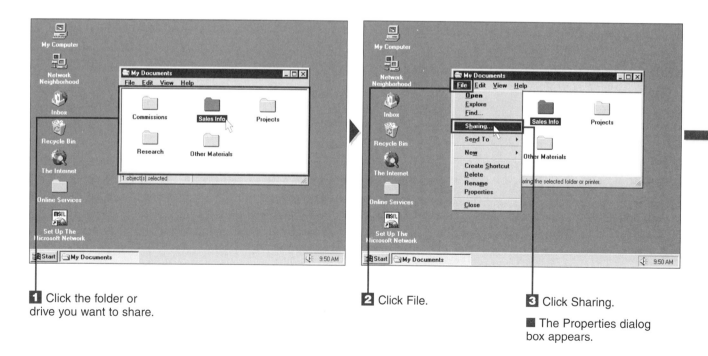

1 Click the folder or drive you want to share.

2 Click File.

3 Click Sharing.

■ The Properties dialog box appears.

TIPS

How can I tell what information and drives on my computer are shared?

You can use Windows Explorer to find out what information and drives on your computer are shared. A hand appears under the icon for a folder or drive you have shared in the Explorer window.

How can I view information about shared folders and drives on other computers on a network?

Double-click Network Neighborhood on the desktop to display a list of computers on the network. Double-click the name of a computer of interest to see what information is shared.

What can I do to prevent other people on a network from seeing which of my folders and drives are shared?

If you do not want other people to see which folders and drives on your computer are shared, change the name of the folder or drive so it ends with a dollar sign ($).

How can I view the comments for shared files?

In the Network Neighborhood window, you can view the comments entered for shared files. Click View and then click Details to display information about each item.

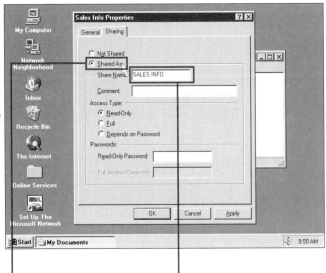

4 Click Shared As to share the information with others on the network (○ changes to ⦿).

■ This area displays the name of the folder or drive you selected. Individuals on the network will see this name.

5 To change the name of the folder or drive, double-click the name and then type the new name.

6 To enter a comment about the folder or drive, click this area. Then type the comment.

CONTINUED

SHARE INFORMATION CONTINUED

Y ou can give individuals on a network one of three types of access to your information.

Read-Only access allows individuals on the network to read, but not change or delete, shared information. Individuals can copy a file with Read-Only access to their own computers and then change the files.

People cannot add files to folders or drives that you have made Read-Only.

Full access allows individuals on the network to read, change and delete shared information. You should not grant Full access to your main hard drive. If someone erases your computer's system files, you may not be able to use your computer.

Depends on Password access is the best way to share your folders and drives. Windows lets you set two passwords. One password allows people to access files you specify as Read-Only. The other password lets people have Full access to your shared information. Using passwords offers some protection against people changing or erasing your files.

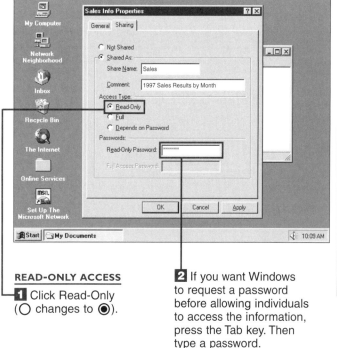

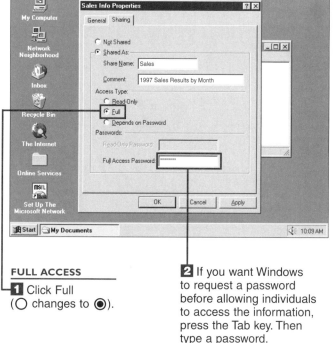

READ-ONLY ACCESS

■1 Click Read-Only
(○ changes to ◉).

■2 If you want Windows to request a password before allowing individuals to access the information, press the Tab key. Then type a password.

FULL ACCESS

■1 Click Full
(○ changes to ◉).

■2 If you want Windows to request a password before allowing individuals to access the information, press the Tab key. Then type a password.

TIPS

NETWORKING

VII

How does sharing information affect the performance of my computer?

When another computer accesses your shared information, it uses your computer to retrieve and then transfer the information through the network. Each time information is transferred through the network by someone accessing your shared files, there is less processing power available and your computer operates more slowly.

How do I stop sharing a folder?

When you no longer want individuals on the network to have access to a folder, perform steps 1 to 4 on page 486, except select Not Shared in step 4. Then click OK.

How can I prevent too many people from accessing my computer at the same time?

You can use passwords to restrict access to the shared information on your computer. Only distribute the passwords to people who need to access your files.

I cannot find one of my shared files. Why not?

If you gave Full access to the file, another person may have deleted the file. Ask everyone with Full access to check their Recycle Bin to see if they can find the file.

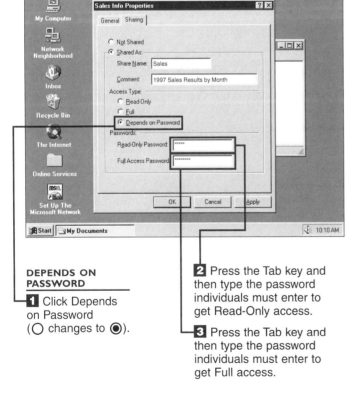

DEPENDS ON PASSWORD

1 Click Depends on Password (○ changes to ●).

2 Press the Tab key and then type the password individuals must enter to get Read-Only access.

3 Press the Tab key and then type the password individuals must enter to get Full access.

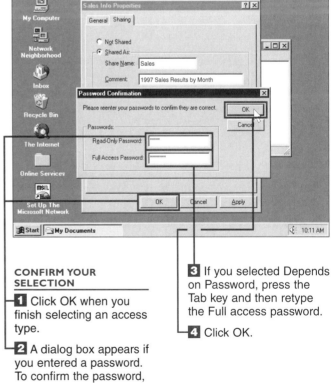

CONFIRM YOUR SELECTION

1 Click OK when you finish selecting an access type.

2 A dialog box appears if you entered a password. To confirm the password, retype the password.

3 If you selected Depends on Password, press the Tab key and then retype the Full access password.

4 Click OK.

489

SHARE A PRINTER

You can share a printer connected to your computer with other individuals on a network.

Sharing printers allows you to save money since each person on the network does not need their own printer.

When sharing a printer, you can assign a name, comment and password to the printer. A descriptive name and comment helps to identify your printer if there are several printers

connected to the network. Other people will be able to see the name and comment when they browse for shared printers on the network.

You should use a printer name that describes where the printer is located, such as "Dan's Office". Choosing a descriptive name will help people distinguish your printer from other printers on the network.

When sharing your printer with other people on a network, you

must make sure that both your computer and your printer are turned on. You must also make sure your printer is accessible when other people need it. For example, if your printer is located in your office, make sure your office door is not locked when people are using your printer.

Before you can share your printer, you must set up your computer to share resources. To turn on file and printer sharing, see page 484.

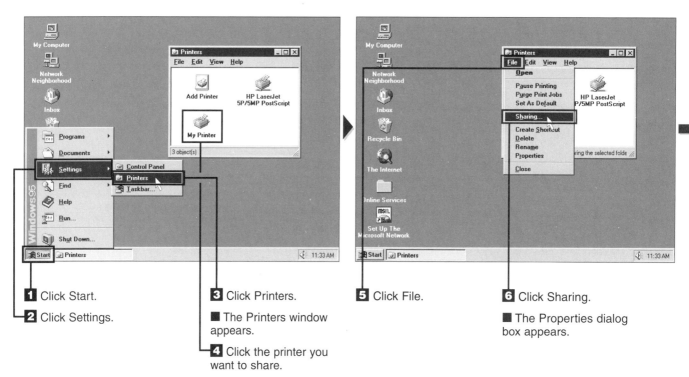

■1 Click Start.

■2 Click Settings.

■3 Click Printers.

■ The Printers window appears.

■4 Click the printer you want to share.

■5 Click File.

■6 Click Sharing.

■ The Properties dialog box appears.

TIPS

How do I restrict access to a printer I am sharing?

You can restrict access by assigning a password that users must enter to send documents to your printer. Only people who know the password will be able to use your printer.

How do I stop sharing a printer?

When you no longer want individuals on the network to use your printer, repeat the steps described below, except click Not Shared in step 7.

How do I connect to a shared printer on the network?

If you want to use a printer on the network, you need to install the printer software on your computer. To install a network printer, see page 492.

Can I hide my printer from other people on the network?

If you do not want other people who use the network to see your printer when they browse for shared printers on the network, type a dollar sign ($) at the end of the name of the printer.

Will sharing a printer affect my computer's performance?

Your computer stores the files sent by other people and then sends the files to your printer. As a result, your computer operates more slowly while other people are using your printer.

NETWORKING

VII

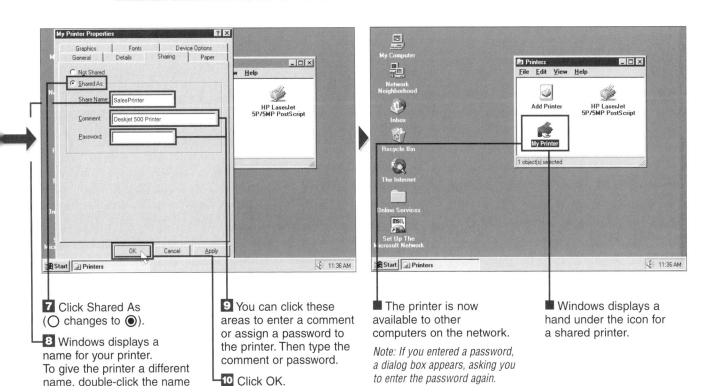

7 Click Shared As (○ changes to ◉).

8 Windows displays a name for your printer. To give the printer a different name, double-click the name and then type the new name.

9 You can click these areas to enter a comment or assign a password to the printer. Then type the comment or password.

10 Click OK.

■ The printer is now available to other computers on the network.

Note: If you entered a password, a dialog box appears, asking you to enter the password again.

■ Windows displays a hand under the icon for a shared printer.

491

CONNECT TO A SHARED PRINTER

You can connect to any printer that is part of your computer network to print your work.

Companies often connect printers to a network to help reduce printing costs. If a company does not have a printer on the network, each person who needs to produce printed copies of their work requires their own printer connected to their computer.

Some printers on a network are attached to computers whose only function is to process print jobs. You can also attach printers with built-in connectors directly to a network cable. Both of these types of printers are dedicated network printers.

Dedicated network printers are usually faster and more reliable than standard printers.

Dedicated network printers can be placed in a central part of an office or building to make it easy for people to retrieve the work they have printed. Many dedicated network printers have extra capabilities not available on standard printers, such as job sorting to help organize print jobs that have been printed by many people.

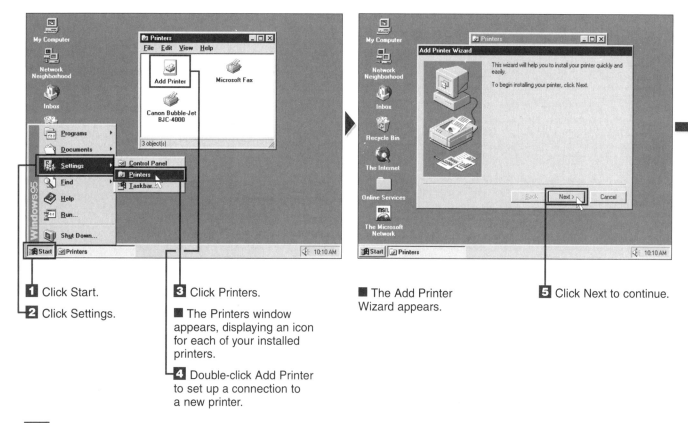

1 Click Start.

2 Click Settings.

3 Click Printers.

■ The Printers window appears, displaying an icon for each of your installed printers.

4 Double-click Add Printer to set up a connection to a new printer.

■ The Add Printer Wizard appears.

5 Click Next to continue.

What is a print queue?

A print queue is a location on a computer or printer where files waiting to print are stored. Printers on a network are often busy and new print jobs have to wait for other jobs to finish printing. You can check the print queue for a network printer to see how busy it is. See page 96.

Will the wizard require more information if I choose to print from MS-DOS-based programs?

Many MS-DOS-based programs must send information to a printer port, called an LPT port. The wizard asks you to specify which LPT port you want to use.

What is a print server?

A print server is a computer on a network that has a shared printer attached to it. A computer used for performing regular office tasks with a standard printer attached can be a print server. A print server can also be a computer that is only used for processing print jobs on the network and is connected to several high-speed laser printers.

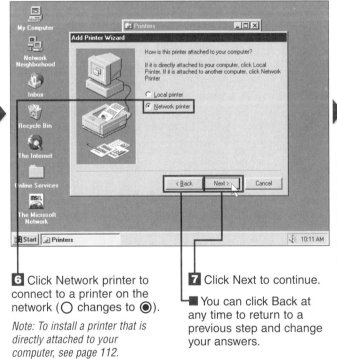

6 Click Network printer to connect to a printer on the network (○ changes to ●).

Note: To install a printer that is directly attached to your computer, see page 112.

7 Click Next to continue.

■ You can click Back at any time to return to a previous step and change your answers.

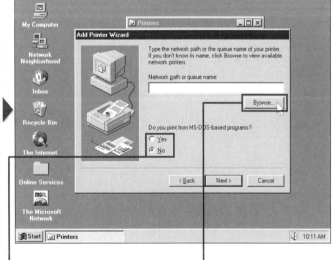

8 Click an option to specify if you print from MS-DOS-based programs (○ changes to ●).

■ Windows asks for the location of the printer you want to connect to.

9 Click Browse to view the available printers on the network.

■ The Browse for Printer dialog box appears.

CONTINUED ▶

CONNECT TO A
SHARED PRINTER CONTINUED

When you print a file, the printer must be able to understand the commands your computer is using to communicate with the printer. A print driver is software that allows Windows to communicate with a printer. Drivers allow Windows to send print jobs to any printer. Windows sends the printing

instructions to the print driver and the print driver translates the instructions into a format that the printer understands.

You may need to specify the manufacturer and model of the network printer to install the appropriate driver. Windows includes most of the popular print drivers. If Windows does

not have the print driver for your printer, you can obtain the driver from the manufacturer of the printer. You should use the most up-to-date driver you can find for the device.

Some people restrict access to a printer by assigning a password.

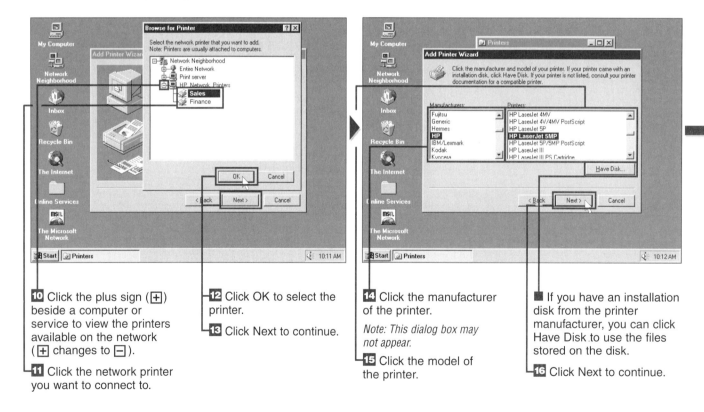

■10 Click the plus sign (⊞) beside a computer or service to view the printers available on the network (⊞ changes to ⊟).

■11 Click the network printer you want to connect to.

■12 Click OK to select the printer.

■13 Click Next to continue.

■14 Click the manufacturer of the printer.

Note: This dialog box may not appear.

■15 Click the model of the printer.

■ If you have an installation disk from the printer manufacturer, you can click Have Disk to use the files stored on the disk.

■16 Click Next to continue.

Why does the printer take a long time to print my files?

Most printers on a network are used by many people and may be used to print large print jobs. These factors may be slowing down the printing of your work.

Can I connect to more than one network printer?

Windows lets you send print jobs to any printer connected to a network, but you can have only one default printer. Windows sends all print jobs to the default printer unless you specify a different printer.

Why am I unable to find the printer I want to connect to?

If you want to connect to a printer that is directly connected to the network, you may need to install a network service before you can access the printer. You should check with your system administrator for more information.

How do I print to a printer on a network?

You can print to a printer on a network using the same methods you use to print to a printer attached directly to your computer.

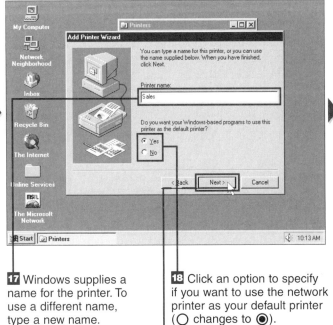

17 Windows supplies a name for the printer. To use a different name, type a new name.

18 Click an option to specify if you want to use the network printer as your default printer (○ changes to ⊙).

19 Click Next to continue.

20 Click an option to specify if you want to print a test page (○ changes to ⊙). A test page will confirm that the printer is set up properly.

21 Click Finish to finish installing the network printer.

■ Windows may ask you to insert the installation CD-ROM disc to complete the installation.

SHARE A FAX MODEM

Windows lets you share a fax modem with other people on a network. A fax modem lets you send documents to fax machines or other computers that have a fax modem. Faxing from your computer allows you to transfer documents that you create on your computer to other people.

Any person who has a fax modem connected to their computer can share the modem with other people on the network. A more common way of sharing a fax modem is to have one computer on the network that is used only for sending faxes.

Sending and receiving faxes uses a lot of computer resources. When someone on the network is using your fax modem to send faxes, your computer will have to process the information. If your computer becomes too slow because other people are using your fax modem, you may have to stop sharing your modem.

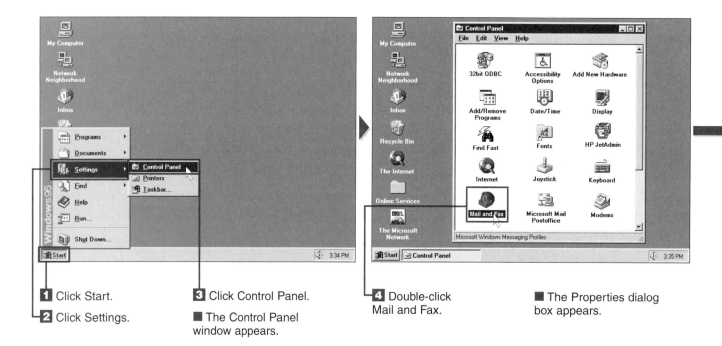

1 Click Start.

2 Click Settings.

3 Click Control Panel.

■ The Control Panel window appears.

4 Double-click Mail and Fax.

■ The Properties dialog box appears.

What must other people do before they can access my shared fax modem?

Before other computers on a network can use a shared fax modem, the computers must be set up to use the shared fax modem. To set up a computer to use a shared fax modem, see page 500.

What should I do when I no longer want other people to share my fax modem?

You can perform the steps described below to stop sharing your fax modem. Perform steps 1 to 8 (☑ changes to ☐ in step 8). Then click OK to close the Microsoft Fax Properties dialog box.

Is there anything I must do before sharing my fax modem?

Before you can use Windows to share a fax modem, you must ensure the fax modem is installed on your computer. See page 350 to install a modem. You must also turn on sharing for your computer. See page 484 to turn on sharing. You also need to set up Microsoft Exchange on your computer. See page 410 to set up Exchange.

5 Click Microsoft Fax.

6 Click Properties.

■ The Microsoft Fax Properties dialog box appears.

7 Click the Modem tab.

■ This area displays the modem(s) installed on your computer.

8 Click this option to allow other people to access the fax modem (☐ changes to ☑).

9 Click Properties to change the sharing options for your modem.

CONTINUED

SHARE A FAX MODEM CONTINUED

When you turn on sharing for a fax modem, you must name the modem. You should use a descriptive name, such as John's Fax, so that other people will be able to identify the modem. The name can contain up to 12 characters, including spaces.

You can also enter a comment you want people on the network to see when browsing for shared equipment. Assigning a comment is useful if the network contains many shared resources.

You must assign Full access to the shared fax modem so other people can use the fax modem.

You can restrict access by assigning a password that people must enter to send documents to the fax modem. Only people who know the password will be able to use the fax modem.

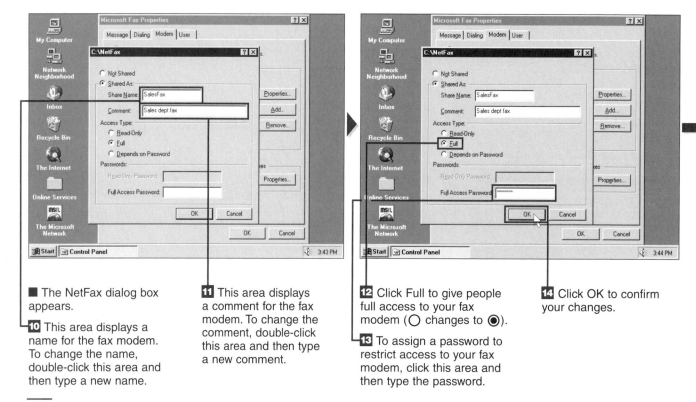

■ The NetFax dialog box appears.

10 This area displays a name for the fax modem. To change the name, double-click this area and then type a new name.

11 This area displays a comment for the fax modem. To change the comment, double-click this area and then type a new comment.

12 Click Full to give people full access to your fax modem (○ changes to ◉).

13 To assign a password to restrict access to your fax modem, click this area and then type the password.

14 Click OK to confirm your changes.

Why are people unable to access my fax modem?

Before people can use your fax modem, your computer must be turned on and logged on to the network. Microsoft Exchange must also be open on your computer.

Can people on the network use my shared fax modem to receive faxes?

Other people cannot use a shared fax modem to receive faxes at their computers. If you receive a fax meant for a colleague on your fax modem, you must print the fax for your colleague or forward the fax by e-mail.

Why should I restrict access to my fax modem?

The main reason to restrict access to your fax modem is to limit the number of people who use your modem to send faxes. If too many people use your fax modem, your computer may become overloaded and you will not be able to use the computer for your own work.

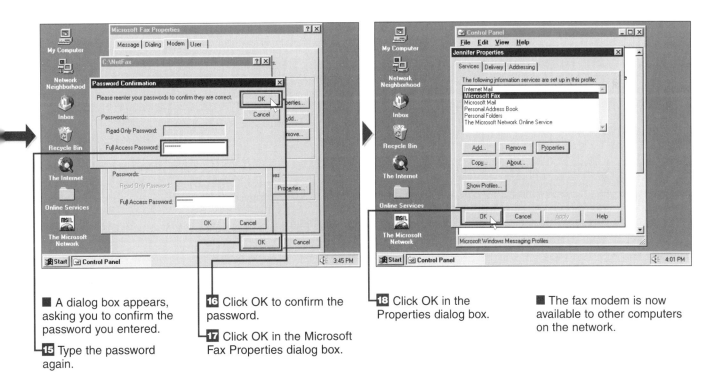

■ A dialog box appears, asking you to confirm the password you entered.

15 Type the password again.

16 Click OK to confirm the password.

17 Click OK in the Microsoft Fax Properties dialog box.

18 Click OK in the Properties dialog box.

■ The fax modem is now available to other computers on the network.

CONNECT TO A SHARED FAX MODEM

Y ou can connect to a shared fax modem that is attached to another computer on a network. You can then use the shared fax modem to send faxes from your computer.

Sending a fax directly from your computer saves you the time of

printing a document and standing in line at the fax machine.

Sharing a fax modem saves money because only one computer on the network needs a fax modem and a dedicated phone line. This saves a business from having to purchase

a modem for each computer on the network.

Before you can connect to a shared fax modem, the owner of the computer with the attached fax modem must turn on sharing for the modem. See page 496 to share a fax modem.

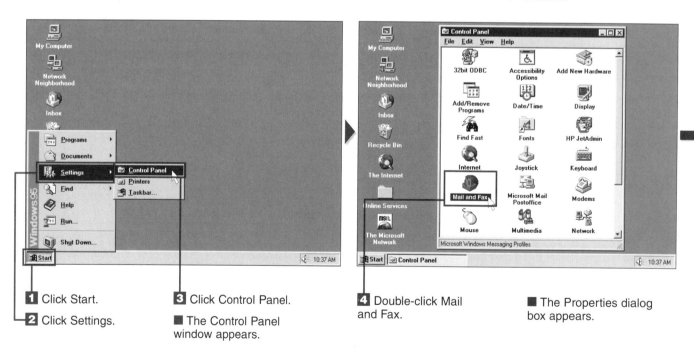

1 Click Start.

2 Click Settings.

3 Click Control Panel.

■ The Control Panel window appears.

4 Double-click Mail and Fax.

■ The Properties dialog box appears.

TIPS

What must I install on my computer before I can connect to a shared fax modem?

Before you can use Windows to connect to a shared fax modem, you must add and set up the Microsoft Fax group on your computer. To add Windows components, see page 580.

What happens when two people send a fax at once?

The shared fax modem will send faxes in the order that it receives them. If the fax modem is busy when you send a fax, the computer attached to the fax modem will store the fax until the modem is ready to send your fax.

Does the person I'm sending a fax to have to be using a fax modem to receive my fax?

A fax modem is compatible with most fax machines. The person who receives the fax may use either a computer attached to a fax modem or a regular fax machine.

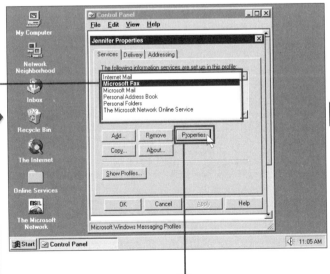

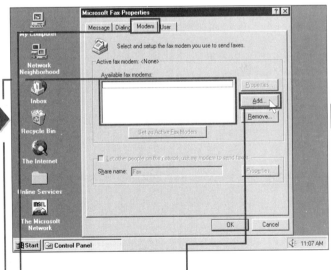

■ This area displays the information services that are set up on your computer.

5 Click Microsoft Fax.

6 Click Properties to change the properties for Microsoft Fax.

■ The Microsoft Fax Properties dialog box appears.

7 Click the Modem tab.

■ This area displays the names of the fax modems installed on your computer.

8 Click Add to add a fax modem.

■ The Add a Fax Modem dialog box appears.

CONTINUED ▶

CONNECT TO A
SHARED FAX MODEM CONTINUED

You must tell Windows the location of the shared fax modem you want to connect to. The location of the fax modem is the name of the computer followed by the name of the shared fax modem, such as "\\BobsComputer\FAX". If you do not know the location of the shared fax modem you want to connect to, ask your system administrator or the person who manages the shared fax modem.

After you finish connecting to a shared fax modem, you can send faxes as if the modem was connected to your own computer.

When someone sends you a fax, the fax will not be sent to your computer. The person who manages the computer with the shared fax modem will have to distribute incoming faxes to the appropriate people.

You can only use a shared fax modem to send faxes. You cannot use a shared fax modem to dial bulletin board services or connect to the Internet.

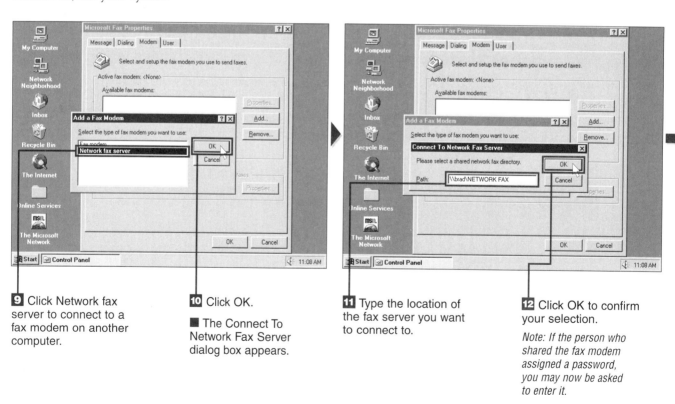

■9 Click Network fax server to connect to a fax modem on another computer.

■10 Click OK.

■ The Connect To Network Fax Server dialog box appears.

■11 Type the location of the fax server you want to connect to.

■12 Click OK to confirm your selection.

Note: If the person who shared the fax modem assigned a password, you may now be asked to enter it.

TIPS

Can all programs use a shared fax modem?

Many older programs, such as MS-DOS or Windows 3.1 programs, may not be able to use a shared fax modem.

How do I disconnect from a shared fax modem?

If you no longer want to use a shared fax modem, display the Microsoft Fax Properties dialog box and then click the Modem tab. Click the fax modem you want to disconnect from and then click the Remove button.

How do I fax a document from my computer?

You can fax a document from most programs that allow you to print. Click the File menu and then click Print. In the Print dialog box that appears, select Microsoft Fax as the printer and then click OK. The Compose New Fax wizard appears to guide you through the process of creating the fax. You can also start the Compose New Fax wizard from within Microsoft Exchange or from the Start menu. See page 452.

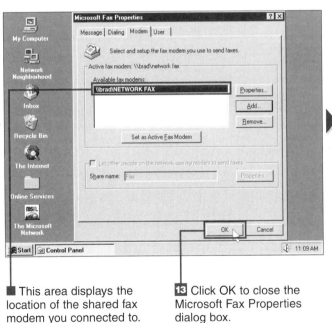

■ This area displays the location of the shared fax modem you connected to.

13 Click OK to close the Microsoft Fax Properties dialog box.

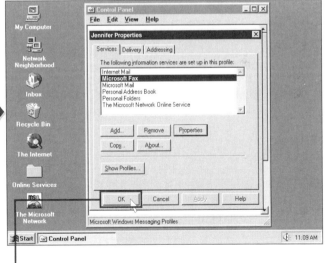

14 Click OK to close the Properties dialog box.

■ You can now use the shared fax modem.

TURN ON USER-LEVEL ACCESS CONTROL

Y ou can specify which people on a network can have access to your shared resources. Shared network resources can include information such as files and folders or devices such as printers and modems.

Share-level access control allows you to assign a password to each resource and give the password to specific people. Using share-level access control is suitable for small networks but can be unmanageable when there are many people who want to access your shared resources.

User-level access control offers better security and is suitable for large networks with dedicated servers. The server controls who can access the network and stores a list of people on the network. You can use the list to determine who you want to be able to access your resources. You can grant access to specific individuals or entire workgroups. The people you select do not need to use a password to access resources you shared.

User-level access control is a more efficient way to give people access to your shared resources on a large network.

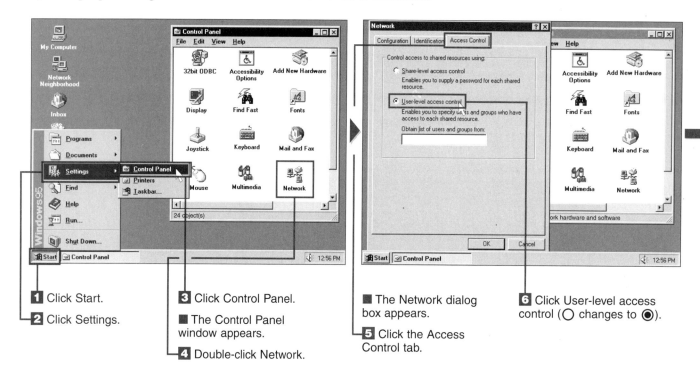

1 Click Start.

2 Click Settings.

3 Click Control Panel.

■ The Control Panel window appears.

4 Double-click Network.

■ The Network dialog box appears.

5 Click the Access Control tab.

6 Click User-level access control (○ changes to ●).

TIPS

What is the name of the network that contains the list of users?

Every network has its own unique name. You will need to know the name of your network before you can turn on user-level access control. If you do not know the name of your network, you should contact your system administrator.

What will happen to my shared resources after I turn on user-level access control?

When you turn on user-level access control, all the resources that you previously shared will no longer be shared. You will have to turn on sharing for each folder and device again if you wish to continue sharing them. To share information, see page 486.

How is the user list created?

Each large network has a computer that controls who can log on to and use resources on the network. This computer is called the domain controller. The domain controller maintains a list of all the users on a network. Before someone can access your shared resources, the domain controller checks this list to see if the person is allowed access.

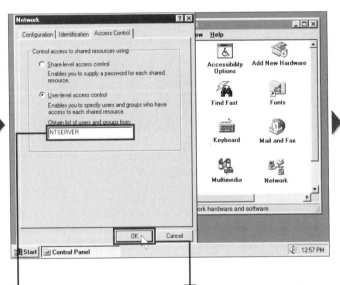

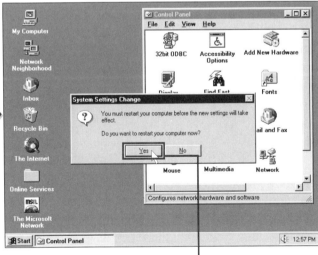

7 Click this area and then type the name of the network or computer where the list of users is stored.

Note: The name of the network or computer may already appear in the area.

8 Click OK.

■ A dialog box may appear, telling you access to shared folders will be lost.

■ The System Settings Change dialog box appears, telling you Windows needs to restart your computer before the new settings will take effect.

9 Click Yes to restart your computer.

ASSIGN ACCESS RIGHTS TO INFORMATION

You can assign access rights to information stored on your computer. Assigning access rights allows you to specify who you want to be able to access your resources and the type of access you want to give. You can change access rights at any time so that only certain people on a network can use your resources.

You must be using a client/server network to assign access rights for other people on the network. A client/server network has a central computer controlling who may access the network. Windows NT and Novell NetWare networks are popular examples of client/server networks.

A central computer, called a server, stores a list of every person on the network. You use this list to determine who you want to be able to access your resources.

You can assign access rights for individuals on the network or entire workgroups. A workgroup is a group of computers on a network that frequently share information.

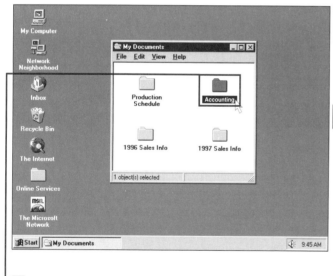

1 Click the folder or drive you want to share.

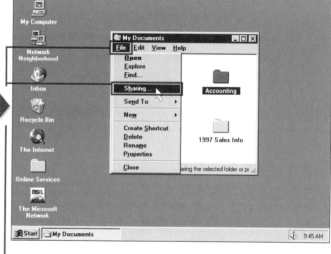

2 Click File.

3 Click Sharing.

■ The Properties dialog box appears.

What must I do before I can assign access rights to information on my computer?

Before you can assign access rights for people on your network, you must turn on user-level access control. Turning on user-level access control allows you to specify which people on your network can access your resources. See page 504.

Which folders and drives on my computer are shared?

You can use the My Computer or Windows Explorer window to determine which folders and drives on your computer are shared. A hand appears under the icon for a shared folder or drive.

How do I stop sharing a folder?

When you no longer want to give people on the network access to a folder, perform steps 1 to 4 starting on page 486, except select Not Shared in step 4. Then click OK.

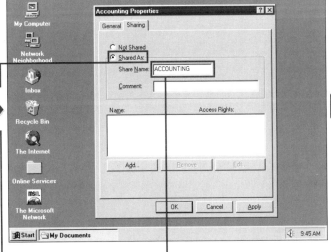

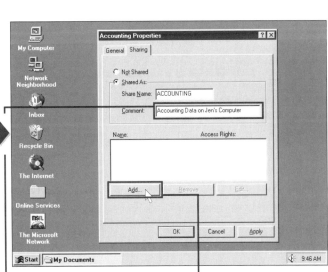

■4 Click Shared As to share the information with others on the network (○ changes to ◉).

■ This area displays the name of the folder or drive you selected. Individuals on the network will see this name.

■5 To change the name of the folder or drive, double-click this area and then type a new name.

■6 To enter a comment about the folder or drive, click this area. Then type the comment.

■7 Click Add to give people on the network access to the information.

CONTINUED ▶

ASSIGN ACCESS RIGHTS
TO INFORMATION CONTINUED

W indows allows you to specify every person and workgroup on the network you want to be able to access your resources. You can select one person, an entire workgroup or several people and workgroups all at once.

When assigning access rights for information on your computer, you can choose the type of access you want to assign.

Read-only access allows a person or workgroup to only read the information in a folder. People cannot change the information on your computer, but they can copy the information to another computer and then change the information.

Full access gives a person or workgroup total control over the information in a folder. Assigning full access rights to information

on a computer is very rare because people on the network will be able to change or even delete the information.

There are also several custom access rights you can assign to people on your network. Assigning custom access rights gives you more control over the type of access people have to your resources.

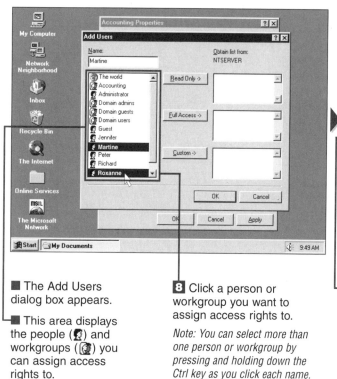

■ The Add Users dialog box appears.

■ This area displays the people (👤) and workgroups (👥) you can assign access rights to.

8 Click a person or workgroup you want to assign access rights to.

Note: You can select more than one person or workgroup by pressing and holding down the Ctrl key as you click each name.

9 Click the access right you want to assign.

10 Repeat steps 8 and 9 until you have selected each person and workgroup you want to assign access rights to.

11 Click OK.

What types of custom access rights can I assign to information?

Read Files access lets people only read your files. The files cannot be changed.

Write to Files access allows people to make changes to your files.

Create Files and Folders access allows people to create new files and folders in the shared folder.

Delete Files access lets people remove the files from your computer. This is a powerful right and should only be given to people you trust.

Change File Attributes access allows people to change the properties of files, such as making a file read-only.

List Files access allows people to view a list of the files in the shared folder.

Change Access Control access lets people change the access rights for files on your computer.

Can I give additional access rights to one person in a workgroup?

Access rights given to individuals take priority over access rights granted to workgroups. For example, you can give read-only access to your entire workgroup and then assign additional rights to one person in the workgroup.

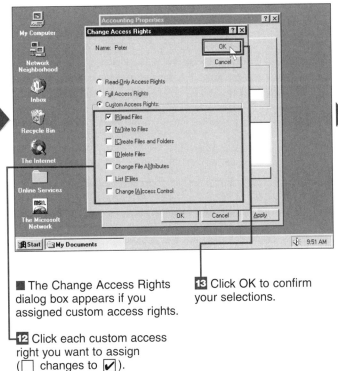

■ The Change Access Rights dialog box appears if you assigned custom access rights.

12 Click each custom access right you want to assign (☐ changes to ☑).

13 Click OK to confirm your selections.

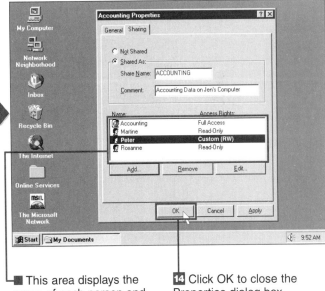

■ This area displays the name of each person and workgroup you assigned access rights to.

14 Click OK to close the Properties dialog box.

INSTALL A NETWORK INTERFACE CARD

A Network Interface Card (NIC) physically connects your computer to a network and controls the flow of information between your computer and the network. When you are attached to a network you can exchange information, such as documents and programs, with other computers on the network. You can also share devices such as printers and CD-ROM drives on the network.

Network interface cards are installed inside a computer. A network interface card has a connector where the network cable attaches.

When buying a network interface card, the card you need depends on the type of cable used on the network you connect to and the amount of information that the cable can transfer at once. A network interface card designed

for Windows 95 that has Plug and Play capabilities will be easier to set up.

The Add New Hardware Wizard helps you correctly install your network interface card. The wizard asks a series of questions and then sets up the network interface card according to the information you provide.

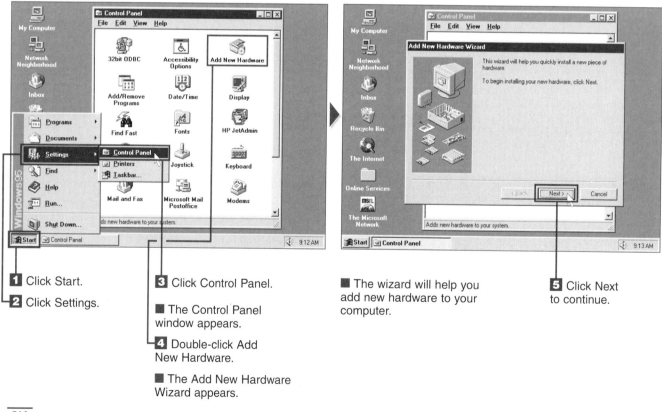

1 Click Start.

2 Click Settings.

3 Click Control Panel.

■ The Control Panel window appears.

4 Double-click Add New Hardware.

■ The Add New Hardware Wizard appears.

■ The wizard will help you add new hardware to your computer.

5 Click Next to continue.

TIPS

My network interface card is already set up on my computer. How did this happen?

If the network interface card was in your computer when you installed Windows 95, your computer may have automatically detected and set up the card for you.

Do I need to use the wizard to install a Plug and Play network interface card?

No. If you add a Plug and Play network interface card to your computer, Windows will automatically recognize and set up the card as soon as you turn on your computer.

Can I install a network interface card in my laptop computer?

Most laptops require a specialized device to connect to a network. Some laptops use a device that connects the laptop through the computer's printer port, called the LPT port. Newer laptop computers have a socket that lets you insert a PCMCIA card, or PC card, to connect to the network.

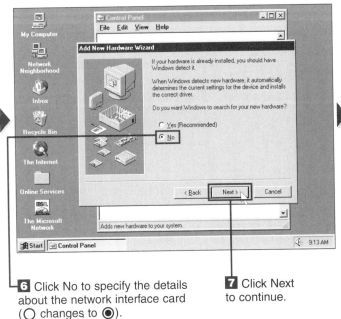

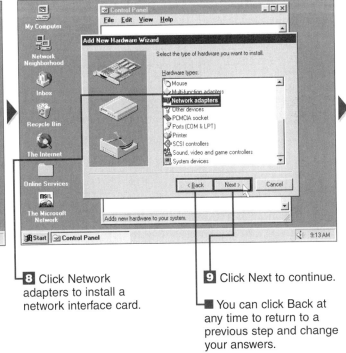

-6 Click No to specify the details about the network interface card (○ changes to ⦿).

Note: Click Yes to have Windows automatically find and install the network interface card for you.

7 Click Next to continue.

-8 Click Network adapters to install a network interface card.

9 Click Next to continue.

■ You can click Back at any time to return to a previous step and change your answers.

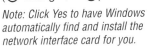

CONTINUED ▶

INSTALL A NETWORK
INTERFACE CARD CONTINUED

You must tell Windows the manufacturer and model of the network interface card you are installing. Windows includes drivers for most models of network interface cards. A driver is a program that enables your computer to communicate with the card.

Windows displays the settings available on your computer that the network interface card can use. You should write down these settings for future reference. If your network interface card is not set up to use the settings, you may need to physically adjust the settings on the card. Most network interface card manufacturers supply a program that allows you to view and change the settings for a card. You should consult the manual for the card before changing any settings.

The Input/Output (I/O) range specifies which area of memory the card uses to communicate with the computer. The Interrupt Request (IRQ) is used to tell the computer when the card needs attention. The Memory Range lets the card communicate directly with your computer's memory to speed up the processing of information.

You will need to use your Windows 95 CD-ROM disc or floppy disks to install the network interface card.

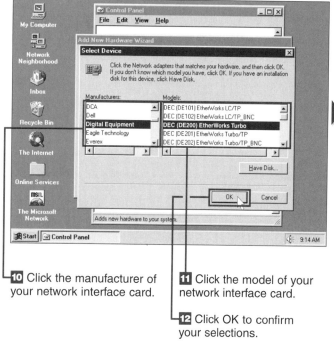

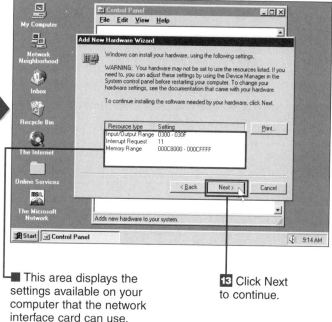

10 Click the manufacturer of your network interface card.

11 Click the model of your network interface card.

12 Click OK to confirm your selections.

■ This area displays the settings available on your computer that the network interface card can use.

Note: The displayed settings depend on the resources available on your computer.

13 Click Next to continue.

Why do I need to enter my computer name and workgroup name?

Windows may ask you to enter your computer name and workgroup name if this information was not previously entered on your computer. If you do not know this information, ask your system administrator.

I installed the network interface card, but now my modem does not work. What happened?

If the settings for the network interface card and the modem are the same, a conflict will occur and the devices will not operate properly. Use the Device Manager to examine the settings for the devices so you can resolve the conflict. See page 624.

Should I use the installation disk included with my network interface card?

If the card is newer than your version of Windows 95, you should use the disk to install the card. The information on the disk will be more up-to-date than the information included with Windows 95. Use the method described below to install the card, except use the Have Disk button to copy the files stored on the disk.

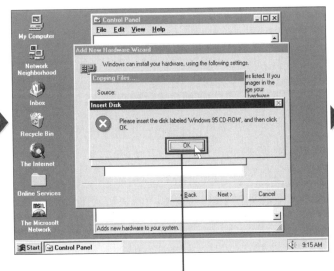

■ A dialog box appears, asking you to insert the Windows CD-ROM disc or a specific floppy disk.

14 Insert the CD-ROM disc or floppy disk into a drive.

15 Click OK to continue.

■ Windows indicates that the software for your network interface card has been successfully installed.

16 Click Finish.

■ A dialog box will appear, asking you to restart your computer. Click Yes to restart the computer.

INSTALL A NETWORK PROTOCOL

Y ou can install a network protocol to allow computers and devices on your network to exchange information. A protocol is a language, or a set of rules, that determines how two computers communicate with each other. A network protocol determines how information transfers from one computer to another on a network.

All computers and devices on a network must use the same protocol before they can communicate with each other. For example, a computer and a network printer must use the same protocol for the computer to successfully send print jobs to the printer.

The type of protocol you must install is often determined by the type of operating system that manages the network. Many network protocols are designed specifically for use with one type of network operating system, such as Novell or Windows NT.

When you install Windows, some network protocols will automatically be installed if your computer has a network interface card. Protocols will also be installed when you add the Dial-Up Networking component.

Windows includes support for the most popular types of network protocols, including IPX/SPX, NetBEUI and TCP/IP.

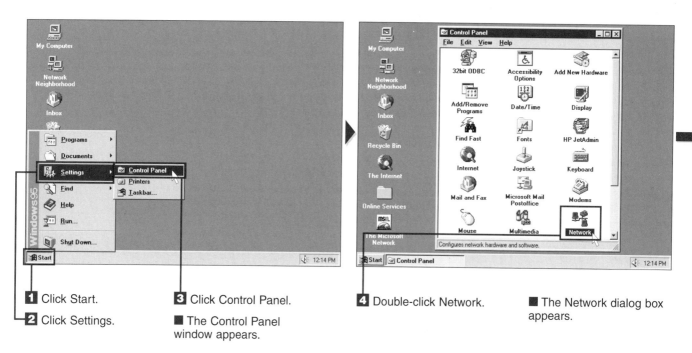

1 Click Start.

2 Click Settings.

3 Click Control Panel.

■ The Control Panel window appears.

4 Double-click Network.

■ The Network dialog box appears.

TIPS

What are the most important features of a protocol?

Error control is a feature that allows a protocol to check for errors in information transferred by a computer on a network. Some protocols try to correct errors by asking the computer to send the information again.

The addressing feature lets a protocol determine where information is to be sent. The addressing feature also makes sure that the information arrives at its intended destination.

Flow control helps regulate the flow of information so slower devices can process information they receive from faster devices on the network.

When should I install a network protocol?

You may need to install a protocol if you want to be able to use network devices such as a printer. You may also need to install a network protocol when the type of network you connect to changes or is upgraded.

NETWORKING

VII

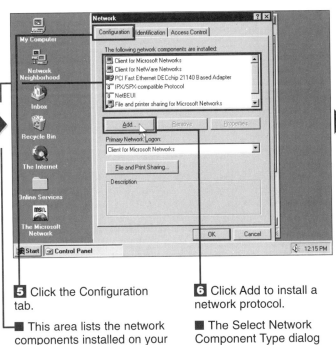

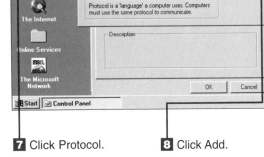

5 Click the Configuration tab.

■ This area lists the network components installed on your computer. Protocols display a cable symbol ( ).

6 Click Add to install a network protocol.

■ The Select Network Component Type dialog box appears.

7 Click Protocol.

8 Click Add.

■ The Select Network Protocol dialog box appears.

CONTINUED ▶

INSTALL A NETWORK PROTOCOL
CONTINUED

When installing a network protocol, you must tell Windows the name of the manufacturer and the type of protocol you want to add.

There are many different types of network protocols you can add to a computer. A network can use several different types of protocols at the same time.

Any device that does not understand a protocol used by a computer on the network will simply ignore the information sent using that protocol.

Protocols may be used for specific tasks on a network. For example, the NetBEUI protocol may be used to control all the information transferred between computers

on the network. The IPX/SPX protocol may be used to send documents to a printer directly connected to the network.

Windows includes software for the most popular protocols. You need to use your Windows CD-ROM disc or floppy disks to add a network protocol.

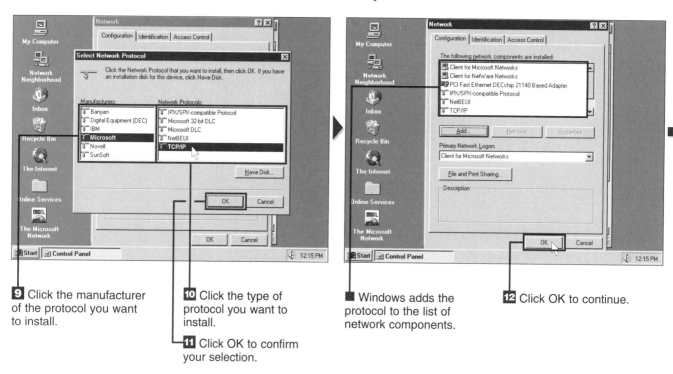

■9 Click the manufacturer of the protocol you want to install.

■10 Click the type of protocol you want to install.

■11 Click OK to confirm your selection.

■ Windows adds the protocol to the list of network components.

■12 Click OK to continue.

Which network protocol should I install?

Internetwork Packet Exchange/ Sequenced Packet Exchange (IPX/SPX) is a popular network protocol used by Novell networks. Most network devices, such as printers, also use the IPX/SPX protocol.

If you are connecting to a Windows 95 network, you can use the NetBIOS Extended User Interface (NetBEUI) protocol developed by IBM. This protocol can be difficult to set up and use on large networks.

Transmission Control Protocol/Internet Protocol (TCP/IP) is the protocol needed to connect to the Internet.

What should I do if the network protocol I want to install does not appear in the list of protocols?

If you purchase a new network device that uses a protocol not supported by Windows, you may have to obtain the appropriate software from the manufacturer of the device. You can use the method described below to install the protocol, except click the Have Disk button to use the disk included with the device.

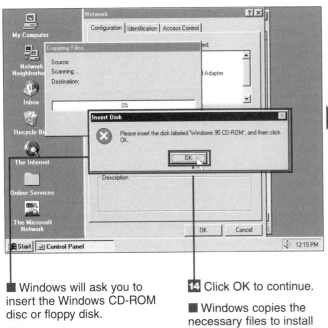

■ Windows will ask you to insert the Windows CD-ROM disc or floppy disk.

13 Insert the CD-ROM disc or floppy disk into the drive.

14 Click OK to continue.

■ Windows copies the necessary files to install the network protocol.

■ The System Settings Change dialog box appears, telling you Windows needs to restart your computer before the new settings will take effect.

15 Click Yes to restart your computer.

INSTALL A NETWORK CLIENT

A network client is software that lets your computer communicate with other computers on a network. You install a network client to help control the flow of information between your computer and other computers.

A network client helps to determine whether information

stays on your computer or is sent to a computer or printer on the network. For example, when you send a document to a printer, the network client will determine if the document will print on a printer attached to your computer or will be sent to another printer on the network. Because the client determines where information

goes, client software is often referred to as a redirector.

A network client also allows a computer using Windows 95 to communicate with a dedicated server on a network. A dedicated server is a computer that supplies information, such as files, to other computers on a network.

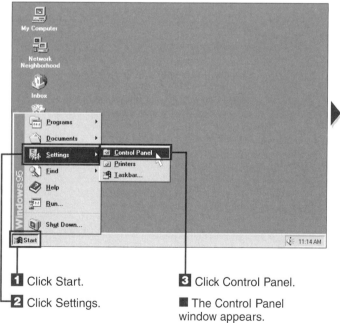

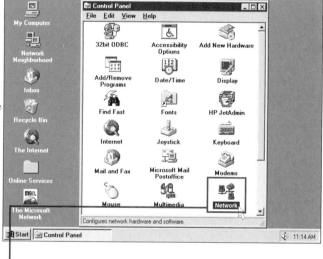

1 Click Start.

2 Click Settings.

3 Click Control Panel.

■ The Control Panel window appears.

4 Double-click Network.

■ The Network dialog box appears.

Why does some network client software already exist on my computer?

If your computer had a network interface card when you installed Windows, some network clients may have been automatically installed. Clients may also be installed when you add the Dial-Up Networking component included with Windows 95.

Will I have to update a network client after I install it?

You usually need to update a network client only when the type of network you connect to changes or is upgraded.

Can I install more than one network client?

Yes. Installing more than one network client allows you to use a wide variety of resources on the network. Many large networks now use more than one type of network to control different resources, such as servers and printers. You can specify a primary client to tell Windows which network client you use most often. See page 522.

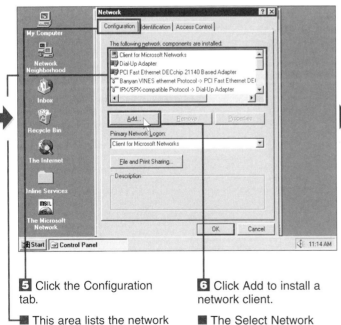

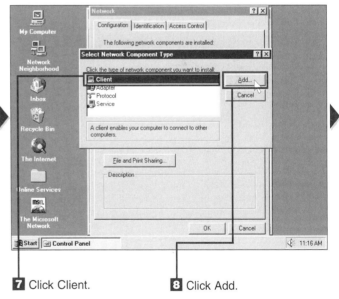

5 Click the Configuration tab.

■ This area lists the network components installed on your computer. Clients display a computer icon (🖳).

6 Click Add to install a network client.

■ The Select Network Component Type dialog box appears.

7 Click Client.

8 Click Add.

■ The Select Network Client dialog box appears.

CONTINUED ▶

INSTALL A NETWORK CLIENT
CONTINUED

When installing a network client, you must tell Windows the name of the manufacturer of the network client and the type of client you want to install.

The type of network you want to connect to determines the type of network client you need.

You should check with your system administrator to confirm that any new client software you wish to install will work with your current network.

Windows 95 includes client software for the most popular types of networks, including Microsoft and Novell. You may

need to use your Windows 95 CD-ROM disc or floppy disks to install the client software.

After you have installed the network client for each type of network you want to connect to, you can access information and devices on the network.

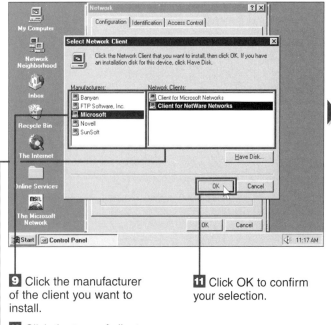

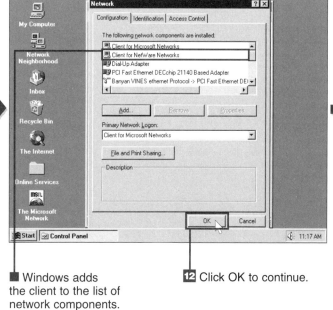

■9 Click the manufacturer of the client you want to install.

■10 Click the type of client you want to install.

■11 Click OK to confirm your selection.

■ Windows adds the client to the list of network components.

■12 Click OK to continue.

TIPS

Which network client should I install?

Windows includes several types of Novell NetWare clients. If you are connecting to a Novell NetWare network, you should contact your system administrator to find out which NetWare client to use.

If the network you want to connect to uses Windows NT, you should use the Client for Microsoft Networks software.

Windows also includes client software for Banyan Vines networks that may be used to connect to this type of network.

I have an installation disk for the client. Should I use the disk to install the client?

If the network client you want to install is newer than your version of Windows 95, you should use the network client installation disk to install the client. You can use the method described below to install the client, except use the Have Disk button to copy the files stored on the disk. Using a disk is safer than using the information supplied by Windows if the information on the disk is more up-to-date than the information supplied by Windows.

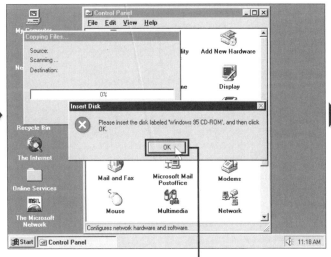

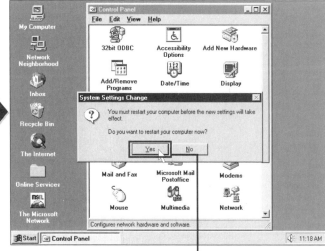

■ Windows may ask you to insert the Windows 95 CD-ROM disc or floppy disk.

13 Insert the CD-ROM disc or floppy disk into the drive.

14 Click OK to continue.

■ Windows copies the necessary files to install the network client.

■ The System Settings Change dialog box appears, telling you Windows needs to restart your computer before the new settings will take effect.

15 Click Yes to restart your computer.

SELECT A PRIMARY
NETWORK CLIENT

Windows lets you choose which network client to use as the primary, or main, network client. A network client is software that allows your computer to communicate with a specific network operating system.

When you start Windows, you need to enter logon information,

such as a password. The primary network client determines which network will check your logon information. When entered correctly, this information allows you to use the network.

When selecting the primary network client, you should choose

the client for the network you use most often. For example, if you frequently use a Novell NetWare network to access files and printers and you use a Microsoft network to occasionally access a database, you should set the Novell NetWare client as your primary client.

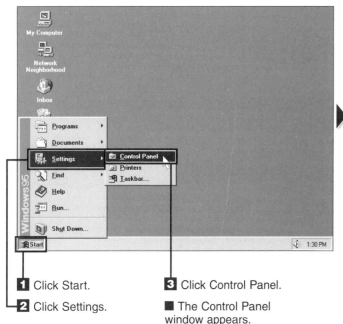

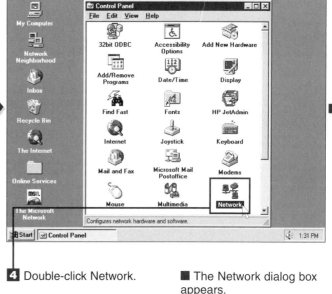

1 Click Start.

2 Click Settings.

3 Click Control Panel.

■ The Control Panel window appears.

4 Double-click Network.

■ The Network dialog box appears.

When would I need to change my primary network client?

Once you set your primary network client, you will rarely need to change the client. If you intend to change network types or will be using another network for more than a few days, it may be helpful to change your primary client.

Why can't I find the client that I want to use as the primary network client?

If the client you want to use as the primary network client is not displayed in the Network dialog box, the client may not be installed on your computer. To install a network client, see page 518.

When selecting a primary network client, you can choose the Windows Logon option. What does this option do?

The Windows Logon option enables you to log on to Windows 95. Using the Windows Logon option will not log you on to any networks. This option is useful if you are currently using a computer that is not connected to a network, such as when you use a portable computer away from the office.

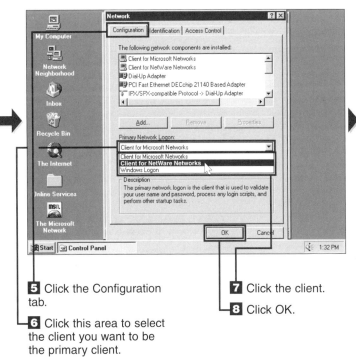

5 Click the Configuration tab.

6 Click this area to select the client you want to be the primary client.

7 Click the client.

8 Click OK.

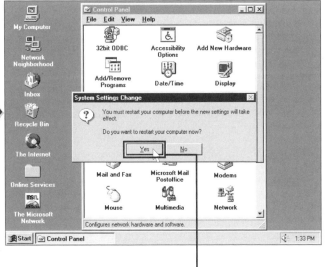

■ The System Settings Change dialog box appears, telling you Windows needs to restart your computer before the new settings will take effect.

9 Click Yes to restart your computer.

CONFIGURE THE MICROSOFT CLIENT

After you install a network client for a Microsoft network, you can adjust the settings for the client to customize the way your computer connects to the network.

You can have Windows automatically connect to your

Windows NT network each time you log on to Windows. You need to tell Windows the name of the server or domain you want to connect to. If you do not know the name of the server or domain, ask your system administrator.

Windows lets you choose between a quick and regular logon to connect to your network. Most computers that are permanently connected to a network use the regular logon option. If you plan to use only a few of the resources on the network, you may want to use the quick logon option.

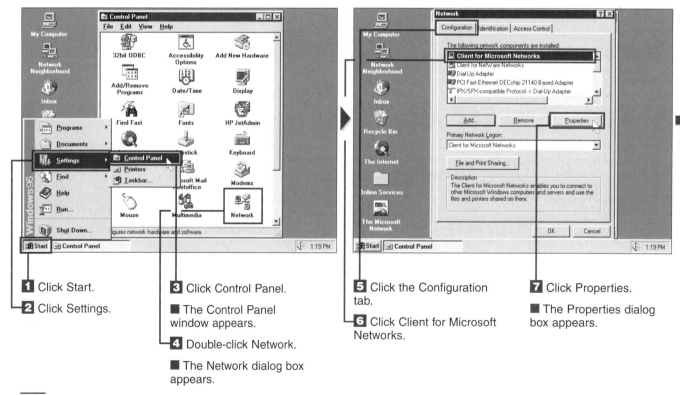

1 Click Start.

2 Click Settings.

3 Click Control Panel.

■ The Control Panel window appears.

4 Double-click Network.

■ The Network dialog box appears.

5 Click the Configuration tab.

6 Click Client for Microsoft Networks.

7 Click Properties.

■ The Properties dialog box appears.

TIPS

What is a network domain?

A network domain is a name given to a collection of related computers on a network. For example, a domain can consist of all computers in a particular department of a business. If a large network consists of many smaller networks connected together, each of the smaller networks is usually a different domain. You need to specify the name of the server or domain if you want Windows to automatically connect you to the network each time you start Windows.

What is the difference between a regular and a quick logon?

A regular logon connects you to each resource on the network every time you start Windows. You will immediately know if each resource is available, but this option increases the time it takes to log on to the network. A quick logon is a faster way to log on to the network because you are only connected to resources when you access them. The quick logon feature is useful if you do not plan to use all of the available resources every time you connect to the network.

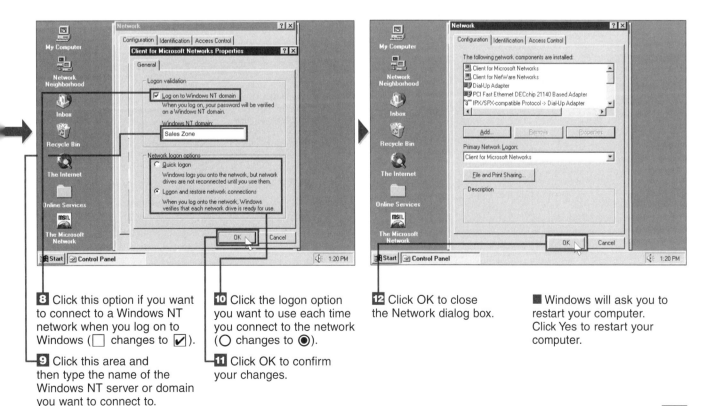

8 Click this option if you want to connect to a Windows NT network when you log on to Windows (☐ changes to ☑).

9 Click this area and then type the name of the Windows NT server or domain you want to connect to.

10 Click the logon option you want to use each time you connect to the network (○ changes to ◉).

11 Click OK to confirm your changes.

12 Click OK to close the Network dialog box.

■ Windows will ask you to restart your computer. Click Yes to restart your computer.

CONFIGURE THE NETWARE CLIENT

After installing a network client for a Novell NetWare network, you may need to adjust the settings of the client to customize the way your computer connects to the network.

A Novell NetWare network can consist of many NetWare servers that store information that

people on the network can access. When configuring the NetWare network client, you need to enter the name of the server you want to connect to each time you log on to the network. If you do not know the name of the server, ask your system administrator.

You can choose to have Windows automatically run logon scripts.

A logon script is a series of instructions that Windows performs when you successfully connect to a NetWare server. The instructions tell Windows what options you want to use. For example, logon scripts often automatically map your network drives.

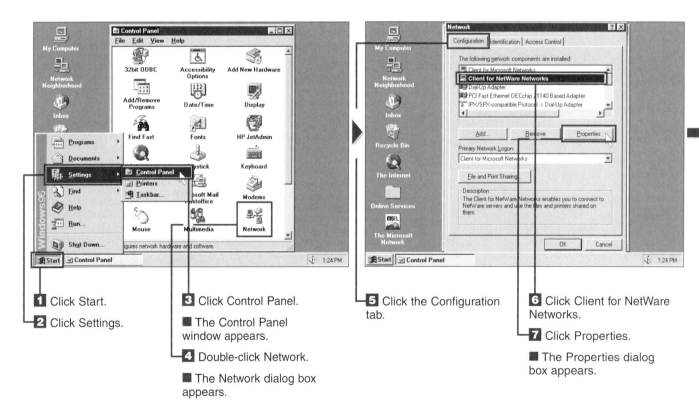

1 Click Start.

2 Click Settings.

3 Click Control Panel.

■ The Control Panel window appears.

4 Double-click Network.

■ The Network dialog box appears.

5 Click the Configuration tab.

6 Click Client for NetWare Networks.

7 Click Properties.

■ The Properties dialog box appears.

TIPS

Can I change the logon scripts?

Most people will not be able to alter their Novell NetWare logon scripts. The logon scripts are written and installed by the system administrator or by the information systems department responsible for the Novell NetWare server.

What is a preferred server?

A preferred server is the Novell NetWare server you connect to each time you log on to the network. The preferred server will check your user name and password and allow or deny you access to the network.

What is a mapped network drive?

A mapped network drive provides a quick way to access information stored on a network. Mapping a network drive assigns a drive letter to a resource on the network so you can work with the information as if the information were stored on your own computer. When configuring the NetWare client, you can specify the drive letter you want Windows to use for your first mapped network drive. See page 480 to create a mapped network drive.

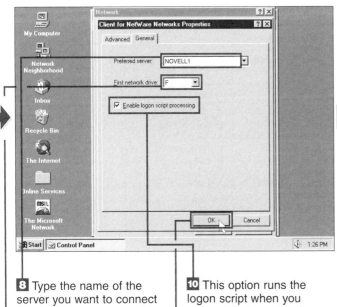

■8 Type the name of the server you want to connect to each time you log on to the network.

■9 This area specifies the drive letter Windows will use for your first mapped network drive. Click ▼ in this area to select another letter.

■10 This option runs the logon script when you connect to the network. Click the option to turn the option on (✔) or off (☐).

■11 Click OK to confirm your changes.

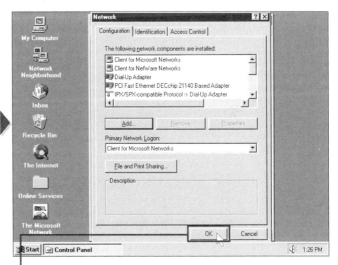

■12 Click OK to close the Network dialog box.

■ Windows will ask you to restart your computer. Click Yes to restart your computer.

MONITOR NETWORK PERFORMANCE USING SYSTEM MONITOR

You can use System Monitor to view information about how your computer is performing on a network.

System Monitor is often used by system administrators to monitor the speed at which parts of a computer, such as a network adapter, process information. This information may help you determine the cause of a problem

your computer is having while connected to the network.

You may want to observe and keep records of how your computer performs when there are no problems. You can use this information in a comparison later on if your computer starts to malfunction. You should monitor your computer's network performance over an extended

period of time to get a better estimate of what normal performance is. A good way to determine if your computer is running properly is to compare it with another computer that is set up in a similar way.

System Monitor remembers which resources you ask it to monitor. The next time you open System Monitor, it will display information about those resources.

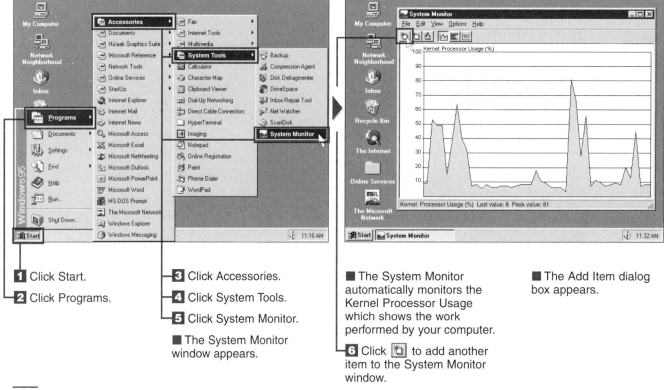

■ Click Start.

■ Click Programs.

■ Click Accessories.

■ Click System Tools.

■ Click System Monitor.

■ The System Monitor window appears.

■ The System Monitor automatically monitors the Kernel Processor Usage which shows the work performed by your computer.

■ Click ▣ to add another item to the System Monitor window.

■ The Add Item dialog box appears.

528

Why isn't System Monitor on my System Tools menu?

System Monitor may not be installed. System Monitor is located in the Accessories group on the Windows 95 CD-ROM disc. To install Windows components, see page 580.

Can I save and print the information displayed by System Monitor?

The only way to print or save any of the information displayed in the System Monitor window is to paste a copy of the screen into a program, such as Microsoft Paint. See page 119.

How do I remove an item from the System Monitor window?

When you no longer want to monitor an item, click the Remove button (🔲) to display a list of items currently shown in the window. Click the item you want to remove and then click OK.

How can I find information about the items displayed in the Add Item dialog box?

Click an item you want to find information about and then click the Explain button. System Monitor will display a brief description of the item you selected.

When should I run System Monitor?

You can run System Monitor all the time, but the program is most useful if you have a problem with your computer's performance on the network. Many people use System Monitor to examine the performance of devices, such as modems, to help them determine whether or not they need to upgrade their computer hardware.

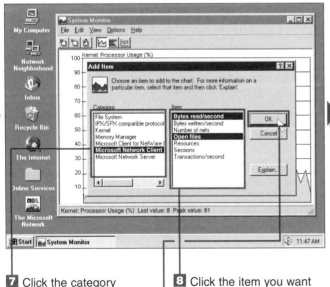

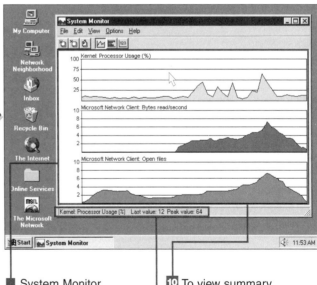

7 Click the category containing the item you want to monitor.

8 Click the item you want to monitor.

Note: You can select multiple items by holding down the Ctrl key as you click each item.

9 Click OK to confirm your selections.

■ System Monitor displays a chart to indicate the activity for each item you are monitoring.

10 To view summary information for an item, click the item.

■ The status bar displays summary information for the item.

USING NET WATCHER

You can use Net Watcher to monitor and manage shared files and folders on your computer.

You can view a list of people who are currently accessing files and folders on your computer to determine how long each person has been accessing your computer and which files they are using. You can also verify that only specific people are using your files. If people you do not want to use your files are accessing files on your computer, you can restrict access to your shared information by using passwords.

Net Watcher can display a list of all the folders you have turned on sharing for. You can also view details about the folders, such as the type of access each shared folder has. Net Watcher can also display a list of shared files on your computer that are currently being accessed by other people.

Monitoring how many people access your shared folders helps you determine how sharing is affecting the performance of your computer. If too many people access the information on your computer, your computer will operate slower.

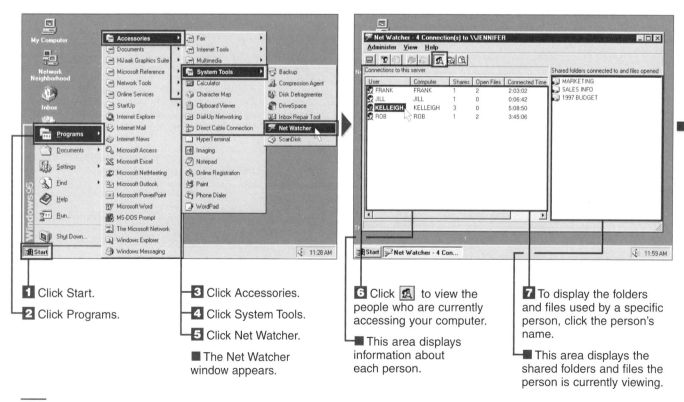

1 Click Start.

2 Click Programs.

3 Click Accessories.

4 Click System Tools.

5 Click Net Watcher.

■ The Net Watcher window appears.

6 Click 🔊 to view the people who are currently accessing your computer.

■ This area displays information about each person.

7 To display the folders and files used by a specific person, click the person's name.

■ This area displays the shared folders and files the person is currently viewing.

TIPS

Why isn't Net Watcher on my System Tools menu?

Net Watcher may not be installed. Net Watcher is located in the Accessories group on the Windows 95 CD-ROM disc. To install Windows components, see page 580.

Why does someone say they cannot access a shared file on my computer?

Many people may use the same user name and password to access shared files and folders on the network. You can use Net Watcher to see who is accessing files on your computer. If a person is already accessing a file, another person may not be able to access the file using the same user name.

I want to turn off sharing for a folder. Is there anything I should do first?

You should use Net Watcher to find out whether people are accessing the folder before you turn off sharing. If you turn off sharing for a folder while someone is accessing it, you may cause the other person's computer to malfunction. You should warn everyone who is accessing the folder to stop using it before you turn off sharing.

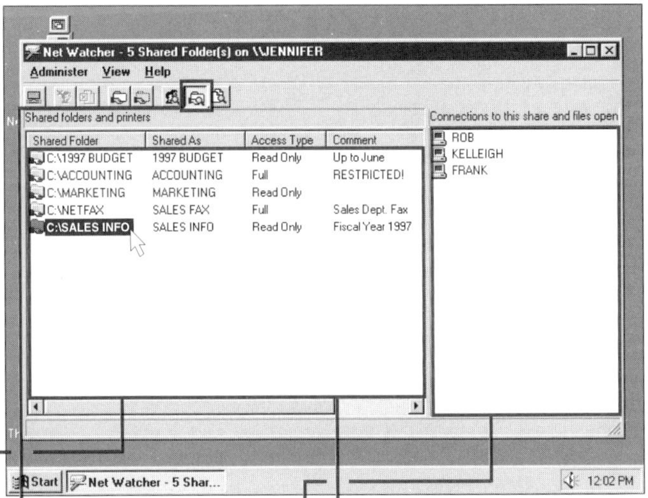

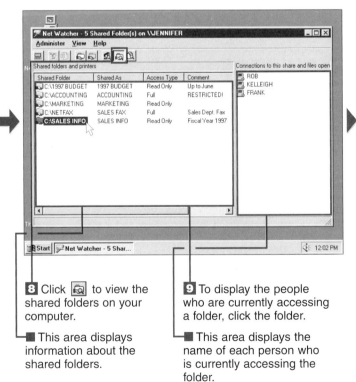

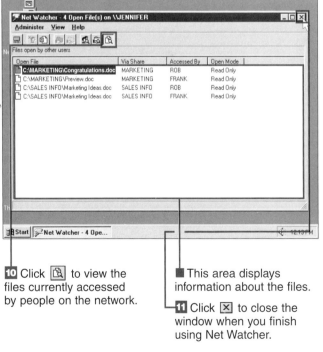

8 Click to view the shared folders on your computer.

■ This area displays information about the shared folders.

9 To display the people who are currently accessing a folder, click the folder.

■ This area displays the name of each person who is currently accessing the folder.

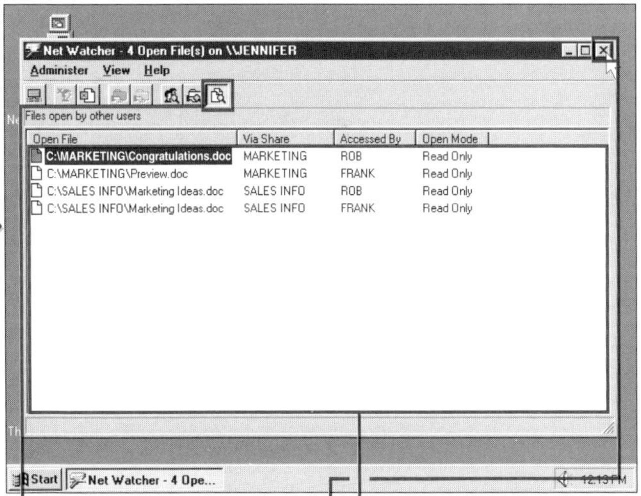

10 Click to view the files currently accessed by people on the network.

■ This area displays information about the files.

11 Click ☒ to close the window when you finish using Net Watcher.

WINDOWS 95 AND THE INTERNET

28) USING MICROSOFT NETMEETING

SET UP A CONNECTION TO A SERVICE PROVIDER

You can use Dial-Up Networking to connect your computer to an Internet Service Provider (ISP). Connecting to an ISP allows you to access the resources available on the Internet.

The Internet is the world's largest computer network. The Internet contains a vast collection of information, including text, images, sounds and videos,

on every subject imaginable. You can use the Internet to exchange messages and information with people all over the world.

An Internet service provider lets people connect to the Internet using a modem and a telephone line. You should use a modem with a speed of at least 14.4 Kb/s to connect to your ISP. A modem speed of 28.8 Kb/s or more is recommended. Make sure you

install your modem before setting up a connection to the ISP. See page 350 to install a modem.

Most service providers are relatively small and offer dial-up access only in small areas, such as a city. Larger ISPs provide access across the country and some even provide access around the world. Large ISPs are useful if you live in a rural area or if you travel frequently.

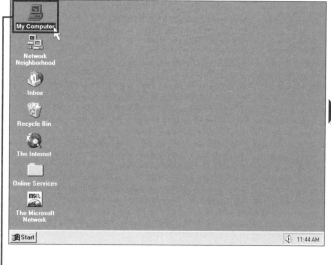

1 Double-click My Computer.

■ The My Computer window appears.

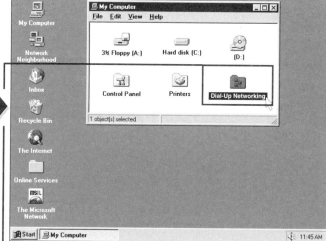

2 Double-click Dial-Up Networking.

Note: If Dial-Up Networking is not available, you must add the Windows component, which is found in the Communications group. See page 580.

■ The Dial-Up Networking window appears.

Note: If the Welcome to Dial-Up Networking dialog box appears, click Next and then skip to step 4.

How much does a connection to the Internet cost?

Most ISPs, and online services like MSN and America Online, charge reasonable rates for access to the Internet. You can usually choose to pay for the amount of time you actually use the Internet or a flat fee for unlimited access.

What name should I use for the computer I want to contact?

When naming a computer, you should use a descriptive name that clearly indicates which computer you are contacting, such as "Internet Account". Descriptive names help you tell one connection from another if you use Dial-Up Networking to connect to more than one computer.

How do I find a local Internet service provider?

When you double-click the Internet icon on your desktop, the Internet Connection Wizard will connect to the Microsoft referral service and provide information about ISPs serving your local area. Many communities have local computer newspapers and magazines. These publications usually have advertisements for Internet service providers. You can subscribe to these publications or check the periodical section of your local library.

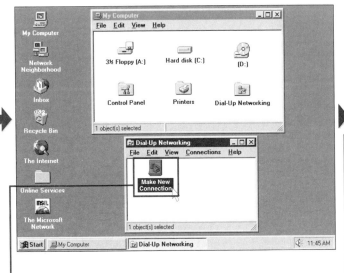

3 Double-click Make New Connection.

■ The Make New Connection dialog box appears.

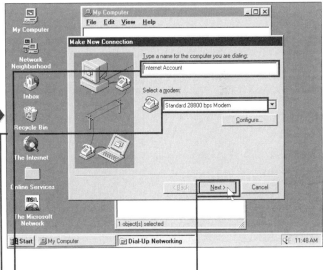

4 Type a name for the Internet service provider's computer you want to contact.

■ This area displays the modem Windows will use to contact the computer.

5 Click Next to continue.

CONTINUED ▶

SET UP A CONNECTION TO A SERVICE PROVIDER

CONTINUED

Before you can connect to an Internet Service Provider (ISP), you must tell Windows about the service provider's computer. Windows will store the information you enter about the computer so you can connect to the computer later on.

Your ISP will provide you with the phone number you need to

dial to connect to the computer. You also need to tell Windows the area code and country you are dialing.

You only need to set up a connection to your service provider's computer once. After the connection is set up, you can dial in to the computer at any time.

Most ISPs have a technical support department you can contact by telephone if you are having problems connecting to the ISP. Before you choose a service provider, you should check to see if its technical support department is available during the hours you usually use your computer, such as evenings or weekends.

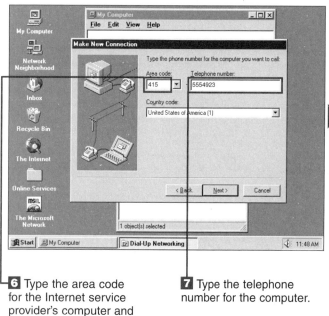

6 Type the area code for the Internet service provider's computer and then press the Tab key.

7 Type the telephone number for the computer.

8 This area displays the code for the country where the ISP is located. You can click this area to change the country code.

9 Click Next to continue.

Before dialing in to my ISP, is there any other information I need to specify?

Before you can dial in to your Internet service provider, you may need to change the settings for the dial-up connection. Most ISPs provide their users with the necessary information, such as the IP address. To change the settings for a dial-up connection, see page 540.

Can I later change the information I entered when setting up a connection?

You can change the information by right-clicking the icon for the connection in the Dial-Up Networking window and then clicking Properties. In the dialog box that appears, you can change the phone number, the country code and the modem you want to use for the connection.

How can I access the connection to my ISP each time I start my computer?

You can create a shortcut for the connection to your ISP and then place the shortcut in the StartUp folder. Each time you start your computer, Windows will display a dialog box that you can use to dial in to your ISP. See page 258 to place an item in the StartUp folder.

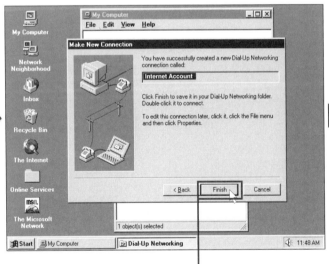

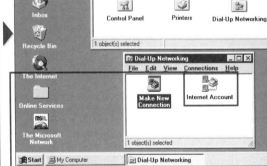

■ A message appears, telling you the connection to the computer has been successfully set up.

10 Click Finish.

■ An icon for the connection appears in the Dial-Up Networking window.

Note: To use the icon to dial in to your Internet service provider, see page 538.

DIAL IN TO A
SERVICE PROVIDER

After you set up a connection to a computer at your Internet Service Provider (ISP), you can dial in to the computer to access the Internet. Windows displays an icon in the Dial-Up Networking window for each connection you have set up. To set up a dial-up connection to an ISP, see page 534.

Windows needs to know your user name and password to dial in to

your ISP. Your service provider should provide you with this information when you set up your account.

Dialing in to an Internet service provider allows you to access a vast number of resources available on the Internet. You can browse through documents on various subjects, exchange electronic mail with friends and colleagues and read messages in newsgroups.

Before you can access information on the Internet, you need a program that allows you to use the services available. For example, Internet Explorer is a program that allows you to access sites on the World Wide Web, exchange e-mail and read newsgroup messages. For information on Internet Explorer, see page 548.

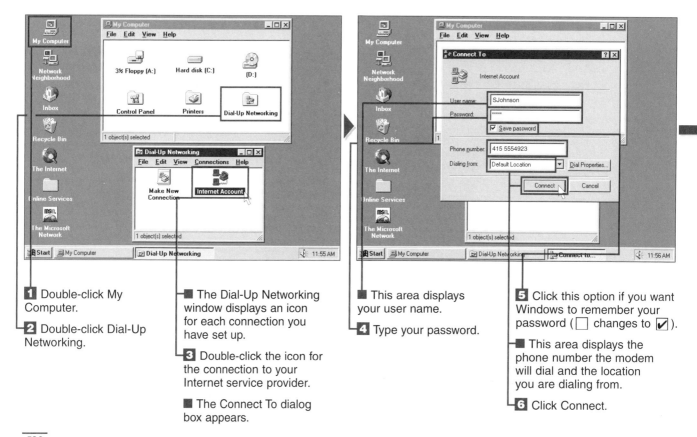

■ 1 Double-click My Computer.

■ 2 Double-click Dial-Up Networking.

■ The Dial-Up Networking window displays an icon for each connection you have set up.

■ 3 Double-click the icon for the connection to your Internet service provider.

■ The Connect To dialog box appears.

■ This area displays your user name.

■ 4 Type your password.

■ 5 Click this option if you want Windows to remember your password (☐ changes to ☑).

■ This area displays the phone number the modem will dial and the location you are dialing from.

■ 6 Click Connect.

TIPS

VIII

Why do I keep getting disconnected when I dial in to my ISP?

Check your ISP's setup information. Although you can connect to most ISPs with the name and password settings provided in the Connect To confirmation dialog box, some service providers may require you to enter your name, password and other information in a terminal window to complete the connection. If you want Windows to display a terminal window after dialing the ISP, right-click the icon for the connection in the Dial-Up Networking window and then click Properties. Click the Configure button and then click the Options tab. Select the Bring up terminal window after dialing option.

How can I test my connection to the Internet?

Windows includes a program called PING that you can use to test a connection with another computer on the Internet. In the MS-DOS Prompt window, type **ping** followed by the name (**www.maran.com**) or IP number (**207.136.66.25**) of the computer you want to communicate with. PING will report how long it takes to send and receive a signal between your computer and the other computer. If PING displays a message stating that the request timed out, the connection is not working. See page 132 to open the MS-DOS Prompt window.

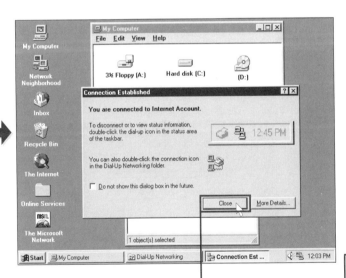

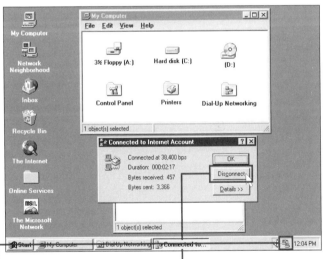

■ A dialog box appears when you are successfully connected.

Note: This dialog box may look different.

7 Click Close to close the dialog box.

Note: If there is no Close button, click ▬ to minimize the window.

END THE CONNECTION

1 Double-click this icon when you want to end the connection with your Internet service provider.

Note: If you minimized the window, click the button for the window on your taskbar.

■ The Connected to dialog box appears.

2 Click Disconnect.

CHANGE SETTINGS FOR A DIAL-UP CONNECTION

E ach dial-up server that you connect to using Dial-Up Networking can have different settings. You must change the settings for each of the dial-up connections you have set up to match the settings of the server you wish to connect to.

You can change the type of dial-up server a connection dials in to. For example, you can choose PPP for a connection to a Windows 95 computer or your Internet Service Provider (ISP).

You can have Dial-Up Networking use the same user name and password you entered when you started Windows to access the network or your ISP.

To increase the security of your password, you can have your computer encrypt the password you use to connect to the dial-up server. The server you connect to must also support encrypted passwords.

The Enable software compression option can help speed up the exchange of information by compressing the data before it transfers between the computers. Compression only occurs if both computers use the same type of compression.

You can specify which network protocols you want your computer to use to exchange information with the server. You can select from the IPX/SPX, NetBEUI or TCP/IP protocols.

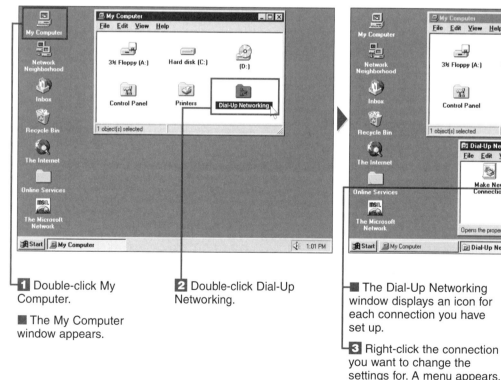

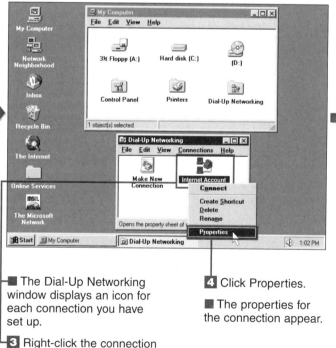

1 Double-click My Computer.

■ The My Computer window appears.

2 Double-click Dial-Up Networking.

■ The Dial-Up Networking window displays an icon for each connection you have set up.

3 Right-click the connection you want to change the settings for. A menu appears.

4 Click Properties.

■ The properties for the connection appear.

What are the most popular types of dial-up servers?

The Point-to-Point Protocol (PPP) server is the most common type of server used for connecting to the Internet. Windows 95 computers that you can dial in to also use PPP. Office networks often set up NetWare Remote Networking (NRN), Windows for Workgroups or Windows NT 3.1 servers to allow people to connect to the office network.

How do I know which settings to select?

The system administrator or owner of the server you are connecting to will be able to tell you which settings to select when changing the settings for a dial-up connection.

How do I know which network protocols to use?

The protocols you need depend on the computer you are connecting to. Computers on a Novell NetWare network use IPX/SPX, while computers on a Microsoft network use NetBEUI. If you are connecting to your ISP, you will use TCP/IP. You should deselect the protocols you do not need for the connection. For example, if you are dialing in to your ISP, turn off the IPX/SPX and NetBEUI options.

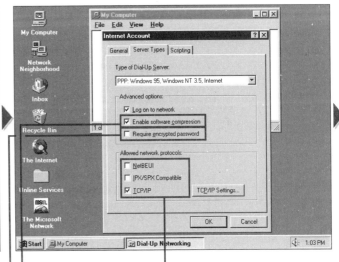

5 Click the Server Types tab.

Note: If the Server Types tab is not available, click the Server Type button.

6 This area displays the type of server the connection dials in to. You can click this area to change the type of server.

■ This option logs you on to the network using the name and password you typed when you started Windows.

■ This option compresses data to speed the transfer of information.

■ This option instructs your computer to only send and receive encrypted passwords for additional security.

■ This area displays the network protocols your computer will use to communicate with the server.

7 You can click an option to turn the option on (☑) or off (☐).

CONTINUED ▶

CHANGE SETTINGS FOR A DIAL-UP CONNECTION CONTINUED

I f you use a dial-up connection to connect to the Internet, you may need to adjust the settings for the TCP/IP protocol. TCP/IP stands for Transmission Control Protocol/Internet Protocol. TCP/IP is the protocol that computers on the Internet use to communicate. You can adjust the TCP/IP settings for each dial-up connection you have set up to the Internet.

Every computer connected to the Internet must have a unique number, called an Internet Protocol (IP) address. The IP address is made up of four numbers separated by periods, such as 254.234.123.65. You can specify the IP address of your computer or have the server you dial in to assign an address. Most computers' IP number is assigned automatically by your Internet service provider.

Most servers require you to enter an address for special computers that help you access computers on the Internet. These computers are called Domain Name Service (DNS) and Windows Internet Name Service (WINS) servers. You can assign the addresses of the name servers yourself or have the server you dial in to assign the addresses.

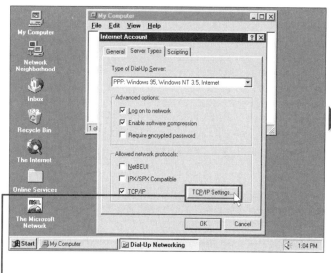

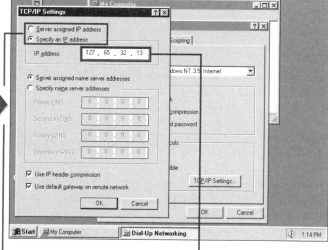

CHANGE TCP/IP SETTINGS

1 Click TCP/IP Settings to change the TCP/IP settings for the connection.

■ The TCP/IP Settings dialog box appears.

2 Click an option to specify if your computer will accept an IP address from the server or will specify its own IP address (○ changes to ●).

3 If you are specifying your own IP address, type the address in this area.

What is a name server?

A name server is a computer that translates names that people can understand and remember, such as www.machine.com, to IP addresses. Domain Name Service (DNS) and Windows Internet Name Service (WINS) servers are the two most common types of name servers found on the Internet.

How often should I change the settings for my dial-up connection?

Once you change the settings for a dial-up connection, you should not have to change them again unless the computer you are dialing in to changes its settings.

Should I use IP header compression?

IP header compression allows the information you transmit between your computer and the other computer to be compressed. This option may result in faster speeds when transmitting information.

Should I use the default gateway?

A gateway is a computer that links two networks together. If information passes from one network to the other, it will have to pass through the gateway that joins the networks. You should always use the default gateway if you want to access the Internet.

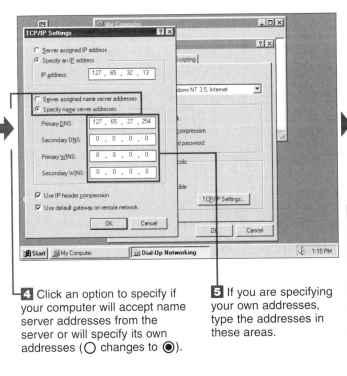

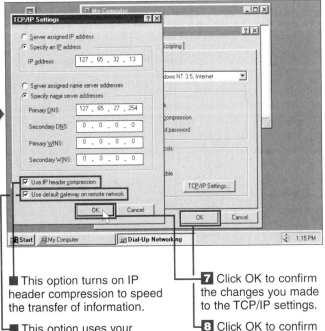

4 Click an option to specify if your computer will accept name server addresses from the server or will specify its own addresses (○ changes to ⦿).

5 If you are specifying your own addresses, type the addresses in these areas.

■ This option turns on IP header compression to speed the transfer of information.

■ This option uses your service provider's gateway so information can travel to the Internet.

6 Click an option to turn the option on (☑) or off (☐).

7 Click OK to confirm the changes you made to the TCP/IP settings.

8 Click OK to confirm all of your changes.

USING THE INTERNET CONNECTION WIZARD

You can use the Internet Connection Wizard to set up a connection to the Internet. The wizard helps you find an Internet Service Provider (ISP) in your area and set up an account.

After setting up an account with a service provider, you can access the resources available on the Internet.

The Internet Connection Wizard comes with OSR2 and is also distributed with Internet Explorer, which you can get at computer stores. If you have access to the Internet, you can get a free copy of Internet Explorer from Microsoft's Web site at www.microsoft.com

During the connection process, you may be asked to insert your Windows 95 installation CD-ROM

disc. You should close any programs running on your computer before starting the wizard since you may need to restart your computer while using the wizard.

You must have a modem installed on your computer to use the wizard to set up a connection. See page 350 to install a modem.

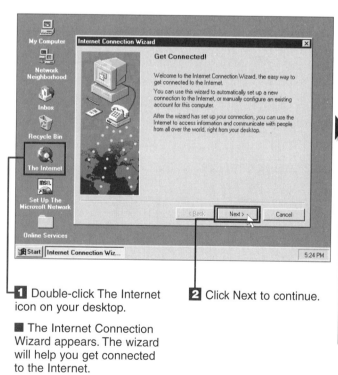

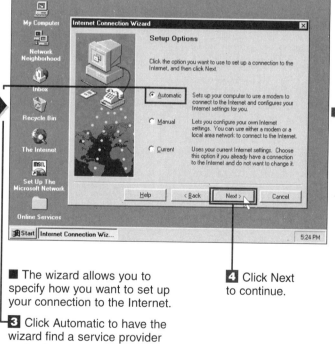

1 Double-click The Internet icon on your desktop.

■ The Internet Connection Wizard appears. The wizard will help you get connected to the Internet.

2 Click Next to continue.

■ The wizard allows you to specify how you want to set up your connection to the Internet.

3 Click Automatic to have the wizard find a service provider and set up a connection for you (○ changes to ◉).

4 Click Next to continue.

VIII

TIPS

I already know the information about the service provider I want to use. Can I set up a connection without having the wizard find a provider for me?

The Internet Connection Wizard will let you specify information about your service provider and the connection you want to set up. Perform steps 1 to 3 below, except select Manual in step 3.

Can I use The Internet icon on my desktop to start a connection I already set up?

If you already have a connection set up and the Internet Connection Wizard starts, perform steps 1 to 4 below, except select Current in step 3.

Why does Internet Explorer start when I double-click The Internet icon on my desktop?

If you previously started the Internet Connection Wizard, double-clicking The Internet icon may not start the wizard. To start the wizard, click the Start button, click Programs, click Accessories, click Internet Tools and then click Get on the Internet.

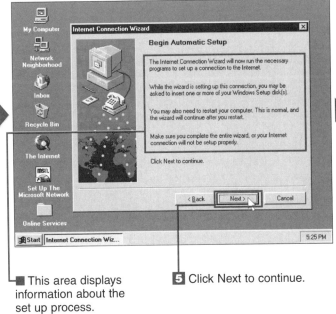

■ This area displays information about the set up process.

5 Click Next to continue.

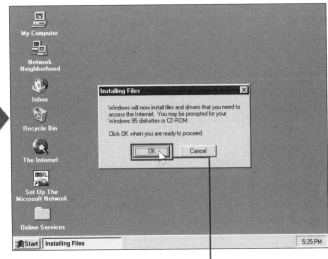

■ A dialog box may appear, indicating that Windows will install the files and drivers you need to access the Internet.

6 Click OK to continue.

CONTINUED ▶

USING THE INTERNET CONNECTION WIZARD CONTINUED

The Internet Connection Wizard asks for your area code and the first three digits of your telephone number to find Internet service providers in your area. Finding a service provider in your area is important so you do not have to pay long-distance charges when you access the Internet.

Microsoft has set up a service that provides a listing of

Internet service providers. The Internet Connection Wizard uses your modem to contact Microsoft and retrieve a list of service providers in your area.

After you select the service provider you want to use, the wizard connects you to the service provider so you can enter information about yourself and the account you want to set up. Most of the service providers

available through the Internet Connection Wizard require you to enter your credit card number.

The Internet Connection Wizard retrieves information about the Internet service provider and the settings needed to configure your computer to connect to the Internet. You will not need to configure the computer yourself.

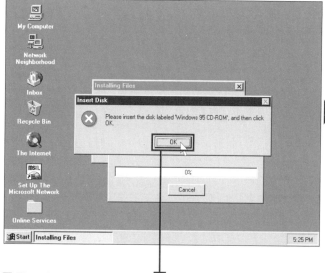

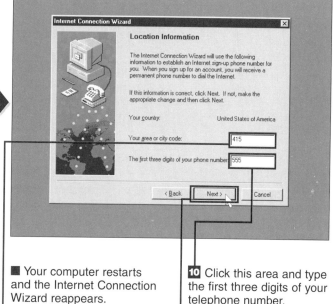

■ The wizard may ask you to insert the Windows CD-ROM disc.

7 Insert the CD-ROM disc into a drive.

8 Click OK to continue.

9 A dialog box may appear, asking you to restart the computer. Click OK to restart the computer.

■ Your computer restarts and the Internet Connection Wizard reappears.

■ This area displays your area code. You can double-click this area to change the area code.

10 Click this area and type the first three digits of your telephone number.

11 Click Next to continue.

How do I connect to my service provider after the connection is set up?

After using the Internet Connection Wizard to set up a connection to a service provider, you can connect at any time. To connect to your service provider to access the Internet, double-click The Internet icon on your desktop.

Why does a dialog box tell me the wizard could not connect to the number dialed?

You may need to adjust the dialing properties for your modem. See page 354 to set the dialing properties for your modem.

Can I find more information about a service provider before I sign up?

When the wizard displays the list of Internet service providers available in your area, you can click More Info beside a service provider to display more information about the provider.

I have to enter my credit card number to set up an Internet account. Is this safe?

Yes. When you set up your Internet account, you are directly connected to the service provider. The information you enter is not transmitted over the Internet.

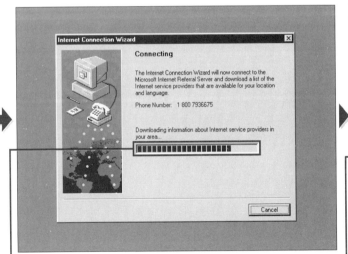

■ The wizard uses your modem to connect to the Microsoft Internet Referral Server and find a list of service providers in your area.

■ This area displays the progress of the transfer of information to your computer.

■ When the transfer is complete, a list of service providers in your area appears.

■12 Click Sign Me Up beside the service provider you want to use to connect to the Internet.

■ The wizard will connect you to the service provider you selected and display a sign-up form.

■13 Follow the instructions on your screen to set up an account with the service provider. Each provider will ask different questions.

START INTERNET EXPLORER

Internet Explorer version 3 is the Web browser included with OSR2. A Web browser is a program that lets you view and explore information on the World Wide Web.

The Web consists of documents, called Web pages, that are connected by hyperlinks. A hyperlink connects text or a picture on one Web page to another Web page. When you

click the text or picture, the other Web page appears on your screen. Hyperlinks allow you to easily navigate through a vast amount of information by jumping from one Web page to another.

Text hyperlinks usually appear underlined and in a different color than the rest of the text on the Web page. Images can contain one or more hyperlinks.

When you move the mouse over a hyperlink, the mouse pointer changes to a hand (☝). You can view information about the hyperlink in the status bar at the bottom of your screen.

A hyperlink you select can display a Web page on the same computer or on any other computer on the Internet.

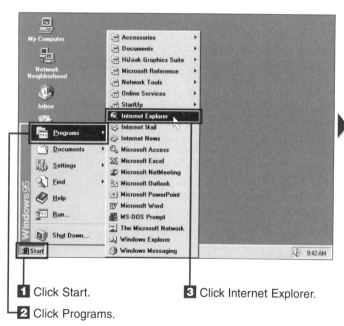

1 Click Start.

2 Click Programs.

3 Click Internet Explorer.

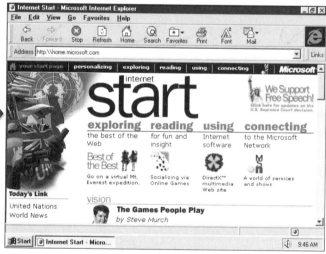

■ The Microsoft Internet Explorer window appears.

Note: If you have not yet connected to the Internet, a dialog box may appear, allowing you to connect.

■ The Microsoft Internet Start page appears when you first start Internet Explorer.

Note: A dialog box may appear, asking you to update your version of Internet Explorer. If you do not want to update your version, click No.

TIPS

I don't have OSR2. How can I get Internet Explorer version 3?

Internet Explorer is available at Microsoft's Web site:
www.microsoft.com/ie

Will a hyperlink always take me to another Web page?

Besides taking you to other Web pages, hyperlinks are also used for tasks such as sending e-mail messages or starting file transfers.

How can I tell when a Web page has fully transferred to my computer?

A Web page is fully transferred when the Internet Explorer logo at the top right of the screen stops moving. Most Web pages consist of several items, such as text, pictures, sound or video. Each item must be transferred to your computer before the page can display properly. The status bar at the bottom of your screen indicates which item is currently transferring.

SELECT A HYPERLINK

■1 Position the mouse ⌖ over a highlighted word or picture of interest (⌖ changes to ⌅).

■2 Click the word or picture.

■ The page connected to the word or picture appears.

WORK WITH WEB PAGES

Internet Explorer provides several toolbar buttons that help you view and work with Web pages.

If a Web page is taking a long time to appear on your screen or is the wrong page, you can stop the transfer of information.

You can move back or forward through the Web pages you have

viewed during your current session of Internet Explorer.

Many Web pages contain information that is constantly being updated, such as news, sports or stock market data. Some Web pages also contain frequently changing images from a live camera. You can transfer a fresh copy of a Web page at any

time to view the most up-to-date information or images.

You can change the size of text in a Web page. There are five font sizes you can choose from. A larger font size displays text more clearly. A smaller font size displays more text on the screen.

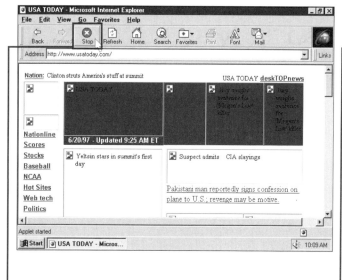

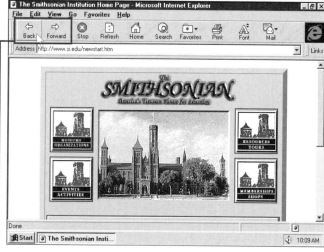

STOP TRANSFER OF INFORMATION

■ The Stop button is red when information is transferring to your computer.

1 Click Stop to stop the transfer of information.

MOVE THROUGH WEB PAGES

1 Click one of these options to move through the Web pages you have viewed.

 Move back

Move forward

TIPS

How can I display or hide the toolbar buttons?

Choose the View menu and then select the Toolbar command.

Can I find a word on a Web page?

In the Edit menu, select the Find (on this page) command.

Why is the Forward button not available?

The Forward button is not available until you use the Back button.

How can I print a Web page?

Click the Print button.

What can I do if a Web page does not transfer completely?

Click the Refresh button to transfer the page again.

How can I choose a new font for the text on a Web page?

Choose the View menu and then select the Options command. Click the General tab and then click the Font Settings button. In the Proportional font drop-down list, select a new font.

Can I save a Web page?

From the File menu, click the Save As File command to name and save a Web page. The images on the Web page will not be saved.

REFRESH A WEB PAGE

1 Click Refresh to transfer a fresh copy of the displayed Web page to your computer.

CHANGE THE FONT SIZE

1 Click Font to change the size of the font in the displayed Web page. Repeat this step until the text on the Web page is the size you want.

DISPLAY A SPECIFIC WEB PAGE

Y ou can display a page on the Web that you have heard or read about. You need to know the address of the Web page you want to display. Each page on the World Wide Web has a unique address, called a Uniform Resource Locator (URL).

You can identify a Web page by the letters www in the address. Most Web page addresses do not make a distinction between upper case and lower case letters, but you should be careful to type the URL exactly. Internet Explorer automatically adds the http:// prefix to an address for you.

When you do not know the exact address for a company's Web page, you can often guess. Large corporations typically use their names in the URL, such as www.kelloggs.com or www.sony.com

1 Double-click this area to highlight the existing Web page address.

2 Type the address of the Web page you want to view and then press the Enter key.

■ You can also click ▼ in this area to display a list of Web page addresses you recently typed. You can then click the Web page you want to view again.

■ The Web page appears on your screen.

DISPLAY HISTORY OF VIEWED WEB PAGES

Internet Explorer keeps track of the Web pages you have recently viewed. You can easily return to any of these Web pages.

The five most recent pages you have visited during your current session of Internet Explorer

appear on the Go menu. Internet Explorer also creates a history list of each Web page you have visited in the last 20 days.

There may be hundreds of pages in your history list. The list displays information such as the title of the page, the Web page

address, the date and time you last visited the page and the date and time the page will be deleted from the history list.

When you find the Web page you want to view, you can use the Go menu or the history list to return to the page.

VIII

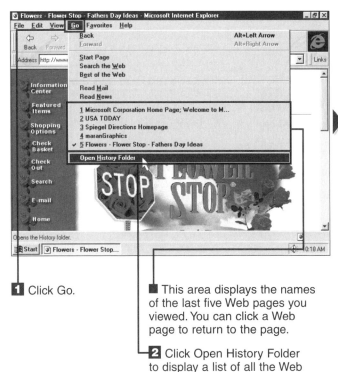

1 Click Go.

■ This area displays the names of the last five Web pages you viewed. You can click a Web page to return to the page.

2 Click Open History Folder to display a list of all the Web pages you have viewed in the last 20 days.

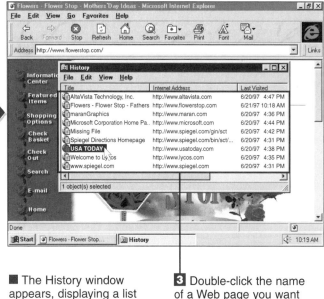

■ The History window appears, displaying a list of the Web pages you have viewed.

3 Double-click the name of a Web page you want to display again.

CHANGE YOUR HOME OR SEARCH PAGE

The home page appears every time you start Internet Explorer. The Microsoft Internet Start page is automatically displayed, but you can select which Web page you want to use as your home page. You can choose a Web page with news and information related to your interests or your work. You can also choose a

Web page that provides links to other Web pages that help you explore the Web and find the resources you are looking for.

You can return to your home page at any time by clicking the Home button on the toolbar.

There are many search and reference pages you can use to look for information on the Web.

You can customize the Search button to provide quick access to the search page you find most useful. You can use a catalog page, like www.yahoo.com, to look through a list of categorized links. You can also use a search engine page, like www.altavista.digital.com, to search Web pages for specific text.

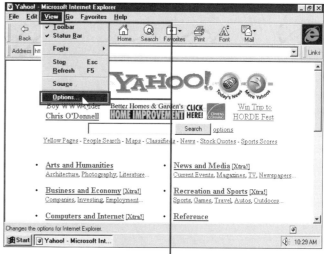

DISPLAY THE HOME OR SEARCH PAGE

1 Click the page you want to view.

Home Page

Search Page

CHANGE THE HOME OR SEARCH PAGE

1 Display the Web page you want to use as your home or search page.

2 Click View.

3 Click Options.

■ The Options dialog box appears.

Can I add more toolbar buttons for Web pages?

The Links section of the toolbar provides five buttons you can customize to display your favorite Web pages. Perform the steps below, selecting a Quick Link from the pull-down menu in step 6.

What makes a good home page?

A good home page is one that loads quickly and provides you with access to the information and resources you need when you are using the Web. You can even use a Web page you created as your home page.

I customized my home and search pages. Can I return them to the original Web pages?

In the Options dialog box, select the Navigation tab. You can use the drop-down list to select your home page, search page or any Quick Link page. Click the Use Default button to reset the page you selected back to the original Web page.

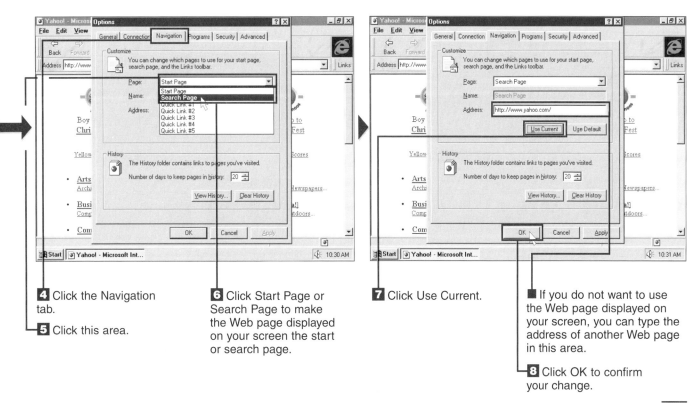

■4 Click the Navigation tab.

■5 Click this area.

■6 Click Start Page or Search Page to make the Web page displayed on your screen the start or search page.

■7 Click Use Current.

■ If you do not want to use the Web page displayed on your screen, you can type the address of another Web page in this area.

■8 Click OK to confirm your change.

ADD WEB PAGES TO FAVORITES

You can create a collection of your favorite Web pages. The Favorites feature allows you to store the addresses of Web pages you frequently visit.

You may want to return to the same Web page several times to investigate the page further or to check for new or updated information.

When you know that you will be returning to a Web page, you can add the page to Favorites so you can quickly access the page later.

When you add a Web page to Favorites, you can give the page a meaningful name that clearly indicates its contents and purpose.

Web page addresses can often be long and complex. Selecting a Web page address from Favorites saves you from having to remember and retype the address. Using Favorites also eliminates the possibility that you will not be able to access a page because you have made a typing mistake in the address.

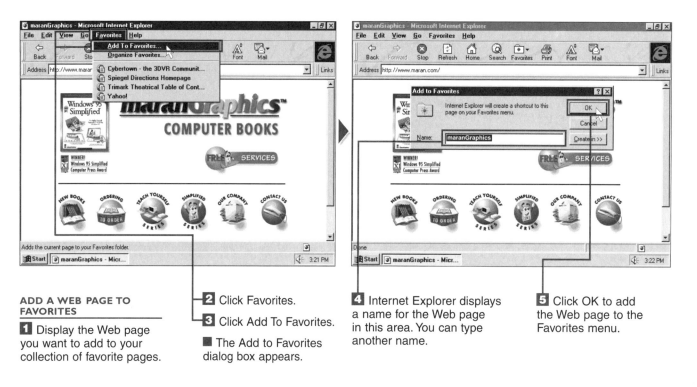

ADD A WEB PAGE TO FAVORITES

1 Display the Web page you want to add to your collection of favorite pages.

2 Click Favorites.

3 Click Add To Favorites.

■ The Add to Favorites dialog box appears.

4 Internet Explorer displays a name for the Web page in this area. You can type another name.

5 Click OK to add the Web page to the Favorites menu.

TIPS

What can I do when my Favorites menu gets too long?

You can organize the Web pages on your Favorites menu into folders and subfolders. Choose the Favorites menu and then select the Organize Favorites command to create and name the folders. You can then drag your Web pages to the folder where you want to store them.

How can I share my favorite Web page with a friend or colleague?

To share a favorite Web page, you can create a shortcut to the Web page and then drag the shortcut into an e-mail message.

Can I create a shortcut to a Web page?

In the File menu, select the Create Shortcut command to create a shortcut to the Web page currently displayed on your screen. Windows places the Web page shortcut on your desktop. When you double-click the shortcut icon, Internet Explorer starts, logs on to the Internet and opens the Web page. You can also drag the shortcut icon to the Start button so you can access the Web page from the Start menu.

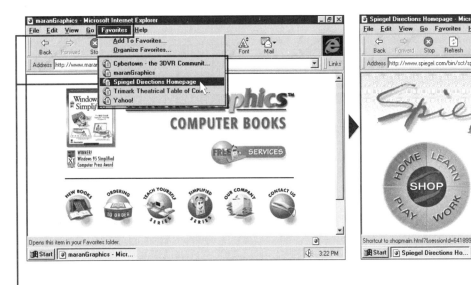

GO TO A FAVORITES WEB PAGE

1 Click Favorites.

2 Click the Web page you want to display.

■ The Web page appears.

INTERNET EXPLORER 4.0

Internet Explorer 4.0 is a major upgrade to previous versions of Internet Explorer and also enhances the way Windows 95 looks and acts. Internet Explorer 4.0 is available free of charge from Microsoft's Web site at www.microsoft.com/ie/ie40. You can download the entire Internet Explorer 4.0 installation kit or download specific components as you need them.

Improved Browsing

Internet Explorer 4.0 remembers the addresses of Web sites you visit. When you start to type the address of a page you previously visited, Explorer completes the address for you. You can keep typing to enter a new address.

The Back and Forward buttons have drop-down lists displaying the Web pages you have visited. To return to a page, you can select the page from the drop-down list instead of repeatedly clicking the Back button.

Internet Explorer 4.0 also features a pane on the left side of the window to help you move through Web pages. For example, when you perform a search, the left pane displays the search results while you view each of the listed pages on the right side. You can also have the left pane display the list of Web sites you have recently visited or your list of favorite Web sites.

Integration with Windows 95

With Internet Explorer 4.0, you can use one window to view the drives, folders and files on your computer and on the network, as well as Web pages and information on the Internet. Internet Explorer 4.0 makes it easier to find and use the information on your computer and on your corporate network or intranet. For example, you can type the name of a drive in Internet Explorer 4.0's address bar to display the files and folders on the drive. When using Internet Explorer 4.0, one click opens any drive, folder or file displayed in the Explorer window.

Active Desktop

You can place Web pages or parts of Web pages on the desktop to view the information without opening your Web browser. For example, you can display current stock prices or sports scores on your desktop. You can also change the entire desktop into a Web page and activate your icons with a single click of the mouse to more easily view information on your computer and the Internet.

Menus and Toolbars

There are several new items on the Start menu, including your Internet Favorites folder. You can drag and drop items in the Favorites and Programs menus to change the order of the items. Internet Explorer 4.0 also includes additional toolbars containing shortcuts to programs and Web sites. You can move the toolbars from the taskbar and place them anywhere on the screen.

E-mail and Newsgroups

Internet mail users will find Outlook Express, the new e-mail program, to be a significant improvement over previous Microsoft Exchange and Internet Explorer e-mail software. Outlook Express supports HTML, so you can send Web pages as e-mail messages. You can use the Find feature to access several Internet white pages directories and find an unknown e-mail address. You can also use Outlook Express to read and post newsgroup messages.

Collaboration and Chatting

Internet Explorer 4.0 includes an upgraded version of Microsoft's collaboration software, called NetMeeting. See page 566 for information on NetMeeting.

Another component of Explorer is Microsoft Chat. This component allows you to communicate directly with other Internet users using a comic strip like format.

Web Page Publishing

Internet Explorer 4.0 now includes software to create Web pages. FrontPage Express is a simple tool for designing and editing Web pages. FrontPage Express is based on the capabilities and features of Microsoft FrontPage, a professional Web page creation program.

Information Updates

Internet Explorer 4.0 lets you use both "push" and "pull" technology to get the information you want. Push technology enables you to have information from sources like Disney, ESPN, Time Magazine and The Wall Street Journal delivered straight to your desktop. You select the type of information you are interested in and how often you want to receive the information.

Internet Explorer 4.0's pull technology can monitor a Web site you specify for updates and download the pages that have changed. You can view the Web pages, including graphics, without having to connect to the Internet.

Internet Security

Internet Explorer 4.0 helps make transferring confidential information on the Internet more secure. Microsoft Wallet lets you store credit card and address information on your computer. People who previously have not wanted to purchase items on the Internet for security reasons can now use Microsoft Wallet to transfer their information on the Internet with confidence.

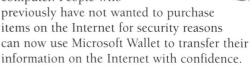

Task Scheduler

The Microsoft Plus! System Agent, now called Task Scheduler, is part of Internet Explorer 4.0. You can schedule tasks or programs to run at times you specify. See page 620 for information on System Agent.

START INTERNET NEWS AND READ MESSAGES

You can use Internet News to read the messages in a newsgroup. A newsgroup allows people with common interests to communicate with each other. There are thousands of newsgroups on every subject imaginable. Each newsgroup discusses a particular topic such as jobs offered, puzzles or medicine.

The name of a newsgroup describes the type of information discussed in the newsgroup. A newsgroup name consists of two or more words, separated by dots (.). The first word describes the main topic. Each of the following words narrows the topic. For example, the rec.bicycles.off-road newsgroup contains messages from off-road bicycle enthusiasts.

New messages are continuously being added to newsgroups. You can read and exchange messages in a newsgroup to learn the opinions and ideas of people around the world. You can browse through messages of interest just as you would browse through a newspaper. Like a newspaper, the message's title tells you what the message is about.

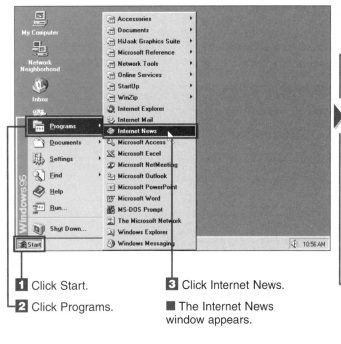

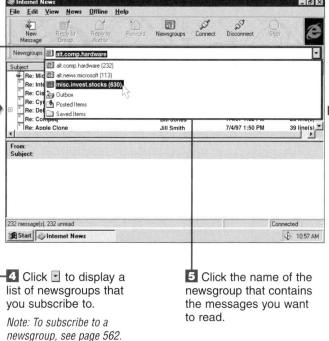

1 Click Start.

2 Click Programs.

3 Click Internet News.

■ The Internet News window appears.

4 Click ⏷ to display a list of newsgroups that you subscribe to.

Note: To subscribe to a newsgroup, see page 562.

5 Click the name of the newsgroup that contains the messages you want to read.

Why do some messages have a plus sign (⊞)?

A plus sign (⊞) indicates the message is part of a series of messages consisting of an initial message and related comments and replies. This is called a thread. You can click the plus sign (⊞) beside a thread to display the related messages.

Should I save a message?

After a few days or weeks, messages are removed from a news server to make room for new messages. When you see a message you want to keep, make sure you print or save the message.

Do I need to set up Internet News before I can use it?

You will need an Internet connection before you can use Internet News. You can use the same Internet connection you use for e-mail and Web browsing. When you start Internet News for the first time, you will need to enter your name and e-mail address. You will also need to enter information about your Internet Service Provider's (ISP's) news server. The news server information should be included with the documentation you received when you signed up with the ISP.

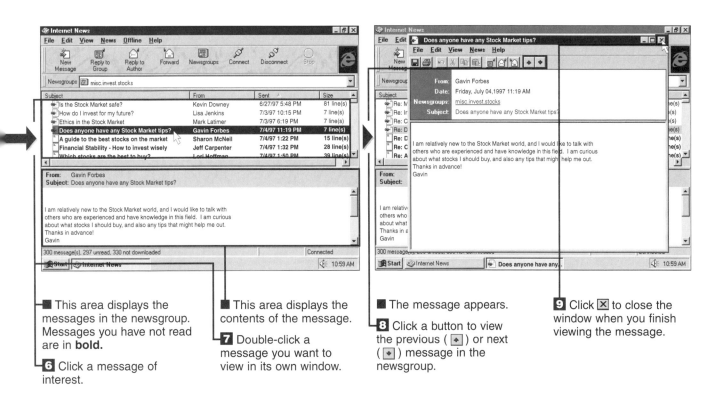

■ This area displays the messages in the newsgroup. Messages you have not read are in **bold.**

6 Click a message of interest.

■ This area displays the contents of the message.

7 Double-click a message you want to view in its own window.

■ The message appears.

8 Click a button to view the previous (▲) or next (▼) message in the newsgroup.

9 Click ☒ to close the window when you finish viewing the message.

SUBSCRIBE TO NEWSGROUPS

You subscribe to a newsgroup when you want to read its messages. If you no longer want to read the messages in a newsgroup, you can unsubscribe from the newsgroup.

Some newsgroups are moderated. In these newsgroups, a person called a moderator reads each message and decides if the message is appropriate for the group. If the message is approved, the moderator posts the message for everyone to read. This

eliminates inappropriate and unnecessary messages. Moderated newsgroups have the word "moderated" at the end of the newsgroup name (example: misc.business. marketing.moderated).

In unmoderated newsgroups, all messages are automatically posted for everyone to read.

The main newsgroup categories include alt (alternative), biz (business), comp (computers),

k12 (kindergarten to grade 12, or education related), misc (miscellaneous), news, rec (recreation), sci (science), soc (social) and talk. There are other newsgroup categories that focus on topics of interest to people living in specific geographical regions, such as aus (Australia) and ca (California).

Newsgroups with the word "binary" in the name are used to exchange files instead of messages.

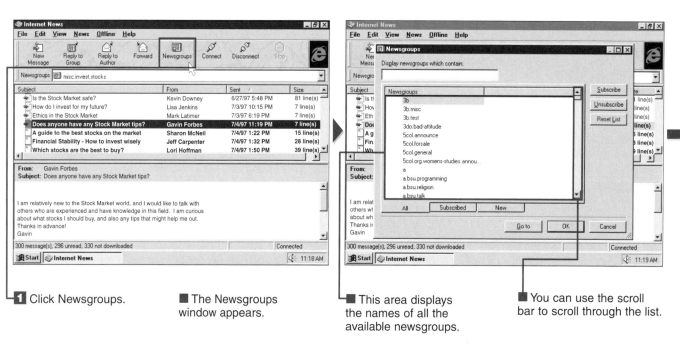

1 Click Newsgroups.

■ The Newsgroups window appears.

■ This area displays the names of all the available newsgroups.

■ You can use the scroll bar to scroll through the list.

Why is my list of newsgroups different from the list shown in this book?

There are always new newsgroups being created. The newsgroups available depend on your Internet Service Provider (ISP). Your ISP may limit the number of available newsgroups because the ISP has a limited amount of storage space or the ISP wants to eliminate newsgroups containing offensive content.

How do I unsubscribe from a newsgroup?

To unsubscribe from a newsgroup you no longer want to read, double-click the newsgroup. The symbol disappears from beside the newsgroup name.

Are there newsgroups designed for beginners?

There are three newsgroups that beginners may find useful: news.announce.newusers, news. answers and news.newusers. questions.

Why do I see only the newsgroups that I have subscribed to?

The Newsgroups window has three tabs. You can view all the available newsgroups, newsgroups you subscribe to and new newsgroups. Click the appropriate tab to view the newsgroups you want.

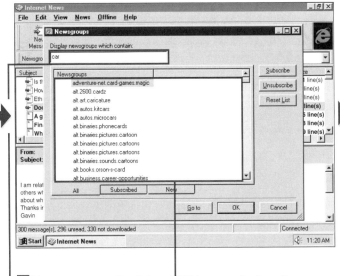

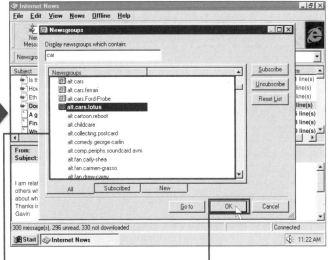

2 You can narrow the list of displayed newsgroups. Click this area and then type a word you want to search for.

■ This area displays the names of the newsgroups containing the word you typed.

*Note: Internet News will display newsgroups containing the word even if the newsgroups are unrelated. For example, searching for **car** will also find child**car**e and **car**toon.*

3 Double-click each newsgroup you want to subscribe to. A symbol () appears beside each newsgroup you select.

4 Click OK to confirm your selections.

SEND AND REPLY TO MESSAGES

You can send a new message to a newsgroup to ask a question or express an opinion. You can also reply to a message to answer a question or supply additional information.

Thousands of people around the world may read a message you send. To practice sending a message and to see what your message will look like, send a test message to the misc.test

newsgroup. If you send a test message to other newsgroups, you may receive unwanted replies or flames.

When you reply to a message, Internet News includes a copy of the original message to help the reader follow an ongoing discussion or series of comments. This is called quoting. The > symbol appears in front of each quoted line. You can delete the

parts of a quoted message that do not directly relate to your reply.

You can send a reply to the author of the message or the entire newsgroup. If your reply would not be of interest to others in a newsgroup or if you want to send a private response, send a message directly to the author instead of to the entire newsgroup.

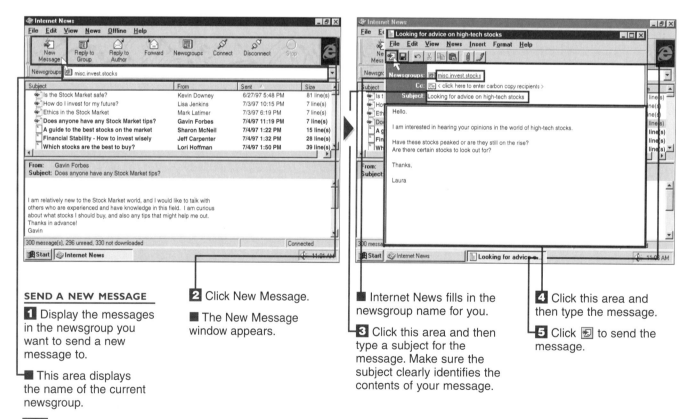

SEND A NEW MESSAGE

1 Display the messages in the newsgroup you want to send a new message to.

■ This area displays the name of the current newsgroup.

2 Click New Message.

■ The New Message window appears.

■ Internet News fills in the newsgroup name for you.

3 Click this area and then type a subject for the message. Make sure the subject clearly identifies the contents of your message.

4 Click this area and then type the message.

5 Click 🔁 to send the message.

Can I forward an interesting message?

Right-click the message and then select Forward by Mail to e-mail the message to a colleague who might be interested.

Do I have to use my real name in my messages?

Many people do not use their real names or real e-mail addresses. Choose the News menu and then click the Options command. Select the Server tab to change the name and e-mail address that appear in your messages. Changing your e-mail address prevents junk mailers from sending you automatic messages. Remember to include your real e-mail address in the body of your message so other readers can contact you.

Can I advertise my company or service in newsgroups where I think readers will be interested?

You should participate and not simply advertise in a newsgroup. To promote your company or service, it is best to send useful information in response to someone's question and include your corporate information at the end of your message.

What is a flame?

When another reader does not like your opinion, they may reply to your message in a negative or hostile manner. These rude messages are called flames. You should ignore flames.

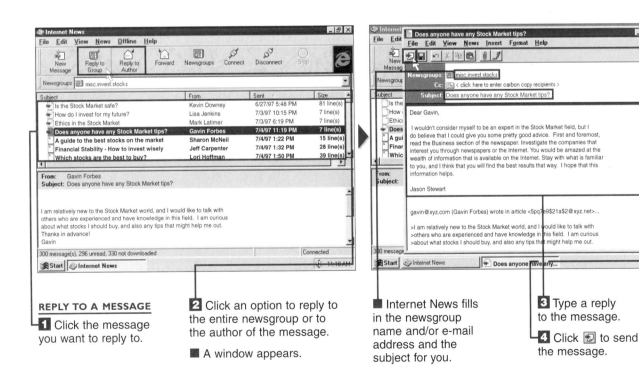

REPLY TO A MESSAGE

1 Click the message you want to reply to.

2 Click an option to reply to the entire newsgroup or to the author of the message.

■ A window appears.

■ Internet News fills in the newsgroup name and/or e-mail address and the subject for you.

3 Type a reply to the message.

4 Click to send the message.

START NETMEETING
AND PLACE A CALL

NetMeeting lets you use a network connection to work with other people. A NetMeeting session can consist of only two people or can be a conference with many participants working together at the same time.

You can connect to people on your company's network or on the Internet. If you are using

the Internet, the Microsoft User Location Service (ULS) helps you find other people running NetMeeting and make a connection. Microsoft has set up six servers you can use to locate other NetMeeting users. If you are planning a NetMeeting session, you and the other participants should agree on which server you will use.

When you place a call, a message is sent and the person you are calling can either accept or ignore the call.

Two people in a NetMeeting session can use voice communication if both participants have sound cards, speakers and microphones. Additional participants cannot use voice communication.

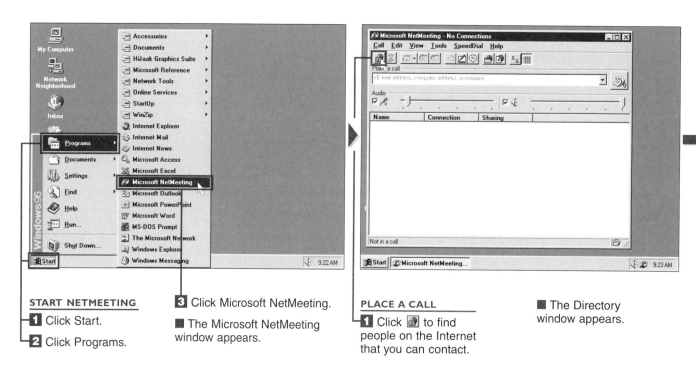

START NETMEETING

1 Click Start.

2 Click Programs.

3 Click Microsoft NetMeeting.

■ The Microsoft NetMeeting window appears.

PLACE A CALL

1 Click 🔲 to find people on the Internet that you can contact.

■ The Directory window appears.

Where can I get NetMeeting?

NetMeeting Version 1 is included in OSR2. You can also get the latest version of NetMeeting free from the Microsoft Web site at www.microsoft.com/netmeeting. NetMeeting Version 2 includes support for video-conferencing and other enhancements.

How do I set up NetMeeting?

The first time you start the program, you will be asked to provide information, such as the name and e-mail address you want people to use to contact you. You can also specify the ULS you want to be listed on. If you have a sound card, NetMeeting will ask you to perform a sound test with your microphone.

Is there an easier way to find the person I want to call?

In the Directory window, you can click a column heading to sort the information in the column.

Can I remove my name from the server?

When your information is listed on the server, you may receive unwanted calls. To avoid this, choose the Tools menu and then select the Options command. Click the My Information tab and then deselect Publish this information in the User Location Service directory (✔ changes to ☐). Then click OK.

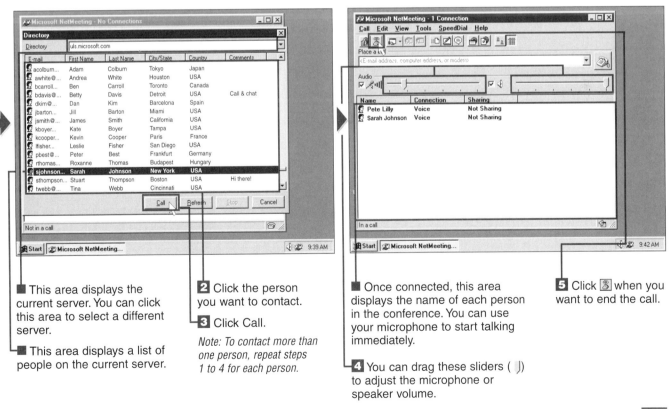

■ This area displays the current server. You can click this area to select a different server.

■ This area displays a list of people on the current server.

2 Click the person you want to contact.

3 Click Call.

Note: To contact more than one person, repeat steps 1 to 4 for each person.

■ Once connected, this area displays the name of each person in the conference. You can use your microphone to start talking immediately.

4 You can drag these sliders (▯) to adjust the microphone or speaker volume.

5 Click ☐ when you want to end the call.

CHAT

You can use Chat to send typed messages to the participants in a NetMeeting conference when voice communication is unavailable. Voice communication can be used by only two participants in a NetMeeting conference. When there are more than two participants, Chat allows all the participants to contribute to the conference.

When one participant starts Chat, the Chat window appears on each participant's screen. When a participant enters a comment, the comment is distributed to all of the participants in the conference. Each line in the Chat window is preceded by the name of the participant who entered the comment. You can prepare your comments or questions and send them to the conference when you are ready.

In a large group, it may be useful to have a moderator or one participant who controls the flow of the Chat.

The Chat can be saved as a file. Saving a Chat is useful when you want to make a copy of the NetMeeting session so that it can be shared with the participants or read by other people.

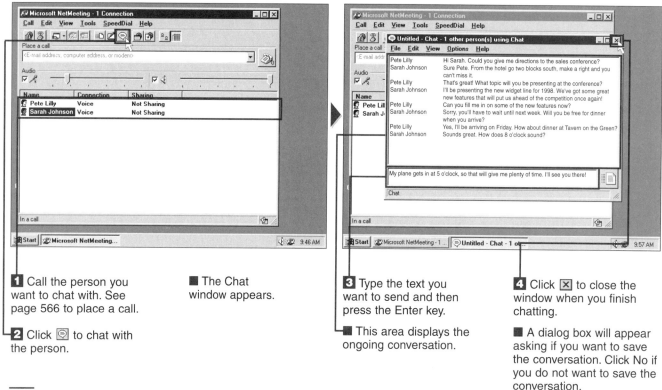

■1 Call the person you want to chat with. See page 566 to place a call.

■2 Click 🗨 to chat with the person.

■ The Chat window appears.

■3 Type the text you want to send and then press the Enter key.

■ This area displays the ongoing conversation.

■4 Click ☒ to close the window when you finish chatting.

■ A dialog box will appear asking if you want to save the conversation. Click No if you do not want to save the conversation.

SEND A FILE

Y ou can send a file to the participants in a NetMeeting session. You can send any type of file, including a document you want to present, a font needed to display a document or a program upgrade.

When you send a file, the file transfers in the background

while you continue to work or chat. You should be very cautious of files you receive from NetMeeting participants you do not know. If you accept a program file, check it with an anti-virus program. You should also use an anti-virus program to check documents with extensions used by

Microsoft Word (.doc) and Excel (.xls). These types of documents may contain macro viruses.

When you send a file, each participant will see a dialog box indicating that the file is being transferred. Each participant can decide whether to keep the file or delete it.

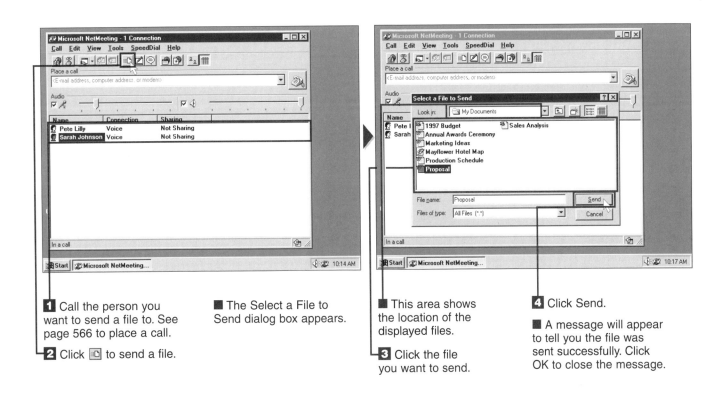

■ 1 Call the person you want to send a file to. See page 566 to place a call.

■ 2 Click 🔲 to send a file.

■ The Select a File to Send dialog box appears.

■ This area shows the location of the displayed files.

■ 3 Click the file you want to send.

■ 4 Click Send.

■ A message will appear to tell you the file was sent successfully. Click OK to close the message.

USING THE WHITEBOARD

The NetMeeting Whiteboard gives all conference participants the opportunity to share and comment on information or pictures on a page. This can help users to describe, create, edit and correct many types of projects.

The Whiteboard is especially useful for displaying and discussing images and designs.

The Whiteboard tools are similar to the tools found in Paint. Users can use the Whiteboard tools to create lines and other basic shapes. Each user also has tools to highlight, underline or place text on the page. The Whiteboard also provides a hand tool that can be used to point out objects on the page.

All the participants can see all of the comments and marks

that are being made on a Whiteboard page. There is no way to tell who is making the changes to the page when there are several users in a NetMeeting conference.

A Whiteboard can contain many pages and you can add new pages at any time. When one participant changes the page, it changes for all users.

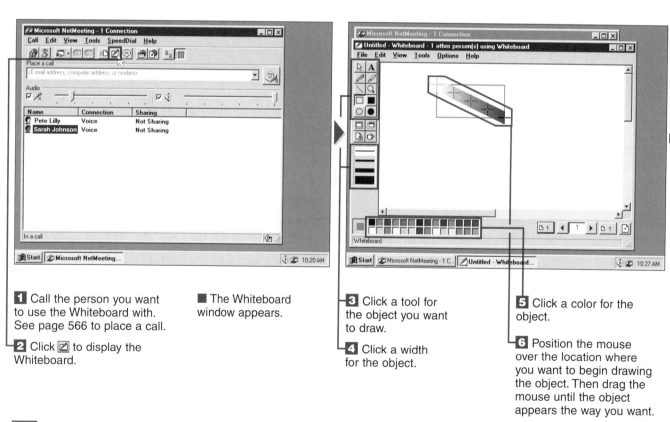

1 Call the person you want to use the Whiteboard with. See page 566 to place a call.

2 Click ☑ to display the Whiteboard.

■ The Whiteboard window appears.

3 Click a tool for the object you want to draw.

4 Click a width for the object.

5 Click a color for the object.

6 Position the mouse over the location where you want to begin drawing the object. Then drag the mouse until the object appears the way you want.

How can I see all the pages in the Whiteboard?

From the Edit menu, select the Page Sorter command. A window appears, displaying miniature images of all of the pages in the Whiteboard. You can delete a page you no longer need, insert a new page or instantly display a specific page.

Can I rearrange the objects on a Whiteboard page?

Click the Select tool (🔲) and then drag the mouse ▷ over the objects you want to move. Then drag the objects to the new location.

Can I place a document on the Whiteboard so all the conference users can see it and make suggestions?

Make the document you want to place on the Whiteboard the active window. In the Whiteboard, click . In the dialog box that appears, click OK to continue. Then click the document you want to display in the Whiteboard.

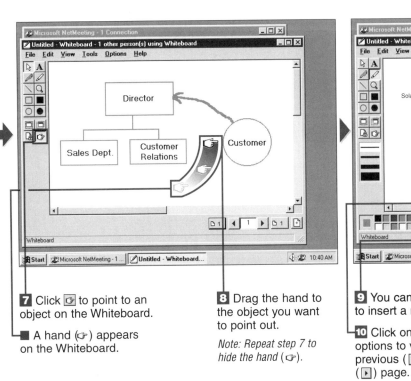

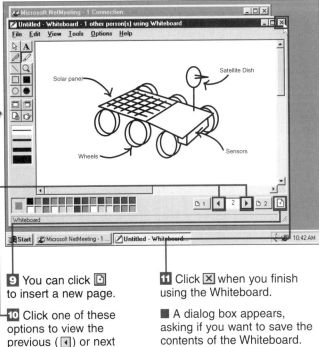

7 Click 🖰 to point to an object on the Whiteboard.

■ A hand (☞) appears on the Whiteboard.

8 Drag the hand to the object you want to point out.

Note: Repeat step 7 to hide the hand (☞).

9 You can click 🖺 to insert a new page.

10 Click one of these options to view the previous (◀) or next (▶) page.

11 Click ✕ when you finish using the Whiteboard.

■ A dialog box appears, asking if you want to save the contents of the Whiteboard. Click No if you do not want to save the contents.

SHARE A PROGRAM

You can use NetMeeting to work interactively and cooperatively with other participants on the same document. When you share a program, every participant in a NetMeeting conference can use the program, even if they do not have the program installed on their computer.

You can let the other participants watch as you work or allow them to work with you in the shared program. You should only let people you trust work with you in a program. Depending on the program you are sharing, a participant could cause damage to your documents or your computer.

When the other conference participants are collaborating with you, any of the participants can take control of the program.

They can use all of the shared program's menus and commands. They can also move the program's window to another location on the screen and resize the window.

All participants should use the same screen resolution and color depth when working in a shared program. A participant with a lower color depth may experience unusual colors.

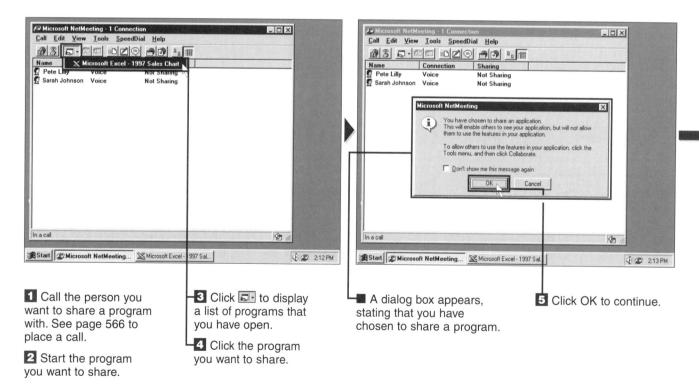

1 Call the person you want to share a program with. See page 566 to place a call.

2 Start the program you want to share.

3 Click 🖻 to display a list of programs that you have open.

4 Click the program you want to share.

■ A dialog box appears, stating that you have chosen to share a program.

5 Click OK to continue.

TIPS

How can I tell who is using the program?

A small box appears above the upper right corner of the program. The box contains the name of the person who is controlling the program.

How can I take control of a shared program?

The initials of the person who currently has control over a program appear as part of the mouse pointer. To take control of a shared program, click the program window.

How do I work alone again?

To turn off collaboration, click .

The shared program is covered with a pattern of gray windows. Why am I unable to see and use the shared program?

The person who is sharing the program is currently using another program. You will only be able to see and use the shared program when it is the active window.

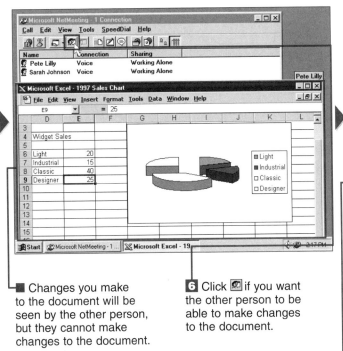

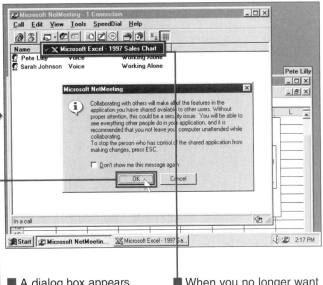

■ Changes you make to the document will be seen by the other person, but they cannot make changes to the document.

6 Click 🖾 if you want the other person to be able to make changes to the document.

■ A dialog box appears, confirming that you are about to allow the other person to make changes to the document.

7 Click OK to continue.

■ When you no longer want to share a program, repeat steps 3 and 4 to remove the check mark (✔) beside the program name.

SECTION IX

INSTALL NEW HARDWARE

When you add capabilities to your computer by installing new hardware, Windows will complete most of the work for you. The wizard guides you step by step through the installation, first detecting and then installing the software needed by the device. You can add hardware to your computer, such as a CD-ROM drive, network card, modem and printer.

You should locate all materials that were included with the hardware, read the manufacturer's instructions and check for readme files before starting. Make sure you also have your Windows 95 CD-ROM disc or floppy disks handy. You should exit all programs because you will likely have to restart your computer.

You will not have to use the wizard if both your computer and the device you want to install

support Plug and Play. Plug and Play devices are automatically detected by the computer. All you have to do is physically install the device. After you restart your computer, Windows will ask for the driver software that enables Windows and the device to communicate.

Even if you do not have a Plug and Play computer, some devices, such as printers, will still Plug and Play.

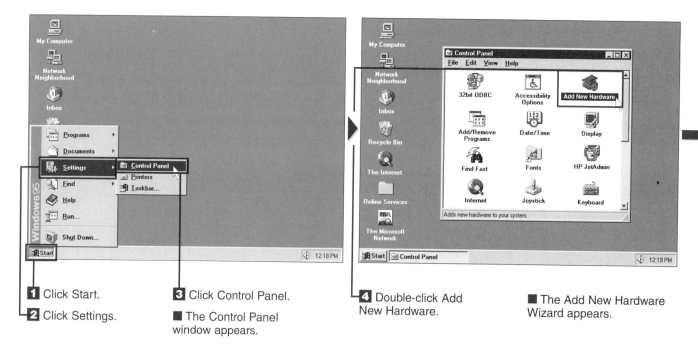

1 Click Start.

2 Click Settings.

3 Click Control Panel.

■ The Control Panel window appears.

4 Double-click Add New Hardware.

■ The Add New Hardware Wizard appears.

TIPS

Where can I find a list of hardware that Windows 95 supports?

If a list was not included when you purchased your computer, use the Windows 95 Hardware Compatibility List located at www.microsoft.com/hwtest

Should I still use the wizard if I know the details about the device and have the installation disks?

Yes. The wizard may simplify the procedure and will install the Windows 95 version of the driver software. This is particularly important for devices you purchased before August 1995. Older drivers may not use the full potential of Windows 95.

How can I tell if my computer supports Plug and Play?

From the Control Panel, double-click System. Select the Device Manager tab and then click the plus sign (⊞) beside System devices to expand the list. If your system has a Plug and Play BIOS, it will be listed here. Even if your computer does not support Plug and Play, Windows may still be able to detect Plug and Play devices.

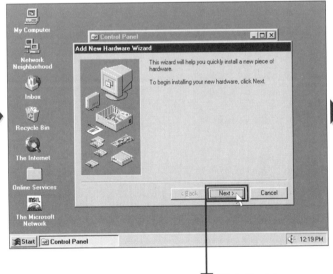

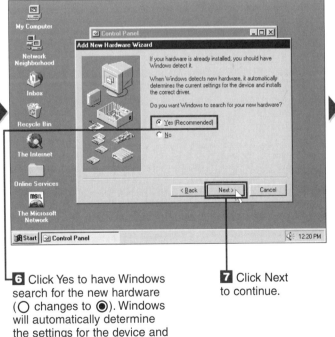

■ The wizard will help you add new hardware to your computer.

5 Click Next to begin installing your new hardware.

6 Click Yes to have Windows search for the new hardware (○ changes to ●). Windows will automatically determine the settings for the device and install the needed software.

7 Click Next to continue.

CONTINUED ▶

INSTALL NEW HARDWARE
CONTINUED

The wizard will take several minutes to check your computer for the new device. If part of the process fails, you should wait until three to five minutes have passed with no disk activity or progress and then restart your computer.

Devices that do not support Plug and Play are referred to as legacy devices. With a legacy device, you may have to provide the driver

software if it is not included with Windows. It is usually worthwhile to install the driver software before installing the hardware. This can help to determine the settings that you will need to use. You may have to adjust the settings on the device to match the settings Windows provides. This can be done by using the device's software or by adjusting the jumpers or switches on the device.

Drivers are only required by certain devices. Basic system items, such as hard drives and RAM, do not require drivers.

There are also specific wizards for adding printers (see page 112) and modems (see page 350). Network cards are covered in more detail on page 510.

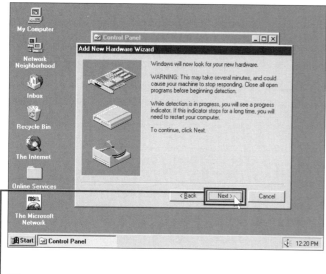

8 Click Next to start searching for the new hardware.

■ The search may take several minutes.

■ This area displays the progress of the search.

Note: You can click Cancel to stop the search at any time.

What should I do if Windows did not find any new hardware?

Windows will offer to start the manual installation process. If you do not know what type of device you are installing, select Other devices from the Hardware types list. This option provides you with a list of computer product manufacturers to help you find the device.

What should I do if I cannot find the driver for an older device?

Call the manufacturer or search the manufacturer's Web site. You can also search the Internet. Even if you have the driver, you should determine if there is a newer version available.

Where can I find out which resource settings, such as IRQs and addresses, are available before I start installing?

You can find this information in the Device Manager. See page 624.

What can I do if the device does not work after it has been installed?

Use Windows Help to start the Hardware Conflict Troubleshooter. This interactive procedure will help you find the problem and suggest solutions.

IX

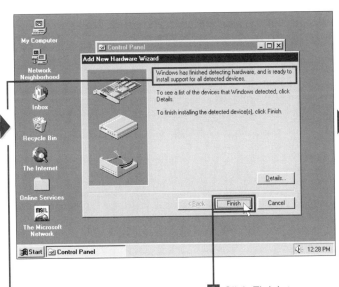

■ This message appears when Windows has finished searching for the new hardware.

Note: You can click Details to see a list of devices that Windows found.

9 Click Finish to finish installing the hardware.

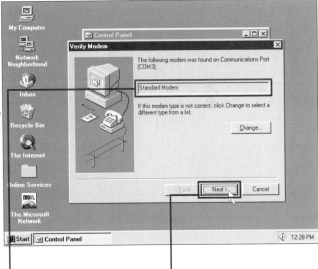

■ This area describes what Windows found.

Note: You can click Change to select a different device from a list if Windows did not find the correct device.

10 Click Next to continue.

■ You may be asked to insert the Windows 95 installation CD-ROM disc or floppy disk and to restart your computer.

■ You can now use your new device.

ADD OR REMOVE WINDOWS COMPONENTS

You can use the Windows 95 CD-ROM disc or floppy disks to add or remove parts of your Windows operating system. You can install components to add additional capabilities and enhancements to your computer. You can also remove components you do not use to free up storage space on your computer.

There are many components of Windows 95 that are not installed on your computer as part of the typical installation. When setting up Windows for the first time, most people do not install all the components included with the program. This avoids taking up storage space with unnecessary components.

Windows displays a list of all the components and indicates which components are not yet installed. Windows provides you with a brief description of each component.

Some components are grouped together. For example, Character Map and Quick View are parts of the Accessories group. Windows uses check boxes to indicate whether all, none or some of the components in a group are installed.

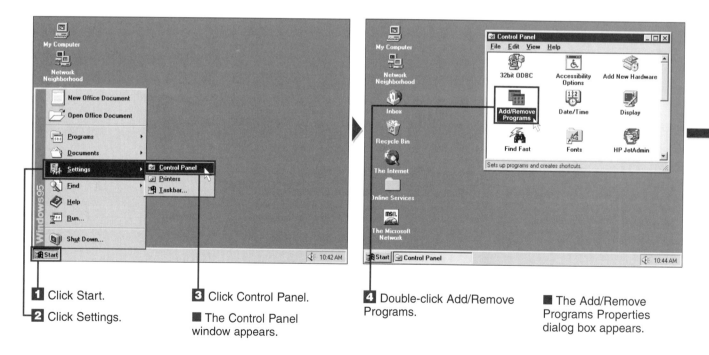

1 Click Start.

2 Click Settings.

3 Click Control Panel.

■ The Control Panel window appears.

4 Double-click Add/Remove Programs.

■ The Add/Remove Programs Properties dialog box appears.

TIPS

I have only the Windows 95 floppy disks. How can I get the extra components?

Some components, such as Quick View and CD Player, are not available on the floppy disks. These are available from the Microsoft Windows 95 Web site. You can access the Web site at the following address:

www.microsoft.com/windows95/info/cdextras.htm

When I installed Windows, why weren't all the components installed?

A typical installation does not install components that are rarely used or are of special interest, like Multilanguage Support. Large components that take up a lot of storage space are also not automatically installed by Windows.

When would I use the Have Disk button?

You use the Have Disk button to install a Windows component that is not listed on the Windows Setup tab. For example, if you download a Windows component from the Internet, you can use the Have Disk button to install the component.

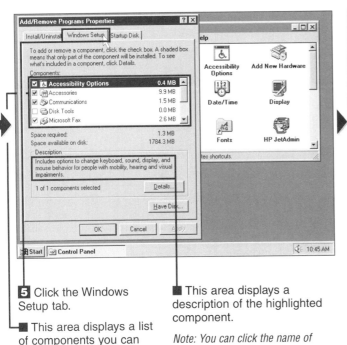

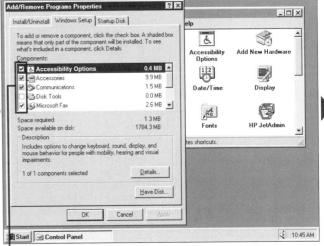

5 Click the Windows Setup tab.

■ This area displays a list of components you can add or remove from your computer.

■ This area displays a description of the highlighted component.

Note: You can click the name of another component to display its description.

■ The box beside each component tells you how much of the component is installed.

☑ All parts of the component are installed.

☑ Some parts of the component are installed.

☐ No parts of the component are installed.

CONTINUED ▶

ADD OR REMOVE WINDOWS
COMPONENTS CONTINUED

There are many useful components that are not part of the typical Windows installation. You can add the components you want with the Windows 95 CD-ROM disc or floppy disks.

The Accessories group has several useful components. The Character Map is invaluable when you need to find a special character that is not available on the keyboard. Quick View

lets you preview the contents of files before you open them. You will also find several games, desktop wallpapers and screen savers in this component.

The Communications group contains Direct Cable Connection to allow you to create a simple network by attaching two computers with a cable.

You can also install the Microsoft Fax component to send and

receive faxes directly from your computer with a fax modem.

The Windows Messaging component manages and stores e-mail messages. Windows Messaging allows you to use and access both Internet and Microsoft Mail, as well as Microsoft Network messages.

You can view all the parts of each group and select the components you want to add or remove.

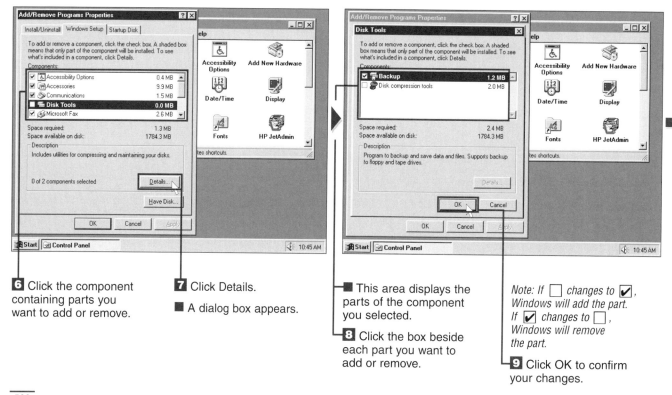

6 Click the component containing parts you want to add or remove.

7 Click Details.

■ A dialog box appears.

■ This area displays the parts of the component you selected.

8 Click the box beside each part you want to add or remove.

Note: If ☐ *changes to* ☑, *Windows will add the part. If* ☑ *changes to* ☐, *Windows will remove the part.*

9 Click OK to confirm your changes.

TIPS

Can I add components to my computer without using the CD-ROM disc every time?

You can copy all the .cab files from the CD-ROM disc to a folder on your hard drive. When Windows asks for the CD-ROM disc, click OK. Then click the Browse button in the Copying Files dialog box and open the folder containing the .cab files.

How can I remove the Briefcase?

Once you install the Briefcase, it cannot be removed.

I wanted to install one component. Why were other parts also installed?

Some components require parts of other components so they will work properly. Windows will automatically install all the parts that are needed.

What is Multilanguage Support?

Multilanguage Support installs the specific fonts and other files needed to allow you to work with and create documents in several non-Western alphabets, including Greek, Polish and Ukrainian. There are five language groups you can choose from.

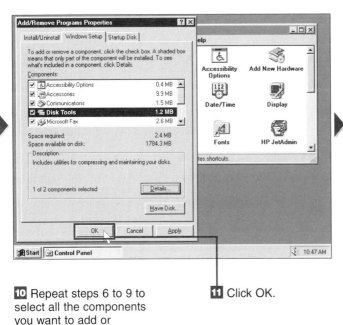

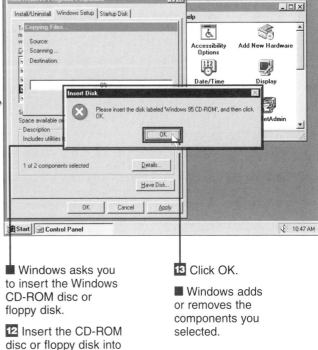

10 Repeat steps 6 to 9 to select all the components you want to add or remove.

11 Click OK.

■ Windows asks you to insert the Windows CD-ROM disc or floppy disk.

12 Insert the CD-ROM disc or floppy disk into the drive.

13 Click OK.

■ Windows adds or removes the components you selected.

INSTALL A PROGRAM

You can use a CD-ROM disc or floppy disk to add a new program to your computer.

Windows 95 programs available on a CD-ROM disc will automatically start an installation program when the CD-ROM disc is inserted.

The installation program asks you questions about your computer and

how you would like to have the program installed. There are three common types of installation. A typical installation sets up the program as recommended for most people. A custom installation allows you to customize the program to suit your specific needs. A minimum installation

sets up the minimum amount of the program needed.

When you finish installing a program, make sure you keep the CD-ROM disc or floppy disks in a safe place. If your computer fails or if you accidentally erase the program files, you may need to install the program again.

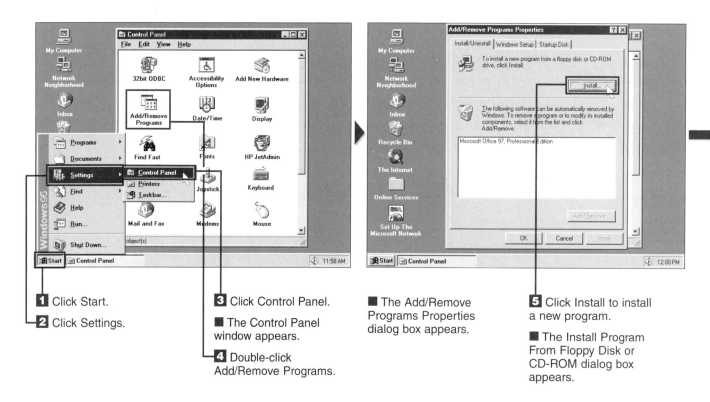

1 Click Start.

2 Click Settings.

3 Click Control Panel.

■ The Control Panel window appears.

4 Double-click Add/Remove Programs.

■ The Add/Remove Programs Properties dialog box appears.

5 Click Install to install a new program.

■ The Install Program From Floppy Disk or CD-ROM dialog box appears.

TIPS

How can I install a program if it does not have an installation program?

If the program does not include an installation program, create a new folder on your computer. Then copy all the files from the installation disk to the new folder. You can run the program from the folder.

I already installed this program for Windows 3.1. Do I need to install it again?

If you have both Windows 3.1 and Windows 95 on your computer, you may need to install the program again to set it up to work properly with Windows 95.

What is a "readme" file?

A "readme" file is a file usually found on the installation disk or CD-ROM disc. This file may contain the latest information about the product or information to help you install the program.

Windows did not find an installation program. What can I do?

If Windows did not find an installation program, you can search for the program using the Browse button. Display the contents of the drive containing the installation disk and look for a file named "setup" or "install".

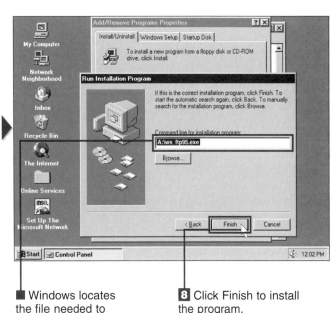

6 Insert the program's first installation floppy disk or CD-ROM disc into a drive.

7 Click Next to continue.

■ Windows locates the file needed to install the program.

8 Click Finish to install the program.

9 Follow the instructions on your screen. Every program will ask you a different set of questions.

REMOVE A PROGRAM

Y ou can remove a program you no longer use from your computer. Removing programs will free up space on your hard drive and allow you to install newer or more useful programs.

Programs designed for Windows 95 appear in a list. You can select the

program you want to remove in the list and have Windows remove the program from your computer.

Windows deletes the files and reverses any settings that were changed when the program was installed. To avoid affecting other programs, Windows may leave

some of the files related to the program on your computer.

When you remove a program, Windows may ask you for the original floppy disks or CD-ROM disc you used to install the program.

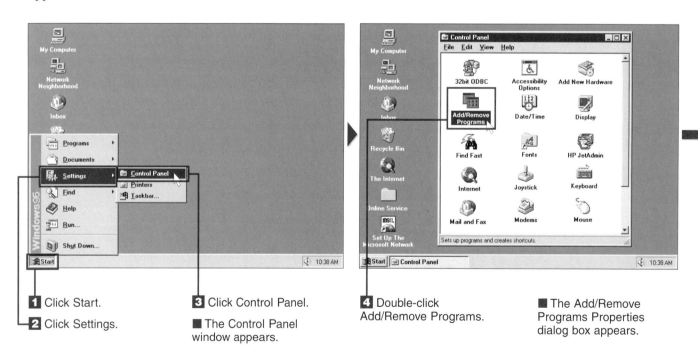

1 Click Start.

2 Click Settings.

3 Click Control Panel.

■ The Control Panel window appears.

4 Double-click Add/Remove Programs.

■ The Add/Remove Programs Properties dialog box appears.

What if I cannot find the uninstall program needed to remove a program?

You can use a commercial uninstall program to delete the files related to a program. You can also delete the program's files yourself. You must be careful to delete only the files for the program you want to remove. You should check the program's documentation to find out which files you can safely remove.

How do I delete the program's shortcut from my desktop?

After deleting a program, you can drag any shortcuts you no longer need to the Recycle Bin.

I have removed a program from my computer but the Start menu still displays the program. How do I remove a program from the Start menu?

To remove a program from the Start menu, see page 254.

How can I remove a program that does not appear in Windows' list?

Older programs, such as those created for previous versions of Windows, will not appear in this list. Check the documentation supplied with the program for instructions on how to remove the program.

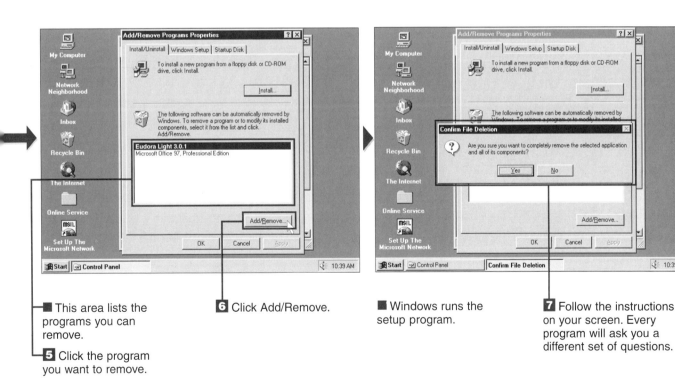

■ This area lists the programs you can remove.

5 Click the program you want to remove.

6 Click Add/Remove.

■ Windows runs the setup program.

7 Follow the instructions on your screen. Every program will ask you a different set of questions.

INSTALL WINDOWS 95

The Setup Wizard helps to ensure that you successfully install Windows 95. It can take 30 minutes to an hour to install and set up Windows.

To install Windows 95, you need the startup disk, the first disk from your previous version of Windows and the Windows 95 floppy disks or CD-ROM disc. If you are using the Windows 95 CD-ROM disc, you will also need your CD-ROM driver disk. To install OSR2, you need the CD-ROM Setup Boot disk and the Windows 95 CD-ROM disc that were supplied with your computer.

Before the installation process starts, your hard drive is checked for errors.

The Setup Wizard displays the Microsoft License Agreement. To continue with the installation, you must accept the terms in the license agreement.

There are three parts to installing Windows. First, the Setup Wizard collects information about your computer. Second, the wizard copies Windows files to your computer. Third, your computer is restarted and the setup is completed.

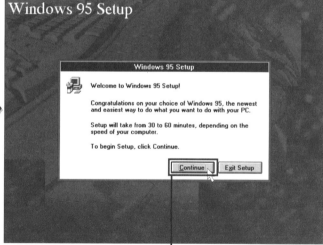

1 Insert your Windows 95 startup disk into drive A.

2 Turn on your computer and insert the Windows CD-ROM disc.

3 Type the letter of your CD-ROM drive followed by a colon (:) and then press the Enter key.

4 Type **setup** and then press the Enter key to start the Setup program.

5 Press the Enter key to check your hard drive for errors.

Note: If your computer has more than one hard drive, press x to continue.

■ The Welcome to Windows 95 Setup screen appears.

6 Click Continue to begin Setup.

■ Setup prepares the Setup Wizard which will guide you through the installation of Windows 95.

What can I do if I do not have the CD-ROM Setup Boot disk or I cannot use it to access my CD-ROM drive?

You can start the computer using the startup disk. For information on the startup disk, see page 636. After the computer is started, you can use the disk supplied with your CD-ROM drive to re-install the CD-ROM software.

What does the license agreement state?

The license agreement states that you must purchase a copy of Microsoft Windows 95 for each computer on which you plan to install and use it.

Can I re-install Windows from a backup?

No, you cannot use a backup until Windows and Microsoft Backup are installed on your computer. You can then use a full system backup to restore most of your other programs and settings.

Can I use the Setup Wizard if I am upgrading from an earlier version of Windows?

The Setup Wizard is also a part of the Windows 95 upgrade kit. You can start the Setup Wizard from the previous version of Windows by double-clicking the Setup file located on the upgrade CD-ROM disc, or floppy disk.

IX

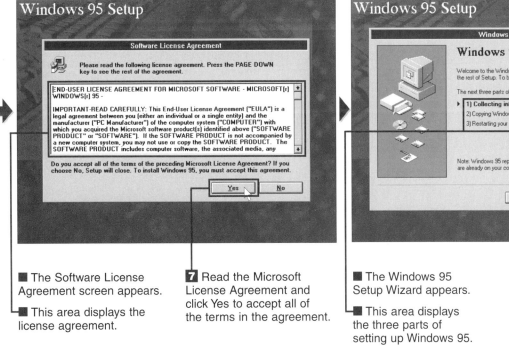

■ The Software License Agreement screen appears.

■ This area displays the license agreement.

7 Read the Microsoft License Agreement and click Yes to accept all of the terms in the agreement.

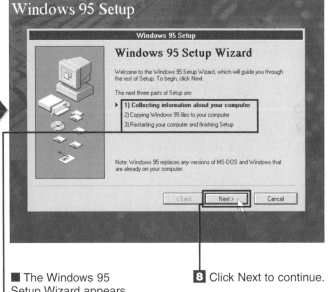

■ The Windows 95 Setup Wizard appears.

■ This area displays the three parts of setting up Windows 95.

8 Click Next to continue.

CONTINUED ▶

INSTALL WINDOWS 95 CONTINUED

The Setup Wizard asks you a series of questions to find out how you want to install Windows.

You can choose the folder, also called a directory, in which Windows will be installed. You should install Windows in the c:\windows folder. Although you can choose another folder, it is not recommended. Some programs may not work properly if Windows is installed in another folder.

You can choose an installation type that reflects your hardware and installs the Windows components you will most likely use. Typical is suggested for most computers. Portable installs components that are useful for mobile computers. Compact installs no optional components, so it is recommended for computers with limited hard disk space. Custom allows you to choose the components that will

be installed and provides greater control for network installations.

You must enter the serial number, also called a CD Key, for your Windows CD-ROM disc. This number is unique and is used for product support. You can find the serial number on the disc's packaging or on the license certificate included with the disc's documentation.

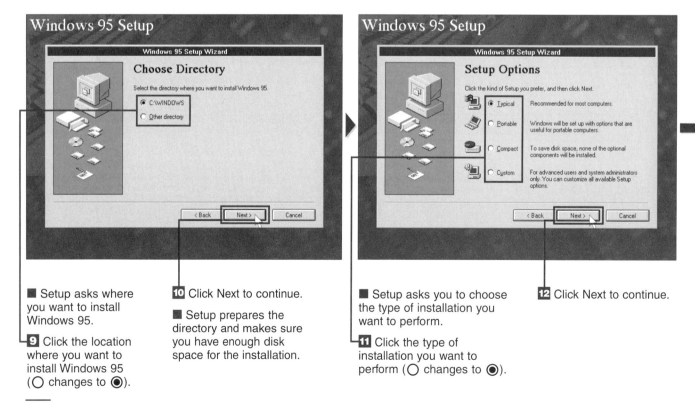

■ Setup asks where you want to install Windows 95.

9 Click the location where you want to install Windows 95 (○ changes to ◉).

10 Click Next to continue.

■ Setup prepares the directory and makes sure you have enough disk space for the installation.

■ Setup asks you to choose the type of installation you want to perform.

11 Click the type of installation you want to perform (○ changes to ◉).

12 Click Next to continue.

Can I change my installation type later?

You can add or remove components after you have installed Windows 95. To add or remove Windows components, see page 580.

Can I proceed without a valid serial number?

If you do not have a valid serial number, the setup process will end without installing Windows. If the number provided with your disc does not work, follow the instructions that appear on your screen. The license agreement requires you to have one serial number for each computer on which you are going to install Windows 95.

Can I choose the Custom installation if I am not an expert?

Anyone can choose the Custom installation. However, unless you are an advanced user, you may have trouble understanding some of the settings you are asked to provide and the options you may have to choose.

Why does Windows want to know my name?

If you have a network card, your name is stored and used during the network setup. This information is also used when you install other programs.

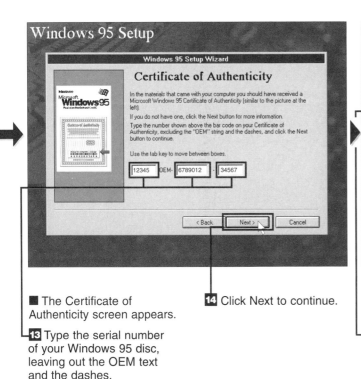

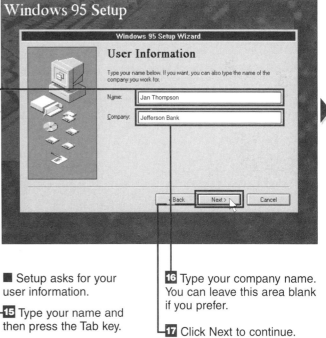

■ The Certificate of Authenticity screen appears.

13 Type the serial number of your Windows 95 disc, leaving out the OEM text and the dashes.

14 Click Next to continue.

■ Setup asks for your user information.

15 Type your name and then press the Tab key.

16 Type your company name. You can leave this area blank if you prefer.

17 Click Next to continue.

CONTINUED ▶

INSTALL WINDOWS 95 CONTINUED

The Setup Wizard analyzes the hardware devices installed on your computer. You can select the types of hardware devices to search for from the list provided by the Setup Wizard. The wizard will not search for devices you have not selected. The search may take several minutes.

Windows includes many components that are not installed by default. Some of Windows' optional components include games, tools and accessories. You can choose the optional components you want to install.

If you already have a Windows startup disk, you do not need to create a new one. If you do not have a startup disk, the wizard helps you create one during the installation. A startup disk is used to start

Windows when the operating system will not start normally. The floppy disk you use to create the startup disk must be able to store at least 1.2 MB of information. If your computer has more than one floppy drive, you should use the A: drive to create your startup disk. The A: drive is used to start the computer when the hard disk cannot.

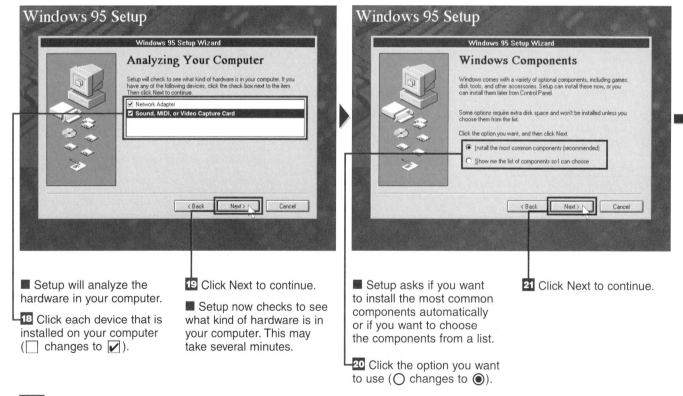

■ Setup will analyze the hardware in your computer.

18 Click each device that is installed on your computer (☐ changes to ☑).

19 Click Next to continue.

■ Setup now checks to see what kind of hardware is in your computer. This may take several minutes.

■ Setup asks if you want to install the most common components automatically or if you want to choose the components from a list.

20 Click the option you want to use (○ changes to ◉).

21 Click Next to continue.

Can I create a startup disk later?

After Windows is installed, you can use the Control Panel's Add/Remove Programs icon to create a startup disk. See page 636.

How much disk space will the optional components use?

When you select the Show me the list of components so I can choose option, the Select Components screen appears. The screen contains information about the amount of space needed by the components you have selected and the amount of space available on your hard disk. The information is updated as you select and deselect components.

What should I do when the Setup Wizard seems to stop while analyzing my computer?

Wait a few minutes. If there is no change on the Progress bar and you do not see the hard drive light flashing, turn off the computer. When you turn the computer back on and start the setup process again, choose the Safe Recovery mode. This gives you the option of skipping the part of the hardware detection process that failed.

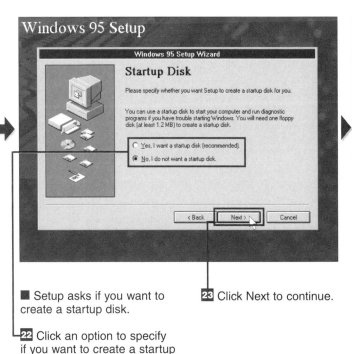

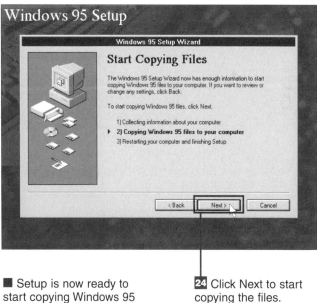

■ Setup asks if you want to create a startup disk.

22 Click an option to specify if you want to create a startup disk (○ changes to ●).

23 Click Next to continue.

■ Setup is now ready to start copying Windows 95 files to your computer.

24 Click Next to start copying the files.

CONTINUED

INSTALL WINDOWS 95 CONTINUED

When the Setup Wizard has finished collecting information about your computer, it copies the Windows operating system files to your computer from the Windows CD-ROM disc. It will take several minutes to copy all the Windows files to your computer. The Setup Wizard takes this opportunity to tell you about the features and benefits of Windows 95.

When all the files have been transferred to your computer, the Setup Wizard restarts your computer to begin the final part of the setup process.

If networking is enabled, you are asked to enter names for your computer and your workgroup, as well as a description. The computer and workgroup names you specify will be stored in your computer's settings. The computer name is used to identify you to others on the network. You should ask your system administrator for the name of your workgroup. The description is used to give people information about your computer, such as its location.

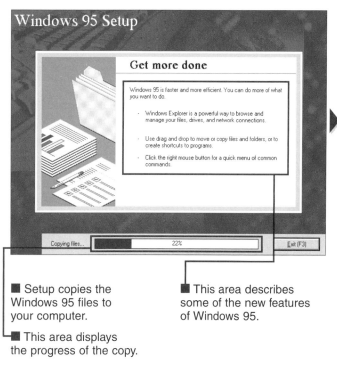

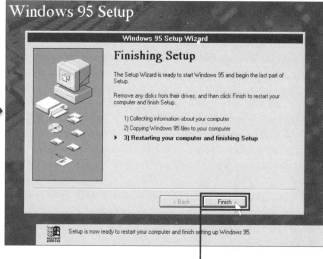

■ Setup copies the Windows 95 files to your computer.

■ This area displays the progress of the copy.

■ This area describes some of the new features of Windows 95.

■ The Finishing Setup screen appears. Setup is ready to start Windows 95 and begin the last part of the setup.

25 Remove any disks from the drives in your computer.

26 Click Finish to restart your computer and complete the installation.

Do I need to turn my computer off or press Ctrl+Alt+Delete to restart the computer?

After you click the Finish button, the Setup Wizard restarts your computer. If your computer does not restart after a few minutes, turn the computer's power off and then on again.

What should I do if I do not know the name of my workgroup?

You can accept the default name which is based on the company name you entered. To change the workgroup name later, in the Control Panel, double-click the Network icon. Use the Identification tab to change the workgroup name, computer name and description.

How much disk space will OSR2 need?

If you choose the Typical setup and do not select any optional components, your Windows folder will be approximately 60 MB. Another 20 MB of files are stored in the Program Files folder. The size of the folders will vary based on the hardware devices that are installed on your computer and the optional components you have chosen.

IX

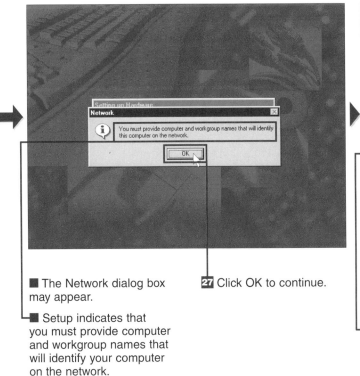

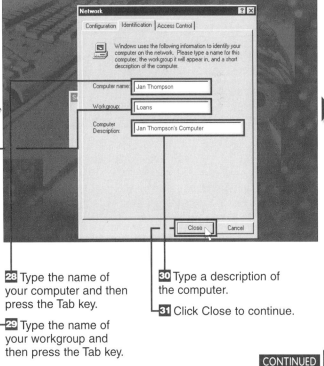

■ The Network dialog box may appear.

■ Setup indicates that you must provide computer and workgroup names that will identify your computer on the network.

27 Click OK to continue.

28 Type the name of your computer and then press the Tab key.

29 Type the name of your workgroup and then press the Tab key.

30 Type a description of the computer.

31 Click Close to continue.

CONTINUED

INSTALL WINDOWS 95 CONTINUED

To finish installing Windows, the Setup Wizard asks for your time zone. Windows uses this information to make adjustments for daylight savings time.

When the Setup Wizard restarts your computer, Windows 95 will start and display the Welcome screen. This screen appears each time you start Windows and presents a tip about Windows. You can click the Windows Tour button or the What's New button on the Welcome screen to find out more about Windows. If you have a modem and you have not already registered your purchase of Windows 95 with Microsoft, you can click the Online Registration button.

If you have a network card, you may be asked to enter a password. Although other people will be able to start and use the computer without the password, they will not be able to access the network.

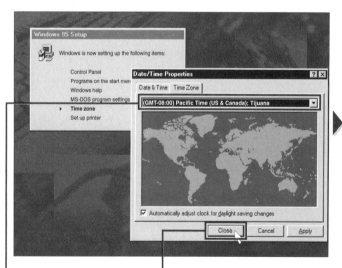

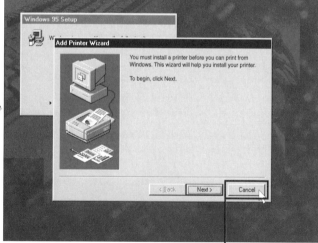

■ The Date/Time Properties dialog box appears.

32 This area displays your time zone. You can click this area to change the time zone.

■ Windows will automatically adjust your computer's clock for daylight savings time.

33 Click Close to continue.

■ The Add Printer Wizard screen appears.

34 Click Cancel if you do not want to install a printer now.

TIPS

What can I do if my hardware devices are not set up properly?

If you have an installation or setup disk for the device, you can use the disk to install the device properly. You can also use the Control Panel's Add New Hardware icon, see page 576. To set up a modem, see page 350.

Can I check if my computer's time is correct while I am selecting the time zone?

Use the Date & Time tab to set the correct date and time. See page 198.

How do I install a printer later?

Click the Start button, select Settings and then click Printers. In the Printers dialog box double-click the Add Printer icon. See page 112.

What happens if I do not enter a password when asked?

Your password will consist of blank spaces. When you start Windows, just press the Enter key when the Enter Network Password dialog box appears.

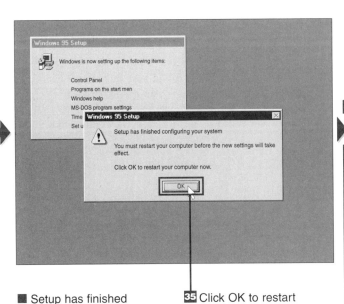

■ Setup has finished setting up your computer.

35 Click OK to restart your computer.

■ The Enter Network Password dialog box may appear.

36 Type your name and then press the Tab key.

37 Type a password. If you do not want to type a password, leave this area blank.

38 Click OK.

Note: If you entered a password, you will be asked to type the password again to confirm the password.

■ You can now use Windows 95.

UPGRADING WINDOWS 95

Since Windows 95 was released in August 1995, Microsoft has made numerous changes and additions to the operating system. There are currently three versions of Windows 95—the original version, version A and version B.

Determine Your Current Version

To determine which version of Windows 95 is installed on your computer, you can refer to the General tab of the System Properties dialog box. See page 298.

If the General tab displays the number 4.00.950, you have the original version of Windows 95. You may have purchased a computer with the original version pre-installed or upgraded from a previous version of Windows. The upgrade version of Windows 95 has not changed since August 1995.

If the displayed number is 4.00.950 a, you have version A. You may have purchased a computer with version A pre-installed or you may have installed Service Pack 1. Service Pack 1 updates the original version of Windows 95 to version A.

If the number on the General tab is 4.00.950 B, you have version B, also called OSR2. OSR2 is only available with the purchase of a new computer.

Microsoft provided versions A and B to computer manufacturers to supply with new computers. These versions are called OEM Service Releases or OSRs.

Service Pack 1

In December 1995, Microsoft released Service Pack 1 to solve some of the problems identified by users of the original version of Windows 95. If you have the original version of Windows 95, you may want to install Service Pack 1. Windows 95 versions A and B both include the service pack upgrade. You can get Service Pack 1 from the Windows 95 Service Packs page at:

www.microsoft.com/windows95/info/
service-packs.htm

Before transferring Service Pack 1 to your computer, you should close all of your programs. If you use Microsoft Plus!, you should also suspend the System Agent. Once you have transferred Service Pack 1, double-click the Setup.exe file to run the update program. After the update program is finished, you will need to restart your computer. When Windows restarts, the General tab of the System Properties dialog box will display the version number 4.00.950 a.

If you wish, you can remove the Service Pack 1 update. To remove a program, see page 586. You can remove all of the Service Pack 1 components except the Password List Update. Even after you remove the service pack, the General tab will still display the version number 4.00.950 a.

System Updates

You can obtain additional fixes and updates, called system updates, which were not included in Service Pack 1. These are useful if you have the original version or version A. You can find the system updates at:

www.microsoft.com/windows95/info/
system-updates.htm

There are several system updates available and each must be transferred and installed on your computer individually. You should transfer and install the fixes or updates for any of the features you use.

Even if you do not want any of the other updates, you should transfer and install the Kernel32 and OLE32 updates, which fix identified bugs.

The Backup Update includes performance enhancements but does not support any additional backup devices.

The MS Fax Cover Page Fix resolves a problem that may disable fax cover pages.

The Internet Mail Service for Windows 95 Release/Update is an upgrade to add Internet Mail services to Exchange.

The Exchange Update for Windows 95 includes several changes and enhancements. In this version, Microsoft Exchange is called Windows Messaging. Windows Messaging is faster and more reliable than the version of Microsoft Exchange included with the original version of Windows 95.

Driver Updates

Hardware manufacturers are continuously changing and improving their drivers. A driver is software that allows Windows to communicate with a specific piece of hardware. No matter which version of Windows you have, you should install the most up-to-date drivers for your hardware devices. Even if your hardware is working properly with the current driver, you may still want to install the new driver. New drivers may include additional capabilities or improve the performance of your hardware. A selection of driver updates is available at:

www.microsoft.com/windowssupport/
default-sl.htm

The drivers are organized into groups that include printer, display, network, modem and audio. These groups do not include all of the available drivers. If you are looking for a new driver for a particular hardware device, you should check the hardware manufacturer's Web site or contact your hardware vendor. For information on updating drivers, see page 630.

CONTINUED ▶

UPGRADING WINDOWS 95 CONTINUED

OSR2 Components

OSR2 was released in September 1996 and contains many enhancements to Windows 95 and version A. OSR2 was designed to work with the newest types of hardware devices and is only available with the purchase of a new computer. Although you cannot obtain the entire OSR2 operating system, individual OSR2 components are available free of charge from Microsoft's Web site at:

www.microsoft.com/windows/
pr/win95osr.htm

OSR2 components provide solutions to Windows problems and offer additional Windows features. None of the components are essential so you can pick and choose, installing only the ones you want.

The most important feature of OSR2, FAT32, is not available for download. FAT32 is a new file system that improves the organization of data on your hard disk to reduce wasted space.

Microsoft has indicated that all of OSR2's features and components will be included in the release of Windows 98, which should be available early in 1998. Some of the items available now include Internet, multimedia, networking and Imaging components.

Internet

Internet programs change so rapidly that the OSR2 components described here may have already been replaced by newer versions. The latest versions can be found at Microsoft's Web site at www.microsoft.com

Internet Explorer 3 contains all of the latest browser features as well as full support for Java and ActiveX. For information on Internet Explorer 3, see page 548.

Internet Mail and Internet News are both part of Internet Explorer. You can use Internet Mail to send and receive e-mail messages. For more information, see pages 410 to 445. If you have already set up Microsoft Exchange to work with your Internet e-mail, you do not need the Mail component from Internet Explorer. You can use Internet News to browse through and participate in newsgroups. For information on Internet News, see pages 560 to 565.

NetMeeting is a program that allows you to collaborate with other Internet users. After contacting other people using NetMeeting, you can have Internet voice conversations, transfer data and view and use a program running on another person's computer. For information on NetMeeting, see pages 566 to 573.

Multimedia

The multimedia enhancements in OSR2 improve the way Windows 95 works with games and videos.

The DirectX enhancements provide your computer with additional graphic, sound and communication capabilities. These enhancements also allow games and other programs to access hardware devices faster.

ActiveMovie is an upgraded version of Media Player. ActiveMovie supports QuickTime and MPEG video formats in addition to Video for Windows.

Networking

Dial-Up Networking Improvements is a useful upgrade if you use a dial-up connection to connect to the Internet. The dial-up networking upgrade includes an improved taskbar icon which allows you to access information about the connection, such as speed and the length of time connected. There are also additional settings in the Dial-Up Networking Connections dialog box. To get Dial-Up Networking Improvements, download the ISDN 1.1 Accelerator Pack. The ISDN Accelerator Pack is available in the Knowledge Base of Microsoft's Web site at www.microsoft.com/kb/default.asp. Search for article Q145987.

Update Information Tool

When upgrading files on your computer, you can use the Update Information Tool to ensure that your upgrade will be successful. This tool can search your computer for all updated files and make sure they are installed properly. The Update Information Tool is available in the Knowledge Base of Microsoft's Web site at www.microsoft.com/kb/default.asp. Search for article Q145990.

Wang Imaging for Windows 95

Imaging allows you to turn paper documents into documents that can be used on your computer. You can use a scanner or a fax machine to read the document into your computer. Once the document is an Imaging document, you can add text or other information to the document. You can also save, print, edit and share Imaging documents. Imaging enables you to open and convert a wide range of graphics file types. For information on Imaging, see page 186.

CONTINUED ▶

UPGRADING WINDOWS 95 CONTINUED
Additional Components

There are many other programs and utilities you can obtain to enhance your version of Windows 95.

PowerToys

You can use PowerToys to gain more control over your computer. PowerToys is a collection of utilities and interface enhancements for Windows 95. You do not have to be an advanced Windows 95 user to use PowerToys' components. PowerToys is available from:

www.microsoft.com/windows/software/
powertoy.htm

Tweak UI

Tweak UI is an important PowerToys component. Tweak UI allows you to control many of Windows' settings. You can set options to automatically log on to your network when Windows starts. You can also change the speed at which cascading menus open when you move the mouse over them. You can clear the Documents section of the Start menu each time you start Windows and prevent CDs from playing automatically. You can control which file types appear when you select New from the right-click menu. Tweak UI helps you remove items from the Control Panel's Add/Remove Programs dialog box. You can also change the appearance of shortcuts and work with special desktop icons.

Taskbar Icons

Some PowerToys components appear as icons on the right side of the taskbar and provide new or additional controls. To make the PowerToys' components appear on your taskbar, you may have to place shortcuts to the components in the StartUp folder. To place items in the StartUp folder, see page 258.

The Desktop Menu icon provides access to the contents of your desktop. When you are working in a program that cannot be minimized, the Desktop Menu icon allows you to access desktop items like My Computer and the Inbox.

The FlexiCD icon provides you with controls to play and stop your audio CDs.

The QuickRes icon lists the graphics modes available for the graphics card and monitor installed on your computer. To change your screen resolution, you can simply click the resolution you want to use. When you use QuickRes, Windows changes the color depth and desktop size without restarting the computer. QuickRes is also included in OSR2.

A second set of PowerToys, called Kernel Toys is also available. These enhancements appeal mostly to people who use MS-DOS programs.

Fonts and Display Enhancements

Microsoft offers a selection of free fonts and font enhancements at www.microsoft.com/truetype. The available fonts include the Webdings symbol font, Trebuchet, Georgia, Verdana, Comic Sans, Arial Black and Impact. These fonts were designed to enhance Web pages, but once installed on your computer, they work with all Windows programs.

When you right-click a font file and select Properties, the Properties dialog box appears and displays the font's basic properties.

The font properties extension adds several new tabs to the Properties dialog box of a font file.

Font smoothing softens the edges of letters to make the text in your programs easier to read. You can turn font smoothing on or off by right-clicking your desktop and selecting Properties. In the Display Properties dialog box select the Plus! tab. Font smoothing works only on computers with HiColor (16 bit) or greater color depth settings.

Dial-Up Networking Upgrade 1.2

Dial-Up Networking 1.2 enhances the security of corporate networks that allow people to dial in to access information. Dial-Up Networking 1.2 includes support for the point-to-point tunneling protocol (PPTP). PPTP allows you to establish a secure connection across the Internet to a private network, creating a Virtual Private Network (VPN).

Dial-Up Networking 1.2 contains all of the Dial-Up Networking Improvements included in the ISDN 1.1 Accelerator Pack and an updated version of WinSock. Dial-Up Networking 1.2 is available from:

www.microsoft.com/ntserver/ info/pptpdownload.htm

Windows 95 Support Assistant

You may find the Windows 95 Support Assistant a very useful upgrade. The Windows 95 Support Assistant contains answers to the most frequently asked questions about Windows 95, sections of the Windows 95 Resource Kit, Knowledge Base articles and troubleshooters. The Support Assistant works like Windows Help. You can get the Windows 95 Support Assistant from:

www.microsoft.com/windows/support/assist.htm

HyperTerminal

HyperTerminal is a program that allows you to connect to another computer using a modem. The upgrade, called HyperTerminal Private Edition, has an auto-redial feature, can resume Zmodem file transfers after a crash and can be used for Internet Telnet connections. You can find the free upgrade at the Hilgraeve Web site at:

www.hilgraeve.com/htpe.html

UTILITIES YOU CAN USE WITH WINDOWS 95

There are many utility programs available on the Internet you can use with Windows 95. You can obtain programs that make computer maintenance tasks easier, protect your computer from viruses and enhance Windows features.

Adobe Acrobat and Acrobat Reader

Adobe Systems Incorporated at www.adobe.com

You can use Adobe Acrobat to create a .pdf or Portable Document Format file that looks the same as your original document. A .pdf file stores all of the font and formatting information with the document. When a user opens the document online, it appears exactly as it was designed. The user does not need to have the program or fonts used to create the document installed on their computer. Acrobat can create .pdf files from any program.

The Acrobat Reader is a program used to view .pdf files. The Acrobat Reader includes the ability to view and print .pdf files directly from a Web browser. This program is free and is available from Adobe's Web site. There are versions of Acrobat Reader for many different operating systems.

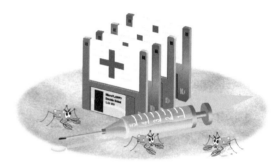

Anti-Virus

McAfee Associates Inc. at www.mcafee.com

You can reduce the risk of a virus infecting your computer by using an anti-virus program. A virus is a program that can cause problems ranging from displaying annoying messages on your screen to erasing all the information on your hard drive.

McAfee offers several anti-virus programs. VirusScan checks for and removes viruses that are already on your computer. To protect against new viruses, VirusScan can also retrieve virus updates on the McAfee Web site. WebScanX provides virus protection for files you download from the Web and for e-mail attachments. BootShield helps to prevent infection from a boot sector disk virus. You can download evaluation versions of these anti-virus programs from the McAfee Web site.

CleanSweep

Quarterdeck Corporation at
www.quarterdeck.com

CleanSweep can help you manage your hard disk
space. The CleanSweep wizards help you find
files that can be removed to free up space on your
hard disk. CleanSweep monitors the number of
times each file is used to determine when a file
is no longer needed. CleanSweep also identifies
duplicate files. You can delete, back up, archive
or move the unneeded files CleanSweep finds.
CleanSweep works with Quick View so you can
display the contents of a selected file.

When you install a program, CleanSweep
monitors your computer so that it can help you
uninstall the program later.

There are safeguards available in CleanSweep that
allow you to undo any unintentional actions.

There is a time-limited trial version of
CleanSweep available at Quarterdeck's Web site.

First Aid

CyberMedia, Inc. at www.cybermedia.com

You can use First Aid to identify and solve
problems with your computer.

First Aid watches for memory and hard drive
problems and can warn you about impending
hard drive failure. First Aid can also back up
and restore your system and configuration files
and provide answers to common questions.

First Aid usually gives you the opportunity to
fix programs that are not responding or to save
your work in a frozen program.

You can use First Aid to analyze and evaluate
your computer for program conflicts and correct
program incompatibilities.

First Aid can update itself using the Internet.
It can also use the Internet to find up-to-date
information from software developers' Web
sites. There is a time-limited trial version
available at CyberMedia's Web site.

CONTINUED ▶

UTILITIES YOU CAN USE
WITH WINDOWS 95 CONTINUED

Norton Utilities 2.0

Symantec Corporation at www.symantec.com

Norton Utilities includes several components to help you with computer maintenance tasks. The Norton System Doctor monitors your computer for potential problems. Norton CrashGuard will try to intercept a potential crash so you can save your work before the program freezes.

Norton Utilities provides advanced tools for hard disk analysis and maintenance. Speed Disk is a disk defragmenter, Protection enhances the Recycle Bin and Space Wizard helps you find and delete unneeded files. There are also several MS-DOS based programs which you can use for emergency recovery.

You can use the Live Update feature to automatically update Norton Utilities from the Symantec Web site. There is no evaluation version available, but you can purchase Norton Utilities from the Web site.

Oil Change

CyberMedia, Inc. at www.cybermedia.com

You can have Oil Change find program updates on the Internet and install them on your computer.

Oil Change identifies the programs installed on your computer and lets you know when a manufacturer provides a free update at their Web site. You can have Oil Change check for new updates as often as you want. You can manually or automatically install the updates Oil Change retrieves.

If an update does not meet your expectations, you can use the Undo feature to remove the update and restore the earlier version of the program.

Oil Change contains some advertising and informs you about trial versions of games, shareware and other programs. You can purchase the Oil Change service for a year. A trial version that finds updates only for Windows 95, Netscape Navigator, Microsoft Internet Explorer and CyberMedia First Aid is available at CyberMedia's Web site.

Paint Shop Pro 4.12

Jasc, Inc. at www.jasc.com

Paint Shop Pro is an inexpensive and easy-to-use graphics program you can use to view, edit and convert images from over 30 image formats. The supported formats include vector drawings like CorelDRAW and bitmap images like Adobe Photoshop and JPEG.

You can use Paint Shop Pro's selection of drawing and painting tools to manipulate and create pictures. Paint Shop Pro also has the tools you need to create images for Web pages, retouch photos and add special effects.

Paint Shop Pro supports the TWAIN standard to work with scanners or other image capture devices. The screen capture feature allows you to select specific areas of the screen and include the mouse pointer.

You can download a shareware version of Paint Shop Pro from the Jasc Web site.

PartitionMagic

PowerQuest Corporation at www.powerquest.com

You can use PartitionMagic to interactively create, format, change and move hard disk partitions. When you use PartitionMagic to modify your partitions, you do not have to back up your data or reinstall the operating system. For OSR2 users who are not currently using FAT32, PartitionMagic's most useful feature is the ability to convert FAT partitions to FAT32. Converting a 1 GB drive to FAT32 may free up 200 MB or more of disk space.

PartitionMagic can create and manage multiple disk partitions. This enables you to install several operating systems on a single hard disk and choose which operating system should start when you turn on your computer.

There is no evaluation version available, but you can purchase PartitionMagic from PowerQuest's Web site.

CONTINUED

UTILITIES YOU CAN USE
WITH WINDOWS 95 CONTINUED

PointCast Network

PointCast Inc. at www.pointcast.com

The PointCast Network transfers the latest news and information to your computer. You can have the PointCast Network send updated information to your computer automatically or only when you ask for it.

You can specify your preferences for local, national and international news. You can also receive information about specific industries, companies, sports, horoscopes and lottery results.

Many well-known publications supply articles to the PointCast Network, such as The New York Times, The Boston Globe, Time Magazine and The Wall Street Journal. The PointCast Network is constantly being upgraded and expanded.

The PointCast SmartScreen feature allows you to use PointCast information as your screen saver.

PointCast sells advertising to pay for the service so you can use it free of charge. You can download the PointCast Network from its Web site. There are specialized versions of the PointCast Network for government, college and Canadian users.

PowerDesk

Mijenix Corporation at www.mijenix.com

PowerDesk includes two utility programs that enhance the Windows 95 interface.

ExplorerPlus replaces Explorer and has the ability to display, open and manage files in .zip and other archive formats. In addition to the folder and file panes, ExplorerPlus can open a third pane using Quick View to display the contents of a file. To simplify drag and drop operations, ExplorerPlus can split its window to view the folders on two drives at the same time.

The PowerDesk Toolbar can float on your screen or be integrated into the taskbar. The toolbar includes launching tools for your favorite programs, a printer selector and computer resource monitors.

There is a time-limited evaluation version of PowerDesk available at Mijenix's Web site.

Quick View Plus

Inso Corporation at www.inso.com

Windows 95 includes Quick View, which allows you to preview a file before you open it. You can extend Quick View's capabilities with Quick View Plus. Quick View Plus accurately displays the fonts, tables, headers, footers, page numbers and embedded graphics in a document. You can preview a document even if you do not have the program used to create the document installed on your computer.

Quick View Plus enables you to preview more file types than Quick View, including Word 97 and Excel 97. You can preview graphic file types like those created in CorelDRAW and Micrografx Designer and image file types such as .jpg, .gif and .tif. You can also use Quick View Plus to work with many compressed file types including .zip.

Quick View Plus can print the documents it displays. You can use the Quick View Plus window to cut and paste items between any of the supported file types.

There is a time-limited trial version of Quick View Plus available at Inso's Web site.

WinZip

Nico Mak Computing, Inc. at www.winzip.com

WinZip compresses files to make it easier and faster to transfer information from one computer to another. Many of the files you transfer to your computer from online services or the Internet are in the .zip format.

WinZip allows you to point and click or drag and drop to view, extract, add, delete and test .zip files.

The Install/Try/Uninstall feature makes it easy to evaluate programs in the .zip format. WinZip lets you try the program. When you are done, WinZip can uninstall the program.

WinZip also supports many other compressed and encoded file formats.

WinZip is shareware and can be downloaded from the Nico Mak Computing Web site. For information on using WinZip, see pages 610 to 613.

USING WINZIP TO WORK WITH COMPRESSED FILES

WinZip compresses, or squeezes, files to make it easier and faster to transfer information from one computer to another. Although WinZip is not included with Windows 95, you will find it essential once you start using online services or the Internet. Many of the files that you transfer, or download, to your computer will be in the .zip format.

Groups of files are often compressed and then packaged into a single .zip file. This saves you from having to transfer each file to your computer individually.

Before you can use a compressed file, you have to "unzip", or separate and decompress, the files.

There are two ways you can use WinZip to work with compressed

files. The WinZip Wizard takes you through the unzipping process step by step. The wizard searches your hard drive for all .zip files. WinZip Classic displays files in a window that resembles a My Computer window. WinZip Classic also provides additional capabilities for advanced users.

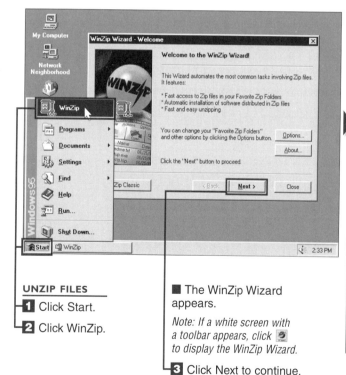

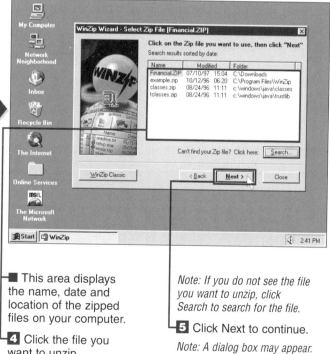

UNZIP FILES

1 Click Start.

2 Click WinZip.

■ The WinZip Wizard appears.

Note: If a white screen with a toolbar appears, click 🔲 to display the WinZip Wizard.

3 Click Next to continue.

■ This area displays the name, date and location of the zipped files on your computer.

4 Click the file you want to unzip.

Note: If you do not see the file you want to unzip, click Search to search for the file.

5 Click Next to continue.

Note: A dialog box may appear. Click yes to continue.

TIPS

How do I get WinZip?

WinZip is available on the Web at www.winzip.com. Select to download the evaluation version and then select the Windows 95 version. If you are using Internet Explorer, you can select the option to save the file to disk. In the Save As dialog box, use the ⬛ button to create a new folder called WinZip. Save the file in the folder you created. WinZip will take a few minutes to transfer to your computer. When the transfer is complete, use Explorer or My Computer to find the file. Double-click the file to start installing WinZip and then follow the instructions on your screen.

Can I unzip a file from a My Computer or Explorer window?

Once WinZip is installed, the program will open when you double-click a file with the .zip extension. In a My Computer or Explorer window, .zip files display the ⬛ icon.

Are there other programs that work with .zip files?

Mijenix PowerDesk and Inso Quick View Plus are two other programs that work with .zip files. For more information about these and other utility programs, see pages 604 to 609.

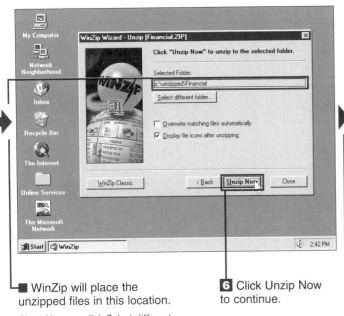

■ WinZip will place the unzipped files in this location.

Note: You can click Select different folder to place the unzipped files in a different location.

6 Click Unzip Now to continue.

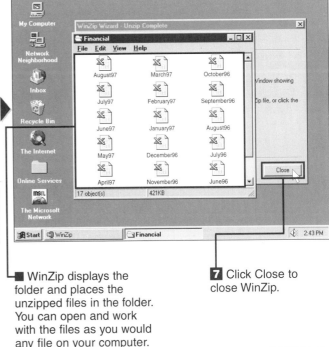

■ WinZip displays the folder and places the unzipped files in the folder. You can open and work with the files as you would any file on your computer.

7 Click Close to close WinZip.

CONTINUED ▶

USING WINZIP TO WORK WITH COMPRESSED FILES CONTINUED

You can combine several files in one compressed .zip file. The .zip file acts like a folder that contains the files you want to send. Zipped files take up less space and are easier to transfer than the original files.

The .zip format is widely used. Many programs have the ability to unzip compressed files when they are received. There are programs available for MS-DOS and previous versions of Windows to open and manage .zip files. When creating a .zip file that will be used on a computer that does not use Windows 95, remember that some operating systems cannot use long file names.

You can create a .zip file to store files on a floppy disk. You can also use WinZip to compress and save documents that you do not often need in an archive. This enables you to keep the files on your hard drive, but the files will take up less space.

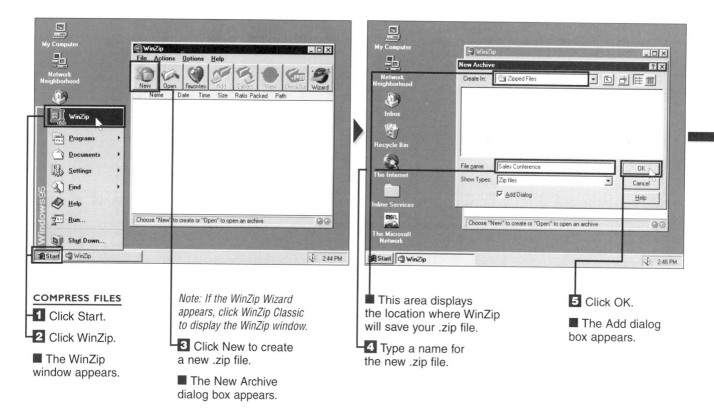

COMPRESS FILES

■1 Click Start.

■2 Click WinZip.

■ The WinZip window appears.

Note: If the WinZip Wizard appears, click WinZip Classic to display the WinZip window.

■3 Click New to create a new .zip file.

■ The New Archive dialog box appears.

■ This area displays the location where WinZip will save your .zip file.

■4 Type a name for the new .zip file.

■5 Click OK.

■ The Add dialog box appears.

How do I add more files to a .zip file?

In the WinZip window, use the Add button to add the files. You can also drag and drop files onto the .zip file from a My Computer or Explorer window.

How do I update the files contained in a .zip file?

Use the Open button to display the contents of the .zip file that needs to be updated. Click Add and use the Action list to select Freshen Existing Files. Then select the files you want to update and click Freshen.

Can I create a .zip file for someone who does not have WinZip?

Display the .zip file you want to change in the WinZip window. Click Actions and select Make .EXE File. When a person who does not have WinZip double-clicks the file, the file will automatically unzip.

What can I do if the .zip file is too big to fit on a single floppy disk?

WinZip Version 6.3 has the capability to store large .zip files over several floppy disks. You can get version 6.3 from the WinZip Web site.

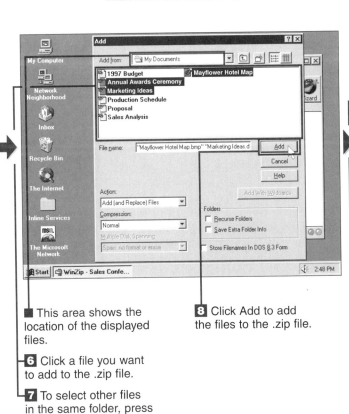

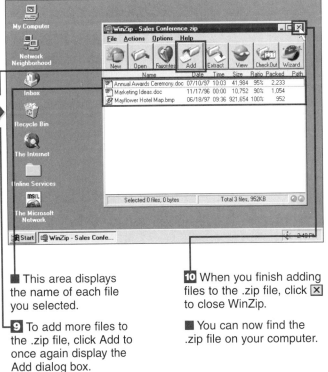

■ This area shows the location of the displayed files.

6 Click a file you want to add to the .zip file.

7 To select other files in the same folder, press and hold down the Ctrl key as you click each file.

8 Click Add to add the files to the .zip file.

■ This area displays the name of each file you selected.

9 To add more files to the .zip file, click Add to once again display the Add dialog box.

10 When you finish adding files to the .zip file, click ☒ to close WinZip.

■ You can now find the .zip file on your computer.

INTRODUCTION TO MICROSOFT PLUS!

Microsoft Plus! is a software package you can install on your computer to enhance Windows 95. Microsoft Plus! makes Windows look and work better and also provides tools to help you connect to the Internet.

Microsoft Plus! is included with some new computers and is available at computer software stores. You can download a free desktop theme from the Microsoft Web site (www.microsoft.com/windows95). Select Using Windows with Microsoft Plus!.

Installation

To run Microsoft Plus! properly, your computer should meet certain minimum requirements. Your computer should have a 486 CPU or better, 8 MB of RAM or more, 25 MB of free hard disk space and a graphics card that can display at least 256 colors. You should consult the Microsoft Plus! packaging for more information.

When you install Microsoft Plus! you will need your Windows CD-ROM disc or floppy disks. The Microsoft Plus! for Windows 95 window may automatically appear when you insert the Microsoft Plus! CD-ROM disc into your drive. From this window you can select Install Plus!. You can also use the Control Panel's Add/Remove Programs icon to install Microsoft Plus!. You can select Custom to install only certain Microsoft Plus! components.

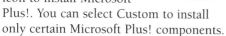

If you decide to uninstall Microsoft Plus!, you should disable System Agent first. Otherwise, you may not be able to successfully remove all the Microsoft Plus! components.

Desktop Themes

A desktop theme provides you with coordinated items such as wallpaper, sounds, mouse pointers and icons that you can use to enhance your desktop. The themes range from the high-tech Inside your Computer to The 60's USA tie-dye experience. You can modify a theme to suit your taste and even mix and match items between different themes. See page 616.

Visual Settings

You can use the visual settings to display full color icons, improve your desktop wallpaper and increase the readability of the text in your programs. See page 618.

System Agent

System Agent can automatically start a program at a date and time you specify. This is useful for running computer maintenance programs that defragment drives or check for disk errors. See page 620.

Dial-up Networking Server

You can set up your computer so you can connect to it from another location using a modem. While connected, you can access files, read network e-mail messages and print documents. Dial-up Networking can be used to stay in touch while you are traveling. This feature is also included in OSR2. See page 366.

Internet Explorer

Internet Explorer is a program used to view Web pages. Although the version included with Plus! is not the most recent, you can use it to access the Microsoft Web site at www.microsoft.com/ie and download the latest version. For information on Internet Explorer, see page 548.

3D Pinball

This pinball game uses advanced sound and graphics for a realistic gaming experience. To play a game of pinball, click the Start button, select Programs and then select Accessories. Click Games and then select Space Cadet Table. To launch a ball, press the spacebar. The longer you hold down the spacebar, the more forceful the launch. You can use the F8 key to define your flipper and table bump keys. Press the Esc key to pause and minimize the game.

DriveSpace 3

The Microsoft Plus! version of DriveSpace is an update to the Windows 95 version, but OSR2 includes the latest version. Computers using the FAT32 file system do not support any version of DriveSpace. For information on DriveSpace, see page 310.

Compression Agent

The Compression Agent optimizes compression and decreases the disk space used by files on drives compressed by DriveSpace 3. HiPack compression improves on standard DriveSpace 3 compression. UltraPack compresses files even more than HiPack. While HiPack and UltraPack increase disk compression, the amount of time it takes your computer to access and use the compressed files is also increased. To take advantage of the Compression Agent, you must leave the computer on while you are not using it. Computers using the FAT32 file system will not be able to use Compression Agent.

Plus! for Kids

Microsoft offers a version of Microsoft Plus! for kids. Plus! for Kids contains a selection of desktop themes designed specifically for children. The package also includes programs children can use to create music, paint pictures and make the computer talk. There are also parental controls to protect children while they are on the Internet.

CHOOSE A DESKTOP THEME

Y ou can choose a desktop theme from Microsoft Plus! to change the appearance of your desktop. Each desktop theme contains several coordinated items including wallpaper, a screen saver, a color scheme, sounds, mouse pointers, icons and fonts.

The themes you can use depend on the number of colors your screen

can display. If your screen can only display 256 colors, you should only use the 256 color themes. If your screen can display more than 256 colors, you can use both the 256 and high color themes. Although you can select a high color theme when your screen can only display 256 colors, you may experience odd color effects and buttons may

not appear to be three-dimensional. You also may not be able to see highlighted selections.

You can personalize a desktop theme by selecting only the theme settings you want to use. You can preview each of the settings before you select the ones you want to use.

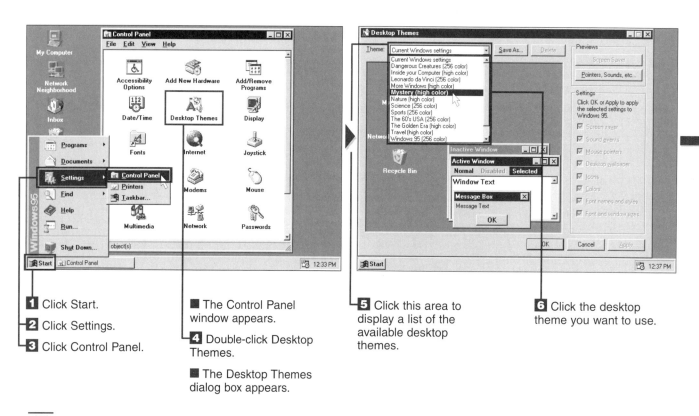

■1 Click Start.

■2 Click Settings.

■3 Click Control Panel.

■ The Control Panel window appears.

■4 Double-click Desktop Themes.

■ The Desktop Themes dialog box appears.

■5 Click this area to display a list of the available desktop themes.

■6 Click the desktop theme you want to use.

How can I change back to my previous desktop?

You must reselect the desktop settings you had before you applied the new desktop theme. The Cancel button will not reverse the new desktop settings after you have applied a change. To display the default desktop, select Windows Default.

How do I change the fonts in my theme to fonts that are easier to read?

Select the Windows Default theme and make sure the Font names and styles setting and the Font and window sizes setting are selected. When customizing your theme, deselect these two settings so you can use the Windows Default font and size settings.

Can I save my personalized desktop theme?

You can use the Save As button to name and save a theme with the settings you have chosen.

Does using a theme have an impact on my computer's performance?

Some computer resources are required to store wallpaper, screen savers, mouse pointers, sounds and other theme elements. Even more resources are used when you choose a high color theme. If you need to increase the performance of your computer, return to the Windows Default theme.

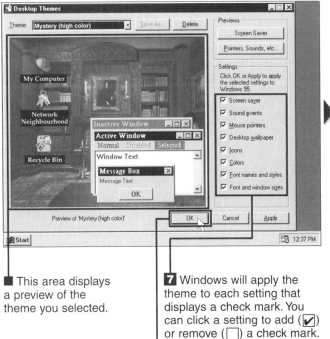

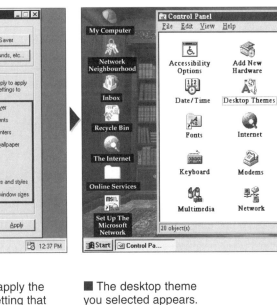

■ This area displays a preview of the theme you selected.

7 Windows will apply the theme to each setting that displays a check mark. You can click a setting to add (☑) or remove (☐) a check mark.

8 Click OK to confirm your changes.

■ The desktop theme you selected appears.

CHANGE VISUAL SETTINGS

You can use Microsoft Plus! to increase the visual appeal of Windows. The Visual settings provide improvements to the way Windows displays icons, wallpaper on your desktop and other details.

The Use large icons setting is designed for high resolution desktops. This setting makes icons appear approximately the same size at a resolution

of 1024x768 as when the standard icons are displayed at 640x480.

You can also use the Show icons using all possible colors setting to display icons using all the colors your computer can display.

The Show window contents while dragging setting makes it simpler to resize windows to display all of their contents perfectly. This setting allows you to see the contents of a window while

you are moving and resizing the window.

The text in a word processor or other program will be easier to read if you use the Smooth edges of screen fonts setting.

Microsoft Plus! can resize your centered wallpaper to fill the entire desktop by using the Stretch desktop wallpaper to fit the screen setting.

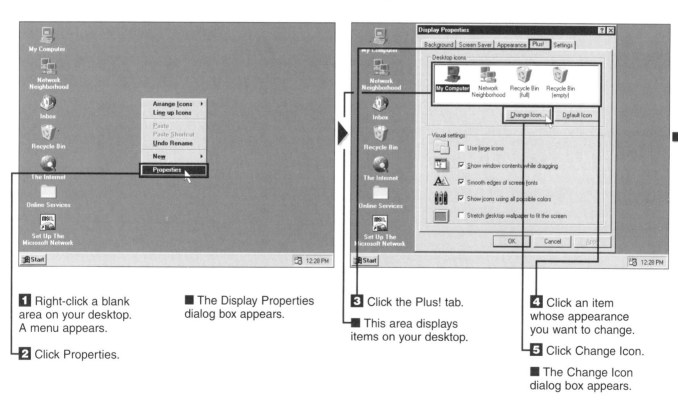

1 Right-click a blank area on your desktop. A menu appears.

2 Click Properties.

■ The Display Properties dialog box appears.

3 Click the Plus! tab.

■ This area displays items on your desktop.

4 Click an item whose appearance you want to change.

5 Click Change Icon.

■ The Change Icon dialog box appears.

Why does my computer seem slower with Plus! installed?

The Visual settings require memory and processor time. If you are using a computer that meets or just exceeds the minimum system requirements to run Plus!, you may notice a considerable slowdown. You can turn off any of the Visual settings to improve the performance of your computer.

The mouse pointer now disappears in the left margin of Word. How can I make the mouse pointer reappear?

Turn off the Show Icons using all possible colors setting (☑ changes to ☐) and the mouse pointer will reappear. This setting may also cause certain mouse pointers to disappear in other programs.

Where can I find more icons on my computer?

To find more icons on your computer, click the Browse button and display the c:\Program Files\Plus!\Themes folder. Each icon in this folder is identified by its theme and purpose.

Why don't the fonts look much better with the smoothed edges?

Fonts will look the best with the highest number of colors displayed on your screen and the highest resolution.

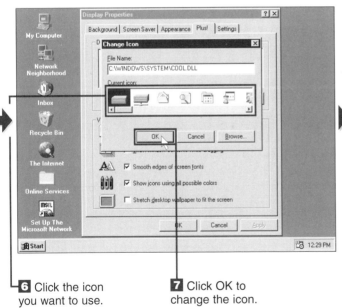

6 Click the icon you want to use.

7 Click OK to change the icon.

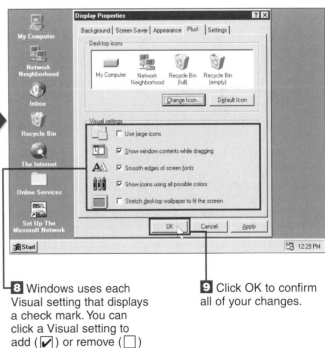

8 Windows uses each Visual setting that displays a check mark. You can click a Visual setting to add (☑) or remove (☐) a check mark.

9 Click OK to confirm all of your changes.

USING SYSTEM AGENT TO SCHEDULE PROGRAMS

You can use System Agent to automatically start a program at a specific date and time. This is useful for running computer maintenance programs that defragment drives or check for disk errors.

System Agent starts each time you start Windows and operates in the background. The System Agent

icon appears on the right-side of the taskbar.

System Agent includes several programs that are already scheduled to run. Low disk space notification checks for low disk space on your hard drive and will notify you if there is less than 20 MB of free space. A standard ScanDisk and a Disk Defragmenter are performed

once a day. System Agent also runs a thorough ScanDisk once a month.

You can add any program or file on your computer to the list of programs that System Agent automatically starts. The program or file you add will be listed in the System Agent window using the description you provide.

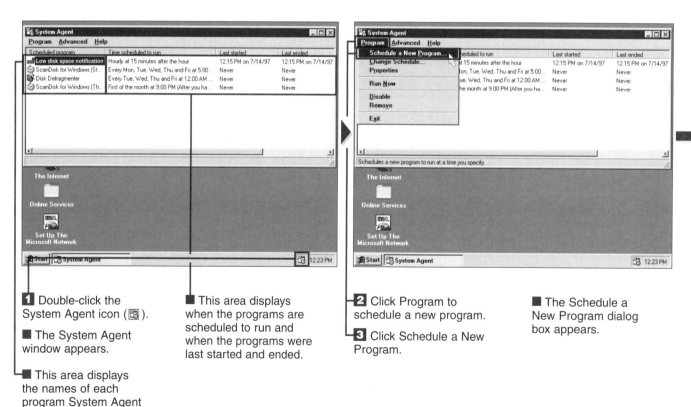

■1 Double-click the System Agent icon ( ).

■ The System Agent window appears.

■ This area displays the names of each program System Agent automatically runs.

■ This area displays when the programs are scheduled to run and when the programs were last started and ended.

■2 Click Program to schedule a new program.

■3 Click Schedule a New Program.

■ The Schedule a New Program dialog box appears.

TIPS

How can I change a program's settings?

Right-click the program and then click Properties. Click the Settings button. You can now specify new settings for the program. The Settings button is only available for Low disk space notification, ScanDisk and Disk Defragmenter.

How do I view System Agent's log?

The log contains information, such as when a program was last started and the result of the operation. You can view the log by choosing the Advanced menu and selecting the View Log command.

How can I set up a backup for System Agent to run?

You must first create a backup set. To create a backup set, perform steps 1 to 5 on page 332. In the Microsoft Backup window, click Settings and then select the Drag and Drop command. Turn off the Confirm operation before beginning option and make sure the Run Backup minimized option and Quit Backup after operation is finished option are both turned on. You can then select the backup set you have created as the program you want to run.

INSTALLING AND TROUBLESHOOTING

IX

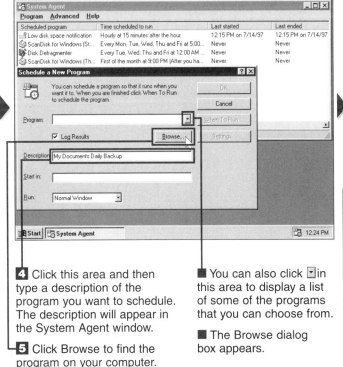

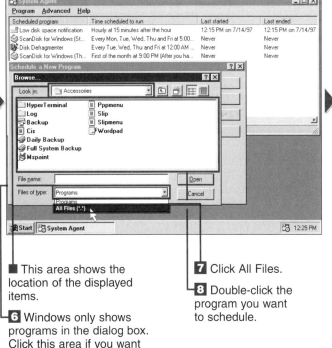

4 Click this area and then type a description of the program you want to schedule. The description will appear in the System Agent window.

5 Click Browse to find the program on your computer.

■ You can also click ▪ in this area to display a list of some of the programs that you can choose from.

■ The Browse dialog box appears.

■ This area shows the location of the displayed items.

6 Windows only shows programs in the dialog box. Click this area if you want to show all the files.

7 Click All Files.

8 Double-click the program you want to schedule.

CONTINUED ▶

621

USING SYSTEM AGENT TO SCHEDULE PROGRAMS CONTINUED

You can specify the conditions under which System Agent will start a program or open a file. You should verify your computer's date and time settings since System Agent monitors the date, time and use of your computer to determine when to start a program.

You can tell System Agent how often to run a program. You can

select daily, weekly or monthly. When you choose a weekly setting, you can select the days of the week you want the program to run.

When you specify the time you want the program to start, you can tell System Agent not to start the program until you have finished using your computer. This is useful if you want to run a program such as Backup at the end of each day,

but you are working late. You can also have System Agent stop running a program when you start using your computer.

System Agent may disable certain functions while it is running a program.

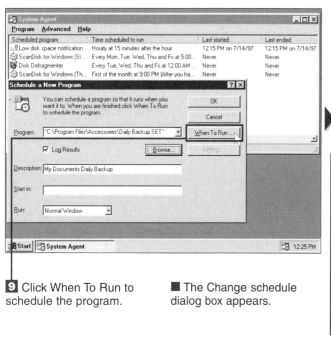

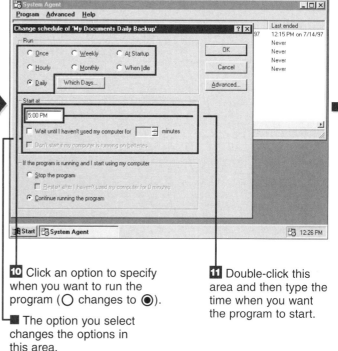

9 Click When To Run to schedule the program.

■ The Change schedule dialog box appears.

10 Click an option to specify when you want to run the program (○ changes to ●).

■ The option you select changes the options in this area.

11 Double-click this area and then type the time when you want the program to start.

How do I stop System Agent?

Right-click the System Agent icon on the taskbar and then select Suspend System Agent to stop System Agent. If you do not want System Agent to start the next time you start Windows, you can select the Advanced menu and then click the Stop Using System Agent command.

Can I restart System Agent?

If you have stopped System Agent, click the Start button, select Programs and then click Accessories. Select System Tools and then click System Agent.

Can I stop a program from running?

To stop a program temporarily, right-click the program and select Disable. To remove the program permanently from your list of scheduled programs, right-click the program and select Remove.

Can I reschedule a program that is already scheduled to run?

To reschedule a program, right-click the program and select Change Schedule. If you want to start the program immediately, you can click Run Now.

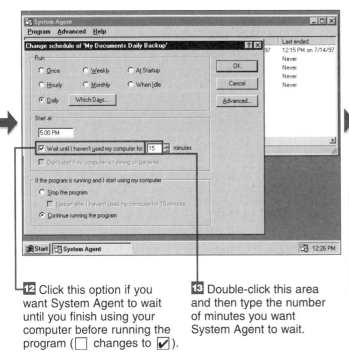

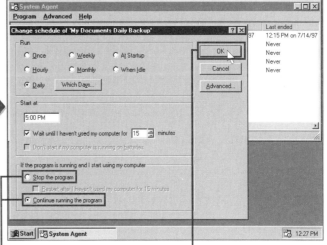

12 Click this option if you want System Agent to wait until you finish using your computer before running the program (☐ changes to ✔).

13 Double-click this area and then type the number of minutes you want System Agent to wait.

14 Click an option to specify whether System Agent should stop the program or continue running the program if you start using your computer while the program is running (○ changes to ⦿).

15 Click OK to finish scheduling the program.

■ The program appears in the System Agent window.

VIEW HARDWARE INFORMATION

If you are having problems with your computer, the Device Manager can help you identify the problem and find a solution.

The Device Manager organizes the types of hardware devices into categories, such as disk drives or monitor. Each category lists the specific hardware devices and the properties of each item in the category. This simplifies the task of identifying and then solving problems with your hardware.

The Device Manager information can be helpful when adding a new hardware device to your computer. You can view which hardware is already installed for your computer.

When you install Plug and Play hardware devices, the Device Manager can change the settings in the hardware and in Windows for you. When you install older hardware devices, you may have to change the hardware settings yourself.

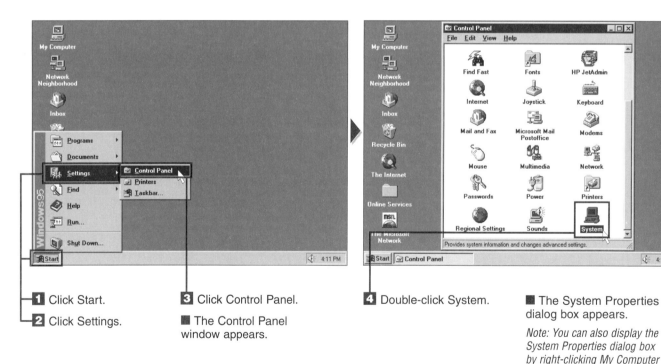

1 Click Start.

2 Click Settings.

3 Click Control Panel.

■ The Control Panel window appears.

4 Double-click System.

■ The System Properties dialog box appears.

Note: You can also display the System Properties dialog box by right-clicking My Computer and selecting Properties.

TIPS

How do I remove a hardware device from my system?

You can remove the highlighted hardware device from your system by using the Remove button in the System Properties dialog box. When you remove a hardware device, all related files are also deleted.

How do I reinstall a hardware device on my computer?

To reinstall a hardware device later, use the Add New Hardware feature in the Control Panel. See page 576.

Can I use the Device Manager in Safe Mode?

If there is a problem with your computer and you must start it in Safe Mode, you can open the Device Manager and display the Computer Properties dialog box to find out what the problem is. An icon with a red X through it indicates the hardware is not working. An icon with a yellow exclamation mark (!) indicates the hardware has a problem, for example, it may not be properly installed.

INSTALLING AND TROUBLESHOOTING

IX

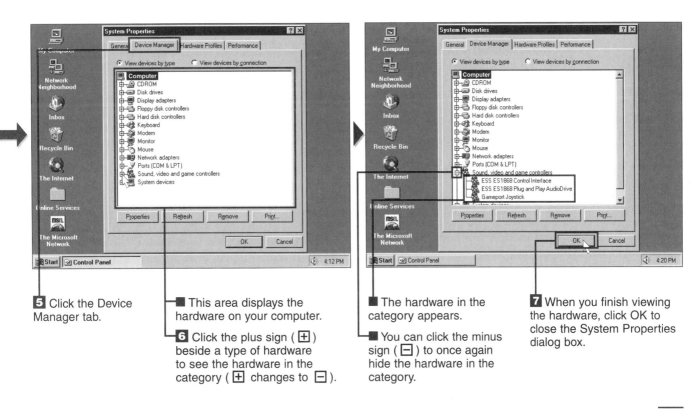

5 Click the Device Manager tab.

■ This area displays the hardware on your computer.

6 Click the plus sign (⊞) beside a type of hardware to see the hardware in the category (⊞ changes to ⊟).

■ The hardware in the category appears.

■ You can click the minus sign (⊟) to once again hide the hardware in the category.

7 When you finish viewing the hardware, click OK to close the System Properties dialog box.

625

VIEW OR CHANGE RESOURCES FOR HARDWARE

Y ou can use the Device Manager to identify which resources on your computer are available to use with new hardware.

There are four main types of resources on your computer including Interrupt Requests (IRQ), Direct Memory Access channels (DMA), Input/Output ports (I/O) and Memory. Some

hardware devices use several resources to run properly.

An IRQ specifies how a device will tell the computer that the device needs attention. The DMA channel lets a device communicate directly with your computer's memory to speed up the processing of information. The I/O address specifies which area of memory a device uses to communicate with

the computer. The Memory resource displays the memory used by each device on your computer.

If the resource settings conflict with the settings for another device, the devices may not work properly. You can view the resources used by a hardware device and find out if there are any conflicts with the device.

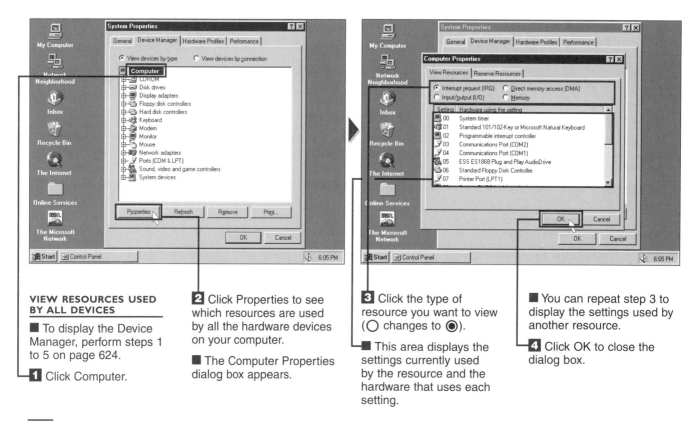

VIEW RESOURCES USED BY ALL DEVICES

■ To display the Device Manager, perform steps 1 to 5 on page 624.

1 Click Computer.

2 Click Properties to see which resources are used by all the hardware devices on your computer.

■ The Computer Properties dialog box appears.

3 Click the type of resource you want to view (○ changes to ⦿).

■ This area displays the settings currently used by the resource and the hardware that uses each setting.

■ You can repeat step 3 to display the settings used by another resource.

4 Click OK to close the dialog box.

What is the best way to resolve hardware conflicts?

Choose the Start menu and select Help. Click the Contents tab and then double-click Troubleshooting. Then double-click "If you have a hardware conflict." Help will ask you questions, open the Device Manager if necessary and help to resolve the hardware conflict.

Can I print my hardware information?

You can use the Print button to print the information you want. The System summary option prints the same information displayed in the Computer Properties dialog box. The All devices and system summary option prints detailed information about hardware devices and the versions of the files being used.

Why is one of my hardware devices listed twice, once with a yellow exclamation mark?

One of the devices could be using an incorrect or older version of the software which is needed to communicate with the hardware device. Select the hardware device and click the Properties button. You can then click the Driver tab to determine which is the latest or most appropriate version for the hardware device.

IX

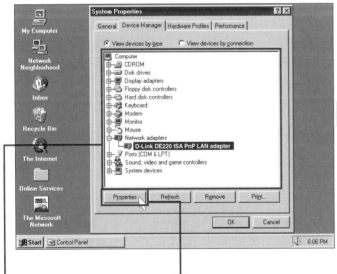

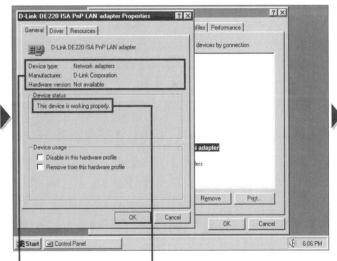

VIEW OR CHANGE RESOURCES USED BY ONE DEVICE

■1 Click a hardware device of interest.

■2 Click Properties to display information about the hardware device.

■ Information about the hardware device appears.

■ This area displays general information about the hardware device.

■ This area tells you if the hardware device is working properly. If there is a problem with the hardware device, Windows will display the type of problem and a suggested solution.

CONTINUED ▶

VIEW OR CHANGE
RESOURCES FOR HARDWARE CONTINUED

I f you have conflicts between your hardware devices, you may need to change some of the resource settings the hardware devices use. The resource settings control the communication between the computer and its hardware devices. Unnecessary changes may create very complicated problems.

Windows can help you find the correct resource settings, but you

need to set up the hardware device so the computer can detect the device. You may have to use the configuration software or read the documentation that came with the hardware device to set up the device properly.

When trying to fix hardware conflicts, it is best to change only one resource setting at a time. There is no way to undo the changes you make. You should

print the current resource settings and make careful notes when making changes. If the problem is not fixed when you change a resource setting, return to the original resource setting before making more changes.

You should not have to change the resources for hardware with Plug and Play or self-configuring capabilities.

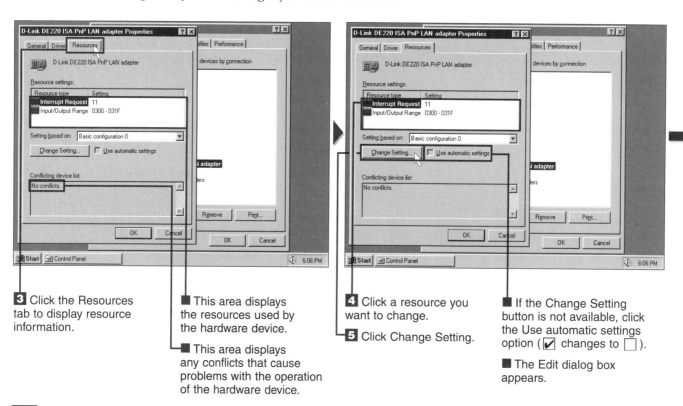

3 Click the Resources tab to display resource information.

■ This area displays the resources used by the hardware device.

■ This area displays any conflicts that cause problems with the operation of the hardware device.

4 Click a resource you want to change.

5 Click Change Setting.

■ If the Change Setting button is not available, click the Use automatic settings option (☑ changes to ☐).

■ The Edit dialog box appears.

Why don't all devices have a Resources tab?

Not all devices use resources directly. For example, the resources for a CD-ROM drive are usually set by the disk controller.

Why does my sound card use two DMA channels?

Your sound card uses two DMA channels to enable your computer to playback and record sound at the same time. This capability is called "duplex" and allows voice communication over the Internet to sound more like a real telephone call.

What can I do if I get an error message saying a resource cannot be modified?

Many devices, such as disk controllers and display adapters, have resource settings that cannot be changed. If you are trying to change a resource setting to fix a conflict, you must resolve it by changing the resource settings for another device.

What can I do if there are no resources available?

You must analyze which devices are using the resources you need and then decide if you are able to remove any of those resources.

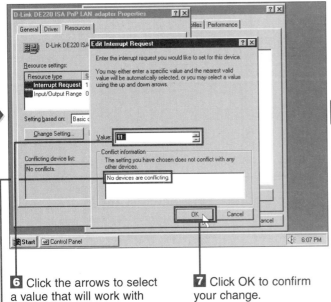

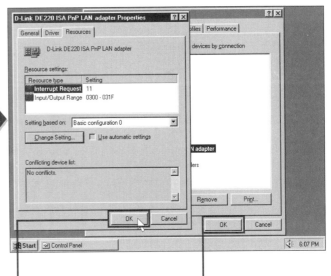

6 Click the arrows to select a value that will work with the hardware device or type a value in the area provided.

■ This area indicates if any conflicts exist with the value you selected.

7 Click OK to confirm your change.

8 Click OK to close the Properties dialog box.

■ A dialog box may appear, warning you Windows will no longer be able to automatically adjust the resource setting. Click Yes to continue.

9 Click OK to close the System Properties dialog box.

■ You may need to restart Windows before the new setting takes effect.

UPDATE DEVICE DRIVERS

Your hardware may work better if you are using the latest version of the software it needs to operate. Hardware devices ranging from your mouse to your modem are all controlled by specific software, called drivers. A driver allows the computer to communicate with and control the device.

When you install a device, Windows checks for the hardware and then installs the appropriate driver from its library. Windows does not include all possible device drivers in its library. If the correct driver is not installed, the device may not work properly.

Even Plug and Play devices may not install correctly. Again, you may have to update the device driver for the hardware to work.

When you purchase a device, the manufacturer may include drivers on a floppy disk. You can also obtain new drivers directly from the manufacturer. Most manufacturers provide the latest drivers in the support area of their Web site. You should particularly check for newer drivers for your video display adapter card. These drivers are frequently updated and improved. The latest driver may be faster and offer more features.

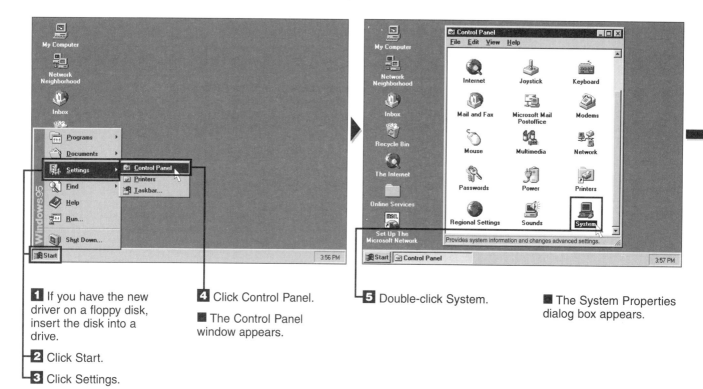

■1 If you have the new driver on a floppy disk, insert the disk into a drive.

■2 Click Start.

■3 Click Settings.

■4 Click Control Panel.

■ The Control Panel window appears.

■5 Double-click System.

■ The System Properties dialog box appears.

What can I do if the device does not have a Driver tab?

In versions of Windows 95 prior to OSR2, some devices, such as modems and monitors, do not have a Driver tab. You can change the settings for many of these devices in the Control Panel. For example, to change a monitor, double-click Display, select the Settings tab and then click the Change Display Type button. To change a modem, you must remove the modem and then reinstall it using the new driver.

Why does my button say "Change Driver" instead of "Update Driver"?

The Change Driver button appears if you do not have OSR2. After you click the button, Windows lists all the drivers included on the Windows 95 CD-ROM disc that may work with the device. If the driver you want to add is on a floppy disk, click the Have Disk button. Then use the Browse button to locate the new driver.

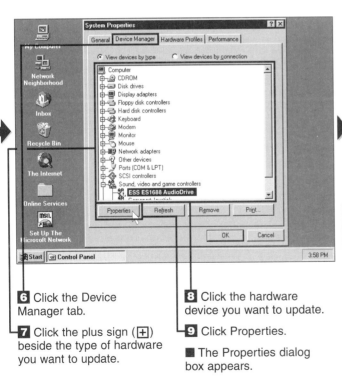

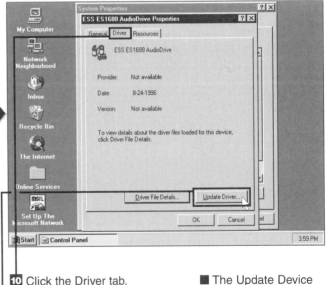

6 Click the Device Manager tab.

7 Click the plus sign (⊞) beside the type of hardware you want to update.

8 Click the hardware device you want to update.

9 Click Properties.

■ The Properties dialog box appears.

10 Click the Driver tab.

11 Click Update Driver to update the driver.

Note: If the Change Driver button is available instead of the Update Driver button, see the Tip above.

■ The Update Device Driver Wizard appears.

CONTINUED ▶

UPDATE DEVICE DRIVERS CONTINUED

The wizard checks your floppy disk for the updated driver. If the driver is not found, you can tell the wizard where the files are located on your computer.

If you are transferring the driver from the Internet, the files are usually in the compressed file format, with the .exe or .zip extension. You must extract, or decompress,

the driver files from the files you downloaded. The extracted files usually contain a readme file, which provides you with information on how to install the driver.

The wizard always looks for a file with the .inf extension. The .inf file contains information that tells Windows how to install the driver. After the wizard reads the .inf file, it will

copy the files Windows needs and adjust the settings that are required by the device. In addition to the .inf file, the wizard may need files from the Windows 95 CD-ROM disc.

When the setup is complete, you will be asked to restart your computer.

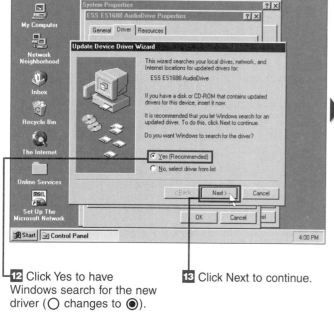

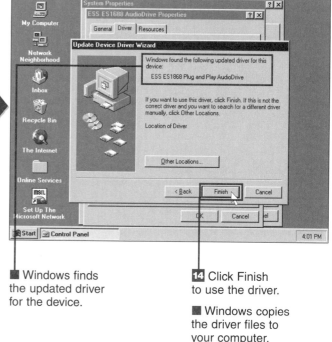

■12 Click Yes to have Windows search for the new driver (○ changes to ◉).

■13 Click Next to continue.

■ Windows finds the updated driver for the device.

■14 Click Finish to use the driver.

■ Windows copies the driver files to your computer.

TIPS

The floppy disk is inserted, so why is Windows still asking me to insert the disk?

The .inf file may refer to folders that do not exist on the floppy disk. If this happens, click OK to display the Copying Files dialog box and then select the Browse button. The Open dialog box displays the name of the file Windows is looking for. To help locate the driver, first try changing the drive letter to A. If this does not work, browse through the folders.

What are my options if the driver does not work? Also, what if the new driver does not work as well as the previous version?

It may be as easy as reinstalling the old driver from the Windows CD-ROM disc. In some cases, it may be necessary to remove the hardware and reinstall it. Before changing anything, always check the information supplied by the manufacturer.

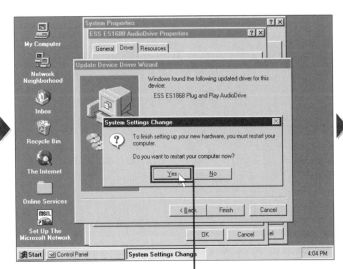

■ A message appears, telling you Windows needs to restart your computer to finish setting up the driver.

15 Click Yes to restart your computer now.

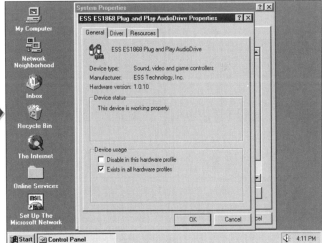

■ The updated device driver is now added to your computer.

■ You can display the new name of the device driver and information about the driver in the Device Manager.

VIRTUAL MEMORY SETTINGS

Virtual memory improves the operation of computers that do not have large amounts of memory, or RAM.

Windows must have at least 4 MB of RAM to function. If your computer has more than 4 MB of RAM, Windows will be able to operate faster and run more programs at the same time. If you do not have more RAM available,

Windows uses part of your hard disk as RAM. This borrowed storage space is called virtual memory. The hard disk space that Windows uses as virtual memory is also called a swap file.

Windows is always busy managing your computer's memory. Whenever you choose a different font, open a new window or begin a task like printing, RAM

is required. When there is no more RAM available, Windows frees up some RAM by placing some of the information in virtual memory. When that information is required again, Windows retrieves the information from virtual memory.

When Windows is using virtual memory, you may notice that your hard drive is accessed more often.

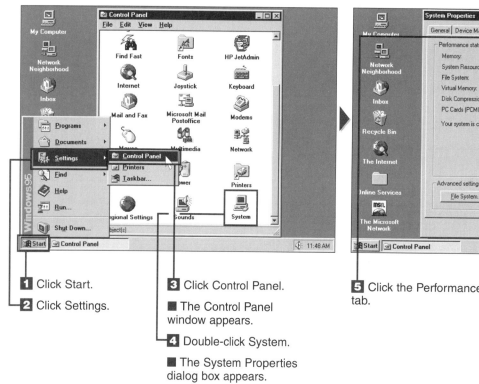

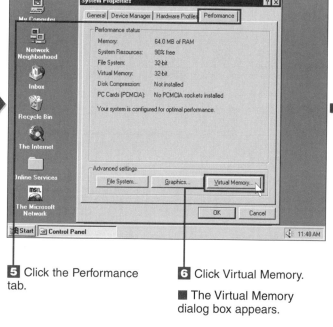

1 Click Start.

2 Click Settings.

3 Click Control Panel.

■ The Control Panel window appears.

4 Double-click System.

■ The System Properties dialog box appears.

5 Click the Performance tab.

6 Click Virtual Memory.

■ The Virtual Memory dialog box appears.

Should I change the virtual memory settings?

In general, you should not change the virtual memory settings. However, you may find that Windows spends less time using the hard drive if you use the same number for the minimum and maximum amount of hard disk space you want to use for virtual memory.

Can I move the virtual memory to a different hard drive?

If you have more than one hard drive, you could move the virtual memory to the fastest drive or to the drive with the most free space.

How much virtual memory do I need?

The amount of virtual memory you need depends on the amount of RAM you have and the number of programs you want to use at one time. If you have 32 MB or more of RAM, try setting the minimum and maximum amount of hard disk space you want to use for virtual memory to 32 MB. If "out of memory" messages start to appear, change the settings to 64 MB.

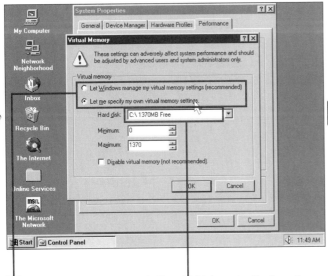

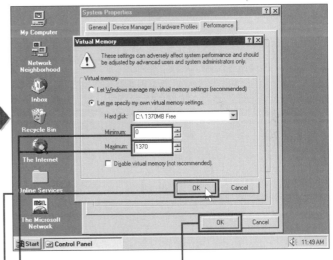

7 Click an option to specify if you want Windows to manage your virtual memory settings or if you want to specify your own (○ changes to ◉).

■ This area displays the hard disk used for virtual memory and the amount of free space on the disk.

8 These areas display the minimum and maximum amount of hard disk space you want to use for virtual memory in megabytes. You can change these values.

9 Click OK to confirm any changes.

Note: If a confirmation dialog box appears, click Yes.

10 Click OK or Close to close the System Properties dialog box.

■ If you change the settings, you must restart your computer.

CREATE A STARTUP DISK

You should create a startup disk and keep it on hand in case you have trouble starting Windows. When you cannot start Windows normally, you can insert the startup disk into your floppy drive to start your computer.

When you use a startup disk to start your computer, a command prompt similar to MS-DOS appears on your screen. You can access several utility programs to try to solve the problem that prevents Windows from starting properly. You will not be able to access your CD-ROM drive or log on to the network.

The floppy disk you use to create the startup disk must be able to store at least 1.2 MB of information. All files currently stored on the floppy disk will be erased when you create a startup disk.

After you have created the startup disk, open the write-protect tab so you do not accidentally delete any files stored on the disk. Make sure you label your startup disk and keep it with your Windows 95 installation CD-ROM disc or floppy disks.

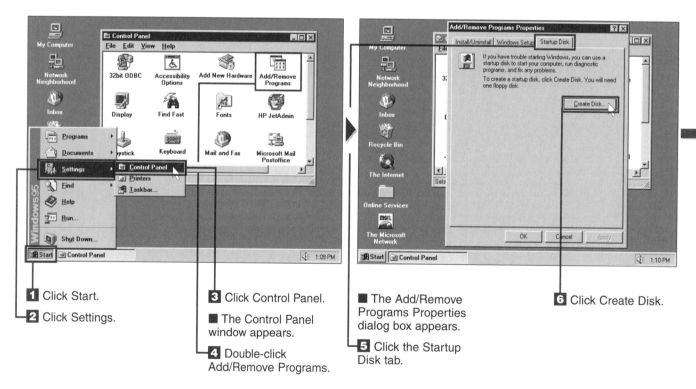

1 Click Start.

2 Click Settings.

3 Click Control Panel.

■ The Control Panel window appears.

4 Double-click Add/Remove Programs.

■ The Add/Remove Programs Properties dialog box appears.

5 Click the Startup Disk tab.

6 Click Create Disk.

TIPS

Which floppy drive should I use when I create my startup disk?

If your computer has more than one floppy drive, you should use the A: drive to create your startup disk.

What is on the startup disk?

In addition to the system files needed to start a command prompt, the startup disk contains several utility programs. ScanDisk checks and repairs hard disk errors. FDISK allows you to partition your hard disk. Format allows you to format your hard disk. Regedit allows you to make changes to your Windows Registry. Edit is a text editor that lets you make changes to text configuration files.

I inserted the floppy disk, but my computer is still trying to start from the hard drive. What can I do?

If your computer does not start from the floppy drive containing the startup disk, consult your computer's manual to find out which settings must be adjusted to start from a floppy drive.

Can I create a startup disk using another Windows 95 computer?

If you have a problem starting Windows and have not created a startup disk, you can create a startup disk using another similar Windows 95 computer.

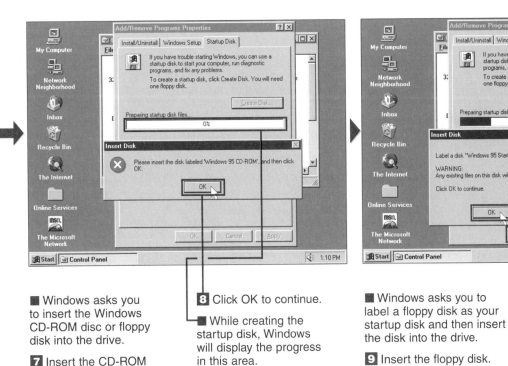

■ Windows asks you to insert the Windows CD-ROM disc or floppy disk into the drive.

7 Insert the CD-ROM disc or floppy disk.

8 Click OK to continue.

■ While creating the startup disk, Windows will display the progress in this area.

■ Windows asks you to label a floppy disk as your startup disk and then insert the disk into the drive.

9 Insert the floppy disk.

10 Click OK to continue.

11 When the startup disk is complete, click OK to close the Add/Remove Programs dialog box.

START WINDOWS IN SAFE MODE

If Windows does not start properly, you can start Windows in safe mode. Safe mode is a limited version of Windows.

Windows may not start properly if you have made inappropriate changes to your computer's setup. For example, you may have incorrectly installed a new device or accidentally changed important

Windows settings. In safe mode, you may be able to correct the problem that prevents Windows from starting normally.

Safe mode uses the minimum capabilities required to run Windows. When you use safe mode, you cannot access CD-ROM drives, tape drives, SCSI devices, printers and devices such as sound cards or modems.

If you need to access the network, you can choose to have safe mode include network support.

Safe mode will not start any of the items in your StartUp folder.

If Windows fails to start properly, your computer may automatically start in safe mode.

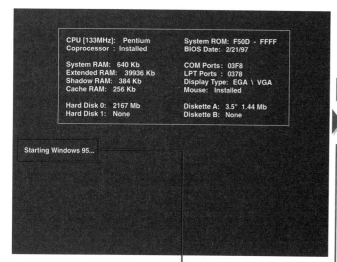

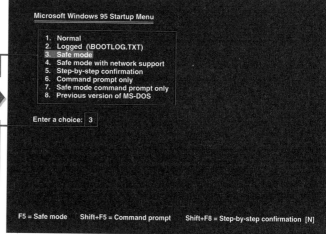

1 Turn on your computer and monitor.

2 Press the F8 key as soon as you see the "Starting Windows 95" message.

■ The Windows 95 startup menu appears. The menu displays a list of choices for starting Windows in different modes.

3 Type the number for the mode you want to use and then press the Enter key.

■ Windows starts in the mode you selected.

When Windows is in safe mode, where should I start looking for the problem?

From the Windows Help window, click the Contents tab and then double-click the Troubleshooting book. Then double-click "If you have a hardware conflict." To use Windows Help, see page 30.

Can I access alternative startup options?

Instead of pressing F8 to display the Windows startup menu, you can access the alternative startup options by using keyboard shortcuts. You can press the F5 key to start Safe mode. You can use Shift+F5 to activate the Command prompt. You can use Shift+F8 to start Step-by-step confirmation.

What are the other options for starting my computer?

A Logged start creates a file on your hard drive that documents the entire startup procedure. This file may allow you to see where a problem is occurring in startup. The Step-by-step confirmation lets you choose which devices to load to start Windows and see where a problem may be occurring. The Command prompt only and Previous version of MS-DOS options start MS-DOS.

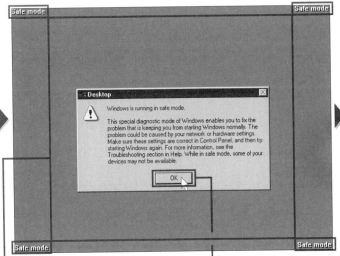

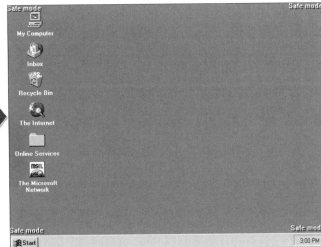

■ A message tells you that Windows is running in safe mode and that some of your devices may not be available.

■ Windows displays the words "Safe mode" at each corner of your screen.

4 Click OK to continue.

■ You can now try to fix the problem that is keeping you from starting Windows normally.

■ When you finish fixing the problem, restart your computer. You should now be able to use your computer as usual.

VIEW AND EDIT CONFIGURATION FILES

You can open and edit setup and configuration files. Configuration files contain the settings required by previous versions of MS-DOS and Windows to start and operate. Some programs designed for these environments may still require these settings. The System Configuration Editor provides a common place to view and edit setup and configuration files.

Config.sys and Autoexec.bat are two files that were used to enable MS-DOS to communicate with devices such as CD-ROM drives and network cards. These files contained the commands which started the driver software used to access and control the devices. By removing these drivers, you can make additional conventional memory available to your MS-DOS applications.

Previous versions of Windows used files with the .ini extension to store settings. These files are still required by older Windows programs, although their settings are duplicated in the Windows 95 registry.

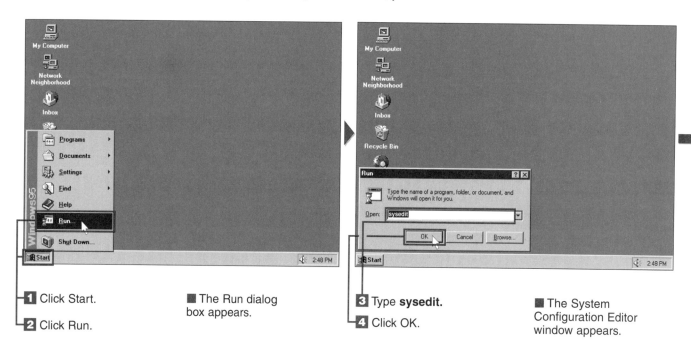

■ **1** Click Start.

■ **2** Click Run.

■ The Run dialog box appears.

■ **3** Type **sysedit.**

■ **4** Click OK.

■ The System Configuration Editor window appears.

When will the changes I make to the Config.sys and Autoexec.bat files take effect?

 You will have to restart your computer for the changes to take effect.

How can I tell what the commands in the Config.sys and Autoexec.bat files do?

Many of the commands are described in the c:\windows folder in the Config.txt and Msdosdrv.txt files.

Can I delete a command from a configuration file?

The commands in a configuration file can be complex and may cause problems if accidentally deleted. In both the Config.sys and Autoexec.bat files, it is wiser to type **rem** and add a space than to delete the commands. If you need to undo the change, you can simply remove the **rem** and the space.

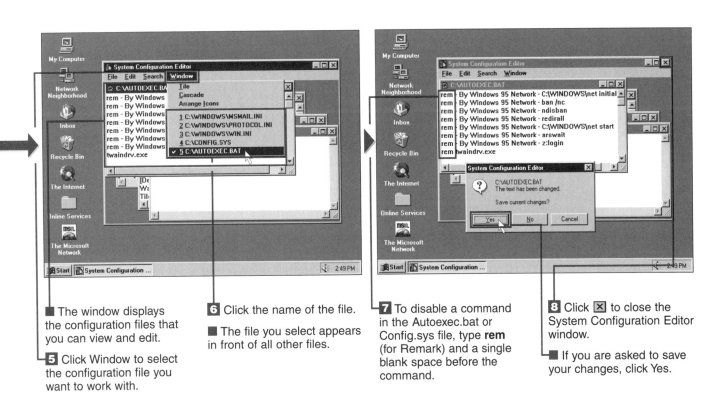

■ The window displays the configuration files that you can view and edit.

5 Click Window to select the configuration file you want to work with.

6 Click the name of the file.

■ The file you select appears in front of all other files.

7 To disable a command in the Autoexec.bat or Config.sys file, type **rem** (for Remark) and a single blank space before the command.

8 Click ☒ to close the System Configuration Editor window.

■ If you are asked to save your changes, click Yes.

START THE REGISTRY EDITOR

The Registry Editor is an advanced tool you can use to view and edit the Registry. The Registry contains information needed to run Windows 95 with your hardware and software.

The contents of the Registry are complex, so you should only use the Registry Editor when absolutely necessary. Before making any changes to the Registry, you should create a backup copy of the Registry and make sure you understand how to restore it.

The Registry contains six main keys, or branches, including two master keys. HKEY_LOCAL_MACHINE contains information about your hardware and software. HKEY_USERS contains information about desktop settings and network connections.

There are also three keys that contain copies of sections of the master keys. HKEY_CLASSES_ROOT contains information about the associations between your

programs and documents. HKEY_CURRENT_USER contains information specific to the current user. HKEY_CURRENT_CONFIG contains information about display and printer settings.

The final main key, HKEY_DYN_DATA, stores data from the computer's RAM including Plug and Play information.

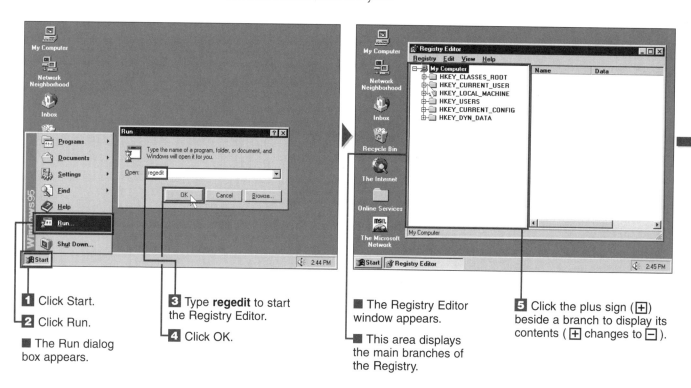

1 Click Start.

2 Click Run.

■ The Run dialog box appears.

3 Type **regedit** to start the Registry Editor.

4 Click OK.

■ The Registry Editor window appears.

■ This area displays the main branches of the Registry.

5 Click the plus sign (⊞) beside a branch to display its contents (⊞ changes to ⊟).

TIPS

What is a key?

Each branch of the Registry is called a key. Each key can contain other keys, as well as values.

How do I back up the Registry?

You can use the Configuration Backup program on your Windows CD-ROM. In the other\misc\cfgback folder, double-click the cfgback.exe file and follow the instructions on your screen. You can create up to nine copies of the Registry. The copies are saved in the Windows folder with the .rbk extension. The Configuration Backup program can also be used to restore the copies of the Registry.

I forgot to back up the Registry! Can I still restore the settings?

You can restore the settings that were used the last time Windows started successfully. These settings are saved in hidden files called System.da0 and User.da0 in your Windows folder. To display the MS-DOS commands and the procedure to restore these files, select the Help menu and then click Help Topics. Click the Contents tab and then double-click the Restoring the registry topic.

What is a value?

A value is the information stored in a key. Each value has a name and data.

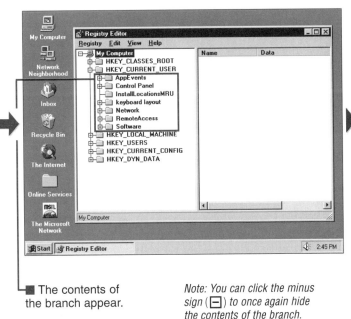

■ The contents of the branch appear.

Note: You can click the minus sign (☐) to once again hide the contents of the branch.

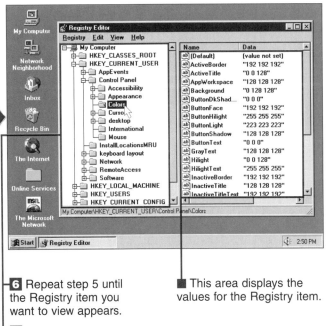

6 Repeat step 5 until the Registry item you want to view appears.

7 Click the Registry item to display its values.

■ This area displays the values for the Registry item.

SEARCH THE REGISTRY

Y ou can use the Registry Editor to find a specific key in the Registry.

The Registry Editor window has two panes, similar to Windows Explorer. The left pane displays the list of keys contained in the Registry. The right pane displays the values, or information, stored in the currently selected key. Looking

for a specific key by browsing through the Registry Editor window can be time-consuming and difficult. The Find feature can help you find information in the Registry.

When you use the Find feature to find a key, you must search for information that is specific to the key you want to find. For example, if you want to find

your screen appearance settings so you can copy them to another computer, search for the name of one of the appearance schemes, such as eggplant.

The Find feature can only search for string data. You will not be able to search for the binary or DWORD formats used in some keys.

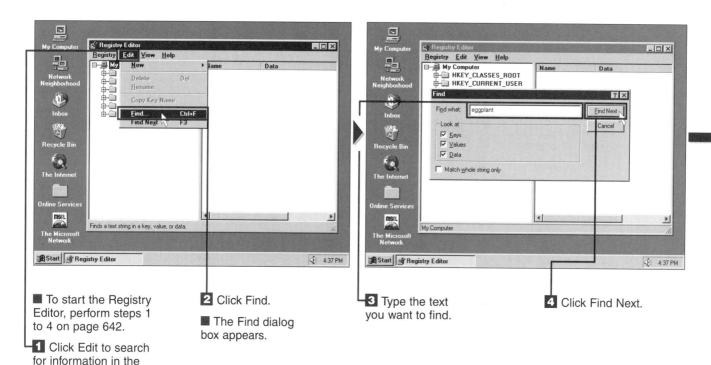

■ To start the Registry Editor, perform steps 1 to 4 on page 642.

1 Click Edit to search for information in the Registry.

2 Click Find.

■ The Find dialog box appears.

3 Type the text you want to find.

4 Click Find Next.

What are the string, binary and DWORD formats?

These are the three data formats used in registry keys. String data appears in quotation marks. Binary data is presented in hexadecimal (hex) format, or pairs of characters and numbers. The DWORD format displays 0x followed by 8 hex characters and a number in parentheses.

The Registry Editor's Find feature is slow. How can I perform faster searches?

You can export the Registry to a text file and then use a word processor like Word to search the Registry. To export the Registry to a text file, see page 648.

What else can I search for with the Find feature?

In addition to keys, you can also search for values and data. To speed up the search, you can specify the type of information you want to search for in the Find dialog box.

I found the key I was searching for. How do I transfer the settings it contains to another computer?

Export the key to a floppy disk. To export a registry file, see page 648. Insert the floppy disk into the other computer. Double-click the file you exported to merge the settings into the Registry of the other computer.

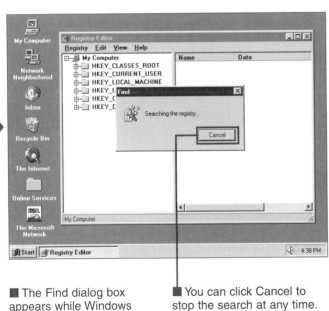

■ The Find dialog box appears while Windows searches the Registry.

■ You can click Cancel to stop the search at any time.

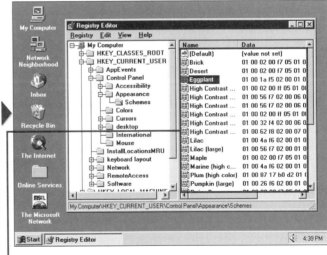

■ This area displays the first item that matches the text you typed.

■ You can press the F3 key to find the next instance of the text in the Registry.

EDIT THE REGISTRY

You can use the Registry Editor to add or change information in the Registry. The Registry Editor does not have an Undo feature and changes are made immediately. If you make a mistake while editing the Registry, Windows may not start. Before making any changes, you should create a backup copy of the Registry.

You can add information to the Registry. For example, you can

have a program start automatically without placing it in the StartUp folder. This is useful if you want to make sure a program is always run when you start your computer.

You can change the information in the Registry. You can change the commands in an existing value or in a value you have added. This is useful if you want to change the behavior of your programs. For example, you can prevent ActiveMovie from closing when

it has finished playing an .avi video file.

Any changes you make to the Registry should be based on tested information from reliable sources. Many computer magazines contain articles about editing the Registry and the changes that are possible. You can also find Web sites and newsgroups containing information about changing the Registry.

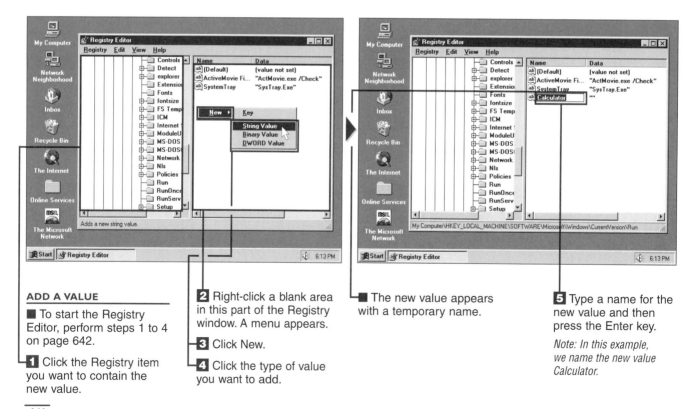

ADD A VALUE

■ To start the Registry Editor, perform steps 1 to 4 on page 642.

1 Click the Registry item you want to contain the new value.

2 Right-click a blank area in this part of the Registry window. A menu appears.

3 Click New.

4 Click the type of value you want to add.

■ The new value appears with a temporary name.

5 Type a name for the new value and then press the Enter key.

Note: In this example, we name the new value Calculator.

Is there another way to make changes to the Registry?

Whenever possible, you should use the Control Panel to make changes to the Registry. You can also use Tweak UI from the PowerToys collection to access a range of otherwise hard-to-adjust registry settings. For information on PowerToys, see page 602.

How can I edit the Registry to prevent ActiveMovie from closing when it has finished playing an .avi file?

In the HKEY_CLASSES_ROOT\ AVIFile\shell\play\command key, double-click the (Default) value and remove /close.

How else can I change a value?

You can turn a value on or off by changing the string data. In the data column, a "0" means the value is off and a "1" means the value is on.

How do I delete a key or value?

Right-click the key or value you want to remove and then select Delete. This is useful if you have removed a program from your computer but it is still listed in the Control Panel's Add/Remove Programs dialog box. To remove the program from the dialog box, delete the program's key from HKEY_LOCAL_MACHINE\SOFTWARE\ Microsoft\Windows\CurrentVersion\ Uninstall.

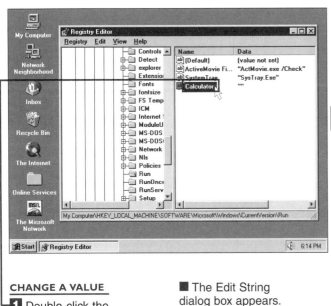

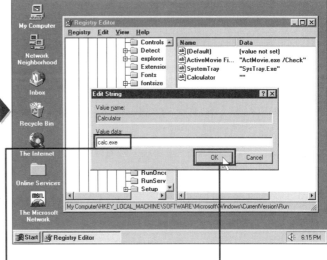

CHANGE A VALUE

■ 1 Double-click the value you want to change.

■ The Edit String dialog box appears.

■ 2 Type the new data for the value.

Note: In this example, the value we change will make Calculator start every time you turn on your computer.

■ 3 Click OK to confirm your change.

EXPORT THE REGISTRY TO A TEXT FILE

You can copy registry settings into a file that can be saved and edited with a word processor. You can copy the entire Registry or just one branch.

You may prefer to use a word processor to edit the Registry since the Registry Editor has a slow Find feature and does not support Find and Replace.

When editing the Registry, keep in mind that the structure of the Registry is complex and its rules for punctuation are complicated. It is easier to make an editing mistake when you use a word processor than when you use the Registry Editor.

You can create a copy of all the registry settings and use the copy as a backup in case there

is ever a problem with your settings.

You can also transfer copied registry settings to another computer. For example, you can export your customized screen color settings to a file. You can then share your screen color settings with a coworker or use them on your home or portable computer.

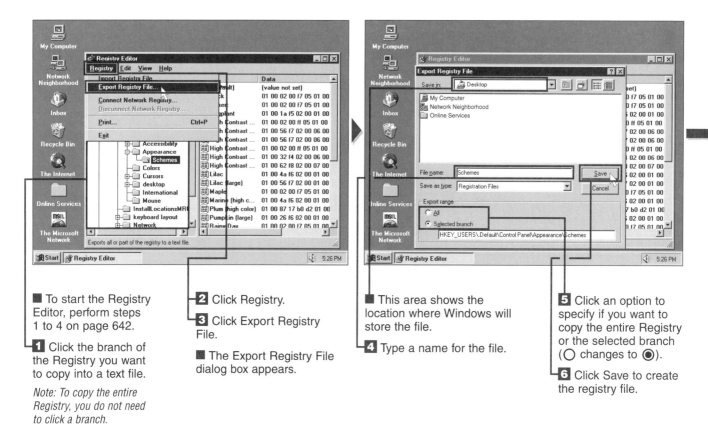

■ To start the Registry Editor, perform steps 1 to 4 on page 642.

1 Click the branch of the Registry you want to copy into a text file.

Note: To copy the entire Registry, you do not need to click a branch.

2 Click Registry.

3 Click Export Registry File.

■ The Export Registry File dialog box appears.

■ This area shows the location where Windows will store the file.

4 Type a name for the file.

5 Click an option to specify if you want to copy the entire Registry or the selected branch (○ changes to ⦿).

6 Click Save to create the registry file.

TIPS

How do I merge the exported file back into the Registry?

If the file has the extension .reg, you can merge the exported file back into the Registry by double-clicking the file. You can also open the Registry Editor, choose the Registry menu and select the Import Registry File command. In the Import Registry File dialog box, click the file you want to import and click the Open button.

What will happen to my current registry settings when I merge the exported file back into the registry?

The contents of the file will overwrite the current registry settings. If the settings in the file do not exist in the Registry, they will be added. If settings exist in the Registry and not in the file, the settings in the Registry will not be affected.

When I double-click an exported registry file, I want to be able to edit it. How can I change the default action from merge to edit?

In your My Computer window, click View and select the Options command. Click the File Types tab. In the Registered file types list select Registration Entries and then click the Edit button. Select the Edit action and then click the Set Default button.

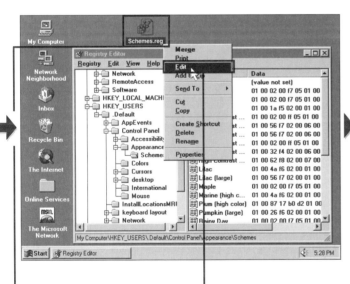

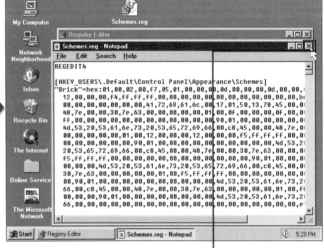

■ Windows creates the registry file.

7 Right-click the registry file. A menu appears.

8 Click Edit to edit the file.

Note: Do not double-click the file since this will merge the information back into the Registry.

■ The registry file appears in Notepad.

Note: A message appears if the file is too large for Notepad to open. Click Yes to use WordPad to read the file.

9 Click ☒ to close Notepad when you finish viewing the file.

INDEX

INDEX

INDEX

DriveSpace
   adjust free space on compressed drive, 316-317
   compress
      drive, 310-315
      part of drive, 318-321
   uncompress drive, 322-325
DriveSpace 3, Microsoft Plus!, 615
DWORD format, Registry, 645

E

echo, add to sound recording, 278
edit
   configuration files, 640-641
      MS-DOS programs, 142-143
   embedded information, 126-127
   fax cover pages, 462-465
   file types, 248-249
   linked information, 130-131
   Registry, 646-647
   scraps, 123
   text, WordPad, 154-155
editable files, faxes, 456-457
electromagnetic radiation (EMR), 346
e-mail
   components, install, 410-415
   compound documents, 131
   Internet Explorer 4.0, 559
   messages
      delete, 301, 434-435
      find, 436-437
      format, 421
      forward, 432-433
      insert files in, 428-429
      move to folder, 438-439
      print, 434
      read, 430-431
      reply to, 432-433
      schedule transfer, 418-419
      send, 420-421
      sort, 434
      view attached files, 429
   painting, 176
embed, information, 124-125

embedded information, edit, 126-127
EMF format, printers, 108-109
empty
      Internet Explorer cache, 300
      Recycle Bin, 72-73, 300
energy, conserve, 400-403
Energy Star computers, 214-215
energy-saving features, 214-215
enterprise network, 469
erase
      part of painting, 173
      tapes, 346-347
error control settings, modem, change, 362-363
Ethernet networks, 471, 472
events, assign sounds to, 260-263
Exchange
      address book
         groups, add, 424-425
         names
            add, 422-423
            select, 426-427
      faxes
         receive, 413
         send, 452-455
         view, 460-461
      install, 410-415
      mail folders, 438-439
         columns
            add, 435
            change width, 435
            delete, 435
      mailboxes
         create, 448-449
         locate, 414
      messages
         color, text, change, 433
         create, 420-421
         delete, 434-435
         find, 436-437
         forward, 432-433
         insert files, 428-429
         move to folder, 438-439
         print, 434

INDEX

INDEX

INDEX

INDEX

INDEX

X

Y

Z